AF840872

The African Union (AU)

The African Union (AU)

Second Edition

Konstantinos D. Magliveras
Gino J. Naldi

This book was originally published as a monograph in the International Encyclopaedia of Laws/Intergovernmental Organizations.

Founding Editor: Roger Blanpain
General Editor: Frank Hendrickx
Volume Editor: Jan Wouters

Wolters Kluwer

Published by:
Kluwer Law International B.V.
PO Box 316
2400 AH Alphen aan den Rijn
The Netherlands
E-mail: international-sales@wolterskluwer.com
Website: lrus.wolterskluwer.com

Sold and distributed in North, Central and South America by:
Wolters Kluwer Legal & Regulatory U.S.
7201 McKinney Circle
Frederick, MD 21704
United States of America
Email: customer.service@wolterskluwer.com

Sold and distributed in all other countries by:
Air Business Subscriptions
Rockwood House
Haywards Heath
West Sussex
RH16 3DH
United Kingdom
Email: international-customerservice@wolterskluwer.com

DISCLAIMER: The material in this volume is in the nature of general comment only. It is not offered as advice on any particular matter and should not be taken as such. The editor and the contributing authors expressly disclaim all liability to any person with regard to anything done or omitted to be done, and with respect to the consequences of anything done or omitted to be done wholly or partly in reliance upon the whole or any part of the contents of this volume. No reader should act or refrain from acting on the basis of any matter contained in this volume without first obtaining professional advice regarding the particular facts and circumstances at issue. Any and all opinions expressed herein are those of the particular author and are not necessarily those of the editor or publisher of this volume.

ISBN 978-90-411-9587-6

e-Book: ISBN 978-90-411-9588-3
web-PDF: ISBN 978-90-411-9589-0

© 2018, Kluwer Law International BV, The Netherlands

All rights reserved. No part of this publication may be reproduced, stored in a retrieval system, or transmitted in any form or by any means, electronic, mechanical, photocopying, recording, or otherwise, without the prior written permission of the publisher.

Permission to use this content must be obtained from the copyright owner. More information can be found at: lrus.wolterskluwer.com/policies/permissions-reprints-and-licensing

The Authors

Konstantinos D. Magliveras graduated from the Law School, University of Athens in 1986. He also graduated LLM from the Exeter University in 1988, LLM by research from the University of East Anglia in 1989, and DPhil from Oxford University in 1998. He was a Lecturer in Law at the Universities of Aberdeen, Sussex, and East Anglia. Currently, he is a practicing lawyer and a member of the Athens Bar Association and he teaches international law at the University of the Aegean.
Konstantinos Magliveras is the author of Parts I and II.

Gino J. Naldi graduated from the Faculty of Law, University of Birmingham in 1978. He was awarded an LLM in 1979 and a PhD in 1984, both from the University of Birmingham. He is a retired university lecturer and is currently an independent scholar in international law and human rights.
Gino Naldi is the author of Parts III to V.

The Authors

Table of Contents

Table of Contents

List of Abbreviations

AAC	African Accounting Council
ACHR	American Convention on Human Rights
ACIRC	African Capacity for Immediate Response to Crises
ACJHR	African Court of Justice and Human Rights
ACSRT	African Centre for Study and Research on Terrorism
AEC	African Economic Community
AFCAC	African Civil Aviation Commission
AFISMA	African International Support Mission in Mali
AHRLR	African Human Rights Law Reports
AIB	African Investment Bank
AIDA	Action Plan for Accelerated Industrial Development of Africa
AJIL	American Journal of International Law
ALSF	African Legal Support Facility
AMF	African Monetary Fund
AMIS	African Union Mission in Sudan
AMISEC	African Union Mission in the Comoros
AMISOM	African Union Mission in Somalia
APA	African Peace Academy
APSA	African Peace and Security Architecture
ATU	African Telecommunications Union
AU	African Union
AUBP	African Union Border Programme
AUC	African Union Commission
AUCIL	African Union Commission on International Law

AUCISS	African Union Commission of Inquiry on South Sudan
AYBIL	African Yearbook of International Law
BASE	African Bureau for Educational Sciences
BCLR	Butterworths Constitutional Law Reports
BIAT	Action Plan for Boosting Intra-Africa Trade
BLR	Botswana Law Reports
BYBIL	British Yearbook of International Law
CAADP	Comprehensive Africa Agriculture Development Program
CAR	Central African Republic
CARMMA	Accelerated Reduction of Maternal Mortality in Africa
CEDAW	UN Convention on the Elimination of Discrimination Against Women
CEMAC	Economic and Monetary Community of Central Africa
CENSAD	Community of Sahelo-Saharan States
CETS	Council of Europe Treaty Series
CFTA	Continental Free Trade Area
CILSA	Comparative and International Law Journal of Southern Africa
CJEU	Court of Justice of the European Union
CM	Organization of African Unity Council of Ministers
COMESA	Common Market for Eastern and Southern Africa
COPAX	Council for Peace and Security in Central Africa
CRC	UN Convention on the Rights of the Child
CSOs	Civil Society Organizations
CSSDCA	Conference on Security, Stability, Development and Cooperation in Africa
Doc.	Document
DRC	Democratic Republic of Congo
EAC	Extraordinary African Chambers
EC	European Community

List of Abbreviations

ECA	United Nations Economic Commission of Africa
ECCAS	Economic Community of Central African States
ECHR	European Convention for the Protection of Human Rights and Fundamental Freedoms
ECJ	European Court of Justice
ECOMIG	Economic Community of West African States' Mission in The Gambia
ECOMOG	Economic Community of West African States Monitoring Group
ECOSOC	United Nations Economic and Social Council
ECOSOCC	Economic, Social and Cultural Council
ECOWAS	Economic Community of West African States
ECR	European Court Reports
ERM	Early Response Mechanism
ETS	European Treaty Series
EU	European Union
EX	Executive Council
FY	Financial Year
HRC	Human Rights Committee
ICC	International Criminal Court
ICCPR	International Covenant on Civil and Political Rights
ICJ	International Court of Justice
ICLQ	International and Comparative Law Quarterly
IDPs	Internally Displaced Persons
IGAD	Intergovernmental Authority on Development
IGO	Intergovernmental Organization
IHRR	International Human Rights Reports
ILM	International Legal Materials
ILO	International Labour Organization
ILR	International Law Reports
JAL	Journal of African Law
LRC	Law Reports of the Commonwealth

LSAC	Labour and Social Affairs Commission
MAES	African Union Electoral and Security Assistance Mission to The Comoros
MINURCAT	UN Mission in the Central African Republic
MINURSO	UN Mission for the Referendum in Western Sahara
MINUSMA	UN Multidimensional Integrated Stabilization Mission in Mali
MISCA	International Support Mission in the Central African Republic
MONUC	UN Observer Mission in the Democratic Republic of Congo
MONUSCO	UN Organization Stabilization Mission in the DRC
MPLA	Popular Movement for the Liberation of Angola
MR	Mauritius Reports
NADAF	United Nations New Agenda for the Development of Africa in the 1990s
NEPAD	New African Partnership for Africa's Development
NGO	Non-governmental Organization
NILR	Netherlands International Law Review
NQHR	Netherlands Quarterly on Human Rights
OAU	Organization of African Unity
OECD	Organization for Economic Cooperation and Development
PAAERD	United Nations Programme of Action for African Economic Recovery and Development 1986–1990
PAIDA	New United Nations and African Union Partnership on Africa's Integration and Development Agenda
PAIPO	Pan-African Intellectual Property Organization
PANWISE	Pan-African Network of the Wise
PAP	Pan-African Parliament
PAPU	Pan-African Postal Union
PATU	Pan-African Telecommunications Union

List of Abbreviations

PIDA	Programme for Infrastructure Development in Africa
PRC	Permanent Representatives Committee
PSC	Peace and Security Council
RADIC	African Journal of International and Comparative Law
REC	Regional Economic Community
SADC	Southern African Development Community
SADR	Sahrawi Arab Democratic Republic
SCSA	Supreme Council of Sports in Africa
UDHR	Universal Declaration of Human Rights
UN	United Nations
UNAMID	United Nation-African Union Misson in Darfur
UNAOU	United Nations Office to the African Union
UNCAC	UN Convention Against Corruption
UNGA	United Nations General Assembly
UNHCR	United Nations High Commission for Refugees
UNMIS	United Nations Mission in Sudan
UNMISS	UN Mission in the Republic of South Sudan
UNSC	United Nations Security Council
UNTS	United Nations Treaty Series
ZaöRV	Zeitschrift für ausländisches öffentliches Recht und Völkerrecht
ZR	Zambia Law Reports

Preface

When our monograph 'The African Union and the predecessor Organization of African Unity' was first published in 2004, it was the only reference work which not only examined and analysed the African Union (AU) in detail but also put it into the necessary context by offering a detailed account of the Organization of African Unity (OAU) as well. Thirteen years later, it continues to be the only monograph to address the AU from an academic perspective and in an exhaustive fashion. Much has happened during this period, and there is no doubt that much more remains to be done. In May 2013, the OAU/AU commemorated its fiftieth anniversary amid fanfare about an African renaissance. Certainly, there is a cause to celebrate but the AU itself acknowledged that work was still needed in many areas, including integration, peace and security, social and economic development, and democratization.

By browsing the AU website, it becomes clear that its activities and operations have expanded considerably and have entered into new spheres of endeavour. All these changes are recorded in the present fourth edition of our monograph, which was partly rewritten to consider the many and important events and developments which have taken place in the African continent. All parts of the monograph have been revisited and updated. Indeed, in some instances, we have changed our argumentation in view of recent developments. As regards the defunct OAU, whose legacy however continues, the reader may wish to consult the first and the second editions of this monograph published in 2004 and in 2009, respectively. Our task has not been easy. Even though the AU has managed to become far more recognizable than the OAU had ever been, there is still not much legal literature on it, although certain aspects with a transnational dimension, e.g., human rights and peace and security, do attract considerable attention. Nevertheless, the relative lack of interest in the AU, its institutions, and the whole range of its activities as such is curious taking into consideration that there has been a renewal of academic interest in African affairs as a whole, especially in Europe. We believe that the AU (and for that matter the African Regional Economic Communities (RECs) as well) deserve to be examined and analysed from a range of different perspectives: institutional, political, legal, economic, financial, and social. We can only hope that the present fourth edition of our monograph is a contribution towards this goal.

The law is stated as we understood it to be in June 2017, although some subsequent events which took place until September 2017 have been recorded.

Konstantinos D. Magliveras and Gino J. Naldi

Part I. History and Evolution: From the Organization of African Unity to the African Union to the United States of Africa

1. It is a well-known fact that the countries of the African continent, with only a very few exceptions, have until recent times been occupied by foreign colonial powers. The course of African history has been and continues to be influenced to a large degree by the centuries' long foreign domination. Before the Second World War, Africa's participation on the international plane was rather negligible and only four states were members of the League of Nations: Egypt (it gained its independence from Great Britain in 1922); Abyssinia-Ethiopia (an ancient kingdom whose sovereignty was recognized when the Treaty of Wichale was concluded with Italy in May 1889; Liberia (founded in 1822, and became a republic in 1847); and the Union of South Africa (created in 1910). In the aftermath of the Second World War, these four countries remained the only independent states in Africa and three of them participated as original United Nation (UN) Members States.[1] When regional organizations were being formed in other continents in the late 1940s (in Europe, the Western European Union (WEU) in 1948 and the Council of Europe in 1949; in the Americas, the Organization of American States in 1948; in the Arab world, the League of Arab States in 1945), Africa consisted mostly of colonies. Consequently, there was no scope for political, economic or other forms of regional cooperation, not to mention integration.

2. However, the situation changed dramatically when, from the late 1950s onwards, the process of decolonization and the parallel move towards political, economic, and cultural self-determination gained momentum and swept most of Africa. The process was not completed swiftly. It took thirty-three years, from 1957, when Ghana declared its independence from Great Britain and was the first African colony to become a sovereign state, to 1990, when Namibia gained its independence from South African occupation. In the period 1957–1963, no less than thirty former colonies became sovereign states. The creation of so many new states, even though they did not share many common features other than their colonial past, did offer the necessary impetus to consider the establishment of a pan-African organization, on the one hand, as a means for consolidating achievements and, on the other hand, as an institutional vehicle for bringing about the much-cherished African unity. Although these discussions,

1. Compare Council of Ministers, *Resolution on Africa's Representation at the United Nations*, OAU Doc. CM/Res. 1 (I) (11 Aug. 1963).

which mainly took the form of ministerial conferences,[2] showed that there was agreement to promote cooperation on the continent, it also became apparent that there was no consensus on the form that it should take. Two opposing groupings surfaced: the Brazzaville Group (from which later the Monrovia Group emerged) represented by Emperor Haile Selassie of Ethiopia, and the Casablanca Group represented by President Kwame Nkrumah of Ghana. The former group, which was constituted of Cameroon, the Central African Republic (CAR), Chad, Congo, Côte d'Ivoire, Benin, Gabon, Mauritania, Madagascar, Niger, Senegal, and Upper Volta (later Burkina Faso), advocated cooperation among African states in various fields and rejected political integration. The latter group, which was composed of Ghana, Guinea, Mali, Morocco, Egypt, and the Provisional Government of Algeria, proposed the creation of a United States of Africa. This proposal was based on the idea of Pan-Africanism, which had dated from the late nineteenth and early twentieth centuries. But this was not the only area of contention among the newly independent African states. They were further divided along the lines of the former colonial power, principally in the Anglophone countries and the Francophone countries, a division that stands until today.[3] Moreover, there were serious disagreements on the issue of their borders, which the European colonial powers had drawn artificially to accommodate their own interests and in clear disregard not only of the prevailing ethnic and tribal divisions but also of obvious geographical considerations.[4]

3. Despite the divergence of opinions, there were a considerable number of issues of common interest (the principal ones being colonialism and apartheid) allowing, on 15 May 1963, the calling of a Preparatory Conference of Foreign Ministers to discuss the creation of a pan-African political organization and to draft its constitutive instrument. A week later, a Conference of the Heads of State and Government of the then thirty-two independent African states took place in Addis Ababa, Ethiopia. On 25 May 1963, the Organization of African Unity (OAU) was born and its Charter was signed by thirty states (Morocco and Togo signed it at later stage).[5] The Charter entered into force on 13 September 1963. In the Preamble, the quest for Pan-Africanism was considerably played down although the following references were made to it:

---

2. Starting in 1958, two entities had met periodically to discuss, *inter alia*, the possible association between African countries: the Conference of Independent African States and the Inter-African and Malagasy Organization. Both ceased functioning after the establishment of the OAU, since they were no longer needed; *see* H.F. Strauch, *Panafrica, kontinentale Weltmacht im Werden? Anfaenge, Wachstum und Zukunft der afrikanischen Einigungsbestrebungen*, (Zürich: Atlantis, 1964), 144 et seq. The first ever Pan-African gathering took place in Manchester, Great Britain, in 1960.
3. *See* C. Clapham, 'Boundaries and States in the New African Order' in *Regionalism in Africa – Integration and Disintegration*, ed. D. Bach (Oxford: James Currey Publishers, 1999), 53; P. Nugent & A.I. Asiwaju (eds), *African Boundaries: Barriers, Conduits and Opportunities* (London: Pinter, 1996).
4. Generally, *see* H. Cohen, *Intervening in Africa: Superpower Peacemaking in a Troubled Continent* (New York: St. Martin's Press, 2000); V. LeVine, *Politics in Francophone Africa* (Boulder, Colorado: Rienner, 2004); A. Andereggen, *France's Relationship with Sub-saharan Africa* (Westport: Praeger, 1994).
5. 479 U.N.T.S. 39; reproduced in 2 I.L.M. (1963) 766 and in G.J. Naldi (ed.), *Documents of the Organization of African Unity* (London: Mansell, 1992), 3.

> [c]o-operation among our States in response to the aspirations of our peoples for brotherhood and solidarity, in a larger unity transcending ethnic and national differences…all African States should henceforth unite so that the welfare and well-being of their peoples can be assured.

At its inception, the OAU stood on two broad premises. The first was the safeguarding and consolidation of the process for liberation, territorial integrity, and sovereignty of the participating countries and the war against neo-colonialism in all its forms. The second was the promotion of links between African states through the establishment of common organs, the two main ones being the Assembly of Heads of State and Government (the supreme organ) and the Council of Ministers (the executive organ).

4. In the 1960s, emerging Africa rested on very fragile foundations with the fight for decolonization continuing and with the newly born independent states fighting for survival, while rejecting involvement in all its forms by the former colonial powers.[6] Given this reality, the structure and the aims of the OAU were rather basic and simplistic, at least compared to other, more sophisticated, regional organizations which had already made their mark in the international society, such as the European Economic Community. Despite these limitations, the importance in creating the OAU laid in that for the first time in African history rivalries and mutual distrust were set aside and a formal institutional entity was established, without outside interference, to address and solve problems, to enhance the much-needed joint cooperation and to allow Africa to speak with one voice on the international plane.

5. Article II(1) of the OAU Charter laid down that it was guided by the following five purposes: promotion of unity and solidarity of the African states; coordination and intensification of the efforts to achieve a better life for the African peoples; defence of Member States' sovereignty, territorial integrity and independence; eradication of all forms of colonialism from the continent; and promotion of cooperation with other parts of the world having due regard to the principles enshrined in the UN Charter. To achieve these goals, Member States agreed in Article II(2) to harmonize their policies in a wide range of fields: political and diplomatic; economic (including transport and communications); educational and cultural; health and sanitation; scientific and technical; as well as defence and security.

6. These purposes were given effect through the observance of seven principles, which were enumerated in Article III and reflected the values and doctrines enshrined in Article 2 of the UN Charter: (a) sovereign equality of the entire membership; (b) non-interference in the internal affairs of other states, irrespective of whether they were Member States or not;[7] (c) respect for the sovereignty and territorial integrity of all states and for their inalienable right to independent existence; (d) settlement of disputes through the traditional peaceful means of negotiation, mediation, conciliation, and arbitration; (e) complete condemnation of political assassination and subversive activities against third countries as instruments of state policy; (f) unqualified dedication

---

6. Compare Council of Ministers, *Resolution on Africa's Non-Alignment*, OAU Doc. CM/Res. 12 (II) (29 Feb. 1964), and Assembly, *Resolution on the Interference of the Internal Affairs of African States*, OAU Doc. AHG/Res. 85 (XIV) (5 Jul. 1977).
7. A.B. Akinyemi, 'The Organization of African Unity and the Concept of Non-Interference in Internal Affairs of Member States', *BYBIL* 46 (1972/1973): 393.

to the total emancipation of those African territories under foreign rule; and (g) affirmation of the policy of non-alignment to any political, ideological or other group.

7. Although, pursuant to Article VI of the Charter, Members pledged to observe these principles scrupulously, the sad truth is that they were breached repeatedly. Through the adoption of declarations and resolutions, the Assembly of Heads of State and Government attempted to give additional credence to the above principles and to make Member States apply them regardless of the circumstances at hand. For example, in September 1967 on account of the serious disruption of Kenyan-Somali relations and Israel's partial occupation of Egypt, which at the time was part of the United Arab Republic, it reaffirmed adhesion to the principle of respect of sovereignty and Member States' territorial integrity.[8] The principle of detachment from any group was partly implemented through the participation of some OAU Member States in the Non-Alignment Movement (NAM), which had surfaced in the mid-1950s and in which Egypt was a leading participant.[9] However, following their independence, most of the states that had been under the domination of Great Britain and France participated in the associations which these countries had set up, namely the British Commonwealth (now the Commonwealth of Nations) and the French Community (Communauté française).[10] The relations with France, which had been particularly strong in the military assistance field, continued throughout the OAU days and have been maintained in the AU era.[11] On occasions, these relations have been to the detriment of the newly independent states. For example, the provisions of the Defence Agreement between, on the one hand, France and, on the other hand, the CAR, Congo (Brazzaville) and the Republic of Chad, which was concluded on 15 August 1960 and entered into force on 13 March 1961, allow France to intervene militarily in these countries and send

---

8. Respectively, *see* Assembly, *Declaration on Kenya-Somali Relations*, OAU Doc. AHG/ST. 1 (IV) and Assembly, *Declaration*, OAU Doc. AHG/ST. 2 (IV) (14 Sept. 1967). It is interesting that the latter Declaration did not name Israel as the occupying force; however later resolutions expressly referred to Israel as the aggressor state, *see* , *inter alia*, Assembly, *Resolution on the Continued Occupation by Israel of Part of the Territory of the Arab Republic of Egypt*, OAU Doc. AHG/Res. 70 (X) (28 May 1973).

9. *See* Council of Ministers, *Resolution of the Council of Foreign Ministers of Non-Aligned Countries*, OAU Doc. CM/Res. 434 (XXV) (25 Jul. 1975) proclaiming non-alignment as one of the fundamental principles of the OAU Charter. Compare Council of Ministers, *Resolution on the Forthcoming Summit Conference of the Non-Aligned Countries*, OAU Doc. CM/Res. 290 (XX) (9 Feb. 1973).

10. *See* W.H. Morris-Jones & G. Fischer (eds), *Decolonisation and After: the British and French Experience* (London: Frank Cass, 1980).Note that, as an association of nations, the French Community was officially terminated in August 1995 when, by virtue of Constitutional Act no. 95-880, the relevant provisions of the French Constitution were abrogated.

11. *See* A. Huliaras, 'Continuity and Change in French Foreign Policy Towards Africa' in *Africa in Crisis*, D. Frost, A. Thomson & T. Zack-Williams (eds) (London: Pluto Press, 2002), 161; P. Manning, *Francophone Sub-Saharan Africa 1880–1995*, 2nd edn (Cambridge: Cambridge University Press, 1999); J. Chipman, *French Power in Africa* (Oxford: Blackwell, 1989).

armed forces to them.[12] A recent example of French military involvement taking the form of intervention was *Operation Serval*, which was lodged in the northern parts of Mali on 11 January 2013.[13]

8. During the Cold War, several African states favoured the Soviet bloc and signed what amounted to security agreements with the USSR; they were rather euphemistically called 'treaties of friendship and cooperation'. Among those concluded, suffice to mention the following six: the Agreement with Egypt, which was signed on 27 May 1971; the Agreement with Somalia on 11 July 1974; the Agreement with Angola on 8 October 1976; the Agreement with Mozambique in April 1977; the Agreement with Ethiopia on 20 November 1978; and the Agreement with the People's Republic of the Congo on 13 May 1981.[14] As the balance in the international community gradually changed and new alliances were struck, some African states abrogated these Agreements, for example, Egypt on 14 March 1976 and Somalia on 13 November 1977.

9. Regarding the borders of the newly independent African states, the OAU had to make a difficult choice between maintaining those inherited from the colonial era (the principle of *uti possidetis*),[15] which did not always mirror ethnic realities, and those that could have been drawn based on equity and pragmatic needs. In the event, the OAU opted for the former solution as the last disruptive option. Thus, the principle of respect for the borders existing at independence was enshrined in the OAU legal order.[16] Although the insistence on colonial borders has led to a considerable number of interstate conflicts, African leaders have maintained that borders' inviolability is one of the 'objectives and principles of the OAU Charter'[17] and that it has 'contributed

12. Reproduced in 821 U.N.T.S. 301; *see* R. Luckham, 'French Militarism in Africa', *Review of African Political Economy* 9 (1982): 55; P. Lellouche & D. Moisi, 'French Policy in Africa: A Lonely Battle Against Destabilization', *International Security* 3 (1979): 108; and N. Bagayoko, *Security Systems in Francophone Africa*, Institute of Development Studies, University of Sussex, Research Report 64 (Brighton, May 2010) at: http://www.ids.ac.uk/files/dmfile/RR64.pdf.
13. *See* P. Melly &V. Darrace, *A New Way to Engage? French Policy in Africa from Sarkozy to Hollande* (London: Chatham House, May 2013), at: https://www.chathamhouse.org/publications/papers/view/191453.
14. *See* T.B. Millar (ed.), *Current International Treaties* (London: Croom Helm, 1984), 474 et seq; K. Somerville, 'The U.S.S.R. and Southern Africa since 1976', *The J. of Modern African Studies* 22 (1984): 73; R.E. Bissell, 'Soviet Military Aid to Africa', *Journal of Contemporary African Studies* 1 (1981): 1; and C. Coker, 'Adventurism and Pragmatism: The Soviet Union, Comecon, and Relations with African States', *Intl Affairs* 57 (1981): 618. For the Agreement with Egypt, *see* 798 U.N.T.S. 184.
15. *See* S.R. Ratner, 'Drawing a Better Line: Uti Possidetis and the Borders of New States', *AJIL* 90 (1996): 590; and S. Lalonde, *Determining Boundaries in a Conflicted World: The Role of Uti Possidetis* (Montreal: McGill-Queen's University Press, 2002), 103 et seq.
16. *See* Assembly, *Borders Disputes among African States*, OAU Doc. AHG/Res. 16 (I) adopted by the First Ordinary Session in July 1964; reproduced in Naldi, *Documents*, 49. Generally, *see* S. Touval, 'The Organization of African Unity and African Borders', *International Organization* 21 (1967): 102; and R.H. Payne, 'Divided Tribes: A Discussion of African Boundary Problems', *New York University Journal of International Law & Policy* 2 (1968): 243.
17. *See* Assembly, *Cairo Declaration on the OAU Mechanism for Conflict Prevention, Management and Resolution*, OAU Doc. AHG/Decl. 3 (XXIX) at para. 14 (30 Jun. 1993).

decisively' to preserving peace and stability.[18] The principle of *uti possidetis* has found express recognition in the *Frontier Dispute Case (Burkina Faso/Mali)*, where the International Court of Justice (ICJ) held that '[i]ts obvious purpose is to prevent the independence and stability of new States being endangered by fratricidal struggles provoked by the challenging of frontiers following the withdrawal of the administering power'.[19] Finally, respect of borders as they existed at on independence was laid down as one of the basic principles of the AU.

10. Many and complex conflicts and disputes between African states plagued the OAU and have continued to pose a challenge for the AU. At a Ministerial Conference on Africa held on 25 September 1997, the UN Security Council noted this fact and expressed its grave concern at the number and intensity of conflicts.[20] The following intra-state and interstate discords, frictions and armed hostilities exemplify this state of affairs.[21] Already in the first years of the OAU's existence, border disputes erupted, on the one hand, between Algeria and Morocco and, on the other hand, between Somalia, Ethiopia and Kenya. The latter lasted until 1967[22] but re-emerged in the 1970s. In 1973, a serious controversy between Rwanda and Burundi broke out, a typical result of the way colonial borders had been drawn. In 1977–1978, insurgents from Angola invaded part of Zaïre, Libya occupied Northern Chad[23] and there was an outbreak of hostilities between Ethiopia and Somalia[24] but also between Ethiopia and Sudan; in the latter case an Ad Hoc Mediation Committee was set up.[25] Moreover, serious disputes erupted between Guinea and Côte d'Ivoire and between Guinea and Senegal.[26] In 1978, the overthrow of Idi Amin of Uganda was partly achieved through the invasion of Uganda by Tanzania (October 1978–April 1979), which led to armed hostilities that lasted until 1981. This incident marked the first time in the OAU's history that a Member State had invaded another in clear disrespect of at least three of the Charter principles: non-interference in the internal affairs of third states, respect

18. *See* Assembly, *Algiers Declaration*, OAU Doc. AHG/Decl. 1 (XXXV) (14 Jul. 1999).
19. ICJ Reports 1986, 554, para. 20 at p. 565.
20. UN Press Release SC/6465 (25 Sept. 1997). The complexity of some of these conflicts is best evidenced by the fact that the UN has set up a Standing Advisory Committee on Security Questions in Central Africa (UNSAC), which met for its forty-second ministerial meeting in 9 Jun. 2016, *see* UN Press Release SG/SM/17833-AFR/3395 (9 Jun. 2016), and for its forty-fourth ministerial meeting on 29 May 2017. For a previous Report on the Committee's activity, *see* UN Doc. A/68/603–S/2013/675 (18 Nov. 2013).
21. Generally, *see* B. Boutros Ghali, *Les conflits de frontières en Afrique (études et documents)* (Paris: Editions techniques et économiques, 1973).
22. *See* Assembly, *Declaration on Kenya-Somali Relations*, OAU Doc. AHG/ST. 1 (IV) (14 Sept. 1967) recording the undertaking of these states to resolve their differences.
23. Assembly, *Resolution on the Libya/Chad Dispute*, OAU Doc. AHG/Res. 94 (XV) (22 Jul. 1978).
24. Assembly, *Resolution on the Somalia/Ethiopia Conflict*, OAU Doc. AHG/Res. 90 (XV) (22 Jul. 1978). Generally, *see* G. Tareke, 'The Ethiopia-Somalia War 1977 Revisited', *International Journal of African Historical Studies* 33 (2000): 635.
25. Assembly, *Resolution on the Somalia/Sudan Dispute*, OAU Doc. AHG/Res. 97 (XVI) Rev. 1 (20 Jul. 1979). Generally, *see* S. Peterson, *Me Against My Brother: At War in Somalia, Sudan and Rwanda* (London: Routledge, 2001).
26. Assembly, *Resolution on Reconciliation between Guinea, Ivory Coast and Senegal*, OAU Doc. AHG/Res. 88 (XV) (22 Jul. 1978).

of sovereignty and territorial integrity, and unreserved condemnation of subversive activities on the part of neighbouring countries. In 1994–1995, conflict situations exploded in Burundi, Somalia, Liberia, Sierra Leone. The genocide in Rwanda also took place. Between 1996 and 1998, there were clashes between Eritrea, Ethiopia and Sudan, while between 1997 and 2000 significant armed hostilities erupted between Ethiopia and Eritrea over border disputes.[27] The latter were terminated by the Agreement of 12 December 2000, which, faithful to the principle of employing peaceful means for the settlement of disputes, established a Boundary Commission and a Claims Commission to adjudicate bilateral claims. The Claims Commission rendered its final award on damages on 17 August 2009. The Boundary Commission issued its decision on delimitation on 13 April 2002, which however does not seem to have been implemented by the two states.[28] Since 2004, the conflict in the Niger Delta has resulted in human loss, while armed clashes at the Djiboutian–Eritrean border in June 2008[29] exemplified that not all matters concerning African borders have been dealt with, especially when, like in this case, the applicable boundary agreement dates from 1900. It is instructive to note that in the twenty-first century the ICJ has given judgments on and/or has heard a considerable number of cases concerning African border disputes, including the following (in chronological order). First, a case concerning the land and maritime boundaries between Cameroon and Nigeria.[30] Second, a disagreement between Benin and Niger concerning the River Niger.[31] Third, a dispute concerning the frontier between Burkina Faso and Niger.[32] Finally, in August 2014, Somalia instituted proceedings against Kenya regarding a maritime delimitation dispute in the Indian Ocean.[33]

11. The OAU was rather ineffective in preventing and solving interstate conflicts and domestic unrest. Arguably, from its inception the Organization was ill-equipped to undertake such missions and to fulfil such roles. Even though under Article XIX of the Charter, Member States had pledged to settle all their disputes by peaceful means and primarily through the Commission of Mediation, Conciliation and Arbitration, this organ never became functional. Fresh impetus to this aspect of the OAU's role was given in June 1993 by means of the Cairo Declaration on the Establishment of a Mechanism for Conflict Prevention, Management and Resolution, which carried out its functions with relative success. It was replaced in early 2004 when the Peace and

---

27. Assembly, *Dispute between Ethiopia and Eritrea*, OAU Doc. AHG/Dec. 130 (XXXIV) (10 June 1998); and Assembly, *Decision on the Conflict between Ethiopia and Eritrea*, OAU Doc. AHG/Dec. 144 (XXXVI) (12 Jul. 2000). Generally, *see* N. Tekeste & K. Tronvall, *Brothers at War: Making Sense of the Eritrean-Ethiopian War* (Oxford: Currey, 2000).
28. UNSC, *Report of the Secretary-General on Ethiopia and Eritrea*, UN Doc. S/2008/40 (23 Jan. 2008) para. 26 and Annex II.
29. A UNSC Statement condemned Eritrea's military action, *see* UN Doc.S/PV.5908, 12 Jun. 2008, p. 2.
30. *See Land and Maritime Boundary between Cameroon and Nigeria* (*Cameroon v. Nigeria*; Equatorial Guinea intervening), Judgment of 10 Oct. 2002, [2002] ICJ Reports 303.
31. *See Frontier Dispute* (*Benin v. Niger*), Judgment of 12 Jul. 2005, I.C.J. Reports 2005, 90.
32. *See Frontier Dispute* (*Burkina Faso v. Niger*), Judgment of 16 Apr. 2013, I.C.J. Reports 2013, 44.
33. *See Maritime Delimitation in the Indian Ocean* (*Somalia v. Kenya*),ICJ Press Release 2014/27, 28 Aug. 2014. A judgment on preliminary objections was handed down in February 2017 finding that the ICJ had jurisdiction to entertain Somalia's application.

Security Council (PSC) of the AU became operative. Even though the Preamble of the OAU Charter referred to the aspiration of African peoples for brotherhood and solidarity (it was repeated in the Preamble of the AU Constitutive Act as the 'noble ideals which guided the founding fathers' of the OAU), the sad truth is that African leaders have chosen to disregard these principles when it has so suited them.

12. Moreover, the OAU had been confronted with a seemingly never-ending series of coups d'état. Even in these instances, the Organization showed that it did not have the capacity or the willingness to intervene. Its usual justification for inactivity was that the unconstitutional overthrow of governments amounted to domestic matters and the OAU could not intervene even if the life of the population was at stake (and invariably it was). This justification emerged from the following two facts: (a) Member States adhered slavishly to the Charter principle of non-interference in the internal affairs of other states; and (b) they usually chose to ignore the serious repercussions of coups d'état not only for the countries involved but also for the neighbouring countries and the African continent at large. For it is a fact that coups d'état are (with only limited exemptions) accompanied by human rights abuses, maladministration and breakdowns in civil society. The OAU attitude was officially reversed during the Thirty-Fifth Ordinary Assembly Session (Algiers, July 1999), which rejected coups d'état as unacceptable and anachronistic acts. The following year, the Assembly adopted the Declaration on the Framework for an OAU Response to Unconstitutional Change of Government, which was a framework for collective response against any regime that had come into power by force instead of being elected through the applicable constitutional procedure. The irony was of course that some of the African leaders who were so eager to condemn them had seized power in coups d'état themselves!

13. Despite the rather ineffective role that the OAU played in conflict resolution, it had considerable success in several other areas, principally, in decolonization and in eradicating racial discrimination and apartheid. For the OAU, decolonization and apartheid were not separate concerns but two interrelated issues, which, as was stated in the Declaration adopted on 1973 on the OAU's tenth anniversary, could be solved by either peaceful means or by military confrontation:

> The liberation of those areas under colonial and racist domination can be achieved either by peaceful means or by armed struggle...we would prefer to achieve our objectives by peaceful means if that were possible. But whether the solution takes the form of intensified military confrontation or negotiations would entirely depend on the response of the racist and colonialist regimes.[34]

Ten years later, in 1984, the OAU repeated the talk of an armed confrontation against the racist African states, but this time the issue was downplayed:

> In the light of the intransigence, ruthlessness, and consistent brutality of the Apartheid regime, both within South Africa and Namibia, we uphold the right of the Liberation Movements and the people they lead to take up arms in pursuance of the struggle for freedom. We continue to express our preference for a peaceful

---

34. *See* Assembly, *Solemn Declaration on General Policy*, OAU Doc. CM/ST. 9 (XXI) (25 May 1973).

> resolution of the Namibian and South African questions as stated in the Lusaka Manifesto. But we are convinced that the peaceful negotiations can only succeed when the Pretoria regime had convincingly demonstrated its acceptance of both the principle and the inevitability of majority rule. One such demonstration would be the unconditional release of imprisoned Liberation Movement leaders, and the subsequent negotiation with the genuine representatives of the South African and Namibian peoples.[35]

It should be noted that the compatibility of the military solution contained in the above references with the UN Charter has been a matter of some contention.[36] In its first year of operation, the OAU established the Coordinating Committee for the Liberation of Africa as a subsidiary organ.[37] Its purpose was to organize diplomatic support for the various liberation movements, which were active in colonized territories, and to channel financial, military, and logistical aid to them. The Assembly dissolved the Liberation Committee in June 1994, even though the continent had been largely decolonized much earlier.[38] Financial assistance to the liberation movements was provided through a Special Fund, which was also set up in 1963 and was maintained by Members States' voluntary contributions. The Fund targeted, *inter alia*, the liberation struggle in Guinea-Bissau, in Angola, and in Mozambique. The OAU internationalized the fight for decolonization, especially in the context of the UN. Thus, in the case of the occupation of Namibia by South Africa, OAU Member States were successful in having judicial action initiated before the ICJ.[39] In the struggle against apartheid, the contribution of the OAU was of pivotal significance. One of its major accomplishments was the sponsoring of the World Conference for Action against Apartheid in 1977, which adopted the Lagos Declaration for Action against Apartheid.[40] The Conference not

35. Assembly, *Declaration on Southern Africa made by the Assembly of Heads of State and Government of the Organization of African Unity*, OAU Doc. AHG/DECL. 1 (XX) (15 Nov. 1984).
36. Generally, *see* C. Dugard, 'The Organization of African Unity and Colonialism: An Inquiry into the Plea of Self-Defence as a Justification for the Use of Force in the Eradication of Colonialism', *ICLQ* 16 (1967): 157; and A. Bikare, *The Compatibility with the United Nations Charter of Support by the Organization of African Unity of Wars of Liberation*, Thesis (John Hopkins University, 1974).
37. OAU Doc. CIAS/Plen.2/Rev.2 (25 Jun. 1963).
38. Assembly, *Resolution on Dissolution of the OAU Liberation Committee*, OAU Doc. AHG/Res. 228 (XXX) (15 Jun. 1994). Note that the AU position is that the United Kingdom continues the unlawful occupation of the Chagos Archipelago denying Mauritius the exercise of its sovereignty over it, Assembly, *Resolution on Chagos Archipelago*, AU Doc. Assembly/AU/Res. 1 (XXV) (15 Jun. 2015). A similar position exists as regards the island of Réunion in the Indian Ocean and France.
39. *See Legal Consequences for States of the Continued Presence of South Africa in Namibia (South West Africa) Notwithstanding Security Council Resolution 276 (1970)*, Advisory Opinion of 21 Jun. 1971, I.C.J. Reports 1971, 16. The Advisory Opinion was requested by the Security Council, whose Res. 276 (1970) of 29 Jul. 1970 had declared that the continued presence of South Africa in the territory of Namibia was illegal and, consequently, all acts taken by its government on behalf of Namibia were invalid.
40. *See Report of the World Conference for Action Against Apartheid*, Lagos, 22–26 Aug. 1977 (New York: United Nations, 1977).

only condemned racial discrimination and segregation but also recognized the legitimate aspirations of the South African population and committed governments to provide support for the liberation movements, which were officially accepted by the OAU. Two years later, the OAU created an ad hoc committee on Southern Africa to mobilize international diplomatic action against the pariah states, namely South Africa and Southern Rhodesia, and to exert pressure on them to abolish the apartheid policies. This entity aligned with the UN Special Committee against Apartheid, which had been set up in 1962 by virtue of General Assembly Resolution 1761(XVII).[41]

14. Although the activities of the OAU were by no means exhausted with decolonization and apartheid, they constituted fundamental aspects of its operations and, even more importantly, they served as themes unifying the whole membership. Suffice to mention the declaration of independence by Zimbabwe in 1980, the achievement of independence by Namibia in March 1990 and the transition to a multiracial and democratic society in the Republic of South Africa in 1994. Undoubtedly, the OAU had not reached the end of its life, for too much work was still required to bring about what the Preamble of the Charter referred to as 'the total advancement of our peoples in all spheres of human endeavour'. In the closing years of the 1990s, African leaders were confronted with many and pressing questions, which, although they could have already been asked, the developments on the international arena had made them more imperative than ever: Had the OAU outlived its usefulness? Could the OAU address effectively the challenges presented by both the post-Cold War age and globalization? Could the OAU enhance Africa's role in an extremely competitive international community? Could the OAU advance social and economic development? Could the OAU promote human rights and democratic reform? These and similar questions were put on the table during the Thirty-Fifth Ordinary Assembly Session, which took place in Algiers in July 1999. It was decided to hold a session specifically dealing with the revitalization of the OAU.[42] The implementation of this proposal came from the least expected quarter: Colonel Muammar Gaddafi, who breaking away from self-imposed alienation in the Organization that had lasted for some twenty years, re-emerged dynamically in the affairs of the continent and invited all African leaders to Libya for deliberations.[43] Gaddafi's plan was grand: the creation of a United States of Africa with a single army, a single currency, and a powerful leadership, which in the initial phase would be entrusted to him. On 8–9 September 1999, the Fourth Extraordinary Assembly Session took place in Sirte, Libya under the theme 'Strengthening OAU Capacity to Enable it to Meet the Challenges of the New Millennium.' Gaddafi's plan did not find favour with Thabo Mbeki, the then President of the Republic of South

41. UNGA Res. 1761(XVII) of 6 November 1962 'on the politics of apartheid of the Government of the Republic of South Africa', para. 5.
42. *See* Assembly, *Decision on the Convening of an Extraordinary Session of the OAU Assembly of Heads of State and Government in accordance with Article 33(5) of its Rules of Procedure*, OAU Doc. AHG/Dec. 140 (XXXV) (14 Jul. 1999).
43. For Libya's comeback, *see* A. Huliaras, 'Qadhafi's Comeback: Libya and Sub-Saharan Africa in the 1990s' *African Affairs* 100 (2001): 5; and Y. Romen, 'Libya's Diplomatic Success in Africa: The Reemergence of Quadhafi on the International Stage' *Diplomacy and Statecraft* 13 (2002): 235.

Africa, who persuaded most of the other leaders to restrict the Session's agenda to revising the OAU Charter to increase efficiency and effectiveness.

15. This was not the first time that the OAU's streamlining had been seriously debated. Attempts had also taken place in 1975[44] and in 1979. In the latter case, the Sixteenth Ordinary Assembly Session (Monrovia, 17–20 July 1979) established a fourteen-member Committee on the Review of the Charter as a subsidiary organ operating within the Secretariat.[45] Its terms of reference were the overhaul of the Organization so as to meet the challenges brought about by the changing international arena and developments in the continent, for example the collapse of dictatorial regimes, the first universal-franchise election in Zimbabwe, the UN plan for self-determination in Namibia, etc. The Committee failed to formulate substantive amendments to the OAU Charter, even though its membership had almost doubled.[46] However, several proposals were successfully carried forward, which, in their turn, led to concrete initiatives. The most notable is the Cairo Declaration Establishing the Mechanism for Conflict Prevention, Management and Resolution, reference to which is made later in the text.

16. At the aforementioned Sirte Extraordinary Session, African leaders sponsored the namesake Declaration, which set out the following aims, most of which centred on the welfare of African peoples:

- to address in an effective manner the new social, political and economic realities as they were emerging both in Africa and in the world;
- to fulfil the African peoples' aspirations for greater unity, as envisaged in the OAU Charter but also in the Treaty establishing the African Economic Community (AEC);
- to revitalize the OAU and to enhance its role to meet the needs of African peoples;
- to eliminate the scourge of conflicts; and
- to harness the human and natural resources of the continent to improve living conditions.[47]

17. The importance of the Sirte Declaration lies in the fact that these aims were not to be realized within the context of the OAU. On the contrary, it was decided to establish a new entity, to be called the 'African Union.' No doubt, the title was coined after the European Union (EU) and its success record which the new pan-African Organization would have liked to emulate. It was further resolved that the AU's guiding principles would be in conformity with the ultimate objectives enshrined in the OAU Charter and in the Treaty establishing AEC. Thus, in Sirte, the Member States declared

44. *See* Council of Ministers, *Resolution on the Establishment of an* Ad Hoc *Committee for the Structured Reform of the OAU*, OAU Doc. CM/Res. 386 (XXIV) (21 Feb. 1975).
45. OAU Doc. AHG/Dec. 111 (XVI) Rev. 1 (20 Jul. 1979).
46. Assembly, *Resolution on the Composition of the Charter Review Committee*, OAU Doc. AHG/Res. 152 (XXII) (30 Jul. 1986), as proposed by the Council of Ministers, *Resolution on the Composition of the Charter Review Committee*, OAU Doc. CM/Res. 1041 (XLIV) (26 Jul. 1986).
47. Assembly, *Sirte Declaration*, OAU Doc. EAHG/Draft/Decl. (IV) Rev.1, at paras 5, 6 and 8 (9 Sept. 1999), reproduced in RADIC 11 (1999): 803.

that the OAU, as originally conceived in the early 1960s, could no longer have served the continent's needs and aspirations and decided to replace it with another, more dynamic, organization capable of safeguarding its achievements and promoting Africa's role in the perplexing and demanding twenty-first century. Yet the AEC was not to be replaced and the Sirte Declaration stipulated that measures had to be taken to accelerate its implementation, including the shortening of the transitory periods envisaged in the Abuja Treaty; the prompt establishment of all organs envisaged therein and especially the Pan-African Parliament (PAP); and the strengthening and consolidation of the African Regional Economic Communities (RECs).

18. It follows that the new organization was not conceived as an 'umbrella' institution with an expanded mandate under which the OAU and the AEC would merge and be given a renewed mandate. In other words, it was not a case akin to the creation of the EU in the early 1990s, where the European (Economic) Community comprised one of its three constituent pillars. African leaders could be criticized for not exploring this avenue at Sirte, especially if the lagging performance of the AEC were to be taken into full account. Although, as is made apparent in Part III of this monograph, the AU commenced its operations with a significant degree of dynamism, the AEC continued its rather aimless course. African states abandoned their economic integration efforts through the AEC and have recently explored other avenues to create a Continental Free Trade Area (CFTA).

19. The task of drafting the AU Constitutive Act was undertaken by a working group comprising lawyers, political scientists, and economists. Its task did not only include offering solutions to such issues as the smooth transition from the OAU to the AU and the functional relationship between the AU organs and those existing in the OAU structure but also the incorporation into the AU of policies, which had been agreed by OAU Summits but had never been implemented. The Republic of South Africa played a significant role in the drafting of the Constitutive Act, which was done in record time by international standards. The insertion of provisions on human rights, the rule of law and democratic principles should be attributed to South Africa. This was a rather risky endeavour, since several regimes (including Libya) had been maintained in power by negating these very rights and principles to their populations. Nevertheless, the Constitutive Act was promptly placed before the Thirty-Sixth Ordinary Assembly Session, which met in Lomé, Togo between 10 and 12 July 2000. Despite some apparent inadequacies in its text, it was approved without many changes.[48] If nothing else, this showed the determination of African leaders to break away from the discredited OAU and to start a new page in their cooperation.

20. The haste to create the AU was also revealed during the Fifth Extraordinary Assembly Session (Sirte, 2 March 2001), which proclaimed its establishment even though at the time the Constitutive Act had not yet entered into force.[49] To declare the advent of a new international organization when its Charter has not come into effect and when there are no provisions on its interim operation during the ratification period is virtually unknown in international law. In particular, Article 28 of the Constitutive

48. 2158 U.N.T.S. 3, reproduced in Appendix I of this monograph, in RADIC 12 (2000): 629, and in RADIC 13 (2005): 25. For analysis, *see* K. Magliveras & G. Naldi, 'The African Union – A New Dawn for Africa?', *ICLQ* 51 (2002): 415.

49. Assembly, *Decision on the African Union*, OAU Doc. EAHG/Dec. 1 (V) (2 Mar. 2001).

Act stipulated that it would enter into force thirty days following the deposit of instruments of ratification by at least two-thirds of OAU Members (i.e., by thirty-six states). On 26 April 2001, Nigeria became the thirty-sixth Member State to do so and, consequently, the Act came into force on 26 May 2001. The actual date of the AU's establishment requires some clarification, as there would appear to be two relevant dates: 2 March 2001 (the day the declaration of establishment was adopted) or 26 May 2001 (the day the Constitutive Act entered into force from a legal point of view). It is submitted that the latter date should be accepted, not least because said declaration was a political act of an undisputed important symbolic character but had no legal consequences from an institutional point of view. The official lodging of the AU was effected in July 2002 when the Inaugural Session of the Assembly took place in Durban, South Africa (*infra* paragraphs 60–61).

21. There can be no doubt that, by deciding to establish the AU, the Member States did not aim at setting up a new institution that was going to be a mere continuation of the OAU by another name. In the words of the OAU Secretary General: '[African leaders] certainly had in mind an organization that would provide a framework for enhanced cohesion, cooperation, integration and strengthened capacity to deal with the crises that face the African continent today.'[50] At the Inaugural Assembly Session, African statesmen 'rededicated' themselves more determinedly to the OAU principles and objectives, 'pledged' to strive more resolutely in pursuing its ultimate goals, and 'reiterated' their commitment to achieving the AU objectives.[51]

22. Fourteen years after inauguration, the AU has made its distinctive mark and the fears that it would be a repetition of the old organization have not materialized. For many years now, the creation answering to the name 'OAU' has been laid to rest. The AU has managed to transform the way African affairs are conducted, although it is true to say that much more has been achieved in areas such as peace and security and considerably less in other areas such as free trade and economic integration, even though the work undertaken in the context of NEPAD, AGENDA 2063, and the Continental Free Trade Agreement, which are examined later in the monograph, should not be underestimated. There is no doubt that a number of favourite conditions have contributed to the important changes achieved over this period. Suffice to mention that most of the continent has enjoyed economic growth at accelerated rates, that the high global prices for the raw materials and commodities produced in Africa have led to increased income for the governments, while the Foreign Direct Investments (FDI) coming not only from Europe and the United States but also from the so-called BRIC countries (Brazil, Russia, India, and China) have been on the rise.[52] At the same time, relations with the former colonial powers and with the EU at large have entered a new phase and a small number of African states (including South Africa, Nigeria, and Libya) have attempted to make their presence felt on the international plane. However,

---

50. *See* Secretary General, *Report of the Secretary-General on the Implementation of the Sirte Decision on the African Union*, OAU Doc. CM/2210 (LXXIV), para. 26 at p. 10 (2001).
51. Assembly, *Durban Declaration in Tribute to the Organization of African Unity and on the Occasion of the Launching of the African Union*, AU Doc. ASS/AU/Decl. 2 (I) (12 Jul. 2002), paras 14 and 15, reproduced in I.L.M. 41 (2002): 1029.
52. J.C. Anyanwu, 'Why Does Foreign Direct Investment Go Where It Goes?: New Evidence From African Countries', *Annals of Economics and Finance* 13 (2012): 425.

for a combination of reasons, including persisting ethnic problems, the recent fall in the prices of commodities and crude oil, the inability to accept and maintain democratic ideals and the rule of law, etc. the much-cherished African renaissance – has still not been materialized. Mentioned for the first time by Nelson Mandela during the Thirtieth Ordinary OAU Assembly Session (Tunis, 13–15 June 1994),[53] the concept of renaissance has been popularized by former President Thabo Mbeki of South Africa as being the third stage in the evolution of post-colonial Africa, the first two being decolonization, and the promotion of democratization.[54] However, the term is used here in a rather different context: with many an African leader of the old generation ousted, the new generation of leaders should pursue collective efforts to create the necessary conditions for breaking away from the ankyloses of the past. This will allow the continent to catch up with the rest of the world and free itself from all kinds of outside interferences and interventions.

23. What follows is a synopsis, in chronological order, of some of the most important events in the history of the OAU and of the AU.[55] It records milestones in the development and evolution of the two institutions, moments of triumph but also of defeat, the various multilateral agreements and other instruments negotiated and adopted under their auspices as well as other events that directly or indirectly have had consequences for their evolution. This record of affairs is based primarily on the work of the Assembly of Heads of State and Government, the highest-ranking organ and policy-making organ and, where pertinent, on the work of other organs as well. Most of the events and documents cited in the following paragraphs are examined and analysed elsewhere in the present monograph. Finally, the current status of the African multilateral treaties and agreements is also noted.

24. Immediately after the establishment of the OAU in 1963, the Coordinating Committee for the Liberation of Africa, the entity responsible for streamlining the efforts for the independence of the territories still under foreign domination, was set up. Moreover, citing Portugal's and South Africa's non-compliance with United Nations Security Council (UNSC) and United Nations General Assembly (UNGA) resolutions on the issue of apartheid and racial discrimination, African leaders resolved to boycott their goods and products and cease the supply of minerals to them.[56] In the First Ordinary Session of the OAU Assembly (Cairo, 17–21 July 1964), African leaders reaffirmed their pledge to the principle of strict observance for the colonial boundaries that were inherited at independence,[57] chose Addis Ababa, Ethiopia and not Accra, Ghana as the organization's headquarters,[58] and established a sub-committee within

53. *See* M. Meredith, *The State of Africa: A History of Fifty Years of Independence* (London: Free Press, 2005), 676 et seq.

54. Thabo Mbeki, *Statement on African Renaissance*, 13 August 1998, at: http://www.unisa.ac.za. Generally, *see* UN Economic and Social Council, *The African Renaissance and the Challenge of Globalization*, UN Doc. E/C.12/2001/WP.1 (2 Mar. 2001).

55. For a more detailed chronology of OAU until the early 1990s, *see* G. Harris, *The Organization of African Unity*, World Bibliographical Series/International Organizations Series, Vol. 7 (Oxford: Clio Press, 1994).

56. Council of Ministers, *Portuguese Colonialism and Apartheid in South Africa*, OAU Doc. CM/Res. 6 (1) (11 Aug. 1963).

57. Assembly, *Border Disputes Among African States*, OAU Doc. AHG/Res. 16 (I) (21 Jul. 1964).

58. Assembly, OAU Doc. AHG/Res. 2 (I) (21 Jul. 1964).

the Secretariat to promote the campaign for economic sanctions against South Africa.[59] Moreover, the person in charge of Angola's National Liberation Front (FNLA) was recognized as the country's legitimate leader,[60] a decision that later caused considerable problems to the smooth functioning of the OAU. Finally, the Protocol establishing the Commission of Mediation, Conciliation and Arbitration, which had been envisaged in Article XIX of the OAU Charter, was adopted and became an integral part of the Charter. Eight French-speaking Member States abstained from the Second Ordinary Assembly Session (Accra, 21–26 October 1965) in protest at the policy of the host state's leader to lend support to rebellious elements in their territories. At the same Session, the Declaration on the Problem of Subversion was adopted, which, *inter alia*, condemned every form of subversion conceived, organized or financed by foreign powers against the OAU and its Member States.[61] On 11 November 1965, the white supremacy regime in Rhodesia (today's Zimbabwe) unilaterally proclaimed its independence as a sovereign state. Even before this declaration of independence, the Assembly had called upon all states and international organizations to withhold recognition of the 'European minority government.'[62] The United Kingdom, the Commonwealth, and the UNs regarded the declaration as illegal, while the UNs imposed the first ever economic sanctions in its history on the former British colony.

25. The Third Ordinary Assembly Session (Addis Ababa, 5–9 November 1966) took no decisions of note. However, the Council of Ministers, the OAU's executive arm, during its Seventh Ordinary Session (Addis Ababa, 31 October–4 November 1966) condemned Rhodesia's proclamation of independence, called upon all Member States and third states to withhold recognition, and strongly condemned 'Britain for her refusal to crush the Southern Rhodesian rebel regime.'[63] On the question of South West Africa (Namibia), the Council considered that the continued domination by South Africa constituted 'an illegal military occupation of an African sister country'.[64] The following year, the OAU was confronted with the Biafran secessionist war in Nigeria. Owing to the serious split between its Member States on whether or not to recognize the self-declared independent state of Biafra (Eastern Nigeria) and their concern to avoid balkanization at a time when the political map of Africa was still being shaped, the Fourth Ordinary Assembly Session (Kinshasa, 11–14 September 1967) considered that the situation was an internal affair and aligned itself with Nigeria's territorial

---

59. Assembly, *Apartheid and Racial Discrimination*, OAU Doc. AHG/Res. 6 (I) (21 Jul. 1964).
60. Assembly, *The Revolutionary Government of Angola in Exile and the Popular Liberation Movement of Angola (MPLA)*, OAU Doc. AHG/Res. 18 (I) (21 Jul. 1964).
61. Assembly, *Declaration on the Problem of Subversion*, OAU Doc. AHG/Res. 27 (II) (25 Oct. 1965).
62. Assembly, *Southern Rhodesia*, OAU Doc. AHG/Res. 25 (II) (25 Oct. 1965).
63. Council of Ministers, *Resolution on Southern Rhodesia*, OAU Doc. CM/Res. 78 (VII) (4 Nov. 1966).
64. Council of Ministers, *Resolution on South West Africa*, OAU Doc. CM/Res. 87 (VII) (4 Nov. 1966).

integrity and unity of.[65] The same Session adopted the Phyto-Sanitary Convention for Africa to prevent the introduction of diseases, insect pests and other threats to plants into Africa. The Convention is quite unique in the sense that it does not contain any provisions about its entry into force; although a single Member State never signed it, it has received ten ratifications (lastly by Burundi in October 1992).

26. Already in 1967, several unresolved incidents, including the border disputes between Somalia, Kenya, and Ethiopia, which had by now lasted almost four years,[66] and the continuing presence of foreign mercenaries in Zaïre (Democratic Republic of Congo (DRC)), had resulted in what was described as the 'crumbling image' of the OAU. In 1967, the Secretariat established the Board of Refugees, which together with the Commission for Refugees, dealt with massive human dislocations in Africa.[67] In 1968, Nigeria was reconciled with those Members supporting secessionist Biafra and the first constitutional crisis in the OAU's history ended. On 15 September 1968, the African Convention on Conservation of Nature and Natural Resources was adopted. It came into effect on 16 June 1969. So far, thirty-two Member States have ratified it (latterly by Guinea in May 2012) and it is interesting to note that it still being signed, e.g., by Equatorial Guinea in January 2011, by Guinea-Bissau in January 2012 and by South Sudan in January 2013. In January 1969, the Constitution of the African Civil Aviation Commission (AFCAC) was opened for signature. It entered into force on 15 March 1972. By the time a Revised Constitution was adopted on 16 December 2009, forty-four Member States had ratified and/or acceded to it. When the Revised Constitution entered into force provisionally on 11 May 2010, the old Constitution was abrogated and superseded. Therefore, the fact that Equatorial Guinea signed the 1969 Constitution on 31 January 2011, by Guinea-Bissau on 27 January 2012 and by South Sudan on 24 January 2013 was probably a procedural mistake, especially since the latter two states signed on the same day the Revised Constitution as well. The Revised Constitution shall enter into force definitely when ratified by fifteen Member States; so far it has had secured only six ratifications (lastly by Cape Verde in September 2015). In January 2017, the AU Assembly adopted an amendment to Article 10(4) of the (Revised) Constitution of AFCAC.[68]

In April 1969, fifteen East and Central African countries issued the Lusaka Manifesto on the Future of southern Africa.[69] The Manifesto was subsequently adopted

65. African leaders reiterated their condemnation of secession in Member States and pointed out that the solution to the present problem is the responsibility of Nigerians themselves, Assembly, OAU Doc. AHG/Res. 51 (IV) (14 Sept. 1967); note that this Resolution did not have a title. *See also* Assembly, *Resolution on Nigeria*, OAU Doc. AHG/Res. 54 (V) (16 Sept. 1968). For the OAU mediation in the Nigerian civil war (1967–1970), *see* T. Princen, *Intermediaries in International Conflict* (Princeton: Princeton University Press, 1992), 186.

66. Assembly, *Declaration on Kenya-Somali Relations*, OAU Doc. AHG/ST. 1 (14 Sept. 1967).

67. Generally, *see* M. Sharpe, 'Organization of African Unity and African Union Engagement with Refugee Protection: 1963–2011', *RADIC* 21 (2013): 50.

68. Assembly, *Decision on the Draft Legal Instruments*, AU Doc. Assembly/AU/Dec. 636 (XXVIII), para. 2 (31 Jan. 2017).

69. For the text with commentary, *see The African Review* (1971): 66; *see* further *African Affairs* 69 (1970): 180.

by the OAU and guided its stance towards South Africa.[70] Moreover, UNGA Resolution 2505(XXIV) of 20 November 1969, brought the Manifesto 'to the attention of all States and of all peoples'. In the meantime, the Council of Ministers, by suggesting that all liberation movements should be required to form a common fighting front and that no assistance be extended to those movements not recognized by the OAU, had indicated that the African struggle against decolonization and racial discrimination had to be under OAU auspices.[71] Finally, on 10 September 1969, the Convention Governing the Specific Aspects of Refugee Problems in Africa was adopted as an effective regional complement to the UN Convention Relating to the Status of Refugees (1951)[72] and its Protocol (1967).[73] All except nine Member States have currently ratified the Convention (South Sudan submitted its ratification instrument in May 2016), which entered into force on 20 June 1974.[74]

27. The 1970s were marked by gross human rights violations orchestrated by dictatorial regimes in Uganda, the CAR, and Equatorial Guinea. In 1971, several Member States (including Gabon, Lesotho, Malawi, and Madagascar) were in favour of dialogue and rapprochement with South Africa, a suggestion that was met with distrust by other Members. In 1972–1973, a series of developments, such as the termination of the civil war in southern Sudan, the rapprochement between, on the one hand, Morocco and Algeria, and, on the other hand, Senegal and Guinea, as well the OAU's tenth anniversary gave a fresh impetus.[75] However, the mass slaughter of Hutus in Burundi went largely unnoticed and the OAU failed to exercise its authority;[76] twenty-two years later, in the genocide of Tutsis by Hutu extremists in Rwanda the Organization, alongside the UN and the international community at large, would once more prove unable to intervene and save human lives. By 1974, the struggle against apartheid, which was organized and directed by the OAU also at the level of the UN through the African Group of Members in the UNGA (it was established in 1964), had intensified on the international plane.[77] The African Group, which was very often succoured by the Arab Group of Members in the UNGA to have the Republic of South

70. Council of Ministers, *Declaration on the Question of Dialogue*, OAU Doc. CM/St. 5 (XVII) (19 Jun. 1971). The *Lusaka Manifesto* should be read together with the *Resolution on Decolonization* and the *Mogadiscio Declaration*, both of which were adopted by the Twenty-Third Ordinary Council of Ministers Session, OAU Doc. CM/Res.350 (XXIII) and CM/ST. 13 (XXIII) (15 Jun. 1974), respectively.
71. Council of Ministers, *Resolution on Decolonization and Apartheid*, OAU Doc. CM/Res. 206 (XIII) (6 Sept. 1969).
72. Entered into force on 22 Apr. 1954, 189 U.N.T.S. 150.
73. Entry into force on 4 Oct. 1967, 606 U.N.T.S. 267.
74. 1001 U.N.T.S. 45.
75. Compare Heads of State and Government, *Solemn Declaration on General Policy*, OAU Doc. CM/ST. 9 (XXI) (25 May 1973). But *see* , Council of Ministers, *Statement on Current Political Issues*, OAU Doc. CM/ST.8/Rev. 2 (XX) (9 Feb. 1973).
76. *See* J.P. Chretien & J.F. Dupaquier, *Burundi 1972: Au bord des genocides* (Paris: L'Harmattan, 2007).
77. Council of Ministers, *Resolution on the Activities of the African Group at the United Nations*, OAU Doc. CM/Res. 351 (XXIII) (11 Jun. 1974), and Council of Ministers, *Resolution on South Africa*, OAU Doc. CM/Res. 428 (XXV) (25 Jul. 1977).

Africa expelled from membership,[78] was instrumental in South Africa's ostracism from the Twenty-Ninth Session (November 1974) and subsequent sessions of the UN General Assembly.[79] On 18 January 1974, the Constitution of the Association of African Trade Promotion Organizations was adopted. Although it came provisionally into force on the day it was opened for signature, it formally entered into force only on 28 March 2012 having secured the required twelve ratifications. Currently, it has been ratified by fifteen Member States (lastly by Burkina Faso in June 2016). In April 1975, the Ninth Extraordinary Council of Ministers Session adopted the Dar-as-Salaam Declaration stipulating that the OAU strategy towards Rhodesia, Namibia, and South Africa should be primarily based on peaceful means and, if these were to fail, resort to armed struggle would be a legitimate course of action.[80] The Extraordinary Session was convened because the collapse of Portugal's dictatorial regime n had immediate effects on its African territories (Angola, Mozambique, Cape Verde) and radically altered the balance of forces in southern Africa and, therefore, the OAU needed to formulate a new common position. Several African leaders boycotted the Twelfth Ordinary Assembly Session (Kampala, Uganda, 28 July–1 August 1975) because they believed that, by meeting there, they were giving respectability to President Idi Amin of Uganda, whose regime had been universally condemned for atrocities and widespread human rights violations. During the Kampala Session, forty-two Members States adopted the Inter-African Convention Establishing an African Technical Cooperation Programme, as the most appropriate method of promoting the employment of African specialists by African states, an early example of the 'African solutions to African problems' line of thinking. The fact that solely six Member States have ratified the Convention (all of them in the twenty-first century), four ratifications short of the required number to enter into force, raises two crucial questions, which happen to concern other OAU/AU treaties as well. The first question is the commitment of Members to ensure that the instruments negotiated and signed under OAU/AU auspices, enter into force and become operative. The second question is to which extent there are valid grounds to continue keeping open multilateral instruments, which were concluded so many years ago and their content no longer corresponds to contemporary realities and needs, in short instruments that ought to have been either abrogated or revised.

---

78. The First Afro-Arab Summit was held in Cairo on 7–9 Mar. 1977. Cooperation was implemented through the following four entities: the Coordinating Commission, the Standing Commission, the Joint Afro-Arab Ministerial Conference, and the Afro-Arab Summit Conference. Generally, *see* Council of Ministers, *Resolution on Afro-Arab Cooperation*, OAU Doc. CM/Res. 770 (XXXIV) (15 Feb. 1980); *Resolution on Afro-Arab Cooperation*, OAU Doc. CM/Res. 781 (XXXV) (28 Jun. 1980); and *Resolution on Afro-Arab Cooperation*, OAU Doc. CM/Res. 1106 (XLVI) (25 Jul. 1987).

79. Council of Ministers, *Resolution on the Expulsion of South Africa from the Twenty-Ninth Session of the United Nations General Assembly*, OAU Doc. CM/Res. 392 (XXIV) (21 Feb. 1975). Generally, *see* K. Magliveras, *Exclusion from Participation in International Organisations – The Law and Practice behind Member States' Expulsion and Suspension of Membership* (The Hague: Kluwer Law International, 1999), 209–222.

80. *See Declaration on Southern Africa*, 10 Apr. 1975, at: http://www.anc.org.za/content/declarations-and-resolutions-organization-african-unity-1963-1994, which was partly endorsed by UNGA Res. 3396 (XXX) of 21 Nov. 1975.

28. Disagreement over the legitimate government of Angola brought to a stalemate the First Extraordinary Assembly Session, which met in Addis Ababa on 10–13 January 1976 solely for determining this very issue.[81] The forty-four voting Members were equally split between the Soviet and Cuba-backed Popular Movement for the Liberation of Angola (MPLA) and the US-backed National Union for the Total Independence of Angola (UNITA), a prime example of the Cold War's so-called proxy wars.[82] The Extraordinary Session collapsed. This complicated the question of Angola's admittance to membership.[83] However, by 2 February 1976 most Members had recognized MPLA leading to express recognition by the OAU and admission on 10 February 1976. Later in the same month, Morocco and Mauritania took over the administration of the Western Sahara territory from Spain (another colonial power that had recently embraced democracy) in negation of the local population's right to self-determination. The Western Saharan issue had always been a crucial test of the OAU's effectiveness and its ability to abide by its lofty principles; until today it remains unresolved even though the de facto presence of Morocco for so many decades has shaped a situation which is hard to ignore. On 29 June 1976, Seychelles acceded to the OAU. The Twenty-Seventh Ordinary Council of Ministers Session (Port Louis, Mauritius, 24 June–3 July 1976) adopted a decision preventing the recognition of the South African Bantustans,[84] while the Thirteenth Ordinary Assembly Session (Port Louis, Mauritius, 2–6 July 1976) denounced as an act of aggression the freeing by Israeli armed forces of their countrymen who were held hostages by Palestinians hijackers in Uganda's Entebbe Airport.[85] Mauritius, as the country which at the time held the OAU Chairmanship, complained before the UNSC for Israel's 'unprecedented aggression' against Uganda. The UNSC deliberated the complaint in early July 1976 but no action was taken.[86] The Thirteenth Assembly also adopted the Cultural Charter for Africa.[87] It came into force with considerable delay on 19 September 1990 and has currently received thirty-four ratifications (lastly by Gabon on 26 September 2007). In the following year, the Fourteenth Ordinary Assembly Session (Libréville, Gabon, 2–5 July 1977) approved the Convention for the Elimination of Mercenarism in Africa. It entered into force on 22 April 1985.[88] Currently, only thirty-two Member States have

81. Note that the previous year an OAU Fact-Finding Commission of Enquiry and Conciliation had been set up, *see* Assembly, *Resolution on the Situation in Angola*, OAU Doc. AHG/Res. 72 (XII) (1 Aug. 1975).
82. *See* J.l. De Maio, 'Plausible Deniability: Proxy Wars in Africa' *Fletcher Security Review* I:II (2014): 35.
83. For the disagreement over Angola's legitimate government, *see* the document titled 'OAU-Angola' released on 12 Jan. 1976 by the Central Intelligence Agency (CIA), at: http://www.faqs.org/cia/index_48.html. *See* further, F. Castro, J. Risquet & G. Garcia Marquez, *Changing the History of Africa: Angola and Namibia* (Melbourne: Ocean Press, 1989).
84. Council of Ministers, *Resolution on Non-recognition of South African Bantustans*, OAU Doc. CM/Res. 492 (XXVII) (3 Jul. 1976).
85. Assembly, *Resolution on Israel Aggression against Uganda*, OAU Doc. AHG/Res. 83 (XIII) (6 Jul. 1976).
86. *See* UNSC Official Records, S/PV. 1939, 9 Jul. 1976.
87. Assembly, *Resolution relating to the Cultural Charter for Africa,* OAU Doc. AHG/Res. 82 (XIII) (6 Jul. 1976).
88. 1490 U.N.T.S. 95.

deposited instruments of ratification (the last four being Algeria on 11 January 2008, Gambia on 9 July 2009, Chad on 27 October 2012, and Guinea-Bissau on 22 January 2015).

29. In July 1978, the discussion at Assembly level on the interference of states from outside the continent in the internal affairs of African states revealed the ideological divide among Member States, when criticism of French and US intervention was counteracted by criticism of Soviet and Cuban involvement leading to cases of instability such as in Angola.[89] It is interesting to note that the Fourteenth Ordinary Assembly Session had adopted an uncontested Decision on the question of outside interference in African affairs which promoted a policy of non-alignment.[90] During 1978, various long-standing interstate conflicts appeared to be coming to a conclusion, including the disputes between Guinea and Ivory Coast and between Guinea and Senegal.[91] However, in other ongoing disputes (e.g., the conflicts between Somalia and Ethiopia,[92] between Ethiopia and Sudan,[93] and between Libya and Chad)[94] the OAU was not a successful mediator. The OAU recognized Mugabe's Patriotic Front as the legitimate government in Zimbabwe (Rhodesia) but appealed to all political parties to participate in the general elections in the hope to avoid a crisis like that of Angola a few years earlier. In 1978/1979, Tanzania invaded Uganda and caused the downfall of the infamous dictator Idi Amin. This led to considerable controversy among Member States which had various consequences. First, it showed the OAU's inability to deal with dictatorial Members violating Charter principles and obligations. Second, it revealed its inability to prevent Members from resorting to extreme measures in their interstate relations (involving the use of force), which were also expressly prohibited. Third, it questioned the notion of absolute sovereignty, which was also enshrined in the Charter. On 2 November 1979, Angola acceded to the OAU.

30. The Second Extraordinary Assembly Session (Lagos, Nigeria, 28–29 April 1980) was convened to discuss Africa's economic revival. It adopted the namesake Plan of Action for the Economic Development of Africa 1980–2000, which was based on the Monrovia Declaration of Commitment.[95] This was a strategy, partly devised by the UN Economic Commission for Africa, for the development and the creation of the

---

89. The discussion of the issue started at the Thirty-First Ordinary Council of Ministers Session (Khartoum, Sudan, 7–18 Jul. 1978) which however rejected a decision tabled as *Draft Resolution on Measures to be Taken against Neo-Colonialist Maneuvers and Foreign Military Intervention in Africa* (OAU Doc. CM/Res. 638 (XXXI)). The matter was then referred to the Fifteenth Ordinary Assembly Session (Khartoum, Sudan, 18–22 Jul. 1978) which failed to reach a decision as well. At the Thirty-First Council of Ministers Session, another decision tabled as *Draft Resolution on the Territorial Integrity of Africa and the Surrounding Islands* (OAU Doc. CM/Res. 676 (XXXI)) was not adopted as fifteen Member States filed reservations and another did not participate in the proceedings.
90. Assembly, *Resolution on the Interference of the Internal Affairs of African States*, OAU Doc. AHG/Res. 85 (XIV) (5 Jul. 1977).
91. Assembly, *Resolution on Reconciliation between Guinea, Ivory Coast and Senegal*, OAU Doc. AHG/Res. 88 (XV) (22 Jul. 1978).
92. Assembly, OAU Doc. AHG/Res. 90 (XV) (22 Jul. 1978).
93. Assembly, OAU Doc. AHG/Res. 93 (XV) (22 Jul. 1978).
94. Assembly, OAU Doc. AHG/Res. 94 (XV) (22 Jul. 1978).
95. Assembly, OAU Doc. EAHG/Res. 1 (II) (29 Apr. 1980).

necessary conditions to encourage economic growth in the agricultural, industry and energy sectors and to protect the environment. The same Session also decided to promote the more active participation of African states in international negotiations, a theme which, many years later, became an objective in the AU Constitutive Act. In June 1980, Zimbabwe acceded to the OAU, an event of immense political importance since it was a turning point in the phasing out of white regimes in southern Africa. The Polisario Front, the political entity representing the indigenous population of Western Sahara, was recognized as the legitimate government by twenty-six out of the then fifty Member States, opening the way for another constitutional crisis in the OAU. In February 1981, after many resolutions issued by the Council of Ministers, the Convention for the Establishment of the African Centre for Fertilizer Development was concluded in the hope to contribute to the stabilization and improvement of Africa's agricultural sector. For some reason, even though the Convention has been signed by thirty-two Member States, it has been ratified by only eight (lastly by Benin and by Burkina Faso in 2016) and has not yet entered into force.

The Eighteenth Ordinary Assembly Session (Nairobi, 24–27 June 1981) adopted the African Charter on Human and Peoples' Rights (also known as the African or Banjul Charter). It entered into force on 21 October 1986. It has become one of the few OAU/AU treaties to be ratified by all Member States, although as of mid-June 2017 Morocco, which as is later explained, acceded to the AU in January 2017, has yet not accepted it. The African Charter constitutes, chronologically speaking, the third regional system for the protection of human rights and has distinctive features separating it from the European and Inter-American counterparts, for example, the notion that people do not only enjoy rights but also owe obligations to fellow people as well as to their countries. Subsequent protocols have augmented both the scope of the protection (adding the rights of women and the rights of older people) and the institutional mechanism of the African Charter (adding a Court of Human Rights). At the same Session, the Assembly's decision to establish an OAU peacekeeping force for Chad marked the first opportunity to involve itself in peacekeeping operations, which, however, ended in an embarrassing failure.[96]

It was also during 1981 that Morocco agreed in principle on holding a referendum in Western Sahara so that the local population could exercise its alienable right to self-determination; the choice offered to the population was either independence or integration with Morocco. Until today, and despite the creation and operation of the UN Mission for the Referendum in Western Sahara (MINURSO),[97] it has not taken place. The UNSC has described the situation as follows:

96. Assembly, *Resolution on Chad*, OAU Doc. AHG/Res. 102 (XVIII) Rev. 1 (27 Jun. 1981), and Council of Ministers, *Resolution on Chad*, OAU Doc. CM/Res. 769 (XXXIV) (15 Feb. 1980). Generally, *see* G. Naldi, 'Peace-Keeping Attempts by the Organisation of African Unity', *ICLQ* 34 (1985): 593; T.M. Mays, *Africa's First Peacekeeping Operation: The OAU in Chad, 1981-1982* (London: Praeger Publishers, 2002).

97. It was established pursuant to UNSC Res. 690(1991) of 29 Apr. 1991. As an annual ritual, MINURCO's mandate is extended for twelve-month periods, *see* UNSC Res. 2285 (2016) of 29 Apr. 2016 and Res. 2351 (2017) of 27 Apr. 2017 extending the mandate until 30 Apr. 2018.

> [t]he Parties [should] continue to negotiate, without preconditions and in good faith, with a view to achieving a just, lasting and mutually acceptable political solution which will provide for the self-determination of the people of Western Sahara in the context of arrangements consistent with the principles and purposes of the Charter of the United Nations[98]

Presumably, the UNSC ought to have added the principles and purposes to be found in the AU Constitutive Act. And this because the Western Sahara saga is characteristic of Africa's emancipation following the withdrawal of colonial powers and it is as much a problem for Africa as it is for the UN. Especially if it is deemed to be a burning issue for the amelioration of relations in the countries of the Arab Maghreb, it is even more an issue to be deal with under AU auspices. Moreover, the successful holding of a referendum in South Sudan in 2011 is sufficient evidence that, despite inherent difficulties, African populations can exercise their right to self-determination without fear of the outcome.

Between 1982 and 1983, the Ordinary Sessions of the Assembly were paralysed for two reasons. The first reason was the Secretary General's decision to admit to membership the Sahrawi Arab Democratic Republic (SADR), the political entity representing the territory of Western Sahara. The second reason was a dispute concerning the legitimate government of Chad. In April 1984, the Constitution of the Association of African Trade Promotion Organizations, which had been adopted on 18 January 1974 and has currently been ratified by fifteen Member States (lastly by Congo in March 2013 and by Burkina Faso in June 2016), came into force.[99] In November 1984, the SADR was officially accepted as the fifty-first Member State, a move that led to Morocco's immediate withdrawal from the OAU. Morocco stayed away when the OAU was transformed into the AU. However, in the summer of 2016 it strongly indicated its wish to apply for membership, which it did later in the same year and was successful. The AU Assembly welcomed Morocco as its fifty-fifth Member State in January 2017 (*infra*, paragraph 57). The Twenty-First Assembly Ordinary Session (Addis Ababa, 18–20 November 1985) strongly urged the USA to reconsider its position and to not withdraw from UNESCO.[100] It also approved Africa's Priority Programme for Economic Recovery 1986–1990, where Member States reaffirmed the primary responsibility for their own economic and social development, identified areas for urgent action and promised to mobilize and utilize domestic resources for achieving the same. The Programme had been preceded by the Declaration on the Critical Economic Situation in Africa which was approved by the Twentieth Assembly Ordinary Session (Addis Ababa, 12–15 November 1984).[101] The UNGA promptly engaged itself

98. *See* UNSC Res. 1971 (2009) of 30 Apr. 2009.
99. Note that, according to the official Status List at: https://au.int/sites/default/files/treaties/7766-sl-constitution_of_the_association_of_african_trade_promotion_organizations.pdf, the Convention came into force on 28 Mar. 2012. However, this is the date that Benin ratified it and became the thirteenth contracting party. However, as its entry into force required twelve ratifications this was achieved when Zambia deposited its instrument of ratification in April 1984.
100. Assembly, *Resolution on UNESCO*, OAU Doc. AHG/Res. 127 (XX) (15 Nov. 1984).
101. Assembly, OAU Doc. AHG/Decl. 2 (XX) (15 Nov. 1984).

in deliberating Africa's economic plight[102] and, in December 1985, it resolved to convene a 'special session to focus, in a comprehensive and integrated manner, on the rehabilitation and medium-term and long-term development problems and challenges facing African countries'.[103] Six months later the special session took place and culminated in the UNs Programme of Action for African Economic Recovery and Development 1986–1990 (PAAERD).[104]

31. On 17 July 1985, the Convention for the Establishment of the African Rehabilitation Institute was adopted with the aim to harmonize the principles and the strategy for disability prevention and the rehabilitation of the disabled. It entered into force on 2 December 1991 and has currently been signed by thirty-one and ratified by twenty-six Member States (the last being Rwanda on 14 July 2010). With economic and financial issues now firmly on the OAU agenda, in July 1985, on the fifth anniversary of the Lagos Plan of Action, the Addis Ababa Declaration on the Economic Situation in Africa was adopted. African leaders resolved to accelerate the implementation of the Lagos Plan and started to debate seriously the problem of the excessive foreign debt incurred by Member States. The Third Extraordinary Assembly Session was convened in November–December 1987 to deliberate the question of external debt, which at the time had reached USD 200 billion. The ensuing document, the African Common Position on Africa's External Debt Crisis, called for a ten-year moratorium. The excessive debt of African countries has remained an issue of considerable concern and many an African state now qualify as Highly Indebted Poor Countries (HIPCs). The appearance of the so-called vulture funds, namely aggressive private creditors who buy sovereign debt at very low prices and, upon maturity, demand to be paid the face value of the debt they hold, has made it a very acute problem. The practice of vulture funds to institute court proceedings against states asking to be awarded the sovereign debt's full-face value attracted the attention of the G-8 group in 2005 (at the time more than USD 1 billion had been awarded by courts to plaintiff vulture funds). The G-8 considered this practice as a major obstacle to its attempts to arrange a debt relief programme for poor countries. Because of these and similar concerns, a few years later, the African Legal Support Facility (ALSF) was created and placed under the auspices of the African Development Bank (ADB) in April 2008. It started operating in 2010.[105] The UNGA also addressed the issue during its Sixty-Eighth Ordinary Session.[106]

A Ministerial Regional Conference on Security, Disarmament and Development in Africa was convened in Lomé in August 1985. It adopted the namesake Declaration

---

102. UNGA Res. 39/29 of 3 Dec. 1984.

103. UNGA Res. 40/40 of 2 Dec. 1985.

104. UNGA A/RES/S-13/2, 1 Jun. 1986, Annex.

105. *See* https://www.afdb.org/en/topics-and-sectors/initiatives-partnerships/african-legal-support-facility/. Following the signing of the Agreement for the Establishment of the African Legal Support Facility (ALSF) by France on 11 Feb. 2013, the number of signatory states reached fifty, of which five are non-African states (France, the United Kingdom, the Netherlands, Belgium and Brazil). France contributed the amount of USD 5 million. *See also* D. Gaspard &V. Renaud, 'Fonds vautours: l'Afrique riposte?', CNCD-11.11.11, 11 August 2009, at: http://www.cncd.be/Fonds-vautours-l-Afrique-riposte#nb9.

106. UNGA Res. 68/304, *Towards the establishment of a multilateral legal framework for sovereign debt restructuring processes*, 9 Sept. 2014.

and Programme of Action, which connected regional security with state commitments to socio-economic development, justice, equity, and human dignity. The Forty-Eighth Ordinary Council of Ministers Session (Addis Ababa, 19–23 May 1988) adopted the Resolution on Dumping of Nuclear and Industrial Waste in Africa, which, *inter alia*, declared the discarding of nuclear and industrial wastes a crime against African peoples and called upon those Member States that had entered into agreements with third countries for their disposal in their territories to terminate them.[107] The last two years of the 1980s were also dominated by the external debt issue[108] to which the question of arrears in the payment of Member States' contributions to the OAU budget was added. The latter, which had become a perennial issue of concern, endangered the financial stability of the OAU and prevented it from carrying out its programmes and projects. Finally, the Fiftieth Ordinary Council of Ministers Session (Addis Ababa, 17–22 July 1989) hailed the creation of another entity fighting racial discrimination, the African Anti-Apartheid Committee, which was described as a Non-Governmental Organization (NGO), and asked the Secretary-General to work out modalities for cooperation with it.[109]

32. The Twenty-Sixth Ordinary Assembly Session (Addis Ababa, 9–11 July 1990) adopted two important documents. The first was the Declaration on the Political and Socio-Economic Situation in Africa and the Fundamental Changes Taking Place in Africa, in which African leaders painted a rather gloomy picture of affairs in the continent and, in particular, as regards its position in the international community. However, they committed themselves to work towards the peaceful and speedy resolution of conflicts. The second instrument was the African Charter on the Rights and Welfare of the Child, which was concluded a year after a similar treaty was finalized by the UNs, the Convention on the Rights of the Child. The Charter entered into force with considerable delay on 29 November 1999 and has currently received forty-seven ratifications (the last being by Swaziland in November 2012).[110] In June 1990, Namibia acceded to the OAU thus ending one of the last chapters of colonialism in Africa. In January 1991, the OAU Conference of Environmental Ministers meeting in Bamako, Mali, adopted the Convention on the Ban of the Import into Africa and the Control of Transboundary Movement and Management of Hazardous Wastes within Africa. The Convention, which entered into force on 22 April 1998, has currently received only twenty-five ratifications (the last two being Burkina Faso in August 2009 and Chad in July 2012) despite the fact that the illegal dumping of hazardous waste in the continent

---

107. Council of Ministers, *Resolution on Dumping of Nuclear and Industrial Wastes in Africa*, OAU Doc. CM/Res. 1153 (XLVIII) (23 May 1988).
108. Council of Ministers, *Resolution on the Convening of the International Seminar on Africa's Common Position on External Debt Crisis*, OAU Doc. CM/Res. 1195 (XLIX) (25 Feb. 1989), and Assembly, *Resolution on Holding an Extraordinary Session of the Assembly of Heads of State and Government on Economic Problems of Africa*, OAU Doc. AHG/Res. 96 (XVI) Rev. 1 (20 Jul. 1989).
109. Council of Ministers, *Resolution on the African Anti-Apartheid Committee*, OAU Doc. CM/Res. 1208 (L) (22 Jul. 1989).
110. 28 I.L.M. (1989) 1456. Generally, *see* T. Kaime, *African Charter on the Rights and Welfare of the Child – A Socio-Legal Perspective* (Pretoria: Pretoria University Law Press, 2009); J. Sloth-Nielsen (ed.), *Children's Rights in Africa: A Legal Perspective* (Aldershot, UK: Ashgate, 2008).

continues unabated.[111] In May 1991, the Kampala Document towards a Conference on Security, Stability, Development and Cooperation in Africa (CSSDCA) was proposed as the first Pan-African attempt to bring together the following four pillars: security, stability, development, and cooperation. While it was forwarded to the OAU Assembly for adoption, Member States received it unenthusiastically which ensured that it was not adopted. Almost a decade later, it was approved by the Thirty-Sixth Ordinary Assembly Session in July 2000.[112]

33. The Twenty-Seventh Ordinary Assembly Session (Abuja, 3–5 June 1991) adopted the Treaty Establishing the AEC, which entered into force on 12 May 1994. It has been signed by all Member States (expect Morocco), the last being Eritrea on 25 April 2012, and has been ratified by forty-nine Members, the last being Gabon in November 2007. The OAU had once before played with the idea of creating a Pan-African economic integration institution to complement its political agenda. Thus, in September 1968 the Council of Ministers had declared that the continent's economic integration was a prerequisite for the realization of the OAU's objectives[113] and, in July 1977 African leaders endorsed the Kinshasa Declaration, which had been adopted by the Eleventh Extraordinary Council of Ministers Session on Economic Development and Cooperation (Kinshasa, DRC, December 1976). The Kinshasa Declaration had called for the establishment of an African Common Market within fifteen to twenty-five years, the required first step towards the creation of the AEC. It was followed by the Monrovia Strategy[114] and the Monrovia Declaration[115] in July 1979, which did not culminate to any concrete results. Even though in the early 1990s the prevailing situation appeared to be much more favourable for pursuing the economic integration through a new entity, which was to become an integral part of the OAU, the AEC has failed to produce any appreciable results and has become a rather obsolete institution. Mainly for this reason that the AEC Treaty is still being signed (by Eritrea in 2012 and by South Sudan in 2013) is noteworthy. In addition to economic integration, a second issue that received considerable attention in the early 1990s was the need to devise and implement an effective mechanism for the settlement of disputes by peaceful means. Thus, the Twenty-Ninth Ordinary Assembly Session (Cairo, 28–30 June 1993) adopted the Cairo Declaration on the Establishment, within the OAU, of a Mechanism for Conflict Prevention, Management and Resolution to revamp the non-operational Commission of Mediation, Conciliation, and Arbitration. The Mechanism carried out

---

111. 30 I.L.M. (1991) 657. Generally, *see* C.N. Eze, 'The Bamako Convention on the Ban of the Import into Africa and the Control of the Transboundary Movement and Management of Hazardous Wastes Within Africa: A Milestone in Environmental Protection' *RADIC* 15 (1997): 208.
112. Generally, *see* F.M Deng & I.W. Zartman, *A Strategic Vision for Africa. The Kampala Movement* (Washington, DC: The Brookings Institution, 2002).
113. Council of Ministers, *Regional Groupings and Market Integration*, OAU Doc. CM/Res. 159 (XI) (12 Sept. 1968).
114. Council of Ministers, *Monrovia Strategy for the Economic Development of Africa*, OAU Doc. CM/Res. 722 (XXXIII) Rev. 1 (2 Jul. 1979).
115. Assembly, *Monrovia Declaration of Commitment of the Heads of State and Government of the Organization of African Unity on Guidelines and Measures for National and Collective Self-Reliance in Social and Economic Development for the Establishment of a New International Economic Order*, OAU Doc. AHG/ST. 3 (XVI) Rev. 1 (20 Jul. 1979).

its mandate relatively successfully and, following the establishment of the AU, the PSC absorbed it. On 24 May 1993, Eritrea acceded to the OAU. However, due to unsurpassable internal problems and strife, Eritrea's participation was kept to a minimum and, therefore, there is some merit in the argument it should not be considered as a fully-pledged Member State.

In the course of 1994, the OAU was not only unable to prevent the Rwandan genocide but also failed to intervene in a forceful manner to bring it to an end. This necessitated the intervention, albeit tardy, by the international community. At the Thirtieth Ordinary Session (Tunis, 13–15 June 1994), the Assembly adopted the following two instruments. First, the Declaration on a Code of Conduct for Inter-African Relations, where fanatism and extremism were rejected as unacceptable means and as detrimental to the promotion of peace and security in the continent.[116] Second, the African Maritime Transport Charter, which entered into force provisionally.[117] Currently, it has been signed by forty and ratified by thirteen Member States (the last being Rwanda on 14 July 2010). The Revised African Maritime Transport Charter was adopted in June 2010 but has not yet entered into force. On 6 June 1994, the Republic of South Africa acceded to the OAU thus ending three decades of hostile relations.

34. While interstate wars and the struggle for liberation from foreign dominance were the OAU's principal concerns in the 1970s and in the 1980s, the 1990s have been dominated by intra-state violence. However, it was only after 1995 that the importance of the OAU possessing its own permanent force to deal with intra-state but also internal disputes and conflicts (at the time, there were clashes in Rwanda, Burundi, Somalia, Liberia, and Sierra Leone) was seriously discussed. But several factors, including the severe shortage of funds, prevented the creation of such a force. On the contrary, peacekeeping operations were (and have continued to be) launched by RECs with a considerable record of success. The Economic Community of West African States (ECOWAS) has played a pivotal role in these operations, most of which have been endorsed by the OAU/AU and approved by the UN Security Council. In June 1995, the Treaty of Pelindaba, which creates a nuclear-weapon-free zone in Africa, was successfully negotiated under the OAU auspices. The Treaty opened for signature in April 1996 and entered into force in force with considerable delay in July 2009. Currently, it has been signed by fifty-one and ratified by forty-one Member States (the last four being the SADR in January 2014, Seychelles in April 2014, Angola in May 2014, and Niger in June 2016).[118] The Treaty, whose Protocols were ratified by Great Britain, France, China and the Soviet Union, could be viewed as the culmination of two previous instruments: the Declaration on the Denuclearization of Africa, which was adopted by the First Assembly Session (Cairo, July 1964)[119] and the UN General Assembly Resolution 3472B (XXX) of 11 December 1975 titled 'Comprehensive

116. Assembly, *Declaration on a Code of Conduct for Inter-African Relations*, OAU Doc. AHG/ Decl. 2 (XXX) (15 Jun. 1994).

117. *See* L. Savadogo, 'La Charte africaine des transports maritime: Principes, règles et techniques' in T.M. Ndiaye and R. Wolfrum (eds), *Law of the Sea, Environmental Law and Settlement of Disputes: Liber Amicorum Judge Thomas A. Mensah* (The Hague: Martinus Nijhoff, 2007) 545.

118. African Nuclear-Weapon-Free Zone Treaty, reproduced in I.L.M. 35 (1996): 702.

119. Assembly, *Denuclearization of Africa*, OAU Doc. AHG/Res. 11 (I) (21 Jul. 1964).

study of the question of nuclear-weapon-free zones in all its aspects.' The latter instrument considered the nuclear weapons free zones as the most effective means for preventing the proliferation of such weapons. In April 1996, the First OAU Ministerial Conference on Human and Peoples' Rights adopted the Grand Bay (Mauritius) Declaration and Plan of Action for the period 1996–2001. The Declaration did not view the protection of human rights on its own but put it into the context of the other problems plaguing domestic and intra-African affairs, such as the lack of a democratic ethos, inadequate governance, corruption, coups d'état resulting in loss of life, internal displacement, etc.[120]

35. In May 1997, the First Continental Conference of African Experts on Anti-Personnel Mines adopted the Kempton Park Plan of Action on a Landmine Free Africa. Endorsed by the Sixty-Sixth Ordinary Council of Ministers Session (Harare, 28–31 May 1997),[121] it committed the continent to the total ban of anti-personnel mines. The following month, the Thirty-Third Ordinary Assembly Session (Harare, 2–4 June 1997) issued a Common Position on the Reform of the Security Council, as a further attempt to establish an African voice on a difficult matter of international concern. The Common Position advocated that, in any future enlargement of the Security Council, Africa ought to be given two permanent seats.[122] The Thirty-Fourth Ordinary Assembly Session (Ouagadougou, 8–10 June 1998) adopted the Protocol to the African Charter on Human and Peoples' Rights on the Establishment of an African Court on Human and Peoples' Rights to complement the supervisory mechanism of the Banjul Charter. Thus, the African human rights system took after the corresponding European system (as originally set up by the Council of Europe) and the Inter-American system (set up by the Organization of American States) where the supervisory mechanism has consisted of a Human Rights Commission and a Human Rights Court. The Protocol entered into force with considerable delay on 25 January 2004. Currently, it has been signed by all Member States except Cape Verde, Eritrea and Morocco but has received only thirty ratifications (the last two being Cameroon in December 2014 and Chad in January 2016). Despite the appalling human rights situation in parts of Africa, the African Court on Human and Peoples' Rights was not promptly operationalized. Moreover, it has attracted a rather limited number of cases even though the rules on *locus standi* have been drafted very widely. Indeed, the first application before the Court was lodged in 2008.[123] While no applications were lodged during 2009 and 2010, as of late the Court appears to attract an increasing number of cases and at the time of writing there were some 100 cases pending before it.[124] The Assembly decision in 2008

120. At: http://www.achpr.org/instruments/grandbay.

121. Council of Ministers, *Report of the Secretary-General on the Issue of Anti-Personnel Mines and International Efforts to Reach a Total Ban*, OAU Doc. CM/Dec.363 (LXVI) (31 May 1997). The Second Continental Conference of African Experts on Landmines took place in September 2004, for the texts emanating from both Conferences, *see* http://www.peaceau.org/uploads/au-mine-action-project-document.pdf.

122. Assembly, *Harare Declaration of the Assembly of Heads of State and Government of the OAU on the Reform of the UN Security Council*, OAU Doc. AHG/Decl. 3 (XXXIII) (4 Jun. 1997).

123. African Court on Human and Peoples' Rights, Application No. 001/2008, *Michelot Yogogombaye v. the Republic of Senegal*, Judgment of 15 Dec. 2009.

124. For information, *see* http://en.african-court.org/index.php/cases/2016-10-17-16-18-21#pending-cases.

to merge it with the AU Court of Justice to create the African Court of Justice and Human Rights (ACJHR), a project that has still not been completed, has arguably deprived the continent of the opportunity to have in place robust judicial organs able to tackle its persisting problems, including the impunity for gross violations of fundamental freedoms (*infra* paragraph 122).

In a move that arguably contradicted fundamental rules of international law, the Thirty-Fourth Assembly Session resolved that Member States should disregard the sanctions imposed by the UN Security Council against Libya under Resolution 748 (1992) of 31 March 1992 and Resolution 883 (1993) of 11 November 1993 for its alleged involvement in the Lockerbie bombing.[125] Resolutions criticizing the UNSC sanctions against Libya were adopted by subsequent Assembly Sessions as well but they did not repeat the express call to disregard them.[126] The Thirty-Fifth Ordinary Assembly Session (Algiers, 12–14 July 1999) approved the Convention on the Prevention and Combating of Terrorism, at the time one of the first regional instruments to address the multifaceted issues of terrorism. The Convention entered into force on 26 December 2002 and has currently been signed by fifty Member States (including South Sudan in January 2013) and ratified by forty-three Members.[127] It is of some interest to note that the Convention envisages an express exception for terrorist acts that are founded on the struggle for liberation or the fight for self-determination. An additional Protocol to the Convention was signed on 2 July 2004 and entered into force on 26 February 2014; it has currently been ratified by seventeen Member States. Following a Decision adopted by the Seventy-Second Ordinary Council of Ministers Session (Lomé, 6–8 July 2000),[128] the OAU convened a Meeting of Experts to consider a Draft Convention on Extradition and a Draft Convention on Mutual Legal Assistance in Criminal Matters. Even though similar instruments have been adopted by most of the African RECs,[129] the AU does not seem to have taken the required action to bring them to completion.

---

125. Assembly, *The Crisis between the Great Socialist People's Libyan Arab Jamahiriya and the United States of America and the United Kingdom*, OAU Doc. AHG/Dec. 127 (XXXIV) (10 Jun. 1998).
126. Assembly, *Decision on the Crisis between the Libyan Arab Jamahiriya and the United States and the United Kingdom*, OAU Doc. AHG/Dec. 134 (XXXV) (14 Jul. 1999); Assembly, *Decision on the Lockerbie Issue*, OAU Doc. EAHG/Dec. 3 (V) (5 Mar. 2001); Assembly, *Decision on the Lockerbie Issue*, OAU Doc. AHG/Dec. 9 (XXXVII) (11 Jul. 2001) & UN Doc. S/2001/1152 (6 Dec. 2001); and Assembly, *Decision on the Lockerbie Issue*, OAU Doc. AHG/Dec. 174 (XXXVIII) (8 Jul. 2002).
127. 2219 U.N.T.S. 179.
128. Council of Ministers, *Decision on the Draft Conventions on Extradition and on Mutual Legal Assistance*, OAU Doc. CM/Dec. 540 (LXXII) (8 Jul. 2000).
129. *See* , *inter alia*, ECOWAS Convention on Mutual Assistance in Criminal Matters of 29 Jul. 1992; Cooperation Agreement between ECOWAS Member States' Police Forces on Investigation in Criminal Matters of December 2002; ECOWAS Convention on Extradition of 1994; IGAD Convention on Mutual Legal Assistance of 2009; SADC Protocol on Mutual Legal Assistance in Criminal Matters of 2002; and Mutual Assistance Pact between the Member States of ECCAS of 2002. It would appear that the first relevant sub-regional legal instrument was the Cooperation Agreement on Police Matters between Benin, Ghana, Nigeria and Togo, signed in Lagos, Nigeria in 1984.

36. 1999 was the year that saw the beginning of the OAU's demise. In June 1999, the now deceased Libyan leader Muammar Gaddafi attended an Assembly Session for the first time in twenty-two years, during which period he had voluntarily abstained because the Organization's criticism of the occupation of northern Chad by his troops. Arguably, Gaddafi returned because he wanted to implement his grand plan and, in particular, to create a new institution, the so-called United States of Africa, with a single currency.[130] The quite original proposals, which Gaddafi was prepared to finance handsomely, were discussed at the Fourth Extraordinary Assembly Session, which took in Sirte on 8 and 9 September 1999 at his invitation. Bringing back memories of the divisions between the Brazzaville Group and the Casablanca Group in the early 1960s on how to proceed with the political integration of the continent, the Extraordinary Session rejected Gaddafi's proposal for the creation of a United States of Africa. Instead the idea of creating a new institution, the AU, to replace the OAU was pushed forward. Moreover, the same Session resolved to accelerate the emergence of the AEC and set the foundations for the creation of a constructive partnership for Africa's regeneration.

37. By the following summer, the drafting of the AU Constitutive Act had been completed and African leaders signed it during the Thirty-Sixth Ordinary Assembly Session (Lomé, 10–12 July 2000). It entered into force on 26 May 2001. The same Session adopted two important Declarations. The first was the Declaration on the Framework for an OAU Response to Unconstitutional Change of Government, based on which, a number of Members, including The Comoros, were excluded from participating in OAU meetings. The second was the Solemn Declaration on the CSSDCA,[131] whose precise purpose was not immediately clear. However, two years later the Memorandum of Understanding (MoU) on Security, Stability, Development, and Cooperation in Africa was adopted to give effect to the Solemn Declaration. The MoU offers clear guidelines on how Member States should pursue its objectives and envisages performance indicators and time-frames.[132] On 1 December 2000, a Ministerial Conference in Bamako adopted the Declaration on an African Common African Position on the Illicit Proliferation, Circulation, and Trafficking of Small Arms and Light Weapons, which found that they threaten peace and security and undermine efforts to improve the living conditions of people.[133] The Declaration, which was endorsed by the Council of Ministers in July 2001,[134] stipulated measures to be taken at the national, regional and continental levels. Fresh impetus to deal with this scourge was given through the conclusion of the Arms Trade Treaty under the auspices of the UN in April 2013 (it was opened for signature on 1 June 2013 and entered into force on 24 December

130. *See* BBC, 'Gaddafi calls for United States of Africa', 20 Aug. 1999, at: http://news.bbc.co.uk/2/hi/africa/425929.stm.
131. *See* Assembly, *CSSDCA Solemn Declaration*, OAU Doc. AHG/Decl. 4 (XXXVI) (12 Jul. 2000).
132. OAU Doc. OAU/CIVILSOCIETY.3 (II) (19 Jul. 2002).
133. At: http://www.un.org/en/africa/osaa/pdf/au/cap_smallarms_2000.pdf.
134. *See* Council of Ministers, OAU Doc. CM/Dec. 599 (LXXIV) (11 Jul. 2001). *See* further, SADC Protocol on the Control of Firearms, Ammunition and other Related Materials, which entered into force on 8 Nov. 2004.

2014).[135] The Fifth Extraordinary Assembly Session (Sirte, Libya, 1–2 March 2001) was convened to give momentum to the AU's establishment. It finally approved the Protocol to the Treaty Establishing the AEC Relating to the PAP, which entered into force on 14 December 2003 and has currently been ratified by forty-eight Member States (South Sudan was the last one to ratify it in January 2014). In June 2014, the Protocol to the Constitutive Act of the African Union (AU) relating to the PAP was concluded; it aims at making PAP a proper AU organ and augments its role by making it at some future stage a *quasi* norms-setting body. In April 2001, the serious problems that the continent encountered by the spread of infectious diseases such as HIV/AIDS and tuberculosis were addressed during an Extraordinary Assembly Meeting, which was held in Abuja, Nigeria.

38. Parallel to these institutional developments, the project for the continent's regeneration was being prepared. During the Thirty-Seventh Ordinary Assembly Session (Lusaka, Zambia, 9–11 July 2001) the so-called New African Partnership for Africa's Development (NEPAD) was presented and unanimously adopted. Its essence is to offer a comprehensive framework for socio-economic development to be realized within the context of the AU. Human rights, conflict resolution and good economic and political governance are at the heart of NEPAD, which only recently has moved towards being institutionally integrated into the AU despite similar attempts over the years.[136] At the same Session, the Convention of the African Energy Commission was adopted. It entered into force on 13 December 2006 and currently has been signed by forty-five and ratified by thirty-two Member States (the last being Swaziland on 6 November 2012). After a fourteen-month transition period, the OAU was replaced by the AU and the last Ordinary Sessions of the Assembly (Thirty-Eighth) and of the Council of Ministers (Seventy-Sixth) took place in Durban in late June and early July 2002, respectively. The First Ordinary AU Assembly Session was held in Durban on 9–11 July 2002 marking the official inauguration of the AU. A brand new chapter in the history of Africa's (primarily) political and (secondarily) economic integration had begun. The Protocol to the Constitutive Act Relating to the Establishment of the PSC was adopted. It came into operation on 26 December 2003 and has currently has been signed by all Member States and ratified by forty-nine Members.

39. The First Extraordinary Assembly Session met in Addis Ababa on 3 February 2003. It approved a Protocol of Amendments to the Constitutive Act without debate. It has still not entered into force having been ratified by only twenty-eight Member States. In May 2003, the First AU Ministerial Conference on Human Rights in Africa adopted the Kigali Declaration, which formed the basis of the continent's revised agenda on human rights.[137] This event was a follow-up to the OAU Ministerial Conference on Human and Peoples' Rights of April 1996, which had adopted the Grand Bay Declaration and Plan of Action. The Second Ordinary Assembly Session (Maputo, Mozambique, 10–12 July 2003) continued with the setting up of the remaining AU organs (it adopted the Protocol of the African Court of Justice, which entered into

135. Currently, it has attracted eighty-six contracting parties, including nineteen African states, for details *see* https://www.un.org/disarmament/convarms/att/.

136. Compare Assembly, *Decision on the Integration of NEPAD into African Union Structures and Processes,* AU Doc. Assembly/AU/Dec. 153 (VIII) (30 Jan. 2007).

137. At: http://www.achpr.org/instruments/kigali/.

force in January 2008 and currently has sixteen contracting parties) and, for some strange reason, it approved again the aforementioned Protocol of Amendments.[138] Moreover, it concluded three important treaties on themes which are of particular interest to Africa. First, the Convention on Preventing and Combating Corruption (it entered into force on 5 August 2006 and currently has thirty-seven contracting parties);[139] the Advisory Board on Corruption was set up on 26 May 2009 under Article 22(1) of the Convention.[140] Second, the revised version of the Convention on Conservation of Nature and Natural Resources, which entered into force in June 2016 having secured the required fifteen ratifications. Third, the Protocol to the African Charter on Human and Peoples' Rights on the Rights of Women in Africa, which came into force promptly on 25 November 2005. It has currently been signed by forty-nine Members with thirty-eight ratifications (the last three being Cameroon in December 2012, Sierra Leone in July 2015, and Algeria in November 2016). Finally, the number of Member States that signed the MoU on the African Peer Review Mechanism (APRM) operating in the context of NEPAD increased to fifteen.[141] In December 2003, with the entry into force of the PCS Protocol, the OAU Central Organ of the Mechanism for Conflict Prevention ceased its operations, which were transferred to the PSC.

40. Initially, the AU addressed the internal conflict in the Sudanese region of Darfur from 2003 onwards by setting up, through the PSC, the severely understaffed AU Mission in Sudan (AMIS I). On 20 October 2004, it was replaced by a considerably larger but still inadequate force (AMIS II) with the mandate to monitor the deteriorating security conditions in the region. Although considerable criticism has been waged against AMIS, it should be regarded as a major improvement compared to the peacekeeping missions of the OAU era. Logistical support was received by the North Atlantic Treaty Organization (NATO) and the EU. As regards NATO, its involvement with AMIS broke new ground in the implementation of the so-called out of area operations. As is later explained, in January 2008, a hybrid UN-AU peace operation succeeded AMIS, the United Nation-African Union Misson in Darfur (UNAMID).[142]

41. On 24 January 2004, the Protocol to the African Charter establishing the African Human Rights Court entered into force and hopes were once more raised that, together with the African Human Rights Commission, it will lead to an effective institutional mechanism for the protection of fundamental freedoms. However, the extremely slow process in operationalizing it in conjunction with the ill-advised decision to merge it with the AU Court of Justice and the fact that only a limited number of

---

138. Reproduced in RADIC 13 (2005): 37.
139. Reproduced in I.L.M. 43 (2004): 5.
140. For the current membership of the Advisory Board and further information on the Regional Anti-Corruption Programme for Africa 2011–2016, *see* http://www.auanticorruption.org/auac/en.
141. Generally, *see* C. Manga Fombad, Z. Kebonang & H. Melber, *AU, NEPAD and the APRM Democratisation Efforts Explored*, Current African Issues No. 32 (Uppsala: Nordiska Afrikainstitutet, 2006). Note that the Assembly has decided that APRM shall be an autonomous entity within the AU system, to operate as a voluntary organisation of Member States exercising autonomy in its financial and budgetary processes, *see* Assembly, *Decision on the Integration of the APRM into the African Union*, AU Doc. Assembly/AU/Dec. 527 (XXIII) (27 Jun. 2014).
142. Established under UNSC Res. 1769(2007) of 31 Jul. 2007, for details *see* http://www.un.org/en/peacekeeping/missions/unamid/.

cases have been filed have so far prevented it from making a significant mark in the continental human rights protection and promotion. It should be noted that there are currently two Member States (Cape Verde and Eritrea) which have not signed the Human Rights Court Protocol and of the remaining membership only twenty-six states have ratified it. Taken on its own, this fact that should question their determination to have in place a regional human rights mechanism able to ensure that the violations of fundamental freedoms and the prevailing ethos of impunity are addressed The Second Extraordinary Assembly Session (Sirte, Libya, 27–28 February 2004) adopted the Declaration on the Challenges of Implementing Integrated and Sustainable Development of Agriculture and Water in Africa. Moreover, it examined the progress towards the adoption of a Non-Aggression and Common Defence Pact. However, as three separate and largely different drafts were proposed (one by the African Union Commission (AUC), the second by the DRC and the third by Libya, the country hosting the Session), it was decided to convene a meeting of government experts to elaborate a single document.[143] Despite this development, the Assembly adopted a lengthy document dealing with similar issues, the Solemn Declaration on a Common African Defence and Security Policy. The Declaration was based on a common perception among African leaders of what is required to be done collectively to ensure that the AU's defence and security interests and goals, as set out in Articles 3 and 4 of the Constitutive Act, are safeguarded in the face of common threats. Finally, the Inaugural and First PAP Session took place in Addis Ababa on 16–18 March 2004.[144] However, as only thirty-eight states had ratified its Protocol at the time, it did not include parliamentarians from all Member States. Even today, there are six Member States which have not ratified it.

The Third Ordinary Assembly Session (Addis Ababa, 6–8 July 2004) adopted a Protocol to the Convention on the Prevention and Combating of Terrorism (1999), which categorically states that 'acts of terrorism cannot be justified under any circumstances'.[145] Following ratification by the SADR in January 2014, the Protocol, which was based on the Dakar Declaration against Terrorism adopted in October 2001,

143. *See* Assembly, *Decision on a Non-Aggression and Common Defence Pact*, AU Doc. Ext/Assembly/AU/Dec. 2 (II) (28 Feb. 2004).

144. *See* Assembly, *Decision on the Launching and the Establishment of the Pan-African Parliament*, AU Doc. Assembly/AU/Dec. 39 (III) (8 Jul. 2004) determining that its seat shall be in South Africa. *See* further the decision that AU organs should be located in different regions on the basis of the principle of geographical distribution, Assembly/AU/Dec. 45 (III) (8 Jul. 2004). *See* further, Assembly, *Decision on the Location of the Headquarters of AU Institutions in various AU Regions*, Assembly/AU/Dec. 64 (IV), para. 2 (31 Jan. 2005).

145. *See* Assembly, *Decision on the Draft Protocol to the OAU Convention on the Prevention and Combating of Terrorism*, AU Doc. Assembly/AU/Dec. 36 (III) (8 Jul. 2004).

secured the required fifteen ratifications and entered into force on 26 February 2014.[146] Currently, only seventeen Member States are contracting parties. The Fourth Ordinary Assembly Session (Abuja, Nigeria, 30–31 January 2005) deliberated and adopted the AU Non-Aggression and Common Defence Pact as a framework for dealing with threats to peace, security and stability but also for providing for mutual assistance vis-à-vis use of force, aggression or threats of aggression.[147] The Pact entered into force on 18 December 2009 and has currently been signed by forty-four and ratified by the clearly inadequate number of twenty Member States (the last two being Comoros in July 2012 and Ethiopia in April 2014). During the same Session, the Assembly recognized the East African Community (EAC) as a REC and, in effect, as one of the blocks in the continental integration process.[148]

Finally, the Assembly deliberated the situation in the Darfur region of Sudan where the fighting between militias groups and armed groups supported by the government in Khartoum since 2003 had led to many tens of thousands of killings and left more than a million homeless and refugees. According to the then US Secretary of State Colin Powell, the killings amounted to genocide,[149] a finding that shortly later was repeated in US domestic legislation, the Darfur Peace and Accountability Act of 2006, signed into law by President George W. Bush on 13 October 2006.[150] Although the Assembly avoided taking sides over the Darfur conflict,[151] it expressly stated that, despite the seriousness of the humanitarian situation in the region, it could not be defined as genocide. At the same time, the Assembly took no measures of substance to address the deteriorating humanitarian situation in Darfur leaving the civilian

---

146. *See also AU Plan of Action on the Prevention and Combating of Terrorism*, which was adopted in September 2002 in Algiers by the AU High-Level Intergovernmental Meeting on the Prevention and Combating of Terrorism in Africa. The Plan of Action promotes practical measures on counter-terrorism and addresses continental security challenges. As part of its implementation, the African Centre for the Study, and Research on Terrorism (ACSRT) was established in 2004 in Algiers, while in July 2011 the Seventeenth Ordinary Assembly Session endorsed the African Model Law on Counter Terrorism, which had been developed by the AU Commission, AU Doc. Assembly/AU/Dec. 369 (XVII)]. *See* further at: http://www.peaceau.org/en/page/64-counter-terrorism-ct.
147. *See* Assembly, *Decision on the Draft African Union Non-Aggression and Common Defence Pact*, AU Doc. Assembly/AU/Dec. 71 (IV) (31 Jan. 2005). Article 1 of the Pact gives a definition of the term 'aggression' and lays down eleven types, including blockage of ports and aerospace, espionage and violent transnational organized crimes.
148. *See* Assembly, *Decision on Granting Accreditation to the East African Community (EAC) as one of the Regional Economic Community of the African Union*, AU Doc. Assembly/AU/Dec. 58 (IV) (31 Jan. 2005).
149. *See* BBC News, 'Powell declares genocide in Sudan', 9 Sept. 2004, at http://news.bbc.co.uk/2/hi/3641820.stm.
150. H.R. 3127, S. 1462, Public Law 109-344, at: https://www.govtrack.us/congress/bills/109/hr3127. On the basis of this and other legislation, successive US administrations imposed sanctions on Sudan, which were considerably eased on 13 Jan. 2017 when President B. Obama signed Executive Order 13761 'Recognizing Positive Actions by the Government of Sudan and Providing for the Revocation of Certain Sudan-Related Sanctions', at: https://www.hsdl.org/?abstract&did=798172. *See* further, https://www.treasury.gov/resource-center/sanctions/Programs/Documents/sudan_fact_sheet.pdf.
151. *See* Assembly, *Decision on Darfur*, AU Doc. Assembly/AU/Dec. 54 (III) (8 Jul. 2004).

population's protection and the armed groups' disarming to the government of Sudan, the very institution that has been accused of being responsible for serious crimes in Darfur. Arguably, the unsatisfactory way the AU has treated the Darfur crisis constitutes a very low point and has shown its limitations in addressing, as an emancipated international organization, intricate matters which are not unique but have been repeated time and time again in Africa. Given that the question of impunity for the crimes committed in Darfur has not been addressed at continental level, as has been argued, this could be seen as denialism on behalf of the AU, which clearly has not only a role to play but also a duty to fulfil.[152] Finally, in September 2004, an Extraordinary Assembly Summit on Employment and Poverty Alleviation in Africa was held in Ouagadougou. It adopted a Declaration, drafted a Plan of Action and established a Follow-up Mechanism committing Member States to place employment at the centre of their socio-economic policies.[153] The Fifth Ordinary Assembly Session (Sirte, Libya, 4–5 July 2005) reaffirmed its previous decision[154] to integrate the AU judicial organ and the African Human Rights Court into a single legal entity, the ACJHR; the first hybrid judicial organ of an international organization mandated to solve disputes among Member States, disputes between them and the organization as well as to act as human rights court.[155]

This Session was dominated by the question of reforming the UN system and promoted a common position in an apparent attempt to let the AU have a voice in multilateral negotiations. The Assembly adopted three relevant documents, the most important being the Sirte Declaration on the Reform of the UN. It, *inter alia*, talked about a 'fairer world based on universalism, equity and regional balance', referred to the General Assembly as a 'world parliament', and called for the establishment of two new entities: a so-called Peace-Building Commission and a new human rights body, which would become a subsidiary organ of the General Assembly and replace the Human Rights Commission.[156] The latter calls were fruitful: the Peace-building Commission was established in December 2005 as an intergovernmental advisory body for post-conflict reconstruction and recovery, while, the following year, the Human Rights Council (HRC) was set up as an intergovernmental body within the UN system mandated to strengthen the promotion and protection of human rights around the world and to address situations of human rights abuses and make

152. *See* K. Magliveras, 'International Organisations and Denialism: The Case of the African Union' in *Denialism and Human Rights*, H. Nelen, J.C.M. Willems & R. Moerland (eds.) (Cambridge: Intersentia 2016), 267.

153. *See* https://www.tralac.org/news/article/5987-extraordinary-summit-of-the-african-union-on-employment-poverty-eradication-and-inclusive-development-ouagadougou-burkina-faso.html.

154. *See* Assembly, *Decision on the Seats of the African Union*, AU Doc. Assembly/AU/Dec. 45 (III) (8 Jul. 2004).

155. *See* Assembly, *Decision on the Merger of the African Court on Human and Peoples' Rights and the Court of Justice of the African Union*, AU Doc. Assembly/AU/Dec. 83 (V) (5 Jul. 2005).

156. *See* Assembly, *Decision on the Expansion of the Follow-Up Mechanism on the Reform of the United Nations*, AU Doc. Assembly/AU/Dec. 87 (V); *Sirte Declaration on the Reform of the United Nations*, AU Doc. Assembly/AU/Decl. 2 (V); and *Resolution on the United Nations Reform: Security Council*, AU Doc. Assembly/AU/Res. 1 (V) (5 Jul. 2005).

recommendations on them.[157] The election of Sudan to HRC membership in 2002 and the assumption of the HRC chairmanship by Libya in 2003, states traditionally accused of widespread abuses of even the most fundamental freedoms, could be criticized as being incompatible with a UN organ dedicated to safeguarding human rights.

At its Sixth Ordinary Session (Khartoum, Sudan, 23–24 January 2006), the Assembly considered the report prepared by a Committee of Seven titled 'An African Union Government: Towards a United States of Africa' and restated that the AU's ultimate goal is the full political and economic integration of the continent leading to the United States of Africa.[158] Prior to this Session, Libya had lodged with the Eighth Ordinary Executive Council Session (Khartoum, Sudan, 16–21 January 2006) six proposals on, *inter alia*, new AU symbols, the establishment of a Pan-African Stock Exchange and the setting up of a fund to alleviate the effects of oil price increases on poor Member States. The proposals were referred to the Assembly for direct deliberation and later forwarded to groups of experts for consideration.[159] Some of them, for example, the revision of insignia and the fund to assist poorer Members with rising oil prices, materialized. Finally, the Assembly noted the proposal for the establishment of an African educational, scientific, and cultural organization and requested the Commission to consider it further.[160] Apparently, the proposal was abandoned. On 12 January 2006, the AU helped the brokering of a Peace Agreement between the fighting sides in the Darfur conflict. The Agreement, apart from the obvious military goals, dealt with the complex issue of human security in the region of Darfur. In order to supervise the implementation of the Agreement, UN Security Council Resolution 1769(2007) of 31 July 2007 authorized the creation of a hybrid UN-AU peace operation (UNAMID) with a predominant African character. The full deployment of UNAMID, which succeeded the AU's own Mission to Sudan (AMIS) on 1 January 2008, was slowed down due to the Sudanese government's tactics. The mandate of UNAMID, one of the largest UN peacekeeping missions ever established, has since been renewed by the Security Council and lastly under Resolution 2296(2016) of 29 June 2016 extending it until 30 June 2017.[161] It consists of up to 15,845 military personnel, 1,583 police personnel and 13 formed police units of up to 140 personnel each.

---

157. For the Peace-building Commission, *see* UN General Assembly Res. 60/180 of 20 Dec. 2005 and UN Security Council Res. 1645(2005) of 30 Dec. 2005; for the Human Rights Council, *see* UN General Assembly Res. 60/251 of 15 Mar. 2006.
158. *See* Assembly, *Decision on the Report of the Committee of Seven Heads of State and Government Chaired by the President of the Federal Republic of Nigeria*, AU Doc. Assembly/AU/Dec. 99 (VI) (24 Jan. 2006).
159. *See* Assembly, *Decision on the Review of Symbols – Flag of the Union, on the Holding of Bilateral Summits Between Africa and other States and on the Non-Assimilation of North Africa into the Middle East with Regard to Nomenclature, Content and Concept*, AU Doc. Assembly/AU/Dec.107 (VI) (24 Jan. 2006).
160. *See* Assembly, *Decision on the Establishment of an African Educational, Scientific and Cultural Organization (AFESCO)*, AU Doc. Assembly/AU/Dec. 110 (VI) (24 Jan. 2006).
161. For previous extensions, *see* UNSC Res. 2063(2012) of 31 Jul. 2012 and Res. 2113(2013) of 30 Jul. 2013. For FY 2012–2013, its budget reached USD 1.51 billion, in FY 2016–2017 it amounted to USD 1.039 billion, *see* UN Doc. A/C.5/70/24, 22 Jun. 2016.

The draft Protocol to the Constitutive Act to create the ACJHR was considered by the Ninth Ordinary Executive Council Session (Banjul, 25–29 June 2006).[162] It decided to refer it to a meeting for Ministers of Justice Ministers and Attorney Generals from Member States and to consider it again at its next Ordinary Session in January 2007.[163] Moreover, it resolved that forthwith there shall be one integrated AU budget: Staff costs, operating expenses, statutory meetings costs and top priority programmes/ projects shall be assessed on Member States, while the remaining programmes costs shall be financed through contributions to be secured from AU partners and donors.[164] The Executive Council also deliberated the draft African Charter on Democracy, Elections, and Governance, whose aim was to consolidate the collective commitments of Member States towards promoting democracy and good governance across the continent.[165] Finally, during this very fruitful Session, the Executive Council endorsed the AU Framework for Post-Conflict Reconstruction and Development, as a strategy towards the consolidation of peace and regeneration in areas emerging from conflict.[166] It also approved the establishment of a Democracy and Electoral Assistance Unit within the Political Affairs Department of the AUC with a special fund attached to it.[167] The latter constituted yet another attempt to secure the continent's stability by tackling the issue of rigged national elections but it was perhaps premature considering that the aforementioned Charter on Democracy had not yet been finalized.

The Seventh Ordinary Assembly Session (Banjul, 1–2 July 2006) adopted the African Youth Charter.[168] It came into force on 8 August 2009 and currently it has been signed by forty-two Member States and has received thirty-eight ratifications (including by Tanzania on 21 March 2013, Ghana on 27 December 2013 and Kenya on 29 January 2014). The Charter seeks to empower the African youth by building their capacity and leadership, while letting them bear responsibilities. Finally, the Assembly dealt with the question of the trial of the former President of Chad, Hissène Habré, who was accused of perpetrating crimes against humanity, war crimes and widespread acts of torture while in power between 1982 and 1990. The Assembly considered his trial as falling with the AU's competence and mandated Senegal, the country to which Habré

162. AU Doc. EX.CL/253 (IX) (2006).

163. *See* Executive Council, *Decision on the Draft Single Legal Instrument on the Merger of the African Court on Human and Peoples' Rights and the Court of Justice of the African Union*, AU Doc. EX.CL/Dec. 283 (IX) (29 Jun. 2006).

164. *See* Executive Council, *Decision on Structure of Budget and Modality of Funding*, AU Doc. EX.CL/Dec. 278 (IX) Rev.2 (29 Jun. 2006).

165. *See* Executive Council, *Decision on the Report of the Ministerial Conference on the African Charter on Democracy, Elections and Governance*, AU Doc. EX.CL/Dec. 288 (IX) (29 Jun. 2006).

166. *See* Executive Council, *Decision on the Establishment and Organization of a Democracy and Electoral Assistance Unit and Fund*, AU Doc. EX.CL/Dec. 300 (IX) (29 Jun. 2006).

167. *See* Executive Council, *Decision on the AU Policy on Post-Conflict Reconstruction and Development,* AU Doc. EX.CL/Dec. 302 (IX) (29 Jun. 2006). For information on the Unit, *see* http://www.au-elections.org/.

168. *See* Assembly, *Decision on the Report of the Ministerial Conference on the African Youth Charter*, AU Doc. Assembly/AU/ Dec. 121(VII) (2 Jul. 2006).

had fled after being overthrown, to prosecute and try him 'on behalf of Africa'.[169] His trial, a major test case of the African states' ability to fight impunity promptly and efficiently, became the subject matter of litigation before international courts. The first was before the Court of Justice of ECOWAS, which in 2010 concluded that that Senegal, in the context of the AU mandate, must put Habré on trial within the framework of a special procedure of an ad hoc nature, as practiced in international law by all civilized nations.[170] The second was before the ICJ, where Belgium had brought an application against Senegal claiming that it must either proceed with his prosecution or extradite him to Belgium. In July 2012, the ICJ upheld the claims advanced by Belgium.[171] After too many twists and turns, Senegal, in agreement with the AU, finally set up within its domestic court system the Extraordinary African Chambers (EAC) to try the international crimes committed in the territory of Chad between June 1982 and December 1990. The Chambers, whose Statute was approved by the Parliament of Senegal on 30 January 2013,[172] commenced operating on 8 February 2013.[173] They are reminiscent of the Extraordinary Chambers in the Courts of Cambodia (ECCC), the prototype of the so-called hybrid criminal courts.[174] In 2013, Habré tried unsuccessfully to halt the EAC proceedings before the Court of Justice of ECOWAS on the ground that they were illegitimate.[175] The trial of Habré before the EAC started on 20 July 2015 and ended on 11 February 2016. Judgment was delivered in May 2016: he was sentenced to life imprisonment having been found guilty of crimes against humanity, war crimes and torture.[176] In June 2016, the judgment was appealed against by lawyers

---

169. *See* Assembly, *Decision on the Hissène Habré Case and the African Union*, AU Doc. Assembly/AU/Dec. 127 (VII) (2 Jul. 2006), para. 5.
170. ECOWAS Court of Justice, *Hissène Habré v. Senegal*, No. ECW/CCJ/JUD/06/10, Decision of 18 Nov. 2010, English translation at: http://jurisafrica.org/html/pdf_ecowa.pdf.
171. ICJ, *Questions Relating to the Obligation to Prosecute or Extradite* (*Belgium v. Senegal*), Merits, Judgment of 20 Jul. 2012, I.C.J. Reports 2012, 422. For commentary, *see* S. Shah in *Human Rights L. R.* (2013) 13: 1.
172. *See Statut des Chambres africaines extraordinaires au sein des juridictions sénégalaises pour la poursuite des crimes internationaux commis au Tchad durant la période du 7 juin 1982 au 1er décembre 1990*, September 2012, unofficial English translation at: http://www.hrw.org/news/2013/09/02/statute-extraordinary-african-chambers. *See* further, S. Williams, 'The Extraordinary African Chambers in the Senegalese Courts. An African Solution to an African Problem?', *Journal of International Criminal Justice* 11 (2013) 1139.
173. For further information, *see* http://www.chambresafricaines.org/.*See* further, Raymond Ouigou Savadogo, 'Les Chambres africaines extraordinaires au sein des tribunaux sénégalais: quoi de siextraordinaire?' *Études internationales* 45:1 (2014) 105.
174. Generally, *see* K. Magliveras, 'Fighting Impunity Unsuccessfully in Africa: A Critique of the African Union's Handling of the Hissène Habré Affair', *RADIC* 22:3 (2014) 420.
175. ECOWAS Court of Justice, *Hissène Habré v. Republic of Senegal*, Decision No. ECW/CCJ/RUL/05/13, 5 Nov. 2013, at: http://www.courtecowas.org (in French).
176. Chambre Africaine Extraordinaire d'Assises, *Le Procuteur Général contre Hissein Habré*, Judgment, 30 May 2016, at: http://www.chambresafricaines.org/pdf/Jugement_complet.pdf; *see* S.A.E. Høgestøl, 'The Habré Judgment at the Extraordinary African Chambers: A Singular Victory in the Fight Against Impunity', *Nordic Journal of Human Rights* 34 (2016):147.

representing Habré. In April 2017, the Appeals Chamber acquitted him of a rape charge but confirmed all other charges and did not alter the sentence of life imprisonment.[177]

42. In the closing months of 2006, relations between the AU and, respectively, the EU and the UN family were given considerable impetus. Thus, on 2 October 2006, the AUC and the EU Commission signed a MoU on the establishment of a partnership to foster twinning and exchange.[178] In November 2006, the UN Secretary-General and the AUC Chairperson concluded the framework for a ten-year AU capacity-building programme highlighting the key areas for cooperation, including institution-building and financial management; peace and security; human development; and food security and environmental protection.[179] A month later, the PSC and the UN Security Council decided to set up a coordination and consultation mechanism, which is operative until today.[180] Finally, in December 2006 the Summit on Food Security in Africa was organized by the UN Food and Agricultural Organization (FAO), the AU, and NEPAD in Nigeria under the theme 'Food Security: an Engine for Growth and Poverty Alleviation in Africa.'[181]

On another front, in December 2006, Ethiopia's military assisted the Transitional Federal Government in Somalia to expel a rebel group known as the 'Union of Islamic Courts.'[182] However, not much later Ethiopia took advantage of the turmoil in Somalia and the lack of an effective government and invaded its territory. It is submitted that, pursuant to the principles enshrined in the AU Constitutive Act, this act amounted to unilateral intervention in another Member State's internal affairs. It was therefore prohibited and the AU ought to have intervened. However, African leaders had only praise for Ethiopia regarding its intervention in Somalia on the invitation of the (legitimate) Transitional Federal Government: they treated it as a positive development and as creating an unprecedented opportunity for lasting peace in the country.[183] In January 2007, with the Ethiopian troops withdrawing, the African Union Mission in

177. Chambre Africaine Extraordinaire d'Assises d'Appel, *Le Procuteur Général contre Hissein Habré*, Judgment, 27 Apr. 2017, at: http://www.chambresafricaines.org. *See* further The Guardian, 'Ex-Chad dictator's conviction for crimes against humanity upheld by Dakar court', 27 Apr. 2017, at: https://www.theguardian.com/world/2017/apr/27/conviction-chad-hissene-habre-crimes-against-humanity-upheld.
178. Generally, *see* N. Pirozzi (ed.), *Strengthening the Africa-EU Partnership on Peace and Security: How to Engage African Regional Organizations and Civil Society* (Rome: Istituto Affairi Internazionali, 2012).
179. *See* Joint Declaration on 'Enhancing UN-AU Cooperation: Framework for the Ten-Year Capacity Building Programme for the African Union', 16 Nov. 2016. Note that on 30 May 2007, during its Forty-First Ordinary Session, the African Human Rights Commission stressed that the Framework's operationalization should also address needs in capacity building and ensure adequate resources.
180. *See* further UNSC Res. 1809(2008) of 16 Apr. 2008 on effective partnerships between the United Nations and regional organizations, particularly the AU, and UN Press Release SC/9301, 16 Apr. 2008, at: http://www.un.org/press/en/2008/sc9301.doc.htm.
181. *See* FAO, *State of Food Insecurity in the World 2006* (Rome, 2006).
182. *See* B. Roggio, 'The Rise & Fall of Somalia's Islamic Courts: An Online History', *The Long War Journal*, 4 Jan. 2007, at: http://www.longwarjournal.org/archives/2007/01/the_rise_fall_of_som.php.
183. *See* Assembly, *Decision on Somalia*, AU Doc. Assembly/AU/Dec. 142 (VIII) (30 Jan. 2007).

Somalia (AMISOM) was formed pursuant to a PSC decision to assist in resolving this long-standing crisis.[184] Despite AMISOM being rather ineffective on the ground, the UN Security Council authorized six-month extensions of its mandate, first under Resolution 1772(2007) of 20 August 2007 and again under Resolution 1801(2008) of 20 February 2008 where it also expressed its intention to consider deploying a UN peacekeeping force to succeed AMISOM. No doubt this would bring into memory the ill-fated UN Operation in Somalia (UNOSOM I), which was created in the early 1990s under UNSC Resolution 751(1992) of 24 April 1992.

In May 2013, UNSC Resolution 2102(2013) established the UN Assistance Mission in Somalia (UNSOM) acting on the recommendations of the UN Secretary General.[185] UNSOM, which became operative in the summer of 2013 and replaced the UN Political Office for Somalia (UNPOS) which had completed its mandate in June 2013, operates alongside AMISOM. Both AMISOM and UNSOM are provided logistic and life support by the UN Support Office in Somalia (UNSOS) set up under UNSC Resolution 2245(2015) of 9 November 2015.[186] Until today, the UNSC has not established is own peacekeeping mission for Somalia, because, as stated in Resolution 2297(2016) of 7 July 2016, it agreed with the UN Secretary-General that conditions in Somalia were not appropriate for its deployment and, therefore, it prolonged AMISOM's mandate until 31 May 2017.[187] The EU has also had a sizeable input in the Somalia situation principally by making available considerable funding. Thus, an AU-EU agreement signed on 20 September 2013 allocated a further financial support to AMISOM in the tune of EUR 124 million from June 2013 to December 2013, bringing its contribution to AMISOM to EUR 411 million since March 2007[188] Also in September 2013, the EU and the Federal Government of Somalia organized a High-Level Conference in Brussels on 'A New Deal for Somalia' where the EU pledged EUR 650 million towards the reconstruction of the country. However, even the ever generous EU cannot maintain its funding for very long and when in 2016 it cut funding to AMISOM it rushed to explain that it should not be misconstrued as a sign of bad relations but the result of competing priorities in Africa and elsewhere.[189]

43. The Eighth Ordinary Assembly Session (Addis Ababa, 29–30 January 2007) appointed the members of the Panel of the Wise, which together with the PSC, the African Standby Force, the Military Staff Committee, and the Continental Early Warning System (CEWS), comprise the so-called African Peace and Security Architecture

---

184. *See* PSC, *Communiqué of the 69th Meeting of the Peace and Security Council*, AU Doc. PSC/PR/Comm (LXIX) (19 Jan. 2007).
185. *See* United Nations, *Letter of the Secretary-General addressed to the President of the Security Council on the findings and observations of the Somalia technical assessment mission*, UN Doc. S/2013/239 (19 Apr. 2013).
186. UNSOS replaced the United Nations Support Office for the African Union Mission in Somalia (UNSOA) established under UNSC Res. 1863(2009) in January 2009, *see* http://unsoa.unmissions.org/.
187. For further details, *see* http://unsom.unmissions.org/.
188. *See* https://eeas.europa.eu/delegations/somalia/1764/somalia-and-the-eu_en#Peace+and+Security.
189. *See* 'EU Reiterates Its Continued Support For AMISOM', 27 Apr. 2016, at: http://amisom-au.org/2016/04/eu-reiterates-its-continued-support-for-amisom/.

(APSA).[190] Moreover, it adopted the African Charter on Democracy, Elections and Governance, which entered into force on 15 February 2012 and has currently been signed by forty-six Member States but has received the unacceptably low number of twenty-four ratifications (the last seven Members to deposit instruments of ratification were Benin on 11 July 2012, Malawi on 24 October 2012, Djibouti on 22 January 2013, Mali on 2 September 2013, Sudan on 16 September 2013, Cote d'Ivoire on 23 November 2013, the SADR on 27 January 2014, and South Sudan on 13 April 2015).[191] Building on previous instruments and similar initiatives, the Charter aims at becoming the main reference point for political reform based on democratic and rule of law ideals. It is often cited in PSC resolutions which are adopted for the purpose of not recognizing regimes which came into power in an undemocratic/unconstitutional manner.

The internal structure of the African Court on Human and Peoples' Rights was approved during the Eleventh Ordinary Executive Council Session (Accra, Ghana, 25–29 June 2007).[192] The Court's first eleven judges had been appointed by the Assembly in January 2006. Moreover, the Executive Council deliberated the modalities of the Africa-EU Summit, which was scheduled to take place in December 2007.[193] It also endorsed the Protocol regulating relations between the AU and RECs,[194] which the Assembly adopted during its Ninth Ordinary Session (Accra, Ghana, 1–3 July 2007).[195] Finally, the Executive Council adopted the Declaration on the African Union Border Programme (AUBP).[196] The AUBP, which comes under the Peace and Security Department (PSD) of the AUC, centres around two principal axes: to delimit and to demark borders where it has not yet been achieved and to develop cross-border cooperation. African Ministers in charge of border issues have adopted the 7th of June of each year as the 'African Border Day' to popularize the importance of the AUBP in promoting peace and integration in the continent. The first African Border Day was celebrated in 2011. Moreover, during the Ninth Ordinary Assembly Session the discussion on forming a politically united continent was consolidated, as a follow-up

---

190. *See* Assembly, *Decision on the Appointment of the Members of the Panel of the Wise*, AU Doc. Assembly/AU/Dec. 152 (VIII) (30 Jan. 2007).
191. *See* Assembly, *Decision on the African Charter on Democracy, Elections and Governance*, AU Doc. Assembly/AU/Dec. 147 (VIII) (30 Jan. 2007).
192. *See* Executive Council, *Decision on the Structure of the African Court on Human and Peoples' Rights*, AU Doc. EX.CL/Dec. 351 (XI) (29 Jun. 2007).
193. *See* Executive Council, *Decision on Africa-European Union Dialogue*, AU Doc. EX.CL/Dec. 355 (XI) (29 Jun. 2007).
194. *See* Executive Council, *Decision on the Protocol on Relations Between the African Union and the Regional Economic Communities (RECs)*, AU Doc. EX.CL/Dec.357 (XI) (29 Jun. 2007). *See* the text of the Protocol at: https://caast-net-plus.org/object/document/239/attach/AU-RECs-Protocol.pdf.
195. *See* Assembly, *Decision on the Protocol on Relations between the African Union and the Regional Economic Communities (RECs)*, AU Doc. Assembly/AU/Dec. 166 (IX) (3 Jul. 2007). For the outcomes of the Ninth Ordinary Assembly Session, see the briefing by the South African Deputy Minister of Foreign Affairs, 16 Jul. 2007, at: http://www.gov.za/s-van-der-merwe-briefing-heads-mission-african-union-summit-outcomes.
196. *See* Executive Council, *Decision on the Conference of African Ministers in Charge of Border Issues held in Addis Ababa, on 7 June 2007*, AU Doc. EX.CL/Dec. 370 (XI) (29 Jun. 2007).

to deliberations at the Tenth Extraordinary Executive Council Session (Durban, South Africa, 8–10 May 2007). On 3 July 2007, Member States adopted the Accra Declaration on the Union Government of Africa, where they resolved to accelerate the continent's economic and political integration and to create an African Common Market with a timeframe shorter than the Treaty establishing the AEC.[197] It should be noted that the political integration, a project which was pushed very hard by Colonel Gaddafi, was finally downplayed in the Accra Declaration. African leaders opted to promote economic integration, a project which has never really got off the ground in Africa.

After many years of delay, the Second Africa-EU Summit took place in Lisbon in December 2007. From the outset, the Summit was surrounded by controversy because Great Britain and other EU Member States had objected (unsuccessfully as it turned out) to the participation of President Mugabe of Zimbabwe because of his totalitarian regime. The Summit resulted in the adoption of a Joint AU-EU Strategy and an Action Plan, which centred on an Africa-EU Strategic Partnership from 2008–2010 concentrating on eight themes covering such diverse topics as human rights, climate change, migration, and space exploration. The first follow-up meeting took place on 4 February 2008 at the AU headquarters. The second meeting was organized in Brussels on 1 April 2008 under the theme 'The Africa-EU Strategic Partnership: Challenges and Prospects.' At the Third Africa-EU Summit, which took place in Libya in November 2010 and centred on investment, economic growth, and job creation, the two sides agreed to continue working on the same eight themes and, therefore, the Second Action Plan (from 2011–2013) has retained them. However, the Second Action Plan has sought to increase policy dialogue and coordination, cooperation on administrative issues, and strengthening the capacity of AU bodies mainly in the areas of human resources, financial resources and statistics.[198] The vigour with which the EU has once again surrounded Africa should have to do not only with the inroads that several emerging economies (principally the BRIC countries (namely Brazil, Russia, India and China))[199] have made in Africa but also with the renewed interest that the USA has taken in the continent.[200] Perhaps it was the first time that Europe had feared that it might lose its primacy in Africa.

The Fourth EU-Africa Summit, which took place on 2–3 April 2014 in Brussels on the theme of 'Investing in People, Prosperity and Peace,' was expected to augment the areas and the intensity of the negotiations. As argued by J.-B. Natame, a high-

197. Text at: http://www.dirco.gov.za/docs/2007/ghan_decl0706.htm. Generally, *see* T. Murithi (ed.), *Towards a Union Government for Africa – Challenges and Opportunities*, Institute of Security Studies Monograph Series, No. 140 (Pretoria, January 2008); B. Yao Gebe, 'The Quest for a Union Government of Africa: Reflections on the Vision and the Realities of Political Integration', *South African J. of International Affairs* 15 (2008): 41.

198. *See* further at: http://africa-eu-partnership.org/en/3rd-africa-eu-summit and for the various documents adopted in the context of the Joint Africa-EU Strategy Action Plan 2011–2013, *see* http://www.africa-eu-partnership.org/sites/default/files/documents/03-jeas_action_plan_en.pdf.

199. Compare Assembly, *Decision on the Africa-South America Summit*, AU Doc. Assembly/AU/Dec.159 (VIII) (30 Jan. 2007); and *Decision on the Africa-China Forum on Cooperation (FOCAC)*, AU Doc. Assembly/AU/Dec. 160 (VIII) (30 Jan. 2007).

200. Generally, *see* A. Huliaras & K. Magliveras, 'In Search of a Policy: European Union and U.S. Reactions to the Growing Chinese Presence in Africa', *European Foreign Affairs Review* 13 (2008): 399.

ranking official with the AUC, on the occasion of the Joint Brainstorming Session on the future of the Joint Africa-EU Strategy held in September 2013, the two sides should not only reflect thoroughly where their partnership stands today but should also discuss the EU's continued engagement as regards, *inter alia*, the current continental frameworks of action. He cited the following frameworks, some of which arguably overlap: the CFTA, the Comprehensive Africa Agriculture Development Program (CAADP), the Programme for Infrastructure Development in Africa (PIDA), the Action Plan for Accelerated Industrial Development of Africa (AIDA), the APSA, the Action Plan for Boosting Intra-Africa Trade (BIAT), and the Accelerated Reduction of Maternal Mortality in Africa (CARMA). There is no doubt that much had changed since the Third Africa-EU Summit in 2010. Many an African country experienced rapid economic growth and there were positive developments in the political front, while the EU was confronted with a damaging financial and banking crisis, which revealed deep rifts and divisions among its membership. The Fourth EU-Africa Summit adopted, *inter alia*, a Roadmap 2014–2017 to complement the Joint Africa-EU Strategy (JAES).[201] While these documents reveal a willingness on behalf of the EU to follow a differentiated relationship towards Africa treating it as a more equal partner, recent challenges faced by the EU (including migratory waves and the initiation of withdrawal proceedings by Great Britain) could question its long-term commitment towards the continent. But until then, the stated EU position is that it wants to deepen its relationship with Africa.[202]

44. On 28 January 2008, the AU and several RECs (including the Community of Sahelo-Saharan States (CENSAD), ECOWAS, and the Intergovernmental Authority on Development (IGAD)) signed a MoU aiming at reinforcing cooperation ties and at coordinating activities. Over and above reviewing the status of those conflicts which, directly or indirectly, were posing threats to peace and security, the Tenth Ordinary Assembly Session (Addis Ababa, 31 January–2 February 2008) dealt with two other major issues. The first issue concerned the Report and Declaration of the Second Conference of African Ministers of Integration (Kigali, 26–27 July 2007). The Assembly endorsed the recommendations and requested Member States to implement them in cooperation with the UN Economic Commission of Africa (ECA), the African Development Bank, and other (undisclosed) development partners.[203] The second issue was the deliberation of the Report on the Audit of the AU, which had been requested by the aforementioned Assembly Session in Accra Summit in July 2007. The Report, which was submitted in mid-December 2007 by an independent group of experts, was the first attempt to examine the effectiveness and the impact of AU programmes, an effort which for some strange reason was associated with the project of political

201. At: http://www.european-council.europa.eu/eu-africa-summit-2014 For the Roadmap and other relevant documents, *see* http://www.consilium.europa.eu/en/meetings/international-summit/2014/04/02-03/. For evaluation of JAES, *see* A. Sherriff & J. Kotsopoulos, 'Africa and the European Union: An Assessment of the Joint Africa-EU Strategy (JAES)' in *Handbook of Africa's International Relations*, T. Murithi (ed.)(Abingdon: Routledge, 2013) 305.

202. *See* European Commission, *The EU-Africa Partnership*, MEMO/15/4808, 22 Apr. 2015, at: http://europa.eu/rapid/press-release_MEMO-15-4808_en.htm.

203. *See* Assembly, *Decision on Economic Integration*, AU Doc. Assembly/AU/Dec. 178 (X) (2 Feb. 2008).

integration and the creation of a Union Government.[204] As the Assembly had not been adequately prepared to appraise the 197-page Report, it authorized the convening within three months of an Extraordinary Executive Council Session to analyse and evaluate it.[205] It was held in Arusha on 7 May 2008. As was perhaps to be expected, the Session did not result in any breakthroughs but repeated the usual rhetoric on how to accelerate the process for setting up the remaining AU organs and to operationalize the AEC.

With at least one-fifth of the AU membership embroiled at the time in domestic strife and transnational conflicts (suffice to mention the DRC, Côte d'Ivoire, Burundi, Sudan, the Comoros, Chad, the CAR, Kenya, Somalia, Ethiopia, and Eritrea) it is no wonder that the AU (just as the OAU before it) was unable to muster the necessary strength and demand its proper place on the international arena as one of the major international political institutions. Six years after its inauguration, there was a huge gap between the goals and the principles stated in the Constitutive Act and the policies adopted and implemented by the AU organs.

The theme of the Eleventh Ordinary Assembly Session (Sharm-El-Sheikh, Egypt, 24 June–1 July 2008) was 'Meeting the Millennium Development Goals on Water and Sanitation.' The Assembly carried on from the previous Session the deliberations on creating a Union Government leading to the United States of Africa (to be abbreviated U.S.A. as well?). The project had to do with the challenges facing the AU: on the one hand, to address effectively the principal African problems through long-term solutions and, on the other hand, to map out an institutional framework that even for the EU would have been considered revolutionary. The former was an urgent task that could not any longer be neglected. The latter was, arguably, of secondary importance. For a number of years now the 'Union Government' project has become a back burner, a fact which should be attributed to the demise of Colonel Gaddafi, the principal underwriter of political integration projects. But such projects were and still are Alptraums motivated by the wishes and the desires of specific African leaders. And there is much point to discuss them if lasting solutions to the scourges devastating Africa have been found. A UN document released in 2008 listed all the conflicts around the globe with which the Security Council had been involved. The document made grim reading as most conflicts were in or about Africa.[206] This situation has continued.[207] Suffice to mention that from January 2011 until December 2013 the Security Council

---

204. *See* African Union, *Audit of the African Union: Towards A People-Centred Political and Socio-economic Integration and Transformation of Africa*, Addis Ababa, December 2007.

205. *See* Assembly, *Decision on the Report of the Executive Council on the Audit of the Union and the Report of the Ministerial Committee on the Union Government*, AU Doc. Assembly/AU/Dec. 185 (X) (2 Feb. 2008).

206. *See* UNSC, *Summary statement by the Secretary-General on matters of which the Security Council is seized and on the stage reached in their consideration*, UN Doc. S/2008/10 (13 May 2008).

207. *See* UNSC, *Summary statement by the Secretary-General on matters of which the Security Council is seized and on the stage reached in their consideration*, UN Doc. S/2013/10 (2 Jan. 2013).

considered at formal meetings the situation in fifteen African states,[208] and in the period from January 2013 until December 2015 in twelve African states.[209]

45. The theme of the Twelfth Ordinary Assembly Session (Addis Ababa, 1–3 February 2009) was 'Infrastructure Development in Africa.' The Assembly was arguably pre-occupied with the international law principle of universal jurisdiction and the fundamentally different way that African states and European states understood and apply it. Universal jurisdiction embodies the principle of international law allowing a state to prosecute and bring to trial the citizens of a third state, who have allegedly committed an array of international crimes, even though the former state may have no link with their perpetration and without breaching state sovereignty. The differing opinions on this principle's applicability resulted in considerable friction between the AU and European states. Moreover, as certain countries (e.g., Belgium and France) had issued arrest warrants against Africans on the basis of this very principle led to problems in bilateral relations. European states have justified the arrest warrants and the legal proceedings against Africans by, *inter alia*, invoking the ethos of impunity prevailing in Africa and that their (alleged) commission amounted to mass violations of human rights which were neither investigated nor prosecuted by African states. Apparently reacting to these accusations, the Assembly suggested that the African Court on Human and Peoples' Rights be empowered to try individuals for egregious criminal offences, namely genocide, crimes against humanity and war crimes.[210] It is not clear whether the Assembly considered the repercussions of such a move to the jurisdiction of other international courts. Regarding the International Criminal Court (ICC) specifically, the consequences would concern those African states which are also contracting parties to the Rome Statute establishing the ICC as well as those situations already at that time referred to the ICC by the UNSC (namely, the situation in Darfur – the situation in Libya was referred in 2011). Given that African states constitute the largest single group of ICC parties and that the ICC deals predominantly with situations in Africa, the implications of this suggestion were significant.

The Twelfth Ordinary Assembly Session also adopted the following three instruments. First, the African Charter on Statistics, which was signed on 4 February 2009. It has currently been signed by thirty Member States and received nine of the fifteen ratifications required to enter into force (the last by Zambia in December 2013).[211] Second, the Statute of the African Union Commission on International Law (AUCIL), which came into force the very day that the Assembly adopted it.[212] Third, the Protocol for the Establishment of the African Investment Bank (AIB), one of the three financial

208. *See* UNSC, *Summary statement by the Secretary-General on matters of which the Security Council is seized and on the stage reached in their consideration*, UN Doc. S/2014/10 (2 Jan. 2014).

209. *See* UNSC, *Summary statement by the Secretary-General on matters of which the Security Council is seized and on the stage reached in their consideration*, UN Doc. S/2016/10 (4 Jan. 2016).

210. *See* Assembly, *Decision on the Implementation of the Assembly Decision on the Abuse of the Principle of Universal Jurisdiction*, AU Doc. Assembly/AU/Dec. 213 (XII) (3 Feb. 2009).

211. *See* Assembly, *Decision on the Draft African Charter on Statistics*, AU Doc. Assembly/AU/Dec. 210 (XII) (3 Feb. 2009).

212. *See* Assembly, *Decision on the Draft Statute of the African Union Commission on International Law*, AU Doc. Assembly/AU/Dec. 209 (XII) (3 Feb. 2009).

institutions envisaged in Article 19 of the Constitutive Act.[213] Currently, it has been signed by twenty Member States and ratified by only two (Congo and Libya). Thirteen more ratifications are required to enter into force.

During its Thirteenth Ordinary Session (Sirte, Libya, 1–3 July 2009) the Assembly was again seized of the saga concerning the 'blatant abuse' by European states of the principle of universal jurisdiction. The Assembly made the novel suggestion that 'an international regulatory body' be set up with the competence to review complaints arising from the abusive exploitation of the universal jurisdiction principle by individual states.[214] The question of the application of universal jurisdiction by European courts targeting Africans has persisted and was one of the issues discussed during the Fourth EU-Africa Summit in April 2014.[215] The Assembly also addressed the aforementioned arrest warrant by the ICC Prosecutor against the President of Sudan Omar al Bashir for allegedly committing crimes against humanity in Darfur. It has since been developed into a major issue of contention between the AU and the ICC.[216] It is submitted that the Assembly's approach was out of line for two reasons. First, because it effectively ordered Member States (including those that have chosen to become contracting parties to the Rome Statute) not to cooperate with the ICC in arresting and surrendering al Bashir to The Hague. Second, because it regarded this arrest warrant as an affront to the dignity, sovereignty and integrity of African states. Undoubtedly, the Assembly, as the highest-ranking organ of an intergovernmental organization, may legitimately show its opposition towards another international institution, namely the ICC. However, to request Member States not to discharge duties owed to the ICC and, at the same time, to neglect addressing the ethos of impunity (especially for the crimes perpetrated in Darfur) is at least problematic.

The Thirteenth Assembly Session also authorized the AU accession to the UN Framework Convention on Climate Change, which was adopted in 1992,[217] and to the Kyoto Protocol, adopted in 1997.[218] It did so by taking advantage of Article 22 of the Framework Convention and Article 24 of the Kyoto Protocol allowing accession by Regional Economic Integration Organizations (REIOs) to these two treaties.[219] The EU had already acceded to both instruments, respectively, in December 1993 and in

213. *See* Assembly, *Decision on the Protocol on the Establishment of the African Investment Bank*, AU Doc. Assembly/AU/Dec. 212 (XII) (3 Feb. 2009).

214. *See* Assembly, *Decision on the Abuse of the Principle of Universal Jurisdiction*, AU Doc. Assembly/AU/Dec. 243 (XIII) (3 Jul. 2009).

215. *See* Fourth EU-Africa Summit, 2–3 Apr. 2014, *Brussels Declaration*, para. 10, at: http://www.nepad.org/content/fourth-eu-africa-summit-2-3-april-2014-brussels-declaration; and *Roadmap 2014-2017*, para. 9, at: http://www.africa-eu-partnership.org/sites/default/files/documents/2014_04_01_4th_eu-africa_summit_roadmap_en.pdf.

216. ICC Pre-Trial Chamber I, *Decision on the Prosecution's Application for a Warrant of Arrest against Omar Hassan Ahmad Al Bashir*, ICC-02/05-01/09-3, 4 Mar. 2009, 48 I.L.M. (2009) 463. The following year a second arrest warrant was issued, ICC Pre-Trial Chamber I, *Second Warrant of Arrest for Omar Hassan Ahmed Al Bashir*, ICC-02/05-01/09-95, 12 Jul. 2010.

217. 1771 U.N.T.S. 107.

218. 2303 U.N.T.S. 148.

219. *See* Assembly, *Decision on the Accession of the African Union to the United Nations Framework Convention on Climate Change (UNFCCC) and the Kyoto Protocol Rev. 1*, AU Doc. Assembly/AU/Dec. 248 (XIII) (3 Jul. 2009).

May 2002. However, until today, the AU has not acceded to either instrument; the AU is among the one hundred intergovernmental organizations which have been admitted as observers to the Framework Convention.[220] The Assembly also authorized[221] the AU to accede to the UN Convention to Combat Desertification in those Countries Experiencing Serious Drought and/or Desertification, Particularly in Africa.[222] Finally, the Assembly adopted a decision dealing with the scourge of coups d'état and the ability to handle them.[223] As regards the stipulations of the decision on enhancing the effectiveness of the AU's response to unconstitutional changes of government, they were a mere repetition of Article 25 of the African Charter on Democracy, Elections and Governance (2007), which at the time had not entered into force. The Assembly considered that the AU was well endowed with an array of instruments to tackle coups d'état and, therefore, the aim was not to elaborate new ones but to promote their effective implementation and, where necessary, to refine, to enrich and to update them. Arguably, the situation was slightly more complicated because the AU did not only have to address the question of Member States' not discharging the obligations flowing from these instruments but also the very high number of (mostly violent) coups d'état, which negated the promotion of peace, security and stability in the continent. Suffice to mention that in a report submitted by the AUC Chairperson to the Special Assembly Session on the Consideration and Resolution of Conflicts in Africa, held in Tripoli, Libya, on 30–31 August 2009, he cited seventeen instances of interstate and intra-state conflicts, coups d'état, etc.[224]

46. Before the commencement of the Fourteenth Ordinary Assembly Session (Addis Ababa, 31 January–2 February 2010) Gaddafi attempted to secure a second term as AU Chairperson but, despite the leverage he exerted on many a Member State, he failed.[225] The Assembly took further measures to enhance the AU effectiveness to respond to coups d'état.[226] Thus, over and above suspending from participation the Member State where the coup took place, it agreed on the following measures. First, the perpetrators shall be barred from participating in the elections to be held to restore constitutional order. Second, sanctions, whose precise content was not given in the decision, shall be implemented against any Member State proven to have instigated

220. *See* http://unfccc.int/parties_and_observers/igo/items/9412.php.
221. *See* Assembly, *Decision on the African Union Accession to the United Nations Convention to Combat Desertification (UNCCD) Rev. 1*, AU Doc. Assembly/AU/Dec. 255 (XIII) (3 Jul. 2009).
222. 1954 U.N.T.S. 3. *See also* UNGA Res. 64/202 of 21 Dec. 2009 titled 'Implementation of the United Nations Convention to Combat Desertification in Those Countries Experiencing Serious Drought and/or Desertification, Particularly in Africa'.
223. *See* Assembly, *Decision on the Prevention of Unconstitutional Changes of Government and Strengthening the Capacity of the African Union to Manage Such Situations*, AU Doc. Assembly/AU/Dec. 253 (XIII) (3 Jul. 2009).
224. *See* Report of the Chairperson of the Commission, *Enhancing Africa's Resolve and Effectiveness in Ending Conflict and Sustaining Peace*, AU Doc. SP/ASSEMBLY/PS/RPT(I) (2009), pp. 12 et seq.
225. *See* A. Huliaras & K. Magliveras, 'The End of an Affair? Libya and Sub-Saharan Africa', *Journal of North African Studies* 16 (2011): 167.
226. *See* Assembly, *Decision on the Prevention of Unconstitutional Changes of Government and Strengthening the Capacities of the African Union to Manage such Situations*, AU Doc. Assembly/AU/Dec. 269 (XIV) Rev. 1 (2 Feb. 2010).

or supported the coup. Third, additional punitive measures, including economic sanctions, could be ordered by the Assembly. It is submitted that, as a whole, these measures, whose legal basis was lacking in the decision, constituted a de facto amendment of the Constitutive Act. This argument is based on that Article 30 thereof stipulates a framework for the AU's response specifically to coups d'état. Moreover, these measures lacked the precision required when punitive measures are imposed on Member States given that, in principle, they violate state sovereignty but are allowed because they have already been agreed and accepted by the whole membership. For example, it is not stipulated which organ shall determine authoritatively that a Member State has instigated a coup d'état against another Member; clearly it should be an impartial and independent organ and one not succumbed to political manipulation, so rife in African affairs. Moreover, to prevent the coup perpetrators from participating in future democratic elections, correct as it might be, is arguably problematic because it could be construed as unacceptable interference in the domestic affairs of the Member State concerned. It should be accepted that it cannot be effected until and unless it is enshrined in its Constitution.

The Assembly also proclaimed 2010 as the Year of Peace and Security in Africa.[227] This was largely a symbolic act. Africa had definitely made overall progress in the reduction of violent conflicts, while democratic and rule of law norms were practiced with increased intensity. However, the situation remained fragile. Future events showed that such initiatives are devoid of purpose if not accompanied by vigorous actions and commitments. One has in mind fighting impunity, famine and illiteracy, promoting closer cooperation between the AU and the RECs but also the RECs among them to achieve economies of scale and reduce waste and committing large funds to self-sufficient well prepared and executed peace and security operations. The coup d'état in Madagascar in March 2009 (*infra*, paragraph 178) is a good illustration how easily the AU's peace and security agenda can be derailed. Even though the Assembly took the rather unusual step to consider the situation both as a separate issue[228] and also in the context of its assessment of those situations posing threats and challenges to peace and security,[229] and despite the country's isolation from the world stage, the AU did not manage to remove from office Andry Rajoelina, the strongman who assumed power in the 2009 coup, until the holding of presidential elections in December 2013. The question of whether in furtherance of the aforementioned Assembly Decision 269(XIV), Rajoelina should not have stood as presidential candidate did not come up because, under pressure from Southern African Development Community (SADC), both Rajoelina and his arch-rival Ravalomanana consented to opt out from the race, as revealed during the Extraordinary Troika Summit of the SADC Organ on Politics, Defence and Security held in Tanzania in January 2013. Their exclusion, together with seven other candidates, from the presidential race was confirmed in August 2013 by the Special Electoral

227. *See* Assembly, *Decision on the Year of Peace and Security in Africa*, AU Doc. Assembly/AU/Dec. 275 (XIV) (2 Feb. 2010).

228. *See* Assembly, *Decision on Madagascar*, AU Doc. Assembly/AU/Dec. 279 (XIV) (2 Feb. 2010).

229. *See* Assembly, *Decision on the Report of the Peace and Security Council on its Activities and the Situation of Peace and Security in Africa*, AU Doc. Assembly/AU/Dec. 268 (XIV) (2 Feb. 2010).

Court, which was formed at the time to assist the organization of the first successful post-coup elections in Madagascar.[230] However the Court did not disqualify Rajoelina as the instigator of the coup but because he had failed to file the required documentation within the prescribed deadline.[231]

Given the rather vague and unclear institutional position of NEPAD within the AU (*supra*, paragraph 38), the Assembly resolved to integrate it into the AU structures and processes. In particular, it established the NEPAD Planning and Coordinating Agency (NPCA) as a technical AU body to replace the NEPAD Secretariat and made the NEPAD Heads of State and Government Orientation Committee (HSGOC) an Assembly sub-committee providing political leadership and strategic guidance on the NEPAD Programme. Finally, it resolved that NPCA's financing will be secured through the ordinary AU budget, through voluntary contributions by Member States and through support by the private sector.[232] Finally, the Assembly adopted the Annexes to the Statutes of the AIB,[233] which had been recommended by the Executive Council a few days earlier.[234] It was decided that the Special Drawing Rights (SDRs) of the International Monetary Fund will be the AIB unit of account until the introduction of an African single currency.

In June 2010, the Panel of the Wise, one of the components of APSA, published its report on how the AU should strengthen its preventive and management role vis-à-vis election-related disputes and conflicts. The report, while acknowledging that elections had become a core ingredient of popular participation in the governance process, cited several principles to be applied, which arguably should be considered as novelty for Africa, e.g., 'rules of orderly political competition' and 'building institutions of competition that are widely accepted by winners and losers'.[235] During the Fifteenth Ordinary Assembly Session (Kampala, Uganda, 25–27 July 2010) the first steps were taken to establish the Pan-African University (PAU), a project that had been proposed by the first African Ministerial Conference on Science and Technology

230. SADC leaders congratulated the Special Electoral Court for its 'bold decision' to disqualify them, *see Communiqué of the 33rd Summit of SADC Heads of State and Government*, Lilongwe, Malawi, 17–18 Aug. 2013, para. 19.

231. *See* The Carter Center, *Legislative and Second Round of Presidential Elections in Madagascar*, Final Report (Atlanta, Georgia, December 2013) 19, at http://www.cartercenter.org.

232. *See* Assembly, *Decision on the Integration of the New Partnership for Africa's Development (NEPAD) into the Structures and Processes of the African Union including the Establishment of the NEPAD Planning and Coordinating Agency (NPCA)*, AU Doc. Assembly/AU/Dec. 283 (XIV) (2 Feb. 2010).

233. *See* Assembly, *Decision on the Annexes to the Statutes of the African Investment Bank*, AU Doc. Assembly/AU/Dec. 286 (XIV) (2 Feb. 2010).

234. *See* Executive Council, *Decision on the Annexes to the Statutes of the African Investment Bank*, AU Doc. EX.CL/Dec. 550 (XVI) (29 Jan. 2010).

235. African Union Panel of the Wise, 'Election-Related Disputes and Political Violence: Strengthening the Role of the African Union in Preventing, Managing, and Resolving Conflict', *The African Union Series* (New York: International Peace Institute, July 2010) at: http://www.peaceau.org/uploads/au-electionviolence-epub.pdf.

in Johannesburg in 2003.[236] The University has seats in three different Member States: in Nigeria, where the concentration is on life and earth sciences, in Kenya on basic sciences, technology, and innovation, and in Cameroon on governance, humanities, and social sciences.[237] The Assembly also adopted the Revised African Maritime Transport Charter, which at the time of writing has attracted only seven out of the fifteen ratifications required to enter into force.[238] Even though the Revised Charter aims at updating the previous treaty adopted in 1994, Member States have continued to become signatory parties to the 1994 treaty (e.g., Angola on 27 January 2012 and Equatorial Guinea on 30 January 2011). This strange development poses the question whether there is a specific reason why Member States continue to prefer the 1994 treaty. Another explanation may have to do with the AU's drive to persuade the membership to sign and ratify as many OAU/AU treaties as possible to ensure, on the one hand, that unratified ones come into force and, on the other hand, that the largest possible number of Member States becomes contracting parties to those already in force. Consequently, it could be argued that the AU wishes to ensure that there is a body of African legal rules which is followed universally, a process which could evolve to something akin to the EU notion of *acquis communautaire*.[239] Finally, it is submitted that, in their eagerness to sign/ratify these treaties, Member States may mistakenly do so with those which are meant to be revised and overhauled.

Moreover, the Assembly examined the commitment to gradually transform the AUC into a new organ, the Authority, in an attempt to strengthen the Organization's institutional architecture and to accelerate the integration process. However, no concrete action was taken other than to request the Commission to prepare and submit the necessary legal instruments.[240] Although the matter was to be discussed at the Assembly Session in July 2012, it was presumably not deemed ripe enough for deliberation. However, it was discussed during the Twentieth Ordinary Session in January 2013, but the Assembly only requested the Commission 'to first make appropriate

---

236. *See* Assembly, *Decision on the Establishment of the Pan-African University*, AU Doc. Assembly/AU/Dec. 290 (XV) (25 Jul. 2010). *See* further, Assembly, *Decision on the Establishment of the Pan-African University*, AU Doc. Assembly/AU/Dec. 391(XVIII) (30 Jan. 2012); Assembly, *Decision on the Establishment of the Pan-African University*, AU Doc. Assembly/AU/Dec. 418 (XIX) (16 Jul. 2012); and Assembly, *Decision on the Amendment of Article 8.2 of the Statutes of the Pan-African University*, AU Doc. Assembly/AU/Dec. 481 (XXI) (27 May 2013).
237. *See* further, First Extraordinary Session of the Conference of Ministers of Education of the African Union (COMEDAF IV+), Nairobi, 11–13 May 2011, Statute of PAU of April 2010, AU Doc. AU/ EXPT/EDUC/3b (IV+). It was amended in January 2016 by the Assembly to ensure that the Council, the highest governing body, becomes more inclusive and representative of the spectrum of stakeholders, *see* Assembly, *Decision on the Specialized Technical Committees*, AU Doc. Assembly/AU/Dec. 589 (XXVI), para. 2 (31 Jan. 2016).
238. *See* Assembly, *Decision on the Adoption of the African Maritime Transport Charter*, AU Doc. Assembly/AU/Dec. 293 (XV) (25 Jul. 2010).
239. It is a body of common rights and obligations binding upon all the EU Members, constantly evolving and comprising, *inter alia*, of the founding Treaties, the EU legislation; the judgments of the Court of Justice; and the agreements and treaties entered into by the EU.
240. *See* Assembly, *Decision on the Transformation of the African Union Commission into the African Union Authority*, AU Doc. Assembly/AU/Dec. 298 (XV) (25 Jul. 2010).

recommendations' on its own strengthening.[241] It should be noted that the whole question of the AU's institutional reform is still open, and one could detect a certain reluctance by African leaders to tackle this pressing issue. In July 2016, the Assembly entrusted Paul Kagame, the Rwandan President, to conduct, in collaboration with the Commission, a study on the AU's institutional reform and on a 'system of governance' capable of addressing the challenges facing it.[242]

During its Fifteenth Ordinary Session, the Assembly also resolved to establish and operationalize the African Petroleum Fund.[243] The idea behind it can be traced to the Seventh Ordinary Assembly Session, which had recognized the need to alleviate the impact of oil prices' increase on poor Member States and had asked for the development of a Strategy for cooperation and solidarity between oil producing and non-oil producing African countries.[244] Moreover, the Cairo Declaration on African Cooperation and Solidarity in the Field of Hydrocarbons, which was adopted on 14 December 2006, promoted further the idea.[245] Even though the Fund has been set up (it is hosted and operated by the African Development Bank), it has not been able to support non-oil exporting African countries because of a lack of contributions, which are voluntary.[246] Interestingly enough, a proposal to levy a tax on hydrocarbons exported by Member States to resource the fund has been proposed but summarily rejected questioning the commitment to allow the Fund play its proper role. Even though the Fund should have liaised with the African Petroleum Producers Association (APPA), the regional platform for petroleum producing states to cooperate, collaborate, and share knowledge and competence, apparently this has not been possible.

Finally, the Assembly discussed for yet another time a perennial problem: the implementation of decisions and resolutions adopted by the principal organs. Although they constitute the legal foundation for the integration process in the continent, there has never been an effective mechanism to supervise the prompt and diligent execution. The Assembly requested that the 'Report on the Implementation of Previous Decisions,' which had been prepared by the Commission, be improved.[247] The new report was submitted to the Executive Council in January 2011 and confirmed the inadequate

---

241. Assembly, *Decision on the Transformation of the African Union Commission into the African Union Authority*, AU Doc. Assembly/AU/Dec. 454 (XX) (28 Jan. 2013), para. 6.

242. Assembly, *Decision on the Institutional Reform of the African Union*, AU Doc. Assembly/AU/Dec. 606 (XXVII) (18 Jul. 2016).

243. *See* Assembly, *Decision on the Establishment and Operationalisation of the African Petroleum Fund*, AU Doc. Assembly/AU/Dec. 307 (XV) (25 Jul. 2010). *See also* Executive Council, *Decision on the Report of the Second African Union Conference of Ministers Responsible for Hydrocarbons (Oil & Gas)*, AU Doc. EX.CL/Dec. 546 (XVI) (29 Jan. 2010).

244. *See* Assembly, *Decision on the Proposal to Establish a Fund within the African Union to Alleviate the Increase in Oil Price on the Poor African Countries and the Coordination of African Oil Policies*, AU Doc. Assembly/AU/Dec. 132 (VII) (14 Dec. 2006). Generally, *see* African Development Bank &African Union, *Oil and Gas in Africa* (Oxford: Oxford University Press, 2009).

245. AU Doc. AU/MIN/OG/Decl. (I) (2006).

246. *See* 'Oil fund for Africa has no money', Ghana Business News, 26 Mar. 2012, at: https://www.ghanabusinessnews.com/2012/03/26/oil-fund-for-africa-has-no-money.

247. *See* Assembly, *Decision on the Implementation of the Previous Decisions of the Executive Council and the Assembly*, AU Doc. Assembly/AU/Dec. 318 (XV) (25 Jul. 2010).

degree of implementation and a tendency to consistently defer their execution.[248] Faced with this situation, it is submitted that the AU should consider adopting the supervisory model of the EU, which entails the work of two organs: the EU Commission, which controls the proper execution of adopted decisions, and the Court of Justice, whose role is to confirm whether Member States have or have not failed to fulfil their obligations and, in the case of repeated infraction, to impose monetary sanctions. Notwithstanding the obvious practical problems that such a system will face in the AU, it should be mentioned that Article 23(2) of the Constitutive Act stipulates that resolutions are binding and envisages the infliction of sanctions by the Assembly against recalcitrant Member States.

47. During its Sixteenth Ordinary Session (Addis Ababa, 30–31 January 2011), the Assembly adopted the African Charter on the Values and Principles of Public Service and Administration, a multilateral instrument promoting the AU agenda on good governance.[249] The Charter, which entered into force on 23 July 2016 (currently signed by thirty-six and ratified by sixteen Member States), aims at improving the way Member States deliver public services and at combating corruption, the latter being one of the scourges plaguing Africa. The operationalization of the African Security and Peace Architecture (ASPA) was also discussed during the Session. ASPA was established by the AU in collaboration with the RECs with terms of reference the prevention, management, and resolution of conflicts in the continent. The EU has contributed significantly to its funding through the EU-African Peace Facility's Capacity Building Component.[250] The Assembly noted the successful conduct of the Amani Africa Exercise in November 2010, whose purpose was to assess the procedures relating to the deployment of the African Standby Force (ASF) and the AUC's capacity to undertake complex peace support operations, and welcomed the support provided by the EU and 'other multilateral and bilateral partners'.[251]

The reliance on external partners does raise the legitimate question if ASPA would survive by using solely African resources or whether it would have to continue depending on the goodwill of a number of non-African states and other international institutions. The challenges faced by complex AU projects like ASPA are multiple. They must address effectively ongoing conflicts, where invariably force must be used, they must also deal with security and peace threats as they develop, and they must initiate reconciliation, stabilization, and reconstruction processes. Given that, on the whole, the UN and its various organs and bodies are unable or unwilling to contribute to these efforts and with the scarcity of resources characterizing the AU but also the African RECs, the dependence on non-African funding is set to continue unabated. However, relevant initiatives taken by individual AU Member States often lead to

---

248. AU Doc. EX.CL/623 (XVIII) (28 January 2011), at: http://www.peaceau.org.
249. *See* Assembly, *Decision on the African Charter on the Values and Principles of Public Service and Administration*, AU Doc. Assembly/AU/Dec. 337 (XVI) (31 Jan. 2011).
250. For details, *see* European Commission, *African Peace Facility, Annual Report 2015* (Luxembourg: Publications Office of the European Union, 2016), 18–21, at: https://ec.europa.eu/europeaid/sites/devco/files/apf-report-2015-en.pdf.
251. *See* Assembly, *Decision on the Report of the Peace and Security Council on its activities and the state of Peace and Security in Africa*, AU Doc. Assembly/AU/Doc. 338 (XVI), para. 3 (31 Jan. 2011).

complications. For example, during the Sixteenth session the Assembly welcomed Egypt's proposal to establish the AU Centre for Post-Conflict Reconstruction and Development.[252] However, subsequently Uganda also offered to host the Centre as well and the two countries have not been able to find an amicable solution.[253] The Centre has apparently never been established.

According to Article 3(i) of the Constitutive Act, one of the AU's principal objectives is to establish the necessary conditions enabling Africa to play its rightful role in the global economy and in international negotiations. To fulfil this objective, the AU has not only promoted bilateral relations with other international organizations but has also attempted to advance the idea of a 'united African voice' during conferences organized at a transnational level. Thus, during its Sixteenth Session the Assembly endorsed the outcome of the Second Africa-Arab Summit, which was held on 10 October 2010.[254] It also welcomed the Declaration and Second Action Plan 2011–2013 agreed during the Third Africa-EU Summit, held in Libya in November 2010.[255] It is no coincidence that both these important events took place in Libya. Indeed, it was Colonel Gaddafi who had played an instrumental role in promoting the AU's foreign agenda. However, with his demise in the summer of 2011 and the country descending into chaos, Libya has been unable to play the pivotal role it used to. Until today, there has not been an African leader who can demonstrate that he is capable to continue and promote the foreign affairs agenda, especially when the world stage continues to be very volatile. Finally, the Assembly endorsed the African Common Position on Climate Change and the African Green Development Fund, which were tabled during the Seventh Conference of Parties to the Kyoto Protocol that met in Durban, South Africa, in December 2011.[256]

The standoff between the AU and the ICC, which, as has been explained, concerned principally the arrest warrant issued against President Al-Bashir, continued with the arrest warrants issued in June 2011 against the then leader of Libya Colonel Gadaffi, his son Saif Al-Islam, and his brother in law Abdullah Al-Senussi.[257] These Warrants of Arrest were the culmination of the investigation carried out by the ICC Prosecutor pursuant to UN Security Council Resolution 1970(2011) of February 2011, which had referred, under Article 13(b) of the Rome Statute, the alleged crimes

252. *See* Assembly, *Decision on the Establishment of an African Union Centre for Post-Conflict Reconstruction and Development (AUCPCRD),* AU Doc. Assembly/AU/Dec. 351 (XVI) (31 Jan. 2011).
253. *See* PSC, *First Progress Report of the Chairperson of the Commission on AU's Efforts on Post-Conflict Reconstruction and Development,* AU Doc. PSC/PR/2/CCCLII, paras 17 et seq. (16 Jan. 2003), at: http://www.peaceau.org.
254. *See* Assembly, *Decision on Africa-Arab Cooperation*, OAU Doc. Assembly/AU/Dec. 343 (XVI) (31 Jan. 2011).
255. *See* Assembly, *Decision on the Africa-European Union Dialogue*, OAU Doc. Assembly/AU/Dec. 344 (XVI) (31 Jan. 2011).
256. *See* Assembly, *Decision on the Sixteenth Conference of Parties to the United Nations Framework Convention on Climate Change and the Sixth Conference of Parties to the Kyoto Protocol*, OAU Doc. Assembly/AU/Dec. 342 (XVI) (31 Jan. 2011).
257. *See* ICC, *Prosecutor v. Muammar Mohammed Abu Minyar Gaddafi, Saif Al-Islam Gaddafi and Abdullah Al-Senussi*, Warrants of Arrest, ICC-01/11-01/11, P.-T. Ch. I, 27 June 2011, at http://www.icc-cpi.int/iccdocs/doc/doc1101339.pdf.

committed during the popular uprising against the Gadaffi regime to the ICC.[258] As in the case of Al-Bashir, the Assembly during its Seventeenth Ordinary Session (Malabo, Equatorial Guinea, 30 June–1 July 2011) considered that these Warrants of Arrest complicated seriously the efforts to find a negotiated political solution to the Libyan crisis and, therefore, decided that Member States shall not cooperate in their execution and requested that the Security Council, under Article 16 of the Rome Statute, defer the ICC proceedings 'in the interest of Justice as well as peace in the Country'.[259] The Assembly discussed additionally the situation in Libya in another resolution,[260] where, without offering compelling legal reasoning, it repeated its request that the Security Council defer its involvement to the African initiative, which was 'the best way of achieving...peace, democracy, the rule of law and national reconciliation in Libya'.[261] Moreover, it considered that the AU's role in the Libyan situation had been recognized by the Security Council in the aforementioned Resolution 1970(2011) and that it was fully consistent with Chapter VIII of the UN Charter concerning regional arrangements for the maintenance of peace and security.

The Assembly's position was prima facie in line with Article 53(1) of the UN Charter. However, the structure of Chapter VIII denotes that, once seized of a situation, the Security Council retains full authority over the measures to be taken to resolve it. Arguably, these measures are not only those envisaged in the UN Charter but also those to be found in other relevant multilateral instruments (in casu, the Rome Statute) and expressly granting powers to the Security Council. Thus, if any relevant action (including enforcement action) were to be pursued by a regional arrangement (in casu, the AU), this could only be undertaken in the context of a Security Council authorization. In these circumstances, the regional arrangement (the AU) should be understood as acting as an agent for the Security Council pursuant to the theory of delegated powers. It was rather clear that in the Libyan situation the Security Council was not prepared to grant any such powers to the AU: it retained all powers and devolved none. On its part, the AU could have perhaps invoked Article 4(h) of the Constitutive Act (it gives it the right to intervene in a Member State pursuant to an Assembly decision when grave circumstances (including war crimes) are present in its territory) to justify an intervention in Libya. This would have tested the unchartered waters of Article 4(g), would have analysed its consistency with the UN Charter's provisions on non-interference in the domestic affairs of states and with the developing theory/principle of the Responsibility to Protect (R2P) and would have created some form of precedence for future situations.[262] However, the outbreak of political transformation in 2010 and the

258. Reproduced in I.L.M. 50 (2011): 287.

259. *See* Assembly, *Decision on the Implementation of the Assembly Decisions on the International Criminal Court*, AU Doc. Assembly/AU/Dec. 366 (XVII) (1 Jul. 2011). In subsequent Sessions, the Assembly reiterated its call on the UNSC to defer ICC proceedings as regards Al-Bashir but also as regards proceedings in the Kenyan situation, *see* , *inter alia*, Assembly, *Decision on the Implementation of the Decisions on the International Criminal Court (ICC)*, AU Doc. Assembly/AU/Dec. 419 (XIX) (16 Jul. 2012).

260. *See* Assembly, *Decision on the Situation in Libya*, AU Doc. Assembly/AU/Dec. 385 (XVII) (1 Jul. 2011).

261. *Ibid.*

262. Compare L. Boisson de Chazournes, *Interactions Between Regional and Universal Organizations: A Legal Perspective* (Leiden/Boston: Brill Nijhoff, 2017), 188 et seq.

ferocity with which it spread to its northern Member States (generally referred to as the 'Arab Spring') showed that the AU was not capable of formulating a coherent response and putting into work the very weapons with which it has been endowed to address such situations (*infra* paragraph 182).

In July 2011, the Assembly deliberated the report submitted by the PSC on its activities.[263] It reiterated the need for greater and better coordinated efforts to promote sustainable peace, security, and stability on the continent 'based on Africa's ownership and leadership'.[264] The reference to 'Africa's ownership' is closely connected to the principle of 'African solutions to African problems,' namely, that the AU, as the pan-African political institution, ought to resolve those issues that are of central importance to the continent through its own actions and means. However, noble as this aim might be, it is clear that the AU has proven time and time again unwilling and unable to tackle the scourges plaguing it and has had to resort to the assistance of other international partners and institutions, including the UN and the EU (although not always in that order).

Furthermore, the Seventeenth Session dealt with a pressing social problem which, although not restricted to Africa, is widely practiced in several African countries: female genital mutilation (FGM). FGM has been condemned and prohibited in all its forms in Article 5 of the Protocol on the Rights of Women in Africa attached to the African Charter on Human and Peoples' Rights (2003), which obliges contracting parties (currently ratified by thirty-six out of the fifty-four Member States) to adopt pertinent legislative measures to be enforced by criminal sanctions. The Assembly supported the proposal tabled by Burkina Faso before the Sixty-Sixth UN General Assembly Ordinary Session to ban FGM worldwide by harmonizing Member States' actions and by strengthening regional and international legal instruments.[265] On 20 December 2012, the UN General Assembly adopted, without a vote, Resolution 67/146 on 'Intensifying global efforts for the elimination of female genital mutilations.' Recognizing that FGM is an irreparable and irreversible abuse of the human rights of woman and girls as well as a threat to their health, it urged UN Member States to condemn all harmful practices, to take all required measures protecting women and girls from this form of violence, to end impunity and to continue observing 6 February as the International Day of Zero Tolerance to Female Genital Mutilation.

Finally, the Assembly adopted a resolution concerning a long-standing feud between two non-AU Member States. In particular, it called upon the United States of America to lift its 'unjustifiable' economic and trade sanctions against Cuba which

263. AU Doc. Assembly/AU/4 (XVII) (2011).

264. *See* Assembly, *Decision on the Report of the Peace and Security Council on its Activities and the State of Peace and Security in Africa*, AU Doc. Assembly/AU/Dec. 369 (XVII), para. 3 (1 Jul. 2011).

265. *See* Assembly, *Decision on the Support of a Draft Resolution at the Sixty-Sixth Ordinary Session of the General Assembly of the United Nations to Ban Female Genital Mutilation in the World*, AU Doc. Assembly/AU/Dec. 383 (XVII) (1 Jul. 2011). Generally, *see* R. Skaine, *Female Genital Mutilation: Legal, Cultural and Medical Issues* (McFarland & Company, 2005); and A. Rahman & N. Toubia (eds), *Female Genital Mutilation: A Guide to Laws and Policies Worldwide* (London and New York: Zed Books, 2000).

had been imposed in the 1960s.[266] An identical resolution had been adopted in a previous session and was adopted subsequently, *inter alia*, during the Twenty-First Ordinary Session in May 2013[267] and the Twenty-Sixth Ordinary Session in January 2016.[268] Even though resolutions to that effect have been issued by the UN General Assembly on a yearly basis since 1992,[269] there is a fundamental difference between their actions because the USA and Cuba participate in the UN and, therefore, its Member States may legitimately take sides in a situation concerning fellow Members. On 27 July 2011, South Sudan acceded to the AU and became the fifty-fourth Member State; on 14 July 2011, it had acceded to the UN as its 193rd Member State.

48. In the transformation from the OAU to the AU the future of the AEC was not properly addressed and in the ensuing years the deadlines mentioned in the founding Abuja Treaty for the step by step process towards economic integration were not met. On the whole, this issue has been a back burner for the AU. The overall negative socio-economic situation in Africa, the fragile state institutions and the constant instability in the peace and security sector have all been inhibiting factors for the promised close economic cooperation to flourish. The Fifth AU Conference of Ministers in Charge of Integration (COMAI V), held in Nairobi in September 2011, gave to the Eighteenth Ordinary Assembly Session (Addis Ababa, 29 January–30 January 2012) the opportunity to discuss developments. The Assembly adopted the first Plan of Action of the Minimum Integration Programme[270] and asked Member States to speed up the integration process and to initiate actions to promote, *inter alia*, the free movement of persons, goods, services and capital, the four cornerstones of any economic integration project. Given that all African RECs have the goal of advancing close economic cooperation among their respective Member States, the Assembly recommended that, in order to accelerate the establishment of the AEC, they be grouped together around two poles of integration. The first pole is to comprise Common Market for Eastern

266. *See* Assembly, *Resolution on the Lifting of the Economic and Trade Embargo imposed on the Republic of Cuba by the United States of America*, AU Doc. Assembly/AU/Res. 1 (XVII) (1 Jul. 2011).

267. *See* , respectively, Assembly, *Resolution on the Lifting of the Economic and Trade Embargo imposed on the Republic of Cuba by the United States of America* AU Doc. Assembly/AU/Res. 1 (XV) (27 Jul. 2010); and Assembly, *Resolution on the Lifting of the Economic and Trade Embargo imposed on the Republic of Cuba by the United States of America*, AU Doc. Assembly/AU/Res. 1 (XXI) (27 May 2013).

268. *See* Assembly, *Resolution on Recent Developments in the Cuba-United States of America Relations*, AU Doc. Assembly/AU/Res. 1 (XXVI) (31 Jan. 2016). Note that the same Session adopted a Declaration asking the USA to terminate its unilateral sanctions against Sudan, *see* Assembly/AU/Decl. 2 (XXVI) (31 Jan. 2016). As mentioned above, on 13 Jan. 2017 President Obama signed a (rather controversial) Executive Order easing sanctions imposed on Sudan, *see* https://www.treasury.gov/resource-center/sanctions/Programs/Documents/sudan_fact_sheet.pdf.

269. For the last two instruments, *see* UNGA Res. 71/5, 26 Oct. 2016, and Res. 70/5, 27 Oct. 2015, both titled 'Necessity of ending the economic, commercial and financial embargo imposed by the United States of America against Cuba'; further, *see* UNGA Res 69/5, 18 Oct. 2014; Res. 68/8, 29 Oct. 2013; Res. 67/4, 13 Nov. 2012; and Res. 66/6/, 25 Oct. 2011, all at: http://www.un.org/en/sections/documents/general-assembly-resolutions/index.html.

270. AU Doc. EX/CL/693 (XX) (2012).

and Southern Africa (COMESA), SADC, and the EAC and the second pole ECOWAS, Economic Community of Central African States (ECCAS), CFN-SAD, and the AMU.[271] Moreover, the Assembly deliberated the report submitted by the AUC on the Seventh Ordinary Session of the Conference of Ministers of Trade, held in Accra, Ghana on 29 November–3 December 2011.[272] The Assembly endorsed the Framework, Road Map and Architecture for Fast Tracking the establishment of the CFTA and the Action Pan for Boosting Intra-African Trade.[273] Considering that the creation of a free trade area is the first major step of any economic integration plan, it is rather strange that the Assembly set the target date for achieving CFTA in 2017 without linking it up with revitalizing the AEC.[274] It was rather obvious that these two projects could not have run independently of each other. It is now certain that the AEC has been abandoned. In July 2016, the Assembly resolved to establish a High-Level Panel of five eminent persons (one from each African region) 'to champion the fast tracking of the CFTA' and asked the AUC to present feasible options to eliminate non-trade barriers among African countries to foster their trade.[275] A Report was submitted for evaluation by the Twenty-Eighth Ordinary Assembly Session in January 2017,[276] which 'took note' of it and mandated Mahamadou Issoufou, President of Niger, to 'champion the process of the CFTA to ensure that the deadline of the end of 2017 is reached'.[277] But it is now obvious that the 2017 target is no longer realistic. The vision for pan-continental economic integration appears to be as elusive and complicated as ever, even though the successful implementation of the stepping stones of Agenda 2063 should increase the likelihood that the vision is turned into reality.[278]

African states have always been very supportive of the Palestinian claim to statehood, even though Palestine is not geographically located in Africa and it could never join the AU. It is noteworthy that during the OAU era the African Committee on the Question of Palestine was set up. This should be attributed to the fact that, since Palestine has been waging a struggle to end Israeli occupation, African states associated

---

271. *See* Assembly, *Decision on African Integration*, AU Doc. Assembly/AU/Dec. 392 (XVIII) (30 Jan. 2012).
272. AU Doc. AU/MIN/TD//Rpt(VII) (2011).
273. AU Doc. EX.CL/700 (XX) (2012).
274. *See* Assembly, *Decision on Boosting Intra-African Trade and Fast Tracking The Continental Free Trade Area*, AU Doc. Assembly/AU/Dec. 394 (XVIII) (30 Jan. 2012). For further developments concerning CFTA, *see* Assembly, *Decision on Boosting Intra-African Trade and fast tracking the Continental Free Trade Area*, AU Doc. Assembly/AU/Dec. 426 (XIX) (16 Jul. 2012).
275. *See* Assembly, *Decision on the Continental Free Trade Area*, AU Doc. Assembly/AU/Dec. 608 (XXVII) (18 Jul. 2016).
276. *See Report on implementation of Assembly/AU/Dec.608(XXVII) on the Continental Free Trade Area and Update on the proposed mechanism for the elimination of non-tariff barriers (NTBs) in the Continental Free Trade Area (CFTA)*, AU Doc. Assembly/AU/4(XXVIII) (2017).
277. *See* Assembly, *Decision on the Continental Free Trade Area*, AU Doc. Assembly/AU/Dec. 623 (XXVIII), para. 4 (31 Jan. 2017).
278. Generally, United Nations Conference on Trade and Development, *African Continental Free Trade Area: Advancing Pan-African Integration – Some Considerations*, UNCTAD/WEB/DITC/2016/5 (New York and Geneva: United Nations, November 2016), at: http://unctad.org/en/PublicationsLibrary/webditc2016d5_en.pdf.

themselves with a political entity fighting for its liberation from alien domination. In a resolution adopted in 1977 the OAU Assembly had asked its Liberation Committee and the Palestine Liberation Organization (PLO) to jointly 'lay down a strategy aiming at liberating Palestine…from Zionist racist colonialism…considering that the cause of Palestine is an African cause'.[279] During its Eighteenth Ordinary Session, the Assembly, noting that Palestine had on 31 October 2011 been accepted as a full Member State in UNESCO, reaffirmed its support for its efforts to obtain full membership in the United Nations' family.[280] Moreover, in 2012 the African group in the UN General Assembly was instrumental in securing that the status of Palestine was upgraded to non-Member observer state.[281] The current AU position on the Palestinian issue was articulated by the Assembly in July 2016; it supported the two-state solution, it demanded the return of Palestinian refugees to their home and properties; and was in favour of the French initiative to hold an international peace conference for relaunching the negotiations to solve the Palestine-Israeli conflict on a specific timeframe.[282]

Furthermore the Eighteenth Assembly Session deliberated again the ongoing stance between the AU and the ICC. One of the problems that had surfaced was that certain AU Member States and ICC parties (Malawi, Djibouti, Chad, and Kenya) had received Sudanese President Al-Bashir in their territories in violation of the aforementioned Arrest Warrants. In December 2011, the ICC reacted by issuing two decisions, which, on the one hand, castigated, respectively, Malawi[283] and Chad[284] for not arresting Al-Bashir even though they had the opportunity to do so and, on the other hand, held that their behaviour was in clear violation of their obligations under the Rome Statute.[285] The Assembly offered political cover to these Member States: it argued that receiving

279. *See* OAU Assembly, *Resolution on the Question of Palestine*, OAU Doc. AHG/Res. 77 (XII) (1 Aug. 1975).
280. *See* Assembly, *Decision on the Situation in Palestine and the Middle East*, AU Doc. Assembly/AU/Dec. 396 (XVIII) (30 Jan. 2012). *See* further, Assembly, *Decision on the Situation in Palestine and the Middle East*, AU Doc. Assembly/AU/Dec. 421 (XIX) (16 Jul. 2012).
281. UNGA Res. 67/19 of 26 Nov. 2012. Note that currently 136 UN Member States have accorded recognition to the State of Palestine, which on 23 Sept. 2011 applied for admission to full membership, *see* UN Doc. A/66/371 – S/2011/592 Annex I (2011). The application is still pending.
282. *See* Assembly, *Declaration on the Situation in Palestine and the Middle East*, AU Doc. Assembly/AU/Decl. 2 (XXVII) (18 Jul. 2016).
283. ICC, *Prosecutor v. Omar Hassan Ahmad Al Bashir, Decision Pursuant to Article 87(7) of the Rome Statute on the Failure of the Republic of Malawi to Comply with the Cooperation Requests Issued by the Court with respect to the Arrest and Surrender of Omar Hassan Ahmad Al Bashir*, Corrigendum, P.-T. Ch. I, ICC-02/05-01/09, 12 Dec. 2011, at: http://www.icc-cpi.int/iccdocs/doc/doc1287184.pdf, reproduced in I.L.M. 51 (2012): 393.
284. ICC, *Prosecutor v. Omar Hassan Ahmad Al Bashir, Decision Pursuant to Article 87(7) of the Rome Statute on the Failure of the Republic of Chad to Comply with the Cooperation Requests Issued by the Court with respect to the Arrest and Surrender of Omar Hassan Ahmad Al Bashir*, P.-T. Ch. I, ICC-02/05-01/09, 13 Dec. 2011, at: http://www.icc-cpi.int/iccdocs/doc/doc1287888.pdf.
285. For analysis of the ICC Decision on Malawi, *see* K. Magliveras & G. Naldi, 'The ICC Addresses Non-Cooperation by States Parties: The *Malawi* Decision', *African J of Legal Studies* 6 (2013): 137; D. Tladi, 'The ICC Decisions on Chad and Malawi. On Cooperation, Immunities and Article 98', *Journal of International Criminal Justice* 11 (2013):199.

Al-Bashir was justified because they were implementing its previous resolutions calling on the entire membership not to cooperate with the ICC as regards his arrest and surrender to The Hague. In effect, the Assembly argued that Member States' obligations flowing from its resolutions take precedence over obligations that they have freely assumed by becoming contracting parties to the Rome Statute.[286]

During the Nineteenth Ordinary Session (Addis Ababa, 15–16 July 2012), the Assembly proposed amendments to the structure of the ACJHR and the PAP. As far as the former organ is concerned, it proposed adding an International Criminal Law Section, a rather complex proposal because the ACJHR has not become operative due to the lack of the required fifteen ratifications for its founding protocol to enter into force.[287] The Assembly decided to ask the AUC to prepare a study on the financial and structural implications resulting from the expansion of jurisdiction to cover international criminal law matters.[288] As regards PAP, the Executive Council had approved during its Twenty-First Ordinary Session (Addis Ababa, 9–13 July 2012) the draft Protocol to the Constitutive Act of the AU relating to the PAP, which had been prepared by the Ministers of Justice of the Member States,[289] with the exception of Article 8.1(a) and Article 8.2 thereof, which dealt with PAP's crucial powers to legislate and to supervise AU activities.[290] Endowing it with these powers would have turned the AU parliamentary organ into an institution resembling the European Parliament. However, the Assembly was not prepared to consent to such a significant augmentation of its role. It resolved that more detailed consultations were required, and the discussion ought to be linked with the progress achieved in the continental integration process. Thus, the Assembly deferred examination of the Draft Protocol.[291] As is later explained in the chapter on the PAP, in June 2014 the Assembly finally approved its new Protocol.

During the same Session, the Assembly pressed for an intensification of efforts to promote its common position on UN Security Council reform and asked Member States to include it as a foreign policy priority.[292] As will be recalled, the African common position was embodied in the Ezulwini Consensus agreed in 2005, which demands no less than two permanent seats with all the prerogatives and privileges of permanent membership (including the right of veto) and, additionally, five non-permanent

286. *See* Assembly, *Decision on the Progress Report of the Commission on the Implementation of the Assembly Decisions on the International Criminal Court (ICC)*, AU Doc. Assembly/AU/Dec. 397 (XVIII) (30 Jan. 2012).
287. *See* G. Naldi & K. Magliveras, 'African Union Debates Adding an International Criminal Law Section to Its Court', *International Enforcement Law Reporter* 28 (2012): 335.
288. *See* Assembly, *Decision on the Protocol on Amendments to the Protocol on the Statute of the African Court of Justice and Human Rights*, AU Doc. Assembly/AU/Dec. 427 (XIX) (16 Jul. 2012).
289. *See Report on the Meeting of Ministers of Justice/Attorneys General on the Review of the Protocol to the Constitutive Act of the African Union Relating to the Pan-African Parliament*, held in Addis Ababa on 14 and 15 May 2012, AU Doc. EX.CL/731 (XXI)b (2012).
290. *See* Executive Council, *Decision on the Protocol to the Constitutive Act of the African Union relating to the Pan-African Parliament*, AU Doc. EX.CL/Dec. 707 (XXI) (13 Jul. 2012).
291. *See* Assembly, *Decision on the Protocol to the Constitutive Act of the African Union relating to the Pan-African Parliament*, AU Doc. Assembly/AU/Dec. 428 (XIX) (16 Jul. 2012).
292. *See* Assembly, *Decision on the Report of the Committee of Ten on UN Reform*, AU Doc. Assembly/AU/Dec. 430 (XIX) (16 Jul. 2012).

seats. As explained by the representative of Mauritius, speaking on behalf of the African Group during the UN General Assembly Sixty-Third Session, the African common position sought to ensure that the continent was fully represented in all UN decision-making organs and especially in the Security Council. Even though Africa was opposed to the veto power, which is enjoyed only by the permanent members, it believed that this power should be made available to all new permanent members for as long as it existed. According to Mauritius, if and when the Security Council is enlarged, the AU should be solely responsible for selecting Africa's representatives and determining the criteria for selection.[293] Reference to the fact that the AU has over-relied on what it has termed 'international partners' for carrying out its various activities has already been made. The AU budget for financial year 2013 exemplified it. In particular, based on the Executive Council proposals agreed at its Twenty-First Ordinary Session,[294] the Assembly adopted a budget totalling USD 278,226,622, of which less than half (USD 122,866,637) was to be assessed to Member States, while the remaining USD 155,359,986 was earmarked for various AU programmes which would have to be funded solely by the 'international partners'.[295]

Finally, the Nineteenth Assembly Session took the unusual step of adopting a declaration concerning the internal situation of a specific Member State, namely Mali, where, in March 2012, army rebels had deposed the democratically elected government of President Amadou Toumani Toure in a coup d'état causing considerable loss of life (*infra* paragraph 180). The Assembly considered, *inter alia*, that the occupation of Mali's northern part by various armed, terrorist, and criminal groups posed a serious threat to the peace, security, and stability in the region and beyond.[296] Two things are noteworthy. First, over and above said declaration, it also condemned the unconstitutional regime in the course of examining the regular PSC report on its activities.[297] Second, the adoption of said declaration does not seem to have served any real purpose other than reproducing verbatim and endorsing the PSC Communiqué on Mali issued on 14 July 2012.[298] The Communiqué urged the UN Security Council and Secretary-General to assist AU efforts and neutralize the situation in Mali. However, given that in paragraph 12 of the Communiqué the PSC had expressed its determination to impose sanctions against those groups perpetuating the crisis and such sanctions had not yet been imposed, the obvious question is why the Assembly did not order them, pursuant to its powers envisaged in the Constitutive Act. It would appear that no sanctions were

293. *See* UNGA, Press Release GA/10786, 18 Nov. 2008.
294. *See* Executive Council, *Decision on the Budget of the African Union for the 2013 Financial Year*, AU Doc. EX.CL/Dec. 696 (XXI) (13 Jul. 2012).
295. *See* Assembly, *Decision on the Budget of the African Union for the 2013 Financial Year*, AU Doc. Assembly/AU/Dec. 438 (XIX) (16 Jul. 2012). On the overall role of 'international partners', *see* S.M. Makinda, F. Wafula Okumu & D. Mickler, *The African Union: Addressing the Challenges of Peace, Security and Governance* (2nd edn., London: Routledge, 2016), 136 et seq.
296. *See* Assembly, *Solemn Declaration on Mali*, AU Doc. Assembly/AU/Decl. 1 (XIX) (16 Jul. 2012).
297. *See* Assembly, *Decision on the Report of the Peace and Security Council on its Activities and the State of Peace and Security in Africa*, AU Doc. Assembly/AU/Dec. 432 (XIX), paras 4–6 (16 Jul. 2002). For the PSC Report, *see* AU Doc. Assembly/AU/6 (XIX) (2012).
298. PSC/AHG/COMM/1 (CCCXXVII) (2012).

ever imposed.[299] And this despite the fact that, on 13 July 2012, the government of Mali had referred the situation since January 2012 to the ICC Prosecutor asking him to investigate, pursuant to Article 14 of the Rome Statute, any alleged crimes committed by these groups. The investigation was officially opened in January 2013: according to the Prosecutor 'the people of Northern Mali have been living in profound turmoil… different armed groups have caused havoc and human suffering through a range of alleged acts of extreme violence'.[300] Fortunately for the population, peaceful elections were held in July and August 2013.[301]

49. The Twentieth Ordinary Assembly Session (Addis Ababa, 27–28 January 2013) was held on the theme 'Pan-Africanism and African Renaissance.' It reflected the fact that 2013 marked the fiftieth anniversary of the OAU establishment. Hailemariam Dessalegn, the Prime Minister of Ethiopia, was elected as AU Chairperson for a one-year term. The Assembly decided to create the Pan-African Intellectual Property Organization (PAIPO).[302] Its Statute was approved in January 2016.[303] The Assembly also requested that the AUCIL – an entity described in the Statute approved by the Assembly in February 2009 as an 'independent advisory organ of the Union in accordance with Article 5(2) of the Constitutive Act' – examine the proposed establishment of an International Constitutional Court and submit its observations and recommendations to the Twenty-Second Ordinary Session (January 2014).[304] The matter, however, was not placed on the agenda of that Session. The Twentieth Assembly also addressed several health issues. In particular, it instructed the Ministers of Health of Member States to come up with concrete and innovative strategies regarding maternal, newborn, and child health. This was associated with the implementation of the so-called Campaign

299. Note that sanctions (taking the form of 'individual measures'), including a travel ban and assets freeze, had been ordered in April 2012 by the PSC against the Mali junta and against those natural persons and entities contributing to the maintenance of the unconstitutional *status quo* and only after sanctions have been ordered by ECOWAS, *see* AU Doc. PSC/PR/COMM(CCCXVI), at paras 7–8 (3 Apr. 2012), at: http://www.peaceau.org/uploads/psc-comm-mali-03-04-2012.pdf.

300. ICC Prosecutor Statement, 16 January 2013, ICC Doc. ICC-OTP-20130116-PR869.

301. *See* The Guardian, 'Mali election won by Ibrahim Boubacar Keïta', 13 Aug. 2013, at: http://www.theguardian.com/world/2013/aug/13/mali-election-ibrahim-boubacar-keita.

302. *See* Assembly, *Decision on the Creation of the Pan-African Intellectual Property Organization (PAIPO)*, AU Doc. Assembly/AU/Dec. 453 (XX) (28 Jan. 2013). *See also* Assembly, *Decision on the Establishment of the Pan- African Intellectual Property Organization*, AU Doc. Assembly/AU/Dec. 138 (VII)) on the need to establish PAIPO (30 Jan. 2007). *See* further, Economic Commission for Africa, *African Union and African Development Bank Group, Assessing Regional Integration in Africa (ARIA VII): Innovation, Competitiveness and Regional Integration*, Addis Ababa, 2016, at: http://www.uneca.org.

303. *See* Assembly, *Decision on the Specialized Technical Committees*, AU Doc. Assembly/AU/Dec. 589 (XVI) (31 Jan. 2016). For analysis, *see* Y. Mupangavanhu 'African Union Rising to the Need for Continental IP Protection? The Establishment of the Pan-African Intellectual Property Organization' 59 *J.A.L.* (2015): 1.

304. *See* Assembly, *Decision on the Establishment of an 'International Constitutional Court'*, AU Doc. Assembly/AU/Dec. 458 (XX) (28 Jan. 2013). For the AUCIL, *see* Assembly, *Decision on the Draft Statute of the African Union Commission on International Law*, AU Doc. Assembly/AU//Dec. 209 (XII) (4 Feb. 2009) and for its Rules of Procedure, *see* AU Doc. AUCIL/Legal/Doc. 4 (III) (April 2011).

on Accelerated Reduction of Maternal and Child Mortality in Africa (CARMMA). The latter, been described as an example of a successful continental initiative with national ownership, was launched during a Special Session of the AU Conference of Ministers of Health (CAMH4), held on the eve of Sixty-Third World Health Assembly in Geneva on 15 May 2010. With the strong backing of the AUC, CARMMA is currently implemented by forty-four Member States.[305] The Assembly also endorsed Nigeria's offer to host in 2013 a follow-up summit meeting on the Abuja Summit on HIV/AIDS, held in 2001. The Summit took place on 12–16 July 2013 and ended with a call for strong commitment of the 'Abuja Actions toward the elimination of HIV and AIDS, tuberculosis and malaria in Africa by 2030.' African leaders noted that the achievements of the last thirteen years in promoting access to medical services depended largely on the political will and commitment by Africa's top leadership.[306]

The Twentieth Ordinary Assembly Session also adopted a declaration of solidarity with Algeria regarding the terrorist attack in In Amenas, the country's third largest gas field operated by British Petroleum (BP), Norway's Statoil, and the national oil company Sonatrach, which started on 16 January 2013 and lasted for four days. What is quite fascinating about the declaration is that the events surrounding the incident were at the time unclear, although the time proximity with the French military intervention in northern Mali on 11 January 2016 (Opération Serval) was suggestive of the attackers' identity.[307] In the event, the Assembly chose to deal with a rather isolated incident in which far more non-Africans than Africans were killed. This was quite extraordinary considering that previous instances of considerable loss of life owed, for example, to post-electoral violence had not attracted the Assembly's attention. In July 2013, US prosecutors charged Mokhtar Belmokhtar, an alleged commander of Al Qaeda's operations in North Africa, with, *inter alia*, kidnapping internationally protected persons

305. *See* Assembly, *Decision on the Reduction of Maternal, Newborn and Child Mortality and Morbidity in Africa*, AU Doc. Assembly/AU/Dec. 461 (XX) (28 Jan. 2013). *See* further *2012 Status Report on Maternal, Newborn and Child Health*, at: http://www.carmma.org/resource/2012-status-report-maternal-newborn-and-child-health. It was the first annual report submitted on these health issues as mandated by the Declaration adopted in July 2010, *see* Assembly, *Actions on Maternal, Newborn and Child Health and Development in Africa By 2015*, AU Doc. Assembly/AU/Decl. 1 (XV) (25 Jul. 2010). For further information, *see* http://www.carmma.org/.

306. *See* Assembly, *Decision on the Hosting of A Special Follow-up Summit on the Abuja 2001 African Union Summit on HIV/AIDS, Tuberculosis and Other Related Infectious Diseases in the Third Quarter (July/August) of 2013*, AU Doc. Assembly/AU/Dec. 464 (XX) (28 Jan. 2013). *See* further, African Union, *Press Release No. 104/2013*, 16 Jul. 2013; and *African Health Strategy 2016 – 2030*, produced by the Department of Social Affairs of the AU Commission, at: http://www.carmma.org/resource/african-health-strategy-2016-2030.

307. *See* Assembly, *Declaration of Solidarity with Algeria following the terrorist attack on Gazier site in Amenas*, AU Doc. Assembly/AU/Decl. 1 (XX) (28 Jan. 2013). Generally, *see* 'Le rescapes d'In Amenas', *Le nouvel Observateur*, 10 Apr. 2013, p. 12; and *The In Amenas Attack Report of the Investigation into the Terrorist Attack on In Amenas. Prepared for Statoil ASA's Board of Directors*, no date, at: http://www.statoil.com/en/NewsAndMedia/News/2013/Downloads/In%20Amenas%20report.pdf.

during the In Amenas incident.[308] On another front, in mid-June 2013, the African Court of Human and Peoples' Rights issued its first decision on merits ruling that Tanzania had breached the provisions of the Banjul Charter by not allowing its citizens to participate without impediments in government positions either directly or through representatives and regardless of party affiliation. The Court also ordered Tanzania to take any necessary constitutional, legislative, and administrative measures to remedy the violations.[309]

50. The second (Twenty-First) Ordinary Assembly Session for 2013 was held in Addis Ababa but not in the months of June or July as is customary. It took place on 26 and 27 May 2013, exactly fifty years after the signing of the OAU Treaty; the Solemn Declaration on the fiftieth Anniversary of the OAU/AU adopted during the meeting, reference to which will be made later on, appears as Appendix 3 to the present monograph. The standoff between the AU and the ICC continued with the Assembly reaffirming that those Member States (e.g., Chad), which had welcomed Sudanese President Al Bashir did so in conformity with its decisions and, therefore, should not be penalized. In this resolution, adopted with the reservation of Botswana, the Assembly stressed the need for international justice to be conducted in a transparent and fair manner to avoid any perception of double standards and requested the AUC, in collaboration with AUCIL, to organize a brainstorming session, as part of the fiftieth OAU Anniversary, on the themes of international criminal justice, peace, justice and reconciliation as well as on the ICC impact in Africa and seek ways to strengthen African mechanisms to deal with African challenges and problems.[310] The Assembly also addressed the AU's difficult financial situation and accepted (with the reservation of Cape Verde) the report on Alternative Sources of Financing prepared by a high-level panel chaired by former Nigerian President Olusegun Obasanjo.[311] The Assembly implemented one of the recommendations contained in the Report and established the AU Foundation accepting voluntary contributions towards financing the AU and called upon Member States, the private sector, donors, philanthropists, and individuals to ensure its operationalization.[312] On 1 February 2014, the Foundation was officially

308. *See* Federal Bureau of Investigation, *Charges Filed in Manhattan Federal Court Against Mokhtar Belmokhtar for His Role in Terror Attack in Algeria and Other Crimes*, 19 Jul. 2013, at: https://archives.fbi.gov/archives/newyork/press-releases/2013/charges-filed-in-manhattan-federal-court-against-mokhtar-belmokhtar-for-his-role-in-terror-attack-in-algeria-and-other-crimes. Belmokhtar was reportedly killed in a US airstrike in Libya in mid-June 2015, *see* http://edition.cnn.com/2015/06/14/world/mokhtar-belmokhtar/.

309. *See* African Court on Human and Peoples' Rights, *Tanganyika Law Society et al. v. The United Republic of Tanzania*, Application Nos 09/2011 and 11/2011, Judgment of 14 Jun. 2013, at: http://en.african-court.org/.

310. *See* Assembly, *Decision on International Jurisdiction, Justice and the International Criminal Court (ICC)*, AU Doc. Assembly/AU/Dec. 482 (XXI) (27 May 2013).

311. *See* Assembly, *Decision on Alternative Sources of Financing the African Union*, AU Doc. Assembly/AU/Dec. 486 (XXI) (27 May 2013). For the Report, *see* AU Doc. Assembly/AU/6(XXI) (2013).

312. *See* Assembly, *Decision on the Establishment of an African Union Foundation for Voluntary Contributions Towards Financing the African Union*, AU Doc. Assembly/AU/Dec. 488 (XXI) (27 May 2013).

launched at AU Headquarters with Jamaica pledging the amount of USD 100,000 to 'underscore the commitment of the Diaspora towards African development'.[313]

Finally, the Assembly adopted a Declaration to mark the fiftieth anniversary from the creation of the OAU, which concentrated on the following eight broad areas: (a) African Identity and Renaissance; (b) the struggle against colonialism and the right to self-determination of people still under colonial rule (the 'unlawful occupation' of the Chagos Archipelago and the Comorian Island of Mayotte as well as the right to self-determination of the people of Western Sahara were specifically mentioned); (c) political, social and economic integration; (d) social and economic development; (e) peace and security (a specific milestone was set to end all wars in Africa by 2020); (f) democratic governance; (g) Africa's destiny by taking ownership of continental issues and providing African solutions to African problems; and (h) promoting Africa's place in the world. Member States pledged to make the above ideals and goals more coherent in domestic development plans and to devise the so-called Continental Agenda 2063 by means of a people-driven process leading to an integrated, people-centred, prosperous Africa at peace with itself.[314] Since then 'Agenda 2063' has become a buzz word for the AU.[315] It was officially adopted by the Twenty-Fourth Ordinary Assembly Session in January 2015[316] and was reaffirmed by its Twenty-Sixth Ordinary Session a year later, where it was described as 'a common continental framework for socio-economic development'.[317] The First Ten-Year Implementation Plan 2014–2023, adopted in 2017, envisages seven aspirations, based on the ideals of Pan-Africanism and the vision of Africa's Renaissance.[318] During the Twenty-Eighth Ordinary Assembly Session, Agenda 2063 was cited in relation to four separate Resolution, which concerned, respectively, achieving a universal health coverage;[319] supporting, encouraging and protecting

---

313. Its office is in Midrand, South Africa, *see* http://www.africaunionfoundation.org/.
314. *See* Assembly, *Solemn Declaration on the 50th Anniversary of the OAU/AU*, AU Doc. Assembly/AU/Decl. 3 (XXI) (26 May 2013), reproduced in Annex III to this monograph.
315. *See* further at: http://au.int/en2/agenda2063.
316. Assembly, *Decision on the Report of the Commission on Development of the African Union Agenda 2063 and the Report of the Ministerial Follow-Up Committee on The Bahr Dar Retreat*, AU Doc. Assembly/AU/Dec. 565 (XXIV) (31 Jan. 2015).
317. Assembly, *Decision on the Domestication of the First Ten-Year Implementation Plan of Agenda 2063*, AU Doc. Assembly/AU/Dec. 588 (XXVI) (31 Jan. 2016). *See* further, Economic Commission for Africa and African Union, Ninth Joint Annual Meetings of the African Union Specialized Technical Committee on Finance, Monetary Affairs, Economic Planning and Integration and the Economic Commission for Africa Conference of African Ministers of Finance, Planning and Economic Development, Meeting of the Committee of Experts, Addis Ababa, 31 Mar.– 2 Apr. 2016, *Draft concept note*, UN Doc. E/ECA/COE/35/Inf/1; AU Doc. AU/STC/FMEPI/EXP/Info.1(II) (27 Jan. 2016).
318. At: http://www.nepad.org/download/file/fid/2947%20.
319. *See* Assembly, *Decision on Universal Access to Immunization as a Cornerstone for Health and Development in Africa*, AU Doc. Assembly/AU/Dec. 624 (XXVIII) (31 Jan. 2017).

Africa-Africa investments;[320] promoting a conflict-free Africa;[321] and repositioning the African Peers Review Mechanism.[322]

The holding of a brainstorming session on AU's relations with the ICC, which had been agreed in May 2013, took place in October 2013 and took the form of an extraordinary Assembly session. There was a lot of speculation as to its outcome and it was even suggested that it might lead to an *en masse* withdrawal of African contracting parties to the Rome Statute establishing the ICC. Although it is highly irregular for the highest-ranking organ of an international organization to dictate to Member States what stance to pursue vis-à-vis another multilateral institution, it would have been the first time that the Assembly would have attempted to do so. The Declaration adopted at the end of the Extraordinary Summit did not call for withdrawal. However, the Assembly did reach several conclusions, which may contradict the rules of international law by imposing upon Member States (and specifically those that have ratified the Rome Statute) duties of a political nature, possibly exceeding its powers and functions. In particular, the Assembly resolved that, in order to safeguard the constitutional order, stability, and integrity of Member States, no charges shall be commenced or continued before any international court or tribunal against any serving African head of state or government or anybody acting or entitled to act in such capacity during their term of office. Moreover, it decided that the ICC trials of Kenyan President Uhuru Kenyatta and Deputy President William Samoei Ruto should be suspended until they have completed their terms of office and that the former should not appear before the ICC until such time as the AU concerns have been adequately addressed by the UN Security Council and the ICC. Finally, it resolved that any AU Member State wishing to refer a case to the ICC (as, e.g., the government of Mali did in July 2012) should first inform and seek the advice of the AU.

It is no doubt problematic that the Assembly has somehow thought that it has the right to prescribe international courts and tribunals (including the Courts of Justice of RECs) not to hear cases brought against serving African heads of state or government. Arguably, this could be construed as giving such individuals) a carte blanche to rule authoritatively and to disregard fundamental freedoms knowing that they shall not be made accountable for as long as they remain in power. It is submitted that this approach is incompatible with 'the AU's unflinching commitment to fight impunity, promote human rights and democracy, and the rule of law and good governance', as reiterated in the Preamble of the Declaration and confirmed in the AU Constitutive Act.[323]

On 30 December 2013, the PSC met for its 411th meeting held at the level of Heads of State and Government. It requested that an African Union Commission of Inquiry on South Sudan (AUCISS) be created. In particular, it asked the AUC, in consultation with the African Human Rights Commission and 'other relevant AU

---

320. *See* Assembly, *Decision on Promotion and Protection of African Investments to Sustain Investment in the* Youth, AU Doc. Assembly/AU/Dec. 625 (XXVIII) (31 Jan. 2017).
321. *See* Assembly, *Decision on the African Union Master Roadmap of Practical Steps for Silencing the Guns in Africa by the Year 2020*, AU Doc. Assembly/AU/Dec. 630 (XXVIII) (31 Jan. 2017).
322. *See* Assembly, *Decision on the Revitalisation of the African Peer Review Mechanism*, AU Doc. Assembly/AU/Dec. 631 (XXVIII) (31 Jan. 2017).
323. *See* Assembly, *Decision on Africa's Relationship with the International Criminal Court (ICC)*, AU Doc. Ext/Assembly/AU/Dec. 1 (12 Oct. 2013).

structures', to urgently establish a Commission to investigate the human rights violations and international humanitarian law abuses committed during South Sudan's armed conflict and to make recommendations on ensuring accountability, reconciliation and healing among all local communities.[324] The AUCISS's Final Report was submitted on 15 October 2014 (but was published exactly a year later). It makes a very interesting read despite the AUCISS's apparent inability to have direct access to primary sources. In particular, the AUCISS complained that it could not reach key witnesses, even though they had previously provided information to other international organizations which had already investigated the conflict.[325] Arguably, the reference was to the Human Rights Division of the UN Mission in the Republic of South Sudan (UNMISS) which had explored and documented events since 15 December 2013 and whose Report had been submitted earlier in 2014.[326] Indeed, there appears to have been considerable friction between them: AUCISS protested that it could not access data in UNMISS's possession despite a UNSC Resolution mandating it to cooperate with AUCISS.

51. The Twenty-Second Ordinary Assembly Session (Addis Ababa, 30–31 January 2014) decided to declare the period 2014–2024 as 'The Madiba Nelson Mandela Decade of Reconciliation In Africa' to promote reconciliation as a means of securing peace, stability and development in the continent as well as 'the lessons learnt from his indelible legacy in the areas of truth, reconciliation and peace building'.[327] The Assembly also took steps in implementing further existing pan-African policies while adopting new ones, e.g., the Maternal New Born and Child Health policy,[328] the 2050 Africa's Integrated Maritime Strategy,[329] the African Capacity for Immediate Response to Crises (ACIRC),[330] the Sharm El Sheikh Commitments on Accelerating Water and Sanitation Goals,[331] etc. Previously, the Twenty-Fourth Ordinary Executive Council Session (Addis Ababa, 21–28 January 2014) had adopted the new Financial Rules and

324. *See* PSC, Communiqué PSC/AHG/COMM.1 (CDXI), 31 Dec. 2013.

325. *See* para. 25 of the Final Report, at: http://www.peaceau.org/en/article/final-report-of-the-african-union-commission-of-inquiry-on-south-sudan.

326. *See* United Nations Mission in the Republic of South Sudan, *Conflict in South Sudan: A Human Rights Report*, 8 May 2014, at: http://www.refworld.org/docid/5371c1924.html.

327. *See* Assembly, *Decision on the Report of the Peace and Security Council on its Activities and the State of Peace and Security in Africa*, AU Doc. Assembly/AU/Dec. 501 (XXII) (31 Jan. 2014), para. 17.

328. *See* Assembly, *Decision on Progress on Maternal New Born and Child Health (MNCH)*, AU Doc. Assembly/AU/Dec. 494 (XXII) (31 Jan. 2014).

329. *See* Assembly, *Decision on the Adoption and Implementation of the 2050 Africa's Integrated Maritime Strategy (2050 AIM Strategy)*, AU Doc. Assembly/AU/Dec. 496 (XXII) (31 Jan. 2014).

330. *See* Assembly, *Decision on the Operationalisation of the African Capacity for Immediate Response to Crises*, AU Doc. Assembly/AU/Dec. 515 (XXII) (31 Jan. 2014). ACIRC was established under Assembly/AU/Dec. 489 (XXI) (2013) as the interim mechanism until the African Standby Force becomes operationalized.

331. *See* Assembly, *Decision on the Report on the Implementation of Sharm El Sheikh Commitments on Accelerating Water and Sanitation Goals in Africa*, AU Doc. Assembly/AU/Dec. 516 (XXII) (31 Jan. 2014).

Regulations (except of Article 22).[332] As has been mentioned, the AU relies on partnerships and financial assistance received by non-African parties. Indeed, had it not been for such funding it would probably have been incapable to operate. The AUC Report on Multilateral Cooperation with respect to Africa's Strategic Partnerships,[333] which was endorsed by the Executive Council,[334] reveals how extensive these links are. Over and above the Africa-EU Partnership, which is explained elsewhere in this monograph, suffice to mention the following events and projects which had taken place at the time: the Tokyo International Conference of African Development (TICAD) Fifth Summit (Yokohama, Japan, June 2013);[335] the Third Africa-Arab Summit (Kuwait, November 2013); the Second Africa-Turkey Summit (Malabo, Equatorial Guinea, November 2014); the Africa-South America (ASA) Partnership, which includes a Financing Mechanism and a Fund for the implementation of agreed specific projects; the Africa-China Process; the Africa-Korea Forum; and the Africa-India Partnership, including the Plan of Action of the Enhanced Framework for Cooperation of the Second Africa-India Forum Summit 2011–2014. Regarding refugees and Internally Displaced Persons (IDPs), another perennial African problem, the Executive Council asked for the implementation of a previous Decision,[336] which had called for doubling (from 2% to 4%) the amount in the AU operational budget destined for emergency humanitarian interventions.[337]

52. The Twenty-Third Ordinary Assembly Session (Malabo, Equatorial Guinea, 26–27 June 2014) approved six multilateral instruments. Three of them concerned the AU's institutional architecture (the Protocol on Amendments to the Protocol on the Statute of the ACJHR, the Protocol on the Establishment of the African Monetary Fund (AMF), and the Protocol to the Constitutive Act of the AU relating to the PAP). The other three broadened the scope of AU's activities (the Convention on Cyber Security and Personal Data Protection, the African Charter on the Values and Principles of Decentralisation, Local Governance and Local Development, and the AU Convention on Cross-Border Cooperation (Niamey Convention)).[338] Most of these treaties are explored elsewhere in the present monograph. Suffice to mention that so far Member States have been most hesitant to sign them let alone ratify them. Clearly, this situation

332. *See* Executive Council, *Decision on the Revised Financial Rules and Regulations of the African Union*, AU Doc. EX.CL/Dec. 784 (XXIV) (28 Jan. 2014).

333. AU Doc. EX.CL/802(XXIV)iv (January 2014).

334. *See* Executive Council, *Decision on the Report of the PRC Sub-Committee on Multilateral Cooperation with respect to Africa's Strategic Partnerships*, AU Doc. EX.CL/Dec. 786 (XXIV) (28 Jan. 2014).

335. Note that TICAD I was held in 1993, TICAD II in 1998, and TICAD III in 2003. For the corresponding Declarations, *see* M. Juma (ed.), *Compendium of Key Documents Relating to Peace and Security in Africa* (Pretoria: Pretoria University Law Press, 2006), 491 et seq.

336. *See* Executive Council, *Decision on the Implementation of the Plan of Action for the Outcomes of the Special Summit on Refugees, Returnees and Internally Displaced Persons in Africa*, Decision EX.CL/Dec. 567 (XVII) (23 July 2010).

337. *See* Executive Council, *Decision on the report of the Sub-Committee on Refugees, Returnees and Internally Displaced Persons in Africa,* AU Doc. EX.CL/Dec. 787 (XXIV) (28 Jan. 2014).

338. Assembly, *Decision on the Protocol and the Statute for the Establishment of the African Monetary Fund*, AU Doc. Assembly/AU/Dec. 517 (XXIII); and *Decision on the Draft Legal Instruments*, AU Doc. Assembly/AU/Dec. 529 (XXIII) (27 Jun. 2014).

poses the question whether Member States have a duty to sign and to ratify those treaties already approved by the Assembly. When the Assembly gives its consent to a treaty's adoption, in effect it is each and every of the Member States that signifies its agreement that the treaty in question be concluded. Therefore, this act of approval does raise legitimate expectations that they will enter into force within a reasonable period of time and that its provisions will benefit those intended.

Regarding the creation of the PAIPO, which the Assembly had already envisaged in a previous resolution,[339] at the Twenty-Third Session it asked the AUC to submit the Draft Statute to the Specialized Technical Committee on Justice and Legal Affairs for consideration.[340] Given that the continent already has two relevant institutions, namely the African Organisation for Intellectual Property (OAPI, created by the Bangui Protocol in 1977) and the African Regional Intellectual Property Organization (ARIPO, created by the Lusaka Agreement in 1976), the obvious question is why the AU should have pressed for another entity in the same field. As has been mentioned (*supra*, paragraph 49), the PAIPO Statute was approved in January 2016. However, on 9 February 2017, the two other Organizations signed a Cooperation Agreement establishing a comprehensive framework for collaboration and the Working Programme for 2017–2018 which was adopted on the same day but does not mention at all the AU dimension.[341] PAIPO was established on the day that the Assembly adopted its Statute and, according to Article 2 thereof, it is an AU Specialized Agency. It follows that AU Member States are *ipso facto* PAIPO Member States, even though Article 13 stipulates that 'Membership to the Organization shall be open to any State, which is a member of the African Union.' The Statute does not elaborate on how membership is to be acquired but it does provide for sanctions to be imposed on recalcitrant Members (Article 19). All Members have the right to withdraw (Article 23). Regarding its linkage with ARIPO and OAPI, Article 16 stipulates that it shall establish and maintain close and continuous working relationships. Thus, there is no indication that PAIPO is to merge with them and/or absorb them at a future date. For the first time since July 2009,[342] the Assembly's agenda contained a topic specifically on maritime piracy, which, even though it does not concern the continent as a whole, has been a point of contention between Western states and certain African states. The decision reached did not actually discuss any of the ramifications of maritime piracy but only took note

339. Assembly, *Decision on the Creation of the Pan-African Intellectual Property Organization*, AU Doc. Assembly/AU/Dec. 453 (XX) (28 Jan. 2013).

340. Assembly, *Decision on Pan-African Intellectual Property Organization (PAIPO)*, AU Doc. Assembly/AU/Dec. 522 (XXIII) (27 Jun. 2014).

341. For details and the relevant documents, *see* H. Muheebwa, 'ARIPO, OAPI To Harmonise Practices On Intellectual Property In Africa', *Intellectual Property Watch*, 21 Feb. 2017, at: https://www.ip-watch.org/2017/02/21/aripo-oapi-harmonise-practices-issues-intellectual-property-africa/.

342. *See* Assembly, *Decision on the Report of the Peace and Security Council on its Activities and on the Peace and Security Situation in Africa*, AU Doc. Assembly/AU/Dec. 252 (XIII), para. 18 (3 Jul. 2009); and Assembly, *Decision to Combat the Payment of Ransom to Terrorist Groups*, AU Doc. Assembly/AU/Dec. 256 (XIII), para. 1 (3 Jul. 2009).

of Togo's proposal to host a Regional Conference on Maritime Piracy and other Criminal Acts Committed at Sea.[343]

53. Not long after the creation of the state of South Sudan, a deadly conflict among the supporters of the main political parties erupted. In February 2015, it was decided to set up an 'independent hybrid judicial body' to prosecute those most responsible for violating international humanitarian law. It culminated to the Hybrid Court for South Sudan (HCSS) and to a new innovative body, the Compensation and Reparation Authority. Their creation was envisaged in Chapter V(3) of the Agreement on the Resolution of the Conflict in South Sudan, signed on 17 August 2015 by the government and various domestic stakeholders under the auspices of the IGAD, one of the RECs. The HCSS was described 'as an African-led and Africa-owned legal mechanism'.[344] It was the second ad hoc criminal court to be created during 2015 to try crimes committed during internal conflicts, the other being the Special Criminal Court (SCC) competent to investigate and prosecute serious violations of international humanitarian law (including crimes against humanity, war crimes and genocide) in the CAR since 2003. In particular, in February 2015, the CAR Council of Ministers voted to establish the SCC and the relevant legislation was promulgated on 3 June 2015.[345] While there is no specific African component in the SCC,[346] it does show the need to have in place a permanent criminal justice system. With the project of the ICL Section of the ACJHR being in limbo, with the ICC often being unable to exercise its role promptly and effectively, and with national judicial systems lacking or crippled, ad hoc internationalized criminal courts appear to be the only answer to ensure (at least) a certain justice. Arguably, these ad hoc courts are rather easily created but their operationalization is far from certain. This derives from the experience of the ad hoc court to try Hissène Habréin Senegal and from the fact that presently there is no indication that either the HCSS or the SCC may become active any time soon. As regards the latter, the Brussels International Conference on the CAR, organized by the EU in November 2016, pledged EUR 2 billion from which to fund, *inter alia*, the SCC.[347] As regards the former, even though there have been continuous reminders that securing accountability in South Sudan is a pressing need, the process moves at an

343. Assembly, *Decision on Maritime Piracy*, AU Doc. Assembly/AU/Dec. 534 (XXIII) (27 Jun. 2014).

344. *See* PSC, 547th Meeting held at the level of Heads of State and Government, PSC/AHG/COMM.3(DXLVII), 26 Sept. 2015, para. 22.

345. *See* Loi Organique N° 15.003 portant creation, organisation et fonctionnement de la Cour Penale Speciale https://rongdhrca.wordpress.com/. *See also* K. Magliveras, 'The Special Criminal Court of the Central African Republic', *International Enforcement Law Reporter* 32 (2016): 69.

346. It was envisaged in the Memorandum of Understanding on Urgent Temporary Measures, signed on 7 Aug. 2014 between the UN Multidimensional Integrated Stabilization Mission in the Central African Republic (MINUSCA) and CAR's transitional government.

347. *See* European Commission, Press Release IP/16/3804, 17 Nov. 2016, at: http://europa.eu/rapid/press-release_IP-16-3804_en.htm.

extremely slow pace.[348] In the summer of 2017, a technical team of the AUC, acting on behalf of the PSC, visited Juba, South Sudan, to confer with the Transitional Government of National Unity on the establishment of the HCSS. The press release issued after the visit recorded that a joint roadmap on its establishment was agreed and the modalities for concluding the process were identified.[349] Neither the contents of the roadmap nor the nature of the modalities were revealed, a clear indication that precious little, if even that, was achieved.

During the Twenty-Fourth Ordinary Session (Addis Ababa, 30–31 January 2015) the Assembly dealt with the consequences of the Ebola virus in the affected Member States (Guinea, Liberia, and Sierra Leone). It asked the Member States to lift all restrictions imposed on them pursuant to the decision of the Extraordinary Executive Council Session of 8 September 2014 calling for the non-closure of borders, and non-stigmatization of their nationals. It also requested that the international financial institutions and partner countries cancel the debt of the affected states to alleviate the virus' impact on their economies and assist in their economic recovery and development; and, presumably as a token measure of solidarity, the Assembly asked the AUC to pay directly to each of these Members the amount of USD 500,000.[350] Finally, it urged the setting up of a High-Level Contact Group composed of Member States, the Commission, the African Development Bank and the UN Economic Commission for Africa to negotiate the terms of debt cancellation in the affected states.[351] On the front of the so-called Arab Spring, the Assembly congratulated Tunisia for the successful democratic transition, after holding free and fair legislative and presidential elections in October and November 2014, and considered 'the successful of the Tunisian experience as possible model for democratization process in Africa'.[352] But African leaders did not ask themselves some obvious questions: why have there not been any more such successful examples; why has Libya been embroiled in a deadly civil war after a 'successful' popular up rise; and why has Egypt relapsed into a totalitarian regime after democratic elections were held in 2012? In an emancipated international organization putting and answering the tough questions is a challenge, but seemingly not so for the AU.

---

348. *See* , e.g., PSC, 609th Meeting, Communiqué, PSC/PR/COMM(DCIX), 30 Jun. 2016, para. 10; and UNSC, Presidential Statement, S/PRST/2016/1, 17 March 2016 and Press Release SC/12761, 23 Mar. 2017, at: https://www.un.org/press/en/2017/sc12761.doc.htm. *See* further, UN Human Rights Council, *Report of the Commission on Human Rights in South Sudan*, UN Doc. A/HRC/34/63, paras 61–64 (6 Mar. 2017).
349. *See* African Union, 'African Union Commission and the South Sudan Transitional Government advance on establishment of the Hybrid Court for South Sudan', Press Release, 22 Jul. 2017, at: https://au.int/sites/default/files/pressreleases/32703-pr-pr-au-south_sudan_technical_meeting-22july2017.pdf.
350. Assembly, *Decision on Ebola Virus Disease (EVD) Outbreak*, AU Doc. Assembly/AU/Dec. 553 (XXIV) (31 Jan. 2015). *See also* Assembly, *Special Declaration Acknowledging the Role of African Volunteers in the Fight Against Ebola*, AU Doc. Assembly/AU/Decl. 4 (XXIII) (31 Jan. 2015).
351. Assembly, *Resolution on Debt Cancellation of Countries Affected by Ebola Virus Disease*, AU Doc. Assembly/AU/Res. 1 (XXIV), para. 4 (31 Jan. 2015).
352. Assembly, *Decision on Democratic Transition in Tunisia*, AU Doc. Assembly/AU/Dec. 568 (XXIV), para. 1 (31 Jan. 2015).

54. The Twenty-Fifth Ordinary Assembly Session (Johannesburg, South Africa, 14–15 June 2015) had the theme 'Year of Women Empowerment and Development towards Africa's Agenda 2063.' The Assembly discussed, as it has been doing in every session for arguably far too many years, the question of the UN Security Council's reform. It reserved the right to determine the criteria for the selection of the two Member States, which it believes must represent the continent as permanent Members.[353] What the decision did not spell out was which entity would make the selection. However, this might not have been an omission because the answer was probably obvious: it would be the Assembly itself. Generally speaking, the Session's agenda was full of administrative matters and recurring themes. However, an important topic, given the scarcity of AU resources and facilities, was the decision to streamline summits and working methods.[354] Taking onboard the Executive Council's recommendations,[355] the Assembly resolved, *inter alia*, to: (a) delineate the decision-making process by it and by the Executive Council and delegate to the latter the power and mandate to take decisions, except on key strategic issues (it did not define which these issues are but a careful reading would suggest the questions of continental integration, peace and security, governance, and financial matters); (b) empower the Specialized Technical Committees (STCs) composed of Member States' Ministers to reach decisions on issues falling under their competence, except on decisions having financial and structural implications and with the provision that if a Member State objects to decision-making by a STC, the Executive Council will consider the relevant decisions; (c) not the repeat the adoption of those decisions already taken at the level of the Executive Council; (d) hold 'closed sessions' meetings to discuss strategic issues, which will be convened 'in a Retreat format'; (e) continue the mode of two (sessions) Summits per year, where one will focus on policy issues with the participation of 'partners' in accordance with the Assembly Rules of Procedure and the other on the implementation of decisions (presumably only the heads of state and government will participate in the latter); and (f) conduct the opening of its sessions in a business-like manner and in accordance with the Rules of Procedure, i.e., only the UN Secretary-General and the President of the State of Palestine (on account of the 'historical African solidarity' with the Palestinian struggle) would be allowed to address them in person, while the other invited guests would have to use 'alternative platforms'. Finally, the Assembly adopted six declarations, one of them dealing with the ever crucial issue of the AU's self-reliance.[356]

55. At the Twenty-Sixth Ordinary Session (Addis Ababa, 30–31 January 2016), the Assembly adopted the impressive number of twenty legal texts, which were a mixture of new multilateral legal instruments (e.g., the Road Safety Charter and the Model Law on Medicine Regulation); additions to existing instruments (e.g., the

353. Assembly, *Decision on the Sixteenth Report of the Committee of Ten Heads of State and Government on the Reform of the United Nations Security Council*, AU Doc. Assembly/AU/Dec. 574 (XXV), para. 8 (15 Jun. 2015).

354. Assembly, *Decision on Streamlining of the AU Summits and the Working Methods of the African Union*, AU Doc. Assembly/AU/Dec. 582 (XXV) (15 Jun. 2015).

355. Presumably this topic was discussed in the context of Executive Council, *Decision on the Report of the Commission on the Review of the Rules of Procedure of the Policy Organs*, AU Doc. EX.CL/Dec. 884 (XXVII) (12 Jun. 2015).

356. Assembly, *Declaration on Self-Reliance*, Assembly/AU/Decl. 5 (XXV) (15 Jun. 2015).

Protocol to the African Charter on Human and Peoples' Rights on the Rights of Older Persons); changes to existing legal instruments (e.g., the Amended Statute of the Pan-African University); changes to Statutes of subsidiary organs / entities / bodies (e.g., the Africa Sports Council; the Legal Aid Fund for the AU Human Rights Organs; the African Science Research and Innovation Council (ASRIC)); and changes to the Rules of Procedure of Specialized Technical Committees (e.g., the Committee on Social Development, Labour and Employment; the Committee on Health Population and Drug Control; and the Committee on Public Service, Local Government, Urban Development and Decentralisation).[357] Eighteen months later, most of these instruments establishing subsidiary or technical organs have not been signed by any Member State raising the rather obvious question, why were they concluded in the first place. Suffice to mention the Statute of the African Minerals Development Centre, the Statute of the Africa Sports Council, and the Statute of the African Science Research and Innovation Council (ASRIC). Even the Protocol to the African Charter on Human and Peoples' Rights on the Rights of Older Persons has been signed by only four states.

Notwithstanding how reluctant Member States appear in signing and ratifying these multilateral instruments, it will submitted that if (a) the AU Constitutive Act and the various Protocols signed pursuant to its provisions, (b) all the treaties and conventions concluded over the years under the OAU/AU auspices, and (c) the various decisions and resolutions adopted by the principal organs (the Assembly, the Executive Council and the PSC) and imposing duties and obligation on the membership are taken as an indivisible whole, they could be regarded as forming a 'African Union law.' The sophistication of this AU law is inferior to, say, the EU law but then the same could be said for other regional intergovernmental organizations. Moreover, the fact that there has never been (and presumably there will not be in the foreseeable future) a functionable AU judicial organ is a very negative development in any attempt to refine AU law and to develop it so as to acquire a norm making status. But, at the same time, it has become rather clear that in certain areas Member States may not act in breach of an African system of rules. A very good example are coups d'état and unconstitutional overthrows of governments, an African scourge, where, as is later explained, the relevant rules are not only applied almost with no exceptions, but the membership accepts their application and act in compliance with them. One is prepared to accept that the AU law is still in its infancy and it has a very long way to go before it is recognized as norms-setting system. But it is a very significant development which deserves to be discussed by AU scholars in depth.

On another front, the Assembly attempted to link up the various decisions adopted by the PSC with the resolutions adopted on similar issues and situations by the UN Security Council. In particular, by invoking Article 7(3) of the PSC Protocol stipulating that Member States have agreed to accept and implement PSC decisions, the Assembly not only concluded that the three African members sitting on the UNSC 'have special responsibility to ensure that the decisions of the PSC are well reflected in the decision-making process of the UNSC on peace and security issues of concern to Africa' but

357. Assembly, *Decision on the Specialized Technical Committees*, AU Doc. Assembly/AU/Dec. 589 (XXVI) (31 Jan. 2016), para. 2. The recommendation to adopt them was made by the Executive Council on the basis of the Report of the First Extraordinary Session of the Specialized Technical Committee on Justice and Legal Affairs, AU Doc. EX.CL/935(XXVIII).

also requested that they present reports to it on their efforts at the UNSC level and on their promotion of common African positions as these have been articulated by the PSC.[358] This demand may actually be against the principle of sincere cooperation which, even though more developed in the law of the EU, it should be considered to be part of the law of international organizations. In the UN Charter this principle is manifested in Article 2(2), which obliges all Member States to fulfil in good faith all their obligations. And if there happens to be a conflict between the UN Charter's obligations and their obligations under another international agreement (in case, under the AU Constitutive Act), Article 103 of the UN Charter expressly states that their obligations under it shall prevail. This provision should be interpreted that if the AU and the UNSC happens to follow completely different policies in a specific matter, the former's Member States have the duty to align with the latter's policy because as UNSC Members they must act having only the UN's best interests at heart. Should they refuse to follow the stance taken by the other UNSC members – and they have every right to do so – they must produce reasons which concern the UN policy itself and not the policy which another international organization (namely, the AU) happens to have adopted. To put it otherwise, the UNSC members must act only in their capacity as members of this organ irrespective of the continent or region in which they are geographically located and the commitments they may have already made in the context of any regional political organization.

56. At the Twenty-Seventh Ordinary Session (Kigali, Rwanda, 17–18 July 2016), the Assembly discussed the continental free movement of people which, as a protected right, is laid down in the African Charter on Human and Peoples' Rights and in the (now defunct) Treaty establishing the AEC (the Abuja Treaty) of 1991. Article 12 of the former, which concerns domestic and transborder migration, guarantees to every individual the right to freedom of movement and residence within the borders of a contracting party as long as he/she abides by its law, the right to leave any country including his/her own, and the right to return to the country of origin. It also guarantees that non-nationals legally admitted in a contracting party may only be expelled by virtue of a decision taken in accordance with domestic law while the mass expulsion of non-nationals forming national, racial, ethnic or religious groups is prohibited. Building on this *acqui*, the Assembly confirmed the decision which had been taken by the Executive Council in January 2016 mandating the AUC to develop the Protocol on Free Movement of Persons in Africa (the target date was set at January 2018),[359] and launched the African Passport, which will be issued by the Commission and the Member States. It asked third states to recognize it as a valid travel document.[360] The Assembly also pressed for the implementation of the CFTA project. It asked the AUC to draft and circulate to Member States negotiating texts on trade in goods and on trade in services while presenting feasible options on the elimination of non-trade barriers

358. *See* Assembly, *Decision on the Activities of the Peace and Security Council and the State of Peace and Security in Africa*, AU Doc. Assembly/AU/Dec. 598 (XXVI) (31 Jan. 2016), para. 24.

359. *See* Executive Council, *Decision on the Mekele Retreat of the Executive Council*, AU Doc. Decision EX.CL/Dec. 908 (XXVIII) (31 Jan. 2017).

360. *See* Assembly, *Decision on the Free Movement of Persons and the African Passport*, AU Doc. Assembly/AU/Dec. 607 (XXVII) (18 Jul. 2016).

among African states to foster continental trade. Finally, it called on Member States to speak with one voice on all issues related to trade negotiations with third parties.[361]

As has been noted above, in May 2016, the African Extraordinary Chambers in Senegal found Hissène Habré, the former dictator of Chad, guilty of most of the charges brought against him. However, regarding the question of victims' reparations, while the Statute of the Chambers does provide for the establishment of a reparation fund, the necessary measures to implement it had not been taken. In particular, the sentencing judge ordered in July 2016 that Habré pay 20 million CFA francs (circa USD 34,000) for each surviving victim of rape and sexual slavery, 15 million CFA francs (circa USD 25,400) for each surviving victim of torture and arbitrary detention, and 10 million CFA francs (circa USD 17,000) for the surviving family members of victims.[362] Thus, the Assembly resolved that the Trust Fund be created under AU auspices and that the AUC together with Chad organize a pledging conference with the participation of as many African and international stakeholders as possible.[363] The reason behind the conference, which apparently has not taken place until today, is that Habré's sequestrated assets are inadequate to satisfy the demands for reparations.[364] In the meantime, none of the eligible victims (who are estimated at more than 4,700) has apparently received any reparation.[365] The matter was not discussed during the January 2017 Assembly Session, which could be explained by the fact that the Appeal Chamber of the African Extraordinary Chambers had still not ruled on the appeal filed by Habré's lawyers against the judgment. As has been noted (*supra*, paragraph 41), in April 2017 the judgment on the appeal was handed down. It ordered, *inter alia*, that Habré pay compensation to 7,396 victims (the applications of 3,489 persons alleging to be victims were rejected) and confirmed the types of reparations and the amounts as decided by the Trial Chamber, giving a total of 82,290 billion CFA francs; and that the proceeds of selling Habré's assets and selling any assets which might recovered subsequently will be used to finance the reparations. The Appeal Chamber, finally, denied the claim advanced by civil parties that Habré must also be ordered to pay collective reparations.

The theme of the Twenty-Seventh Ordinary Session was 'The African Year of Human Rights with Particular Focus on the Rights of Women'. The Assembly expressed its determination to protect and promote human rights as embodied in the Protocol on the African Charter on Human and People's Rights on the Rights of Women in Africa (the Maputo Protocol) and in the Solemn Declaration on Gender quality in Africa,

---

361. Assembly, *Decision on the Continental Free Trade Area (CFTA)*, AU Doc. Assembly/AU/Dec. 608 (XXVII) (18 Jul. 2016).
362. Note that the victims' lawyers lodged an appeal challenging the amounts afforded for compensation which were considered inadequate and only the number of eligible victims. On 27 Apr. 2017, the Appeals Chamber upheld the decision on reparations and quantified the total amount of Habré's criminal responsibility at 82,290 billion CFA francs.
363. Assembly, *Decision on the Hissene Habre Case*, AU Doc. Assembly/AU/Dec. 615 (XXVII) (18 Jul. 2016).
364. Generally, *see* Justice Hub, *Victims' Lawyers Start Battle to Seize Habré's Millions*, 4 Aug. 2016, at: https://justicehub.org/article/ex-chadian-dictator-hissene-habre-ordered-pay-millions-victims.
365. Generally, *see* C. Sperfeldt, 'The Trial Against Hissène Habré: Networked Justice and Reparations at the Extraordinary African Chambers', *The International Journal of Human Rights*, published online, 17 Aug. 2017.

adopted during its Third Ordinary Session (Addis Ababa, 6–8 July 2004). Member States 're-committed' themselves to expedite the ratification, domestication and implementation of the Maputo Protocol (six states have currently not ratified it), and called upon the AUC to introduce measures and modalities to support the establishment of capacities and processes to monitor domestication efforts.[366] Arguably, the proper organ to do so is the African Commission on Human and Peoples' Rights and to ask the AUC to undertake this task is unnecessary duplication of efforts. Finally, the Assembly took decisions towards boosting the financing of the AU, a question whose importance cannot be underestimated. After many years of discussions, different proposals and a large measure of inaction, it was resolved, starting 2017, to institute and implement a 0.2% levy 'on all eligible imported goods' into Africa as the measure which will create sufficient income to finance the budget of the Operational Programme and the budget of peace support operations. As regards the practical aspects, the amounts to be collected by the levy will be automatically paid by national administrations into the account opened for the AU with the Central Bank of each Member State for the purpose of transmitting each Member's assessed contribution to the AU. Moreover, the AUC was asked to study the management of African mineral resources bearing in mind how revenue may be optimized through harmonization of royalties and fiscal regimes.[367]

57. The Twenty-Eighth Ordinary Assembly Session (Addis Ababa, 30–31 January 2017) had the theme 'Harnessing the demographic dividend through investments in the youth'. Before it, the Thirtieth Executive Council Ordinary Session had taken place between 25 and 27 January 2017 and, before it, the Thirty-Third Permanent Representatives Committee Ordinary Session between 22 and 24 January 2017.[368] While the discussion of the AU's financing was meant to have been continued from the last Session, the Assembly simply recorded that some (unnamed) Members had started implementing the collection of the levy on imported goods and that some other (unnamed) Members faced challenges.[369] The question of the AU's relationship towards the ICC was again the dominant issue. Despite formal reservations entered by Cabo Verde, Nigeria, Senegal and Liberia, the Assembly adopted the ICC Withdrawal Strategy[370] and asked Member States to consider implementing its recommendations. As in the second half of 2016 Burundi, the Republic of South Africa, and The Gambia had notified their withdrawal from the ICC, the Assembly regarded them as 'pioneer

366. Assembly, *Declaration of the Assembly on the Theme of the Year*, AU Doc. Assembly/AU/Decl. 1 (XXVII) Rev. 1 (18 Jul. 2016).

367. Assembly, *Decision on the Outcome of the Retreat of the Heads of States and Government, Ministers of Foreign Affairs and Ministers of Finance on the Financing of the African Union*, AU Doc. Assembly/AU/Dec. 605 (XXVII) (18 Jul. 2016).

368. For the agenda of these organs, *see* https://www.au.int/web/en/documents/20170125/agenda-or-program-28th-au-summit-meetings.

369. Assembly, *Decision on the Implementation of the Financing of the Union*, AU Doc. Assembly/AU/Dec. 641 (XXVIII) (31 Jan. 2017).

370. *See Withdrawal Strategy Document*, Draft 2, Version, 12.1.2017, at: https://www.hrw.org/sites/default/files/supporting_resources/icc_withdrawal_strategy_jan._2017.pdf.

implementers of the Withdrawal Strategy'.[371] However, subsequent events proved that this jubilation was rather premature: The Gambia, whose former President Yahya Jammeh had announced in November 2016 the intention to withdraw from the Rome Statute, changed course when the new President, Adama Barrow, advocated that the withdrawal process will be terminated and the country will follow a rapprochement with international institutions (including the Commonwealth), while, in February 2017, the High Court in South Africa degreed that that the notice to withdraw from the ICC was unconstitutional and, therefore, invalid, because the government had failed to consult Parliament.[372] In April 2017, the South African government officially withdrew its notice of withdrawal. Finally, the Assembly expressed its deep concern at the slow pace of ratification of the 2014 Malabo Protocol to the ACJHR.[373]

The Assembly also considered a topic introduced by Ethiopia titled 'Universal Access to Immunization as a Cornerstone for Health and Development in Africa,' which is closely linked to the Pharmaceutical Manufacturing Plan for Africa (PMPA), whose implementation calls for investing in the continent's capacity to develop and produce vaccines.[374] In the meantime, it asked Member States in partnership with all relevant stakeholders (presumably this means the World Health Organization) to negotiate with manufacturers the provision of vaccines at affordable prices.[375] During its previous Session (July 2016), the Assembly had resolved to establish the AU Special Fund on the Prevention and Combating Terrorism and Violent Extremism in Africa and had entrusted the drafting of its Statute to the AUC.[376] It now decided to submit the draft Statute to the Specialized Technical Committee on Justice and Legal Affairs for consideration.[377] However, the Assembly adopted the Statute of the African Union Mechanism for Police Cooperation (AFRIPOL), which, when it becomes operative,

371. Assembly, *Decision on the International Criminal Court*, AU Doc. Assembly/AU/Dec. 622 (XXVIII), paras 8 and 6 (31 Jan. 2017). *See* further, M. Ssenyonjo, 'State Withdrawal Notifications from the Rome Statute of the International Criminal Court: South Africa, Burundi and the Gambia' *Criminal Law Forum*, 2017, https://doi.org/10.1007/s10609-017-9321-z.
372. North Gauteng High Court, Pretoria, *Democratic Alliance v. Minister of International Relations and Cooperation and Others (Council for the Advancement of the South African Constitution Intervening)*, Case no. 83145/2016, Order, 22 Feb. 2017, [2017] ZAGPPHC 53, at: http://saflii.org/za/cases/ZAGPPHC/2017/53.html.
373. *See* Assembly/AU/Dec. 622 (XXVIII), *supra* 371, para. 4.
374. *See* AU Commission and United Nations Industrial Development Organization, *Pharmaceutical Manufacturing Plan for Africa (PMPA): Business Plan*, Addis Ababa, November 2012, at: http://apps.who.int/medicinedocs/documents/s20186en/s20186en.pdf.
375. Assembly, *Decision on Universal Access to Immunization as a Cornerstone for Health and Development in Africa*, AU Doc. Assembly/Dec. 624 (XXVIII) (31 Jan. 2017).
376. Assembly, *Decision on the Establishment of an African Union Special Fund on Prevention and Combating Terrorism and Violent Extremism in Africa*, AU Doc. Assembly/AU/Dec. 614 (XXVII) (18 Jul. 2016).
377. Assembly, *Decision on the African Union Special Fund on the Prevention and Combating of Terrorism and Violent Extremism in Africa*, AU Doc. Assembly/AU/Dec. 627 (XXVIII) (31 Jan. 2017).

will no doubt deal with terrorism and Extremism.[378] Until now (September 2017), no Member State has signed it.

It is submitted that the regular PSC Activity Report examined by the Assembly revealed the degree of turmoil that continues to hamper the continent's ability to overcome its chronic problems. The Assembly referred to the following issues: post-election crisis in The Gambia; ethnic tensions in South Sudan; lack of stabilization of Somalia; the political crisis in DRC; (lack of) national reconciliation in Libya; (lack of) peace and reconciliation in Mali; no lasting peace in Sudan and no security of civilians in Darfur; the strife in Burundi; political differences in Guinea-Bissau; the conflict in Western Sahara; and (lack of) reconciliation in the CAR.[379] The Assembly did not actually take any concrete action to deal with any of these situations. It simply reviewed events since the last PSC Activities Report, commended the work undertaken by it, by other AU organs and by the RECs, and appealed to the international partners to continue providing political, financial, and logistical support. That the Assembly avoids taking specific measures to deal with issues negating peace and security and having a very heavy toll on human life is no longer problematic, it is unacceptable. To an outside observer, the Assembly gives the impression that it has become a toothless organ, dangerously following the steps of the disgraced OAU Assembly ('a club of dictators', as it was referred to). Should a major crisis befall the continent, it could prove incapable to handle it promptly and effectively.

The Assembly also discussed the long overdue issue of the AU's institutional reform. Based on the Report titled 'The Imperative to Strengthen our Union: Proposed Recommendations for the Institutional Reform of the African Union' and on comments received by Member States, it agreed to the following five goals: (a) focus on key priorities with continental scope priorities; (b) realign AU institutions to deliver against those priorities; (c) connect the AU to its citizens; d) manage AU business efficiently and effectively at political and operational levels; and (e) finance the AU sustainably and with the full ownership by Member States. The day-to-day coordination and realization of these goals will be undertaken by a new Reform Implementation Unit to be created within the AUC, the latter also being instructed to devise a mechanism ensuring that 'legally binding decisions and commitments are implemented by Member States'.[380] Arguably, several of the proposed changes will require the amendment of the Constitutive Act. Suffice to mention the following: strengthening and enforcing the sanctions mechanism; making participation in AU deliberations contingent on observing Summit decisions; establishing a troika arrangement composed of the outgoing, the current, and the incoming Chairpersons; reforming the PSC (as will be recalled the PSC is not mentioned in the Constitutive Act as it was created after the AU's inauguration); and applying the principle of subsidiarity in the relations between

378. Assembly, *Decision on the Draft Legal Instruments*, AU Doc. Assembly/AU/Dec. 636 (XXVIII), para. 2 (31 Jan. 2017).

379. Assembly, *Decision on the Report of the Peace and Security Council on its Activities and the State of Peace and Security in Africa*, AU Doc. Assembly/AU/Dec. 629 (XXVIII) (31 Jan. 2017).

380. Assembly, *Decision on the Outcome of the Retreat of the Assembly of the African Union on the Institutional Reform of the African Union*, AU Doc. Assembly/AU/Dec. 635 (XXVIII) (31 Jan. 2017).

the AU, RECs, Regional Mechanisms (RMs), and Member States. Further amendments to the Constitutive Act and but also to legal instruments might be required if such reform measures as to review and clarify the roles and functions of the PAP and of the 'African Union judicial organs' are undertaken. It is rather unclear if the latter term also covers the African Commission on Human and Peoples' Rights and the African Court on Human and Peoples' Rights considering the long-standing determination that they should be firmly imbedded into the AU's institutional architecture. However, the Declaration on the Commemoration of the Tenth Anniversary of the Operationalization of the African Court on Human and Peoples' Rights, which the Assembly adopted during the same Session, had nothing to say in this regard.[381] Therefore, one can only wait and see if and how this goal will be implemented.

The most important item on the agenda was no doubt Morocco's official application to accede to the AU. Many observers of AU affairs were no doubt surprised when King Mohammed VI in July 2016 made known the intention to return.[382] Several Member States were apparently not thrilled with this development prompting the Legal Counsel to provide a legal opinion.[383] The Assembly decision accepting the application does not reveal how many Member States agreed and how many; reportedly, thirty-nine Members expressed their agreement in writing and nine voted against. The decision is also silent on whether accession was conditional or with reservations but from its wording one could detect that no strings were attached:

> [Morocco's accession] provides the opportunity to reunite the African community of states around the Pan-African core values of the Founders of solidarity, unity, freedom and equality, in accordance with the Principles and Objectives of the Constitutive Act. This will strengthen the ability of the African Union to find African solutions to African problems.[384]

Morocco became the fifty-fifth Member State when it deposited its instrument of accession to the Constitutive Act on 31 January 2017. At a time when there is a leadership crisis in the AU and those Members which in the past had played a pivotal role (including Libya, Egypt, and South Africa) are no longer able or willing to do so,

381. Assembly, *Declaration on the Commemoration of the Tenth Anniversary of the Operationalization of the African Court on Human and Peoples' Rights*, AU Doc. Assembly/Decl. 2 (XXVIII) (31 Jan. 2017).

382. It took the form of Royal Message handed over to the Chadian President and then AU Chairperson Idriss Deby, *see* http://themoroccantimes.com/2016/07/20237/morocco-join-african-union. Note that in February 2017 Morocco told the Economic Community of West African States (ECOWAS) that it will be seeking full membership, a move arguably signifying deeper relations with other African states. In June 2017, ECOWAS leaders gave the go ahead but decided that the implications of Morocco's membership still needed to be considered before it could formally join, *see* BBC News, 'Ecowas agrees to admit Morocco to West African body', 5 Jun. 2017, at: http://www.bbc.com/news/world-africa-40158089.

383. *See* ISS Peace and Security Council Report, 'Morocco's plans to join the AU a legal conundrum', 9 Sept. 2016, at: https://issafrica.org/pscreport/on-the-agenda/moroccos-plans-to-join-the-au-a-legal-conundrum.

384. Assembly, *Decision on the Admission of the Kingdom of Morocco to the African Union*, AU Doc. Assembly/AU/Dec. 639 (XXVIII), para. 3 (31 Jan. 2017).

Morocco could very well fulfil this role. The conflict in Western Sahara would no doubt prove to be a major issue of contention. Its description as 'a non-self-governing territory', an anathema to Morocco, and the insistence that a self-determination referendum for the people must be held,[385] a development that Morocco has managed to prevent until now, could lead to a clash between it and a large group of Member States. Lest it be forgotten, many an African state still regard Morocco as a colonial power suppressing fellow Africans. To that extent, there is a credible possibility that those which disagreed with Morocco's accession will oppose its assuming a larger role, especially if it immediately pursues a policy to disrupt the participation of the SADR in AU affairs or even have it excluded completely from the Organization. There are already signs that this is Morocco's intention. In March 2017, Morocco failed to attend a PSC meeting on the situation in Western Sahara even though it had been invited.[386] The PSC asked it 'to extend the necessary cooperation in conformity with the … Constitutive Act' and, presumably to accommodate a hostile Morocco, it resolved to reactivate the Ad hoc Committee of Heads of State and Government on the conflict in Western Sahara, which had been established by the OAU Assembly in July 1978.[387] Moreover, some days later, a meeting between the AU and the UN Economic Commission for Africa (ECA) was postponed because Morocco demanded the exclusion of SADR as it is does not participate in ECA. Given that SADR does not participate in any international organization and institution bar the AU and has not become a contracting party to any multilateral treaty bar the OAU/AU ones, should Morocco pursue this policy of disruption with vigour, it will soon be (at least diplomatically) isolated.[388] The AU should treat this as a matter of concern and urgently come up with a solution.

58. If one might have thought that the following observations were made by an African to assess the current situation in the continent:

> No single internal factor has contributed more to the present socio-economic problems in the Continent than the scourge of conflicts within and between our countries. They have brought about death and human suffering, engendered hate and divided nations and families. Conflicts have forced millions of our people into a drifting life as refugees and internally displaced persons, deprived of their means of livehood, human dignity and hope. Conflicts have gobbled-up scarce resources, and undermined the ability of our countries to address the many compelling needs of our people.

he would have been surprised to find out that they were included twenty-four years ago in the Cairo Declaration adopted in June 1993 to create the OAU Mechanism for Conflict Prevention, Management and Resolution, the predecessor of the PSC. Since the 1990s, the average annual economic loss of African countries as a result of wars, civil strife, and insurgencies has been estimated at USD 18 billion. Considering that

---

385. *See* Assembly/AU/Draft/Dec. 8 (XXVIII), *supra* para. 10.

386. PSC, Communiqué, PSC/PR/COMM(DCLVIII), 20 Mar.2017, at: http://www.peaceau.org/en/article/communique-of-the-668th-meeting-of-the-peace-and-security-council-of-the-african-union-au-on-the-situation-in-western-sahara.

387. *See* OAU Doc. AHG/Res. 92 (XV) (22 Jul. 1978).

388. *See* further, The Economist, 'Western Sahara: The never-ending dispute', 25 Feb. 2017, p. 30.

the current total population of Africa has exceeded 1.2 billion people, conflicts have cost to each and every African USD 15 every year. But, as eloquently argued by a previous Commission Chairperson, armed conflicts should also be viewed as 'the destruction of hope' for the children that remain uneducated, for the women who suffer abuse but also for the skilled persons who leave their countries because of the conflicts.[389] And these are not all the problems and the challenges that the AU has been mandated to tackle on behalf of its now fifty-five Member States following the accession of Morocco.

389. *See* Report of the Chairperson of the Commission, *Enhancing Africa's Resolve and Effectiveness in Ending Conflict and Sustaining Peace*, AU Doc. SP/ASSEMBLY/PS/RPT(I) (2009), para. 83 at p. 22.

Part II. The African Union

Chapter 1. Transition from the OAU to the AU

59. The Constitutive Act of the AU, which entered into force on 26 May 2001, did not expressly stipulate that the replacement of the OAU was a case of succession between international organizations. This followed from the wording of Article 33(1) thereof, the clause dealing with the question of transition, which, on the one hand, provided that the Constitutive Act would replace the OAU Charter and, on the other hand, referred to the devolution of all OAU assets and liabilities to the AU. It was not clear from the wording of Article 33(1) whether the arrears owed to the OAU from unpaid budgetary contributions were to be regarded as Member States' debts to be paid to the AU. In the balance sheet of 31 December 2002, which showed the OAU assets and liabilities to be transferred to the AU, the sum of USD 21 million representing arrears in contributions had been written off for two reasons. The first was that it was highly unlikely that they would ever be recovered. The second reason was, without such a provision, the balance sheet would not have reflected the prevailing at the time financial situation.[390] There was disagreement among AU organs as to how this issue ought to be handled. The AUC took the view that all arrears ought to be considered as dues owed and measures be taken to claim them. On the other hand, the Permanent Representatives Committee (PRC), namely the organ composed of the Member States' representatives appointed to the AU, regarded that they should be written off entirely.[391] This reaction was rather to be expected as it was in the Member States' best interests not to pay them. In the event, the latter recommendation was approved by the Executive Council and no effort was made to persuade recalcitrant Member States to even pay a part of the monies owed.[392]

60. Pursuant to Article 33(1), once the Constitutive Act had entered into force, the OAU Charter was to remain operative for a transitional period of one year or for any further period that was determined by the Assembly. Therefore, the transitional period ought to have lasted until 26 May 2002. However, the Thirty-Seventh Ordinary Assembly Session (Lusaka, July 2001) decided, 'due to the magnitude of the tasks to

390. *See Report of the Fifth Ordinary Session of the Advisory Sub-Committee on Administrative, Budgetary and Financial Matters on the Report of Ernst & Young*, AU Doc. EX/CL/69 (IV) (2004).
391. *See* Permanent Representatives Committee, Seventh Ordinary Session, 12–13 Mar. 2004, AU Doc. PRC/Rpt (VII), 8.
392. *See* Executive Council, *Decision on the Balance Sheet of the African Union as at 31 December 2002*, OAU Doc. EX/CL/Dec. 75 (IV) (16 Mar. 2004).

be performed and bearing in mind the need for consultations with Member States', to extend it to mid-July 2002.[393] As it turned out, setting the transition period to just under fourteen months (May 2001–July 2002) was a most ambitious goal and failed to take into consideration the following parameters which complicated the procedure. First, Member States had a varying degree of adaptability to new state of affairs that the AU was bringing about. Second, as it turned out, not all OAU Member States had ratified the Constitutive Act by the time the transition period had expired. Third, there were extraneous circumstances in several Member States (e.g., ongoing armed hostilities, breakdown of state functions, etc.) preventing the smooth cooperation between the whole membership, a fundamental condition for completing promptly the transition. Fourth, the OAU lacked the necessary manpower, facilities and expertize for undertaking such a massive project, which involved reconstituting an organization that had existed for almost forty years and setting up of fifteen organs, most of which did not previously exist.

61. The transition from the OAU to the AU was supervised by the Secretary-General and the Eminent Persons Advisory Panel, a group of experts convened for this specific purpose. On 8 May 2002, the Panel recommended that the transition period be extended, a view shared by the Secretary General. Although it was generally expected that African leaders would agree with the recommendation, at the end of the day it was decided to proceed as planned, that is, to inaugurate the AU in July 2002. There is no doubt that considerations of pragmatism drove this decision. A delay in launching the AU would have tarnished its image and might have dealt a severe blow to the continent's morale at a crucial moment.[394] However, with the benefit of hindsight one cannot but criticize the decision to keep the transition period shorter than longer, not least because even today not all organs envisaged in the Constitutive Act are in operation.

62. The methods used to set up the various AU organs could be classified in four separate categories. The first concerns those organs (namely, the Assembly of Heads of State and Government, the Executive Council, the Commission, the Specialized Technical Committees, and the PRC), whose establishment and functioning was expressly laid down in the Constitutive Act. For this category no further action was required on behalf of the Member States. The second category relates to those organs (namely, the PAP (an organ originally envisaged in the AEC Treaty), the African Court of Justice and the Financial Institutions), whose setting up required the negotiation, conclusion, and adoption of corresponding protocols by the Member States.[395] This is a method not generally found in international institutions and, particularly, in regional Intergovernmental Organizations (IGO) of a politico-economic nature. The Protocol of the PAP was concluded in March 2001 and entered in force in December 2003, while the Protocol on the African Court of Justice was concluded in July 2003 and entered into force in February 2009 (*see infra* paragraphs 122 et seq. regarding its still pending merger with the African Court on Human and Peoples' Rights). As regards

393. *See* Assembly, *Decision on the Implementation of the Sirte Summit Decision on the African Union*, para. 15, OAU Doc. AHG/Dec. 160 (XXXVII) (11 Jul. 2001).

394. *See* the Acts of the Symposium on *African Union and the New Pan-Africanism: Rushing to Organize or Timely Swift?* in *Transnational Law & Contemporary Problems* 13/1 (2003): 1.

395. For the Pan-African Parliament, *see* Art. 17(2), for the Court of Justice, *see* Art. 18(2), and for the Financial Institutions, *see* Art. 19 of the Constitutive Act.

the Financial Institutions, so far the Protocol on the AIB and the Protocol on the AMF have been concluded (respectively, in February 2009 and June 2014) but have not yet come into force; the Protocol on the African Central Bank has not yet been concluded. The Constitutive Act did not stipulate the number of ratifications necessary for each of these protocols to enter into force. Even though one would assume that they would require the same number as the Constitutive Act itself (namely, two-thirds of the OAU Member States), they actually contain different stipulations. Thus, the PAP Protocol requires a simple majority of the total membership (at the time of its conclusion it meant twenty-eight ratifications), while the Protocol on the Court of Justice and the Protocol on the AIB require only fifteen ratifications, which incidentally is the usual number of ratifications for OAU/AU treaties and conventions to come into force.

A few general comments on these Protocols should be made. First, as the relevant provisions in the Constitutive Act give only a basic description for the above organs, the protocols' drafters were given a very broad mandate to determine the scope of their functioning and activities. To that extent, it is probably open to question whether the original wishes of African leaders have been followed. Second, said protocols would apply only to those Member States which choose to ratify them. In effect, two classes of organs have been created: (a) those established directly by the Constitutive Act and to which all Member States participate as contracting parties to the Act and (b) those which have been set up by protocols and to which only the Member States that have become contracting parties to the relevant protocol/s participate. This rather awkward situation was amply manifested in March 2004 during the Inaugural Session of the PAP where only thirty-eight Member States took part. Currently, there are still seven states which have not ratified it. Even though these include countries where basic state functions have collapsed and/or are facing serious domestic strife (Somalia, Eritrea, DRC, etc.), the question cannot be avoided if PAP should be regarded the 'pan-African' entity that it proclaims to be. Third, to the extent that they introduce new rules and principles, these protocols do not modify the Constitutive Act de jure, because they were not adopted as protocols amending it under Article 32 thereof as well. Nevertheless, they have resulted in many and important de facto changes. A practical consequence of this situation is for example that even if the PSC is one of the most prominent and active organs, its existence is not acknowledged in the Constitutive Act.

63. It will be argued that the Constitutive Act has given to the Assembly the authority to adopt the protocols setting up the organs falling into this second category without necessitating their prior ratification to enter into force. The argument could be advanced that, since they were already envisaged in the Constitutive Act, the Assembly was authorized (and mandated for that matter) to conclude the relevant protocols and that they would come into force immediately after adoption. Since, however, these protocols require their prior ratification by a specific number of Member States, the latter have effectively been given the opportunity to decide whether they wish their operationalization, a desire manifested by ratifying the respective protocol. But was this the real aspiration of the Constitutive Act's drafters? To put it otherwise, it would be improper to reach the conclusion that Member States have been offered the opportunity to determine anew whether these organs should actually be set up. However, as things have developed, this is what has happened: by being asked to ratify these protocols, several Member States have chosen not to approve them and, consequently, not to participate in them. And in some cases they have not even shown any commitment to ensure that the respective treaties will enter into force at some future stage, as evidenced for example by the Protocol on the AIB which, eight years after its conclusion, has only attracted five ratifications.

Thus, the AU membership has effectively been divided into two categories: those states which have ratified the protocols and are bound by the decisions adopted by the respective organs and those which have not ratified them. This is clearly unacceptable. It leads to a de facto permission to pursue membership a la carte: with the exception of those organs, which were expressly established and set up by the Constitutive Act (the Assembly, the Executive Council, and the Commission) participation in the other organs is subject to the Member States' discretion whether or not to ratify the applicable protocols. It is a basic rule of the law of international organizations is that all Member States must be bound by all decisions taken by all organs.

64. The third category actually concerns only one organ, the Economic, Social and Cultural Council (ECOSOCC). Its establishment required an Assembly resolution laying down its functions, powers, composition and organization. This was done during the Third Ordinary Assembly Session (Addis Ababa, 6–8 July 2004).[396] Finally, the fourth category concerns those organs that the Assembly has decided to create pursuant to the power granted under Article 5(2) of the Constitutive Act. Until today, two such organs have been established. The first is the PSC. It was set up through the adoption of a separate Protocol attached to the Constitutive Act.[397] The second is the AUCIL. It was set up through a Statute, which was adopted by the Executive Council during its Fourteenth Ordinary Session in January 2009[398] and was approved by the Assembly at its Twelfth Ordinary Session in February 2009.[399] The Statute is not attached to the Constitutive Act.

65. The procedure for setting up the organs is laid down in the third paragraph of Article 33 of the Constitutive Act, which reads as follows:

> Upon the entry into force of this Act, all necessary measures shall be undertaken to implement its provisions and to ensure the establishment of the organs provided for under the Act in accordance with any directives or decisions which may be adopted in this regard by the Parties thereto within the transitional period stipulated [in Article 33(1)]

This is arguably a rather vague and badly drafted provision that gives rise to a number of problems and questions. First, it diminished the importance of the transitional period, because it referred solely to 'directives or decisions' adopted during that stage and not

396. *See* Assembly, *Decision on the Economic, Social and Cultural Council (ECOSOCC)*, AU Doc. Assembly/AU/Dec. 48 (III) (8 Jul. 2004).

397. Note that the setting up of the PSC is envisaged in Art. 9 of the Protocol on Amendments to the Constitutive Act of 2003, which inserted a new Art. 20*bis* in the Constitutive Act. If and when the Protocol enters into force, the PSC will join those organs that are expressly laid down in the Constitutive Act.

398. AU Doc. EX.CL/478 (XIV) a (30 Jan. 2009).

399. *See* Assembly, *Decision on the Draft Statute of the African Union Commission on International Law*, AU Doc. Assembly/AU//Dec. 209 (XII) (3 Feb. 2009).

that the implementation and execution of such instruments would also have to be effected within the same deadline. Second, by using passive voice the drafters did not elaborate on whether it will be the Member States or the AU itself (presumably acting through the Assembly) which will proceed with realizing the Act's provisions and the setting up of the organs. This is a crucial question because, as the wording of Article 33(3) contains what would appear to be a legally binding obligation, it should be determined upon whom the burden falls and, in particular, whether the Member States are under a duty to give effect to any 'necessary measures' adopted. Third, the reference to 'directives or decisions' might be against the rule of the law of international organizations stipulating that Member States may not deal with issues relating to their organization but outside its formal structure. To put it otherwise, given that the Constitutive Act's entry into force had legally created the AU, any 'directives or decisions' should not have been reached by the Member States themselves but only through the Assembly. And this because, pursuant to Article 6(2) thereof, it is the 'supreme' AU organ where all Members are represented. Consequently, has the general competence to adopt all required measures. Fourth, considering that the Constitute Act's entry into force required ratification by two-thirds of OAU Member States, it could have reasonably been expected (and indeed this is what happened) that not all states would be able to ratify it on time and be allowed to participate in the adoption of the relevant decisions.

66. The official launching of the AU was scheduled to take place in mid-July 2002 and was planned to coincide with the e Assembly's inaugural session. However, there was still one state which had not ratified the Constitutive Act (Madagascar) and another which, even though it had ratified it, had not deposited the instrument of ratification (Guinea-Bissau).[400] Therefore, as these two states could not have participated in the AU, the delicate issue of permitting them to be present in the Assembly's inaugural session was raised. It was argued by certain Member States that, since they were part of the OAU whose assets and liabilities were being transferred to the AU, they should be allowed to attend as observers. Other states advanced the rather impossible argument that, since they had signed the Constitutive Act, they had already the status of AU Member State. The matter was referred to the Acting Legal Counsel for an opinion. He was categorical that, since they had not completed the ratification process or had not acceded to the Constitutive Act, its provisions were not binding upon them and, consequently, they had neither rights nor obligations. In the event, it was decided that the Council of Ministers would invite them under the status of 'prospective Members'.[401]

This solution was nothing more than a legal machination, which could only be explained by the importance attached to the presence of all OAU Members at the launching of the AU. Moreover, it was probably driven by the expectation that by then they would have completed the ratification process. However, as Madagascar deposited

400. T. Maluwa, 'International Law-Making in Post-Colonial Africa: The Role of the Organization of African Unity', *Netherlands International Law Review* 49 (2002): 81, 101–102 might be wrong in writing that the DRC had also not ratified the Act, as it had deposited its ratification on 9 Jul. 2002; *see List of States which Have Signed, Ratified/ Acceded to the Constitutive Act of the African Union as at 26 November 2002*, OAU Doc. CAB/LEG/23.15 (2002).

401. *See Report of the Fifteenth Ordinary Session of the Committee of Ambassadors and Other Plenipotentiaries*, OAU Doc. Cttee/AMB/Rpt (XV) at paras 83–86 (30 Jun. 2002).

its instrument of ratification on 10 June 2003 (it had ratified the Act five days earlier) and Guinea-Bissau on 7 July 2003,[402] the fact that they were treated as full Members (Guinea-Bissau was even allowed to sign the Protocol establishing the PSC on 9 July 2002, which incidentally it ratified in December 2011) is highly questionable. To conclude, by affording these states the status of 'prospective Members', the AU, even though it secured, from a political perspective, the participation of all states, arguably committed unconstitutional acts.

402. *See Report of the Interim Chairperson of the Commission on the Status of AU Treaties as at 17 June 2003*, AU Doc. EX/CL/36 (III) (2003), and the Constitutive Act's ratification table that appears on the AU website.

Chapter 2. Objectives and Principles

67. The Constitutive Act follows the structure of the OAU Charter and contains the AU objectives (Article 3) separately from its principles (Article 4). There are fourteen objectives laid down covering an extremely broad spectrum of activities primarily in the fields of political cooperation and economic integration. They range from greater unity and solidarity between the countries and peoples of Africa, to the promotion of peace, security and stability, on the one hand, and democratic principles and good governance, on the other hand, to the protection of human rights, to coordination and harmonization between the RECs and the AU, etc. Moreover, the objectives include the creation of the necessary conditions enabling the continent to play its rightful role in the global economy and in international negotiations, while advancing and defending common positions on those issues that are of shared interest. A good example is the UN reform and specifically the restructuring of the Security Council, where Africa has been pressing to reverse the fact that it is the only continent without a permanent seat. Thus, the Sirte Declaration on the Reform of the UN of July 2005 adopted the Common African Position calling, *inter alia*, for 'the allocation of two permanent seats to Africa with all the privileges, including the right of veto, and five non-permanent seats on the Security Council',[403] even though there has been no consensus as to which Member States should hold the permanent seats.[404]

Since then, the promotion of the Common Position has been entrusted to the Committee of Ten Heads of State and Government on the Reform of the UN Security Council.[405] During the Fourteenth Ordinary Assembly Session (2010) the issue was discussed in some detail on the basis of a Committee Report but no specific action was taken other than to reiterate the call to all Member States to 'ensure that Africa speaks with one voice' on this issue.[406] Three years later, when the Assembly discussed the matter anew, no concrete decisions were reached. The Committee of Ten has now become a regular fixture. In July 2016, its Eighteenth Report was examined by the

---

403. *See* Assembly, *Sirte Declaration on the Reform of the United Nations*, AU Doc. Assembly/ AU/ Decl. 2 (V) (5 Jul. 2005). Two further instruments were adopted on the same day: Assembly, *Resolution on the United Nations Reform: Security Council*, AU Doc. Assembly/AU/ Resolution 1 (V); and Assembly, *Decision on the Expansion of the Follow-Up Mechanism on the Reform of the United Nations*, AU Doc. Assembly/AU/Dec. 87 (V). *See* further Executive Council, *The Common African Position on the Proposed Reform of the United Nations: The Ezulwini Consensus,* AU Doc. Ext/EC.CL/2 (VII) (8 Mar. 2005).

404. *See* D. Bourantonis & K. Magliveras, 'The Enlargement of the UN Security Council: Reflections from the Current Debate', *Politics* 22 (2002): 24, 27. For the African position vis-à-vis the enlargement of the Security Council in the mid-1990s, *see* D. Bourantonis, *The History and Politics of UN Security Council Reform* (Abingdon: Routledge, 2005), 59–60. For an earlier Decision on the rotation of the two seats, *see* Assembly, *Modalities of Rotation for Two Seats Being Claimed by Africa on the Enlarged Security Council*, OAU Doc. AHG/Dec. 129 (XXIV) (10 Jun. 1998).

405. *See* Assembly, *Decision on the Reform of the United Nations Security Council*, AU Doc. Assembly/AU/Dec. 184 (X) (2 Feb. 2008).

406. *See* Assembly, *Decision on the Reform of the United Nations Security Council*, AU Doc. Assembly/AU/Dec. 285 (XIV) (2 Feb. 2010).

Assembly, which repeated verbatim the demand: Africa's full representation in the Security Council cannot be with less than two permanent seats with all the prerogatives, privileges and the veto right attached as well as five additional non-permanent seats (apparently the number has in the meantime been reduced to two). The insistence on the veto power was explained in the following terms: while Africa is opposed, in principle, to the veto power, it is a matter of common justice that it should be made available to all permanent members. Finally, to correct the historical injustice that the African continent continues to endure through its non-representation on the UNSC, Member States were asked for the umpteenth time to include it in their foreign policy priorities and in discussions with non-African partners.[407] It would appear that several non-African UN Member States are supporting the African position judging from the statements made in November 2016 at the podium of the UN General Assembly, which made an attempt to rejuvenate the stalled reform project.[408] Even though follow-up intergovernmental negotiations on UNSC reform were held in February 2017 during the Seventy-First UNGA Ordinary Session,[409] it is very doubtful if the composition of the UNSC's permanent membership will ever change for a very simple reason: the existing permanent Members must decide to dilute considerably their existing power before they accept newcomers.

Regarding AU objectives, some are vague (e.g., 'to promote cooperation in all fields of human activity to raise the living standards of African peoples'), others are rather devoid of meaning (e.g., 'to promote sustainable development at the … cultural level') and others express nothing more than wishful thinking (e.g., 'to promote … the integration of African economies'). Finally, the Protocol on Amendments of February/July 2003 added three new objectives as subparagraphs (i), (p), and (q) to Article 3: First, the effective participation of women in decision-making in all areas. Second, the development and promotion of common policies on trade, defence, and foreign relations ensuring the defence of the continent's interests and strengthening its negotiating position. Third, the encouragement of the African Diaspora's full participation in building up the AU and its recognition as an important stakeholder.[410] The dynamics of the Diaspora were addressed during the Global African Diaspora Summit, which took place in South Africa on 25 May 2012 with the participation of African Caribbean and South American leaders.[411] The Summit culminated to the so-called Five Legacy Projects, which were endorsed by the Assembly in July 2012. A

407. *See* Assembly, *Decision on the Reform of the United Nations Security Council*, AU Doc. Assembly/AU/Dec. 616 (XXVII) (18 Jul. 2016).

408. *See* the statements of, *inter alia*, Norway and Belgium, UN Press Release, *Updated Security Council Must Reflect Changing Global Reality, Member States Say, as General Assembly Debates Ways to Advance Progress on Reform*, UN Doc. GA/11854, 7 Nov. 2016, at: https://www.un.org/press/en/2016/ga11854.doc.htm.

409. For updated information, *see* http://www.un.org/pga/71/tag/security-council-reform/.

410. On the African Diaspora, *see* , *inter alia*, Executive Council, *Decision on the Definition of the African Diaspora*, AU Doc. EX.CL/ Dec. 173 (VI) (28 Jan. 2005); Executive Council, *Decision on the Definition of the African Diaspora*, AU Doc. EX.CL/Dec. 221 (VII) (2 Jul. 2005); and Executive Council, *Decision on the First African Union Diaspora Ministerial Conference*, EX.CL/Dec. 386 (XII) (29 Jan. 2008).

411. *See Declaration of the Global African Diaspora Summit*, AU Doc. Diaspora/Assembly/AU/Decl (I) (25 May 2012).

South African proposal to establish self-funding Technical Committees of Experts for the implementation of these projects was adopted by the Assembly in May 2013.[412] The next Summit took place in November 2015, where it was argued that the Diaspora should be considered the sixth region of Africa.[413]

68. While OAU objectives were almost exclusively concerned with political issues, the AU broke away from this tradition. The Constitutive Act has advanced all kinds of economic and developmental questions and topics promoted democratic principles and institutions as well as issues which in the 1990s had started to appear in the constitutive instruments of international organizations, namely, the democratic principle, good governance and popular participation. That the popular participation was included in the Act should not be underestimated, since it marked a significant change in Member States' attitude. Whereas previously there was almost no institutionalized cooperation between the OAU and NGOs and the civil society at large (possibly because of suspiciousness towards NGO activities),[414] this policy of exclusion was partly overturned with the African Charter for Popular Participation in Development and Transformation (1990)[415] and was further consolidated with the aforementioned Sirte Declaration of September 1999, which expressly referred to involving African peoples and 'their grassroots organizations'.

This aspect of the Sirte Declaration, which, as will be recalled, also decided to establish the AU, was carried on to the Constitutive Act, whose seventh recital puts forward 'the need to build a partnership between governments and all segments of civil society … in order to strengthen solidarity and cohesion among our peoples'. Almost two years later, the First OAU/Civil Society Conference took place in June 2001 and a follow-up Second Conference in Addis Ababa on 11–14 June 2002 to establish a mechanism facilitating and deepening the interface among the continent's civil society and the AU.[416] Since then, this interface has largely been institutionalized twofold: through the setting up of the ECOSOCC, envisaged in Article 22 of the Constitutive Act as an AU advisory organ composed of different social and professional groups, and through the New Economic Partnership for Africa's Development (NEPAD).[417] As was noted by the AUC, the decision to establish ECOSOCC signifies

412. *See* Assembly, *Decision on the Implementation of the Global African Diaspora Legacy Projects*, AU Doc. Assembly/AU/Dec. 478 (XXI) (27 May 2013).
413. African Union, Economic Cultural Social and Cultural Council, Global Africa Diaspora Stakeholder Convention, 19–22 Nov. 2015, Washington DC and Maryland, USA, *Official Report*, at: http://www.globalafricadiaspora.org.
414. *See* E. Gyimah-Boadi, 'Civil Society in Africa', *Journal of Democracy* 7 (1996): 118.
415. The Charter, which was a declaration of intent, was adopted in February 1990 at the International Conference on Popular Participation in the Recovery and Development Process in Africa held under the auspices of the UN Economic Commission for Africa in Arusha, text in UN Doc. A/45/427 (22 Aug. 1990). *See also*, S.J. Kpundeh (ed.), *Democratization in Africa: African Views, African Voices* (Washington, DC: National Research Council / National Academy Press, 1992), 34–36.
416. *See* T. Murithi, *The African Union: Pan-Africanism, Peacebuilding and Development* (London: Ashgate, 2005) 117–118.
417. *See* A. De Waal, 'What's New in the "New Partnership for Africa's Development"?', *International Affairs* 78 (2002): 463.

the will to make the AU 'a tool to build a new equilibrium between state and non-state actors on solid foundations'.[418]

69. The aforementioned objectives are to be materialized and implemented pursuant to the sixteen principles that are laid down in Article 4 of the Constitutive Act. Some of these principles are repetition of those set out in Article III of the OAU Charter and include the fundamental doctrines of sovereign equality between all Member States, the peaceful resolution of disputes and the non-intervention in the internal affairs of other states. However, many and significant new objectives were added and it is particularly worthwhile to note (again) the participation of African peoples in AU activities, the establishment of a common defence policy, the promotion of self-reliance within the framework of the Union, the advancement of gender equality and of social justice and, last but not least, the condemnation and rejection of political assassination, acts of terrorism, subversive activities and of unconstitutional changes of government. Finally, the Protocol on Amendments of February/July 2003 added the principle of restraining Member States from entering into any treaty or alliance incompatible with AU principles and objectives as Article 4 subparagraph (q) and the principle of prohibiting Member States from allowing the use of their territory as a base for subversion against other Members as Article 4 subparagraph (r). The latter echoes Article III(5) of the OAU Treaty and it was probably the drafters' omission to include it in the Constitutive Act.

70. A number of observations should be made in relation to the Article 4 principles. First, arguably two doctrines that are essential to the functioning of all international organizations were omitted: (a) that Member States shall fulfil in good faith all the obligations assumed by ratifying the Constitutive Act;[419] and (b) that Member States shall facilitate the achievement of AU tasks and shall abstain from any measure that could jeopardize the attainment of its objectives.[420] It should be noted that the latter doctrine (the so-called solidarity clause) has been partly covered by the aforementioned Protocol on Amendments, which inserted Article 4(q) in the Constitutive Act.

71. The second observation relates to the principle of condemnation and rejection of acts of terrorism. It was inserted in a strict and unqualified manner even though some quarters of the international community would justify terrorist activities if they were undertaken against totalitarian regimes; if the right to self-determination has been unlawfully negated; or where regimes have come into power by forcibly overthrowing

418. *See* Commission of the African Union, *Vision of the African Union and Missions of the African Union Commission*, Final Draft, March 2004, 31.

419. Compare Art. 2(2) of the UN Charter; Art. 4(3) of the Consolidating Version of the Treaty on European Union, Official Journal of the European Union, 26 Oct. 2012, C 326/13.

420. Compare Art. 4(3) of the Consolidating Version of the Treaty on European Union.

legitimate governments.[421] Indeed, in the Algiers Declaration of July 1999, African leaders accepted the connection between acts of terrorism and the legitimate struggle 'waged by peoples for freedom and self-determination'.[422] Considering that contemporary African history has been marked by a continuous struggle against colonialism, dictatorships, and human rights abuses, that Member States have directly interfered in the internal affairs of other Members (even though the OAU and the AU would not be prepared to admit that much) and that the term 'terrorism' has many political shades and has not yet received a universally acceptable legal definition, it is submitted that the AU should think again the strictness of this principle. Arguably, it should reconsider the legitimacy of terrorist activities directed against governments which have come into power by quashing the rule of law and by abolishing democratic institutions and also terrorist acts perpetrated against foreign occupation troops. Moreover, this strict principle would appear to be against the OAU Convention on the Prevention and Combating of Terrorism of July 1999 (in force since December 2002), whose Article 3(1) expressly stipulates that:

> the struggle waged by peoples in accordance with the principles of international law for their liberation or self-determination, including armed struggle against colonialism, occupation, aggression and domination by foreign forces shall not be considered as terrorist acts.

However, it could be counter-argued that, in view of the Protocol to the Terrorism Convention, concluded in July 2004 and in force since February 2014, the provision of Article 3(1) does no longer represent the AU position. And this because the fifth preambular paragraph of the Protocol reads: '[The Member States of the African Union] convinced that acts of terrorism cannot be justified under any circumstances … .'[423] Therefore, there would appear to be a prima facie conflict between the Constitutive Act, the Terrorism Convention, and the Protocol raising a point of interpretation. However, the three instruments in question stipulate separate methods for resolving disputes on interpretation. Thus, Article 26 of the Constitutive Act envisages resort to the African Court of Justice (now, the ACJHR) pending the establishment of which the Assembly shall be responsible) Article 22 of the Convention envisages amicable solution between the disagreeing parties, failing which resort to the ICJ or to arbitration and, finally, Article 7 of the Protocol is an amalgamation of the other methods: it

---

421. *See* further *Convention on Combating International Terrorism*, adopted by the Organization of the Islamic Conference on 1 Jul. 1999 (now the Organization of Islamic Cooperation (OIC)), at: http://ww1.oic-oci.org/english/convenion/terrorism_convention.htm; *Kuala Lumpur Declaration on International Terrorism*, adopted by the Extraordinary Session on Terrorism of the Islamic Conference of Foreign Ministers, 1–3 Apr. 2002, UN Doc. A/56/911 – S/2002/362 (8 Apr. 2002); and Twenty-Ninth Session of the Islamic Conference of Foreign Ministers, Res. No. 6/29-LEG on the OIC Convention on Combating International Terrorism (27 Jun. 2002). Note that thirty African countries participate in the OIC.
422. *See* Assembly, *Algiers Declaration*, OAU Doc. AHG/Decl. 1 (XXXV) (14 Jul. 1999), reproduced in RADIC 11 (1999): 788.
423. Compare Executive Council, *Decision on Terrorism*, AU Doc. Ext/EX/CL/Dec. 4 (III) (24 May 2003), which rejected the perpetration of terrorism in all its forms and recalled Africa's stand to unequivocally condemn all terrorist acts.

stipulates that, should the difference not be settled amicably, either party may refer it to the ACJHR, but if either or both parties do not participate in said Court, they may refer it to the ICJ for a settlement in conformity with the latter's Statute. Finally, reference should be made to a 2010 Assembly resolution expressing the AU's determination to fight any form of terrorism.[424]

72. The third observation relates to the fact that the well-versed principle of non-intervention in the internal affairs of Member States during the OAU years has been qualified by providing for a right of intervention. The Constitutive Act, the only multilateral instrument currently containing the right of an international institution to intervene in such express terms in its Member States, envisages the following two instances. The first is laid down in Article 4(h), as amended by the Protocol of February/ July 2003. It could be described as involuntary intervention in the sense that the targeted Member State must endure it and cannot object to it. Article 4(h), a provision reflecting the collective inability during the OAU era to deal effectively with numerous cases of genocide and ethnic cleansing,[425] endows the AU with the right to intervene on the basis of an Assembly, following a PSC recommendation, when grave circumstances (i.e., war crimes, genocide, crimes against humanity as well as a serious threat to legitimate order) are present in a Member State and it is necessary to restore peace and stability. What constitutes a threat to legitimate order in the context of domestic affairs should be treated as a legal and not as a political matter and, consequently, it ought to be ultimately determined, in case of dispute, by the ACJHR (once it becomes operative).

73. The second instance is voluntary intervention in accordance with Article 4(j) of the Constitutive Act. It stipulates that Member States have the right to request AU intervention to restore peace and security. The wording of this provision raises a point of interpretation: is intervention to be demanded only by the Member State concerned or could any other Member request it? An AU Legal Adviser has argued for the latter interpretation by offering a grammatical interpretation of Article 4(j). According to him, this provision 'refers to Member States and not to a member State, and therefore does not restrict the right to request intervention of the Union to the member State concerned'.[426] Even though this interpretation moves towards expanding the ambit of Article 4(j) (undoubtedly this could lead to protecting the population of Member States from civil strife, human rights violations, etc.), it is submitted that it could lead to unwanted consequences. Thus, it might be used as a weapon by a Member State to create internal problems in another state or to support a minority in that state. In such instances, the Member invoking Article 4(j) should be required to show an adequate and justifiable legal interest. Moreover, there is nothing to suggest that the drafters of the Constitutive Act wanted such a significant departure from the way the

---

424. *See* Assembly, *Decision on the Prevention and Combating of Terrorism*, AU Doc. Assembly/ AU/311 (XV) (27 Jul. 2010).

425. *See* B. Kioko, 'The Right of Intervention under the African Union's Constitutive Act: From Non-Interference to Non-Intervention', *International Review of the Red Cross* 85 (2003), No. 852: 807; D. Kuwali, 'The End of Humanitarian Intervention: Evaluation of the African Union's Right of Intervention', *African Journal of Conflict Resolution* 9 (2009): 41.

426. Kioko, *ibid.*, 817.

OAU Mechanism for Conflict Prevention and Management operated.[427] Finally, Article 4(j) introduces several supranational elements, which the AU arguably does not currently possess.

74. The modalities of AU involvement pursuant to either Article 4(h) or to Article 4(j) have not been laid down in the Constitutive Act. Especially, in the case of Article 4(j) it does not even specify which would be the competent organ to order it. Following the adoption of the Rules of Procedure of the Assembly, it is clear that both actions require its prior decision.[428] However, with the advent of the PSC (it commenced operations in 2004) the situation has changed. In particular, as regards Article 4(h), the PSC is able to recommend to the Assembly intervention on behalf of the AU, while, as regards Article 4(j), it has been mandated to approve the modalities for intervention once the Assembly has reached the relevant decision.[429] Another issue left unresolved is whether the AU involvement could take the form of armed intervention on its own volition. Leaving aside, instances where this would be absolutely necessary under the circumstances (e.g., to prevent a genocide), it would be questionable. Thus, were it undertaken to address breaches of regional peace and security, it should require the UN Security Council's prior authorization, as stated in Article 53(1) of the UN Charter. It is a well-known fact that the Security Council has been endowed to function as the primary guardian of international peace and security, the notion of having 'primary responsibility' as laid down in Article 24 of the UN Charter. On numerous occasions, the Security Council has emphasized that it considers itself competent to deal not only with issues of international peace and security, as expressly stipulated in Article 24 of the UN Charter, but with regional peace and security and/or internal conflicts as well.[430] Finally, it should be noted that the ASF has been established to enable the PSC perform its responsibilities vis-à-vis deploying of peace support missions and (direct) intervention pursuant to Article 4(h) and Article 4(j). Even though, until today, the ASF is not fully operational,[431] the fact that military intervention may be ordered and undertaken by the AU cannot be ruled out.[432]

If that were to happen, the question arises whether the targeted Member State or rather its government in power is obligated to accept the intervention, especially if it were to take the form of a peacekeeping force approved by the Assembly. Such an incident played out in January 2016, when African leaders wanted to send a peacekeeping force to Burundi to tackle the civil war which had cost of life of 300,000 people.

---

427. For analysis *see* K. Magliveras & G. Naldi, *The African Union* (Alphen aan den Rijn: Kluwer Law International, 2009), 59 et seq.
428. *See* Art. 9(1) of the Constitutive Act in conjunction with Rule 4(1) of the Rules of Procedure of the Assembly. *See also* T. Maluwa, 'Reimagining African Unity: Some Preliminary Reflections on the Constitutive Act of the African Union', *African Yearbook of International Law* 8 (2002): 29.
429. *See* Art. 7(1) of the Protocol establishing the Peace and Security Council.
430. As the examples of Somalia, Rwanda, and Sudan clearly show. Generally, *see* N.M. Blokker & M. Kleiboer, 'The Internationalization of Domestic Conflict: The Role of the UN Security Council', *Leiden Journal of International Law* 9 (1996): 7.
431. In October and November 2015, Operation Amani Africa II was deployed in South Africa as the first major field exercise. ASF is composed of composed of multidisciplinary contingents having both civilian and military components.
432. *See* Art. 13 of the Protocol establishing the Peace and Security Council.

However, despite the grave circumstances they were not willing to invoke the right to intervene in a Member State pursuant to an Assembly decision as stipulated in Article 4h of the Constitutive Act. This decision would have legitimatized military intervention in Burundi. Burundian President Pierre Nkurunziza objected to the peacekeeping force presumably because it would have disrupted his plans to enjoy a third consecutive term in office, which was not sanctioned by the Constitution. Arguably, given Burundi's violent history, African leaders should not have heeded to the President and should have promptly invoked Article 4h. However, the Assembly decided to dispatch a high-level delegation to consult with the government as well as other with other Burundian actors on how the AU could contribute to stabilization and the resolution of the crisis.[433] Six months later, nothing had changed in the situation in Burundi but the Assembly was still not prepared to discuss the possibility of ordering forceful measures.[434] Finally, in January 2017, the Assembly urged the government of Burundi to sign the MoU on the deployment of the authorized 200 AU Human Rights Observers and Military Experts in the country.[435] At the time of writing, the MoU had still not been signed.[436]

75. The above considerations beg the question whether the AU, in its present form, constitutes a regional arrangement within the meaning of Chapter VIII of the UN Charter. Articles 52–54 thereof allow the existence of arrangements dealing with the maintenance of peace and security in a manner appropriate for regional action, provided that they act under the primacy of the Security Council and in accordance with the relevant UN Charter provisions. Such arrangements, which have included, *inter alia*, NATO, the League of Arab States, the Warsaw Pact (before its dissolution), the Western European Union (as conceived in the late 1940s and early 1950s), and the Organization of American States (OAS), could be understood as agencies and/or acting

433. Assembly, *Decision on the Activities of the Peace and Security Council and the State of Peace and Security in Africa*, AU Doc. Assembly/AU/Dec. 598 (XXVI) (31 Jan. 2016), para. 13.
434. Assembly, *Decision on the State of Peace and Security in Africa*, AU Doc. Assembly/AU/Dec. 612 (XXVII) (18 Jul. 2016), para. 1.
435. Assembly, *Decision on the Report of the Peace and Security Council on its Activities and the State of Peace and Security in Africa*, AU Doc. Assembly/AU/Dec. 629 (XXVIII), 31 Jan. 2017, para. 9.
436. *See also*, UNSC, *Report of the Secretary-General on Burundi*, UN Doc. S/2017/165, 23 Feb. 2017; and *Security Council Press Statement on Situation in Burundi*, UN Doc. SC/12750, 13 Mar. 2017.

as agents of the UN Security Council.[437] Although the answer at the time the AU was on the drawing table should have been in the negative, as it did not possess the structures that are characteristic of such arrangements, the entry into force in December 2003 of the Protocol establishing the PSC and the wide powers and functions entrusted to it in conjunction with the way the PSC has performed its mandate clearly leads to the conclusion that it is now a Chapter VIII regional arrangement. The first major AU action was setting up in 2004 AMIS, a peacekeeping force operating in the region of Darfur. The following year, UNSC Resolution 1590 (2005) of 24 March 2005 requested that the United Nations Mission in Sudan (UNMIS) 'closely and continuously liaise and coordinate at all levels' with AMIS.[438]

Although there is a growing rapport between the UN and the AU in addressing collective security challenges in the continent,[439] the two institutions may understand their priorities differently. The Security Council has recognized that in some cases it may authorize the AU to deal with such challenges,[440] while the AU has called upon

---

437. In order to define and make more concrete its relationship with regional arrangements, the UNSC has adopted over the years numerous instruments, including the following of particular interest to Africa: Res. 1269(1999) of 19 Oct. 1999 on the responsibility of the Security Council in the maintenance of peace and security, reproduced in 39 I.L.M. (2000) 238; Res. 1308(2000) of 17 Jul. 2000 on the responsibility of the Security Council in the maintenance of peace and security; Res. 1625(2005) of 14 Sept. 2005 on threats to international peace and security; Res. 1631(2005) of 17 Oct. 2005 on cooperation between the United Nations and regional organizations for the maintenance of international peace and security; Presidential Statement of 20 Sept. 2006 on cooperation between the United Nations and regional organizations in the maintenance of international peace and security, UN Doc. S/PRST/2006/39 (20 Sept. 2006); and Presidential Statement S/PRST/2009/11 (5 May 2009). *See* further the open UNSC debate 'Cooperation between the United Nations and regional and sub-regional organizations: peace operations – the United Nations-African Union partnership and its evolution', held in December 2014, UN Doc. S/2014/879 (9 Dec. 2014) and UN Doc. S/PV.7343 (16 Dec. 2014). *See also* the following UNGA instruments: Res. 60/1, *2005 World Summit Outcome*, 16 Sept. 2005, para. 68(h); Res. 55/2, *United Nations Millennium Declaration*, 18 Sept. 2000, para. 28; and Res. 49/57, *Declaration on the Enhancement of Cooperation between the United Nations and Regional Arrangements or Agencies in the Maintenance of International Peace and Security*, 9 Dec. 1994.
438. *See also* UNSC Res. 1564 (2004), 18 Sept. 2004. Note that, without expressly saying so, UNSC Res. 2320(2016) of 18 Nov. 2016 considers that, as a regional mechanism, the AU comes under Chapter VIII of the UN Charter.
439. Based on the *Declaration on Enhancing UN – AU Cooperation: Framework for the Ten-Year Capacity-Building Programme of the African Union*, signed in Addis Ababa between the UN Secretary-General and the Chairperson of the AU Commission on 16 Nov. 2006, UN Doc. A/61/630, 12 Dec. 2006. *See also* United Nations, *Report of the African Union-United Nations panel on modalities for support to African Union peacekeeping operations*, UN Doc. A/63/666-S/2008/813 (31 Dec. 2008).
440. For the developing dynamics of the relationship, *see* UNSC, Presidential Statement of 28 Mar. 2007 on the relationship between the United Nations and regional organizations, in particular the African Union, in the maintenance of international peace and security, UN Doc. S/PRST/2007/7 (28 Mar. 2007); UNSC Res. 2033(2012) on Cooperation between the United Nations and regional and sub-regional organizations in maintaining international peace and security (12 Jan. 2012); and UNSC, *Report on the activities of the Ad Hoc Working Group on Conflict Prevention and Resolution in Africa for the period January-December 2013*, UN Doc. S/2013/778 (30 Dec. 2013).

the UN to fund its peacekeeping operations.[441] A UN Secretary-General Report issued in April 2008 may have blurred the issues when it referred to 'the potential for misunderstanding and misrepresentation concerning the meaning and scope of [UN-AU] partnerships'.[442] On 16 April 2008, the Republic of South Africa, taking advantage of holding the rotating monthly UNSC Presidency, organized a high-level meeting on the security challenges facing Africa. The PSC participated in the meeting. Even though this was an excellent opportunity to appraise the situation, address the then multifaceted problems (e.g., the deployment of the UN-AU hybrid mission in Darfur), and negotiate a working relationship between the UN and the AU, the UNSC instrument adopted later on the same day failed to offer pertinent answers. In November 2016, the Security Council said that the UN-AU partnership should further develop into a systematic and strategic partnership adapted to the continent's complex security challenges.[443] It culminated into the signing on 19 April 2017 of a Joint UN-AU Framework for Enhancing Partnership in Peace and Security between the Secretariats of the two Organizations at the UN Headquarters in New York.[444]

76. Before the advent of the AU in 2002, several RECs had already come into the ambit of Article 52 of the UN Charter and, importantly, they had established a tradition of peacekeeping at a sub-regional level. The most important of the RECs, in terms of activities, was ECOWAS. Although it was established in 1975 as a regional economic integration organization,[445] it gradually acquired a collective security dimension which brought it under Chapter VIII of the UN Charter. In particular, ECOWAS adopted on 22 April 1978 a Non-Aggression Protocol prohibiting Member

441. *See* , *inter alia*, Assembly, *Decision on the Activities of the Peace and Security Council of the African Union and the State of Peace and Security in Africa*, para. 6, AU Doc. Assembly/AU/Dec. 408 (XVIII) (30 Jan. 2012); Assembly, *Decision on the Activities of the Peace and Security Council of the African Union and the State of Peace and Security in Africa*, para. 17, AU Doc. Assembly/AU/Dec. 177 (X) (2 Feb. 2008); and Assembly, *Decision on the Activities of the Peace and Security Council of the African Union and the State of Peace and Security in Africa*, AU Doc. Assembly/AU/Dec. 145 (VIII) (30 Feb. 2007).

442. *See* United Nations, *Report of the Secretary-General on the relationship between the United Nations and regional organizations, in particular the African Union, in the maintenance of international peace and security*, UN Doc. S/2008/186 (7 Apr. 2008). *See* further United Nations, *Concept paper on the relationship between the United Nations and regional organizations, in particular the African Union, in the maintenance of international peace and security*, UN Doc. S/2007/148 (14 Mar. 2007).

443. *See* UNSC Res. 2320(2016), *supra* . *See* further Security Council, *Report of the Secretary-General on strengthening the partnership between the United Nations and the African Union on issues of peace and security in Africa, including the work of the United Nations Office to the African Union*, UN Doc. S/2016/780 (13 Sept. 2016).

444. *See* AU Commission, Directorate of Information and Communication, Press Release N° 060/2017, 18 Apr. 2017. *See* further, UNSC, *Report of the Secretary-General on options for authorization and support for African Union peace support operations*, UN Doc. S/2017/454, 26 May 2017, para. 4, and the discussion at the UNSC on 19 Jul. 2017 (8006th Meeting), UN Doc. SC/12915. For the Framework's text, *see* https://unoau.unmissions.org/sites/default/files/signed_joint_framework.pdf.

445. *See* the Treaty of Lagos establishing ECOWAS of 28 May 1975, reproduced in 14 I.L.M. (1975) 1200. A Revised Treaty was signed in Cotonou, Benin on 24 Jul. 1993 and entered into force on 30 Jul. 1995, reproduced in 35 I.L.M. (1996) 660; RADIC 8 (1996): 187.

States to use force as a means for settling disputes, on 29 May 1981 it concluded the Protocol on Mutual Assistance in Defence, which came into force in October 1987, later it established the Defence and Security Commission (CDC), and, finally, on 10 December 1999 it concluded the Protocol relating to the Mechanism for Conflict Prevention, Management, Resolution of Conflicts, Peacekeeping and Security, which created a Mediation and Security Council.[446] Presently, ECOWAS implements the so-called Vision 2020 where peace and collective regional security is one of its building blocks.[447] In December 1989, ECOWAS created a peacekeeping force, the Economic Community of West African States Monitoring Group (ECOMOG), which has been deployed with considerable success in the territory of several Member States. At an international level, ECOMOG has attracted attention for its involvement in the civil wars in Liberia (1990–2005),[448] which was approved and endorsed by the UN Security Council,[449] in Sierra Leone (1997–2005),[450] in Guinea-Bissau (1998–1999)[451] as well as for its efforts to promote reconciliation in Côte d'Ivoire and to organize democratic presidential and legislative elections in the country (2005–2010).[452] Reference should also be made to the ECOWAS Conflict Prevention Mechanism, which has incorporated

---

446. *See* ECOWAS Decision A/DEC.11/10/98, which was approved by Member States in Abuja, Nigeria on 31 Oct. 1998. The Protocol entered provisionally into force upon signature; *see* A. Abass, 'The New Collective Security Mechanism of ECOWAS: Innovations and Problems', *Journal of Conflict and Security Law* 5 (2000): 211. Generally, *see* A. Adebajo & I. Rashid (eds), *West Africa's Security Challenges – Building Peace in a Troubled Region* (London: Lynne Reiner, 2004); and M. Pitts, 'Sub-Regional Solutions for African Conflict: The ECOMOG Experiment', *Journal of Conflict Studies* 19 (1999): 49.
447. *See* ECOWAS Vision 2020 Towards a Democratic and Prosperous Community, at: http://www.ecowas.int/about-ecowas/vision-2020/.
448. *See* K. Kufuor, 'The Legality of the Intervention in the Liberian Civil War by the Economic Community of West African States', *RADIC* 5 (1993): 525. Generally, *see* J. Boulden (ed.), *Dealing with Conflict in Africa: The United Nations and Regional Organizations* (New York: Palgrave Macmillan, 2003); and C. Borgan, 'The Theory and Practice of Regional Organization Intervention in Civil Wars', *New York University Journal of International Law& Policy* 26 (1994): 797.
449. *See* , *inter alia*, UNSC Res. 788(1992) of 19 Nov. 1992; Res. 856(1993) of 10 Aug. 1993; Res. 866(1993) of 22 Sept. 1993; Res. 911(1994) of 21 Apr. 1994; Res. 950(1994) of 21 Oct. 1994; Res. 1083(1996) of 27 Nov. 1996' Res. 1100(1997) of 27 Mar. 1997; Res. 1116(1997) of 27 Jun. 1997; Res. 1343(2001) of 7 Mar. 2001, reproduced in 40 I.L.M. (2001) 1024; Res. 1497(2003) of 1 Aug. 2003; and Res. 1626(2005) of 19 Sept. 2005.
450. For the relevant UNSC instruments, *see* , *inter alia*, Res. 1132(1997) of 8 Oct. 1997; Res. 1315(2000) of 14 Aug. 2000; Res. 1385(2001) of 19 Dec. 2001; Res. 1400(2002) of 28 Mar. 2002; Res. 1470(2003) of 28 Mar. 2003; Res. 1508(2003) of 19 Sept. 2003; Res. 1562(2004) of 17 Sept. 2004; and Res. 1626(2005) of 19 Sept. 2005.
451. For the relevant UNSC instruments, *see* , *inter alia*, Res. 1216(1998) of 21 Dec. 1998; and Res. 1233(1999) of 6 Apr. 1999.
452. For the relevant UNSC instruments, *see* , *inter alia*, Res. 1609(2005) of 24 Jun. 2005; Res. 1633(2005) of 21 Oct. 2005; Res. 1708(2006) of 14 Sept. 2006; Res. 1721(2006) of 1 Nov. 2006; Res. 1765(2007) of 16 Jul. 2007; Res. 1782(2007) of 29 Oct. 2007; Res. 1795(2008) of 15 Jan. 2008; Res. 1865(2009) of 27 Jan. 2009; and Res. 1880(2009) of 30 Jul. 2009. Generally, *see* A. Orahbelashvili, *Collective Security* (Oxford: Oxford University Press, 2011), 294 et seq.

traditional African mediation notions such as the Council of Elders.[453] Finally, the Organization has deployed a military force, the Economic Community of West African States' Mission in The Gambia (ECOMIG), to support peace and stability in the country following the friction caused in December 2016 when the presidential election was won by the party in opposition. The UNSC has endorsed it under Resolution 2337(2017) of 19 January 2017 and has held that the government bears primary responsibility for protecting human rights as well as the civilian population. On 5 June 2017, ECOWAS extended the mission in The Gambia for another year for which extension the EU contributed the amount of EUR 5 million.[454]

Other RECs having a collective security dimension include the SADC, the ECCAS and the Economic and Monetary Community of Central Africa (CEMAC), which shares characteristics with ECCAS. SADC acquired a regional security dimension in two phases. First, though the conclusion on 14 August 2001 of the Protocol on Politics, Defence, and Security Cooperation, which established the namesake Organ. Second, through the signing on 26 August 2003 of a Mutual Defence Pact. Regarding ECCAS, a Non-Aggression Pact was signed on 9 September 1994. Following its reactivation in 1999, ECCAS adopted on 24 February 2000 the Protocol Relating to the Establishment of a Council for Peace and Security in Central Africa (COPAX).[455] The Protocol, which envisages that COPAX includes the Defence and Security Commission (CDC), the Multinational Force of Central Africa (FOMAC) and the Early Warning Mechanism of Central Africa (MARAC), entered into force in early 2004. In 2008, it was decided that the Multinational Force maintained by CEMAC (FOMUC) be taken over by COPAX,[456] while in October 2007 the Multinational Force deployed in the CAR had been transferred to ECCAS.

---

453. *See* UNSC Res. 1197(1998) of 18 Sept. 1998, para. 7.

454. *See* http://www.externalpartners.ecowas.int/eu-to-finance-ecowas-ecomig-force-in-the-gambia/.

455. *See* A. Meyer, *Peace and security cooperation in Central Africa: Developments, Challenges and Prospects*, Discussion Paper 56 (Nordiska Afrikainstitutet, Uppsala, 2011); H. Besada (ed.), *Crafting an African Security Architecture: Addressing Regional Peace and Conflict in the 21st Century* (London: Routledge, 2016) 196–198.

456. *See Final Communiqué of the Council of Ministers of COPAX*, 27 Feb. 2008, at: http://www.ceeac-eccas.org.

Chapter 3. Admission to and Withdrawal from the AU: The Amendment of the Constitutive Act – The Question of Unratified OAU/AU Treaties

77. As far as admission to AU membership in concerned, there are two relevant provisions in the Constitutive Act. The first is Article 27(1) stipulating that it is open to signature and accession only by OAU Member States. The second is Article 29 stipulating that, after the Constitutive Act has entered into force, any interested African state may notify the Chairman of the Commission of its intention to be admitted as a Member State for which it will have to accede to the Constitutive Act. Once a state's intention has been received, the Chairman would communicate the notification to all Member States, which shall decide by a simple majority. This provision is almost identical to the admission to membership clause in Article XXVIII of the OAU Charter. However, one notable difference is that the Constitutive Act does not expressly confer upon African countries the right to become AU Members, as was the case under Article IV of the OAU Charter.[457] The fact that the states capable of becoming original AU Members were restricted to those which were at the time OAU Members served to emphasize the continuity between them and the fact that the former institution succeeded the latter. The practical effect of Article 27(1) was that Morocco, which withdrew from the OAU in November 1985, could not have signed the Constitutive Act in July 2000. Although in the previous editions of this monograph it was argued that Morocco did not appear willing to seek membership,[458] in the summer of 2016 the situation changed dramatically and, as already mentioned, in January 2017 its application for membership was accepted by the majority of Member States and became the fifty-fifth Member State.

Before Morocco, the Republic of South Sudan has become fifty-fourth Member State. On 27 July 2011, the AU Commission Chairperson announced that thirty-three Member States, including the Republic of Sudan, had submitted their written communications supporting South Sudan's admission application. Its accession was rather exceptional and presumably it was induced by the need to consolidate its statehood, following the territory's secession from the rest of Sudan. Secession was achieved when the population freely and fairly exercised its right to self-determination in a referendum held on 9–15 January 2011. Already at its Sixteenth Ordinary Session (January 2011) the Assembly had adopted a Declaration on Sudan indirectly promising AU accession.[459] When the Constitutive Act was drafted, the opportunity was there to lay down which conditions ought to be met before a state's request for admission was examined. One such condition (and indeed an obvious one) would be that it is considered to be capable of fulfilling the obligations and the duties emanating from membership.[460] Arguably, the Republic of South Sudan, being a newly created state, could not have

457. For analysis, *see* K. Magliveras & G. Naldi, *The African Union* (Alphen aan den Rijn: Kluwer Law International, 2009), 41 et seq.

458. *See ibid.*, p. 45.

459. *See* AU Doc. Assembly/AU/Decl. 3 (XVI).

460. Compare Art. 4(1) of the UN Charter.

met this condition if the necessary state institutions and procedures were not in place. For example, it was only in late 2012 that South Sudan adopted the necessary legislative procedures for signing and ratifying treaties and conventions. South Soudan submitted the ratification instrument to the African Charter on Human and Peoples' Rights in May 2016 but has still not ratified its Protocol on the Rights of Women in Africa and the African Charter on the Rights and Welfare of the Child (it signed both instruments in January 2013). The bloodshed in the country due to the hostilities between government forces and the opposition is a constant reminder of the value of not only subscribing to but also upholding these and similar instruments.[461]

78. Regarding observer status in the AU and the rules of accreditation, in July 2005, the Executive Council adopted the Criteria for Granting Observer Status and a System of Accreditation,[462] while previously it had determined that states as well as IGOs outside Africa could in principle be granted accreditation and this status would confer them the right to attend public sessions and to receive documents of general circulation.[463] These criteria also apply to NGOs and, currently, more than fifty NGOs have been granted observer status. When the NGO Lions Club International applied for observer status, the Executive Council withheld its decision and, at the same time, asked the PRC to reconsider the criteria for granting AU observer status within the Union.[464] Apparently, the matter was never resolved. Finally, it should be noted that the Assembly has allowed representatives of the African Diaspora to follow its meetings as observers.[465]

79. Article 31(1) of the Constitutive Act, almost a repetition of Article XXXI of the OAU Charter,[466] expressly stipulates that Member States have the unfettered right to renounce and, consequently, to terminate their membership by forwarding a written notification to that effect to the Commission Chairperson. According to Article 31(1), at the end of one year, commencing from the date of the written notification, 'the Act shall cease to apply with respect to the renouncing State, which shall thereby cease to belong to the Union', unless the notification has in the meantime been withdrawn. During the twelve-month period, the withdrawing Member is obliged to comply with the provisions of the Constitutive Act and to discharge all its duties and

461. Compare AU Commission of Inquiry on South Sudan, Final Report, 15 Oct. 2014, para. 375 at p. 116, at: http://www.peaceau.org/uploads/auciss.final.report.pdf.

462. *See* Executive Council, *Decision on the criteria for granting observer status and a system of accreditation to the AU*, AU Doc. EX.CL/Dec. 230 (VII) (2 Jul. 2005). For the draft text, *see* AU Doc. EX.CL/195 (VII) Annex IV (May 2005).

463. *See* Executive Council, *Decision on the criteria for granting observer status and a system of accreditation to the AU*, AU Doc. EX.CL/Dec. 168 (VI) (28 Jan. 2005). For the OAU criteria, *see* OAU Doc. CAB/LEG/117/82, adopted by the Fourteenth Ordinary Assembly Session (Libreville, 5 Jul. 1977).

464. *See* Executive Council, *Decision on the application by Lions Club International for accreditation with the AU*, AU Doc. EX.CL/Dec. 238 (VIII) (21 Jan. 2006). For the text of the application, *see* AU Doc. EX.CL/212 (VIII).

465. *See* AU Doc. Assembly/AU/Res. 1 (XVIII) (July 2012). For the AU Commission Protocol Services Division's list of accredited non-African states and International Organisations as of April 2015, *see* African Union Commission and New Zealand Ministry of Foreign Affairs and Trade, *African Union Handbook* (2016), 167–168.

466. *See* Magliveras & Naldi, *supra* , 45–46.

obligations (Article 31(2)). It is submitted that this obligation, which was not included in the OAU Charter but, in varying forms, has been inserted in the constitutive instruments of international organizations for almost 100 years,[467] is unlikely to bc legally enforceable. Thus, it will probably become another toothless provision and it will be up to the withdrawing Member State to fulfil its obligations, especially to pay in full any outstanding budgetary contributions.

In a most puzzling move, Article 12 of the Protocol on Amendments of February/July 2003 deleted Article 31. Although it is not unusual for constitutive instruments not to include a withdrawal clause,[468] there is no previous experience with abrogating the right of Member States to withdraw. Clearly, if a Member State is determined to terminate its membership, it will do so even if the constitutive instrument does not contain a relevant clause. If one attempted to explain why it was imperative to remove Article 31, one could possibly suggest the wish to emphasize that AU membership is perpetual and that it will operate in perpetuity. Indeed, this was offered as an explanation why in 1957 the Treaty of Rome establishing the European Economic Community had no withdrawal clause and why this continued throughout its evolutionary process and despite the fundamental institutional changes. It was only in 2004 when the draft Treaty Establishing a Constitution for Europe overturned this understanding by permitting Member States to withdraw subject to concluding an agreement with the EU.[469] The draft Treaty was never ratified by the required number of states and further negotiations led to the Treaty of Lisbon, which was signed in December 2007 and entered into force in 2009. The Treaty of Lisbon, while it differed in several respects from the draft Constitution for Europe, it did include a withdrawal clause,[470] which for the first time was invoked by the United Kingdom in March 2017.

80. Notwithstanding the existence of Article 31 and the apparent right of Member States to withdraw, the question could be posed if the AU itself or individual Members could block the withdrawal of a third Member whose government has seized power in a coup d'état or through other unconstitutional means and irrespective of whether violence was used or not. In particular, suppose that such a government was, by virtue of Article 30 of the Constitutive Act, suspended from participating in AU activities and, in order to antagonize the AU and show that it will not be intimidated, announced its withdrawal and, once the twelve-month period of notice had lapsed, it officially declared that it no longer has the status of a Member State. In these circumstances, could the other Member States and/or the AU treat the act of withdrawal as null and void on the ground that the unconstitutional government cannot legally bind the state

467. Starting with Art. 1(3) of the Covenant of the League of Nations of 1919; K. Magliveras, 'Withdrawal from the League of Nations Revisited' *Dickinson Journal of International Law* 10 (1991): 25.

468. The classic example is the UN Charter, whose drafters feared that the mass exodus of states from the League of Nations could have been replicated if withdrawal was expressly allowed. However, the understanding is that Member States may not withdraw but will not be prevented from seceding if there are compelling reasons.

469. *See* Art. I-60 of the draft Treaty Establishing a Constitution for Europe.

470. *See* Art. 50 of the Treaty on European Union. The problems surrounding the application of this clause have already arisen following the referendum on withdrawal in the United Kingdom on 23 Jun. 2016.

in question on the international plane and, consequently, continue to treat it as a Member State and demand that it fulfil all its membership's obligations and duties? The answer should be in the negative, because withdrawal would appear to occur automatically and be tantamount to secession from membership. Moreover, the AU does not seem to be able to examine either the legality of the intention to withdraw or the legitimacy of the act of secession, even though, if and when the ACJHR commences its operation, these questions could form the subject matter of a request for an advisory opinion in accordance with Articles 53 et seq. of the Protocol establishing the Court. However, if the unconstitutional regime were to be overturned and replaced by a legitimate government within a reasonable period of time following the expiration of the twelve-month period, it could be argued that the AU, acting though the Assembly, could determine that the membership had never been terminated and, should the new regime wish to re-establish ties with the AU, it is not required to seek membership anew under Article 29 of the Constitutive Act.

81. The procedure for the amendment and revision of the Constitutive Act is laid down in Article 32 of the Constitutive Act, which is rather like the corresponding clause in the OAU Charter (Article XXXIII), and in Rule 28 of the Rules of Procedure of the Assembly. Any Member State may submit its proposals to the Chairman of the Commission, who is instructed to transmit them to the other Members within thirty days. The Assembly will then examine the proposals within a period of one year and the Executive Council will give its advice on them. Amendments or revisions will be adopted by the Assembly by consensus or, failing which, by a two-thirds majority and shall be submitted to all Member States for ratification under domestic constitutional procedures. Amendments shall enter into force after two-thirds of the membership have ratified them. This provision signifies that, once the amendments have entered into force, they become mandatory upon any Members which had voted against them. Although this provision ensures that the amended Constitutive Act will be binding upon all Members, it could prove to be problematic if certain Members are unwilling to follow the adopted changes.

82. As already mentioned, so far there has been one attempt to modify the Constitutive Act. The fact that it was deemed necessary so soon after its entry into force could be explained by the haste with which the Constitutive Act was drafted.[471] Although the Protocol on Amendments was approved by the First Extraordinary Assembly Session (Addis Ababa, 3 February 2003) without any debate,[472] it was adopted again by the Assembly at the Second Ordinary Session on 11 July 2003. The only difference between the two texts would appear to be that in the latter the clause on withdrawal was deleted. Arguably, this situation raises several pertinent legal questions, including which would have been the effect if some Member States had

471. *See* E. Baimu & K. Sturman, 'Amendment to the African Union's Right to Intervene', *African Security Review* 12(2) (2003): 37, 38–39, offering a different explanation, namely that the aim was to prevent the alienation of Libya, which in July 2002 was unsuccessful in pushing through its own amendments to the Constitutive Act. *See* further, T. Maluwa, 'Fast-Tracking African Union or Making Haste Slowly? A Note on the Amendments of the Constitutional Act of the African Union', *Netherlands International Law Review* 51 (2004): 195.

472. *See Report of the First Extraordinary Session of the Assembly of the African Union*, AU Doc. EX/Assembly/Rpt (I) (3 Feb. 2003) at para. 23.

already ratified the February 2003 version before the Second Ordinary Assembly Session had taken place. The Decision of July 2003 approving the changes has not dealt with these considerations; it simply stated that 'The Assembly adopts the Protocol on the amendments to the Constitutive Act,'[473] while the protocol itself expressly stipulates that it was adopted by both Sessions.

83. The Protocol on Amendments contains cosmetic changes in the wording of the Constitutive Act. For example, the words 'founding fathers' in Article 2 and the words 'Chairman of the Assembly' in Article 6 are substituted, respectively, by the gender-neutral words 'founders' and 'Chairperson,' while the term 'working languages' in Article 25 is replaced by the term 'official languages'. Moreover, it endows the AU with a security dimension by including the PSC to the AU primary organs and by extending the AU's powers in this area. To avoid unnecessary duplication, the various changes to be brought about by the Protocol, if and when it enters into force, are discussed in the appropriate sections of the present monograph. Currently, the Protocol has been signed by fifty Member States and has received twenty-eight ratifications. It will enter into force when ratified by thirty-six states. While one cannot foresee when this will happen (the last two ratifications were by Congo on 27 December 2012 and by Guinea-Bissau on 4 January 2012),[474] arguably it can no longer play the role for which it was adopted in the first place. It is only advisable that Member States opt for abrogating this Protocol and, taking stock of institutional and other developments during the first fourteen years of AU operations, negotiate a new Protocol of Amendments. In particular, the negotiations ought to take into account the new organs which have been added to the AU architecture and/or commenced operations after the Constitutive Act's entry into force (e.g., the PSC, the PAP, the PRP, possibly the AIB, etc.), update the AU principles and values, ensure that there are no inconsistencies between the Constitutive Act and the Rules of Procedure of the various organs, make the provisions on sanctions more concrete, include provisions on the AU's privileges and immunities, etc. In January 2016, the Assembly decided, on the one hand, to 'revise and review the Constitutive Act of the AU for it to be an effective legal instrument to accelerate, facilitate and deepen the efficiency and the integration process on the continent' and, on the other hand, to empower individuals to directly petition the African Court on Human and Peoples' Rights on the implementation of the decisions taken by the AU policy organs provided that such individuals come from Member States, which are contracting parties to the 1998 Protocol establishing the African Human Rights Court and have also accepted its jurisdiction to receive communications from individuals in conformity with Article 36 of the Protocol.[475] Although it is not immediately clear why the African Human Rights Court will be competent to rule on such cases unless they direct concern Decisions having a specific human rights content, one can reasonably gather that the Assembly is effectively asking the population of Member States to supervise whether their governments give full effect to the decisions adopted by the

473. *See* Assembly, *Decision on the Amendments to the Constitutive Act*, AU Doc. Assembly/AU Dec. 26 (II) (11 Jul. 2003). The text of the Protocol is reproduced in RADIC 13 (2005): 37.

474. For the ratification by Rwanda, *see* Law No. 19/2004 of 19 Jul. 2004 published in Official Gazette No. special of 20 Aug. 2004.

475. *See* Assembly, *Decision on Streamlining of the African Union Summits and the Working Methods of the African Union*, AU Doc. Assembly/AU/Dec. 597(XXVI) (31 Jan. 2016), para. 2.

Assembly, the Executive Council, the PSC, etc. Finally, the question of the overall AU institutional reform was discussed on 16 July 2016 during a retreat of Heads of State and Government, of Foreign Affairs Ministers and of Finance Ministers, held in Kigali, Rwanda. Although the outcome was apparently never made public, the Assembly in its July 2016 Session resolved to entrust the preparation of a study on this question to Paul Kagame, the President of Rwanda, who will then submit a report on proposed reforms aiming at 'put[ing] in place a system of governance capable of addressing the challenges facing the Union'. In carrying out this task, Kagame has been given a free hand to make use of any expertise of his choice; however, the participation of the civil society in this project not specifically envisaged.[476]

84. While not directly concerned with the questions of membership, the fact that many a treaty concluded during the OAU era but also under the AU's auspices have not been ratified by the required number of Member States and, therefore, have not entered into force should also be addressed. Arguably, the inability to become operative has to do mostly with the attitude of the membership towards these multilateral instruments. The vast majority of OAU/AU treaties have been adopted by the Assembly (i.e., by the representatives of the Member States) and, thereafter, Member States have been expected to sign, to ratify or to accede to them. The fact that most of these treaties have been adopted without facing opposition would suggest that Member States were prima facie willing to become contracting parties within a reasonable period of time. However, reality has been quite different and often Member States have been reluctant to even sign them. Arguably, the long period of time elapsed since these treaties were negotiated and adopted partly negates their aims and usefulness because they no longer reflect the current state of affairs. Even though updating and revising them would be the logical step to take, this has happened in only a few cases. At the same time, Member States have continued to sign and/or to ratify instruments which had been concluded many years ago and are clearly outdated. To offer examples of treaties which have still not entered into force: the Inter-African Convention Establishing an African Technical Cooperation Programme(concluded in August 1975, lastly ratified by Gambia in July 2009 and lastly signed by Angola in January 2012); and the Convention for the Establishment of the African Centre for Fertilizer Development(concluded on 1 July 1985, lastly ratified by Zimbabwe in July 2012, twenty-six years after signing it, and lastly signed by Guinea-Bissau in January 2015).

But, even in instances where a new and revised instrument was concluded, the fact that it only entered into force after a very long period of time having lapsed, arguably defies the purpose of adopting it in the first place. Thus, the revised version of the African Convention on the Conservation of Nature and Natural Resources was adopted in July 2003 (the original was concluded in September 1968) but it only attracted the last of the required fifteen ratifications, the usual number of ratifications envisaged in OAU/AU treaties, in the summer of 2016 (*supra*, paragraph 39). Despite the fact that fifteen ratifications is not such an onerous condition to meet (it corresponds to something more than one fourth of the current AU membership), the ratification rate of OAU/AU treaties has always been rather low. In turn, this has hampered the AU's ability to function in areas where the close and coordinated cooperation of

476. *See* Assembly, *Decision on the Institutional Reform of the African Union*, AU Doc. Assembly/AU/Dec. 606 (XXVII) (18 Jul. 2016).

Member States is required, e.g., in the case of the African Nuclear-Weapon-Free Zone Treaty which was signed in 1996 and came into force only in July 2009; currently fourteen Member States are not contracting parties.

Over the years, the Executive Council has, on the one hand, appealed to Member States as well as to the PAP to expedite the ratification process and, on the other hand, instructed the Commission to undertake a review of OAU/AU treaties.[477] A Conference of Ministers of Justice and of Attorneys General, which was held in Kigali, Rwanda, between 27 October and 4 November 2008 took up this specific issue. Its recommendations have since shaped considerably the AU policy in this area, including the suggestion that Member States commence the process of ratification within one year from the adoption of each treaty and the decision to institutionalize the so-called AU Treaty Signing Week in the month of December of each year.[478] In January 2012, the Executive Council authorized the establishment of a Ministerial Committee on the challenges of ratification/accession and implementation of the OAU/AU treaties. This Committee was created within the context of the fiftieth anniversary of the OAU in 2013. On another note, it is characteristic of the difficult financial situation which he AU has been facing that the Executive Council noted that its establishment will not involve any financial implications [for the AU]'.[479]

477. *See* Executive Council, *Decision on the Report of the Status of OAU/AU Treaties*, AU Doc. EX.CL/Dec. 352 (XI) (29 Jun. 2007); *Decision on the Status of Signature and Ratification of OAU/AU Treaties*, AU Doc. EX.CL/Dec. 390 (XII) (29 Jan. 2008).

478. *See* Executive Council, *Decision on the Status of Signature and Ratification of OAU/AU Treaties and the Harmonization of Ratification procedures*, AU Doc. EX.CL/Dec. 459 (XIV) (30 Jan. 2009).

479. *See* Executive Council, *Decision on the Status of Signature and Ratification of OAU/AU Treaties*, AU Doc. EX.CL/ Dec. 705 (XXI) (13 Jul. 2012). Generally, *see* T. Maluwa, 'Ratification of African Union Treaties by Member States: Law, Policy and Practice', *Melbourne Journal of International Law* 13 (2012):1; T. Maluwa, 'Beyond Rhetoric: Commitment to and Ratification of African Human Rights and Human Rights-Related Treaties' in *Law Politics and Rights – Essays in Memory of Kader Asmal*, T. Maluwa (ed.)(Leiden/Boston: Martinus Nijhoff, 2014), 58.

Chapter 4. Imposition of Punitive Measures by the AU

85. Unlike the OAU Charter, which did not stipulate at all punitive action against recalcitrant Member States, the Constitutive Act contains elaborate provisions in this respect. This impressive shift in attitude was arguably brought about by reality: Member States (and some of them consistently) were (often deliberately) violating or failing to observe their various obligations. Thus, African leaders appeared to be determined to deal with them by allowing the infliction of sanctions and other penalties of a punitive nature. While there are three different provisions in the Constitutive Act dealing with recalcitrant Members, it should be noted that their stipulations have been augmented by the Rules of Procedure of the Assembly and, therefore, it could legitimately be asked whether the Constitutive Act has been indirectly amended.

The first provision is Article 23(1), which empowers the Assembly to determine the sanctions to be imposed upon any Member State defaulting in paying its contributions to the AU budget. The content of Article 23(1) is very strict. Unlike the relevant provisions in other constitutive instruments (they usually follow the prototype embodied in Article 19 of the UN Charter), where the infliction of sanctions requires that the Member in question has been in arrears for more than two years, the Assembly is mandated (it does not have the discretion) to impose the following punitive measures on any Member State defaulting for any amount of contributions: denial of its right to speak at meetings; denial of right to vote; denial of right to present candidates for any AU position and professional post; and denial of the right to benefit from any AU activities or commitments. Clearly, there is a grading severity in these measures, in the sense that to refuse the right to vote is evidently far more important than not being allowed to address meetings; equally to deny activities and commitments is more significant than the right to present candidates for professional posts. Even though it is not expressly stipulated in the Constitutive Act, there is a general rule of law pertaining to IGOs that the sanctions to be imposed must be proportional to the seriousness of the infraction. Therefore, if, for the sake of argument, the denial of AU benefits to a Member State is the toughest sanction, it should be inflicted when the state in question has repeatedly, consistently, and deliberately failed in paying its budgetary contributions.

Rule 35 of the Assembly Rules of Procedure partly answers these issues, but the question should again be put whether a secondary instrument, such as a set of Rules of Procedure, may effectively lead to the modification and the de facto amendment of the Constitutive Act. In particular, Rule 35 stipulates that, on the basis of recommendations by the Executive Council and the PRC as well as on the basis of information provided by the Commission, the Assembly shall act differently depending on whether the arrears in payment amount to two but not exceeding five years of assessed contributions or amount to more than five years. In the former case, the Member State in question shall suffer the following: suspension of its right to speak, of its right to vote, and to receive documentation at AU meetings; of its right to offer to host sessions of the Assembly and the Executive Council; and of its right to present candidates for Union positions and posts. In the latter case, its right to have contracts of employment of its nationals renewed and to receive AU funds for new projects in its territory shall be suspended. A temporary lifting of sanctions is envisaged when the recalcitrant Member has paid at least 50% of outstanding arrears and payment has been made thirty days before the next scheduled session of the Executive Council.

86. Arguably, Article 23(1) of the Constitutive Act and Rule 35 do not consider the fact that at any given time a considerable number of African countries are facing chronic economic and financial problems and, consequently, that the non-payment of budgetary contributions could be attributed to a situation akin to force majeure and not be treated as a deliberate act of disregarding their obligations. It should be noted that the constitutive instruments of the AEC and of certain African RECs not only envisage this possibility but expressly exonerate such states from the obligation to pay financial contributions.[480] Therefore, it is suggested that the AU should lay down in any future Protocol of Amendments a mechanism whereby Member States facing significant economic problems or hardship would either be alleviated, wholly or partly, of their obligation to pay up their contributions or have the payment suspended without suffering in the enjoyment of their membership rights and privileges. It should be mentioned that in a number of instances temporary and exceptional exemptions have been granted (e.g., to Sierra Leone in July 2003[481] or to the DRC in January 2012 but with conditions attached).[482] However, as in the case of the OAU, these are rather ad hoc arrangements and it is questionable whether they could be treated as creating a precedence.

The importance which must be attached to engaging all Member States, rich and poor, in the political and socio-economic integration promised by the AU cannot be underestimated. Therefore, it is crucial not to prevent the full participation in the Union activities of those Members, which can justify, on objective grounds, their inability to fulfil their financial obligations. By reading the list of states that have been on the sanctions list over the years it becomes immediately obvious that some of them fall into the category of countries being objectively unable to pay contributions. However, it will be submitted that the AU should not treat those Member States that deliberately owe contributions solely through the imposition of punitive measures. On the contrary, it should consider how other international organizations have addressed this issue (e.g., by imposing accrued interest on arrears[483] or by setting off the arrears against sums owed by the organization to the recalcitrant Member) and act accordingly.

---

480. Generally, *see* K. Magliveras, 'African International Organisations: Suspension and Expulsion of Members', *Australian International Law Journal* (1999): 158, 169–170. For example, Art. 171 of the COMESA Treaty (1994) stipulates the non-payment of budgetary contributions when public or natural calamities or exceptional circumstances have gravely affected the economy of a Member State.

481. *See* Executive Council, *Decision on the Report of the Sub-committee on Contributions*, AU Doc. EX/CL/Dec. 25 (III) (8 Jul. 2003).

482. *See* Executive Council, *Decision on the Contributions of Member States' to the Budget of the African Union*, AU Doc. EX.CL/ Dec. 673 (XX) (27 Jan. 2012).

483. *See* Art. 33.3 of the Convention of the International Telecommunications Union, as currently in force following the amendments adopted by the Plenipotentiary Conference in 2014. It stipulates that 'The amounts due shall bear interest from the beginning of the fourth month of each financial year of the Union at 3% (three per cent) per annum during the following three months, and at 6% (six per cent) per annum from the beginning of the seventh month', at: http://search.itu.int/history/HistoryDigitalCollectionDocLibrary/5.21.61.en.100.pdf.

87. Article 23(1) of the Constitutive Act should be read in conjunction with its second paragraph. The latter, on the one hand, stipulates that any Member State failing to comply with AU decisions and policies may be subjected to further sanctions, such as the denial of transport and communications links with fellow Member States, and, on the other hand, empowers the Assembly to determine the imposition of any other 'measures of a political and economic nature'. A first point to clarify is whether the Article 23(2) sanctions are over and above those envisaged in the first paragraph. In other words, whether a Member defaulting in its financial obligations may face the sanctions envisaged in both paragraphs. The answer should be in the negative, as the principle of specialization should apply. Thus, Article 23(1) is the only provision dealing with punitive measures to be imposed for contributions in arrears.

88. The wording of Article 23(2) is inordinately unclear. By effectively giving the Assembly a carte blanche to establish additional political or economic punitive measures, the drafters may have opened a dangerous door to political manoeuvring. In particular, the Assembly may be driven to consider incidents of non-compliance on a case-by-case basis instead of applying in similar instances predetermined rules. Undoubtedly, Article 23(2) lacks the legal clarity that is required of constitutive instruments of international institutions and may violate the principles of legitimate expectations and legal certainty, which run through the law of international institutions. Notwithstanding these considerations, it should be noted that the Assembly will probably be subject to checks and balances in implementing its Article 23(2) powers, since any Member which has a vested interest in disputing the legality of the sanctions imposed would be able to resort to the AU judicial organ and file an action akin to judicial review.

89. A final point arising from Article 23(2) is whether the additional measures to be determined by the Assembly could ever go as far as ordering the expulsion of the recalcitrant Member State. The answer should be in the negative, because the wording of this provision refers exclusively to punitive measures of a political or economic nature. Even though expulsion could be described as a measure of political character, it is submitted that the term 'political' in the context of Article 23(2) does not cover measures bearing upon the membership status. Finally, it is interesting to note that the OAU Secretariat has indicated that, since the Constitutive Act does not provide for expulsion, it follows that the Assembly lacks the required legal basis for ordering it.[484]

Rule 36 of the Assembly Rules of Procedure, which corresponds to Article 23(2), does not shed any light on the above questions. The gist of Rule 36, which arguably contradicts the spirit of Article 23(2), is that, upon the Executive Council's recommendation, the Assembly shall record that a Member State has not, without good and reasonable cause, complied with AU decisions and policies and shall determine the sanctions to be imposed. However, the wording of the third paragraph of Rule 36:

> [3.] When taking any decision in this regard, the Assembly shall stipulate the time frame for compliance and indicate when the failure to comply with that

---

484. *See Report of the Meeting of OAU Permanent Representatives and Experts on the African Union*, 21–25 January 2002, Addis Ababa, Ethiopia, at para. 27.

> decision will trigger the sanctions regime provided for under Article 23(2) of the Constitutive Act and this Rule.

would suggest that sanctions are not automatic but the Member in question shall first be given the opportunity to observe the decision and, only if he does not, will the sanctions be imposed. Finally, Rule 36, in a rather cryptic manner, stipulates that Members under sanctions are entitled to present their case to the Assembly. Presumably the object of this move would be to ask the Assembly to lift or vary the sanctions.

90. The third instance for the imposition of punitive measures is when governments have come into power through unconstitutional means.[485] According to Article 30 of the Constitutive Act, such governments 'shall not be allowed to participate in the activities of the Union'. This provision is in line with the aforementioned principle of condemnation and rejection of unconstitutional changes of government. Moreover, it was influenced by developments since the early 1990s in a number of international organizations where the realization of the democracy principle (i.e., states must be governed by regimes subscribing to the rule of law, fundamental freedoms must always be protected, and undemocratic overthrows of governments are not tolerated) has led to the inclusion of similar clauses in their constitutive instruments. Suffice to mention two examples. First, the Protocol of Washington of 14 December 1992, which amended the Charter of the Organization of American States (OAS) by adding a new Article 9 to it.[486] Second, Article 7 of the Treaty on EU and Article 309 of the Treaty Establishing the European Community (EC), which were inserted by the Treaty of Amsterdam of 1997;[487] following the entry into force of the Lisbon Reform Treaty, which revised the EU Treaties in 2009, the relevant provisions are laid down in Article 7 of the Consolidated Version of the Treaty on EU.

91. The gist of Article 30 is that only those governments coming into power through unconstitutional means and not the Member States in question shall be prevented from participating in AU activities. Thus, the membership of the relevant states is not affected or compromised and once constitutionality returns, full involvement will resume. Considering that Article 30 does not stipulate which organ will be competent to order non-participation, it is submitted that the process is an automatic one and this is signified by the words 'shall not be allowed'. To put it otherwise, contrary to the aforementioned provisions of Article 23, the sanction of non-participation does not involve political discretion. If this submission were correct, the AU would be required to establish authoritatively and to the satisfaction of at least the majority of Member

---

485. *See* J. Grauvogel, K. Newbery &C. von Soest, *Stabilität durch regionale Sanktionen in Afrika?*, German Institute of Global and Area Studies, GIGA Focus Afrika 3, 2013, at: http://www.ssoar.info/ssoar/handle/document/34799.

486. The Protocol is reproduced in 33 I.L.M. (1994) 1005; for commentary, *see* K. Magliveras, *Exclusion from Participation in International Organisations: The Law and Practice Behind Member States' Expulsion and Suspension of Membership* (The Hague: Kluwer Law International, 1999), 171–174. *See also* the Inter-American Democratic Charter, adopted by the OAS on 11 Sept. 2001, reproduced in 40 I.L.M. (2001) 1289.

487. Reproduced in *Official J. of the Eur. Communities* 1997, C 340 1. For analysis, *see* K. Magliveras, *The Adoption of Punitive Measures by the European Community and the European Union Against Recalcitrant Member States: Analysis, Criticism and Some Proposals*, European Public Law Series, vol. VII (Athens: European Public Law Center, 1999), 45–67.

States that the government in question did come into power through unconstitutional means. Although the Assembly would probably assume this function, in its capacity as the plenary organ encompassing the whole membership, one could also suggest two reasons why the AU judicial organ should be called upon to decide it. First, the determination would have to be based on legal grounds and there would be no place for political considerations. Second, as the determination would be a judicial pronouncement, it would have the legally binding effect of an ACJHR decision (when it becomes operative).

92. Article 30 does not offer any guidance on the ambit of the unconstitutional government's non-participation in Union activities. As has already been indicated, it will not bring about the suspension of the membership of the Member State in question. It is rather a measure of a punitive nature aiming at putting considerable pressure on the relevant government to restore constitutional normality and the rule of law. It is submitted that the scope of non-participation includes the sanctions referred to in Article 23(1) of the Constitutive Act but not those envisaged in the second paragraph of the same Article, because the latter are measures of a general nature and not directly related to Union activities. Finally, it should be accepted that for as long as an unconstitutional government is not allowed to participate in the proceedings of the Union, all obligations of the Member in question shall remain intact and, consequently, it will be obliged to continue paying its budgetary contributions, to give effect and to comply with mandatory Assembly decisions, etc.

Rule 37 of the Assembly Rules of Procedure, the provision corresponding to Article 30, has considerably augmented the latter's arguably insufficient content and some of its provisions run contrary to the submissions made here. More specifically, the fourth paragraph of Rule 37 lays down a five-stage procedure for dealing with unconstitutional changes of government. It should be noted that the following actions are to be jointly taken by the Assembly Chairperson and the Commission Chairperson: (a) on behalf of the AU, condemn coups d'état promptly and demand that constitutional order be reinstated immediately; (b) convey a clear and unequivocal warning that the illegal change of government shall neither be tolerated nor recognized; (c) ensure consistency in the action to be taken against the unconstitutional regime at the bilateral, sub-regional and international levels; (d) request the PSC to convene and discuss the matter; and (e) suspend the Member in question from the AU and from participating in its organs at once, provided that such non-participation shall not affect its membership and its obligations towards the organization. As far as the sanctions against the unconstitutional regime itself are concerned, the fifth paragraph of Rule 37 endows the Assembly to inflict the following measures in a non-exclusive fashion. First, visa denials for the perpetrators of the unconstitutional change (and presumably their entourage as well). Second, restrictions in the contacts between the illegal regime and the governments of the other Member States. Third, trade restrictions. Fourth, the sanctions provided for in the aforementioned Article 23(2) and in the Assembly Rules. Fifth, any additional sanctions that might be recommended by the PSC. Finally, the sixth paragraph of Rule 37 entrusts the Commission Chairperson with a specific role in assisting the peaceful reinstatement of the democratic order. It could be described as a mixture of mediation and good offices. In particular, the Chairperson is asked to, *inter alia*, establish appropriate contacts with the perpetrators without recognizing or legitimizing them and to enlist the contribution of African leaders and personalities as a conduit for securing cooperation between the perpetrators and the AU.

Chapter 5. Organs

93. According to Article 5(1) of the Constitutive Act, the AU comprises the following organs: The Assembly of Heads of State and Government, the Executive Council, the PAP, the Court of Justice, the Commission, the PRC, the Specialized Technical Committees, the Economic and Cultural Council, and the Financial Institutions. This array of organs would suggest that the AU has been modelled on the EU. Fifteen years after the AU's operationalization it has become clear that the large number of organs and the fact that the Assembly has been empowered to establish new ones under Article 5(2) of the Constitutive Act have posed significant hurdles which arguably the AU has not yet addressed in a coherent and effective manner. However, it is an undisputed fact that the AU has been endowed with all the necessary organs to carry out its diverse duties and mission.

94. As has been explained (*supra* paragraph 62), the Constitutive Act did envisage which will be the organs of the AU but for the majority of them (principally, those organs that did not appear in the OAU Treaty) it postponed their immediate operation until, for each of these organs, a separate Protocol had entered into force laying down its functions, powers, composition, etc. The Fifth Extraordinary OAU Assembly Session (Sirte, 1–2 March 2001) entrusted to the next Ordinary Session to, *inter alia*, prepare the necessary Protocols.[488] To that effect, the OAU Secretary-General prepared a report, which was submitted to the Seventy-Fourth Ordinary Session of the OAU Council of Ministers (Lusaka, Zambia, 5–8 July 2001).[489] At its Thirty-Seventh Ordinary Session (Lusaka, 9–11 July 2001), the OAU Assembly mandated the OAU Secretary-General to undertake the necessary consultations with Member States to elaborate the modalities for launching the AU organs and to prepare their Rules of Procedure giving priority to the 'key Organs', namely the Assembly of Heads of State and Government, the Executive Council, the Commission and the PRC.[490] That the OAU Assembly did not consider the Court of Justice to be a 'key Organ' was undoubtedly characteristic of an international organization that was not used to have a judicial organ embedded in its operation.

§1. The Assembly of Heads of State and Government

95. Article 6(2) of the Constitutive Act, proclaims the Assembly to be the supreme organ of the AU. It is composed of all Heads of States or Government or their duly accredited representatives. Unlike the OAU Assembly which was meeting in ordinary session once a year, since 2004 the AU Assembly has followed the practice (which is not envisaged in the Constitutive Act or in its Rules of Procedure)[491] of two

488. *See* Assembly, *Decision on the African Union*, OAU Doc. EAHG/Dec.1 (V) (2 Mar. 2001).
489. OAU Doc. CM/2210 (LXXIV) (July 2001).
490. Assembly, *Decision on the Implementation of the Sirte Summit Decision on the African Union*, OAU Doc. AHG/Dec. 1 (XXXVII), para. 4 (11 Jul. 2001).
491. The *Rules of Procedure of the Assembly* were adopted in July 2002 pursuant to Art. 8 of the Constitutive Act, AU Doc. ASS/AU/2(I)-a, reproduced in RADIC 13 (2005): 41.

sessions per year, one in the winter time (usually January) and the other in the summer time (usually June). In most cases one of the two sessions takes place in Addis Ababa, the headquarters of the AU, but this is not a norm; for example, both sessions in 2012 were held in Addis Ababa. Usually, a Member State will take the initiative and propose that the next session be held in its territory. This diplomatic move has the advantage of offering prestige to the proposing Member but also the disadvantage that it has to cover most of the associated costs. Theoretically all Member States may become proposers but in reality a number of them cannot afford the cost while in others (e.g., Somalia, South Sudan, Eritrea, Mali, etc.) the security situation is so complicated that it is not realistic to host Assembly sessions. Another trend, which by now has become the norm, is to build sessions around a specific theme, which is topical or of particular importance to Africa. Thus, the Tenth Ordinary Assembly Session (Addis Ababa, 31 January–2 February 2008) concerned the 'Industrial Development of Africa,' while the July 2008 Session concerned 'Water and Sanitation'. The theme for the whole of 2016 was 'The African Year of Human Rights with Particular Focus on the Rights of Women.'[492] Finally, the theme of the January 2017 Session was 'Harnessing Demographic Dividend through investments in the Youth.'[493] Moreover, occasionally special summits have been scheduled to deal with pressing issues but they have not always materialized. Thus, the special summit of Heads of State and Government scheduled for November 2008 to deal with refugees, returnees and IDPs and to adopt the Convention for the Protection and Assistance of IDPs in Africa[494] took place a year later in Kampala, Uganda, where the IDP Convention was approved on 23 October 2009.[495]

Any Member State may request the holding of an extraordinary session, which must be met with the approval of two-thirds of all Member States within the period specified by the Commission Chairperson. Thus, if a state does not reply on the request within the deadline set by the Commission this is understood as a negative vote (Article 6(3) of the Constitutive Act and Rule 11). Pursuant to the Protocol on Amendments of 2003, the initiative of holding extraordinary sessions lies with the Assembly Chairperson as well. Decisions, except for procedural matters, are reached by consensus, failing which, by a two-thirds majority (Article 7(1)). Interestingly enough, the corresponding Rule 30 does not refer to consensus and subjects all decisions on substantive issues to a 'secret ballot of Member States eligible to vote'. Recently, the

---

492. *See* Assembly, *Declaration of the Assembly on the Theme of the Year*, AU Doc. Assembly/AU/Decl. 1 (XXVII) Rev.1 (19 Jul. 2016). It was induced by the fact that the UN Secretary-General had included water and sanitation among the topics in Africa's priority development agenda. *See* further, Executive Council, *Decision on the Proposal to Make Water and Sanitation the Theme of the July 2008 Summit*, AU Doc. EX.CL/Dec. 392 (XII) (29 Jan. 2008).

493. *See* Assembly, *Decision on the Dates and Venue of the 28th Ordinary Session of the Assembly of the African Union*, AU Doc. Assembly/AU/Dec. 620 (XXVII) (19 Jul. 2016).

494. *See* Executive Council, *Decision on the Situation of Refugees, Returnees and Internally Displaced Persons in Africa*, AU Doc. EX.CL/Dec. 381 (XII) (29 Jan. 2008).

495. *See* Executive Council, *Decision on the Situation of Refugees and Internally Displaced Persons in Africa*, AU Doc. EX/CL/Dec. 413 (XIII) (28 Jun. 2008); *Decision on the Report on the Situation of Refugees Returnees and Internally Displaced Persons in Africa*, AU Doc. EX/CL/Dec. 462 (XVI) (30 Jan. 2009); *Decision on the Report on the Situation of Refugees Returnees and Internally Displaced Persons in Africa*, AU Doc. EX.CL/Dec. 494 (XV) Rev.1 (30 Jun. 2009).

Assembly agreed to hold an extraordinary summit not as a separate decision but as one of the resolutions adopted while reviewing peace and security in the continent. In particular, the Twenty-Fifth Ordinary Session (Johannesburg, June 2015) resolved, *inter alia*, to hold in Lomé, Togo, an extraordinary Summit on Maritime Security and Safety and Development in Africa,[496] which could also be considered as a follow-up to the AU Integrated Maritime Strategy adopted in 2012. It was postponed so as to ensure adequate preparations and, in January 2016, it was resolved to take place on 15 October 2016 and only after preparatory sessions of the PRC and the Executive Council were preceded.[497] It culminated in the adoption of a binding Charter on maritime security and safety. The Extraordinary Summit's website described it: '[a] diplomatic victory for Togo. The conference – the first large-scale conference for 30 years – was conducted in exemplary fashion and went off without a hitch'.[498]

96. The Office of the Assembly Chairperson is established under Article 6(4) of the Constitutive Act. Although it is to be held for one-year periods by a Head of State or Government, who was elected following consultations among Members, the OAU practice that the Head of State in whose territory the session takes place becomes Chairperson has been continued. Thus, Thabo Mbeki of South Africa became Chairperson from July 2002 to July 2003, Joaquim Chissamo of Mozambique from July 2003 to July 2004, and Olusegun Obasanjo of Nigeria from July 2004 to January 2006. However, this understanding was disrupted during the Sixth Ordinary Session (Khartoum, 23–24 January 2006). Many African leaders objected to Sudanese President Omar Hassan Al-Bashir assuming the Chairmanship on account of his government's direct involvement in the civil war waged in the south of the country (the area that later became the Republic of South Sudan) and in the Darfur region. The opposition was strong enough to disrupt the meeting in reminiscence of similar events during the OAU years. In the event, the Sudanese President accepted the postponement of his term until 2007, a gesture which in the African tradition of exaggeration was demonstrated as 'a true reflection of [his] great sense of responsibility and leadership'.[499]

It was further resolved that a committee would be instructed to examine the implementation of a rotation principle in the years to come.[500] In the event, Denis Sassou-Nguesso of Congo became Chairperson until January 2007. In the following year there was apparently no discussion of the Sudanese President assuming the Chairmanship, which went to John Kofi Agyekum Kufuor of Ghana. He was followed by Jakaya Kikwete, the President of Tanzania, in January 2008, and by the now deceased Colonel Gaddafi in January 2009. He was followed by Bingu wa Mutharika from Malawi (he took office on 31 January 2010), by Teodoro Obiang Nguema Mbasogo

496. *See* Assembly, *Decision on the Report of the Peace and Security Council on its Activities and the State of Peace and Security in Africa*, AU Doc. Assembly/AU/Dec. 583 (XXV), para. 22 (15 Jun. 2015).

497. *See* Assembly, *Decision on the Extraordinary African Union Summit on Maritime Security and Safety and Development in Africa*, AU Doc. Assembly/AU/Dec. 593 (XXV) (30 Jan. 2016).

498. *See* http://www.african-union-togo2015.com/en/accueil.

499. *See* Assembly, *Declaration of the Assembly of the African Union*, AU Doc. Assembly/AU/Decl. 2 (VI) (24 Jan. 2006).

500. *See* Assembly, *Recommendation of the Committee on the Chairmanship of the African Union*, AU Doc. Assembly/AU/Recommendation (VI) (24 Jan. 2006).

from the Equatorial Guinea (31 January 2011), by Yayi Boni from Benin (29 January 2012), by Hailemariam Desalegn from Ethiopia (27 January 2013), by Mohamed Ould Abdcl Aziz of Maritania (30 January 2014); Robcrt Mugabc of Zimbabwc (30 January 2015), Idriss Déby of Chad (30 January 2016), and Alpha Condé of Guinea (30 January 2017). Although the Constitutive Act did not elaborate on the Chairperson's duties, these were laid down in Rule 16 of the Assembly Rules of Procedure. In particular, he/she is responsible for a number of procedural duties, such as convening sessions, submitting to vote matters under discussion, and, in-between sessions, acting as the AU representative 'in conformity with the fundamental objectives and principles enshrined in the Constitutive Act'. Interestingly enough, the Protocol on Amendments 2003 has inserted a new Article 7*bis* to the Constitutive Act laying down the Chairperson's functions, which include the convening of other organs' meetings.

97. The Assembly's powers and functions are contained in Article 9(1) of the Constitutive Act and in Rule 4 of the Assembly Rules of Procedure. They are in line with the powers traditionally exercised by the supreme organs of international organizations. In particular, it determines the AU's common policies; considers and acts upon reports and recommendations issued by other organs; considers requests from African states seeking membership; monitors the implementation of and compliance with AU policies and decisions; adopts the budget; directs the Executive Council on the management of conflicts, war, and other emergency situations and the restoration of peace; appoints the Commission members and determines their functions; and appoints the judges to serve at the Court of Justice and terminates their appointment (it has never become operationalized). Finally, as already mentioned, Article 5(2) of the Act authorizes the Assembly to decide on the establishment of other organs. This provision is repeated in Article 9(1), which stipulates that '[t]he functions of the Assembly shall be to...establish any organ of the Union'. It is submitted that the latter is a badly drafted clause, because surely the Assembly cannot set up any of the organs envisaged in Article 5(1) but solely supplementary ones. So far, only the PSC has been expressly established pursuant to Article 5(2).

98. It is submitted that Article 9(2) of the Constitutive Act, which stipulates that the Assembly may delegate any of its powers and functions to any other organ, is problematic because of its wide formulation. Although it might be conceivable to hand over specific powers (e.g., delegating to the ACJHR (when it becomes operative) the power to ensure that Member States comply with AU decisions (as is the case in the EU)), it is submitted that there is array of other powers and functions which should never be delegated on the ground that they express the whole membership's will and, consequently, they should be exercised solely by the Assembly. An example of delegation of specific powers, which however might be explained by considerations of urgency and pressure, is the authorization granted by the Second Ordinary Assembly Session (Maputo, 10–12 July 2003) to the Executive Council to adopt the necessary measures for the operationalization of the PSC, including the election of its first members and the adoption of its Rules of Procedure.[501]

99. The powers and functions contained in Article 9 are supplemented with further powers envisaged in other provisions of the Constitutive Act. The most important

501. *See* Assembly, *Decision on the Operationalization of the Protocol Relating to the Establishment of the Peace and Security Council*, AU Doc. Assembly/AU/Dec. 11 (II), para. 8 (12 Jul. 2003).

are: (a) the imposition of sanctions on recalcitrant Member States (Article 23 of the Constitutive Act), (b) until the operation of the AU's judicial organ (initially the African Court of Justice and thereafter presumably the ACJHR), the interpretation of the Constitutive Act (Article 26), a power which has apparently never been exercised despite the existence of lacunae in its text as argued in the present monograph; and (c) the deliberation and the adoption of amendments to the Constitutive Act (Article 32(3)–(4)).

100. It should be noted that the Assembly has not followed to the letter the aforementioned provisions and it has adopted new practices. The following examples will illustrate this argument. First, there is a growing tendency to let the Executive Council reach decisions of importance, even decisions on institutional matters, which are then rubber-stamped by the Assembly. Thus, the Twelfth Ordinary Executive Council Session (Addis Ababa, 25–29 January 2008) elected the new Commissioners[502] and recommended them for appointment to the Tenth Ordinary Assembly Session, which simply consented to the recommendation.[503] Second, as already mentioned, the ordinary Assembly sessions, which are held at six-month intervals, have a central theme of common interest to the membership and the Member State hosting the session is asked to hold various high-level meetings on this theme. Third, the OAU practice to set up committees with limited participation of heads of state and government (usually ranging between seven and ten members and coming from Africa's five regions) and to entrust them with the elaboration of common positions in selected topics has been carried on to the AU and their use has been augmented. These entities are not established pursuant to the aforementioned Article 5(2) but are rather ad hoc institutional arrangements giving to the Assembly a measure of flexibility as regards the mandate, the terms of reference, setting the timeframe for submitting the deliverables, prolonging the mandate, etc. Suffice to mention the Committee of Seven Heads of State and Government on the United States of Africa, the seven-member Committee on the Chairmanship of the AU, and the Committee of Twelve Heads of State and Government on the AU Government (Uganda, South Africa, Tanzania, Nigeria, Ethiopia, Cameroon, Gabon, Egypt, Libya, Botswana, Senegal, and Ghana), which was created in 2008.

§2. The Executive Council and the Specialized Technical Committees

101. According to Article 10 of the Constitutive Act and Rule 3 of its Rules of Procedure,[504] the Executive Council is composed of the Ministers of Foreign Affairs or any other Ministers duly accredited by the governments of the Member States. It meets at least twice a year in ordinary session and in extraordinary session when so

502. *See* Executive Council, *Decision on the Election of AU Commissioners*, AU Doc. EX.CL/Dec. 414 (XII) (29 Jan. 2008).
503. *See* Assembly, *Decision on Appointment of AU Commissioners*, AU Doc. Assembly/AU/Dec. 190 (X) (3 Feb. 2008).
504. *See Rules of Procedure of the Executive Council*, adopted during the First Ordinary Assembly Session in July 2002, AU Doc. ASS/AU/2 (I)-b, reproduced in RADIC 13 (2005): 55.

requested by a Member State and approved by a two-thirds majority of the total membership. Extraordinary sessions have been held, *inter alia*, in the following cities: Sun City, South Africa (21–25 May 2003), Addis Ababa (12–16 March 2004, 6 December 2004, and 7–8 March 2005), Khartoum (19 January 2006),[505] Arusha (8 May 2008), Tripoli (15–16 April 2009), and Addis Ababa (11 October 2013). The Sixteenth Extraordinary Session also took place in Addis Ababa on 8 September 2016 and concerned the Ebola Virus Disease Outbreak.[506] As is made clear in Article 13(2) of the Constitutive Act, the Executive Council is an organ subsidiary to the Assembly. It is mandated to consider issues referred to it by the Assembly and, moreover, to monitor the implementation of AU policies and decisions.

102. Its main task is to coordinate and take decisions on policies in areas which are of common interest to the Member States. Article 13(1) of the Constitutive Act refers to twelve such areas, whose common characteristic is that they concern economic and social issues rather than political issues. To that end, the third paragraph of Article 13 stipulates that the Executive Council may decide to delegate its powers and functions to any of the Specialized Technical Committees. The areas of common interest are quite diverse and include: foreign trade; energy and industry; agriculture; water resources; protection of the environment and humanitarian action; transport and communications; education, culture, and health; science and technology; immigration matters; and social security. Decisions are reached by consensus, failing which by a two-thirds majority of Member States. It is not known whether the Executive Council has ever resorted to vote taking and the text of the approved decisions does not reveal any dissenting Member States. According to Article 11 of the Constitutive Act, the same majority constitutes a quorum at all meetings.

103. Although, as already mentioned, the Assembly is empowered to direct the Executive Council regarding the management of conflicts and similar situations, Article 13 of the Constitutive Act does not envisage any corresponding competence for the Executive Council. The situation becomes more complicated because the PSC, the organ charged with the primary duty to handle such situations, was not originally envisaged in the Constitutive Act but was created through the Protocol of July 2002. Even though the Protocol on Amendments of 2003 could have dealt with this situation (after all it added the PSC to the AU organs), it failed to do so. It is submitted that the Assembly, when exercising its right to delegate powers pursuant to Article 9(2), is entitled to involve the Executive Council in the management of conflicts and the restoration of peace in the territory of Member States, while the Executive Council shall be obliged to act in accordance with the Assembly directions. Even though it has apparently never happened, were a Member State to dispute the validity of the actions undertaken, the AU judicial organ should be competent to rule on the matter. On previous occasions, when the Executive Council addressed instances of civil war and

505. It took place while the Eighth Ordinary Executive Council Session was ongoing (it lasted from 16–21 Jan. 2006) and dealt exclusively with budgetary matters.

506. *See* AU Doc. Ext/EX.CL/Dec. 1 (XVI) (8 Sept. 2014).

interstate strife (e.g., Somalia,[507] Cote d'Ivoire,[508] Burundi,[509] Liberia,[510] and the DRC),[511] its relevant decisions did not contain action requiring implementation but rather reviewed the situations at hand and recorded developments. During the last seven years, the Executive Council has not deliberated cases relating to peace and security, presumably because it is now considered the purview of the PSC, and has concentrated on examining the reports on activities submitted by other AU organs (both primary and subsidiary) and electing the members of various organs.

104. A practice that has been carried on from the OAU is for the Executive Council to meet before the biannual ordinary sessions of the Assembly and in the same venue as the Assembly. This practice has the obvious advantage that there is continuity between the sessions of these two organs. However, considering that a large number of issues are primarily determined during the Executive Council meetings, this practice means that for the period of six months which usually lapses between two Assembly sessions there is no meeting of the two most important organs. Consequently, if serious matters that arise would have to wait until the next scheduled meeting or be addressed at an extraordinary session. However, if the Executive Council were to hold its meetings in-between the Assembly sessions, for example, three months after each Assembly session, it would have been possible to have every three months a session of either of them. There would be obvious advantages in this arrangement and given that the Assembly may delegate powers and functions to the Executive Council it would be possible to have the meetings of Heads of State and Government only once yearly and making significant savings in resources and funding

105. Article 14(1) of the Constitutive Act establishes seven Specialized Technical Committees, covering the AU's non-political activities: (a) the Committee on Rural Economy and Agricultural Matters; (b) the Committee on Monetary and Financial Affairs; (c) the Committee on Trade, Customs and Immigration Matters; (d) the Committee on Industry, Science and Technology, Energy, Natural Resources and Environment; (e) the Committee on Transport, Communications and Tourism; (f) the Committee on Health, Labour and Social Affairs; and (g) the Committee on Education, Culture and Human Resources. These committees are subordinate to the Executive Council, which is empowered to restructure them or to establish new ones. They are composed of Ministers or senior officials from the Member States responsible for sectors falling within their respective areas of competence. The functions of these Committees are set out in Article 15 of the Constitutive Act. They include the preparation of AU projects and programmes, ensuring that they are coordinated and harmonized, and the submission to the Executive Council, on their own initiative or at the latter's request, of reports and recommendations relating to the implementation of the Constitutive Act's relevant provisions. The process of setting up the Specialized Technical Committees has been extremely slow. In July 2003, the Executive Committee

507. *See* , *inter alia*, AU Doc. EX.CL/Dec. 270 (XIII) (21 Jan. 2006).
508. *See* , *inter alia*, AU Doc. Ext/EX/CL/Dec. 12 (III) (25 May 2003); and EX.CL/Dec. 271 (XIII) (21 Jan. 2006).
509. *See* , *inter alia*, AU Doc. Ext/EX/CL/Dec. 13 (III) (25 May 2003).
510. *See* , *inter alia*, AU Doc. Ext/EX/CL/Dec. 11 (III) (25 May 2003).
511. *See* , *inter alia*, AU Doc. Ext/EX/CL/Dec. 8 (III) (25 May 2003).

requested the PRC to submit a report on the issue,[512] while, during its Eleventh Extraordinary Session (Arusha, 6–7 May 2008), it requested that they be established pursuant to Article 14(3) of the Constitutive Act and that their number be finalized by the PRC and the Commission. The meeting, originally scheduled for the summer of 2008, was postponed to November 2008.

In the end, the Fourteenth Ordinary Assembly Session in February 2009 decided to 'reconfigure' the Specialized Technical Committees as follows:

(1) Committee on Agriculture, Rural Development, Water and Environment.
(2) Committee on Finance, Monetary Affairs, Economic Planning and Integration.
(3) Committee on Trade and Industry and Minerals.
(4) Committee on Transport, Transcontinental, and Interregional Infrastructures, Energy and Tourism.
(5) Committee on Gender and Women Empowerment.
(6) Committee on Justice and Legal Affairs.
(7) Committee on Social Development, Labour and Employment.
(8) Committee on the Public Service, Local Government, Urban Development and Decentralization.
(9) Committee on Health, Population and Drug Control.
(10) Committee on Migration, Refugees and IDPs.
(11) Committee on Youth, Culture and Sports.
(12) Committee on Education, Science and Technology.
(13) Committee on Communication and ICT and.
(14) Committee on Defence, Safety and Security.

It also requested that the Commission avoid overlap and ensure coherence and harmony with its own portfolios.[513] Based on a report prepared by the Commission itself,[514] in July 2011 the Assembly adopted, in principle, the proposed detailed activities of the Committees, resolved that each Committee should meet at the level of ministers and experts once every two years (with the exception of the Committees on Finance, Monetary Affairs, Economic Planning and Integration, on Gender and Women Empowerment, and on Defence and Security which are to meet once a year in ordinary session), and decided that the Commission be responsible for convening and servicing all their meetings so as to ensure synergy with other AU organs.[515] Finally, in June 2015, the Assembly decided, on the one hand, to empower the Specialized Technical Committees (STCs) of Ministers to take decisions on issues falling under their competence with the exception of decisions having financial and structural implications

512. *See* Executive Council, *Decision on the Launching of the Specialized Technical Committees*, AU Doc. EX/CL/Dec. 72 (III) (8 Jul. 2003).
513. *See* Assembly, *Decision on the Specialised Technical Committee (STCS)*, AU Doc. Assembly/AU/Dec. 227 (XII) (3 Feb. 2009).
514. *See* AU Doc. Doc. EX.CL/666 (XIX) (2011).
515. *See* Assembly, *Decision on the Specialised Technical Committee (STCS)*, AU Doc. Assembly/AU/Dec. 365 (XVII) (1 Jul. 2011).

and, on the other hand, that the Executive Council should consider STC decisions at the request of Member States.[516]

106. It should be noted that, as originally envisaged, the Specialized Technical Committees were the same sectoral Committees which were created in accordance with Article 25(1) of the Treaty Establishing the AEC. Their main difference would appear to be that the AU Committees are mandated to report directly to the Executive Council, whereas the AEC Committees were accountable to the Economic and Social Commission, which in turn reported to the Council of Ministers. However, as is elsewhere explained, the AEC does not appear to be any longer functionable.

107. Moreover, it should be noted that during the OAU era, several Conferences at ministerial level had been set up to deal with specific issues. There are similarities between these conferences and the Specialized Technical Committees. The following five examples could be cited. First, the Labour and Social Affairs Commission (LSAC), which was organized jointly with the International Labour Organization (ILO) and has the characteristic to IL tripartite participation comprising representatives of governments, employers and workers). Second, the Conference of Ministers of Health, organized jointly with the World Health Organization. Third, the Conference of Ministers of Industry, organized jointly with the ECA, the United Nations Industrial Development Organization (UNIDO), and the Regional Office for Africa of the Food and Agricultural Organization (FAO). Fourth, the African Population Commission set up jointly with the African Development Bank (ADB) and the ECA in 1994. Fifth, the Ministerial Conference on Drug Control, which adopted a Plan of Action for 2002–2006 in cooperation with the UN International Drug Control Programme.[517] In January 2008, the AU launched a Plan of Action on Drug Control and Crime Prevention (2008–2012), which, upon its expiration, was substituted with a Plan of Action on Drug Control (2013–2017).[518] Finally, in February 2009 the Assembly adopted a resolution on the drug trafficking threat for the continent; it acknowledged that it was becoming a major challenge to security and governance and requested the AUC and the RECs to intensify their actions to address it effectively.[519]

108. As there was a danger in duplication of the operation of the Specialized Technical Committees and these Ministerial Conferences and considering that similar organs exist in the RECs, a rationalization and streamlining of activities was required. Thus, in 2001 the Lusaka Assembly Summit mandated the Secretary-General to look

516. *See* Assembly, *Decision on Streamlining of the AU Summits and the Working Methods of the African Union*, AU Doc. Assembly/AU/Dec. 582 (XXV), para. 1. For the current composition of STCs, *see* African Union Commission and New Zealand Ministry of Foreign Affairs and Trade, *African Union Handbook 2016*, 45–46.

517. *See* UN Doc. AFR/410 – SOC/NAR/843 (14 May 2002). *See also* Executive Council, *Decision on the Report of the 2nd Session of the Ministerial Conference on Drug Control in Africa*, AU Doc. EX.CL/Dec. 169 (VI) (28 Jan. 2005). The functions of the UN Programme have in the meantime been assumed by the UN Office on Drugs and Crime, http://www.unodc.org.

518. *See* AU Doc. CAMDC/EXP/2(V) (October 2012). The current Plan is, available at: http://studylib.net/doc/5494568/au-plan-of-action-on-drug-control-2013-2017.

519. *See* Assembly, *Decision on the Threat of Drug Trafficking in Africa*, AU Doc. Assembly/AU/Dec. 239 (XII) (3 Feb. 2009). The problem seems to be particularly acute in West and Northern Africa, *see* , *inter alia*, the February 2014 position of the US Department of State, which is responsible for rolling out the US Strategy to Combat Transnational Organized Crime.

into these issues and come up with pertinent suggestions.[520] A year later, the Durban Summit specifically requested the Secretary-General to determine the position of the African Population Commission[521] and of the LSAC within the AU structure.[522] However, this streamlining was never achieved. Today an increasing number of ministerial bodies and institutions are active and a lot of business is transacted through them.[523] Apart from the LSAC,[524] the Conference of Ministers of Health,[525] and the African Population Commission (APC),[526] suffice to mention the following two entities: (a) the African Ministerial Conference on Housing and Urban Development (AMCHUD);[527] and (b) the African Energy Commission (AFREC),[528] which was established by the namesake Convention adopted in Lusaka, Zambia, on 11 July 2001.[529]

---

520. Assembly, *Decision on the Implementation of the Sirte Summit Decision on the African Union*, OAU Doc. AHG/Dec. 160 (XXXVII), para. 9 (11 Jul. 2001).
521. Assembly, *Decision on the Place of the African Population Commission in the African Union*, OAU Doc. AHG/Dec. 176 (XXXVIII) (8 Jul. 2002).
522. Assembly, *Decision on the Place of the OAU Labour and Social Affairs Commission in the African Union*, OAU Doc. AHG/Dec. 177 (XXXVIII) (8 Jul. 2002).
523. Compare Executive Council, *Decision on the Specialized Technical Committees (STCs)*, AU Doc. EX.CL/Dec. 921 (XXIX) (15 Jul. 2016).
524. The First Ordinary Session of the Labour and Social Affairs Commission was held in Mauritius in April 2003 (*see* Executive Council Decision EX/CL/Dec. 49 (III) (8 Jul. 2003)), the Second Ordinary Session in Cotonou on 20 Apr. 2004, the Third Ordinary Session in 2005 (*see* Executive Council Decision EX.CL/Dec. 201 (VII) (2 Jul. 2005)), the Fourth Ordinary Session in April 2006 in Cairo, the Fifth Ordinary Session in Addis Ababa on 16–21 Apr. 2007, and the Sixth Ordinary Session in Addis Ababa on 21–25 Apr. 2008. Generally, *see* Commission, *Report of the Chairperson of AU Commission on the Activities Falling within the Competence of the Labour and Social Affairs Commission* (May 2007–April 2008), AU Doc. LSC/EXP/2 (VI) (2008). The Ninth Ordinary Session was held in Addis Ababa on 8–12 Apr. 2013. A special session took place in Namibia in April 2014 under the theme 'Employment, Poverty Eradication and Inclusive Development'.
525. Executive Council, *Decision on the Report of the First Ordinary Session of the AU Conference of African Ministers of Health*, AU Doc. EX/CL/Dec. 50 (III) (8 Jul. 2003).
526. The Fifth Ordinary Session of its General Assembly took place in 2005; *see* Executive Council Decision EX.CL/Dec. 202 (VII) (2 Jul. 2005). The Sixth Ordinary Session was held in Johannesburg on 16–17 Jul. 2007; for the Declaration adopted, *see* AU Doc. ACP/Draft/Decl. (VI) (17 Jul. 2007), at: http://partners-popdev.org/docs/declarations/Johannesburg_declaration07.pdf For its Rules of Procedure, *see* http://www.un.org/popin/oau/rulesprc.htm. *See* further the Addis Ababa Declaration on Population and Development in Africa Beyond 2014 adopted on 4 October 2013, at: http://www.unfpa.org.
527. Executive Council, *Draft Decision on the Report of the First Session of the African Ministerial Conference on Housing and Urban Development (AMCHUD)*, AU Doc. EX/CL/Dec. 200 (VII) (2 Jul. 2005). The Fifth Ministerial Conference took place in Chad in February 2014, *see* http://mirror.unhabitat.org/categories.asp?catid=839.
528. *See* Conference of the African Union Ministers in Charge of Energy, *Algiers Declaration on the Official Launching of the African Energy Commission*, 15–17 Feb. 2008, AU Doc. AU/EXP/ EN/Decl. (III) Rev. (2008).
529. Convention of the African Energy Commission, at: http://afrec-energy.org/En/convention.html.

§3. The Pan-African Parliament (PAP)

109. The creation of PAP, the parliamentary organ envisaged in Article 17 of the Constitutive Act, had already been among the organs to complement the AEC under Article 14 of the Treaty establishing the AEC.[530] Like the parliamentarian organs operating in the framework of RECs,[531] PAP's purpose is to ensure the full participation of African peoples in the continent's development and economic integration. The Constitutive Act did not contain any provisions on its composition, powers, functions, and organization but, as is true with other organs, left the details to be defined in a future protocol. But more importantly it failed to deal with the relationship between the PAP and the namesake organ of the AEC Treaty. However, the fact that the wording of the aforementioned two provisions is almost identical would suggest that the drafters intended that the two organs be unified, merged and a single parliamentarian entity serve both the AEC and the AU. The Protocol to the Treaty establishing the AEC relating to the PAP was adopted by the Fifth Extraordinary OAU Assembly Session (Sirte, 2 March 2001) and, following its ratification by a simple majority of Member States, entered into force on 27 November 2003.[532] It is a rather strange instrument as it was drafted in the AEC's context but was amended to incorporate the necessary changes to function as an AU organ. The Parliament, which according to Article 2(2)

530. The attempts in the context of the AEC were never pursued thoroughly; e.g., in March 1999, the Fourth Ordinary Session of the AEC Council of Ministers played with the idea of setting up a Consultative Forum of African Parliamentarians as a prelude to creating the proper PAP, *see* AEC Doc. CM/AEC/Regl.1 (IV), para. 2 (23 Mar. 1999), at: http://archive.au.int/collect/auassemb/import/English/CM%20Draft%20AEC%20Regl%201%20IV_E.pdf.

531. The first African attempt to set up a parliamentarian organ within an intergovernmental organization was the East African Legislative Assembly (EALA), envisaged as an organ of the East African Community and Common Market; *see* Art. 56 of the Treaty for East African Co-Operation, concluded on 6 Jun. 1967; reproduced in I. Brownlie, *Basic Documents on African Affairs* (Oxford: Clarendon Press, 1971), 63. Following the rejuvenation of EAC through the namesake Treaty of 30 Nov. 1999, in force on 7 Jul. 2000, EALA was formally inaugurated on 30 Nov. 2001 as an independent organ. Moreover, Arts 6 and 13 of the Revised Treaty of ECOWAS envisaged the creation of a Community Parliament as a forum for dialogue, consultation and consensus for representatives of the peoples of West Africa and as a vehicle to promote regional integration. The founding Protocol was signed on 6 Aug. 1994 and entered into force on 14 Mar. 2002. Other parliamentary entities currently in operation include the Network of Parliamentarians at the Economic Community of Central African States (ECCAS), the Interparliamentary Committee at the West African Economic and Monetary Union (UEMOA), and the Parliamentary Forum at the Southern Africa Development Community (SADC).

532. *See* OAU Assembly, *Decision on the Draft Protocol to the Treaty Establishing the African Economic Community Relating to the Pan-African Parliament*, OAU Doc. EHAG/Dec.2 (V) (2 Mar. 2001). The text of the Protocol is reproduced in RADIC 13 (2005): 86. For an early analysis of the Protocol, *see* K. Magliveras & G. Naldi, 'The Pan-African Parliament of the African Union: An Overview', *African Human Rights Law Journal* 3 (2003): 222. *See* further, K. Magliveras & A. Huliaras, 'Understanding Success and Failure in the Quest for Peace: The Pan-African Parliament and the Amani Forum', *The Hague Journal of Diplomacy* 11 (2016): 275. Currently, the Protocol has been ratified by forty-eight Member States. Eritrea is the only Member State not to have signed it; however, given that its National Assembly has apparently not met since 2002, the participation of parliamentarians from Eritrea would be a moot point.

of the Protocol is the representative of the peoples of Africa, held its inaugural session in March 2004. Its Rules of Procedure were approved by the Second Ordinary PAP Session (Mindrad, South Africa, 16 September–1 October 2004) and were amended in October 2011.[533]

110. Each Member State participating in the PAP is entitled to five members, at least one of whom must be a woman.[534] Pursuant to Article 5 of the Protocol, members shall either be elected or designated by national legislatures, be it parliaments or other deliberative bodies, from among their members. A former PAP President, Gertrude Mongella, complained in May 2007 that the membership keeps on changing between sessions on account of national general elections taking place during the in-between periods[535] and has cited it as a ground preventing the PAP from establishing strong foundations. Article 6 specifies that members shall vote in their personal and independent capacity and, consequently, they should not receive directions from governments or other state bodies. Under Article 7, holders of domestic executive or judicial posts are specifically barred from participating in the PAP. No uniform electoral procedure is envisaged. It is ultimately expected that its members will be elected by universal adult suffrage,[536] no doubt a lofty aim which, presently, has only been achieved in the context of the EU. However, developments so far do not suggest that the PAP will evolve into a fully democratically elected body.[537] This could call into question the AU's own stated commitment to democracy, popular participation and good governance, which, as explained, are enshrined in Article 3(g) and (h) of the Constitutive Act. Although in accordance with Article 4(3) of the Protocol parliamentarians must reflect the diversity of political opinions in national legislatures, there would appear to be no restraint on dictatorial regimes to manipulate the nomination process.

111. As Africa experiences elections which cannot be described as free and fair even by basic standards, it will be suggested that provision ought to have been made to exclude parliamentarians, who were elected by means of fraudulent, violent or highly undemocratic elections and/or elected or appointed following a coup d'état, which has been condemned by the AU and other international institutions. It is submitted that the Protocol or the Rules of Procedure should have included a provision akin to Rule 8 of the Rules of Procedure of the Parliamentary Assembly of the Council of

533. At: http://www.panafricanparliament.org/pap-resolutions.

534. Article 4(2) of the Protocol. This reflects the AU's commitment to promote adequate gender representation, which in effect means securing that there will be women parliamentarians irrespective of domestic laws in Member States; *see* Art. 4(1) of the Constitutive Act.

535. This occurs because, pursuant to Art. 5(3) of the Protocol, a PAP member's term runs concurrently with his/her term of office in the national legislature.

536. According to Art. 2(3) of the Protocol, the transition to universal suffrage will not occur automatically but will necessitate an amendment to the Protocol to that effect. The 2014 PAP Protocol, reference to which is made later on, has not made any advances towards universal suffrage, no doubt a very progressive step for African nations.

537. Nevertheless, the European Court of Justice's *dictum* in Case 138/79 *Roquette Frères v. Council* [1980] E.C.R. 3333 at para. 33 referring to the 'fundamental democratic principle that the peoples should take part in the exercise of power through the intermediary of a representative assembly' would appear to be met by the PAP in its present status.

Europe.[538] It stipulates that the credentials of a national delegation may be challenged *in toto* on the grounds that the basic principles guiding the Council of Europe, namely the rule of law and the enjoyment by all people of human rights and fundamental freedoms, are seriously violated in the territory of the Member State in question.

112. The proper place for envisaging this possibility would be Article 5 of the PAP Protocol, which in conjunction with Rule 8 of the Rules of Procedure, lays down the instances leading to vacation of seats in the PAP. These include: death; resignation; inability to perform one's duties for reasons of physical or mental incapacity; removal on grounds of misconduct; when the parliamentarian ceases to be a member of the national legislature; or when he/ she is recalled by the national legislature; and automatically when the parliamentarian's Member State has withdrawn from the AEC.[539] The manner to fill vacant seats is not addressed in the Protocol. The Rules of Procedure envisage that, depending on the circumstances, the Member State of the parliamentarian shall be notified accordingly, and it will then be up to it to arrange for the replacement. Unlike the Parliamentary Assembly of the Council of Europe, there are no substitute parliamentarians.

113. Pursuant to Articles 8(1) and 9(1) of the Protocol, parliamentarians exercising their functions shall enjoy in the territory of all Member States, respectively, the immunities and privileges extended to Member States' representatives under the OAU General Convention on the Privileges and Immunities and the Vienna Convention on Diplomatic Relations as well as parliamentary immunity. Parliamentarians shall, therefore, not be liable to civil or criminal proceedings, arrest, imprisonment or damages for anything said or done within or outside the PAP provided they are discharging their duties. The scope of Articles 8(1) and 9(1) has been augmented in Rule 10 of the Rules of Procedure. However, Rules 11–12 allow the PAP to waive immunity on the ground of committing a criminal offence. The request for waiver shall be heard by the Permanent Committee on Rules, Privileges, and Discipline.

114. The PAP meets in ordinary session at least twice a year[540] and in extraordinary session at the request of two-thirds of parliamentarians, the Assembly or the Council.[541] The quorum for a meeting is a simple majority.[542] Notwithstanding the fact that each parliamentarian has one vote, the general rule is that decisions are reached by consensus.[543] Failing that, however, decisions could be taken by a two-thirds majority of all the members being present and voting.[544] This rule reflects the general AU position that majority vote shall be employed if consensus cannot be achieved.[545] Procedural matters

538. The Rules of Procedure were adopted under Parliamentary Assembly Res. 1202 (1999) in November 1999 and lastly amended under Res. 2182 (2017), at: http://assembly.coe.int/nw/xml/RoP/RoP-XML2HTML-EN.asp.
539. *See* Art. 19 of the Protocol and Rule 8(1)(g) and discussion *infra* para. 120.
540. Article 14(2) of the Protocol. These sessions may last a month. It should be noted that, according to Art. 16, the Parliament may convene in the territory of any Member State at the latter's invitation.
541. Article 14(3) of the Protocol.
542. Article 12(11) of the Protocol.
543. Article 12(12) of the Protocol.
544. Unless stipulated to the contrary in the Rules of Procedure, *see* Art. 12(12) of the Protocol.
545. Compare Art. 7(1) of the Constitutive Act referring to the Assembly.

are decided by a simple majority of those present and voting.[546] In the event of a tie, the presiding official has the casting vote.[547]

115. PAP is meant to provide a forum for African people and their grass-roots organizations to become more involved in deliberations and decision-making on African problems and challenges. Its objectives include facilitating the implementation of AU/AEC policies, promoting human rights and democracy, encouraging good governance, transparency, and accountability in Member States, promoting peace, security and stability, advancing economic recovery, assisting cooperation among RECs, and assisting cooperation and stability in Africa.[548] Accordingly, PAP has been authorized to discuss and make recommendations on issues relating to human rights, democracy, and good governance, to harmonize the laws of Member States, to make recommendations advancing AU/AEC objectives, to promote the AU/AEC in the Member States, and to harmonize the policies and programmes of RECs.[549] As regards the budget, the PAP can draw it up, discuss it but not adopt it as long as it has no legislative powers.[550] Moreover, the Protocol envisages that the PAP has the function of discussing the AEC budget and 'make recommendations thereon prior to its approval to the Assembly'.[551] Other PAP powers include to request AU/AEC officials to attend its sessions and to produce documents.[552] Finally, it has been authorized to perform such other functions as it deems appropriate to achieve its objectives.[553] This latter provision could potentially be of significance because, if used boldly and imaginatively, it could turn functions into real powers.[554] Given that the PAP is composed of the peoples' direct representatives, no doubt it could invoke its legitimacy vis-à-vis the Assembly, regardless if this would lead to tense relations between them. However, a power struggle as the one that has taken place in the EC between the European Parliament and the Council of Ministers during the 1980s and the 1990s, a struggle that sometimes was brought before the European Court of Justice (ECJ),[555] is not envisaged.[556] Under Article 12(13) of the Protocol, the PAP has been authorized to establish any committees that it deems necessary. Currently, the following ten Permanent Committees are in operation and their functions correspond to those of the AU

546. Unless stipulated to the contrary in the Rules of Procedure, *see* Art. 12(12) of the Protocol.
547. *Ibid.*
548. Article 3 of the Protocol.
549. Compare Art. 11 of the Protocol setting out its functions and powers.
550. Article 11(2) in conjunction with Art. 15(2) of the Protocol. Until then, its budget is approved by the Assembly.
551. Article 11(2) of the Protocol. Note that the corresponding provision in the Rules of Procedure (Rule 4(g)) refers to examining and debating the AU budget, which should be regarded as being separate from the AEC budget.
552. Article 11(5) of the Protocol.
553. Article 11(9) of the Protocol.
554. Note that this possibility has been played down in Rule 4(i) and Rule 5(f), which stipulate that the PAP may exercise functions and powers that are of an incidental or auxiliary nature.
555. *See* , *inter alia*, European Court of Justice, Case 13/83 *European Parliament v. Council* [1985] E.C.R. 1513; Case C-70/88 *European Parliament v. Council* (The Chernobyl Case) [1990] E.C.R. 2041; and Case C-21/94 *Parliament v. Council* [1995] E.C.R. I – 1827.
556. *See also* T. Demeke, 'The New Pan-African Parliament: Prospects and Challenges in View of the Experience of the European Parliament', *African Human Rights Law Journal* 4 (2004): 53.

Specialized Technical Committees: the Committee on Rural Economy, Agriculture, Natural Resources, and Environment; the Committee on Monetary and Financial Affairs; the Committee on Trade, Customs, and Immigration Matters; the Committee on Cooperation, International Relations, and Conflict Resolutions; the Committee on Transport, Industry, Communications, Energy, Science, and Technology; the Committee on Health, Labour, and Social Affairs; the Committee on Education, Culture, Tourism, and Human Resources; the Committee on Gender, Family, Youths, and People with Disabilities; the Committee on Justice and Human Rights; and the Committee on Rules, Privileges, and Discipline.

116. The following two examples serve to illustrate the kind of the issues that the PAP has sought to address. The first example concerns the PAP Committee on Rural Economy, Agriculture, Natural Resources, and Environment, which during the second half of 2007 undertook a fact-finding mission to Côte d'Ivoire to establish the facts on an incident concerning toxic waste dumping in December 2006; the aim was to make recommendations to the Assembly so as to avoid repetition of such events. In the second example, a member from the South African Parliament tabled in May 2007 a motion calling for a fact-finding mission to Zimbabwe to investigate matters relating to human rights protection, good governance, transparency and the rule of law arguing that the mission was pertinent to the PAP's mandate. The motion was put to the vote and 149 parliamentarians voted in favour, twenty voted against and three abstained. Arguably, even though the PAP does not possess direct rights in this area, the above mandate emanates from Rule 4(b) of its Rules of Procedure, which envisages that it shall promote fundamental freedoms as well as consolidate democratic institutions and culture in all Member States. However, such a mandate would appear to fall also within the ambit of the African Commission on Human and Peoples' Rights,[557] begging the question whether there should be some sort of cooperation between them.[558] Indeed, the overlap of mandates between the various AU organs and entities is a matter that the AU should address as a matter of urgency.[559] Finally, it should be mentioned that the PAP will spare no effort to make its presence felt and to be involved in as many initiatives as possible. Thus, in a regional meeting held in Rwanda in late May 2008 on the African Charter on Democracy, Election, and Governance, the PAP delegation of the proposed that it acts as promoter for the Charter's ratification and popularization processes. According to a commentator, PAP resolutions and recommendations are often very brief, insufficiently substantiated, poorly drafted and leave much room for improvement.[560] True as this argument is, it should be observed that the rather low quality of draftsmanship extends also to the decisions of other AU organs. In particular, as regards the Assembly and the Executive Council the situation is indeed dramatic because their decisions are meant to be binding instruments creating duties for Member States and, therefore, require legal clarity and precision. To that extent the AUC on

557. *See* Art. 45(1)(a) of the African Charter on Human and Peoples' Rights.

558. Compare *ibid.*, Art. 45(1)(c).

559. In the present case, considering that the situation in Zimbabwe has security implications for the region, the Peace and Security Council might have a role to play; Compare Art. 18 of the PSC Protocol delineating its relationship with the PAP.

560. *See* F. Viljoen, *International Human Right Law in Africa*, 2nd edition (Oxford: Oxford University Press, 2012), 175.

International Law could have a vital role to play in assisting AU organs to improve the quality of their instrument.

117. As mentioned, pursuant to Article 11(7) of the Protocol, the PAP has been entrusted with facilitating coordination and harmonization of policies and programmes of RECs and the other African parliamentary fora.[561] This objective is further elaborated in Article 18, which arguably has a wider ambit, as it envisages that the cooperation shall extend to cover national parliaments or other deliberative organs operating in Member States as well. Apparently, the envisaged cooperation is nothing more than the possibility for the PAP to convene annual consultative meetings with the other entities to 'discuss matters of common interest'. However, there would appear to be no major institutional hindrance if representatives from the parliamentary organs of RECs were invited to participate, at least as observers, at all its sessions.[562] Suffice to mention that Rule 5(d) provides that the PAP could issue invitations to the representatives of RECs in order to 'furnish explanations on issues affecting or likely to affect the life of the African Union'.

118. During the initial (undefined in terms of duration) stage, it was decided that the PAP powers will only be consultative and advisory. However, it is expected that through an evolutionary proceed it will acquire legislative powers as well. This derives from the combined reading of Articles 2(3) and 11 of the Protocol. However, the wording of these provisions raises issues of interpretation because the former provision talks about the Member States deciding by an amendment to the Protocol, while the latter talks about legislative powers to be defined by the Assembly. Given the state of affairs in the continent as well as the fact that democracy has still to flourish in many an African country, it was probably considerations of pragmatism that dictated the decision not to grant legislative powers to the PAP from the onset. However, this evolutionary process is imperative, as the full and effective functioning of the PAP would only be beneficial and would confer democratic legitimacy to the AU. It should be noted that the Seventh Ordinary PAP Session, which ended on 19 May 2007, recommended to the Assembly that it be transformed into a legislative organ within the AU's evolutionary process towards the creation of a Union Government.

119. The powers of the PAP were enhanced by the Protocol establishing the African Court of Justice, adopted by the Assembly in July 2003. These favourable for the PAP provisions were carried on to the 2008 Protocol and the appended Statute, which as has been explained, merged it with the African Court on Human and Peoples' Rights to create the ACJHR. In particular, under Article 29 of the ACJHR Statute, the PAP is entitled to submit cases relating, e.g., to the interpretation and application of the Constitutive Act, the interpretation, application and validity of all AU treaties, as

561. Compare Rule 4(e) and Rule 5(b), (d) and (e) of the Rules of Procedure.

562. Compare Arts 4(2)(a) and 6(2) of the AEC Treaty envisaging collaboration with the RECs, which was formalized by the Protocol on the Relationship between the African Economic Community and the Regional Economic Communities of 25 Feb. 1998, reproduced in RADIC 10 (1998):157. *See* further Art. 6(2)(f)(v) of the AEC Treaty envisaging the harmonization and coordination process to be achieved during the AEC's fifth and final stage of creation (originally scheduled to be completed by 2034), and OAU Assembly, *Relaunching Africa's Economic and Social Development: The Cairo Agenda for Action*, OAU Doc. AHG/Res. 236 (XXXI) (26 Jun. 1995) which considered the achievement of regional economic integration a top priority.

well as to decisions issued by other AU organs. Equally, were the PAP to misuse its powers, an action could be brought against it before the ACJHR by the other organs. Finally, under Article 53 of the ACJHR Statute, PAP has also been granted the right to ask the ACJHR to issue advisory opinions on any legal question. Arguably, were these provisions to be used constructively by the PAP once the ACJHR has become operative, it could strengthen its position considerably in the AU institutional architecture.

120. As has been noted, Article 19 of the PAP Protocol deals with parliamentarians from a contracting party which has withdrawn from the AEC and stipulates that they shall automatically cease holding their office. The corresponding provision in the Rules (Rule 8(1)(g)) refers to withdrawal from the AU and not from the AEC, presumably because the Rules, without explaining why, regard that the AEC has been incorporated in the AU and does no longer exist (Eritrea signed the AEC Treaty in 2012 and South Sudan in 2013). For as long as the AEC is not officially dissolved, this argument is very difficult to be sustained because participation in the AEC is distinct from AU participation. Indeed, at the time of the AU's inauguration, there were six AU Member States which were not AEC Members.[563] Today, AEC membership is five states short of AU membership (not counting Morocco). Moreover, Article 19 does not specifically confer upon contracting parties the right to withdraw from the Protocol but only sets out the consequences when they have withdrawn from the AEC. Arguably, the PAP Protocol, as a legal instrument, is separate from the AEC Treaty and Member States cannot be compelled to become contracting parties to it. Therefore, Article 19 ought to have stipulated that withdrawal from the Protocol is independent of withdrawal from the AEC Treaty.

121. As has been explained, even though the PAP Protocol was prepared based on the AEC Treaty's mandate, it regulates a principal AU organ. Given the aforementioned ensuing problems, the sensible thing had always been to disassociate it from the AEC and act solely as the AU parliamentary organ. Thus, in 2009 the Assembly requested the Commission to initiate a review process in consultation with the PRC and the PAP.[564] In May 2011, the Fifth Meeting of the Government Experts on the Legal Instruments on the Transformation of the AUC into AU Authority and on Review of the Protocols relating to the Pan-African Parliament and the African Court on Human and Peoples' Rights adopted a draft Protocol to replace the 2001 Protocol.[565] After it was reviewed by the Ministers of Justice and the Attorneys General of Member States in mid May 2012,[566] the Executive Council approved it except of Article 8.1(a) and 8.2, the provisions on PAP's legislative and oversight powers. It recommended that it be deferred in line with developments in the African integration process.[567] In January

563. Namely Djibouti, Equatorial Guinea, Eritrea, Gabon, Somalia and Swaziland; *see List of Countries which Have Signed, Ratified/Acceded to the Treaty Establishing the African Economic Community as at 26 September 2002*, AU Doc. CAB/LEG/28.1 (2002).

564. *See* Assembly, *Decision on the Review of the Protocol Relating to the Pan-African Parliament (PAP)*, AU Doc. Assembly/AU/Dec. 223 (XII) (3 Feb. 2009).

565. *See* Draft Protocol to the Constitutive Act of the African Union Relating to the Pan-African Parliament, AU Doc. Exp/Legal/AUC-Auth./4(V) (May 2011).

566. AU Doc. EX.CL/731(XXI)b (May 2012).

567. *See* Executive Council, *Decision on the Protocol to the Constitutive Act of the African Union Relating to the Pan-African Parliament*, EX.CL/ Dec. 707 (XXI) (13 Jul. 2012).

2013, the Assembly adopted the recommendation.[568] Presumably because national sovereignty continues to be the determining factor in how African leaders approach political integration,[569] the PAP's legislative and oversight powers caused considerable contention among them. This draft Protocol was discussed in the previous edition of this monograph.[570] It was finally accepted by the Assembly in June 2014.[571] Until the very end, Article 8 proved to be a most contentious matter. It was the only issue that the First Ministerial Meeting of the Specialized Technical Committee on Justice and Legal Affairs, held Addis Ababa in mid May 2014, was asked to deliberate.[572] Finally, the Executive Council recommended to the Assembly that Article 8(1) be worded as follows:

(a) The Assembly shall determine the subjects/areas on which the Pan-African Parliament may propose draft model laws;
(b) *The Pan-African Parliament may on its own make proposals on the subjects/ areas on which it may submit or recommend draft Model Laws to the Assembly for its consideration and approval.*[573]

At the time of writing, fifteen Member States have signed the Protocol and five have ratified it (Mali was the first to ratify it in April 2015 and Togo the last in August 2016). Even though, according to Article 23, it shall into force when approved by a simple majority of Member States (currently, twenty-eight), several its salient features will be discussed. Pursuant to Article 27(1), it shall replace the 2001 Protocol. The obvious question, which has not been addressed in the new Protocol, is whether participation will be restricted to those parliamentarians coming from only the contracting parties to the 2014 Protocol or from all forty-eight Member States, which have presently approved the 2001 Protocol. Under the former solution, which appears to be the correct one from a legal point of view, the new PAP will operate with parliamentarians from the first twenty-eight contracting parties. The Protocol does not stipulate the parallel operation of both the old and new PAP. On the contrary, Article 2(1) refers to the continuation of the existing PAP (there will be no legal succession as such) pursuant to the new rules while Article 27(2) stipulates that the term of office of PAP Members shall terminate no later than one year after the 2014 Protocol's entry into force.

As regards the contentious Article 8, it limits considerably the PAP's legislative powers. In particular, the first paragraph thereof envisages that it shall be the AU

568. *See* Assembly, *Decision on the Protocol to the Constitutive Act of the African Union relating to the Pan-African Parliament*, AU Doc. Assembly/AU/Dec. 455 (XX) (28 Jan. 2013).
569. *See* O. Nzewi, *The Challenges of Post-1990 Regional Integration in Africa: Pan-African Parliament*, Centre for Policy Studies, Policy Brief 57, Johannesburg, April 2009, p. 11.
570. *See* K. Magliveras &G. Naldi, *The African Union* (Alphen aan den Rijn: Wolters Kluwer, 2014), para. 116.
571. Protocol to the Constitutive Act of the African Union Relating to the Pan-African Parliament, *see* Assembly, *Decision on the Draft Legal Instruments,* AU Doc. Assembly/AU/Dec. 529 (XXIII) (27 Jun. 2014).
572. *See* AU Doc. STC/Legal/Min/7(I) Rev.1 (2014) at: https://www.yumpu.com/en/document/view/36432612/7mkd9bh2g/3.
573. *See* Executive Council, *Decision on the Draft Legal Instruments*, AU Doc. EX.CL/Dec. 835 (XXV) (24 Jun. 2014), para. 3.

legislative organ but it shall have no law-making powers of its own. On the contrary, it will be the Assembly which shall determine the subjects or the areas in which the PAP may propose draft model laws, which will presumably be adopted by the Assembly itself if it so wishes. But, at the same time, the PAP is also entitled, on the one hand, to propose such subjects and areas and, on the other hand, to recommend draft model laws for the Assembly's consideration and approval. Clearly the outcome of compromises, this provision could prove unworkable if there is no sincere rapport between the two organs. The new PAP will acquire the consultative and oversight powers laid down in Article 8(2). They include to receive and consider reports of AU organs, provided they are referred to it by the Executive Council and the Assembly; debate but not adopt its own budget and the AU budget and make recommendations on them; discuss any matter relevant to the AU and make pertinent recommendations; promote AU programmes and objectives in Member States; receive, consider, and submit opinions on draft legislative instruments and international agreements as may be referred to it by the Executive Council and the Assembly (a function arguably overlapping with the mandate of the AUCIL); and liaise with the parliamentarian bodies of Member States and of RECs on issues concerning the AU and regional integration.

The PAP is also authorized to carry out any other activities which it deems appropriate to achieve the objectives of Article 3 of the new Protocol. These objectives have been unchanged from the 2001 Protocol, and, *inter alia*, include the following: giving a voice to African people and the African Diaspora, while encouraging the latter's full participation in African affairs;[574] facilitating the effective implementation of AU policies; promoting human rights and democracy; encouraging good governance, respect for the rule of law, transparency and accountability; promoting peace, security, and stability; encouraging collective self-reliance and economic recovery; strengthening African solidarity, cooperation, and development, and building a sense of common destiny; and encouraging national parliaments to ratify and to implement AU treaties into their legal systems. A new provision on how the PAP is to exercise its powers and functions has been inserted as Article 8(3). It is another restrictive provision because, while it may carry out fact-finding, inquiry and observer missions, it may do so if not in conflict with the mandate of other organs. The priority to be given to other organs may be acceptable in the case of fact-finding missions to establish e.g., peace violations (the PSC should have priority on account of its mandate and/or the Commission if so instructed by the Assembly) but not as regards e.g., observer missions to report on electoral processes in the territory of contracting parties. Moreover, the question of duplication of efforts and complementarity comes into play. Clearly the AU should adopt guidelines to that effect which should not be based on an assumed superiority of one organ over another but which organ can carry out the mission more effectively, economically, and faster.

As has been mentioned (*supra*, paragraph 112), the clause in the 2001 Protocol on the circumstances justifying the vacation of parliamentarians' seats did not include those elected through fraudulent, violent or highly undemocratic elections or appointed by a regime which came to power in a coup d'état and similar situations. The 2014

574. *See* B.R. Dinokopila, 'The Pan-African Parliament and African Union Human Rights Actors, Civil Society and National Human Rights Institutions: The Importance of Collaboration', *African Human Rights Law Journal* 13 (2013): 302.

Protocol overturns this omission and Article 6(3)(h) stipulates that the seat of a PAP Member shall become vacant if the holder represents a contracting party which has been suspended from participating in AU activities. Arguably, this provision means that parliamentarians from a Member State which participates in the PAP will not only be denied participation but their seats will be considered to be untaken for as long as the state in question remains suspended as regards AU activities, a sanction provided for in Article 30 of the Constitutive Act (*supra*, paragraphs 90–92). However, it is rather unclear if parliamentarians will be allowed to speak at meetings, to vote, etc. if the state they come from has been subjected to sanctions imposed by the Assembly pursuant to Article 23(1) of the Constitutive Act for having defaulted in paying budgetary contributions.

The 2014 Protocol also creates new institutions, a necessary step since the PAP will no longer be an AEC organ.[575] Thus there will be a Bureau (Article 12) and a Secretary-General (Article 13). The former will be responsible for developing policies to manage and administer the PAP's affairs and property. The latter will be the Head of the Secretariat, the Accounting Officer and will also responsible for day-to-day activities. Moreover, the fact that the PAP will operate as a proper AU organ led to the insertion of a new Article 20 in the Protocol to regulate relations with other organs. Thus, the Assembly Chairperson will deliver a speech on the state of the AU at each inaugural session of the PAP, the Commission and other organs will present their Activity Reports to the PAP, while the latter will forward its own Activity Report to them. Presumably, this exchange of Reports is not meant to be a mere formality but issues of substance ought to be deliberated and there is room for a meaningful exchange of opinions at an institutional level. Finally, the 2014 Protocol does not solve satisfactorily the question of interpretation of its provisions. While Article 21 thereof provides that it will be interpreted by the ACJHR, the drafters deleted the reference in the corresponding Article 20 of the 2001 Protocol stipulating that, pending its establishment, matters of interpretation will be resolved by the Assembly acting by a two-thirds majority. Given that it cannot be prognosed whether the Protocol establishing the ACJHR will come into force before the 2014 Protocol, theoretically speaking the new PAP could become functionable without the ACJHR being able to deliver authoritative decisions on issues of interpretation, which could concern important legal issues.

§4. The African Court of Justice and Human Rights (ACJHR)

122. The process for establishing the AU's judicial organ, the African Court of Justice (ACJ), was explained in some detail in the second edition of the present monograph.[576] The ACJ Protocol was adopted in July 2003 and entered into force in February 2009. However, in July 2008, the Assembly decided to merge it with the African Court on Human and Peoples' Rights. To that end, it adopted the Protocol on

575. To that extent, the aforementioned Art. 19 of the 2001 Protocol on withdrawal from the AEC and the effect on parliamentarians was deleted from the new Protocol.

576. For analysis, *see* K. Magliveras & G. Naldi, *The African Union* (Alphen aan den Rijn: Kluwer Law International, 2009) paras 177–187.

the ACJHR (2008 Protocol),[577] which at the time of writing had only secured five out of the required fifteen ratifications (another twenty-five Member States have signed it). Since the AU has apparently abandoned the project of operationalizing the ACJ, even for the provisional period until the 2008 Protocol comes into force, it is only the ACJHR that will be examined here. The present authors maintain their argument that the merger between the ACJ and the African Human Rights Court was ill-advised and that it would lead to complicated institutional problems.[578] If and when the 2008 Protocol enters into force, the ACJHR will operate on the basis of its provisions as well as the Statute which has been appended to the Protocol.

123. According to Article 2(1) of the Statute, the ACJHR will be 'the main judicial organ of the African Union'.[579] Article 16 thereof stipulates that it will comprise a General Affairs Section, which corresponds to the ACJ jurisdiction,[580] and a Human Rights Section, which corresponds to the jurisdiction of the African Court on Human and Peoples' Rights.[581] The former section will be competent to hear all cases except those expressly reserved for the latter. Either section may constitute chambers. A third section, the 'International Criminal Law Section,' is envisaged in the Malabo Protocol adopted in June 2014 and will be examined later.[582] Each Section will be entitled to refer any case it has received to the Full Court for consideration. Pursuant to Article 20 of the Statute, the ACJHR will hold ordinary sessions, which will be determined on an annual basis, and extraordinary sessions, to be convened at the discretion of the President or at the request of most judges.

124. The ACJHR will have both contentious jurisdiction (Article 28 of the Statute) and advisory jurisdiction (Articles 53–56 of the Statute). The former will comprise all legal disputes relating to: (a) the interpretation and application of the Constitutive Act; (b) the interpretation, application or validity of other OAU/AU Treaties and subsidiary legal instruments adopted within their framework; (c) the interpretation and the application of the African Charter on Human and Peoples' Rights (the Banjul Charter) and its Protocol on the Rights of Women in Africa, of the Charter on the Rights and Welfare of the Child, as well as of any other legal instrument pertaining to human rights, even if it is a non-African instrument but provided it has been ratified by the contracting parties concerned; (d) any question of international

577. *See* G. Muigai, 'From the African Court on Human Rights and Peoples' Rights to the African Court of Justice and Human Rights' in *The African Regional Human Rights System. 30 Years After the African Charter on Human and Peoples' Rights*, M. Ssenyoujo (ed.) (Leiden: Martinus Nijhoff Publishers, 2012), 265.

578. Magliveras & Naldi, *The African Union*, *supra* paras 188–191.

579. For further analysis of the ACJHR with extensive references to bibliography, *see* G. Naldi & K. Magliveras, 'The African Court of Justice and Human Rights: A Judicial Curate's Egg', *International Organizations Law Review* 9 (2012): 383.

580. *See* G. Naldi, 'Aspects of the African Court of Justice and Human Rights' in *International Law and Dispute Settlement: New Problems and Techniques*, D. French, M. Saul, & N.D. White (eds) (Oxford: Hart Publishing, 2010), 321.

581. *See* G. Naldi, 'The Role of the Human Rights Section of the African Court of Justice and Human and Rights' in *Protecting Human Security in Africa*, A. Abass (ed.)(Oxford: Oxford University Press, 2010), 284.

582. Protocol on Amendments to the Protocol on the Statute of the African Court of Justice and Human Rights, signed on 27 Jun. 2014, not yet in force.

law; (e) all acts, decisions, regulations and directives adopted by AU organs; (f) all matters specifically stipulated in any other agreement, which has been concluded among contracting parties or concluded with the AU; (g) the existence of any fact which, if established, would constitute a breach of an obligation owed to a contracting party or to the AU; and (h) the nature or extent of the reparation to be made for the breach of an international obligation.

According to Article 29(1) of the Statute, the persons and entities entitled to submit cases on any issue or dispute stipulated in Article 28 fall into three categories. First, the contracting parties to the 2008 Protocol. Second, the Assembly, the PAP and other AU organs (e.g., the Executive Council, the Commission, and the PSC) provided that the Assembly has so authorized them. Third, AU employees, who in accordance with Regulation 14 of the AU Staff Regulations and Rules,[583] have appealed against a decision rendered in the context of a labour dispute with the AU. The first category could be described as privileged applicants, i.e., they may approach the ACJHR on any dispute falling within the ambit of its general jurisdiction, which could also include human rights violations. However, as far as alleged violations of human rights are specifically concerned, Article 30 of the Statute contains a very broad *locus standi* clause encompassing the following six categories of applicants. First, the contracting parties to the 2008 Protocol. Second, the African Commission on Human and Peoples' Rights.[584] Third, the African Committee of Experts on the Rights and Welfare of the Child. Fourth, the 'African Intergovernmental Organizations' which have been accredited to the AU or to its organs, a term which should be understood as synonymous to RECs. In this respect, it should be noted that the Court of Justice of ECOWAS has stated that it has been assigned responsibility for protecting human rights, including those enshrined in the Banjul Charter,[585] the East African Community (EAC) has contemplated adding jurisdiction on human rights to its Court of Justice[586] but finally backed down,[587] while in the case of the SADC Tribunal its pronouncements on human rights issues largely

583. They were adopted in 2010, *see* Assembly, *Decision on the Staff Regulations and Rules*, AU Doc. Assembly/AU/Dec. 305 (XV) (27 Jul. 2010).

584. *See* M. Hansungule, 'African Courts and the African Commission on Human and Peoples' Rights' in *Human Rights in Africa – Legal Perspectives on their Protection and Promotion*, A. Boesl & J. Diescho (eds)(Windhoek: Konrad Adenaueur Stiftung, 2009), 233, 253–255.

585. *See* ECOWAS Community Court of Justice, *Hadijatou Mani Koraou v. Republic of Niger*, Judgment No. ECW/CCJ/JUD/06/08, 27 Oct. 2008, paras 41–42; AHRLR (2008): 182, at: http://www.refworld.org/docid/496b41fa2.html, discussed by H. Duffy, '*Hadijatou Mani Koroua v. Niger: Slavery Unveiled by the ECOWAS Court*' *Human Rights Law Review* 9 (2009): 151–170. *See also* Supplementary Protocol A/SP.1/01/05 Amending the Preamble and Arts 1, 2, 9 and 30 of Protocol A/P.1/7/91 Relating to the Community Court of Justice and Art. 4 para. 1 of the English Version of the Said Protocol, which was signed on 19 Jan. 2005 and inserted new Arts 9(4) and 10(d) in the Protocol of the ECOWAS Court of Justice, at: http://www.courtecowas.org/site2012/pdf_files/supplementary_protocol.pdf.

586. *See* S. Lawena, 'The Human Rights Jurisdiction of the East African Court of Justice: Challenges and Prospects', *Journal of African and International Law* 6 (2013):119; S. Kingah, *Regional Courts and Human Rights in the Developing World*, UNU-CRIS Working Papers W-2013/11, pp. 7–8, at: http://cris.unu.edu/regional-courts-and-human-rights-developing-world.

587. *See* Communiqué of the 16th Summit of EAC Heads of State, Nairobi, Kenya, 20 Feb. 2015, para. 9.

led to its demise in its original form in 2010.[588] Fifth, African National Human Rights Institutions. Sixth, individuals or NGOs accredited to the AU or to its organs but subject to the satisfaction of the conditions envisaged in Article 8 of the 2008 Protocol. In particular, Article 8(3) states that '[a]ny Member State may … make a declaration accepting the competence of the Court to receive cases under Article 30(f) [of the Statute] involving a State which has not made such a declaration'. It is not clear what the intention of the drafters was. Were the intention to allow the ACJHR to receive petitions from individuals and NGOs contingent upon contracting parties making a separate optional declaration, then it should have stipulated that the ACJHR would not receive any petition involving a contracting party which has not made such a declaration. However, if indeed a separate declaration is required, then it might lead to negation of justice because contracting parties with a record of serious human rights abuses are highly unlikely to accept the ACJHR's jurisdiction in this respect. Finally, it should be emphasized that, under the Statute, a complainant is not required to be the victim of the alleged human rights violation. Thus, the drafters have opted for the Inter-American human rights system, which is based on a *laissez-passer* attitude and, pursuant to Article 44 of the American Convention on Human Rights (ACHR), it allows (almost) anyone to file a petition alleging violations. The justification for such extensive standing has been based on the fact that in the ACHR contracting parties there exists poverty, lack of education, lack of legal assistance, while human rights defenders are often hindered from pursuing petitions for alleged violations (that much is also true for African states).[589] However, it is not clear whether, once operative, the ACJHR will allow petitions amounting to *actio popularis*, as the African Commission on Human and Peoples' Rights has permitted when interpreting the Banjul Charter's admissibility requirements.[590]

125. As far as the incidental jurisdiction is concerned, the Statute covers provisional (interim) measures, intervention, and reparations but does not cover preliminary objections and friendly settlement. Regarding provisional measures, Article 35(1) of the Statute authorizes the ACJHR to indicate, *proprio motu* or at the request of a litigant party, any measures necessary to preserve the respective rights of litigant parties. Although it breaks away from the corresponding provisions governing other international courts (it does not require the existence of extreme gravity and urgency and/or the need to avoid irreparable harm as preconditions to ordering provisional

588. Generally, *see* G. Naldi & K. Magliveras, 'The New SADC Tribunal – or the Emasculation of an International Tribunal', *Netherlands Journal of International Law* 63 (2016): 133.

589. *See* F. Viljoen, 'Admissibility under the African Charter' in *The African Charter on Human and Peoples' Rights: The System in Practice, 1986-2000*, M.D. Evans & R. Murray (eds) (Cambridge: Cambridge University Press, 2002), 61, 75. *See also Contribution of the International Federation for Human Rights (FIDH) and the World Organisation Against Torture (OMCT) before the African Commission on Human and Peoples' Rights*, Fifty-Third Ordinary Session, Banjul, Gambia, 9–23 Apr. 2013, under agenda item 9: 'Situation of human rights defenders', 13 Apr. 2013, at: http://www.omct.org/human-rights-defenders/statements/2013/04/d22227.

590. *See* , *inter alia*, African Commission on Human and Peoples' Rights, *Article 19 v. Eritrea*, Communication No. 275/2003, *22nd Activity Report 2006–2007*, annex II, para. 65; AHRLR (2007): 73; and *The Social and Economic Rights Action Center and the Center for Economic and Social Rights v. Nigeria*, Communication No. 155/96, *15th Activity Report 2001–2002*, para. 49; AHRLR(2001): 60.

measures), its brief content leaves many questions unanswered, which presumably will be addressed in the ACJHR Rules of Procedure. Suffice to mention the following four questions. May a request for provisional measures be submitted to the ACJHR at the same time as the main proceedings are instituted? Should the ACJHR satisfy itself that it has jurisdiction, prima facie or otherwise, before ordering provisional measures? What is going to happen if another entity (e.g., the African Commission on Human and Peoples' Rights) has already adopted interim measures in the context of the same dispute? Will the orders prescribing provisional measures be legally binding? The latter is a perennial question for international courts and tribunals. It can only be hoped that the ACJHR will follow the trend of, *inter alia*, the ICJ, the Inter-American Court of Human Rights, and the European Court of Human Rights, which have established that such orders enjoy binding effect and litigant parties must obey them and act according to their stipulations.

Article 49(1) of the Statute allows any Member State or any AU organ to petition the ACJHR to intervene, provided that it has a legal interest in the outcome of the case and could be affected by the judgment to be given. There is no guidance in the Statute as to precise content of the term 'legal interest' and as to the required degree of interest. The ACJHR might be influenced by the practice of other international courts, such as the ICJ, which has applied a strict policy.[591] The fact that Article 49 refers to 'Member States,' if read in conjunction with Article 1 of the Statute, would suggest that the whole AU membership is entitled to request intervention, irrespective of whether they are contracting parties to the 2008 Protocol or not. Moreover, all AU organs have the opportunity to intervene and can do so without the Assembly's prior authorization. It is commendable that Article 49(2) stipulates that the interpretation to be given by the ACJHR will be binding upon the Member State/s or the AU organ/s which were allowed to intervene. This will potentially prevent speculative intervention, especially in interstate litigation that might have been politicized. Finally, as regards intervention in cases concerning the interpretation of treaties, the Statute distinguishes between the interpretation of the Constitutive Act (Article 50) and the interpretation of 'other treaties' (Article 51). According to Article 50(3), the decisions concerning the interpretation and application of the Constitutive Act will be binding on all Member States and AU organs, notwithstanding that not all of them might have intervened by taking advantage of the opportunity offered under Article 50(2). In contradistinction, the interpretation to be given in another treaty will be binding only on those contracting parties and/or AU organs which opted to exercise their right to intervene.

126. The issue of reparations is dealt with in Article 281(h) of the Statute. It allows the ACJHR, acting at the request of a litigant party, to determine the nature and the extent of the reparations to be made or the 'fair compensation' to be paid by the

---

591. *See* Art. 81(2)(a) of the ICJ Rules of Procedure requiring the intervening state to indicate the interest of a legal nature that will be affected. In *Case Concerning Sovereignty over Pulau Litigan and Pulau Sipadan (Indonesia/Malaysia),* Application by Philippines to Intervene, Judgment of 23 Oct. 2001, *I.C.J. Reports 2001*, p. 575, the ICJ explained the meaning of an 'interest of a legal nature'. *See* further, ICJ, *Obligations concerning Negotiations relating to Cessation of the Nuclear Arms Race and to Nuclear Disarmament* (*Marshall Islands v. United Kingdom*), General List No. 160, Judgment of 5 Oct. 2016, at: http://www.icj-cij.org/docket/files/160/19198.pdf.

losing party for breaching its obligations. Moreover, Article 45, which deals specifically with situations where the ACJHR has established a violation of human rights by the respondent state, authorizes it to order 'any appropriate measures' so as to remedy the situation, including granting fair compensation. Arguably, the wording of this provision leads to the conclusion that the ACJHR has the discretion to make an award on its own motion provided that a human rights violation has been established. Moreover, the ACJHR has a broad mandate to order suitable remedies, of which fair compensation is only one of the options. Thus, it could order consequential measures requiring parties to adopt positive measures to rectify the situation and avoid the infraction's repetition in the future. It is unclear whether the Statute envisages restitution in kind as a remedy. However, it could be covered by the concept of 'reparations' and be deemed to form part of the general structure of Article 45. Equally, what constitutes 'fair compensation' will have to be determined by the ACJHR presumably on a case to case basis. Suffice to mention that the African Commission on Human and Peoples' Rights has in the past accepted the principle of compensatory damages as a form of indemnity.[592] Finally, there exists the considerable practice of the Inter-American Court of Human Rights on reparations with ample examples of the nature and the forms that they may take.[593]

127. Regarding the ACJHR's incidental jurisdiction, the drafters have not covered the issues of preliminary objections and amicable or friendly settlement. Regarding the former, based on established practice of international litigation, it cannot be ruled out that the ACJHR's jurisdiction will not be challenged. Therefore, it is rather curious that the ability to determine its own jurisdiction (the so-called principle of *Kompetenz-Kompetenz*) has not been envisaged in the Statute. However, considering that 'the inherent power of a tribunal to interpret the text establishing its jurisdiction' has long been recognized as a principle of international law,[594] the ACJHR should be in the position to assert this implied capacity if and when necessary. Regarding the latter omission, it is rather problematic that the Statute does not envisage amicable or friendly settlements, especially as concerns the competence of the Human Rights Section and given that it is envisaged in the African Court on Human and Peoples' Rights. If, once operative, the ACJHR wanted to adopt procedures for friendly settlement, presumably it will do so by including them in the Rules of Procedure. However, it is submitted that the Rules should not be used as a vehicle for adding new processes, if these were not already envisaged in the 2008 Protocol.

---

592. *See* , *inter alia*, African Commission on Human and Peoples' Rights, *Malawi African Association, Amnesty International, Ms Sarr Diop, Union Interafricaine des Droits de l'Homme and RADDHO, Collectif des Veuves et Ayant-droit, and Association Mauritanienne des Droits de l'Homme v. Mauritania*, Communication Nos 54/91, 61/91, 98/93, 164/97-196/97, and 210/98, Decision of 11 May 2000, *13th Activity Report 1999–2000*, OAU Doc. AHG/222 (XXXVI), p. 138); *AHRLR* (2000): 149. *See also* G. Naldi, 'Reparations in the Practice of the African Commission on Human and Peoples' Rights', *Leiden Journal of International Law* 14 (2001): 681.

593. Generally, *see* Human Rights Clinic at the University of Texas School of Law, *Collective and Moral Reparations in the Inter-American Court of Human Rights*, November 2009, at: https://law.utexas.edu/wp-content/uploads/sites/11/2015/04/2009-HRC-Cambodia-CollectiveReparations.pdf.

594. *See* , *inter alia*, ICJ, *Norwegian Loans Case (France v. Norway)*, Judgment of 6 Jul. 1957, Separate Opinion of Judge Lauterpacht, *I.C.J. Reports 1957*, pp. 9, 34.

128. The wording of Article 53(1) of the Statute stipulating that, the ACJHR has the competence to issue advisory opinions suggests that they will be given by the Full Court and not by the respective Section. Advisory opinions may be issued (i.e., the ACJHR has only a discretion) on any legal question when requested by the Assembly, the PAP, the Executive Council, the PSC, the ECOSOCC, the Financial Institutions or any other AU organ so authorized by the Assembly (e.g., the Commission, and the Specialized (Technical) Committees). It follows that contracting parties will be barred from requesting advisory opinions. Although this is also the case with the judicial organs of other international organizations having a primarily political nature, including the ICJ, it is regrettable that the AU Member States (and not just those which are contracting parties to the 2008 Protocol) will be unable to do so. There is no compelling reason why organs such as ECOSOCC are expressly permitted to seek advisory opinions but not Member States. While, traditionally, the advisory opinions of transnational courts (e.g., the ICJ and the Inter-American Court of Human Rights) have been non-binding, over time their content has been regarded as influential judicial pronouncements. Thus, if the ACJHR opinions were to be followed consistently by AU organs, they could lead to an important body of legal principles to be applied across the continent. Regarding the advisory jurisdiction's procedural aspects, it follows from Articles 55 and 56 of the Statute that the ACJHR will be guided by the procedure applicable in contentious cases (including delivering separate or dissenting opinions).

In exercising its various heads of jurisdiction, the law to be applied by the ACJHR is laid down (presumably in descending order) in Article 31(1) of the Statute:

(a) The Constitutive Act.
(b) International treaties, whether of general or particular content, which have been ratified by litigant parties.
(c) International custom, as evidence of a general practice accepted as law.
(d) General principles of law recognized either universally or by African states.
(e) Judicial decisions, academic writings and decisions issued by AU organs but only as subsidiary means for the determination of the rules of law in a specific case, and
(f) Any other law relevant to the case under consideration.

Moreover, under Article 31(2), it will have the power to decide a case *ex aequo et bono* should the litigant parties so agree.

129. Other procedural issues of note include the following. Pursuant to Article 36 of the Statute, contracting parties will be represented by agents, with the assistance of counsel if necessary, while the AU organs with *locus standi* before the ACJHR will be represented by the Commission's Chairperson. On the contrary, the African Commission on Human and Peoples' Rights, other African IGOs and the Member States' national human rights institutions will be represented by a person of their choice. The same applies to individuals and NGOs. Regrettably, the Statute does not provide for free legal representation in the interests of justice, a significant oversight especially in cases involving human rights violations and given that the African Court on Human and Peoples' Rights does envisage legal aid. All persons appearing before the ACJHR are guaranteed the protection necessary for properly discharging their functions and duties, a welcome development since arbitrary detention, ill-treatment, and disappearances for defying national authorities are all too common in parts of Africa. However, this does not address how individuals (e.g., complainants and witnesses) will be protected from reprisals in the territory of contracting parties which appear as respondents before the ACJHR. In such situations, the ACJHR could and should use creatively its competence to indicate provisional measures under the aforementioned Article 35 of the Statute. Pursuant to Article 41 of the Statute, if a litigant party fails to appear or does not defend the case against it, the ACJHR is authorized to consider the case and give its judgment. However, it will first satisfy itself that it has jurisdiction, then that the claim is well-founded in fact and in law, and. finally, that due notice was given to the defaulting party. Presumably because the non-appearing party is likely to prejudice its case, it is offered ninety days from the date of notification of the default judgment to lodge an objection against it.

The provisions concerning judgments in contentious cases are laid down in Articles 42 et seq. of the Statute. Judgments will be taken by a majority, will be reasoned, will be read in open court (but no provision is made as regards their publication), while separate and dissenting opinions may be attached. Compared to other international courts, Article 43(1) innovates in that it requires the ACJHR to render its judgment within ninety days once deliberations have been completed. Pursuant to Article 46(2), judgments rendered by a section or by the Full Court will be final. This should be interpreted as not allowing appeals. Although appealing against a judgment given by the Full Court might be inappropriate (taking into account the position in other international courts as well), to challenge a Section's judgment before the Full Court should perhaps be contemplated if and when the ACJHR becomes operative.

According to Article 47 of the Statute, litigant parties may ask the ACJHR to interpret the meaning and scope of a judgment if a dispute over it has arisen. No deadline is envisaged for this procedure. Article 48 authorizes the ACJHR to review its judgments in the light of new facts subject to a number of conditions. These include that the application is lodged no later than six months after the new facts' discovery, which if known at the time might have influenced the ACJHR's determination, that it is lodged not later than ten years from the judgment, and that the party claiming revision has already complied with the judgment. Regarding compliance, Article 46(3) stipulates that litigant parties will not only be obliged to comply with the judgment promptly but also guarantee its execution. However, whether parties will actually comply or not is a matter that cannot be influenced by the ACJHR. And this because, like other international judicial organs, it will have no power to enforce its judgments. Should a party fail to comply, Article 46(4) directs the ACJHR to refer it to the Assembly for a decision. But how will non-compliance be monitored? Presumably, this is another matter to be addressed in the Rules. It will be submitted that the best means will be for the losing party/ies to notify the ACJHR and/or the Assembly of the measures taken to give effect to judgments. Under Article 47(6), failure to comply with a judgment empowers (but does not compel) the Assembly to impose sanctions pursuant to the aforementioned Article 23(2) of the Constitutive Act.

130. Article 3(1) of the Statute stipulates that the ACJHR will be composed of sixteen judges, to be divided equally between the General Affairs Section and the

Human Rights Section. However, this choice of number is problematic. For example, in those judicial organs of international organizations where the number of judges is not equal to the number of Member States, their number is invariably odd so as to avoid ties when delivering judgments. This obvious advantage will not be available in the case of the ACJHR. Taking into consideration that, as has been explained, the entry into force of the 2008 Protocol necessitates fifteen ratifications, at the exact moment that the ACJHR will become operative the number of judges will exceed the number of contracting parties. This situation will remain so until there is a sixteenth ratification of the 2008 Protocol. However, since Article 3(2) of the Statute prohibits two judges to be nationals of the same state, it is unclear from which contracting party the sixteenth judge will be appointed.

Article 7(1)(2) of the Statute envisages a two-stage procedure for confirming judges: initially they will be elected by the Executive Council in a secret ballot and, thereafter, appointed by the Assembly. It is neither clear what this two-stage procedure serves nor which is the legal basis. It is not to be found in any similar judicial body of an international organization. Moreover, it is not to be found in the Constitutive Act, whose Article 9(1)(h) envisages the appointment of judges as a function reserved for the Assembly. Article 13(1) of the Constitutive Act describes the Executive Council's functions as coordinating and taking decisions in areas of common interest to Member States, ranging from foreign trade to immigration to science and to technology. However, it could be counter-argued that the Assembly may delegate it to the Executive Council pursuant to Article 9(2) of the Constitutive Act. In that case, the Executive Council would directly appoint judges without first electing them. Finally, the Statute does not stipulate whether the Assembly is obliged to accept the election (thus making their appointment a rubber-stamp exercise) or whether it could (wholly or partly) challenge it and, in the latter case, how the procedure will proceed. Admittedly, this is not very likely to happen considering that the Executive Council is made up of the Member States' foreign ministers. However, this is not an excuse for not regulating quite obvious eventualities.

Finally, according to Article 7 of the Statute, the election of judges will require a two-thirds majority of all AU Member States with voting rights. Therefore, until and unless the whole AU membership has ratified the 2008 Protocol, non-contracting parties will vote in a matter which, arguably, is not of direct concern to them. Moreover, they could potentially use their vote to support friendly countries or in exchange of favours and benefits given to them by those contracting parties promoting their nationals to be elected to the ACJHR. Pursuant to Article 10(3), the same procedure will apply in case of vacancies resulting from death, resignation or removal from office. Finally, Article 7(4) stipulates that Africa's regions and its principal juridical traditions (presumably, the civil, Roman-Dutch, common, and Islamic legal systems) must be represented on the ACJHR.

131. In 2010 the AU started discussing adding a third Section to the ACJHR, the 'International Criminal Law Section' (ICL Section). It started with the Assembly calling for a feasibility study to empower the African Court on Human and Peoples' Rights to try international crimes.[595] The determining factors for African states to seek

595. *See* Assembly, *Decision on the Abuse of the Principle of Universal Jurisdiction*, AU Doc. Assembly/AU/Dec. 292 (XV), para. 5 (27 Sept. 2010).

a localized solution to the question of international criminal justice are, on the one hand, Africa's disenchantment with the ICC and the fact that it almost exclusively focuses on the continent[596] and, on the other hand, the controversy over the ICC arrest warrants issued against African dignitaries, including President Al-Bashir of Sudan and the late Colonel Gaddafi.[597] One could brush away this attempt on two grounds. First, despite Article 4(h) of the Constitutive Act, the AU lacks a clear and developed agenda on international criminal justice. Second, the existence of the ICC has made such moves superfluous, because the largest part of the international community (including the majority of African states) have decided that the ICC should be the principal multilateral judicial entity to deal with breaches of war crimes, crimes against humanity, etc. and tasked with fighting impunity. In other words, it is submitted that the choice had already been made to put in place an overarching multilateral institution with the potential to acquire global jurisdiction rather than having regional judicial institutions. Although any regional organization is entitled to have its own criminal justice tribunal (provided that it has been expressly granted the necessary powers to create it), arguably it should have very good reasons to do so and, moreover, it should show to be able to meet the standards set by the ICC.

132. In May 2012 a Draft Protocol on Amendments to the Protocol on the Statute of the ACJHR was produced for consideration by the Assembly.[598] Its purpose was to add the ICL Section and to grant to the ACJHR 'original and appellate jurisdiction' to hear cases referred by, *inter alia*, RECs and other international organizations. The Draft Protocol did not address the following legal technicality. Since the 2008 Protocol setting up the ACJHR had not yet entered into force, amendments to it and to the Statute could not be contemplated before it became operational, since Article 58(2) of the Statute stipulates that proposed amendments will be adopted by the Assembly only '*after* the Court has given its opinion on it' (emphasis added). Arguably, this is another manifestation of the rather careless approach towards the judicial organ. After

596. Generally, *see* K. Magliveras & G. Naldi, 'The International Criminal Court's Involvement with Africa: Evaluation of a Fractious Relationship', *Nordic Journal of International Law* 82 (2013): 417.

597. *See* K. Magliveras & G. Naldi, 'The International Criminal Court and the African Union: A Problematical Relationship' in *The International Criminal Court and Africa*, C. Jelloh & I. Bantekas (eds)(Oxford: Oxford University Press, 2017), 111.

598. *See* Meeting of Government Experts and Ministers of Justice/Attorneys General on Legal Matters, 7–11 and 14–15 May 2012, Addis Ababa, Ethiopia, *Draft Protocol on Amendments to the Protocol on the Statute of the African Court of Justice and Human Rights*, AU Doc. Exp/Min/IV/Rev. 7 (15 May 2012).

further elaboration,[599] the Protocol was approved by the Assembly in June 2014 (the 'Malabo Protocol').[600]

133. The ICL Section is mirrored on the ICC. It will be composed of a Pre-Trial Chamber, a Trial Chamber and an Appellate, or Appeals, Chamber. A novelty is the establishment of a Defence Office to ensure the rights of suspects, the accused and any other person entitled to legal assistance.[601] The Assembly is authorized to establish, within the ACJHR's jurisdiction, a Trust Fund to provide legal aid and assistance to the victims of crimes or human rights violations and their families.[602] The Court may order any kind of property collected through fines or forfeiture to be transferred to the Trust Fund.[603] Decisions of the Pre-Trial Chamber or the Trial Chamber may be appealed to the Appellate Chamber by the Prosecutor or by the accused. Cases will be brought by the Prosecutor, who may initiate investigations *proprio motu*, following a referral by a contracting party, by the Assembly or by the PSC.[604] It is not clear whether crimes committed in the territory of non-contracting parties might be referred to the ICL Section. With regard to jurisdictional competence, contracting parties automatically accept the ICL Section's jurisdiction upon ratification of the Malabo Protocol, while non-contracting parties may do so on an ad hoc basis by means of a declaration. The jurisdiction *ratione materiae* of the ICL Section is far broader than that of the ICC, perhaps overly ambitious. In addition to the core international crimes of aggression,[605] genocide, crimes against humanity and war crimes, its jurisdiction also includes the crime of unconstitutional change of government, mercenarism, piracy, terrorism, corruption, money laundering, drug trafficking, trafficking in persons and the illicit exploitation of natural resources amongst others.[606] Even though addressing this criminal behaviour is a reflection of African concerns and priorities, not all of them are generally categorized as international crimes. Thus, while coups d'état constitute a violation of Article 4(p) of the Constitutive Act, it is rather premature to claim that they are contrary to general international law, provided that they do not negate directly the principle of

599. *See* Assembly, *Decision on the Progress Report of the Commission on the Implementation of the Decisions on the International Criminal Court*, AU Doc. Assembly/AU/Dec. 493 (XXII), para. 13 (31 Jan. 2014).
600. *See* Assembly, *Decision on the Draft Legal Instruments*, AU Doc. Assembly/AU/Dec. 529 (XXIII) (27 Jun. 2014), currently signed by nine Member States with no ratifications. For analysis, *see* G. Naldi & K. Magliveras, 'The African Union's International Criminal Court: An Appraisal', *African Yearbook of International Law* 21 (2015) 297; G. Werle & M. Vormbaum (eds), *The African Criminal Court – A Commentary on the Malabo Protocol* (The Hague: T.M.C. Asser Press, 2016).
601. *See* Arts 19*bis*, 221A, 22B and 22C of the ACJHR Statute, as amended by the Malabo Protocol.
602. Compare the Trust Fund for Victims (TFV) provided for in Art. 79 of the ICC Rome Statute. It became operative in 2007.
603. *See* Art. 46M of the ACJHR Statute, as amended by the Malabo Protocol.
604. *Ibid.*, respectively, Arts 34A(1), 46G, and 29)1)(b).
605. *Ibid.*, Art. 28M defines the crime of aggression.
606. *Ibid.*, Art. 28A.

self-determination.[607] Moreover, although the Convention on Mercenarism in Africa (*supra*, paragraph 28) condemns mercenarism as an international crime, it is unclear whether it is also prohibited under customary international law.

Finally, a number of OAU/AU treaties do require contracting parties to pass legislation designating certain acts and practices as criminal offences, which, arguably, do not amount to international crimes.[608] The question could, therefore, be legitimately posed whether they amount to 'most serious crimes of concern to the international community', at least as understood in Article 5(1) of the Rome Statute. As regards jurisdiction *ratione personae*, the ICL Section will be able to prosecute natural persons but also legal persons, which includes corporations but not states.[609] The inclusion of corporate legal liability is welcome in the era of globalization and in light of the sometimes questionable practices pursued by multinational corporations. Notwithstanding the increasing trend to impose human rights standards on transnational corporations,[610] there are problems given the limited international legal personality recognized to multinational companies.[611] The principle of complementarity, which constitutes the bedrock of the ICC, also applies to the ICL Section.[612] Therefore, it will only have competence when and if the domestic courts of contracting parties are unwilling or unable to prosecute alleged perpetrators.

134. The Malabo Protocol does not contain a savings clause and the important question of the relationship between the ACJHR and the ICC is not addressed. In effect, African contracting parties to both the Rome Statute and the ACJHR Statute as amended by the Malabo Protocol may be faced with the awkward question of conflicting obligations. In line with customary law over incompatibility between successive treaties on the same subject matter, as reflected in Article 30(3) of the Vienna Convention on the Law of Treaties (1969), the ACJHR Statute, when it enters into force, would be

---

607. In *Sir Dawda K. Jawara v. Gambia,* Communication Nos 147/95 and 149/96, 13th *Activity Report 1999–2000*, para. 73; AHRLR (2000) 107, the African Commission on Human and Peoples' Rights relied on the internal dimension of self-determination to uphold democratic values and to condemn military coups. It held that the military coup that overthrew Gambia's democratic system 'was a grave violation of the right of the Gambian people to freely choose their government as entrenched in Art. 20(1) [of the Banjul Charter]'.

608. For example, Art. 9(2) of the OAU Convention on the Ban of the Import of Hazardous Wastes into Africa and on the Control of their Transboundary Movements within Africa (1991), and Art. 5(1) of the AU Convention on Preventing and Combating Corruption (2003).

609. Article 46C of the ACJHR Statute, as amended by the Malabo Protocol.

610. Generally, *see* UN Sub-Commission on the Promotion and Protection of Human Rights, *Norms on the Responsibilities of Transnational Corporations and Other Business Enterprises with Regard to Human Rights*, UN Doc. E/CN.4/Sub.2/2003/12/Rev.2 (2003). The Norms were drafted between 1999 and 2003 and were approved by Res. 2003/16 of the UN Sub-Commission on the Promotion and Protection of Human Rights on 13 Aug. 2003; For analysis, *see* D. Weissbrodt & M. Kruger, 'Norms on the Responsibilities of Transnational Corporations and Other Business Enterprises with Regard to Human Rights', *American Journal International Law* 97 (2003): 901; and D. Kinley & R. Chambers, 'The UN Human Rights Norm for Corporations: The Private Implications of Public International Law', *Human Rights Law Review* 6 (2006): 452.

611. *See* P. Malanczuk, *Akehurst's Modern Introduction to International Law* 7th rev. ed. (Routledge, London, 1997), 100–103.

612. *See* Art. 46H of the ACJHR Statute, as amended by the Malabo Protocol.

deemed to prevail over the Rome Statute. However, if the ICC were to rule that it has jurisdiction over an African situation, as it was conferred by a UN Security Council resolution in accordance with Article 13(b) of the Rome Statute,[613] and a clash arose between an African state's obligations under the ACJHR Statute and a suitable ICC decision, the latter would probably prevail. This argument flows from the wording of Article 103 of the UN Charter.

135. It is a worrisome development that, even though the 2003 Protocol setting up the African Court of Justice entered into force in February 2009, it was never operationalized and, therefore, the wish of the AU membership was not honoured. Due the convoluted manner by which this affair was handled, the AU does not presently have a functionable judicial organ. Moreover, given that Members States have stopped signing the 2008 Protocol (Madagascar was the last to sign it on 31 January 2014) let alone ratify it (Liberia was the last to do so in February 2014), the question could validly be put if the ACJHR will ever become reality. In the meantime, many and complicated legal issues remain unanswered. Even though Article 27 of the Constitutive Act stipulates that, pending the establishment of the African Court of Justice (presumably this provision should now be read 'pending the establishment of the ACJHR'), matters of interpretation arising from the Constitutive Act's application or implementation will be submitted to the Assembly, which shall decide by a two-thirds majority, fifteen years later, the Assembly is unable (and presumably unwilling) to act accordingly. Thus, the Assembly has not assumed its prescribed *quasi*-judicial role.

In the course of 2013, the AU continued its policy to create judicial organs. More specifically, the Twentieth Ordinary Assembly Session took onboard a proposal by the then Tunisian President Marzouki to establish an International Constitutional Court as 'an advisory and jurisdictional body responsible for ensuring the respect and promotion of democratic principles, human rights and the rule of law', ultimately leading to the abolition of dictatorships. The Assembly requested the AUCIL to examine the matter and to address recommendations to its Twenty-Second Ordinary Session in January 2014.[614] Judging from the proposal, one could not see any major differences from the scope and jurisdiction of the African Human Rights Commission and the African Human Rights Court working in unison with the PSC.[615] In the January 2014 Session the proposal was not placed on the Assembly's agenda. Moreover, in January 2014 the Executive Council deplored the fact that, fourteen years after the Protocol setting up the African Human Rights Court (in reality it was sixteen years) was adopted, only twenty-six Member States had ratified it and only seven had filed declarations

---

613. *See* ICC, Pre-Trial Chamber I, *Prosecutor* v. *Omar Hassan Ahmad Al Bashir,* Decision Pursuant to Art. 87(7) of the Rome Statute on the Failure of the Republic of Malawi to Comply with the Cooperation Requests Issued by the Court with respect to the Arrest and Surrender of Omar Hassan Ahmad Al Bashir, Corrigendum, ICC-02/05-01/09, 13 Dec. 2011, para. 36, reproduced in I.L.M. 51 (2012): 393.

614. *See* Assembly, *Decision on the Establishment of an 'International Constitutional Court'*, AU Doc. Assembly/AU/Dec. 458 (XX) (28 Jan. 2013). Marzouki made the same proposal in a speech delivered in the UN General Assembly on 27 Sept. 2012.

615. *See* further, House of Commons, International Courts: Constitutional and Administrative Law: Written question 12816, answered on 29 Oct. 2015, at: http://www.parliament.uk/business/publications/written-questions-answers-statements/written-question/Commons/2015-10-21/12816/.

allowing individuals and NGOs to lodge cases before it.[616] Arguably, this signifies that African states are most willing to establish judicial organs but, at the same time, are unwilling to operationalize them. Until today, there was no follow-up to the Tunisian proposal.

§5. The Commission

136. A Commission is set up under Article 20 of the Constitutive Act. Its structure, functions and regulations were left to be determined by the Assembly. The Commission is composed of a Chairperson, the deputy/ies and the Commissioners. They are assisted by the necessary staff headed by the Chief of Staff. Although the number of Commissioners was not laid down in the Constitutive Act, it was decided to be the following eight: The Commissioner for Political Affairs; the Commissioner for Social Affairs; the Commissioner for Trade and Industry; the Commissioner for Economic Affairs; the Commissioner for Peace and Security; the Commissioner for Infrastructure and Energy; the Commissioner for Human Resources, Science, and Technology; and the Commissioner for Rural Economy and Agriculture. Notwithstanding that Article 20(1) of the Constitutive Act stipulates that the Commission shall be the AU Secretariat, in 2001 the OAU Secretary-General had argued that its operation ought to be different from the OAU Secretariat. In particular, he advocated that the Commission ought to be given the vital mandate and authority to initiate programmes and assist Member States in their implementation as well as to take decisions in order to carry out the Assembly's general directives.[617] It would appear that, on this occasion, the Secretary General's views were taken seriously into account. Thus, Article 3 of the Commission Statutes, which the Assembly approved in July 2002, lays down more than thirty areas of activities. Suffice to mention the following functions: the implementation and the monitoring of the decisions taken by other organs; the elaboration of common African positions on a variety of issues; and acting as the custodian of the Constitutive Act, its protocols and the treaties and legal instruments adopted under OAU/AU auspices.[618]

Article 33(4) of the Constitutive Act stipulates that the OAU Secretariat was to act as the interim AU Secretariat pending the establishment of the Commission. Pursuant to this provision, the First Ordinary Assembly Session resolved to designate the then OAU Secretary-General Amara Essy, the Assistant Secretaries General, and the staff of the OAU Secretariat as the Interim Commission and extended their mandate to July 2003.[619] On 16 September 2003, Alpha Oumar Konare, former President of Mali, was elected as the new Chairperson. He served until early 2008, when the Tenth Ordinary Assembly Session (Addis Ababa, 31 January–2 February 2008) elected, by a two-thirds majority, his successor Jean Ping, the Vice Prime Minister and Minister of Foreign

616. *See* Executive Council, *Decision on the 2013 Activity Report of the African Court on Human and Peoples' Rights*, EX.CL/Dec. 806 (XXIV), para. 10 (28 Jan. 2014).

617. *See* Secretary General, *Report of the Secretary-General on the Implementation of the Sirte Decision on the African Union*, OAU Doc. CM/2210 (LXXIV), para. 27 at p. 11 (2001).

618. *See Statutes of the Commission of the African Union*, AU Doc. ASS/AU/2(I)-d (2002), reproduced in RADIC 13 (2005): 74.

619. *See* Assembly, *Decision on the Interim Period*, AU Doc. ASS/AU/Dec.1 (I) (10 Jul. 2002).

Affairs of Gabon. The same Session elected Erastus Mwenda, a citizen of Kenya and Secretary-General of COMESA, as Deputy Chairperson to replace Patrick Mazimhak from Rwanda.[620] On 16 July 2012, Dr Nkosazana Dlamini-Zuma, a South African minister of state and ex-wife of the South African President Jacob Zuma, was elected as Chairperson, marking the first time that a female person was chosen to hold a post of such significance in the continent.[621] Unlike previous occasions where the decision was a rather rubber-stamp procedure, this was a most contested process: Dlamini-Zuma secured her election against the incumbent Chairperson Jean Ping after three voting rounds and following a deadlocked vote in January 2012(the Summit extended existing Commission members' terms of office until its next ordinary session).[622] Some commentators interpreted this event as showing that finally the AU started functioning as a proper intergovernmental organization. However, it will be submitted that it also showed that Member States continue casting votes according to predetermined patterns (e.g., the Anglophone states voting in favour of their 'own' candidate and against the candidate preferred by the Francophone states) and neglecting which are the AU's best interests. The Twenty-Seventh Ordinary Assembly Session (Kigali, Rwanda, July 2016) ought to have elected the new Chairperson (Dlamini-Zuma did not include herself in the nomination process because she wanted to return to South African politics)[623] but proved to be another thriller as none of the three contenders for the position obtained the required two-thirds majority, after seven rounds of voting. As a result, the Assembly decided to suspend the election and extend the term of office of Commission Members until new elections were held in January 2017, and reopened the nomination process.[624] Five contenders emerged, all experienced in foreign affairs and with a fair representation of women: Pelonomi Venson-Moitoi (Foreign Minister of Botswana), Moussa Faki Mahamat (Foreign Minister of Chad), Agapito Mba Mokuy (Foreign Minister of Equatorial Guinea), Amina Mohamed (Foreign Minister of Kenya), and Bathily Abdoulaye from Senegal (currently the UN special envoy for Central Africa). A Western-style public debate with live broadcast was held on 9 December 2016 among them, while according to rumours a group of (unnamed) Member States were seeking that the second round of the election process to be also deadlocked.[625] On 30 January 2017, a secret ballot cast during the Twenty-Eighth Ordinary Assembly Session elected Moussa Faki as the new Chairperson, ending an impasse which could have obstructed the AU's functioning.

---

620. Assembly, *Decision on Elections of Chairperson and Deputy Chairperson*, AU Doc. Assembly/AU/Dec. 189 (X), and AU Press Release No. 21/2008 (1 Feb. 2008).
621. *See* Assembly, *Decision on Election of the Chairperson of the African Union (AU) Commission*, AU Doc. Assembly/AU/Dec. 445 (XIX) (16 Jul. 2012). Thereafter, Mr Erastus J.O. Mwencha was elected as Deputy Chairperson, *see* AU Doc. Assembly/AU/Dec. 446 (XIX) (16 Jul. 2012).
622. AU Doc. Assembly/AU/Dec. 414 (XVIII).
623. *See* A. Harding, 'Nkosazana Dlamini-Zuma: What Next for African Union boss?', *BBC News*, 30 Jan. 2017, at: http://www.bbc.com/news/world-africa-38795674.
624. *See* Assembly, *Decision on the Election of Members of the Commission*, Assembly/AU/Dec. 610 (XXVII) (18 Jul. 2016).
625. *See* V.S. Makhan, 'Election of the Chairperson of the African Union Commission: The AU at a Crossroads', *Pambazuka News*, 15 Dec. 2016, at: https://www.pambazuka.org/pan-africanism/election-chairperson-african-union-commission-au-crossroads.

137. In 2014, the Commission had 1,444 staff both at Headquarters and regional offices. The principal seat is in Addis Ababa and the Headquarters Agreement between the AU and Ethiopia was signed on 25 April 2008[626] The Commission operates on the basis of the following values: Respect for diversity and team work; 'Think Africa above all'; transparency and accountability; integrity and impartiality; efficiency and professionalism; and information, and knowledge-sharing. It is built around a number of 'Departments', some of which were carried on from the OAU, while others were newly established.[627] Currently it comprises the following twenty-one Departments reporting to the Office of the Chairperson through the Chief of Staff: The Bureau of the Chairperson; the Bureau of the Deputy Chairperson; the Department of Peace and Security; the Department of Political Affairs; the Department of Infrastructure and Energy; the Department of Social Affairs; the Department of Human Resources, Science and Technology; the Department of Trade and Industry; the Department of Rural Economy and Agriculture; the Department of Economic Affairs; the Office of the Secretary to the Commission; the Directorate of Administration and Human Resources Development; the Directorate of Conference Services; the Directorate of Programming, Budgeting, Finance and Accounting; the Directorate of Strategic Policy Planning, Monitoring and Evaluation; the Directorate of Women, Gender and Development; the Office of the Internal Auditor; the Office of the Legal Counsel; the Medical Services Directorate; the Directorate of Information and Communication; and Protocol Services. Moreover, the Commission acts the AU's legal representative in its relations with third states and other international institutions. It maintains offices in New York, Geneva, and Washington, DC, while its Brussels Office acts as the Permanent Mission to the EU and the ACP.[628]

The first ever group of Commissioners was appointed by the Second Ordinary Assembly Session in July 2003. They were (in brackets their country of nationality and portfolio): S. Djinnit (Algeria, Peace and Security); J. Joiner (Gambia, Political Affairs); B. Zoba (Congo, Infrastructure and Energy); P. Gawanas (Namibia, Social Affairs); S. Agrebi (Tunisia, Human Resources); El. Tankeu (Cameroon, Trade and Industry); and R. Kurwijila (Tanzania, Rural Economy and Agriculture).[629] The second group was assigned by the Executive Council at its Fourth Ordinary Session in March 2004, acting under delegation of power by the Assembly: N. Assayed (Libya, Human Resources, Science and Technology); and M. Mkwezalamba (Malawi, Economic Affairs).[630] In this first election process, two things stand out: the majority were women

626. *See* Executive Council, *Criteria for Hosting the AU Organs*, AU Doc. EX/CL. 195 (VII) Rev.1 Annex III, July 2005; the Criteria were endorsed by the Fifth Ordinary Assembly Session in July 2005.

627. *See* Executive Council, *Report of the 3rd Ordinary Session of the Executive Council on the Proposed Structure, Human Resource Requirements and Conditions of Service for the Staff of the Commission of the African Union and their Financial Implications*, AU Doc. EX/CL/39 (III) (8 Jul. 2003).

628. *See* further, African Union Commission and New Zealand Ministry of Foreign Affairs and Trade, *African Union Handbook 2016*, 67 et seq.

629. *See* Assembly, *Decision on Appointment of AU Commissioners*, AU Doc. Assembly/AU/ Dec.28 (II) (4 Jul. 2003).

630. *See* Executive Council, *Decision on Election and Appointment of AU Commissioners*, AU Doc. EX/CL/Dec. 80 (IV) (16 Mar. 2004).

and there were no persons from South Africa, Egypt, and Nigeria, the traditional 'big' African states. On 3 February 2008, the Tenth Ordinary Assembly Session (Addis Ababa, 31 January–2 February 2008) elected the second group of Commissioners. According to portfolio, they were: Peace and Security, Ramtane Lamamra (Algeria); Political Affairs, Julia Dolly Joiner (Gambia); Infrastructure and Energy, Elham Mahmood Ahmed Ibrahim (Egypt); Social Affairs, Bience Philomina Gawanas (Namibia); Human Resources, Science and Technology, Jean Pierre Onvehoun Ezin (Benin); Trade and Industry, Elizabeth Tankeu (Cameroon); and Economic Affairs, Maxwell Mkwezalamba (Malawi).[631] Regarding the Commissioner of Rural Economy and Agriculture, the election was postponed to conform to the AU rules in respect to regional and gender balance. The Assembly authorized the Executive Council to elect and appoint the Commissioner in question.[632] As the Eastern region had not proposed a female commissioner during the election, said post was reserved for a female candidate from that region.[633] During its Eleventh Extraordinary Session (Arusha, 6–7 May 2008) the Executive Council appointed Ms Tumusiime Rhoda Peace.

138. The third group of Commissioners was appointed by the Assembly in July 2012 following the aforementioned contested vote on the election of the Commission Chairperson. Again, it proved impossible to conclude the process during that 2012 Session and for this reason two Commissioners were elected by the Executive Council and appointed by the Assembly during, respectively, the Twenty-Second and the Twentieth Ordinary Session in January 2013. They were: R. Lamamra (Algeria) Peace and Security; A.L. Abdullahi (Nigeria) Political Affairs; Elham Mahmood Ahmed Ibrahim (Egypt) Infrastructure and Energy (for a second term); M.S. Kaloko (Sierra Leone) Social Affairs; F.H. Acyl (Chad) Trade and Industry; and Tumusiime Rhoda Peace (Uganda) Rural Economy and Agriculture (for a second term)[634] as well as M. De-Paul Ikounga (Congo) Human Resources, Science and Technology; and A. Mothae Maruping (Lesotho) Economic Affairs.[635] It is submitted that, even though not envisaged in the Commission Statutes, the Executive Council should forward the names of the proposed Commissioners to the PAP for consideration. Naturally, any PAP comments would not binding but the fact that the organ representing (even indirectly) the peoples of Africa has expressed its opinion would no doubt give more credence to the process and increase its legitimacy.

139. In January 2013, Erastus Mwencha, the then Deputy Chairperson, outlined the Commission's strategic plan for the period between 2014 and 2017. Its overall aims were to improve, to strengthen and to maintain accountability while ensuring

---

631. *See* Assembly, *Decision on Appointment of AU Commissioners*, AU Doc. Assembly/AU/Dec. 190 (X) (2 Feb. 2008) and Executive Council, *Decision on Appointment of AU Commissioners*, AU Doc. EX/CL/Dec. 414 (XII) (29 Jan. 2008).

632. *Ibid.*

633. *See* AU Press Release No. 22/2008 (1 Feb. 2008).

634. *See* Assembly, *Decision on the Appointment of the Commissioners of the African Union*, AU Doc. Assembly/AU/Dec. 447 (XIX) (16 Jul. 2012).

635. *See* Executive Council, *Decision on the Election of the Commissioner for Human African Union*, AU Doc. EX.CL/Dec. 761 (XXII) (25 Jan. 2013) and Assembly, *Decision on the Election of the Commissioner for Human Resources, Science and Technology and the Commissioner for Economic Affairs of the African Union*, AU Doc. Assembly/AU/Dec. 467 (XX) (28 Jan. 2013).

operational efficiency. Moreover, to achieve sustainable financing and to promote synergies with the other AU organs, with the RECs but also with other multilateral institutions (or 'stakeholders' in the AU jargon) such as the African Development Bank and the UN Economic Community for Africa. According to the Deputy Chairperson, the strategic plan was developed pursuant to the SMART model, which has the following attributes: Specific, Measurable, Achievable, Realistic, and Timely.[636] The way the Executive Council addressed the strategic plan during its Twenty-Second Ordinary Session could be described as lukewarm: it requested the Commission 'to closely and continuously engage the Permanent Representatives Committee…in the further development of the Plan'.[637] However, during the same Session the Executive Council revisited the strategic plan when it considered, as a separate agenda item, the Commission's Activity Report for 2012, where it renewed 'its commitment to provide all necessary support to the Commission through the allocation of adequate human and financial resources to enable it to effectively carry out its mandate'. It was agreed to hold an Extraordinary Session in April 2013 at AU Headquarters to consider 'urgent strategic issues', namely the Draft 2014–2017 Strategic Plan of the Commission, the Draft 2063 AU Strategic Framework, the preparations for the OAU/AU fiftieth Anniversary, the question of the proliferation of AU structures and institutions, and the question of the implementation of adopted decisions.[638] It was finally held as the Fourteenth Extraordinary Session on 8 April 2013.

§6. The Permanent Representatives Committee (PRC)

140. According to Article 21 of the Constitutive Act, the PRC is composed of the Member States' permanent representatives or other plenipotentiaries accredited to the AU. The origins of this organ could be traced to the Committee of Ambassadors and other established by the Sixty-First Ordinary Session of the OAU Council of Ministers (Addis Ababa, 23–27 January 1995) as an auxiliary organ mandated with the preparation of Council meetings.[639] Unlike the other AU organs, the Constitutive Act did not stipulate how the PRC's structure, functions and regulations were to be determined. However, in July 2002, during the First Ordinary Assembly Session, the Executive Council adopted its Rules of Procedure presumably under the authority of being the organ to which the RPC is responsible.[640] Considering that the permanent representatives act as agents of their respective countries, it is questionable whether

636. *See* AU Commission, Directorate of Information and Communication, *AU Echo*, Issue 06, 28 Jan. 2013, p. 8.

637. *See* Executive Council, *Decision on the Development of the African Union Commission Strategic Plan 2014-2017*, AU Doc. EX.CL/Dec. 734 (XXII) (25 Jan. 2013).

638. *See* Executive Council, *Decision on Decision on the Activity Report of the Commission*, AU Doc. EX.CL/Dec. 758 (XXII) (25 Jan. 2013).

639. *See* Council of Ministers, *Resolution on the Methodology of the Sessions of the Council of Ministers*, OAU Doc. CM/Res. 1557 (LXI) (27 Jan. 1995).

640. *See* Assembly, *Rules of Procedure of the Permanent Representatives' Committee*, AU Doc. ASS/AU/2 (I)-c (10 Jul. 2002), reproduced in RADIC 13 (2005): 67. There would not appear to be a logical explanation why the Rules were adopted and approved by the Executive Council while the text indicates that they were adopted during a meeting of the Assembly.

the RPC, as an organ, should be regarded as being answerable to the AU as a whole. An associated question is whether the ACJHR, once it becomes operative, will have jurisdiction over the RPC. However, considering that the ACJHR's competence extends only to acts, decisions, regulations and directives issued by AU organs and that Rule 26 of the RPC Rules of Procedure stipulates that its decisions shall be recommendations until adopted by the Executive Council, the conclusion could be reached that they lack any legally binding effect. Consequently, they should not be subjected to judicial review by the ACJHR.

141. A closer examination of Rule 4 of the PRC Rules of Procedure, which sets out its powers and functions, reveals that it acts principally as an organ complimentary to the Executive Council. In particular, it is mandated to prepare its meetings, its agenda and draft decisions, to monitor the implementation of the policies and decisions adopted by the Executive Council (a task for which arguably the Commission could have also been responsible), to make recommendations to the Executive Council on matters relating to administrative, budgetary and financial matters and, generally, to consider any matter assigned to it by the Executive Council. Furthermore, the PRC has been authorized to examine and make recommendations to the Financial Report issued by the Commission as well as to the report prepared by the Board of External Auditors and it may set up sub-committees or working groups as deemed necessary. Finally, as regards functions, which are not directly or indirectly connected to the Executive Council, the PSC has been asked to facilitate communication between the Commission and the capitals of the Member States and to participate in the preparation of the calendar of AU meetings. While all Member States are entitled to be represented on the PRC, it principally functions as a Bureau consisting of a chairperson, three vice-chairpersons and a rapporteur. These positions are occupied by the same Member States sitting on the Assembly Bureau and on the Executive Council Bureau and serve for one-year periods. The PRC meets in ordinary session at least once a month in Addis Ababa, in extraordinary sessions when required, in closed sessions, and reaches decisions by two-thirds majority, failing which by consensus. It has a number of sub-committees, including the Advisory Sub-Committee on Administrative, Budgetary And Financial Matters, the Sub-Committee on Audit Matters, the Sub-Committee on Contributions, the Sub-Committee on Economic And Trade Matters, the Sub-Committee on Headquarters and Host Agreements, the Sub-Committee on Multilateral Cooperation and Strategic Partnerships, the Sub-Committee on Refugees, Returnees and IDPs in Africa, the Policy Sub-Committee of the Special Emergency Assistance Fund for Drought and Famine Relief in Africa, etc.

142. The practice has developed whereby PRC meetings kick off Assembly Sessions. For example, the Twentieth Ordinary Assembly Session, which was held under the theme of 'Pan-Africanism and African Renaissance', commenced on 21 January 2013 with the convening of the Twenty-Fifth Ordinary PRC Session. During the two-day meeting, the PRC members exchanged views, *inter alia*, on specific reports which had been prepared by a number of sub-committees; on the progress report concerning the AUC's draft Strategic Plan 2014–2017; on the report concerning NEPAD; on the Special Emergency Fund for Drought and Famine in Africa; on the Headquarters Agreement with Ethiopia; on the revision of the Commission Rules of Procedure concerning the election of its members; and on various other working documents and draft decisions which had been placed on the agenda of Twenty-Second Ordinary Executive Council Session (24 and 25 January 2013). In order to show the extent to which the resolutions adopted by the Executive Council in January 2013 had already been negotiated at PRC level (a fact indicating that a lot of work takes place behind closed doors during PRC meetings), only the following decisions had not been discussed at PRC level: those dealing with matters concerning the Commission, with reports submitted by various ministerial conferences, by the African Human Rights Commission and by the African Human Rights Court, and those concerning the election of members of various AU organs.

§7. The Economic, Social and Cultural Council (ECOSOCC)

143. Article 22 of the Constitutive Act creates ECOSOCC, which bears more than a simple resemblance to the European Economic and Social Committee, one of the advisory organs operating in the EU, which describes itself as 'a bridge between Europe and organised civil society'. ECOSOCC is an advisory organ composed of different social and professional groups active in Member States. It facilitates the principle stated in the third indent of Article 4 of the Constitutive Act, namely the participation of African people and the civic society at large in all AU activities. It should be noted that Articles 90 and 91 of the AEC Treaty provide for the establishment of consultative mechanisms between, on the one hand, the AEC and, on the other hand, African NGOs and socio-economic organizations and associations. The purpose of these mechanisms is to encourage and ensure their involvement in the integration process while allowing the AEC to mobilize their technical and financial support. To that extent, the OAU Secretary-General had suggested that ECOSOCC could also double as the consultative mechanism envisaged in the AEC Treaty and urged Member States to reconsider its structure, format and other procedural questions.[641] His remarks reinforce the submission made in this monograph, namely that the urgency with which the Constitutive Act was adopted did not allow for a proper and in-depth analysis of the consequences of having a complicated institutional architecture.

144. Although the Assembly was empowered to determine the functions, powers, composition, and organization of ECOSOCC, it delegated this authority to the Executive Council. In May 2003, the draft Statutes of ECOSOCC were presented.[642] At its Third Ordinary Session (Maputo, Mozambique, 4–12 July 2003), the Executive Council requested the Commission Chairperson to submit revised draft Statutes before its Fourth Ordinary Session in March 2004.[643] With considerable delay, the Statutes were adopted in 2005.[644] According to Articles 3 and 4 thereof, ECOSOCC is composed of the following entities: social groups representing women, children, disabled persons,

641. *See* Secretary General, *Report of the Secretary-General on the Implementation of the Sirte Decision on the African Union*, OAU Doc. CM/2210 (LXXIV), paras 30 and 31 at p. 12 (2001).

642. *See Draft Statutes of the Economic, Social and Cultural Council of the African Union*, AU Doc. Exp/Draft/ECOSOCC Statutes/Rev. 2 (14 May 2003).

643. *See* Executive Council, *Decision on the Report of the Interim Chairperson on the Operationalization of ECOSOCC*, EX/CL/Dec. 21 (III) (8 Jul. 2003).

644. At: http://au.int/en/documents/30971/statutes-economic-social-and-cultural-council-au-ecosocc.

etc.; professional groups such as associations of artists, engineers, teachers, lawyers, chambers of commerce, etc.; NGOs; organizations of workers and employers; and religious and cultural organizations. The maximum number of participating Civil Society Organizations (CSOs) has been set at 150. Each Member State shall be represented by two organizations, whereas the remaining shall be allocated to the African Diaspora (twenty), to organizations operating at regional level (ten) and at continental level (eight), and, finally, six organizations will participate in an ex officio capacity. Articles 5 and 6 of the Statutes lay down the modalities and the specific eligibility for ECOSOCC members to be elected. The term in office runs for four years and members are entitled to re-election only once. As far as the functions of ECOSOCC are concerned, Article 7 of the Statutes stipulates, *inter alia*, the following: to contribute, through advise, to the effective translation of the AU objectives, principles, and policies into concrete programmes and the evaluation thereof; to undertake studies recommended by other AU organs and submit recommendations accordingly; to contribute to the promotion of popular participation, sharing of best practices and expertise, and to the realization of the AU vision and objectives; to contribute to the promotion of human rights, the rule of law, good governance, democratic principles, gender equality and child rights; to promote and support the efforts undertaken by institutions engaged in reviewing the future of Africa and forging Pan-African values; and, finally, to foster and consolidate partnership between the AU and CSOs through effective public enlightenment, mobilization and feedback on AU activities.

145. Unlike the other AU organs which are unitary, that is, they are not made up by separate entities, ECOSOCC has its own institutional architecture and is composed of a General Assembly, a Standing Committee, Sectoral Cluster Committees, and a Credentials Committee. The Assembly has adopted its own Rules of Procedure. There is also a Secretariat, which is located at the AU Headquarters in Addis Ababa. The General Assembly is the highest decision and policy-making body. All ECOSOCC members participate in it. It meets once every two years in general session and has been entrusted with the following tasks and duties: electing the eighteen members of the Standing Committee for a term of two years and overseeing its work; electing a Bureau composed of a Presiding Officer and five Deputy Presiding Officers for two years on the basis of equitable geographical distribution and rotation, including one from the Africa Diaspora; preparing and submitting advisory opinions and reports (including reports on the AU budget); and approving the Code of Ethics and Conduct for the CSOs affiliated to or working with the AU.

The role of the Standing Committee is to run ECOSOCC in-between sessions of the General Assembly. It consists of the Presiding Officer and the other members of the Bureau, the Chairpersons of the ten Sectoral Cluster Committees as well as of two representatives of the AUC. Its functions are auxiliary to those of the General Assembly and include coordinating ECOSOCC work; preparing and submitting annual reports to the Assembly; and determining the criteria and the modalities for granting observer status to ECOSOCC. The Sectoral Cluster Committees operate as the key mechanisms of ECOSOCC in formulating opinions and offering input in AU policies, programmes, and activities. To that end, the subject matter of the ten Clusters mirror the main areas of work of the AU and the Directorates at the Commission, for example, Peace and Security; Political Affairs (including human rights; rule of law, democratic and constitutional rule; and humanitarian assistance); Infrastructure and Energy; Social Affairs and Health; Trade and Industry; Rural Economy and Agriculture; Women and Gender, etc. Finally, the Credentials Committee is composed of representatives of the CSOs from each of Africa's five regions and the African Diaspora, one nominated representative for special interest groups (e.g., vulnerable groups, the aged, the physically challenged, and people living with HIV/AIDS) and two representatives of the Commission.

146. The process towards operationalizing the General Assembly by electing its first members proved lengthy. The role of the Credentials Committee was instrumental in completing the procedure for the General Assembly.[645] Although ECOSOCC was officially launched in Dar-es-Salam, Tanzania, in September 2008,[646] and the first meeting of its General Assembly was held in December 2008,[647] not all components and necessary instruments were promptly completed and adopted, revealing a degree of ineffectiveness on behalf of the AU, quite problematic considering that it represents a whole continent.[648] The elections for the Second ECOSOCC General Assembly took place in December 2014.[649] For Financial Year 2013, ECOSOCC was allocated USD 1,015,372 from the AU budget. For purposes of comparison, USD 972,336 was allocated to the Advisory Board on Corruption, USD 587,275 to AUCIL, and USD 10,492,998 to PAP. Interestingly enough, ECOSOCC was the only organ which in the 2013 budget did not receive any funds secured from the so-called international partners,[650] and it still does not receive funding from them. In Financial Year 2014, ECOSOCC saw its funding curtailed (down to USD 993,710), while other organs will see their funding augmented significantly, e.g., the Advisory Board on Corruption (increased to USD 1,507,857) and the PAP (increased to USD 14,292,124).[651] For Financial Year 2017, ECOSOCC's funding will slightly increase to USD 1,119,557 but it pales compared to the Advisory Board on Corruption which will see its funding go up to USD 2,396,246. Even though there is some merit in the argument that ECOSOCC's functions could also be performed by other organs, this should not be regarded as a reason for not investing in it. The submission made in the present monograph, namely that the AU's institutional architecture was not properly thought of, was overly ambitious and still remains unsustainable, applies even more so to ECOSOCC. Unless and until the AU

---

645. *See* Executive Council, *Decision on the Report on the Interim Standing Committee of the Economic, Social and Cultural Council (ECOSOCC)*, AU Doc. EX.CL/Dec. 384 (XII) (29 Jan. 2008).
646. *See* Executive Council, *Decision on the Economic, Social and Cultural Council (ECOSOCC)*, AU Doc. EX.CL/Dec. 477 (XIV) (30 Jan. 2009).
647. *See* Executive Council, *Decision on the Economic, Social and Cultural Council (ECOSOCC)*, AU Doc. EX.CL/Dec. 508 (XV) Rev.1 (1 Jul. 2009).
648. Compare Executive Council, *Decision on the Economic, Social and Cultural Council (ECOSOCC)*, AU Doc. EX.CL/Dec. 633 (XVIII) (28 Jan. 2011) and *Decision on the Economic, Social and Cultural Council (ECOSOCC)*, EX.CL/Dec. 656 (XIX) (28 Jun. 2011).
649. For the results, *see* https://au.int/web/sites/default/files/newsevents/workingdocuments/27443-wd-members_of_2nd_general_assembly_of_ecosocc_kenya_december_2014.pdf.
650. *See* Executive Council, *Decision on the Budget of the African Union for the 2013 Financial Year*, AU Doc. EX.CL/ Dec. 696 (XXI) (13 Jul. 2012).
651. *See* Executive Council, *Decision on the Budget of the African Union for the 2014 Financial Year*, AU Doc. EX.CL/ Dec. 767 (XXIII) (23 May 2013).

commences a soul-searching exercise regarding its institutional set up and its Member States realize that they cannot afford to finance all organs, the AU should not treat organs in a discriminatory fashion. It would not be unthinkable to expcct that the Second ECOSOCC General Assembly would strive to achieve a better position in the constellation of AU organs. However, the following extract from the Statement by the Presiding Officer of the Second General Assembly on the occasion of its inauguration is rather apocalyptic that it is not going to happen:

> As members of the wider African Union family we would normally require parity of treatment with our esteemed colleagues in other commensurate organs in defense of the dignity of the African Civil society community but this 2nd ECOSOCC General Assembly will serve the interests of the wider African people and commit itself to the development and integration project of the African continent.[652]

§8. The Financial Institutions

147. Article 19 of the Constitutive Act establishes three financial institutions: the African Central Bank (it was also envisaged in the final stage of creating the AEC), the AMF, and the AIB.[653] The Constitutive Act has neither laid down their aims and purposes nor guiding principles for their operation leaving everything to be defined in future protocols. As has been argued elsewhere in this monograph, the lack of even setting out the basic regulatory aspects for these and other organs should question the seriousness of the AU's founding fathers to achieve their lofty promises. Despite calls to set them up (e.g., during the Extraordinary Executive Council Session in May 2008), the Protocol on the AIB was adopted in February 2009 and the Protocol on the AMF in June 2014. Neither has entered into force. The Protocol on the African Central Bank has apparently not been negotiated because it presupposes an up and running AMF.

I. The African Investment Bank (AIB)

148. The Protocol establishing the AIB was adopted by the Twelfth Ordinary Assembly Session on 4 February 2009.[654] A Statute containing the substantive provisions for the AIB's operations has been appended to the Protocol. Both will enter into force

652. At: https://www.auecosocc.org/resources.
653. These institutions should not be confused with the African Development Bank, which is a multilateral financial institution set up in 1964. Its current membership comprises all African states as well as twenty-six states from the Americas, Europe and Asia (the so-called non-regional Members).
654. *See* Assembly, *Decision on the Protocol on the Establishment of the African Investment Bank*, AU Doc. Assembly AU/Dec. 212 (XII) (3 Feb. 2009).

on the same day.[655] According to Article 3 of the Protocol, the purpose of the AIB is to foster economic integration and development through investments in development projects in line with AU objectives. Article 4 lays down its four functions, which concern both the public and the private sectors. First, to offer financing in accordance with banking principles. Second, to advance regional economic integration among contracting parties. Third, to support the strengthening of private sector activities. Fourth, to assist the modernization of the rural sector in low-income contracting parties. Article 5 stipulates that its seat will be in Tripoli, Libya. This was in line with the policy pursued by the late Colonel Gaddafi to use his country's wealth to house the headquarters of various AU organs in Libya and, at the same time, to employ this policy as a vehicle to augment his stature within the AU. If the OAU and the AU over many years had one single paymaster this was without any doubt Gaddafi. However, given the precarious political and economic situation in Libya since the uprising of February 2011 and the disintegration of the country, it is highly unlikely that these commitments could be met.

149. Article 7 of the Protocol envisages the procedure for the AIB's dissolution; it involves a recommendation by the plenary organ, the General Assembly of shareholders, and a discretionary decision by the AU Assembly, which will also determine the terms and the conditions of the dissolution. While the Protocol does not envisage withdrawal, Article 16 of the Statute provides that 'Any member may withdraw from the Bank at any time by delivering a notice in writing to the Bank at its Headquarters.' Withdrawal will become effective and, consequently, membership will cease at least six months after the notification was lodged. Until that time, the withdrawing contracting party will remain liable for all direct and contingent obligations to the AIB. The Statute does not explain how these obligations will be honoured. As has been noted when examining withdrawal from the AU, it is a perennial issue to ensure that withdrawing Members fulfil all their duties and obligations before it becomes effective. Article 18 of the Statute contains provisions on the settlement of accounts with shareholders having ceased to be Members: the remaining contracting parties will purchase the former Members' shares. It is submitted that the Statute could have envisaged that, before such purchase takes place, the AIB will set off any sums owed by the former Members with the shares they hold, a scenario offering two possibilities. First, the AIB would get ownership in a number of shares enough to cover the sums owed to it and subsequently sell them to other Members (possibly at a discount) and recover the sums owed. Second, the sale and purchase of shares would go ahead but the Members acquiring them would not pay directly to the former Member their whole value but only what remains after subtracting the sums owed to the AIB.

The fact that the Statute, on the one hand, stipulates the dissolution of the AIB and, on the other hand, allows contracting parties to withdraw should be considered problematic. And this because the AIB (as well as the other two Financial Institutions), pursuant to Article 5(1) in conjunction with Article 19 of the Constitutive Act, are principal AU organs. To put it otherwise, the AIB is *not* an organ that the Assembly

655. According to Art. 9(1), the Protocol is open only to AU Member States. Fifteen ratifications are required to enter into force. At the time of writing, only five instruments of ratification had been deposited (the first three being those of Libya, Congo and Benin) and twenty-two Member States had signed it.

has decided to establish in accordance with the power vested in it under Article 5(2) of the Constitutive Act. It follows that the decision to dissolve it would be tantamount to dissolving any other principal AU organ through a mere Assembly resolution. This is not in line with the law of international organizations prescribing that the dissolution of principal organs (as opposed to terminating subsidiary or auxiliary organs) must follow the procedure for amending or revising the founding instrument, in casu Article 32 of the Constitutive Act. Moreover, it dictates that Member States are not to withdraw at wish from only one organ but only from the international organization as a whole. Thus, it would be possible for a Member State to withdraw from the AU but continue participating in the AIB. Although the Protocol and Statute treat the AIB as a separate institution possessing full international personality (Article 23 of the Statute), in reality it does not have this status but remains an AU principal organ. Thus, from a legal point of view, the AIB is not identical or equal to e.g., the International Bank for Reconstruction and Development (IBRD) or the International Monetary Fund (IMF), which, although part of the UN family as Specialized Agencies, were established as autonomous international institutions and where UN Member States do not have an entitlement to membership.[656] Arguably, this problematic state of affairs is the direct result of completing the AU's institutional architecture in multiple stages.

150. Article 6 of the Statute envisages two separate types of membership, even though the Protocol does not mention it. The first (Article 6(1)) comprises only states and, in particular, those AU Member States, which have resolved to become contracting parties to the Protocol. As has already been argued, their participation in the Protocols to the Constitutive Act setting up AU organs ought to be obligatory and not discretionary. The second (Article 6(2)) comprises considerably different shareholders: (a) public financial institutions incorporated in the territory of contracting parties; (b) nationals or legal entities registered in contracting parties with 51% of the capital owned by nationals of the relevant contracting party, as well as the African Diaspora; and (c) financial institutions established in the context of RECs.[657] The division in two types of membership is reflected in the capital of the AIB (the authorized initial capital was set at the rather high amount of USD 25 billion to be divided into 2.5 million shares with a par value of USD 10,000 each.) Thus, according to Article 7 section 2(3) of the Statute, contracting parties will subscribe to 'A' shares, which will represent at least 75% of total capital stock,[658] while all other Members will subscribe to 'B' shares, not to exceed 25% of total capital stock. Strangely enough, the Statute does not stipulate how the 'other Members' will accede to the AIB. The only relevant provisions are

---

656. According to Art. II(2) of the IBRD Articles of Agreement, 'Membership shall be open to other members of the [IMF], at such times and in accordance with such terms as may be prescribed by the Bank'; Art. II(2) of the IMF Articles of Agreement is similar: 'Membership shall be open to other countries at such times and in accordance with such terms as may be prescribed by the Board of Governors.'

657. It would appear that no such institutions are currently operating in RECs. Indeed, investment is not an area where RECs have primary but only incidental competence. *See* , *inter alia*, the SADC Protocol on Finance and Investment, which was adopted in August 2006 and entered into force in April 2010.

658. For the individual Member States' subscriptions to the authorized capital stock and the corresponding voting power, *see* , respectively, Annex A and Annex B of the Statute.

Article 7 section 2(4) providing that the number of 'B' shares will be determined by the AU Assembly and Article 7 section 2B(1) reading: 'Entities as referred under Article 6(2) eligible for membership shall subscribe to "B" shares.' Finally, Article 13 section 1(2) on the powers and functions of the General Assembly, reads '... (g) Decide on the admission of new members and conditions of this admission, as provided in Article 5 of this Statute'.[659] While the reference to 'Article 5' is obviously a typing error (the relevant provision is Article 6), it does not elaborate on how the first 'other Members' envisaged in Article 6(2) will join.

151. One of the General Assembly's powers will be to elect the members of the Board of Directors, which together with the President, complete the AIB's institutional structure. Like all other decisions, it will require a double majority of shares and shareholders, with the majority of shares prevailing in the event of a tie. The AIB President, who will be appointed by the General Assembly, is designated as the Chief Executive and Legal Representative (Article 13 section 3(1) of the Statute). There exists a considerable degree of delegation of powers between these three organs. However, the way it has been stipulated is rather problematic. In particular, according to Article 13 section (1) paragraph 3, the General Assembly is empowered to delegate all or some of its powers to the Board as necessary 'with the exception of those listed in paragraph 2 of this section'. Considering that it is exactly paragraph 2 that lays down the General Assembly's powers, it is unclear which powers may be delegated. In its turn, the Board is entitled, pursuant to Article 13 section (2) paragraph 7, to delegate its own powers to the AIB President, with the exception of the power to elect its own Chairperson. As most of the Board of Directors' powers are of a sensitive nature (e.g., deciding on loans 'granting, preparing the General Assembly sessions, approving the AIB's annual budget, etc.), arguably they should not be delegated to the President, whose role is quite different.

152. A broad reading of Article 13 leads to the conclusion that it might be possible for the President to carry out those General Assembly's powers delegated to the Board of Directors, in effect a succession of handing over powers. Article 17 of the Statute, the clause on suspension of Members failing to fulfil their obligations, offers an illustration. The General Assembly has the discretion to order suspension (the Statute does not lay down which are the precise obligations that failure to meet them could lead to suspension). One year later, the participation of the suspended Member will automatically cease unless the General Assembly decides to restore it to good standing. Taking into account that the power to suspend and to restore to good standing is not envisaged in Article 13 section (1) paragraph 2, the General Assembly may delegate either or both powers to the Board of Directors. But it is a basic rule of the law of international organizations that decisions on membership issues should always be adopted by the highest-ranking organ, in casu the General Assembly.

There are further problematic aspects of Article 17. Thus it creates a mechanism for imposing sanctions on recalcitrant Member States without linking it up with the general provision on punitive measures laid down in the aforementioned Article 23(2) of the Constitutive Act. In effect, Article 17 should be considered as *lex specialis*.

659. According of Art. 13 of the Statute, the General Assembly will consist of the shareholders, namely the Members irrespective of whether they are states, individuals or companies, or their representatives.

Moreover, if suspension was ordered under Article 17, no further sanctions may be imposed under Article 23(2), as this would violate the double jeopardy/*ne bis in idem* rule. Furthermore, Article 17(3) allows suspended Members to withdraw from the AIB. Notwithstanding the arguments advanced above why withdrawal from the AIB is inappropriate, it is rather awkward to offer recalcitrant Members the opportunity to 'save face' and withdraw. While they will lose access to AIB services and benefits, governments could use secession for purposes of domestic consumption and conveniently blame it on AIB tactics and behaviour.

II. The African Monetary Fund (AMF)

153. In June 2014, the Assembly adopted the Protocol and Statute on the AMF.[660] These texts had already been approved by the Specialised Technical Committee (STC) on Justice and Legal Affairs, which had met in May 2014 at the level of Experts and then at the level of Ministers of Justice and Attorneys Generals.[661] The text of the Protocol is almost identical to AIB Protocol and the issues concerning dissolution, withdrawal, and suspension of membership are treated in the same way. To avoid unnecessary repetitions, the arguments advanced above apply, *mutatis mutandis*, here as well. The Statute has drawn rather heavily from the Articles of Agreement of the Arab Monetary Fund concluded in April 1976.[662] Unlike the AMF, the Arab Monetary Fund is an independent international financial institution and only affiliated to the League of Arab States. The AMF will not be the first African experiment in regional monetary issues: the West African Monetary Institute was established in Accra, Ghana, in January 2001 and became operational two months later.[663]

The AMF Headquarters will be in Yaoundé, the capital of Cameroon. According to Article 3 of the Protocol, its purpose is to foster macroeconomic stability, sustainable shared economic growth, and balanced development in the continent to facilitate the effective integration of African economies. The objectives, laid down in Article 2 of the Statute, are quite ambitious and include: correcting disequilibria in contracting parties' balances of payments; ensuring stability of exchange rates among their currencies and mutual convertibility; promoting African monetary cooperation to facilitate economic integration and economic development; assisting contracting parties to design and implement debt management policies; promoting African financial markets and the settlement of commercial debts; and establishing a clearing system for trade transactions. These objectives will be fulfilled through the following functions and activities: enabling trade; encouraging capital flows; providing short-term and medium-

660. *See* Assembly, *Decision on the Protocol and the Statute for the Establishment of the African Monetary Fund*, AU Doc. Assembly/AU/Dec. 517 (XXIII) (27 Jun. 2014), reproduced in 54 I.L.M. 507 (2015).

661. *See* Executive Council, *The Report, the Draft Legal Instruments and Recommendations of the Specialized Technical Committee on Justice and Legal Affairs*, AU Doc. EX.CL/846 (XXV) (2014), at: https://www.justsecurity.org/wp-content/uploads/2014/07/Legal-Instruments-Adopted-in-Malabo-July-2014.pdf.

662. At: http://www.amf.org.ae.

663. For further information, *see* http://www.wami-imao.org/.

term credit facilities to sustain balances of payments; offering technical assistance and policy advice; cooperating with other international financial institutions, and conducting periodic consultations with contracting parties on economic policies.

Unlike the AIB, Article 4 of the Statute restricts membership to those AU Member States which have ratified the Protocol. Yet, like the AIB, there is considerable reluctance among Member States to become parties; at the time of writing, only seven have signed and none has ratified it.[664] It is rather difficult to explain why even Cameroon has not yet signed it. When a delegation from the AUC visited the country in November 2014, it made it clear that since the AMF will be headquartered in Yaoundé prompt ratification could set the pace for others Member States to follow.[665] As not only fifteen ratifications are required but also 25% of the minimum paid up capital must have been deposited to become operationalized, any prognosis on when this might happen is bound to be unreliable. For this reason, any discussion to which extent the AMF could or would weaken the IMF position and role in Africa is premature. At the same time, one should entertain the thought whether the AMF's operationalization could be hastened if it were to act as the IMF's African arm.[666]

Pursuant to Article 28, any disputes concerning the Statute's interpretation or application shall be resolved amicably within a time limit of one year, failing which they may be referred to the AU Court of Justice. But since, as explained above, this organ has never been operationalized (wrongly Article 28 mentions that it has not been established), any unresolved disputes are to be submitted to the Assembly, whose determination will require a two-thirds majority. Article 28 does not explain if these are to be only interstate disputes and/or also disputes between the AMF and contracting parties.

The authorized (i.e., the maximum) share capital shall be USD 22.640 billion, denominated in shares of USD 100 each. The capital subscription calculation for each of the contracting states is envisaged in Annex 2 of the Statute. It will be determined taking into account their GDP and population and using a mathematical formula. The subscription to the capital given as a percentage is also the number of voting rights that each party will have, the total being 500,000 voting rights. South Sudan will have the smallest capital subscription (0.57%) resulting in 2,829.81 voting rights while the Republic of South Africa shall the most voting rights (40,249.06) by subscribing to 8.05% of the capital. The majority of parties will subscribe to less than 1.5% of the capital but South Africa, Nigeria, Egypt and Algeria will hold between them more than 25% of the voting rights, which, as will be explained, effectively gives them the opportunity to run the AMF according to their wishes.

154. Institutionally, the AMF will comprise a Board of Governors, a Board of Directors, and a Managing Director. As regards the former, according to section 1 of Article 10 of the Statute, each party will be represented by a Governor or alternate

664. *See* http://www.au.int/en/sites/default/files/treaties/7805-sl-protocol_on_the_establishment_of_the_african_monetary_fund_8.pdf.

665. *See* G. Bainkong, 'Cameroon: AU Campaigns for Ratification of African Monetary Fund Statutes', *all Africa*, 19 Nov. 2014, at: http://allafrica.com/stories/201411190492.html.

666. Compare International Monetary Fund, *On the IMF's Role and Activities in Af*rica, Speech by Thomas C. Dawson, Director of External Relations, 28 Apr. 2013, at: https://www.imf.org/en/News/Articles/2015/09/28/04/53/sp042803.

Governor, who has to be the Finance Minister or the Central Bank Governor. Its mandate is to oversee the AMF. It will meet at least once every year and will have the 'highest executive powers'. These include confirming the members of the Board of Directors; to appoint the Managing Director, who must have the nationality of a contracting party but not be a member of either Boards; and to admit new members, also determining the conditions of their admission. This is a rather curious provision because the aforementioned Article 4 stipulates that, upon ratification of the Protocol, participation in the AMF is automatic. Indeed, it could not have been otherwise because the AMF is a principal AU organ and all Member States have a right to join it.

According to section 2 of Article 10 of the Statute, the Board of Directors will be composed of the Managing Director, the Permanent Members, five Substantive Directors, one for each region of Africa, and five Alternate Directors, again one per region.[667] It shall meet at least once every quarter. Under section 3 thereof, only those parties having at least 4% of voting rights shall be allowed to hold a permanent seat. But given the mathematical formula in Annex 2, there will be only four parties able to become permanent Members (clearly an unacceptable small number). However, it is submitted that, if the threshold was lowered to 2.3% of voting rights, six more states would be entitled to permanent seats, a total of ten (a more acceptable number). Moreover, it would appear that there is a possibility which the drafters did not take into consideration: that none of the first fifteen states to ratify the Protocol will have at least 4% of voting rights, in which case there would be no permanent seats in the Board of Directors, a situation which could affect the taking of decisions. But as this is a matter to be addressed in the AMF Rules and Regulations, which will be adopted when it becomes operationalized, no answer can be given at this stage. The Board of Directors will be responsible for adopting the Code of Conduct; take decisions on lending conditions and borrowing terms; approve the annual report; approve the conclusion of cooperation agreements with other similar international institutions; and approve the annual operating budget.

The Managing Director, whose role is to administer the AMF, is also its Chief Executive and legal representative. He is assisted by several Deputy Managing Directors to whom all or part of his duties may be delegated. He is entitled to attend the Board of Governors meetings, to anticipate in the deliberations but not to vote. His main duties are laid down in section 3 of Article 10 of the Statute: recruit, appoint and discipline AMF staff; implement the Statute and the Boards of Governors and Directors' decisions; prepare the annual budget; sign agreements on behalf of the AMF; and carry out those duties assigned by the Board of Governors. Article 11 of the Statute stipulates that the Code of Conduct concerns the Managing Director and the staff, who promise that while performing their duties they shall neither accept nor receive instructions from governments or other authorities (presumably the central banks of contracting parties). Equally, parties undertake to respect the 'exclusive nature of the responsibilities' of the Managing Director and staff and refrain from even seeking to influence them. Should the Managing Director fail to comply with his duties and obligations, the Board of Governors will establish an ad hoc Committee to recommend what action be taken.

667. These are geographical regions defined in OAU Council of Ministers Resolution CM/Res. 464 (XXVI), adopted in March 1976.

Other procedures are envisaged when a Deputy Managing Director or staff are found to be in breach of obligations.

If a contracting party were to violate any of the obligations towards the AMF, the Board of Governors may suspend both its voting rights and borrowing rights. Article 13(2) of the Statute stipulates that this organ will determine the conditions for suspension, while Article 14(2) provides that the suspended party shall remain liable for any outstanding loans extended by the AMF and for any other commitments towards it. Finally, the Board of Directors is entitled under Article 15 to temporally suspend the extension or release new or existing credit facilities to any contracting party until 'outstanding issues have been resolved', while Article 16 permits the Board of Governors to terminate the operations of the AMF but its resolution must be 'duly adopted by the Assembly of the Union'.

§9. The Peace and Security Council (PSC)

155. The idea of establishing a pan-African entity to deal with security issues and breaches of the peace had been debated for many years in the OAU. However, it was never set up as most Member States were not in favour fearing that it would encroach upon their sacred sovereignty.[668] When the Central Organ of the OAU Mechanism for Conflict Prevention, Management, and Resolution was created in 1993 under the Cairo Declaration,[669] the discussion was apparently abandoned. However, with the advent of the AU it was decided to institutionalize the ad hoc operations of the Central Organ and to incorporate it into the new Organization by turning it into a proper organ pursuant to Article 5(2) of the Constitutive Act; it stipulates that the Assembly has the power to create new organs. Thus, on 9 July 2002, the First Ordinary Assembly Session adopted the Protocol establishing the PSC, whose entry into force required ratification by the majority of Member States.[670] It swiftly came into effect on 26 December 2003 and, pursuant to Article 22 thereof, it replaced the 1993 Cairo Declaration and superseded the OAU instruments relating to the Conflict Prevention Mechanism and in conflict with the Protocol. To that extent the PSC, whose First Session took place on 16 March 2004, should be considered as the successor to the Mechanism. At the time of writing, there were still five Member States which have not ratified the Protocol (CAR, Cape Verde, DRC, Liberia, and South Sudan). Somalia was the last to submit its instrument of ratification on Christmas Eve of 2013. Finally, pursuant to the Protocol of Amendments to the Constitutive Act of 2003, which, as has been explained, has not yet entered into force, the PSC has been included as one of the main AU organs.

---

668. *See* OAU Secretary General, *Report of the Secretary-General on Conflicts in Africa*, OAU Doc. CM/1710 (LVI), June 1992, reproduced in RADIC 4 (1992): 1072, 1076–1077.

669. At: http://www.dipublico.org/100609/oau-declaration-on-a-mechanism-for-conflict-prevention-management-and-resolution-cairo-declaration/.

670. The Protocol is reproduced in RADIC 13 (2005): 96. The PSC Rules of Procedure were adopted by the Executive Council on behalf of the Assembly in March 2004, *see* Executive Council, *Decision on the Operationalization of the Peace and Security Council*, AU Doc. EX/ CL/Dec. 79 (IV) (16 Mar. 2004).

156. As regards the relationship between the PSC and the contracting parties to the 2002 Protocol, this is based on the notion of agency. In particular, Article 7(2) thereof stipulate: 'The Member States agree that in carrying out its duties under the present Protocol, the PSC acts on their behalf.' This provision echoes Article 24(1) of the UN Charter, which provides that the Member States agree that any action taken by the Security Council when performing its duties, pursuant to the duty to maintain international peace and security, shall be considered to have been on their behalf.

However, there is a difference between the two provisions: While Article 24(1) was based on the premise that UN Member States had conferred the primary responsibility to preserve peace and security specifically to the Security Council, the same is not true as regards the PSC. Three reasons justify this conclusion. First, the PSC was not envisaged as an AU original organ and still remains an Assembly created body. Second, in view of this fact, the functions relating to what is generally referred to as 'peace and security' were initially given to the Assembly, as revealed by Article 9(1)(g) of the Constitutive Act which allows the Assembly to give instructions to the Executive Council 'on the management of conflicts, war and other emergency situations and the restoration of peace'. The inference is that the Assembly enjoys original powers in this area, which it may delegate to the Executive Council. Although practice shows that this aspect of the Executive Council's mandate is now completely entrusted to the PSC, it is submitted that the principal responsibility as regards 'peace and security' still rests with the Assembly, which in any given case could take the necessary measures to address the situation. Third, the description of the PSC in Article 2(1) of the Protocol as 'a standing decision-making organ for the prevention, management and resolution of conflicts' does not alter the previous arguments. In conclusion, the notion of agency has different legal foundations in the UN Security Council and in the PSC. Notwithstanding these considerations, the consistent practice of the Assembly, as the highest-ranking organ representing all Member States and having a general mandate to act, is that when the PSC takes measures, especially of a punitive nature, it acts on behalf of the entire membership. Indeed, it would appear that in the thirteen years that the PSC has been active the Assembly has never objected or criticized its actions.

157. Although the 2002 Protocol does not expressly lay down that the PSC should be regarded as a regional arrangement in the maintenance of international peace and security within the meaning of Chapter VIII of the UN Charter,[671] this derives both from the Preamble and several provisions, including Article 17(1) which stipulates that the PSC shall cooperate and work closely with the UN Security Council. To that end, representatives from the two entities met in Addis Ababa on 17 June 2007 in the context of implementing the ten-year capacity-building programme, which had been concluded between the UN Secretariat and the AUC. At the end of the session, an MoU was signed committing them to the development of a stronger and more structured relationship on conflict prevention, management and resolution, peacekeeping and peace-building, including post-conflict reconstruction and development, to sharing

671. Strictly legally speaking, it is not correct to term the PSC as a 'regional arrangement' in the sense that only the African Union could be regarded as an arrangement, while the PSC is simply the organ (or one of the organs) authorized to achieve the pacific settlement of regional (or sub-regional or localized) disputes.

information on conflict situations and to holding joint meeting at least once a year.[672] Moreover, the PSC figured prominently in the Solemn Declaration on a Common African Defence and Security Policy, which was adopted by the Second Extraordinary Assembly Session (Sirte, 27–28 February 2004),[673] as one of the main actors in implementing the AU's defence and security agenda.

Finally, reference should be made to the Ezulwini Framework for the Enhancement of the Implementation of Measures of the African Union in Situations of Unconstitutional Changes of Governments in Africa, adopted during a Retreat of the PSC held in Ezulwini, Swaziland in December 2009.[674] The principal purpose of the Ezulwini Framework was to implement a previous PSC Decision establishing a Committee on Sanctions,[675] in conformity with Article 8(1) of the PSC Protocol. The Committee is meant to complement the AU efforts to combat and prevent unconstitutional changes of government was resolved and operates with five PSC members appointed on the basis of regional representation. Its mandate is to monitor and make recommendations on the execution of sanctions already ordered by the PSC. Sanctions are to be imposed in a graduated manner from the moment a coup d'état has taken place. The functioning of this Committee appears to be similar to the ad hoc Sanctions Committees established by the UN Security Council to control compliance by Member States with resolutions ordering mandatory punitive measures under Chapter VII of the UN Charter.

158. Moreover, the PSC Protocol delineates the relationship between the PSC and the African (sub) regional mechanisms for conflict prevention, management, and resolution by subjecting the latter to what appears to be the former's superior authority. In particular, Article 16(1) thereof provides that '[t]he Regional Mechanisms are part of the overall security architecture of the [African] Union, which has the primary responsibility for promoting peace, security and stability in Africa'. It will be argued that these are rather false premises, because on many an occasion the AU has shown that it is unable, incapable or unwilling or a combination thereof to tackle urgent issues affecting peace and stability in parts of the continent, to promote an ethos of accountability, to combat impunity; and to ensure that all Africans are treated as equals irrespective of status, wealth and origin. Indeed, as has been maintained, the attitude shown by the AU could result in denialism as regards tackling matters over which it does have 'primary responsibility'.[676] Notwithstanding these observations, Article 16 of the Protocol instructs the PSC and the AUC Chairperson to harmonize and coordinate the regional mechanisms' activities so that their actions are consistent with the AU objectives

---

672. Compare Assembly, *Decision on Enhancing UN-AU Cooperation: Framework for the Ten-Year Capacity-Building Programme for the African Union*, AU Doc. Assembly/AU/Dec. 140 (VIII) (30 Jan. 2007).

673. At: http://www.peaceau.org/uploads/declaration-cadsp-en.pdf and reproduced in M. Juma, *Compendium of Key Documents Relating to Peace and Security in Africa*(Pretoria: Pretoria University Law Press, 2006), p. 100. Generally, *see* O.A. Touray, 'The Common African Defence and Security Policy', *African Affairs* 104 (2005): 635.

674. At: http://www.peaceau.org/uploads/ezulwini-framework-english.pdf.

675. *See* PSC, Communique of the 178th Meeting of the Peace and Security Council, PSC/PR/COMM.3(CLXXVIII), 13 Mar. 2009.

676. *See* K. Magliveras, 'International Organisations and Denialism: The Case of the African Union' in *Denialism and Human Rights*, H. Nelen, J.C.M. Willems & R. Moerland (eds) (Cambridge: Intersentia, 2016) 267.

and principles. It is rather difficult to justify, from a strictly legal point of view, the subjecting of organs already in existence and belonging to different IGOs(namely the RECs) and having separate international legal personality to the jurisdiction of an organ, which has been set up in the context of another, separate, international organization (namely the AU).

The fact that the membership, respectively, in the AU and in these regional mechanisms invariably coincides is of no relevance, because, unlike the AEC, there is no institutional rapport between the AU and the RECs which have established these mechanisms. Even if it were argued that the AU was conceived as the supreme political and security institution in Africa, its relationship with the other mechanisms cannot be similar to that established under Articles 52 et seq. of the UN Charter, namely the relationship existing between the Security Council and the peace and security regional arrangements. Notwithstanding these considerations, in 2008 the AU and the RECs concluded an MoU on peace and security, whose Article II describes it as a binding legal instrument.[677] This is an interesting contention because, apparently, the MOU did not require to be approved by the plenary organs of the participating organizations; under Article XXVI it came into force upon signature by five of the participating parties, including the AUC. Adherence to the principles of subsidiarity, complementarity and comparative advantage guides the MOU's operation.[678]

159. Pursuant to Article 2(2) of the Protocol, the PSC is composed of the following five separate entities. First, the so-called Panel of the Wise, which according to Article 11 is a body advising PSC on all issues relating to the promotion and maintenance of peace and stability. It is made up by five leading African personalities from various segments of society, each representing an African region. They are expected to intervene early in the outbreak of a dispute and attempt to solve it through discreet diplomacy. The first members of the Panel were appointed during the Eighth Ordinary Assembly Session (Addis Ababa, 23–30 January 2007) for three years: Salim Ahmed Salim, former OAU Secretary General; Brigalia Bam, Chairperson of the Independent Electoral Commission (IEC) of South Africa; Ahmed Ban Bella, former President of Algeria; Elisabeth K. Pognon, President of the Constitutional Court of Benin; and Miguel Trovaoda, former President of Sao Tome and Principe.[679] Although there was considerable delay in the Panel becoming operative (the modalities for its functioning were adopted in April 2008), it has been active in a number of activities

677. *See Memorandum of Understanding on Cooperation in the Area of Peace and Security between the African Union, the Regional Economic Communities and the Coordinating Mechanisms of the Regional Standby Brigades of Eastern Africa and Northern Africa.* Note that the certified copy of the MOU at: http://www.peaceau.org/uploads/mou-au-rec-eng.pdf, does not state on which month and day of 2008 it was adopted, while the MOU, as published by the AU Commission in June 2008, at: https://issafrica.s3.amazonaws.com/site/uploads/AUMOURECSJUN08.PDF, indicates that it was signed in 2007.

678. *See* father J. Akokpari & S. Ancas, 'The African Union and Regional Economic Communities: A Partnership for Peace and Security' in *Handbook of Africa's International Relations*, T. Murithi (ed.), (Abingdon: Routledge, 2014) 73.

679. *See* Assembly, *Decision on the Appointment of the Members of the Panel of the Wise*, AU Doc. Assembly/AU/Dec. 152(VIII) (30 Jan. 2007).

including pre-election assessment missions.[680] The current composition expiring in 2017 is as follows: Central Africa is represented by Albina Faria de Assis Pereira Africano, special advisor to the President of Angola; Eastern Africa by Speciosa Wandira Kazibwe, former Vice President of Uganda; Northern Africa by Lakhdar Brahimi, formerly the Arab League and UN Special Envoy for Syria; Southern Africa by Luisa Diogo, former Prime Minister of Mozambique; and Western Africa by Edem Kodjo, former Prime Minister of Togo and former OAU Secretary-General.

Second, a Continental Early Warning System (CEWS), which pursuant to Article 12 of the Protocol is the body facilitating the anticipation and prevention of conflicts.[681] It is responsible for data collection and analysis. It is also mandated to cooperate closely not only with the observation and monitoring systems that RECs have put in place but also with the UN and its agencies, with research centres and academic institutions, and with NGOs. Based on the Framework for the Operationalization of the CEWS, adopted in 2006 and endorsed by the Tenth Ordinary Executive Council Session held in January 2007, it was meant to be fully operational by the end of 2009. However, due to a number of reasons (limited human resources, lack of training, under-funding, and lack of coordination with the Early Warning Systems (EWS) of RECs), it has rather been unable to turn early warning into concrete action.[682] It is submitted that the latter issue should be addressed by the AU as there is no formal structure allowing relevant information to reach those taking the decisions at the earliest possible time. This state of affairs does question the very essence of EWS. Recently an attempt has been made to enlist the assistance of civil society organizations in making the CEWS more effective.[683]

Third, an African Standby Force (ASF), which according to Article 13 of the Protocol is a body composed of multidisciplinary civilian[684] and military contingents (of roughly 15,000 troops) for rapid deployment of peace support missions and intervention pursuant to Article 4(h) and (j) of the Constitutive Act. In short, it should act as the AU's peacekeeping arm to manage complex operations.[685] In essence, ASF forces are contributed by the following five sub-regional standby forces operating in

680. For AU documents on its work, *see* http://www.peaceau.org/en/resource/93-organ-panel-of-the-wise.

681. *See* J. Cilliers, *Towards a Continental Early Warning System for Africa*, ISS Paper 102 (Pretoria: Institute of Security Studies, April 2005).

682. Compare UNSC Res. 65/283 of 17 Jun. 2011 titled 'Strengthening the role of mediation in the peaceful settlement of disputes, conflict prevention and resolution', where at para. 16 the UNSC welcomed the AU efforts in developing its mediation capacities and structures, including its early warning assessment systems.

683. *See* 'Early Warning: CSOs' Drive on Conflict Prevention in Africa', *This Day* (Nigeria), 17 Nov. 2016, at: http://www.thisdaylive.com/index.php/2016/11/17/early-warning-csos-drive-on-conflict-prevention-in-africa/.

684. *See* C. de Coning & Y. Kasumba (ed.), *The Civilian Dimension of the African Standby Force*, African Union Commission/ African Centre for the Constructive Resolution of Disputes (ACCORD), 2010, at: http://www.zif-berlin.org/fileadmin/uploads/ueber_zif/dokumente/The_Civilian_Dimension_of_the_African_Standby_Force.pdf.

685. For an unsuccessful attempt to create a defence force during the OAU era, *see* Council of Ministers, *Resolution of the Establishment of the OAU Defence Force*, OAU Doc. CM/Res. 867 (XXXVII) (26 Jun. 1981).

the context of RECs, namely the East African Standby Force (EASF); the ECOWAS Standby Force (ESF); the ECCAS Standby Force; the North African Regional Capability (NARC) Standby Force; and the SADC Standby Force (SSF). Fourth, a Military Staff Committee (MSC), which hierarchically comes under the ASF. Pursuant to Article 13(8)(12) of the Protocol, it will advise and assist the PSC in all questions relating to military and security requirements for the promotion and the maintenance of peace and security. Fifth, a Peace Fund, which according to Article 21 of the Protocol is a special fund to provide the necessary financial resources for peace support missions and other operational activities (*infra*, paragraphs 166–167). Over and above these entities, the PSC has also been authorized to establish subsidiary bodies and sub-committees. Finally, it should be noted that the AUC has been mandated to support the PSC logistically through its relevant Directorate, a fact which could lead to duplication of efforts and depletion of the limited recourses available.

In line with the PSC Protocol and the aforementioned MoU of 2008 between the AU and RECs, in June 2012, the Panel of the Wise agreed to establish a Pan-African Network of the Wise (PANWISE). The purpose of this entity is to bring under one umbrella (and presumably under AU leadership as well) the following organs operating in the context of separate African institutions: the AU Panel of the Wise; the ECOWAS Council of the Wise; the COMESA Committee of Elders; the SADC Mediation Reference Group and Panel of Elders; the IGAD Mediation Contact Group; as well as any other similar structure to be set up in the future in another REC. Its operation shall be based on the Framework for the Operationalization of the PANWISE, which was meant to be submitted for consideration to the AU and the respective RECs during 2013.[686] As it becomes obvious, the necessary qualifications for individuals to gain membership in it are to have reached a certain age and have the status of elders. This insistence on the age of members derives from indigenous African custom and traditions, pursuant to which elders are called upon to offer advice, to mediate between the parties to a dispute, and to undertake other conflict prevention measures. While even in contemporary Africa such methods continue to be official practice in several states (e.g., Ghana, Lesotho, and Rwanda), the question should be asked whether peace and security problems encountered in almost all parts of the continent go not require the participation, whether on an equal basis or not, of a younger generation of experienced and competent technocrats, who could very well come from the African Diaspora.

As has already been submitted, the abundance of organs is a theme characterizing the whole AU institutional architecture. However, in the case of the PSC it should seriously be questioned whether it is viable to have different structures operating on the basis of separate rules and at a financial cost that the AU can ill-afford and, consequently, has to appeal (time after time) to the international community for assistance.[687] It is further submitted that African conflicts and the various threats to peace and security that the continent has been experiencing require centralization and not decentralization and, in that respect, RECs have a significant role to apply. Given the multitude of institutions active in the field of peace and security and the invariable

686. *See* AU Commission, Directorate of Information and Communication, *AU Echo*, Issue 06, 28 Jan. 2013, p. 10.

687. Compare Assembly, *Decision on the African Standby Force (ASF) and the Military Staff Committee (MSC)*, AU Doc. Assembly/AU/Dec. 35 (III) (8 Jul. 2004).

lack of (human and financial) resources it might be more appropriate to reinforce the role of RECs even if this meant the downgrading of AU's role.

160. Article 7 of the PSC Protocol lays down the multifaceted powers with which it has been endowed. The most important are the following: to undertake peacemaking and peace-building functions; to authorize the deployment of peace missions; to recommend to the Assembly intervention in a Member State in case of grave circumstances; to institute sanctions in cases of unconstitutional change of governments; to implement the AU common defence policy; to take appropriate action where a Member's independence and sovereignty is threatened by acts of aggression; and to exercise any powers that might be delegated to it by the Assembly. The power to introduce sanctions for coups d'état would appear to be problematic in view of the Assembly's primary responsibility to impose punitive measures pursuant to Article 23 of the Constitutive Act. Generally speaking, the charters of international organizations stipulate that the imposition of sanctions is the prerogative of the highest-ranking organ encompassing all Member States; in the case of the AU, this would be the Assembly. As has been noted (*supra*, paragraphs 90 et seq.), the regime for the imposition of sanctions against illegal regimes is not without problems. The adoption, variation and rescinding of punitive measures by the PSC without (at least ex post facto) approval by the Assembly should be regarded as a problematic state of affairs and arguably is not consistent with the AU's institutional architecture. If the ACJHR ever become operative and a Member State, which has been the object of PSC sanctions, were to challenge their legality before it, it is submitted that these considerations will surface.

161. Pursuant to Article 5(2) of the PSC Protocol, the Assembly has been empowered to elect its Members by applying the principles of equitable regional representation and rotation as well as by applying a number of other criteria. However, until now Members have been elected by the Executive Council under delegation of powers and subsequently appointed by the Assembly.[688] The first Members elected on 15 March 2004, were Gabon, Ethiopia, Algeria, South Africa, and Nigeria (for a three-year term) and Cameroon, Congo, Kenya, Sudan, Libya, Lesotho, Mozambique, Ghana, Senegal, and Togo (for a two-year term).[689] At the Twelfth Ordinary Executive Council Session (Addis Ababa, January 2008), the following ten Members were appointed drawn from the continent's five regions: from Central Africa, Burundi and Chad; from Eastern Africa, Rwanda, and Uganda; from Northern Africa, Tunisia; from Southern Africa, Swaziland, and Zambia; and from Western Africa, Benin, Burkina Faso, and Mali.[690] They joined the following five, which had been elected by the Executive Council and appointed by the Assembly in January 2007: Ethiopia (representing the Eastern Africa region), Algeria (North), Angola (South), Gabon (Central), and Nigeria

688. For the first such delegation of powers, *see* Assembly, *Decision on the Operationalization of the Protocol Relating to the Establishment of the Peace and Security Council*, AU Doc. ASS/AU/Dec. 16 (II) (12 Jul. 2003).

689. Executive Council, *Decision on the Election of Members of the Peace and Security Council*, AU Doc. EX/CL/81 (IV) (16 Mar. 2004).

690. Subsequently they were appointed by the Assembly, *see* Assembly, *Decision on Election of Ten (10) Members of the Peace and Security Council of the African Union*, AU Doc. Assembly/AU/Dec. 183 (X) (2 Feb. 2008).

(West).[691] In the current decade, Angola, Egypt, Guinea, Cameroon, Cote d'Ivoire, Congo Republic, Djibouti, Tanzania, Gambia, and Lesotho were elected and appointed in January 2012 for two-year terms effective from March 2013, while Libya, Equatorial Guinea, Kenya, Nigeria, and Zimbabwe were elected for three-year terms as from April 2013).[692] The most recent appointments were made in January 2016. Five Members were appointed for a three-year term as of 1 April 2016, as follows: DRC (representing the Central Region), Kenya (Eastern Region), Egypt (Northern Region), Zambia (Southern Region), and Nigeria (Western Region), while the following ten Members for a two-year term as of 1 April 2016: Burundi and Chad (Central Region), Rwanda and Uganda (Eastern Region), Algeria (Northern Region), and Botswana and South Africa (Southern Region).[693]

The participation of certain Members (including Zimbabwe) in the PSC should raise some concern, since they arguably do not meet the standards on the rule of law and the protection of human rights as enshrined in the aforementioned Article 5(2) of the Protocol.[694] But then again, a lot could be said about the participation of some states not subscribing to these principles in multilateral entities, such as the UN HRC, whose goal is no other but to safeguard and promote them. Thus, it could be argued that a trend has been established whereby the participation of states in transnational bodies dealing with the rule of law, human rights, democratic ideals, and the like does not depend on whether they actually subscribe to these principles. And this because membership in such bodies is based on candidate states securing the backing of a populous group of states (e.g., the African group) which is adequate to have them elected. Thus, non-democratic or totalitarian states, which invariably fail to protect and/or violate fundamental freedoms, choose to support similar states to be elected to membership. Given that it is probably impossible to officially brand the Member States of any international organization as 'undemocratic' or 'totalitarian' and, on this ground, to disallow them to stand as candidates, the phenomenon of such states being elected to organs, which aim at preventing such violations, will continue despite such efforts as the UN Democracy Caucus, a loose association of UN Member States which subscribe to the standards of the 2000 Warsaw Declaration[695] and support candidates with good human rights records.[696]

---

691. *See* Assembly, *Decision on Election of Five (5) Members of the Peace and Security Council of the African Union*, AU Doc. Assembly/AU/Dec. 149 (VIII) (30 Jan. 2007).
692. *See* , respectively, Assembly, *Decision on the Election of Ten (10) Members of the Peace and Security Council of the African Union*, AU Doc. Assembly/AU/Dec. 411 (XVIII) (30 Jan. 2012) and Assembly, *Decision on the Election of the Five Members of the Peace and Security Council of the African Union*, AU Doc. Assembly/AU/Dec. 468 (XX) (28 Jan. 2013).
693. Assembly, *Decision on the Election of the Fifteen (15) Members of the Peace and Security Council of the African Union*, AU Doc. Assembly/AU/Dec. 594 (XXVI) (31 Jan. 2016).
694. *See* J. Vorrath, *Imbalances in the African Peace and Security Architecture*, Stiftung Wissenschaft und Politik, Comments 29, September 2012, pp. 1, 3, at: http:///www.swp-berlin.org.
695. Final Warsaw Declaration: Toward a Community of Democracies, 27 Jun. 2000, at: https://2001-2009.state.gov/g/drl/rls/26811.htm.
696. *See* US Department of State, *United States Participation in the United Nations: A Report by the Secretary of State to the Congress for the Year 2006*, January 2008, p. 88, at: https://www.state.gov/p/io/rls/rpt/c25829.htm.

162. The PSC functions on a continuous basis and, therefore, all its Members are required to be represented at AU headquarters. It holds closed sessions (Article 8(9) of the Protocol). Although this is also the case with the UN Security Council, the secrecy with which closed meetings is associated has often been criticized as running contrary to the notion of an open international society, a criticism which is gradually gaining ground. Given that often there is secrecy in domestic decision-making processes, it is not difficult to replicate it in international dealings.[697] However, it is important to note that Article 8(10) envisages open meetings as well, in which case any CSO involved or interested in the matter under consideration may be invited to participate, without vote, in the discussion. This provision as well as Article 20 of the Protocol, which urges the PSC to encourage NGOs and other community-based organizations to participate in the common effort to promote peace and security in Africa, should be viewed in furtherance of the Constitutive Act's request that the civil society be involved in African affairs. In December 2008 in Livingstone, Zambia, the PSC held a retreat to discuss appropriate mechanisms for its interaction with civil society organizations. The outcome was the Livingstone Formula, which has become the latter's gateway in issues of peace, security and stability.[698] Thus, on 26 March 2013, the PSC during its 364th Meeting devoted an Open Session on the theme 'Women and Children in situations of violent conflict in Africa: Contribution and Role of Women,' which was held pursuant to a previous decision on 30 March 2010 (223rd meeting).[699] Moreover, on 19 August 2013 (391st meeting), the PSC held an Open Session on the occasion of the World Humanitarian Day, where it was briefed on the protection of civilians and the humanitarian situation in the CAR and the DRC by the AUC, the UNs, other partners, the civil society, and the Institute for Security Studies. Interestingly enough, the latter describes itself as 'an African organisation which aims to enhance human security by providing independent and authoritative research, expert policy analysis and advice, and training and technical assistance'.[700]

163. Each Member of the PSC has one vote with the exception of those Members, which happen to be parties to a conflict or to a situation under consideration. The term 'party' is not defined in the Protocol and this could lead to questions of interpretation. Let us assume for the sake of argument that, as it often happens in African affairs, State A, which is embroiled in a belligerency situation with State B, accuses State C, a PSC Member, that it has aided and abetted State B, a fact strenuously denied by State C. Would State C be considered a 'party' to the conflict and, consequently, denied participation in the deliberations and during voting time? Notwithstanding that this is an issue to be resolved by the other PSC Members, it could derail discussions and prevent the prompt solution of the conflict.

164. Decisions are reached by consensus failing which by a two-thirds majority of the Members present and voting. Considering that ten Members constitute a quorum

697. *See* United States Senators Daniel Patrick Moynihan and Ron Wyden, *Secrecy in International and Domestic Policy Making: The Case for More Sunshine* (United States Senate, October 2000) at: https://fas.org/sgp/library/wyden.html.

698. AU Doc. PSC/PR/Comm (CLX), at: http://www.au.int/en/sites/default/files/documents/30974-doc-psc_conclusion_-_livingstone.pdf.

699. *See* PSC, Press Statement, AU Doc. PSC/PR/BR.(CCCLXIV) (26 Mar. 2013).

700. *See* PSC, Press Statement, AU Doc. PSC/PR/BR.(CCCXCI) (19 Aug. 2003).

(Article 8(13) of the Protocol), decisions could be taken by seven Members, that is, by less than half of its membership and almost one-eighth of the total AU membership. Arguably, some doubts could be raised about thc authority such decisions carry, especially as regards those instituting sanctions or dealing with sensitive issues pertaining to the sovereignty of Members States embroiled in armed conflict or in a civil war. Even though a strict adherence to consensus could easily result in paralysis and be counter-productive, it is submitted that the most important decisions should be taken by no less than, say, ten Members and be subsequently forwarded to the Assembly for approval. It should be noted that, from the beginning of its operations, the PSC has adopted the policy of issuing only communiqués and press releases at the conclusion of its meetings and not decisions and resolutions as the other organs, thus not revealing whether decisions were unanimously approved or whether one of more Members disagreed or abstained.

165. According to Article 7(3) of the Protocol, all Member States are obliged to accept and implement PSC decisions. This is a rather curious provision as it attaches a strict obligation to all Member States irrespective of whether they have ratified the Protocol or not. As has been explained, there are still Member States which have not ratified it and it is doubtful whether they will do so it in the foreseeable future.[701] Moreover, considering that, the PSC was not envisaged as an original AU organ but was created later under the authority of Article 5(2) of the Constitutive Act, the validity of any decisions dealing with non-contracting parties could be challenged. Indeed, it is a fundamental rule of the law of international organizations that participating states are legally bound by the decisions of organs only to the extent that have already accepted their jurisdiction and competence, a rule that is evidently not satisfied in the present circumstances.

166. For the PSC to operate efficiently and effectively and to bring to fruition its goals it is imperative that it possesses adequate financial resources. It relies primarily on the Peace Fund, the continuation of the fund which had financed the operations of the OAU Central Organ since June 1993. The Peace Fund is supported by appropriations from the regular AU budget (originally it did exceed 6% of the regular AU budget), voluntary contributions by Member States (although it is doubtful whether even a dozen states could be reasonably expected to afford sizeable funding), and other sources within Africa (defined as the private sector, the civil society and individuals), through fund raising and by voluntary contributions from sources outside Africa.[702] During the Special Assembly Summit, held in Tripoli in August 2009, Member States agreed to increase the contribution to the Peace Fund to 12% of the regular budget. However, with hindsight, doubling the contribution was considered not feasible and, therefore, during the Sixteenth Ordinary Executive Council Session (Addis Ababa, January

701. Note that on occasions the PSC has dealt with conflicts and situation concerning Member States which are not contracting parties, e.g., with the situation in Somalia during its Seventy-Third Meeting on 19 Mar. 2007.

702. Thus, on 1 Nov. 2002, it was announced that Japan contributed USD 200,000 towards the Peace Fund; *see* AU Press Release No. 45/2002. Moreover, on 31 Dec. 2003, Finland and the AU signed an agreement, according to which the former contributed EUR 750,000 to the Peace Fund until December 2005; *see* AU Press Release No. 122/2003. In mid-December 2012 Russia contributed USD 2 million.

2010), it was agreed to maintain the target of 12% but implement it over a period of three years starting from 2011. This development should be viewed in the light of the fact that several Member States default on their compulsory budget contributions threatening, *inter alia*, the PSC's ability to function effectively and carry out its mandate. It is of interest to note that the Protocol allows the PSC to resort to the UN to secure financial and logistical support. However, given the perennial pecuniary UN problems and its policy not to afford direct funding to regional peace and security institutions, realistically speaking, the PSC cannot rely on it.

167. Despite their pledges, Member States never channelled anything near the 6% of the regular AU budget to the Peace Fund. Apparently, over many years they financed it with only 2%. Thus, and given the lack of voluntary contributions from Member States, the remaining funding has had to be secured from international donors. However, an evaluation of APSA undertaken in 2013 did not reveal the fundamental role played by non-African funding.[703] At its 582nd Meeting held on 14 March 2016, the PSC welcomed that during the Twenty-Fifth Ordinary Assembly Session (Johannesburg, 14–15 June 2015) resolved 'to enhance ownership of the budget of the Union' and that Member States should finance, *inter alia*, 25% of the peace and security budget, incrementally over a five year period.[704] Moreover, in July 2016 the Assembly determined that the Peace Fund shall be structured around three so-called Windows: The first Window will concern Mediation and Preventive Diplomacy; the second will concern Institutional Capacity and the third will concern Peace Support Operation.[705] The latter Window should take up most of the resources leaving the other two Windows underfunded. To offer an illustration, the cost of maintaining AMISOM (with an approved strength of more than 22,000 uniformed personnel) is estimated at USD 900 million per year, which exceeds the AU budget for FY 2017 (it stood at USD 782 million)! According to a Report on the challenges surrounding the financing of peace activities submitted in the summer of 2016 by the AU High Representative for the Peace Fund presented:

> The percentage contribution from the regular budget has only reached 7%. This is mainly because of high levels of arrears and late payments of Member States' assessed contributions. While some AU Member States have made additional voluntary contributions to the Peace Fund, these payments are irregular and unpredictable. As a result, the Fund is highly dependent on external partners[706]

---

703. *See* A. Vines, 'A Decade of African Peace and Security Architecture', *International Affairs* 89 (2013): 89, 99.

704. *See* PSC Press Statement, PSC/PR/BR.(DLXXXII), 14 Mar. 2016. The Assembly decision concerned possible alternative sources for securing the adequate funding of the AU budget, AU Doc. Assembly/AU/Dec. 561 (XXXIV).

705. Assembly, *Decision on the Outcome of the Retreat of the Heads of States and Government, Ministers of Foreign Affairs and Ministers of Finance on the Financing of the African Union*, AU Doc. Assembly/AU/Dec. 605 (XXVII), para. 5b (18 Jul. 2016).

706. *See* AU Peace Fund Silencing the Guns, *Securing Predictable and Sustainable Financing for Peace in Africa*, Report, August 2016, para. 20, at: http://www.peaceau.org/uploads/auhr-progress-report-final-020916-with-annexes.pdf.

As has been noted (*supra*, paragraph 56), in July 2016 the Assembly took concrete measures to address the perennial problem of inadequate AU financing by creating a 0.2% levy on the importation of goods into Africa. Regarding specifically the Peace Fund, it was resolved to have it endowed from this levy with an initial amount of USD 325 million rising to USD 400 million in 2020. Each of the five African regions is expected to contribute an equal amount to the Peace Fund.[707]

Contributions from the EU and from individual Member States have always been instrumental to maintain PSC activities. However, accepting EU funding should pose a moral dilemma to those countries blaming the former European colonial powers for most of Africa's plagues. On 2 April 2003, the AU and the EU signed a EUR 12 million financial agreement, of which EUR 10 million was earmarked for supporting the peace and security agenda. Moreover, in July 2003, the Second Ordinary Assembly Session, had requested that the EU examine the possibility of setting up a Peace Support Operation Facility to fund peacekeeping operations carried out under AU authority.[708] Promptly, the EU created the Peace Facility for Africa with an initial endowment of EUR 250 million to support African-led peace support operations and enhance the institutional capacities of the AU and the RECs in peacekeeping and conflict prevention for a period of three years.[709] In April 2006, the EU Council determined to extend it until 2010 and allocated the amount of EUR 300 million.[710] Later, the funding of the Peace Facility was increased to EUR 440 million. In June 2004, the AU Mission in Sudan (AMIS) became the first peacekeeping operation to be supported by the Peace Facility; originally it received EUR 12 million; an additional EUR 40 million was pledged by the EU Council in May 2007.[711] During its life, the Peace Facility has supported, *inter alia*, peacekeeping efforts in the CAR (FOMUC), in Somalia (AMISOM), and in the African Union Mission in the Comoros (AMISEC), while some EUR 30 million were committed for capacity-building. The African Peace Fund (APF) envelope under the Tenth European Development Fund (EDF)[712] stands at EUR 600 million and is broken down into two tractions of EUR 300 million each, one for the Action

707. *See* Assembly/AU/Dec. 605 (XXVII), *supra* .
708. *See* Assembly, *Decision on the Establishment by the European Union of a Peace Support Operation Facility for the African Union*, AU Doc. Assembly/AU/Dec. 21 (II), para. 5 (12 Jul. 2003).
709. *See* ACP-EC Council of Ministers, *Decision 2003/3 of 11 December 2003 on the use of resources from the long-term development envelope of the ninth EDF for the creation of a Peace Facility for Africa*, Official J. of the Eur. Communities (OJ) L 345 of 31 Dec. 2003.
710. *See* EU Council, *Regulation 617/2007/EC of 14 May 2007 on the implementation of the 10th European Development Fund under the ACP-EC Partnership Agreement*, OJ L 152 of 13 Jun. 2007, and ACP-EC Council of Ministers, *Decision No 2/2007 of 25 May 2007 allowing additional bilateral contributions, to be managed by the Commission, in support of the objectives of the African Peace Facility*, OJ L 175 of 5 Jul. 2007.
711. *See* European Commission, *Bulletin of the European Union 5-2007*, point 1.34.40, and *Bulletin of the European Union 6-2007*, point 1.34.72.
712. EDF was created in 1957 by the Treaty of Rome establishing the European Economic Community and is the EU's main instrument challenging development aid to African, Caribbean and Pacific (ACP) states.

Programme 2008–2010 and the other for the Action Programme 2011–2013.[713] The current 11th EDF initially foresaw a total contribution of EUR 750 million to the African Peace Facility but another EUR 150 million was allocated in December 2015 due to increased needs. Finally, Denmark made a voluntary contribution of EUR 1.24 million specifically for AMISOM, which until December 2015 had received a total of EUR 901.2 million from European sources.[714] By the end of 2016, more than EUR 2.1 billion had been allocated in total to the African Peace Fund since its creation, of which EUR 1.9 billion had been contracted through it.[715]

168. Regarding contributions from the international community (bar the EU), reference could be made to a joint project between the AUC and the Regional Bureau for Africa of the United Nations Development Programme (UNDP). On 15 May 2003, it agreed on a USD 7.2 million project titled 'Support for the Implementation of the Peace and Security Agenda of the African Union' to run until October 2013. It is a follow-up to a UNDP supported project dating from 1997 and titled 'Capacity Building for the OAU Mechanism for Conflict Prevention, Management and Resolution.' The financial input of UNDP amounted to USD 2 million, while other donors (including Germany, Norway, Sweden, Canada and the Netherlands) committed themselves to cover the remainder. This is an overarching scheme with specific objectives (e.g., to improve the management skills and the technical level of staff at the Commission's Directorate of Peace and Security) but states may finance other actions as well. Thus, on 17 March 2006 Japan and the UNDP signed a USD 2 million agreement, whereby the former agreed to finance an AU plan to demobilize, disarm, rehabilitate, and reintegrate young ex-combatants in the war-torn Great Lakes region.

169. It has been argued that the AU is unable to provide for its peace and security agenda, especially when the UN is unwilling to deploy its missions.[716] It is submitted that this approach does not appreciate either how international organizations really work or the importance to be placed on cooperation and good willing by Member States allowing the organization in question to perform its mandate without obstacles and barriers. Moreover, if the UN were to play an active role in an African situation, the states which would contribute personnel to any (peacekeeping) mission to be deployed would rather be same as if the mission had been set up by the AU itself. Indeed, African states expect that only African will partake in such missions. Apparently, it is a question of trust (or mistrust when it comes to non-Africans). The reality is that there are only that many African states which can realistically afford to participate in any African peacekeeping mission. However, the PSC should be considered adequately endowed to achieve its goals. Its wide-ranging powers are unprecedented. Despite African states insisting to uphold their sacred sovereignty, which in practice means

713. Generally, *see European Commission, Annual Report 2011 – The African Peace Facility*, no date, at: https://ec.europa.eu/europeaid/annual-report-2011-african-peace-facility_en.

714. *See* European Commission, *Annual Report 2015 – he African Peace Facility*, July 2016, 11, at: http://www.africa-eu-partnership.org/sites/default/files/documents/apf-report-2015-en.pdf.

715. *See* European Commission, *Annual Report 2016 – The African Peace Facility*, July 2017, 7, at: http://www.africa-eu-partnership.org/sites/default/files/documents/apf_ar2016_en_v1_web.pdf.

716. *See* E. Yemisi Omorogke, 'Can the African Union Deliver Peace and Security?', *Journal of Conflict & Security Law* 16 (2011): 35.

that that only rarely do they act in unison, the PSC has managed to push through decisions adopted unanimously. Indeed, if the PSC were to become the indispensable organ in the area of peace and security that the continent so urgently requires, it must be allowed to carry out its functions without external interferences, while Member States must comply with its decisions and demands promptly and in full. This does not mean that the PSC should be without checks and balances: clearly its actions (and omissions of that matter) should be open to scrutiny, review and annulment by the AU's judicial organ. To build an efficient working relationship and a relationship of mutual trust, it is important that Member States enjoy the right to resort to an independent and impartial judicial body, express their grievances and expect a legal determination. Given the lack of a functioning judicial organ in the AU, the PSC appears to be without legal checks, especially when it orders sanctions and other measures of a punitive nature. This is deplorable for a modern intergovernmental organization which should be resilient to tackle the many challenges it has been facing since its establishment.

170. The constitutional crisis in The Comoros in the period 2007–2008 presents a good illustration of the way the PSC operates. Perhaps the small size of the Comoros and the fact that its role in the AU is negligible could be reasons not to show any interest in this situation. However, there are three reasons making it a case of particular interest. First, it was a situation which could not have led either to a regional African security threat or to a breach of the peace between Member States. Second, like so many other African states, the Comoros has been facing unending internal problems of a constitutional and an institutional nature. Third, over and above the PSC, there was an involvement of other entities, whose relationship with the AU ought to be analysed. The Union of the Comoros Islands, which is made up by the Autonomous Islands of Grande-Comoros, Anjouan, and Mwali, gained its independence from France on 6 July 1975. Since then the country has been plagued by more than twenty coups d'état. In December 2001, a new Constitution was promulgated, which provides for a rotating presidency among the islands as well as a separate Union president and grants more autonomy to each of the islands.[717] When the Union President called for the election of the islands' presidents to take place on 10 June 2007, the PSC authorized the deployment of the African Union Electoral and Security Assistance Mission to The Comoros (MAES), which included civilian personnel but also a police and a military component with forces coming from the Republic of South Africa (which later played the role of coordinator in the regional efforts to solve the crisis), Senegal, the Sudan, and Tanzania.[718] The deployment of MAES was financially assisted by the League of Arab States, of which the Comoros has been a Member State since 1993.[719]

A few days before the elections, the President of The Comoros decided to postpone them for a week in the island of Anjouan, because the prevailing conditions were not conducive for holding free, fair and transparent elections. Even though it could be argued that this was an internal affair of a Member State, the PSC issued a Communiqué where it 'took note' of this decision, 'endorsed' the assessment that the

---

717. At: http://www.wipo.int/wipolex/en/details.jsp?id=8667.

718. *See* Peace and Security Council, Seventy-Seventh Meeting, Communiqué PSC/MIN/Comm.1 (LXXVII), 9 May 2007.

719. *See Africa Research Bulletin: Politics, Social and Cultural Series*, vol. 44, 171134-17115A (July 2007).

conditions in Anjouan did not guarantee democratic voting and indicated that the results of any elections that might held against its decision would not be recognized by the AU and the international community.[720] In the event, the island's authorities held the vote on 10 June 2007 as scheduled. General Mohamed Bacar, who had held the office from 2002 to 2007, won 73% of the vote. Notwithstanding that the other four candidates boycotted the elections and the result was never recognized by the Union government, he was sworn-in on 14 June 2007. As the crisis with the 'de facto' authorities in Anjouan could not be resolved, a so-called Ministerial Committee of the Countries of the Region on The Comoros was established and coordinated by South Africa and with the participation of Tanzania, Mozambique, Mauritius, Seychelles, Kenya, and Madagascar. Although it would appear that at the time its setting up was not sanctioned by the PSC or any other AU organ, the Committee met twice on 19 June 2007 and on 8–9 July 2007.[721] The Committee formulated a number of recommendations for which the PSC expressed its full support.[722] The recommendations did not receive the expected positive response from the 'de facto' authorities in Anjouan and in mid-August 2007 the PSC 'deplored the intransigence displayed' and the lack of cooperation with the regional initiative.[723]

According to the PSC Communiqué issued in October 2007, the fact that the 'illegal authorities of Anjouan' had continued to reject the Ministerial Committee's recommendations in conjunction with the fact than 'any further delay in the resolution of the crisis would further destabilize' the country led the PSC to 'reiterate' its determination to ensure that the Anjouanese authorities comply fully and unconditionally with, *inter alia*, the demands of the countries of the region. It also approved the further recommendations that the Ministerial Committee had submitted on 18 September 2007 and decided that Member States shall impose against the 'illegal authorities of Anjouan' for an initial period of forty-five days, namely prevent the entry into their territories of the authorities and all other persons constituting a threat to the peace and security in the Comoros and freeze their financial assets. It also resolved to review the mandate of MAES and instructed it to support the implementation of the above sanctions, establish in Anjouan an internal security force, and facilitate the restoration of the central government's authority in the island. Finally, it created a follow-up mechanism consisting of two of its Members (Angola and Senegal) as well as representatives of the countries of the region, the Union government, and the AUC.[724] The PSC extended twice the imposed sanctions and the mandate of MAES until 22 February 2008 'pending

720. *See* Peace and Security Council, Communiqué PSC/PR/COMM (LXXVIII), Seventy-Eighth Meeting, 9 Jun. 2007.

721. Note that in the past the OAU Council of Ministers had recommended to the U Assembly the taking of military measures against the Anjouanese separatists and had requested the countries of the region, under Republic of South Africa's coordination, to take all appropriate steps, *see* Council of Ministers, *Decision on the Com*oros, OAU Doc. CM/Dec. 523 (LXXII) Rev. 1 (8 Jul. 2000). The Assembly approved the recommendations and authorized the countries of the region and the Central Organ to determine the modalities of the military measures to be taken, Assembly, *Decision on the Comoros*, OAU Doc. AHG/Dec. 149 (XXXVI) (12 Jul. 2000).

722. *See* PSC, Press Statement PSC/PR/PS (LXXXII), Eighty-Second Meeting, 23 Jul. 2007.

723. *See* PSC, Communiqué PSC/PR/COMM (LXXXVII), Eighty-Seventh Meeting, 13 Aug. 2007.

724. *See* PSC, Communiqué PSC/PR/COMM (XCV), Ninety-Fifth Meeting, 10 Oct. 2007.

the envisaged ministerial meeting of the countries of the region that would review the situation and submit recommendation on the way forward'.[725]

The role played by the Ministerial Committee in the crisis requires clarification: it did not confine itself to the role of intermediary or conciliator but moved on to formulate concrete recommendations, which were converted into PSC policy. Even though the South African Foreign Ministry has claimed that the Committee was mandated by the AU to facilitate peace and national reconciliation in the Comoros, this was not apparently corroborated by the action of AU organs. On the contrary, judging by the PSC actions, arguably it 'delegated' the handling of the situation to the Ministerial Committee and was happy to go along with its suggestions. Given the geography of the Comoros and domestic strife since independence, the constitutional crisis could have not escalated into a regional security threat. Therefore, it is submitted that the PSC felt that it had to ensure that the presidential elections in the islands would be held in a free and transparent manner and, to that end, it established MEAS. However, as the voting in Anjouan took place as planned and the crisis escalated, the PSC was only happy to let the Ministerial Committee take the initiative, work out the solutions that seemed appropriate to its members and, subsequently, to back up the Committee's work by adopting the necessary decisions. The way the PSC handled this incident cannot but beg the question if it would have followed the same course of action had it not been for a small and poor archipelago country.

Reference should also be made to the way the Assembly dealt with the Comoros situation during its Tenth Ordinary Session (Addis Ababa, 31 January–2 February 2008) as it addressed it on two different instances. The first was in the course of examining the report submitted by the PSC on its activities for the year 2007. The second was as a separate matter on the agenda. In the first instance, the Assembly simply expressed its full support for the efforts 'in pursuant of the pertinent decisions of the PSC with a view to restoring State authority in Anjouan and put a definite end to the crisis from the attitude of Anjouan's illegal authorities'.[726] But in the second instance it referred specifically to the MAES, avoided making any reference to the aforementioned Ministerial Committee and, finally, urged the UN Security Council to adopt a resolution endorsing the sanctions already imposed by the PSC.[727] Considering that, as argued above, the Comoros crisis could not have posed a threat on regional peace and security, the Assembly's attempt to get the Security Council involved is questionable, unless the aim was to seek, even belatedly, its approval and legitimation. However, given that the Security Council had not already addressed the situation in question, it was rather improbable that it would approve the PSC's punitive measures. Apparently, the Security Council had never in the past dealt with the Comoros and, when the resolutions adopted by the Islamic Conference of Foreign Ministers in June

---

725. *See* OSC, Communiqué PSC/PR/COMM (CII), Hundred-Second Meeting, 26 Nov. 2007, and Communiqué PSC/PR/COMM (XVII), Hundred-Seventh Meeting, 21 Jan. 2008.

726. *See* Assembly, *Decision on the Activities of the Peace and Security Council of the African Union and the State of Peace and Security in Africa*, AU Doc. Assembly/AU/Dec. 177 (X) (2 Feb. 2008).

727. *See* Assembly, *Decision on the Situation on The Comoros*, AU Doc. Assembly/AU/Dec. 186 (X) (2 Feb. 2008).

2004 were submitted to it,[728] the matter was brought to its attention but was not discussed.[729]

Based on the presumed authorization contained in Decision Assembly/Dec. 186(X), on 25 March 2008 Operation 'Democracy in The Comoros' was launched by Comorian forces backed by Tanzania, the Sudan, Libya, and Senegal (France and the USA provided transportation and logistics support) and removed the 'illegal regime' of General Bacer from power.[730] With constitutional order restored in Anjouan, new elections were planned and, to that effect, on 30 April 2008, the PSC extended for six months the MAES mandate, which was, *inter alia*, requested to provide 'assistance in the establishment of an internal security force in Anjouan'.[731] The first round of the election for the President of the Autonomous Island of Anjouan took place on 15 June 2008. When a few weeks later, the Eleventh Ordinary Assembly Session met in Sharm El Sheikh, Egypt (30 June–1 July 2008), it did not discuss the PSC actions.[732]

171. As has been mentioned, one of the roles of the PSC is to address promptly unconstitutional changes of government. Most of the incidents handled by the PSC are summarized below in chronological order.[733] Emphasis has been placed in recording any additional action undertaken and measures taken by other AU organs as well as any relevant action by the competent REC. Finally, where pertinent, the issues surrounding the PSC practice are also discussed.

I. Central African Republic (March 2003–June 2005)

172. Following the coup d'état in the CAR on 15 March 2003, the Central Organ of the OAU Mechanism for Conflict Prevention, Management, and Resolution met immediately and decided at its Nineteenth session to suspend the CAR from AU activities.[734] In June 2005, the PSC, which had in the meantime replaced the Central Organ, considered that the holding of legislative and presidential elections in the country had marked the return to constitutional rule and resolved to lift the suspension.[735] It will be submitted that, legally speaking, there was an irregularity in the PSC dealing with this situation, because the CAR had chosen not to ratify the 2002 Protocol establishing the PSC (it still has not ratified it) and, consequently, the PSC should not be regarded as competent to deal with Member States which effectively have not recognized it. On the contrary, the lifting of the sanctions should have been determined

---

728. *See* UN Doc. S/2004/582 and Corr. 1 (15 Jul. 2004).
729. *See* UNGA, *Report of the Security Council 1/8/2004 – 31/7/2005*, UN Doc. A/60/2, p. 186 (2005).
730. PSC, Press Statement PSC/PR/BR (CXVII), 117th Meeting, 28 Mar. 2008.
731. *See* PSC, Communiqué PSC/PR/COMM (CXXIV), 124th Meeting, 30 Apr. 2008.
732. *See* Assembly, *Decision on the Report of the Peace and Security Council*, AU Doc. Assembly/AU/Dec. 193 (XI) (1 Jul. 2008).
733. For situations during the OAU era, *see* K.O. Kufuor, 'The OAU and the Recognition of Governments in Africa: Analyzing Its Practice and Proposals for the Future', *American University International Law Review* 17(2002): 369.
734. *See* OAU Doc. Central Organ/MEC/AMB/Comm. (XC) (17 Mar. 2003).
735. *See* AU Doc. PSC/PR/Comm (XXXIII) – (ii) (24 Jun. 2005).

by the Assembly, it being the highest-ranking AU organ and the one having primary responsibility in the broad area of peace and security.

II. Togo (February 2005–May 2005)

173. Following the death of President Gnassingbé Eyadéma on 5 February 2005, the armed forces assumed power, revised the Constitution and committed other acts, which the PSC regarded at its Twenty-fourth Meeting held a few days later as blatant and unacceptable violation of the Lomé Declaration on the Framework for an OAU Response to Unconstitutional Change of Government, which the OAU Assembly had adopted in July 2000,[736] the AU principles, and the 2002 Protocol.[737] The PSC demanded that the armed forces refrain from interfering in the political life on pain of suffering sanctions if they did not restore constitutional legality. Two weeks later, the PSC condemned the 'constitutional modifications' carried out by the armed forces, which were 'intended to legally window dress the coup d'état', 'confirmed' the suspension of the de facto authorities from participating in AU activities, and requested the AUC to ensure its scrupulous implementation.[738] It is submitted that the PSC could not but have ordered suspension because, on 19 February 2005, the ECOWAS had imposed its own sanctions against the illegal regime, which were far stricter than to merely suspend participation.[739] In this case, it would appear that the PSC trailed the ECOWAS. Thus, the latter, on account of the country's return to constitutional legality, lifted all sanctions on 26 February 2005 and the PSC followed suit three months later.[740]

III. Mauritania (August 2005–April 2007)

174. On 3 August 2005, a military coup d'état deposed President Maaouya Ould Sid'Ahmed Taya while he was abroad. Taya himself had come to power through a (bloodless) coup in December 1984. Thereafter, he introduced a democratic Constitution (July 1991) and organized the first multi-party elections (April 1992), which he won and kept winning. Therefore, the question arose whether Taya's regime ought to have been regarded a 'constitutional' regime, the overthrow of which through a military coup d'état could not be condoned, or whether it remained 'unconstitutional'. When it met the following day, the PSC did not discuss this issue but moved to suspend

---

736. *See* OAU Doc. AHG/Decl. 5 (XXXVI) (12 Jul. 2000).
737. *See* AU Doc. PSC/PR/Comm(XXIV) (7 Feb. 2005).
738. *See* AU Doc. PSC/PR/Comm(XXV) (25 Feb. 2005).
739. The sanctions were based on Art. 45 of the ECOWAS Protocol A/SP1/12/01 on Democracy and Good Governance Supplementary to the Protocol relating to the Mechanism of Conflict Prevention, Management, Resolution, Peacekeeping and Security, which was adopted on 21 Dec. 2001 and entered into force on 20 Feb. 2008, reproduced in S. Ebobrah & A. Tanoh (eds), *Compendium of African Sub-Regional Human Rights Documents* (Pretoria: Pretoria University Law Press, 2010), 203. Generally, *see* F. Cowell, 'The Impact of the ECOWAS Protocol on Good Governance and Democracy', *RADIC* 19 (2011): 331.
740. *See* AU Doc. PSC/PR/Comm(XXX) (27 May 2005).

Mauritania from AU activities until constitutional order was restored.[741] The elections in March 2007, which culminated to the democratic election of President Sidi Mohamed Ould Cheikh Abdallahi, in conjunction with the positive recommendation by the AUC Chairperson,[742] led the PSC to lift 'the suspension measure' in April 2007.[743]

IV. Mauritania (August 2008–June 2009)

175. In August 2007, the Mauritanian President Abdallahi named General Abdel Aziz, the leading figure behind the August 2005 coup, as his Chief of Staff. On 6 August 2008, the Presidential Guard arrested the President, the Prime Minister, and the Minister of the Interiors. Mauritania was to be governed by an eleven-member High Council of State, headed by General Aziz, until new presidential elections were held as soon as possible. The PSC met the following day: it condemned the coup d'état, demanded the release of those arrested and that their dignity be respected, ordered the restoration of constitutional order but did not order the unconstitutional authorities' suspension from AU activities. On the contrary, it cited Article 30 of the Constitutive Act, the Lomé Declaration, and the Protocol establishing the PSC and held that these instruments 'provide in particular for the automatic suspension of the participation of the country concerned in the activities of the AU until the restoration of constitutional order' (emphasis added).[744] Effectively the PSC was saying that it was unnecessary to actually order the illegal authorities' suspension because it is a sanction imposed automatically and, consequently, does not require an express decision to that effect.

It is submitted that the argument that there is automaticity in Article 30 of the Constitutive Act making the illegal regimes' suspension redundant cannot be sustained. On the contrary, the wording of Article 30 suggests that the AU is under an obligation to do so and has no discretion because there are no circumstances justifying the use of unconstitutional means for coming into power. But this is not tantamount to saying that suspension is automatically applied without a prior decision to that effect. Moreover, Article 7(1) of the 2002 Protocol, on the one hand, authorizes the PSC to institute sanctions in cases of unconstitutional changes of government and, on the other hand, imposes upon it the duty to do so. Article 7 does not cite Article 30 of the Constitutive Act but only the Lomé Declaration, whose wording suggests that there might be discretion in ordering suspension:

> [F]ollowing the initial response of condemning the unconstitutional change by the Central Organ [now the PSC]: (a) A period of up to six months should be given to the perpetrators of the unconstitutional change to restore constitutional order. During the six month period, the government concerned should be suspended from participating in the Policy Organs of the OAU [now the AU] (emphasis added).

741. *See* AU Doc. PSC/PR/Stat.(XXXVI)-(ii) (4 Aug. 2005).
742. *See Report of the Chairperson of the Commission on the Evolving Developments in the Islamic Republic of Mauritania*, AU Doc. PSC/PR/2(LXXVI) (10 Apr. 2007).
743. *See* AU Doc. PSC/PR/Comm(LXXVI) (10 Apr. 2007).
744. *See* AU Doc. PSC/PR/Comm(CLIV) (7 Aug. 2008).

In late September 2008, the PSC held its 151st Meeting at the fringe of the UN General Assembly Annual Session in New York. After noting the lack of progress in the case of Mauritania, it linked it with the fact that Mauritania (under the overthrown regime) was the first Member State to ratify the African Charter on Democracy, Elections, and Governance in July 2008. It is not clear why the Charter was invoked: if the PSC had wanted to infer that the illegal regime was additionally bound by the Charter, this was a wrong because at the time it had not entered into force and did not produce any legal effects. Finally, the PSC resolved to declare null and void all constitutional and legislative measures adopted by the military authorities and issued an ultimatum: either unconditionally restore President Abdallahi to power by 6 October 2008 or 'the authors of the coup d'état and their civilian supporters' would face 'sanctions and isolation'.[745] A month after the deadline had expired, the PSC met to consider the situation. Surprisingly, it did not impose sanctions but requested the AUC to propose urgently concrete measures on the basis of its September 2008 Communiqué and the Lomé Declaration.[746] The Commission recommended that, if by 5 January 2009 no progress was made, the PSC consider imposing limited and targeted sanctions, including travel restrictions on and freezing the assets of all civilian personnel, military personnel, and economic operators, whose actions maintained the illegal regime in power.[747] Finally, it suggested that the UN Security Council be encouraged to assess the impact of the concerted international measures taken to restore constitutional order pursuant to the Presidential Statement of 19 August 2008 on Mauritania and to consider additional measures. In that statement,[748] the Security Council had condemned the overthrow of the democratically elected government; demanded the immediate release of President Abdallahi and the restoration of democratic institutions; recognized the important role played by the AU and the support given by regional and international partners; commented the UN Secretary General's involvement through his Special Representative for West Africa Said Djinnit, who had been appointed in February 2008;[749] called on all UN Member States to assist in restoring constitutional order; and resolved to monitor developments.

At its 163rd Meeting in December 2008, the PSC espoused the AUC's recommendations and repeated them almost verbatim with one exception: the sanctions were to be imposed if by 5 February 2009 the constitutional order had not been fully restored. Presumably, the deadline was extended by one month because, in the meantime, Abdallahi had been released, a move showing some progress towards returning to constitutional normalcy.[750] The PSC met on the day the ultimatum expired and resolved that the aforementioned sanctions had entered into force, that all AU Member States must scrupulously implement them, and that the Commission must monitor their effective implementation. Moreover, it stressed that the sanctions were not an end by themselves but should be accompanied by diplomatic efforts to ensure prompt return

745. *See* AU Doc. PSC/MIN/Comm.2(CLI) (22 Sept. 2008).
746. *See* AU Doc. PSC/PR/Comm(CLVI) (11 Nov. 2008).
747. *See Report of the Chairperson of the Commission on the Situation in Mauritania*, AU Doc. PSC/MIN/3 (CLXIII) (22 Dec. 2008).
748. *See* UN Doc. S/PRST/2008/30 (19 Aug. 2008).
749. *See* UN Doc. SG/A/1121 – BIO/3964 (28 Feb. 2008).
750. *See* AU Doc. PSC/MIN/Comm.3(CLXIII) (22 Dec. 2008).

to constitutional order. These efforts were to be undertaken by the AU and its partners and involve all Mauritanian parties.[751] One of the main problems surrounding the implementation of sanctions imposed against an undefined group of individuals is to determine their identity.

In March 2009, the PSC distinguished among three groups of targeted individuals: (a) the members of the High Council of State; (b) the members of the government; and (c) all other persons, whether civilians or military, whose activities were designed to maintain the unconstitutional *status quo*. Even though the identities of those falling into the first and second categories were largely clear, this was not the case for the third category. The task was entrusted to the AUC: it had to present the three lists by 24 April 2009.[752] On 4 June 2009, a political solution culminated to the Dakar Framework Agreement envisaging, *inter alia*, the formation of a national transitional unity government. The Agreement proved adequate for the PSC to declare that Mauritania had returned to constitutional order, to lift the suspension from participation in AU activities and to cancel the sanctions.[753] Interestingly enough, the PSC did not wait for the presidential elections, which were scheduled for July 2009, as the most appropriate sign to conclude authoritatively that democratic institutions were again fully observed. The results of the free and fair elections held on 18 July 2009 was an interesting lesson for the AU because it showed that the population does not always turns its back to those violating democratic norms: 52% of the electorate voted for Aziz to become the new president, the very individual who had orchestrated the coups d'état in August 2005 and in August 2008.

V. Guinea (December 2008–December 2010)

176. On 22 December 2008, President Lansana Conté died. Elements of the armed forces took advantage and, under the command of Captain Moussa Dadis Camara, staged a bloodless coup d'état suspending the Constitution and state institutions. A few days later, the PSC condemned it. Although one would have expected that the new authorities' participation in AU activities would have been automatically suspended (as in the case of Mauritania in August 2008), it did not happen. The PSC Communiqué simply stated that the perpetrators and those committing human rights' violations would be held accountable and dealt with accordingly.[754] Less than a week later, the PSC suspended the new regime's participation in AU activities and reaffirmed its determination to take, in due course, all other measures envisaged in the Lomé Declaration to accelerate the process of return to constitutional order.[755] Arguably, the PSC delayed the imposition of sanctions for purposes of political expediency; it would appear that ECOWAS was not convinced that the coup d'état was such a bad a thing for a country suffering from misrule for so many years. President Conte had been in power for twenty-four years having staged his own coup in 1984. The Executive

751. *See* AU Doc. PSC/PR/(CLXVIII) (5 Feb. 2009).
752. *See* AU Doc. PSC/PR/COMM(CLXXXII) (24 Mar. 2009).
753. *See* AU Doc. PSC/MIN/COMM.(CXCVI) (29 Jun. 2009).
754. *See* AU Doc. PSC/PR/Comm(CLXIV) (24 Dec. 2008).
755. *See* AU Doc.PSC/PR/Comm(CLXV) (29 Dec. 2008).

President of ECOWAS, Mohammed Ibn Chambas, had expressed to the BBC his surprise that the coup enjoyed support among political parties, civilians, and trade unions.[756] However, on 10 January 2009, an ECOWAS Authority Extraordinary Session held in Nigeria ordered the suspension of participation of the new regime in its activities pending free and fair elections. The following month, the Twelve Ordinary Assembly Session (Addis Ababa, 1–4 February 2009) supported the decisions taken by the PSC.[757]

In mid-September 2009, the PSC reviewed the situation in Guinea. In view of lack of any positive developments, it decided to impose 'appropriate' sanctions against Captain Camara, who had assumed the office of President of the National Council for Development and Democracy (NCDD), and against a number of other individuals, both civilian and military. However, the sanctions were not imposed with immediate effect but targeted individuals were given one month to comply with the demands.[758] Before the deadline had expired, the PSC asked the AUC, in collaboration with ECOWAS and other AU partners, to finalize the measures to be taken and to produce the list of the relevant individuals.[759] In the meantime, Guinea was facing a rapidly deteriorating political, security and human rights situation. On 28 September 2009, security forces under NCDD authority massacred 150 peaceful pro-democracy demonstrators and engaged in mass rapes. It was obvious that the deadline would not be observed. In late October 2009, the PSC requested the Commission, in close collaboration with ECOWAS and the International Contact Group on Guinea (ICG–G), to take all necessary measures for the targeted sanctions' implementation (principally denial of visas, travel restrictions and freezing of assets) against the President, members of NCDD, government ministers as well as civilians and military personnel involved in maintaining the unconstitutional *status quo*. The Commission was asked to circulate the list identifying these individuals within a week. Finally, as in previous occasions, the PSC moved to universalize the adopted sanctions by communicating them to the UN Security Council and to 'all other AU partners', in case of the EU, the Organization of the Islamic Cooperation, the International Organization of La Francophonie, and the League of Arab States.[760]

At the time, the PSC did not have much room for manoeuvring because on 17 October 2009, an ECOWAS Authority Extraordinary Session had discussed, *inter alia*, the massacre. It resolved to work with the AU on a 'regime of targeted sanctions' against those individuals deliberately preventing return to constitutional order as well as to impose an arms embargo on Guinea pursuant to the ECOWAS Convention on Small Arms and Light Weapons, their Ammunitions, and Related Materials, which

756. *See* BBC News, 'African Union bars Guinea on coup', 29 Dec. 2008, at: http://news.bbc.co.uk/go/pr/fr/-/2/hi/africa/7802803.stm.
757. *See* AU Assembly, *Decision on the Resurgence of the Scourge of Coups d'état in the Africa*, Assembly/AU/Dec. 220 (XII) (4 Feb. 2009).
758. *See* AU Doc. PSC/PR/Comm(CCIV) (17 Sept. 2009).
759. *See* AU Doc. PSC/PR/BR.1(CCVI) (15 Oct. 2009).
760. *See* AU Doc. PSC/AHG/COMM.2(CCVII) (29 Oct. 2009).

incidentally had entered into force on the day of the massacre.[761] Finally, it asked for the AU's support in implementing and enforcing the sanctions.[762] In early December 2010, free and fair elections led to the election of a new civilian President and, later in the same month, all AU sanctions were lifted.

VI. Niger (August 2009–March 2011)

177. On 4 August 2009, a constitutional referendum took place asking the population whether it agreed to dissolve the state of Niger and create the so-called Sixth Republic of Niger with a presidential system of government. Even though the Constitutional Court had already ruled that the plan was illegal, the referendum returned a majority for the 'yes' vote and President Mamadou Tandja changed the constitutional regime. The opposition regarded it as a coup d'état aiming at turning Niger into a dictatorship. The ECOWAS reacted first and during the aforementioned Extraordinary Authority Summit of October 2009 imposed two of the sanctions stipulated in Article 45(2) of the Supplementary Protocol on Democracy and Good Governance: first, to refuse supporting Niger's candidates for elective posts in international organizations and, second, to refuse to organize ECOWAS meetings in Niger. Moreover, it threatened that if Tandja failed to comply with its decisions, this would lead to 'the automatic and immediate imposition of [the] full sanctions [of Article 45]' and the case would be referred to the AU for similar action.[763] The PSC considered the developing situation in Niger on 29 October 2009 where it did not pronounce on the legality of the new constitutional regime but endorsed the ECOWAS decision.[764] Thus, the PSC, by endorsing the ECOWAS sanctions, concurred that Tandja's actions had violated the Constitution and had resulted in a very serious political crisis but, for whatever reason, it chose not to expressly denounce him. Although in early February 2010, the Fourteenth Ordinary Assembly Session called upon all parties in Niger to cooperate fully with the mediator, who had been appointed by the ECOWAS,[765] it was too late. The rapidly deteriorating situation culminated, on 18 February 2010, to a coup d'état staged by the military. It resulted in the formation of a junta (the Supreme Council for the

761. This Convention, signed on 14 Jun. 2006, at: https://www.sipri.org/node/2934, analysis by I. Berkol at: http://archive.grip.org/, should not be confused with similar treaties adopted by other RECs, e.g., the Protocol on the Control of Firearms, Ammunition and Other Related Materials in the Southern African Development Community (SADC) Region (signed on 14 Aug. 2001, in force since November 2004), the Central African Convention for the Control of Small Arms and Light Weapons, their Ammunition, Parts and Components that can be used for their Manufacture, Repair or Assembly (the Kinshasa Convention, adopted in April 2010, in force on 8 Mar. 2017); and the Nairobi Protocol for the Prevention, Control and Reduction of Small Arms and Light Weapons in the Great Lakes Region and the Horn of Africa (adopted on 21 Apr. 2004).

762. ECOWAS Press Release No. 111/2009, 17 Oct. 2009, at: http://news.ecowas.int.

763. ECOWAS Press Release No. 111/2009, 17 Oct. 2009, at: http://news.ecowas.int.

764. AU Doc. PSC/AHG/Comm.3(CCVII) (29 Oct. 2009).

765. *See* Assembly, *Decision on the Report of the Peace and Security Council on its Activities and the State of Peace and Security in Africa*, AU Doc. Assembly/AU/Dec. 268 (XIV) Rev.1, para. 21 (2 Feb. 2010).

Restoration of Democracy (CSRD)), which promised to turn Niger into an example of democracy and good governance and save the population from poverty and corruption. Reportedly, the population was not against the overthrow of President Tandja and the opposition Co-ordination of Democratic Forces for the Republic (CFDR), a coalition of political parties, trade unions and human rights groups formed in 2009 to protest against the constitutional changes, welcomed this development.[766]

The following day, the PSC convened for the 216th Meeting. It condemned the government's overthrow and decided 'in accordance with the relevant legal instruments of the AU' to suspend Niger's participation in all AU activities until the restoration of constitutional order, which was defined 'as the internal situation [which] stood before the referendum of 4 August 2009'.[767] Since the PSC regarded the August 2009 referendum as unconstitutional, it is submitted that it ought to have reacted at that time and condemn it. The formation of the junta was dissociated from the referendum. Therefore, the PSC dealt simultaneously with two different events – the military coup d'état and Tandja's attempt to remain in power through unconstitutional means – in a rather unsatisfactory way. The PSC also referred to the decision on Prevention of Unconstitutional Changes of Government and Strengthening of the Capacity of the AU to Manage such Situations, which the Assembly had adopted a few weeks earlier during its Fourteenth Ordinary Session.[768] Even though the decision's stated purpose was to revamp the way the AU addressed coups d'état, in reality it failed to enhance the AU's effectiveness, failed to propose any new strategy, and merely repeated the provisions of Article 25 of the Charter on Democracy, Elections and Governance.

It would appear that the Assembly considered that, from a regulatory point of view, the AU was adequately equipped to tackle coups d'état and therefore, the aim should be to focus on promoting efficient implementation and, where necessary, refinement of the legal regime. Thus, the decision emphasized the need for a comprehensive approach based on zero tolerance for coups d'état and violations of democratic standards. Moreover, it stipulated that, in addition to the sanction of suspending participation in AU activities, the following four measures shall be applied. First, perpetrators shall be barred from any elections held to restore constitutional order in the Member State concerned. Second, sanctions shall be ordered against any Member State proven to have instigated or supported coups d'état in another Member's territory. Third, the Assembly shall order additional punitive measures, including economic sanctions. Fourth, Members shall not recognize the de facto authorities. Finally, the decision called on all non-African international institutions not to grant accreditation to de facto authorities and not take actions undermining AU efforts to restore constitutional legality.

To return to the situation in Niger, with the active involvement of ECOWAS, parliamentary elections were held in October 2010 followed by presidential elections between January and March 2011. In mid-March 2011, the PSC decided to cancel the

---

766. *See* BBC News, 'African Union suspends Niger after military coup', 20 Feb. 2010, at: http://news.bbc.co.uk/2/hi/africa/8525665.stm.

767. *See* AU Doc. PSC/PR/COMM.2(CCXVI) (19 Feb. 2010).

768. *See* Assembly, *Decision on the Prevention of Unconstitutional Changes of Government and Strengthening the Capacities of the African Union to Manage such Situations*, AU Doc. Assembly/AU/Dec. 269 (XIV) Rev.1 (2 Feb. 2010).

suspension of Niger's participation in AU activities.[769] A week later, the thirty-ninth ECOWAS Authority Ordinary Session also lifted sanctions. In the present case, the PSC was prepared to leave the initiative to ECOWAS and to Nigeria, its most important Member State, and be a follower rather than leading the way as it should have done.

VII. Madagascar (March 2009–January 2014)

178. The political crisis in Madagascar, the longest in the AU history, started with a rather minor incident: in December 2008 the government of President Marc Ravalomanana closed a TV station owned by Andry Rajoelina, the Mayor of the capital. Rajoelina accused him of authoritarianism and organized a public demonstration, which attracted tens of thousands of people but resulted in several days of rioting, burning and looting leaving at least 100 people dead. When Rajoelina announced that he was taking over the government and forming a parallel cabinet, Ravalomanana removed him from office and the Mayor found refuge in the French embassy. With mounting pressure and the death toll rising, on 17 March 2009, Ravalomanana announced that he was handing power to the military, which almost immediately allowed Rajoelina to form a transitional government with a promise to hold elections.

The PSC met promptly to discuss the situation. It condemned the unconstitutional change of government; noted that it 'mark[ed] another serious setback in the ongoing democratization processes on the continent and reinforce[d] the concern over the resurgence of the scourge of coups d'état'; and resolved to suspend Madagascar from participation in AU activities.[770] On 30 March 2009, the situation was also discussed during an Extraordinary Summit of the SADC Summit of Heads of State and Government. It condemned the illegal ousting of the democratically elected government and called for an immediate restoration of constitutional order; decided not to recognize the Rajoelina regime because the Malagasy Constitution, the SADC Treaty's core principles and values, the AU Constitutive Act and the UN Charter had been violated; and, without citing any legal basis, suspended Madagascar '[f]rom all Community's institutions and organs until the return of the country to constitutional normalcy with immediate effect'.[771] At the end of April 2009, the inaugural meeting of the International Contact Group on Madagascar (ICG–M) took place. This ad hoc entity comprised of representatives from a wide array of actors: the AU, the COMESA, the EU, the Indian Ocean Commission, the International Organization of la Francophonie, the SADC, the UN, the Member States holding the Chair at the AU and the PSC, the African states elected to the Security Council as non-permanent members as well as the latter's permanent members. The ICG–M has been instrumental in maintaining open channels with the Rajoelina regime at difficult times.

During the summer of 2009, two important events occurred. First, Rajoelina formed the 'government of National Unity', excluding, however, all other political

769. *See* AU Doc. PSC/PR/COMM(CCLXVI) (16 Mar. 2011).
770. *See* AU Doc. PSC/PR/COMM(CLXXXI) (20 Mar. 2009).
771. The Communiqué is available at http://www.sadc.int. For criticism of the SADC handling, *see* International Crisis Group, *Implementing Peace and Security Architecture (II): Southern Africa*, Africa Report No. 191, 15 Oct. 2012, pp. 14–16, at: http://www.crisisgroup.org.

powers. Second, the Maputo Agreements were signed on 9 August 2009 among the principal Malagasy political stakeholders. Revised on 6 November 2009, they contained a roadmap for a peaceful and consensual transition to constitutionality. In September 2009, the PSC threatened the Rajoelina regime and its supporters with 'appropriate measures, including targeted sanctions', if they failed to implement the terms of the Maputo Agreements.[772] In mid-February 2010, the PSC repeated the threat to impose sanctions. But this time they were to be automatically applied, if by 16 March 2010 'the de facto authorities borne out of the unconstitutional change' did not implement fully the Maputo Agreements and the Addis Ababa Additional Act.[773] Never before had the PSC threatened such wide-ranging and comprehensive sanctions, which included:

(a) a travel ban against the de facto authorities and all other followers of the 'Rajoelina camp' whose actions impeded AU and SADC efforts to restore constitutional order. At its own initiative or upon request and on a case-by-case basis, the PSC reserved the power to grant, on humanitarian grounds, exemptions;
(b) freezing of the funds and other assets of all individuals and entities contributing to the maintenance of the unconstitutional *status quo* and impeding AU and SADC efforts. Again, the PSC could determine whether exemptions could be granted; and
(c) diplomatic isolation of the de facto authorities. This was to be effected through concerted action by the other Member States, which were mandated to challenge the de facto authorities' participation in the activities of non-African international organizations, including the United Nations and its Specialized Agencies.

Unlike precious instances, where the PSC had imposed sanctions against individuals and entities but had not established in advance their identity, in the present case it requested the AUC to compile, in close collaboration with the SADC, the relevant lists before the sanctions had entered into force. When the ultimatum expired, the PSC convened for its 221st Meeting. It noted that the Rajoelina regime had not complied with its obligations and decided that the sanctions had come into force as of 17 March 2010 against those individuals whose names appeared in the list attached to the Communiqué issued.[774] However, in July 2010, when the PSC discussed next the situation in Madagascar, it was clear that, despite their sweeping nature, the sanctions coupled with the Rajoelina regime's suspension from AU activities were not having the desired effects. With no other ammunition left, the PSC stressed the need for renewed efforts to ensure that sanctions are scrupulously implemented and called on the international community to assist in strengthening their effectiveness and on international organizations to coordinate their action.[775] The Assembly also discussed the situation during its Seventeenth Ordinary Session in June 2011. As no tangible proposals on forcing the Rajoelina regime to abide by constitutional principles were tabled, its response was reduced to calling upon the SADC and the AU to continue

772. *See* AU Doc. PSC/PR/BR(CCII) (10 Sept. 2009).
773. *See* AU Doc. PSC/PR/COMM.1(CCXVI) (19 Feb. 2010).
774. *See* AU Doc. PSC/PR/BR(CCXXI) (17 Mar. 2010).
775. *See* AU Doc. PSC/PR/COMM-2(CCXXXVII) (21 Jul. 2010).

working together for a consensual and sustainable solution to the crisis, in full compliance with the relevant AU instruments on unconstitutional changes of government.[776] A week later, the PSC met to give effect to the Assembly's Decision but took no concrete action.[777]

During 2012 and 2013 there were various attempts to organize elections in Madagascar and to return the country to constitutional normalcy. In the end, the first round of presidential elections was successfully held on 25 October 2013 and the second round, together with legislative elections, took place on 20 December 2013. The final results on the second round were announced in early January 2014. In September 2013, based on the fact that the timetable for elections appeared to be on track, the PSC resolved to immediately lift the sanctions which had been imposed on 109 Malagasy 'political personalities', pursuant to the aforementioned Communiqués of 19 February and 17 March 2010.[778] However, as regards the resumption of the country's participation in AU activities, the PSC decided to postpone it after the elected President had assumed his duties[779] His inauguration on 25 January 2014 satisfied it that democratic normalcy was achieved and, at its 415th meeting, held two days later, the PSC invited Madagascar to immediately resume its participation in the activities of the AU.[780] An Extraordinary SADC Summit lifted the suspension as well.[781] It has been suggested that the Charter on Democracy, and in particular Article 25(4) prohibiting perpetrators of coups d'état to partake in elections held to restore the democratic order, had a role to play in ending the impasse.[782] Considering that Madagascar was not a party to the Charter (and still is not despite signing it on 31 January 2014), it is open to doubt to which extent the fighting sides were swayed by its stipulations.

This protracted coup d'état in Madagascar clearly showed the limitations of the AU's machinery to address unconstitutional overthrow of governments even if acting in consort with RECs. Arguably if the political turmoil had taken place in previous decades it could have resulted in the de facto authorities remaining in power for much longer or even being considered as a legitimate (or legitimized) regime. However, the trend towards democratization in Africa has no doubt changed attitudes and has allowed populations to be given the opportunity to choose freely who will govern them.

---

776. *See* AU Doc. Assembly/AU/Dec. 369 (XVII) (1 Jul. 2011).
777. *See* AU Doc. PSC/PR/BR.(CCLXXXIII) (6 Jul. 2011 & 12 Jul. 2011).
778. *See* AU Doc. PSC/PR/COMM.(CCCXCIV) (5 Sept. 2013).
779. This was in line with the position adopted in a previous Communiqué, *see* AU Doc. PSC/MIN/COMM.(CCCLXVIII), para. 10 (22 Apr. 2013).
780. *See* AU Doc. PSC/PR/COMM.(CDXV) (27 Jan. 2014).
781. *See* http://sadc.int/files/1413/9109/9609/Communique_of_the_SADC_Extraodinary_Summit_-_January_2014.pdf.
782. S. Choudhry & S. Bisarya, 'Regional Organizations and Threats to Constitutional Democracy from Within: Self Coups and Authoritarian Backsliding' in *Rule of Law and Constitution Building: The Role of Regional Organizations*, International Institute for Democracy and Electoral Assistance (ed.), (Stockholm: 2014) 183, 195.

VIII. Côte d'Ivoire (December 2010–April 2011)

179. Even though elections in November 2010 had ousted President Laurent Gbagbo, he refused to recognize the results, as proclaimed by the IEC and certified by the Special Representative of the UN Secretary-General appointed pursuant to UNSC Resolution 1765(2007) of 16 July 2007. It was not the first time that Côte d'Ivoire had been embroiled in political turmoil following presidential elections: in 2005, the AU had appointed the then President of South Africa, Thabo Mbeki, as Mediator and, while the PSC had expressed its willingness, upon his recommendation, to impose appropriate sanctions against those blocking the constitutional process,[783] no sanctions were ever imposed. When it became clear that the President-Elect, Alassane Ouattara, was prevented from exercising his authority, first, the ECOWAS and, then, the AU responded swiftly. On 7 December 2010, an Extraordinary ECOWAS Authority Session told Gbagbo that he must go.[784] A few days later, the PSC decided to suspend Côte d'Ivoire's participation in AU activities until Ouattara had assumed power.[785] Despite universal condemnation, Gbagbo was refusing to cede power and the country was driven to chaos and anarchy with heavy casualties among the population. The PSC met twice at the level of Heads of State or Government in January 2011 and in March 2011 but did not adopt any sanctions (a rather indirect threat was made in the latter meeting but was never materialized).[786] However, the UN Security Council ordered sanctions under Resolution 1975(2011) of 30 March 2011.[787] In particular, the Security Council imposed targeted sanctions on five high-ranking officials, including Gbagbo.

The impasse ended when in mid-April 2011 Gbagbo was placed under house arrest. Following the assumption of power by President Ouattara, the AUC issued a report where it argued that it was necessary to lift the suspension so as to 'help consolidate the positive development recorded in Côte d'Ivoire, while allowing it to

---

783. *See* AU Doc. PSC/Min/Comm.(XXXIV)–(ii) (3 Jul. 2005).

784. *See also* ECOWAS Authority Extraordinary Session, *Final Communiqué*, 24 Dec. 2010, threatening to use legitimate force to oust Gbagbo, ECW/CEG/ABJ/EXT/FR./Rev.0, para. 10, at: http://www.ecowas.int. *See* further J. Dubé Gagnon, 'ECOWAS's Right to Intervene in Côte d'Ivoire to Install Alassane Ouattara as President-Elect' *Notre Dame J. of Int'l & Comparative L.* III (2013) 51 claiming that ECOWAS had no power to interfere.

785. *See* AU Doc. PSC/PR/COMM.1(CCLII) (9 December 2010). For criticism of the AU's handling of the affair, *see* E. Abatan &Y. Spies, 'African Solutions to African Problems? The AU, R2P and Côte d'Ivoire', *South African Journal of International Affairs* 23 (2016): 21.

786. *See* AU Docs PSC/AHG/COMM(CCLIX) (28 Jan. 2011) and PSC/AHG/COMM.1(CCLXV) (10 Mar. 2011).

787. The UNSC had expressed its readiness to impose targeted measures against those individuals threatening the peace process, obstructing the work of the United Nations Operation in Côte d'Ivoire (UNOCI) or committing serious human rights violations, *see* Press Statement on Côte d'Ivoire, UN Doc. SC/10105-AFR/2079, 8 Dec. 2010, at: https://www.un.org/press/en/2010/sc10105.doc.htm. Further, *see* UNSC Res. 1946(2010) of 15 Oct. 2010.

make its contribution to the attainment of the objectives of our Union'.[788] On 21 April 2011, the PSC cancelled the suspension noting that this decision 'will help consolidate the positive development recorded in Côte d'Ivoire, while allowing it to make its contribution to the attainment of the objectives of our Union'.[789] It should be noted that the ICC has assumed competence to investigate the crimes committed during the period of post-election violence between December 2010 and April 2011 and prosecute those allegedly responsible. Thus, in November 2011, former President Laurent Gbagbo was transferred to ICC custody and in February 2003 the charges brought against him as indirect co-perpetrator for crimes against humanity were confirmed; in February 2012 a Warrant of Arrest was issued against his wife Simone Gbagbo for the same alleged crimes (she is not currently in ICC custody), and in December 2011, a Warrant of Arrest was issued against Charles Blé Goudé, who was described not only as being 'part of Mr Gbagbo's inner circle' but also as his mouthpiece and 'spin doctor'. He surrendered to ICC custody on 27 March 2014 and on 11 December 2014 he was committed to trial. The cases against Laurent Gbagbo and Charles Blé Goudé were joined on 11 March 2015 and the trial commenced on 28 January 2016.[790] The trial is currently ongoing.[791]

IX. Mali (April 2012–October 2012)

180. In March 2012, army rebels deposed the democratically elected government of Malian President Amadou Toumani Toure in a coup d'état causing considerable loss of life. The PSC convened promptly and given that Mali had also been confronted with rebellion by armed groups in its northern territory, it regarded that the situation was not only posing a threat to national unity and territorial integrity but also to regional peace and security.[792] A few days later, the PSC ordered the immediate suspension of Mali from AU activities.[793] After the ECOWAS had adopted its own punitive measures against the insurgents on 27 March 2012,[794] sanctions were also ordered by the PSC in early April 2012. In particular, the PSC decided to impose 'individual measures',

788. *See Report of the Chairperson of the Commission on the Situation in Cote d'Ivoire*, AU Doc. PSC/PR/2 (CCLXXIII), 21 Apr. 2011. Note that in July 2011 Gbagbo challenged the legality of the house arrest before the ECOWAS Court of Justice, which held that it was illegal, arbitrary and violated Art. 6 of the African Human Rights Charter, *Simone & Michel Gbagbo v. Cote d'Ivoire*, Decision No. ECW/CCJ/JUD/03/13, 22 Feb. 2013, at: http://www.courtecowas.org (in French).
789. *See* AU Doc. PSC/PR/2 (CCLXXIII) (21 Apr. 2011), para. 18.
790. *See* further, Statement *of ICC Prosecutor at the Commencement of Trial in the case against Messrs. Laurent Gbagbo and Charles Blé Goudé*, 28 Jan. 2016, at: http://www.icc-cpi.int.
791. Note that Côte d'Ivoire signed the ICC Rome Statute on 30 Nov. 1998 but ratified it only on 15 Feb. 2013.
792. *See* AU Doc. PSC/PR/COMM(CCCXI), 20 Mar. 2012.
793. *See* AU Doc. PSC/PR/COMM(CCCXV), 23 Mar. 2012.
794. ECOWAS Authority Extraordinary Summit, *Final Communiqué*, 27 Mar. 2012, ECOWAS Press Release No. 083/2012 (27 Mar. 2012), at: http://news.ecowas.int. It also established the Contact Group of Mali, composed of Benin, Burkina Faso, Côte d'Ivoire, Liberia, Niger, Nigeria and Togo.

including a travel ban and asset freeze, against the junta but also against other individuals and entities deemed to be contributing to the maintenance of the unconstitutional status quo. It also 'recalled' that, pursuant to Article 25(5) of the African Charter on Democracy, Elections, and Governance, coup d'état perpetrators are liable to prosecution.[795] However the implementation of the AU sanctions seems to have been delayed because the list of targeted individuals was not promptly finalized.

It should be observed that the Malian case should be distinguished from previous instances of coups d'état, because, over and above the issue of the culpability of those responsible for the loss of life, there was also the culpability for severe attacks against religious and historic buildings, many of which are protected as UNESCO World Heritage sites. In early July 2012, the UN Security Council emphasized the cultural dimension of the rebellion and argued that these attacks could constitute violations of international law possibly falling under the Rome Statute establishing the ICC.[796] Two weeks later, the government of Mali, as a contracting party to the Rome Statute since 16 August 2000, referred 'the situation in Mali since January 2012' to the ICC Prosecutor and requested its investigation because domestic courts were unable to prosecute alleged perpetrators.[797] It was also in July 2012 that the PSC, for the first time ever, asked the African Commission on Human and People's Rights[798] to investigate the human rights situation in northern Mali since January 2012, and 'to submit a comprehensive report with concrete recommendations on the way forward'.[799] Both investigations are ongoing.[800]

It was also in mid-July 2012 that the situation in the northern part of Mali was discussed in the context of the Nineteenth Ordinary Assembly Session. Instead of issuing a decision, the Assembly adopted a Solemn Declaration on Mali which, *inter alia*, authorized the PSC to take all appropriate measures on behalf of the entire AU membership.[801] However, developments were swift: on 20 August 2012, a Government of National Unity was formed and this led the PSC to declare, a fortnight later, its readiness to review its decision on suspending Mali from participation in AU organs.[802] Arguably, the PSC could have lifted the suspension at its September 2012 meeting. However, it probably wanted to play it safe and wait for more concrete progress. But when the UN Security Council adopted Resolution 2071(2012) on 12 October 2012 and, *inter alia*, called on regional and international organizations, including the AU, to provide as soon as possible coordinated assistance, expertise, training and capacity-building to the Malian armed and security forces, the PSC could not have continued maintaining the suspension and, on 24 October 2012, it was lifted.[803] Finally, it is

795. *See* AU Doc. PSC/PR/COMM(CCCXVI), 3 Mar. 2012.
796. UNSC Res. 2056(2012) of 5 Jul. 2012, para. 16.
797. ICC Press Release, ICC-OTP-20120718-PR829, 18 Jul. 2012.
798. For previous Resolutions of the African Human Rights Commission on Mali, *see* Res. 209 (24 Feb. 2012) and Res. 217 (3 May 2012), at: http://www.achpr.org.
799. *See* AU Doc. PSC/AHG/COMM/1(CCCXXVII), para. 15 (14 Jul. 2013).
800. For subsequent Resolutions of the African Human Rights Commission on Mali, *see* Res. 238 (24 Jul. 2013) and Res. 258 (5 Nov. 2013).
801. *See* AU Doc. Assembly/AU/Decl. 1 (XIX), para. 16(e) (16 Jul. 2012).
802. *See* AU Doc. PSC/PR/COMM(CCCXXXII), 4 Sept. 2012.
803. *See* AU Doc. PSC/MIN/COMM.2(CCCXXXIX), para. 6 (24 Oct. 2012).

important to note that the ICC is also investigating alleged crimes committed in Mali since January 2012 and coming under its ambit following the referral of the situation to the ICC by the Malian government in July 2012.[804]

X. Guinea-Bissau (April 2012–April 2014)

181. A(nother) coup d'état took place in Guinea-Bissau on 12 April 2012, two weeks before the second round of the presidential elections which had been scheduled for later that month. The first round had been deemed free and fair. A week later, the PSC suspended, with immediate effect, the country's participation in AU activities until the effective restoration of constitutional order. Moreover, invoking the frequency of coups d'état in Guinea-Bissau and using as legal basis the African Charter on Democracy Elections and Governance, it requested the AUC, in consultation with the ECOWAS and (unnamed) AU partners, to submit within two weeks proposals on additional sanctions, against the perpetrators and their civilian and military supporters, including a travel ban and an asset freeze.[805] But a week later, the PSC met and, *inter alia*:

> Request[ed] the Commission, in view of the refusal of the coup perpetrators to respond positively to the calls from the AU, ECOWAS, the CPLP [Community of Portuguese Speaking Countries] and the UN Security Council and other members of the international community, for the restoration of constitutional order, to compile and disseminate to all Member States, after appropriate consultations, the list of the members of the military junta and their military and civilian supporters, for application of the individual measures mentioned in paragraph 6 of communiqué PSC/PR/COMM(CCCXVIII).[806] Council call[ed] on all Member States to fully implement these sanctions. Council further request[ed] the Commission to expedite, in consultation with ECOWAS, the finalization of its proposals on additional sanctions to be imposed on members of the junta and their military and civilian supporters (emphasis added)[807]

804. *See* ICC Office of the Prosecutor, *Situation in Mali. Art. 53(1) Report*, 16 Jan. 2013, at: http://www.icc-cpi.int. It is rather interesting to question whether the UNSC ought to have referred the situation in Mali to the ICC, as it did with Darfur and Libya. Clearly there are merits in the suggestion of Togo, made during the UNSC discussion in October 2012 on promoting the rule of law and maintaining peace and security with a special focus on the ICC, that to achieve impartiality, consistency and transparency, it should establish clear criteria for determining which situations should be referred to the ICC and which not, *see* UN Doc. S/PV. 6849, p. 21 (17 Dec. 1012).
805. *See* AU Doc. PSC/PR/COMM(CCCXVIII), para. 6 (17 Apr. 2012).
806. Compare UNSC Res. 2048(2012) of 18 May 2012 imposing a travel ban on five junta members and establishing a Sanctions Committee to monitor implementation. The UNSC was influenced by the Report submitted by the UN Secretary-General on the situation in Guinea-Bissau following the coup d'état, UN Doc. S/2012/280 (30 Apr. 2012).
807. *See* AU Doc. PSC/MIN/COMM/1(CCCXIX), para. 8 (24 Apr. 2012).

The wording of the text raises again the aforementioned issue of the automaticity of AU sanctions. And this because the envisaged 'individual measures' had not actually been imposed at the previous PSC Meeting but were treated as if they had been imposed. Moreover, although the Nineteenth Ordinary Assembly Session, reference to which has been made, discussed the situation in Guinea-Bissau in the context of reviewing PSC activities (as it did with the situation in Mali),[808] it only condemned the coup d'état[809] and did not adopt a separate instrument (as it did with Mali). The progress of the transitional organs in Guinea-Bissau towards restoring constitutional order divided ECOWAS and the AU on whether to maintain the sanctions imposed: at the end of June 2012, ECOWAS suspended them and called for lifting Guinea-Bissau's exclusion from AU activities.[810] But in January 2013, the PSC decided to maintain them.[811] On 17 July 2013, the ECOWAS Mediation and Security Council reiterated the call that the AU recognize the ongoing transition process and urged 'international partners' to consider lifting sanctions and resume bilateral cooperation.[812] Later on the same day, the Forty-Third Ordinary ECOWAS Authority Session repeated the call emphatically.[813] However, it turned out that the AU was right to continue excluding it because, at the time, the planned Presidential and legislative elections were considerably delayed, a fact also criticized by the UN Security Council.[814] The elections finally took place on 13 April 2014 and, three days later when the new President had assumed office, the PSC invited Guinea-Bissau to resume its participation in AU's activities.[815]

XI. The (So-Called) Arab Spring (Tunisia, Egypt, Libya) and the Problem of Very Long Serving Heads of State (2010/2011 – Today)

182. Judging by events, the AU was rather ill prepared to handle the uprisings in its northern Member States, even though there were good reasons to believe that the pro-democracy trend which had been developing in other parts of the continent would engulf the autocratic and dictatorial North Africa as well. Indeed, a high-level meeting organized by the PSC in April 2014 noted the weaknesses and gaps in the AU's normative framework which had impacted its response to the uprisings.[816] While the PSC did condemn the violence which followed the popular uprisings in Tunisia, in Egypt, and in Libya and asked the incumbent regimes to honour the legitimate

808. *See* Assembly, *Decision on the Report of the Peace and Security Council on its Activities and the State of Peace and Security in Africa*, AU Doc. Assembly/AU/Dec. 432 (XIX), para. 4 (16 Jul. 2012).
809. *Ibid.*, para. 7.
810. *See* UNSC, *Report of the Secretary-General on the restoration of constitutional order in Guinea-Bissau*, UN Doc. S/2012/704, para. 14 (12 Sept. 2012), at: http://www.un.org/en/sc/documents/sgreports/2012.shtml.
811. *See* AU Doc. PSC/PR/COMM(CCCLI), para. 6 (16 Jan. 2013).
812. *See* ECOWAS Press Release, No. 208/2013, 17 Jul. 2013, at: http://news.ecowas.int.
813. ECOWAS Press Release, No. 210/2013, 17 Jul. 2013.
814. *See* Statement by the President of the Security Council, UN Doc. S/PRST/2013/19 (9 Dec. 2013).
815. AU Doc. PSC/PR/COMM.(CDXXIX), 16 Apr. 2014, para. 8.
816. PSC, Press Statement of the 432nd Meeting, PSC/PR/BR.(CDXXXII), 29 Apr. 2014.

aspirations of their populations,[817] an important question of substance vis-à-vis democratic governance in Africa was not addressed. Given that the relevant AU instruments (including the Constitutive Act, the PSC Protocol, and the African Charter on Democracy Elections and Governance) talk only about democratic change of government, the question not tackled (or avoided for political reasons) was whether these uprisings (or rebellions) resulted in undemocratic regime changes. It is submitted that the answer should be in the affirmative. One should remember that the international community never challenged the authority of President Zine El Abidine Ben Ali, of President Hosni Mubarak and of Colonel Gaddafi, always accepted them as the legitimate representatives of their states, always transacted with them, and always held them responsible for criminal acts committed by their states. That they run their countries as autocrats, as dictators, with no respect for human rights and fundamental freedoms was a well-known fact but other states and international organizations (including the AU as is later explained) never challenged the validity of the credentials issued by their regimes, inadvertently accepting that democratic and undemocratic / totalitarian countries simply co-exist on the global plane.

In particular, the aforementioned AU instruments fail to stipulate if the undemocratic overthrow of dictatorial/unconstitutional regimes (especially when violence has been used) could, under CERTAIN circumstances, be treated as a legitimate act. However, the fact remains that, while these instruments regard all coups d'état to be *a priori* illegal, a sizeable number of African states have been ruled for so many years by tyrants and despots. It follows that, when adopted, these instruments did not acknowledge what the real status of democratic governance in the continent was. On the contrary, they rather assumed that all African states had functional constitutional regimes in power and, therefore, to be unconstitutionally overturned (forcefully or not) does constitute an illegal act. At the beginning of 2014, there were at least six heads of state with extremely long periods in office: Teodoro Obiang Nguema Mbasogo of Equatorial Guinea (in office for thirty-six years), José Eduardo dos Santos of Angola (thirty-six years), Robert Mugabe of Zimbabwe (twenty-seven years), Paul Biya of Cameroon (thirty-three years), Yoweri Museveni of Uganda (twenty-eight years), and Blaise Compaoré of Burkina Faso (twenty-six years). At the beginning of 2017, five of them were still in office, allowing the argument that they have long exceeded what should be democratically accepted and tolerated. The only President who lost power in the meantime was Compaoré in October 2014 when hundreds of thousands took to the streets of Burkina Faso to complain for his attempt to prolong his office. He was forced to resign.[818] As of late, certain African leaders have promoted the idea of becoming 'Presidents for Life' despite strong opposition from the population. Thus, the decision by President Pierre Nkurunziza of Burundi to seek in 2015 a third term in office at all

817. *See* , *inter alia*, PSCPR/COMM.(CCLXI), 23 Feb. 2011.
818. *See* 'Burkina Faso general takes over as Compaore resigns', *BBC News*, 1 Nov. 2014, at: http://www.bbc.com/news/world-africa-29851445.

costs (the Constitution does not allow it) resulted in violence and many killings,[819] while Presidents Dennis Sassou Nguesso of Congo-Brazzaville and Paul Kagame of Rwanda put in motion the procedure to extend the length of their office.[820] Finally, President Joseph Kabila of DRC wanted to follow suit when his second term in office was to expire at the end of 2016.[821] He was not successful and on 31 December 2016 he signed an AU facilitated political agreement with his opponent Étienne Tshisekedi on the DRC's consensual management of the country until the next parliamentary and legislative elections which must be organized no later than December 2017. Until then, Kabila will remain President but he is obliged to ensure a peaceful transfer of power to the winner of the presidential election in which he may not be a contender.[822]

In the discussion of what constitutes democratic governance in Africa and when the undemocratic overthrow of a legitimate government may be condoned, events in Egypt after the overthrow of the Mubarak regime by popular uprising, the formation of the Mohamed Morsi government in June 2012 through democratic elections, and its non-democratic overthrow by means of military intervention in July 2013 are of particular interest, not least because the AU reacted differently from other international organizations. In the beginning of the uprises in North African the PSC was quick to side with those fighting the incumbent regimes and to express its solidarity. More specifically, in a Communiqué issued in February 2011 the PSC 'took note of the ardent aspirations of the Egyptian people … for change and the opening of the … political space … to democratically establish and designate institutions that are truly representative and respectful of human rights and freedoms'.[823] Two aspects stand out. The first is that AU organs had not in the past questioned seriously the legitimacy of incumbent regimes. This begs the question how was it that Mubarak, who had ruled as a dictator for almost thirty years and, according to the Communiqué, his regime did not respect fundamental freedoms and, therefore, it was not representative of Egyptians, was permitted to participate in the AU for so long. To put the question otherwise: what was the material difference between the Mubarak and the 'illegal authorities' in another African state which had assumed power by forcefully overthrowing the previous totalitarian regime? Because in the latter case, as has been seen from the coups d'état examined in the previous pages, the 'illegal authorities' were not only suspended from

819. In the event, he won the July 2015 Presidential elections and is currently serving the third consecutive term but the domestic strife has continued unabated, Compare UNSC Res 2248(2015) of 12 Nov. 2015, 2279(2016) of 1 Apr. 2016, and, more recently, 2303(2016) of 29 Jul. 2016. The latter's lack of implementation was lamented in a UNSC Statement in March 2017, *see* UN Doc. SC/1275 (13 Mar. 2017), at: https://www.un.org/press/en/2017/sc12750.doc.htm.

820. In October 2015, the necessary constitutional amendments were overwhelmingly approved by a referendum in Congo-Brazzaville and by the Rwandan Parliament. *See* generally, K. Sieff, 'Obama's Push for Democracy in Africa Runs Up Against 'Presidents for Life'', *The Washington Post*, 2 Dec. 2015, at: http://www.washingtonpost.com.

821. K. Roth &I. Sawyer, 'Joseph Kabila Forever: The Dangers of an Extended Presidency in the Democratic Republic of the Congo', *Foreign Policy*, 28 Jul. 2015, at: http://foreignpolicy.com/2015/07/28/joseph-kabila-forever-congo-president-extend-term/.

822. Compare Statement by the President of the UNSC, UN Doc. S/PRST/2017/1, 4 Jan. 2017, and Res. 2277(2016) of 30 Mar. 2016.

823. UN Doc. PSCPR/COMM.(CCLX), 16 Feb. 2011.

AU activities but often sanctions were imposed against the coup leaders and their associates.

The answer should lie in the fact that, when at the turn of this century democratic values were embedded in the AU as guiding principles, Member States ought to have put words into deeds and abandon the long-held view that undemocratic regimes are acceptable and could remain in office. In other words, the AU membership had been presented with a choice: either commence a long and arduous process towards democratization or maintain the status quo of undemocratic regimes. Evidently, they chose the latter, which has resulted in totalitarian governments being perpetuated, often with devastating effects for the populations. This situation is reminiscent of one of the major issues which the OAU founders had to address. It concerned the borders of then newly independent African states and the dilemma whether to redraw them to accommodate the local populations' desires or keep them as determined by the colonial powers to suit their own needs. Faithful to the principle of international law that newly independent states should maintain the borders existing before independence (*uti possidetis juris*), they chose the latter. And this choice has led to many anomalies and conflicts plaguing African until today.

The second aspect is that when the Communiqué was issued in mid-February 2011 the uprising in Egypt was still a domestic matter.[824] It did not pose a threat to regional peace and security and no war crimes or crimes against humanity had arguably taken place. Putting this state of affairs into the context of the Constitutive Act, it should be noted that Article 4(g) thereof expects Member States not to interfere in the internal affairs of another country. Moreover, Article 4(h) endows the AU with the right to intervene in a Member State but only when grave circumstances (defined as war crimes, genocide and crimes against humanity) are present. Arguably the PSC used the apparent violation by the Mubarak regime of the commitments Egypt had assumed as a contracting party to the Constitutive Act (promote democratization and good governance, respect for human rights, etc.) to dispute the regime's legality. By doing so, it is submitted, the PSC intervened in Egypt's domestic affairs.

The Egyptian uprising culminated to democratic elections in July 2012 returning Mohammed Morsi of the Muslim Brotherhood as the first democratically elected President. Five months later a free and fair referendum approved the new Constitution[825] but a year later he was overturned and the Constitution was suspended. While the new military-controlled regime apparently had the support of a considerable part of the population, both the EU and the UN chose to play politics: they failed to outrightly denounce the army orchestrated coup d'état and to demand the return to constitutional

824. For an overview, *see* O. Varol, 'The Democratic Coup d'Etat',*Harvard International Law Journal* 53 (2012): 291.

825. For unofficial translation, *see* http://constitutionaltransitions.org/wp-content/uploads/2013/05/Egypt-Constitution-26-December-2012.pdf.

normalcy but signalled their readiness to work with the new regime.[826] However, the PSC treated it as an illegal seizure of power. On 5 July 2013, it issued a Communiqué where, after recalling that the relevant AU instruments on unconstitutional change of government 'provide[d] for the automatic implementation of specific measures whenever an unconstitutional change of Government occurs', it suspended Egypt form participating in the AU until restoration of the constitutional order. The PSC also emphasized the AU's solidarity with the Egyptian population as well as its commitment to 'support long-term efforts to address the structural problems facing Egypt'.[827] In effect the PSC followed the relevant instruments to the letter without taking into consideration the ideological struggle which dominated these events, namely the Islamist regime run by Morsi versus the lay regime run by the military.[828]

The PSC justified the suspension on the ground that the Egyptian Constitution did not condone the overthrow of a democratically elected President.[829] Arguably, no democratic constitution would ever excuse such an act. However, more importantly, constitutions are domestic legal instruments having a legal effect within the boundaries of the respective state and, therefore, their stipulations should, in principle, not be invoked to justify imposing punitive measures by an intergovernmental organization. To put it otherwise, were the Egyptian Constitution to tolerate undemocratic acts would this have prevented the PSC from exercising its powers as it thought fit? The answer should be in the negative because the PSC draws its mandate and its legitimacy from multilateral instruments which are founded on the collective agreement of all Member States to promote and protect democratic values. To that extent, it could be argued with some persuasion that these instruments stand higher than domestic constitutions. But even if one agreed that the PSC acted correctly as regards the events of July 2013, one cannot but accuse it of double standards. And this because, while it overlooked the totalitarian rule during the Mubarak era, it was quick to suspend the participation of the military backed regime in the AU, even though it was clear that increasingly a substantial part of the population supported it. Thus, when in late May 2014 the planned presidential elections took place, Abdel Fatah el-Sisi, the former chief of the Egyptian army, overwhelmingly won them with 96% of the votes cast,[830] a percentage that does

826. *See* Statement by EU High Representative Catherine Ashton on developments in Egypt, 3 Jul. 2013, at:http://eeas.europa.eu/delegations/egypt/press_corner/all_news/news/2013/20130704_en.htm and Statement by the UN Secretary-General, who, even though he regarded that the 'military interference in the affairs of any State is of concern', was happy not to condemn it as long as an 'inclusive approach' was taking place, UN Press Release SG/SM/15151-AFR/2657, 3 Jul. 2013, at: http://www.un.org/press/en/2013/sgsm15151.doc.htm.

827. AU Doc. PSC/PR/COMM.(CCCLXXXIV), 5 Jul. 2013, paras 6 and 9.

828. Compare E. Hellquist, *Regional Organizations and Sanctions Against Members – Explaining the Different Trajectories of the African Union, the League of Arab States, and the Association of Southeast Asian Nation*s, Freie Universität Berlin (KFG Working Paper Series, No. 59, January 2014) 14, at: http://userpage.fu-berlin.de/kfgeu/kfgwp/wpseries/WorkingPaperKFG_59.pdf.

829. *See* Art. 6 of the Constitution of 2012 stipulating that the political system is based, *inter alia*, on the peaceful transfer of power.

830. *See The Guardian*, 'Abdel Fatah al-Sisi won 96.1% of vote in Egypt presidential election, say officials', 2 Jun. 2014, at: https://www.theguardian.com/world/2014/jun/03/abdel-fatah-al-sisi-presidential-election-vote-egypt.

bring to mind non-democratic electorate processes. The military regime had already drafted a new Constitution, which was approved by a referendum held on 14 and 15 January 2014 and considered to be free and fair.[831]

On account of these political developments, it was difficult and politically inexpedient for the PSC to press for Egypt's continued exclusion from AU activities. In particular, the PSC would need to explain why these events did not amount to restoration of constitutional order in the country. Clearly this position would have been hard to sustain and the PSC was already criticized for the way it had handled the change in government in July 2013. Thus, in June 2014, two weeks after el-Sisi was elected President, it adopted a Communiqué resolving to lift the suspension of participation and invited Egypt to immediately resume its seat.[832] By following to the letter the provisions of the AU instruments against coups d'état, the PSC may have fulfilled its role and mandate but, in retrospect, its action could have been questioned, especially since, as has been explained, other international organizations never took an expressly negative stance *vis-à-vis* the perpetrators of the July 2013 coup. This reality should explain the fact that in the June 2014 Communiqué the PSC was so eager to defend its actions by reaffirming 'the correctness of its decision characterising the events of 3 July 2013 in Egypt as falling under the definition of unconstitutional changes of Government as stipulated in the relevant AU instruments'.[833]

At the same time, the adoption of the Communiqué had to overcome a hurdle of some importance: both Article 25(4) of the Charter on Democracy and the Assembly Decision on Prevention of Unconstitutional Changes of Government[834] stipulate that the perpetrators of coups d'état are not to be allowed to participate in any elections held to restore constitutional order. Evidently the problem was that, since el-Sisi had come to power in a manner conflicting with the aforementioned Article 6 of the Constitution of 2012(effectively it amounted to a coup d'état), he could not have been a contender in the May 2014 presidential elections.[835] From a legal perspective, the PSC could not have bypassed these prohibitions: rules are rules and may not be varied according to prevailing circumstances. Nevertheless, there might be political considerations diluting legal normativity. Thus, a compromise solution was necessary, one which would allow Egypt to resume participation but would not compromise the PSC's authority as the Member States' constitutional watchdog. In the event, the PSC lifted Egypt's suspension but only 'on the understanding that this does not constitute a precedent in terms of adherence' to the relevant AU instruments.[836] In other words, the PSC let it be known that this was an extraordinary case justifying extraordinary

831. For the official AU record of events in Egypt since January 2011, *see* PSC, *Final Report of the African Union High-Level Panel for Egypt*, PSC/AHG/4.(CDXVI), 17 Jun. 2014, at http://www.peaceau.org/uploads/auhpe-report-egypt-16-06-2014.pdf.

832. AU Doc. PSC/PR/COMM.2(CDXLII), 17 Jun. 2014, para. 8, at: http://www.peaceau.org/uploads/psc-com-442-egypt-17-06-2014.pdf.

833. *Ibid.*, para. 2.

834. Assembly/AU/Dec. 269 (XIV) Rev.1, *supra* .

835. Under Art. 5 of the Amended Constitution of 2014 the political system is based on the peaceful rotation of power, *see* the unofficial translation provided by the State Information Service of Egypt, at: http://www.sis.gov.eg/Newvr/Dustor-en001.pdf.

836. PSC/PR/COMM.2(CDXLII), *supra* .

treatment. When ten days later the Assembly discussed the work of the PSC during the first semester of 2014, it did not touch upon this rather crucial and delicate issue but only noted with satisfaction Egypt's return.[837] The question of when would an undemocratic change of government be regarded as 'popular uprising' and, consequently, the new regime would not be suspended from participating in AU activities and its perpetrators and supporters would not face punitive measures was left unanswered, even though the PSC was of view that it ought to be dealt with at the level of AU Heads of State and Government.[838]

Regarding the general handling of the 'Arab Spring', the AU, and especially the PSC, have been criticized for not applying (particularly in the case of the Libyan uprising with its heavy toll on human life) Article 4(h) of the Constitutive Act. As it will be recalled, it permits the AU to intervene in the territory of a Member State if grave circumstances are present.[839] As is well-known, Article 4(h) is considered to be a manifestation of the Responsibility to Protect (R2P), a concept developed by the UN[840] but not without ambiguities.[841] As argued elsewhere in the present monograph, the application of Article 4(h) is surrounded by a number of issues, which for present purposes raise the following questions. First, should the AU have devised a specific set of rules for the purposes of coups d'état? Second, irrespective of Article 4(h), could the AU, acting through the Assembly and/or the PSC have applied the R2P concept directly?[842] Third, does the AU have an independent right to hold the alleged perpetrators of humanitarian and human rights' violations which took place during popular revolts personally accountable?

The situation in Libya offers a good illustration because, over and above the proceedings pursued domestically, the ICC has opened an investigation pursuant to the referral made in February 2011 by the UN Security Council under Resolution

---

837. Assembly, *Decision on the Report of the Peace and Security Council on its Activities and the State of Peace and Security in Africa*, AU Doc. Assembly/AU/Dec. 536 (XXIII), 27 Jun. 2014, para. 8.
838. PSC/PR/COMM.2(CDXLII), *supra* para. 9.
839. *See* , *inter alia*, J.F. Mutton, 'Article 4(h) and the Citizen's Right to be Protected' in *Africa and the Responsibility to Protect – Article 4(h) of the African Union Constitutive Act,* D. Kuwali & F. Viljoen (eds)(London: Routledge, 2014), 97, 105 et seq.; A. Girmachew, *A Study of the African Union's Right of Intervention Against Genocide, Crimes Against Humanity and War Crimes* (Nijmegen: Wolf Legal Publishers, 2011). Specifically, as regards the Arab Spring, *see* K.N. Obse, 'The "African Spring" and the Question of Legitimacy of Democratic Revolution in Theory and Practice', *Human Security Perspectives* 10 (2014): 232, 265.
840. *See* UNGA Resolution 60/1, *World Summit Outcome*, 16 Sept. 2005, paras 138–139.
841. *See* J. Genser & I. Cotler, *The Responsibility to Protect* (Oxford: Oxford University Press, 2012), 28 et seq.
842. While it has been argued that R2P is widely acknowledged within the AU, N. Zähringer, 'Norm Evolution Within and Across the African Union and the United Nations: The Responsibility to Protect (R2P) as a Contested Norm', *South African Journal of International Affairs* 20 (2013): 187, arguably this is quite separate from actually invoking it, applying it, and implementing it during a specific situation.

1970(2011).[843] Thus, could the AU have initiated criminal proceedings against, on the one hand, dignitaries of the old regime (including Saif Al-Islam Gaddafi, the son of the late Colonel Gaddafi)[844] and, on the other hand, those allegedly responsible for killing civilians loyal to the Gaddafi regime?[845]

These are not purely theoretical questions. It is true that after the Gaddafi regime's demise the AU has not apparently attempted to discuss what actually happened during the uprising,[846] but has been content to leave the matter to be handled by others despite the consequences for neighbouring countries.[847] Only in January 2016 did it decide to establish the High-Level Committee of Heads of State and Government,[848] as had been agreed by the PSC eighteen months earlier to support peace and reconstruction in Libya.[849] However, if the aforementioned Protocol attaching an International Criminal Law Section to the ACJHR (Malabo Protocol) and the annexed Statute had entered into force, the ICL Section would have been competent to adjudicate criminal prosecutions brought against individuals allegedly involved in unconstitutional changes of government. To that extent, the AU would have been directly involved, alongside the ICC and domestic criminal proceedings.[850] Although not stated in the Malabo Protocol, the ICL Section fulfils Article 25(5) of the Charter on Democracy stipulating that the illegal acts envisaged therein may also be tried before the AU Court. Indeed, under new Article 28(F) of the ACJHR Statute, the international crime of unconstitutional changes of government goes far beyond coups d'état and covers additionally the refusal of a government to relinquish power following free and fair elections as well as Constitutional amendments which are considered to be incompatible with democratic principles.

843. *See* ICC, Pre-Trial Chamber I, ICC-01/11-01/11, *The Prosecutor v. Saif Al-Islam Gaddafi and Abdullah Al-Senussi*. Further *see* , K.D. Magliveras, 'Recent Developments in the 'Situation in Libya' and the Trial of Saif Al-Islam Gaddafi', *International Enforcement Law Reporter* 28 (2012): 294.

844. In late July 2015 he was sentenced to death by a court in Tripoli, *see* http://www.theguardian.com/world/2015/jul/28/saif-al-islam-sentenced-death-by-court-in-libya-gaddafi-son.

845. *See* generally, E. O'Shea, 'Responsibility to Protect (R2P) in Libya: Ghosts of the Past Haunting the Future', *International Human Rights Law Review* 1 (2012): 173.

846. The UN organized two investigations, *see Report of the International Commission of Inquiry to investigate all alleged violations of international human rights law in the Libyan Arab Jamahiriya*, UN Doc. A/HRC/17/44, 1 Jun. 2011, and *Report of the International Commission of Inquiry on Libya*, UN Doc. A/HRC/19/68 (8 Mar. 2012).

847. These are principally the Ministerial Committee of Libya's Neighbours and the International Contact Group for Libya (ICG-L). *See* Assembly, *Decision on the Report of the Peace and Security Council on its Activities and the State of Peace and Security in Africa*, AU Doc. Assembly/AU/Dec. 583 (XXV), 15 Jun. 2015, para. 17.

848. Assembly, *Decision on the Activities of the Peace and Security Council and the State of Peace and Security in Africa*, AU Doc. Assembly/AU/Dec.598(XXVI), 31 Jan. 2016, para 21.

849. PSC Communique, AU Doc.PSC/MIN/COMM.(CDLIX), 23 Sept. 2014, para. 17.

850. *See* K. Magliveras, 'African Human Rights Court Castigates Libya for Violating Saif Al-Islam Kadhafi's Rights to Liberty and Security of Person', *International Enforcement Law Reporter* 32 (2016): 306.

Of the three North African states where the Arab Spring erupted only Tunisia has so far achieved a transition to a democratic regime.[851] The PSC did not intervene in the situation in Tunisia and although it condemned the excessive use of force against the demonstrators, resulting in deaths, it took no action.[852] Based on this and other statements,[853] the question has been asked whether, in reality, the AU continued to recognize the incumbent regimes or was in favour the populations' democratic aspirations,[854] which, by necessary implication, negated the legitimacy of the former. It is submitted that for the AU the parallel anti-establishment uprisings in North Africa (and in the case of the League of Arab States in the Middle East as well) could not have been coped with effectively because the relevant procedures and mechanisms are only meant to address single instances of unconstitutional change of government and not repetitive situations having similar characteristics. Regional political organizations are always wary of such incidents because, from a certain point onwards, repetitive events could lead to paralysis.

§10. The African Union Commission on International Law (AUCIL)

183. The Statute of the AUCIL was adopted by the Executive Council at its Fourteenth Ordinary Session in January 2009[855] and came into force, upon its approval by the Assembly, the following month.[856] The AUCIL was created as an 'independent advisory organ' of the AU pursuant to the provision on the establishment of subsidiary organs (Article 5(2) of the Constitutive Act). Its functions, objectives and structure have been defined in the Statute and elaborated in its Rules of Procedure.[857] The setting up of the AUCIL was originally envisaged in Article 14 of the AU Non-Aggression and Common Defence Pact, adopted in January 2005, in force in December 2009. In

851. A new Constitution was adopted on 26 Jan. 2014, English translation at: http://www.constituteproject.org. Article 2 stipulates that Tunisia is based on the will of the people and the supremacy of law (rule of law), a provision which cannot be amended.
852. PSC, Press Statement, PSC/PR/COMM.2(CCLVII), 15 Jan. 2011.
853. PSC, Communique, PSC/PR/COMM.(CCLX), 16 Feb. 2011 regarding the situation in Egypt; Communique PSC/PR/COMM(CCLXI), 23 Feb. 2011 regarding the situation in Libya.
854. *See* M. Eriksson &K. Zetterlund, *Dealing with Change: EU and AU Responses to the Uprisings in Tunisia, Egypt and Libya* (Swedish Defence Research Agency, Report No. FOI-R-3589-SE, January 2013) 38, at: http://www.foi.se.
855. *See* Executive Council, *Decision on the Draft Statutes of the African Union Commission on International Law*, AU Doc. EX.CL/Dec. 474 (XIV) (30 Jan. 2009). For the text of the Statute, *see* https://www.au.int/en/treaties/statute-african-union-commission-international-law. For details, *see* the UN Audiovisual Library of International Law at: http://legal.un.org/avl/ls/Kilangi_RO.html#.
856. *See* Assembly, *Decision on the Draft Statute of the African Union Commission on International Law*, AU Doc. Assembly/AU//Dec. 209 (XII) (4 Feb. 2009).
857. *See* AU Doc. AUCIL/Legal/Doc. 4 (III). The Rules were adopted by the Executive Council and revised by the AUCIL during its Third Ordinary Session (23 Mar.–1 Apr. 2011). However, in 2016 the Assembly adopted a document titled 'Rules of Procedure of the African Union Commission on the International Law', *see* Assembly, *Decision on the Specialized Technical Committees*, AU Doc. Assembly/AU/Dec. 589 (XXVI), para. 2 (31 Jan. 2016).

particular, contracting parties undertook to establish the AUCIL and decided that its objectives shall be to study legal matters pertaining to the protection of peace and security in Africa, including the demarcation of borders. Moreover, according to Article 11 of the Pact, the AUCIL together with the African Peace Academy (APA) and the African Centre for Study and Research on Terrorism (ACSRT) were asked to assist the PSC in its activities. It would appear that the APA has not yet been established, while the ACSRT was established in accordance with the provisions of the AU Action Plan for the Prevention and Fight against Terrorism in Africa, which was agreed by the AU High-Level Intergovernmental Meeting on the Prevention and Combating of Terrorism in Africa in Algiers in September 2002. The ACSRT was inaugurated on 13 October 2004 and its seat is in Algeria.[858] However, the AUCIL was additionally envisaged (albeit with considerably augmented objectives) in the Report of Experts on the Review of OAU/AU Treaties, which was discussed during the Fifth Ordinary Executive Council Session in 2004.[859] By taking note of the proposal to establish it and by requesting the Commission to come up with proposals,[860] effectively, the Executive Council disassociated the AUCIL's further development from its role as envisaged in the Non-Aggression and Common Defence Pact. As stated in the Preamble of the Statute, the need for establishing the AUCIL was reaffirmed by the Assembly in Decision 66(IV) of January 2005. This is clearly a mistake because Decision 66(IV) was concerned solely with the situation in the DRC and its relations with Rwanda. In fact, the only reference by the Assembly was in Decision 118(VII) adopted in July 2006, requesting the Commission and the PRC to, *inter alia*, elaborate the document on the AUCIL establishment and submit a report to the Executive Council in January 2007.[861]

The AUCIL consists of eleven members, who are nationals of Member States and serve in their personal capacity. They are elected for a period of five years (re-election for another term is possible) by secret ballot. Pursuant to Article 13 of the Statute, members may resign (there is no requirement to give reasons) and may be suspended or removed from office upon the recommendation of two-thirds of the other members, if they are deemed to be unable to continue meeting the required conditions of office. The Statute does not stipulate which organ will be competent to decide on the recommendation and has left it to be determined in the Rules of Procedure. The latter do not contain any relevant provisions. However, this is not the only omission: according to Article 11 of the Statute, the act of the election of members is also governed by the Rules but no such provisions have been included. In the event, the first members

858. Note that in October 2010 the Chairperson of the AU Commission appointed the AU Special Representative for Counter-Terrorism Cooperation, who also acts as the Director of ACSRS.

859. *See* AU Doc. EX.CL/95 (V) (2004).

860. *See* Executive Council, *Decision on the Meeting of the Experts on the Review of OAU/AU Treaties*, AU Doc. EX.CL/Dec. 129 (V), para. 5 (3 Jul. 2004).

861. *See* Assembly, *Decision on the Draft Single Instrument on the Merger of the African Court on Human and Peoples' Rights and the Court of Justice of the African Union*, AU Doc. Assembly/AU/Dec. 118 (VII) (2 Jul. 2006).

were elected by the Executive Council in June 2009,[862] and their appointment was effected by the Assembly during its Thirteenth Ordinary Session the following month.[863]

The AUCIL objectives are laid down in Article 4 of the Statute. Its activities include the codification of international law, which is further elaborated in Article 6; the progressive development of international law (Article 5); the revision of existing OAU/AU treaties (Article 8); the teaching and dissemination of international law (Article 9); and the carrying out of studies on legal issues of interest to the AU and the Member States (Article 7). Regarding the codification of international law, the functions to be performed by the AUCIL are similar to those of the UN International Law Commission (ILC), which was created as a subsidiary organ of the Sixth Committee of the UN General Assembly's in 1948. Indeed, under Article 25(3) of the Statute, the AUCIL is mandated to establish close cooperation with the ILC in order to promote international law in Africa. On 17 July 2012, representatives from the AUCIL visited the ILC in Geneva.[864]

The AUCIL shall act upon the requests for codification submitted by the Assembly and other (not named in the Statute) organs, shall prepare drafts in the form of Articles and, through the Executive Council, shall submit them to the Assembly together with commentaries. Following consultations with Member States, the AUCIL shall submit to the Assembly a final draft report and recommend that the Assembly undertake one of the following: take no action; take note of the report; adopt the report; or recommend to Member States the conclusion of a convention based on the report. However, according to Article 6(12) of the Statute, the Assembly may refer the draft report back to the AUCIL for reconsideration and further elaboration. In January 2013, and in the context of the Twentieth Ordinary Assembly Session, the AUCIL President said that its work has dealt with a broad aspect of legal issues, including the harmonization of ratification procedures in Member States (presumably this would require considerable changes in national constitutions); the immunity of states officials under the Rome Statute of the ICC (as already explained, a particularly thorny issue in Africa given the arrest warrants that the ICC has issued against African dignitaries); the revision of OAU/AU Treaties (clearly a daunting task); the juridical basis for reparations for slavery in the African continent (a long-standing theme that the AU has arguably not pursued actively); a Model Law assisting Member States in implementing the provisions of the Kampala Convention on IDPs; and a definition of the crime of unconstitutional change of governments.[865]

The Eleventh Ordinary Session was held in Cairo in October 2015, the first ever session outside the AU Headquarters. The considered a number of ongoing studies, including the Continental Legal Framework on Migration, a review of the African Charter on the Rights and Welfare of the Child, the Continental Legal Framework on Piracy, and the African Convention on Judicial Cooperation and Mutual Legal Assistance.

---

862. *See* Executive Council, *Decision on Election of Members of the African Union Commission on International Law (AUCIL)*, AU Doc. EX.CL/Dec. 498 (XV) (30 Jun. 2009).

863. *See* Assembly, *Decision on the Report on the Election of Members of The African Union Commission on International Law*, AU Doc. Assembly/AU/Dec. 249 (XII) (3 Sept. 2009).

864. *See* UN Doc. A/CN.4/SR.3146 (13 Aug. 2012).

865. *See* AU, Directorate of Information and Communication, Press Release N°18 / 20th AU Summit, 25 Jan. 2013.

To the best of one's knowledge, the work of AUCIL is not widely disseminated and in a rather cryptic resolution in July 2016 the Executive Council requested that it focuses its reports in line with its mandate, namely the development and codification of international law, and to align AU treaties with the vision of Agenda 2063. It is not easy to decipher whether the Executive Council was showing its displeasure with the topics the AUCIL has been considering or with the priorities it has set. However, as it further urged Member States to pay greater attention to AUCIL activities and to participate in its deliberations,[866] the conclusion can be reached that the AUCIL still operates in the AU fringes and does not have a mainstream role.

866. *See* Executive Council, *Decisions on the Activity Report of the African Union Commission on International Law (AUCIL)*, AU Doc. EX.CL/Dec. 932 (XXIX) (15 Jul. 2016).

Chapter 6. Privileges and Immunities

184. The Constitutive Act is silent on the question of privileges and immunities. However, given that the AU has substituted the OAU (namely, the case of succession between two international organizations where the latter was established to specifically succeed the former), it can be assumed that the totality of the privileges and immunities enjoyed by the OAU were transferred in toto to the AU. As the OAU Charter did not contain any clauses on privileges and immunities, a General Convention on the Privileges and Immunities of the OAU was adopted on 25 October 1965.[867] The Convention, whose provisions follow closely the Convention on the Privileges and Immunities of the UN,[868] has a rather obscure and peculiar clause as regards its entry into force. Thus, Article X provides that it is submitted to every Member State for accession, which would be effected by the respective Head of State and Government's signature and the very act of signing would imply its immediate entry into force. This clause has led to some strange consequences. First, it has still not come into force for the entire membership, only forty-one states have ratified it. Second, over and above the unacceptable situation that not all Member States have recognized the AU's privileges and immunities, there are also other practical problems. To mention one example, the Republic of South Africa, which has not signed the Convention, hosts the seat of the PAP. Even though Article 9 of the Protocol establishing the PAP stipulates that 'The Pan-African Parliamentarians shall enjoy parliamentary immunity in each Member State', clearly this provision has no application in those Member States which have chosen not to become contracting parties to the Protocol. The matter has also been dealt with in Article 9 of the Host Country Agreement between the AU and the Government of the Republic of South Africa on the Seat of the PAP, concluded in 2004.[869] It stipulates that the PAP, its members, the Clerk and the Deputy Clerks shall enjoy full diplomatic immunities as provided for in the 1965 Convention as well as in the Vienna Convention on Diplomatic Relations of 1961.[870] It follows that South Africa is obliged to guarantee specific privileges and immunities not as a contracting party to the 1965 Convention but only because it ratified the Host Country Agreement. Equally, the Member States, which are not contracting parties to the 1965 Convention but have ratified the PAP Protocol, must secure parliamentary immunity as an obligation emanating only from the latter.

185. Article I of the Convention stipulates that the OAU (now the AU) possesses international legal personality (an issue on which both the OAU Charter and the AU Constitutive Act are silent) and has the capacity to enter into contracts, including the acquisition and disposal of movable property and the lodging of legal proceedings. Under Article II, the AU premises and assets enjoy immunity from every form of legal

867. 1000 U.N.T.S. 393, reproduced in Naldi, *Documents*, 38. For further details, *see* K. Magliveras & G. Naldi, *The African Union* (Alphen aan den Rijn: Kluwer Law International, 2009) para. 99.
868. Signed on 13 Feb. 1946, 1 U.N.T.S. 16.
869. Reproduced in Republic of South Africa, Government Gazette, Vol. 471, 22 September 2004, No. 26816.
870. Entered into force on 24 Apr. 1964, 500 U.N.T.S. 95.

proceedings, except when the AU itself has waived immunity, are inviolable and may not be searched, confiscated or expropriated. In accordance with Article III, the AU, its income, assets, and properties are exempt from all direct taxes, from import and export duties as well as from quantitative restrictions on imports and exports in respect of goods used for official purposes and from customs duties in respect of publications. Even though the Convention does not exempt AU from sales taxes, when it has acquired property on a large-scale for official use, the Member States, in whose territory the acquisition has taken place, are directed to refund all taxes paid.

186. Article V of the Convention concerns the privileges and immunities of Member States' representatives[871] attending the meetings of the AU principal and subsidiary organs. Thus, they will enjoy the following: immunity from personal arrest or detention and from any legal process in respect of opinions expressed and acts performed in the exercise of their official functions; inviolability for their documents and the right to use diplomatic bags; exemption of their families from any immigration restrictions and alien registration; and exemption from currency and exchange restrictions, including custom duties on goods imported and sales tax. Interestingly enough, the complete freedom of speech and opinion and the immunity from legal proceedings will continue to be accorded even when representatives have ceased acting as ones. The provision of Article V(4) merits particular mention. It stipulates that these privileges and immunities are not accorded to representatives for their personal benefit but in order to protect the independent discharge of their functions in the AU. Consequently, Member States are placed under the duty to waive the immunity of their representatives, when they believe that the exercise of immunity would impede the course of justice.

187. Article VI of the Convention dealing with AU officials is not applicable to all categories of officials but only to those which are specified by the OAU Secretary-General (now the Commission Chairperson) and approved by the Assembly.[872] Their immunities and privileges resemble those of Member States' representatives. Additionally, officials are exempt from taxation on their salaries and emoluments and, in times of international crisis, are accorded the same repatriation facilities as diplomatic envoys.[873] Article VI(3) stipulates that the Commission Chairperson shall enjoy, in addition, 'the privileges and immunities, exemptions and facilities accorded to diplomatic envoys'. The immunity granted to officials may be waived by the Commission Chairperson in instances like those applying to Member States' representatives. In their turn, the Chairperson's immunities may be waived by the Council of Ministers (now the Executive Council). Finally, the AU must cooperate at all times with Member States' appropriate authorities to assist the proper administration of justice, to ensure that police regulations are observed and that its officials do not abuse the privileges and immunities accorded to them.

---

871. The term 'representatives' has been given a rather broad interpretation and covers not only delegates but also deputy delegates, advisers, technical experts and secretaries of delegations; *see* Art. V(6) of the Convention.

872. Experts performing missions for the OAU are not included in the term 'officials'. On the contrary, their privileges and immunities are regulated separately in Art. VII of the Convention and are similar to those granted to representatives of foreign governments.

873. Compare Art. 44 of the Vienna Convention on Diplomatic Relations.

188. Article IX of the Convention contains the dispute settlement clause. Four different categories of disputes are envisaged. The first concerns those arising out of contracts or other disputes of a private law nature to which the AU is a party (e.g., acquisition of land or the construction of new buildings). The second category concerns disputes involving any AU official enjoying immunity and provided that such immunity has not been waived by the Chairperson of the Commission. In these two categories, Article IX does not prescribe specific dispute settlement mechanisms but stipulates that the AU shall make provisions for appropriate modes of settlement. The third category deals with disputes arising out of the interpretation or application of the Convention, irrespective of the parties involved. These are to be settled by arbitration through the OAU Commission on Mediation, Conciliation, and Arbitration, unless the parties have agreed to a different settlement method. Given that this organ does no longer exist (it was established by virtue of a protocol attached to the OAU Charter in 1964),[874] the provision should be considered as inoperative. However, a different conclusion might be reached on the basis of Article 28 of the Protocol establishing the ACJHR, which stipulates that the ACJHR's jurisdiction encompasses, *inter alia*, the interpretation, application or validity of any treaty adopted within the framework of the OAU/AU. Therefore, it could be assumed that, if the conditions for *locus standi* are fulfilled, such disputes could be adjudicated by the ACJHR once it becomes operative. Finally, the fourth category also involves disputes relating to the Convention's interpretation or application but only between the AU and a Member State. These shall be settled by negotiation or any other agreed method, failing which, they shall be submitted to an arbitral tribunal for ad hoc arbitration. The tribunal shall consist of three arbitrators, one of whom shall be named by the Commission Chairperson, the other by the Member State concerned and the third by the arbitrators themselves. There are no reported cases dealing with private law litigation involving the AU or with disputes concerning the interpretation and application of the Convention.

189. When the Convention was adopted in 1965, there were no OAU specialized agencies in operation. However, their subsequent establishment raised the question of whether the Convention applied to their personnel as well. This led the Assembly to adopt in June 1980 an Additional Protocol to extend privileges and immunities to such personnel. In line with the Convention, the Additional Protocol was not opened for signature by the Member States but was submitted to each of them for accession, as stipulated in Article 10(1) of the Additional Protocol. Thus, its entry into force did not require its ratification by a certain number of signatory parties but, once a Member State had deposited the instrument of accession, it came into force between that Member and the OAU (now, the AU). So far, only eight Member States have deposited instruments of accession (the last being Congo on 8 August 2012). The immunities and privileges granted to officials of the specialized agencies depend on whether the nationality of the official is that of a Member State (Article 2) or of another state (Article 3). The former enjoy far more immunities compared to the latter: they are immune from any legal proceedings in respect of words spoken and written; exempt from taxation on emoluments paid; immune from arrest and detention; from national service obligations; from immigration restrictions and alien registration, etc. Finally, Article 5 stipulates that the OAU/AU may issue laissez-passer to an Agency's officials, which must be

874. Reproduced in 3 I.L.M. (1964) 1116.

recognized and accepted as valid travel documents by Member States, while Article 6 provides that it may issue travel certificates to those officials who are not nationals of a Member State. The last specialized agency created by the OAU was the African Energy Commission. Article 19 of the Convention establishing the Commission (adopted on 11 July 2001 and entered into force on 13 December 2006) does not mention the Additional Protocol but stipulates that the Commission, its property and assets as well as its staff shall enjoy in the territory of each contracting party (there are now thirty-two) the privileges and immunities provided for in the Convention.

It is clear that the AU has not paid the attention it should have to the issue of privileges and immunities. The fact that the Convention and the Additional Protocol have not been accepted by all Member States is in itself problematic. Moreover, it is very doubtful if they cover the current needs of the AU. In particular, the fact that the AU's institutional architecture is very different from that of the OAU is adequate reason to advocate the drafting of new rules, which would have to take the form of a new treaty substituting the existing two instruments and cover additionally the totality of the organs (principal and subsidiary) which have been established since 2002 pursuant to the Constitutive Act.

Chapter 7. Finances

190. Unlike OAU, in the AU the financial year coincides with the calendar year (January to December). As regards the size of AU budgets, they have been considerably increased compared to OAU budgets given that the AU has to finance not only considerably more organs but also considerably many more activities and programmes. Thus, the budget for financial year (FY) 2004, which the Second Ordinary Assembly Session approved in July 2003, was set at USD 43 million,[875] compared to USD 35.6 million for FY 2003.[876] During the Fourth Ordinary Assembly Session (Addis Ababa, 4–8 July 2004), the Commission asked for a USD 570 million budget for FY 2005 but it was denied. In the event, the Assembly did not reach a decision but authorized the Executive Council to consider and adopt the budget at an extraordinary session.[877] Five months later, the Sixth Extraordinary Executive Council Session met: the approval of the budget was the sole agenda item. It adopted a USD 158.384 million budget, a four-fold increase compared to the previous year, of which USD 63 million represented operational costs to be shared among Member States as assessed contributions, while the remaining amount represented the 'Programme-Budget', which Member States were asked to cover on a voluntary basis.[878]

191. The scale of budgetary assessments had been under review since 2002. In July 2003, the Executive Council followed the conclusions of the Ad Hoc Ministerial Committee on the Review of the Scale of Assessment and recommended to the Assembly new rates with an 8.25% upper ceiling and two low floors of 0.25% and 0.75%. Moreover, it recommended that, as an exception, Algeria be granted, due to the natural disasters it had faced, a five year grace period during which it would continue to pay its contributions based on the previous rate of 7.25%.[879] Although the Second Ordinary Assembly Session approved the Executive Council's recommendations,[880] some Member States indicated that their new assessment rates were too high and requested a review.[881] This proved to be a contentious issue.[882] However, the report prepared by

875. *See* Assembly, *Decision on the Programme-Budget for the Year 2004*, AU Doc. Assembly/AU/Dec. 8 (II) (12 Jul. 2003), which was based on the recommendations of the Executive Council, AU Doc. EX/CL/26 (III) Rev. 1 (4 Jul. 2003).

876. *See* Assembly, *Decision on the Budget for the Period January–August 2003 and the Budget for the Period September–December 2003*, AU Doc. Assembly/AU/Dec. 7 (II) (12 Jul. 2003).

877. *See* Assembly, *Decision on the Draft Programme Budget for the 2005 Financial Year*, AU Doc. Assembly/AU/Dec. 47 (III) (8 Jul. 2004).

878. *See* Executive Council, *Decision on the Reprioritized Priority Programme, the Solidarity Budget and the 2005 Programme-Budget*, AU Doc. EXT/EX.CL/Dec. 1 (VI) (6 Dec. 2005).

879. *See* Executive Council, *Recommendation on the Review of the Scale of Assessment of the African Union*, AU Doc. EX/CL/Dec. 35 (III), which was based on AU Doc. EX/CL/40 (III) (4 July 2003). Note that Egypt attached a reservation.

880. *See* Assembly, *Decision on the Review of the Scale of Assessment of the African Union*, AU Doc. Assembly/AU/Dec. 31 (II) (12 Jul. 2003).

881. *See Report of the Sub-Committee on Contributions*, AU Doc. EX.CL/70 (IV) (2004).

882. *See* Executive Council, *Decision on the Scale of Assessment*, AU Doc. EX.CL/Dec. 191 (VI) (28 Jan. 2005).

the aforementioned Ad Hoc Ministerial Committee,[883] was approved by the Seventh Ordinary Executive Council Session (Sirte, 28 June–2 July 2005)[884] and was adopted by the Fifth Ordinary Assembly Session (Sirte, 4–5 July 2005).[885] The revised Scale of Assessment, effective 1 January 2006, was based on the principle of the Member States' capacity to pay and featured an upper ceiling of 15% with no floor rate. Algeria, Egypt, Libya, Nigeria, and South Africa offered to contribute 15% of the regular budget each. As the result, 75% of the regular budget was to be covered by only five Member States, while the remaining forty-eight Members were asked to pay between them the remaining 25% of the budget. To offer two examples, Ethiopia's contribution was set at 0.63% and Botswana's at 0.83% of the budget.[886]

192. Despite the new Scale, disagreement among Member States persisted prompting the Fifth Ordinary Assembly Session to authorize the convening of another extraordinary Executive Council session to resolve the matter. It took place in Khartoum on 19 January 2006 and approved the budget for financial year 2006, which amounted to USD 129.6 million. As in previous years, the budget was divided into an assessed part of USD 69.4 million for operational costs to be to be contributed by all Member States, and a voluntary part (the 'Programme-Budget') to be financed on a voluntarily basis by Member States and with the support of non-African states. South Africa appended a reservation to the resolution objecting to dividing the budget, as it that it was contrary to the AU Financial Rules and Regulations. In its opinion, it should have been presented as a joint, composite budget and assessed to all Member States.[887] FY 2007 budget was set at USD 133 million, which in absolute numbers was lower than the 2006 budget because it also included the costs associated with the PAP (circa USD 6.4 million) and the African Court on Human and Peoples' Rights (circa USD 2.4 million).[888] Finally, FY 2008 budget was approved by the Twelfth Ordinary Executive Council Session (Addis Ababa, 25–29 January 2008). It was again a separated budget totalling USD 140 million, of which USD 106.5 million were assessed to the Member States pursuant to the 2005 Scale of Assessments, USD 32.4 million were earmarked for AU programmes to be secured by the so-called international partners, and USD 1 million came from arrears in contributions.[889]

193. As the Scale of Assessments is to be reviewed every three years, in July 2010, a new Scale was adopted by the Seventeenth Ordinary Executive Council Session

883. *See* AU Doc. EX.CL/192 (VII) (2005).

884. *See* Executive Council, *Decision on the Scale of Assessment*, AU Doc. EX.CL/Dec. 223 (VII) (2 Jul. 2005).

885. *See* Assembly, *Decision on the Scale of Assessment*, AU Doc. Assembly/AU/Dec. 88 (V) (5 Jul. 2005).

886. *See* Executive Council, *Statement of Contributions of Member States to the African Union Budget as at 12 June 2006*, AU Doc. EX.CL/249 (IX) (25 Jun. 2006).

887. *See* Executive Council, *Decision of the Eighth Extraordinary Session of the Executive Council on the Budget for 2006*, AU Doc. Ext/EX.CL/Dec. 1 (VIII) (19 Jan. 2006).

888. *See* Assembly, *Decision on the Budget of the African Union for 2007*, AU Doc. Assembly/AU/Dec. 154 (VIII) (30 Jan. 2007), which was based on the recommendations of Executive Council, *see* Executive Council, *Decision of the Tenth Ordinary Session Council on the Budget for 2007*, AU Doc. EX.CL/Dec. 340 (X) (26 Jan. 2007).

889. *See* Executive Council, *Decision on the Draft Budget for the AU Commission for 2008*, AU Doc. EX.CL/Dec. 378 (XII) (29 Jan. 2008).

to cover FY 2011–2013. It followed the recommendations of the Ministerial Committee on the Review of the Scale of Assessments, namely that the new scale with a ceiling of 13.271% and without a floor rate be introduced. Moreover, it asked those Member States with the capacity and the ability to pay over and above their assessed contribution to do so. Thus, Algeria, Egypt, Libya, Nigeria, and South Africa agreed to contribute 13.271% of the budget each, another five Member States agreed to pay more than 1% of the budget each, while the remaining membership was to pay less than 1% each. The latter included Burundi (0.063% of the budget), the Comoros (0.034%), Djibouti (0.075%), Gambia (0.037%), Liberia (0.037%), South Sudan (0.016%), San Tomé and Principe (0.010), and Seychelles (0.067%).[890]

The Twenty-Second Ordinary Executive Council Session (Addis Ababa, 21–25 January 2013) adopted the Scale of Assessments for FY 2014–2016 based on a maximum rate (ceiling) of 12.898% without the imposition of a minimum (floor) rate. Moreover, it endorsed the recommendation of the Ministerial Committee on the Review of the Scale of Assessment that South Sudan be assessed at 0.599% and agreed that the assessed contribution of Sudan be fixed temporarily at 2%, both with effect from January 2012. Finally, the Executive Council asked the PRC to review the statutory contributions of small island Member States, to take into account their vulnerability, as well as to make suitable recommendations as regards the minimum amount to be paid by Member States in arrears of contributions to avoid sanctions.[891] The Scale of Assessments for FY 2016–2018, approved by the Assembly in January 2016, envisages three tiers. The first concerns Nigeria, South Africa, Egypt and Algeria, each having to pay 12% of the budget, i.e., USD 20,391 million for FY 2016. The second concerns thirteen Member States and ranges between 8% (Angola) and 1,141% (Uganda) giving a total of 37,478% of the budget. All other Member States are in the third tier, which ranges from 1,095% (Gabon) to 0,017% (San Tome and Principe), which had to pay USD 28,888 for FY 2016. This new Scale reflects the voluntary decision of four states to increase the assessed contributions: Cote d'Ivoire to 3% (almost double the previous assessment), Ethiopia to 4%, Kenya to 4.1% and Chad to 0.942%.[892] According to the Assembly, the currently applicable scale is based 'on the principles of solidarity, equitable payment and capacity to pay', and ensures that no single Member State country bears a disproportionate share of the budget.[893]

In May 2013, the Twenty-Third Executive Council Ordinary Session approved a total regular budget of USD 308 million for FY 2014: USD 137.8 million as AU operating costs and USD 170.1 million for AU programmes.[894] Rather unprecedented

---

890. *See* Executive Council, *Decision on the Scale of Assessment*, AU Doc. EX.CL/Dec. 582 (XVII) (23 Jul. 2010).
891. *See* Executive Council, *Decision by the Ad Hoc Ministerial Committee on the Scale of Assessment*, AU Doc. EX.CL/Dec. 756 (XXII) (25 Jan. 2013).
892. *See* Assembly, *Decision on the Scale of Assessment and the Implementation of Alternative Sources of Financing the African Union*, AU Doc. Assembly/AU/Dec. 602 (XXVI) (31 Jan. 2016).
893. *See* Assembly, *Decision on the Scale of Assessment and Alternative Sources of Financing the African Union*, AU Doc. Assembly/AU/Dec. 578 (XXV), paras 2 and 4 (15 Jun. 2015).
894. *See* Executive Council, *Decision on the Budget of the African Union for the 2014 Financial Year*, AU Doc. EX.CL/Dec. 767 (XXIII) (23 May 2013).

for international organizations, most funds were to be secured from international partners (in the tune of USD 170 million) and only USD 126 million were to be assessed to Member States (with the remaining funds coming mostly from existing AU financial resources). The case of the NEPAD is very illustrative: of the total allocated budget of USD 36 million, only USD 4.4 million would be paid by Member States. The significant financial resources offered by international partners probably explains why NEPAD's funding exceeded considerably the funding of the PAP (USD 14.3 million) as well as of the African Human Rights Commission and of the African Human Rights Court (in total USD 14.2 million). In the case of these three organs, the Member States' assessments were considerably higher than the funds to be offered by international partners. However, the overall financial contribution to be made by the international partners is not restricted to the above figure. And this because the Executive Council also approved a (separate) budget to cover: (a) Special Projects in the tune of USD 24.2 million; (b) the so-called Pass-Through Funds (USD 90.5 million); and (c) Technical Assistance (USD 37.7 million), giving a total of USD 152.4 million, to be 'mobilized' from non-African partners. Finally, it authorized the AUC to 'mobilize' even more funds from the international partners, this time for closing until the end of 2013 the funding gap of USD 78.1 million in the 'Programmes-Budget'. In conclusion, the total amount which the AU would seek to secure from its partners exceeded USD 400 million until the end of FY 2014.

Dividing the budget into two amounts, one to be assessed on Member States and the other to be raised from international partners, has become of permanent fixture for the AU. The budget for FY 2017 has been set at USD 782,108 million, broken down into USD 488,525 million as Operating Budget and USD 293,582 million as Programmes. In particular, USD 205,149 million will be assessed on Member States and USD 576,958 million will be raised from international partners. To give an illustration of how the budget is to be distributed, the AUC will receive USD 348,8 million, the PAP USD 22 million, the African Human Rights Court USD 10.3 million, the African Human Rights Commission USD 5.5 million, ECOSSOC USD 1.1 million, NEPAD USD 41.4 million, the AUCIL USD 731,000, the Advisory Board on Corruption USD 2.3 million, and the PSC USD 1 million. Finally, AMISOM, the only AU peace operation currently active, will receive USD 335,9 million to be raised solely from international partners.[895]

194. As was the case with the OAU, the AU continued to be plagued by arrears in the payment of the financial obligations. In February 2003, outstanding contributions amounted to USD 42.5 million, which included outstanding assessed contributions from January to December 2002 of USD 10.2 million.[896] By December 2004, Member States had paid only USD 26 million out of the USD 43 million budget for FY 2004.

---

895. *See* Executive Council, *Decision on the Budget of the African Union for the 2017 Financial Year*, AU Doc. EX.CL/Dec. 919 (XXIX) (15 Jul. 2016). For the FY 2016 budget, *see* Executive Council, *Decision on the Budget of the African Union for the 2016 Financial Year*, AU Doc. EX.CL/Dec. 873 (XXVII) (12 Jun. 2015) and for the FY 2015 budget *see* Executive Council, *Decision on the Budget of the African Union for the 2015 Financial Year*, AU Doc. EX.CL/Dec. 813 (XXV) (24 Jun. 2014).

896. *See* National Assembly of the Republic of South Africa, Question No. 36 to the Minister of Foreign Affairs, 19 Mar. 2003.

On account of the chronic problem of under-funding, the AU has attempted to seek alternative sources of funding. A report, which was prepared by the Interim Chairperson to deal with this matter,[897] was transmitted to Member States for consideration, while the Executive Council set up a Commission to promote this idea.[898] The latter failed to make any headway because its first two meetings in December 2003 and in February 2004 were not held due to lack of quorum.[899] A select group of fifteen experts from Member States was then established to discuss the report and submit views by 31 May 2004.[900] Apparently, these efforts did not lead at the time to any concrete results, characteristic perhaps of the AU's inability to handle promptly and efficiently issues of major importance affecting its operation.

195. Regarding the imposition of sanctions against Members in arrears, the Third Ordinary Executive Council Session, acting on the basis of the Report of the Sub-Committee on Contributions,[901] determined that eight Members (Guinea-Bissau, Liberia, CAR, DRC, San Tomé and Principe, Seychelles, Somalia, and the Comoros) shall remain under sanctions; determined that the sanctions imposed on Niger be lifted; and decided that a temporary and exceptional exemption be granted to Sierra Leone.[902] This decision raised a number of issues. First, pursuant to Article 23(1) of the Constitutive Act, the competent organ for imposing sanctions on Member States in arrears is the Assembly. As there was apparently no delegation of power to the Executive Council, the legal basis for these sanctions was at least ambiguous. Second, since the sanctions against most of the above-mentioned Member States were originally imposed under OAU rules,[903] it was rather inappropriate that the AU maintained them without reaching its own separate resolutions. Third, it was unclear which punitive measures of those envisaged in Article 23(1) were actually imposed, since they differ from OAU sanctions.

196. The Executive Council has continued to impose sanctions against Member States in arrears despite the fact that a good number of them have been facing internal turmoil and strife of such magnitude that their involvement in AU activities has been problematic (reportedly, certain countries have been unable to pay the expenses of their representatives to attend AU meetings). Thus, during its Eighth Extraordinary Session (Khartoum, 19 January 2006) the Executive Council affirmed that eight

---

897. *See Report of the Interim Chairperson on Alternative Sources of Funding the African Union*, AU Doc. EX/CL/24 (III) (2003).

898. *See* Executive Council, *Decision on the Synoptic Report on Alternative Sources of Funding the African Union*, EX/CL/Dec. 22 (III) (8 Jul. 2003).

899. *See Progress Report of the Chairperson of the Commission on the Implementation of Decision EX.CL/Dec.22(III) on Alternative Sources of Funding the African Union*, AU Doc. EX.CL/71 (IV) (2004).

900. *See* Permanent Representatives Committee, Seventh Ordinary Session, 12–13 Mar. 2004, AU Doc. PRC/Rpt (VII), 9–10, and Executive Council, *Decision on the Alternative Sources of Funding the African Union*, AU Doc. EX/CL/Dec. 77 (IV) (16 Mar. 2004).

901. *See* AU Doc. EX/CL/27 (III) (2003).

902. *See* Executive Council, *Decision on the Report of the Sub-Committee on Contributions*, AU Dec. EX/CL/Dec. 25 (III) (4 Jul. 2003). Sanctions were maintained by virtue of Executive Council, *Decision on the Report of the Sub-Committee on Contributions*, AU Doc. EX/CL/Dec. 76 (IV) (16 Mar. 2004).

903. *See* , *inter alia*, OAU Council of Ministers, Decision CM/Dec. 2 (LXXIV), adopted at its Seventy-Fourth Ordinary Session in July 2001.

Members will continue to be under sanctions (CAR, DRC, Eritrea, Guinea-Bissau, Sao Tomé and Principe, Somalia, Liberia, and Seychelles, i.e., almost the same states which were under OAU sanctions); imposed sanctions on Benin, Cape Verde, Côte d'Ivoire, Guinea, and Mauritania; lifted sanctions imposed on Niger, Djibouti and Gabon, which had paid the arrears in contributions; and, finally, determined that Sierra Leone shall not be subjected to sanctions for as long as it honoured the agreed payment schedule.[904] Two years later and with only twenty-nine Member States being up to date with the payment of contributions to the general budget, the situation had not changed considerably with the exception that Liberia and Somalia were no longer in the list of Member States under sanctions.[905]

It is of some interest to note that there have been instances where several Member States, against whom sanctions were lifted (they had cleared their arrears from previous years), failed to keep up payments to the budget and, consequently, found themselves again the target of sanctions. For example, although the Eleventh Ordinary Executive Council Session (Accra, 25–29 June 2007) had cleared Guinea-Bissau and the CAR (they had paid arrears up to FY 2004, had partially paid for FY 2005 and therefore were not for more than two years in arrears),[906] they failed to continue paying outstanding contributions for FY 2006 and, therefore, the Twelfth Ordinary Executive Council Session (Addis Ababa, 25–29 January 2008) reinstated the sanctions. In early 2008, the following Member States were under sanctions: Guinea-Bissau, the CAR, Cape Verde (it did not present the repayment schedule that the Executive Council had requested in June 2007), the DRC, Eritrea, San Tomé and Principe, and Seychelles.[907]

Arguably, these states did not choose not to fulfil their AU budgetary obligations but their precarious politico-economic situation led to arrears in other international organizations as well, including the UN. Thus, in January 2008 eight of the fifteen UN Member States, whose arrears had reached the stage where their voting rights in the General Assembly were suspended under Article 19 of the UN Charter, were African states under AU sanctions as well.[908] Equally, during the UN General Assembly's Sixty-Seventh Session (2012) there were five African states (CAR, the Comoros, Guinea-Bissau, Sao Tome and Principe, and Somalia) falling into the scope of Article 19. However, the General Assembly decided that this was due to conditions beyond their control and allowed them to participate in voting.[909] During the General Assembly's

904. *See* Executive Council, *Decision of the Eighth Extraordinary Session of the Executive Council on the Contributions by Member States*, AU Doc. Ext/EX.CL/Dec. 2 (VIII) (19 Jan. 2006).
905. *See* Executive Council, *Decision on the Contributions of Member States*, AU Doc. EX.CL/Dec. 379 (XII) (31 Jan. 2008).
906. *See* Executive Council, *Decision on Contributions*, AU Doc. EX.CL/Dec. 377 (XI) (29 Jun. 2007). *See also* Permanent Representatives Committee, *Report on the Status of Contributions by Member States*, AU Doc. EX.CL/337 (XI) (2007).
907. *See* Decision EX.CL/Dec. 379 (XII), *supra* . The Decision was based on *Report on the Contributions of Member States*, AU Doc. EX.CL/369(XII)c (2008).
908. *See* United Nations, *Letter dated 18 January 2008 from the Secretary-General to the President of the General Assembly*, UN Doc. A/62/657 (21 Jan. 2008), and UNGA Res. 62/1 of 15 Oct. 2007. In the case of Benin and Cape Verde, the amount of USD 20,000 each would have reinstated them to good standing.
909. *See* UNGA Res. 67/2 of 11 Oct. 2012 and Official Records, Sixty-seventh Session, Report of the Committee on Contributions, Supplement No. 11, UN Doc. A/67/11 (2012).

current Seventy-first Session (2016–2017) it was again these states (except CAR) against which Article 19 was not applied on account of conditions beyond their control.[910]

197. Lately, the situation has ameliorated and the number of Member States under sanctions for being in arrears has diminished. Thus, the aforementioned Twenty-Second Ordinary Executive Council Session imposed sanctions only on Guinea-Bissau and Madagascar and decided that Somalia's temporary exemption from sanctions be maintained.[911] However, this is not on its own a clear indication that the remaining Member States have been paying all assessed contributions on time, because, as will be recalled, the sanctions under Article 23(1) of the Constitutive Act are triggered only when they have been in arrears for more than two years. Thus, in July 2016 the Executive Council expressed again its concern, on the one hand, over Member States' non-compliance with paying assessed contributions as and when due and, on the other hand, 'the persistent pattern of arrears which is impacting adversely on the [AU's] financial situation'.[912]

Since 2013, there have been renewed efforts in securing alternative sources for financing the AU. In the course of 2013, a panel of African dignitaries under the chairmanship of Olusegun Obasanjo, the former President of Nigeria, produced a report to that effect, which was approved by the Twenty-First Ordinary Assembly Session (Addis Ababa, 26–27 May 2013). The Assembly committed itself to 'self-reliance in the mobilization of resources in the financing of the AU programmes to avert undue dependency' (presumably the reference to dependency concerned the international partners, whose contributions, as has been explained, keep the AU largely operating). However, as it is characteristic of the Assembly when facing difficult issues requiring complex decisions, no concrete measures were taken but deliberations were postponed for its Twenty-Second Ordinary Session (January 2014) by which time the ministers of finance ought to have come up with concrete proposals.[913] The matter was not placed on that session's agenda. After many delays, the Assembly dealt with it in earnest in July 2016. Resolving that the AU must be 'financed in a predictable, sustainable, equitable and accountable manner with the full ownership by its Member States', it took the following measures. First, it created a 0.2% levy on all eligible goods imported into Africa to finance the operational, programme, and peace support operations budgets starting from 2017. The amounts collected from the levy are to be automatically paid by the national administrations into an account to be opened for the AU with the Central Banks of each Member State; the relevant amounts shall be transmitted to the AU in accordance with each state's assessed contribution. Second,

910. *See* UNGA Res. 71/2 of 3 Oct. 2016; *See also* UNGA Res. 70/2 of 12 Oct. 2015 and Res. 69/2 of 22 Sept. 2014.

911. *See* Executive Council, *Decision on Contribution of the African Union Member States towards the 2012 Budget of the African Union*, AU Doc. EX.CL/Dec. 731 (XXII) (25 Jan. 2013).

912. *See* Executive Council, *Decision on the Oversight and Accountability Mechanism(s)*, AU Doc. EX.CL/Dec. 931 (XXIX), para. 5 (15 Jul. 2016).

913. *See* Assembly, *Decision on Alternative Sources of Financing the African Union*, AU Doc. Assembly/AU/Dec. 486 (XXI) (27 May 2013). *See* further, Executive Council, *Decision on Alternative Sources of Financing the African Union*, AU Doc. EX.CL/Dec. 760 (XXII) (25 Jan. 2013).

it instructed the Commission to put in place strong oversight and accountability mechanisms to ensure that resources are effectively and prudently used. Third, it instructed the Commission to complete the AU's ongoing institutional reform paving in the attainment of all AU objectives and the careful use of resources. Fourth, it decided that, when preparing the annual budget, a Committee of Ministers of Finance comprising ten Member States, representing Africa's five regions, will participate, a move which presumably aims at giving to the membership more direct say over the budget at the drafting stage.[914]

914. Assembly, *Decision on the Outcome of the Retreat of the Heads of States and Government, Ministers of Foreign Affairs and Ministers of Finance on the Financing of the African Union*, AU Doc. Assembly/AU/Dec. 605 (XXVII), para. 5 (18 Jul. 2016).

Part III. Activities

Chapter 1. Settlement of Disputes

198. One of the guiding principles of the OAU was the peaceful settlement of disputes.[915] In fact, it has been observed that 'the principle of the peaceful settlement of international disputes has been recognized and accepted as a binding principle of international law by African States'.[916] To facilitate its commitment to dispute settlement the OAU had available to it various institutional and informal arrangements. In the former category was the Commission of Mediation, Conciliation, and Arbitration[917] but it never become operational as African States regarded formal dispute settlement procedures with suspicion.[918] Rather, resort to diplomatic or political procedures was for many years the preferred mode of dispute settlement.[919] Indeed, the OAU was distinctive for its lack of a judicial organ. These modes of dispute settlement proved to be remedial and reactive and therefore failed in general to address the root causes of many disputes, ultimately proving inadequate as preventative problem solvers. All in all these efforts often yielded disappointing results.[920]

199. In establishing a Mechanism for Conflict Prevention, Management, and Resolution in 1993 the OAU proclaimed its readiness to adopt a more resolute approach

915. Charter of the Organization of African Unity Arts III(4), XIX (25 May 1963), 479 U.N.T.S. 39, 2 I.L.M. 766 (1963). The latter provision required the Member States to settle *all* their disputes by peaceful means. *See Democratic Republic of Congo v. Burundi, Rwanda and Uganda,* Communication No. 227/99, 20th Activity Report 2005–2006, paras 66, 74–75; *Association Pour la Sauvegarde de la Paix au Burundi v. Tanzania, Kenya, Uganda, Rwanda, Zaire and Zambia,* Communication No. 157/96, 17th Activity Report, 2003–2004. Cooperation between the OAU and the UN was common in this area, B. Boutros-Ghali, *Confronting New Challenges* (New York: United Nations, 1995), 340–341.
916. T. Maluwa, 'The Peaceful Settlement of Disputes among African States, 1963–1983: Some Conceptual Issues and Practical Trends', *I.C.L.Q.* 38 (1986): 299.
917. *See* K.D. Magliveras & G.J. Naldi, *The African Union* (The Hague: Kluwer Law International, 2009), paras 74–79.
918. Maluwa, 305–307.
919. T. Maluwa, *International Law in Post-Colonial Africa* (The Hague: Kluwer Law International, 1999), 241. *See* generally J.G. Merrills, *International Dispute Settlement* (3rd edn, Cambridge: Cambridge University Press, 1998), Chs 1, 2, 4.
920. Maluwa, International Law in Post-Colonial Africa, 241–245.

to dispute settlement.[921] The Mechanism, designed to be preventative and proactive, put in place an institutional framework for the peaceful and speedy resolutions of disputes.[922] Its primary objective was the prevention of conflicts, with the emphasis on anticipatory and preventive measures; it was therefore directed to undertake confidence-building measures and peacemaking functions.[923] It was also designed to prevent conflicts escalating. Prompt and decisive action should have acted as a deterrent to conflicts and preclude the need to resort to complex peacekeeping operations. The Mechanism's record was mixed[924] and with the advent of the AU, the Mechanism became an organ of the AU.[925]

200. The AU is similarly committed to the settlement of disputes. The 'peaceful resolution of conflicts' is one of its founding principles.[926] The AU thus inherited the Mechanism from the OAU but which was soon transformed into the PSC.[927] This transformation was necessitated by the need to enhance the AU's conflict resolution and management capacities and to establish an operational structure for the more effective implementation of the relevant decisions. To this end the APSA was established as the continent's overarching strategic security framework to enhance continental and regional capabilities for the prevention, management and resolution of conflict, including post-conflict reconstruction and peace-building, of which the PSC is but one element.

---

921. Declaration of the Assembly of Heads of State and Government on the Establishment Within the OAU of a Mechanism for Conflict Prevention, Management and Resolution (the Cairo Declaration), 6 R.A.D.I.C. 158 (1994).
922. Cairo Declaration para. 14, reaffirmed the OAU's commitment to the principle of peaceful settlement of disputes in Africa. The Mechanism was described as 'a new and deliberate attempt to institutionalize the *political* means of dispute settlement in preference to *legal* mechanisms', Maluwa, International Law in Post-Colonial Africa, 249. *See* further Magliveras & Naldi, paras 74–79.
923. Cairo Declaration paras 15, 19, 22.
924. *See* Magliveras & Naldi, paras 232–233.
925. At its Thirty-Seventh Ordinary Session in Lusaka, Zambia, in July 2001, Decision AHG/Dec.160 (XXXVII), the OAU Assembly incorporated the Mechanism as one of the organs of the AU in accordance with the Constitutive Act of the African Union, Art. 5(2) (26 May 2001), 2158 U.N.T.S. 3.
926. Constitutive Act, Art. 4(e). *See also* Fifteenth Anniversary Solemn Declaration para. E, Assembly, Twenty-First Ordinary Session, 26 May 2013; Agenda 2063, Assembly, *Decision on the Report of the Commission on Development of the African Union Agenda 2063*, AU Doc. Assembly/AU/Dec. 565(XXIV) (30–31 Jan. 2015).
927. *See* Protocol Relating to the Establishment of the Peace and Security Council of the African Union (9 Jul. 2002), https://www.au.int/en/treaties, C. Heyns & M. Killander (eds), *Compendium of Key Human Rights Documents of the African Union* (6th ed., Pretoria: Pretoria University Law Press, 2016), 17. The PSC Protocol entered into force on 26 Dec. 2003 and the PSC became operational in 2004, *see supra* para. 155. By June 2017 it had been ratified by fifty-one States. Note that the Protocol on Amendments to the Constitutive Act Art. 5 (9 Jul. 2002), https://www.au.int/en/treaties, Heyns & Killander, 12, not yet in force, classifies the PSC as one of the organs of the AU. For fuller discussion of the PSC *see supra* paras 155–171; F. Viljoen, *International Human Rights Law in Africa* (Oxford: Oxford University Press, 2007), 205–211.

201. According to Article 2(1) of the PSC Protocol the PSC is a 'standing decision-making organ for the prevention, management and resolution of conflicts'.[928] Additionally, it is a 'collective security and early-warning arrangement to facilitate timely and efficient response to Conflict and crisis situations in Africa'. As such the PSC is the organ that co-operates with relevant regional mechanisms and the UN.[929] The objectives of the PSC include, according to Article 3 of the PSC Protocol, promoting peace, security and stability in Africa, anticipating and preventing conflicts, undertaking peacemaking and peace-building functions, promoting and implementing peace-building and post-conflict reconstruction activities, and promoting and encouraging democratic practices, good governance and the rule of law, and protecting human rights.[930] According to Article 4 of the PSC Protocol, its guiding principles include the peaceful settlement of disputes and early responses to crisis situations.

202. The functions of the PSC, according to Article 6 of the Protocol, include the promotion of peace, security and stability in Africa, early warning and preventive diplomacy,[931] peacemaking, including the use of good offices, mediation, conciliation and enquiry, peace support operations,[932] peace-building and post-conflict reconstruction[933] and humanitarian action and disaster management.[934] It has the power, under Article 7, *inter alia*, to anticipate and prevent disputes and conflicts, to undertake peacemaking and peace-building functions, to authorize and mount peace support missions, to follow-up the progress towards the promotion of democratic practices, good governance and the rule of law, and the protection of human rights, and to support and facilitate humanitarian action.[935]

203. Since the PSC became operational it has been active in a number of spheres, including Peace Support Operations (PSOs).[936] These include peacekeeping, capacity-building, maintaining public order and mediation activities. One significant development, based on Article 12 of the PSC Protocol, is the Continental Early Warning System (CEWS) mandated to anticipate and prevent conflicts. It has an intelligence-gathering capacity to warn the PSC on threats to peace and security, and advises on courses of action. Another important body is the Panel of the Wise, established under Article 11 of the PSC Protocol, to support the PSC's mission, particularly in the area of conflict

928. *See also* Protocol on Amendments to the Constitutive Act Art. 9.
929. PSC Protocol Arts 16 and 17.
930. Another AU organ that has a role in promoting peace, security and stability in Africa is the Pan-African Parliament, Protocol Establishing the African Economic Community relating to the Pan-African Parliament Art. 3(5) (2 Mar. 2001), https://www.au.int/en/treaties, Heyns & Killander 14. The Protocol entered into force on 14 Dec. 2003. It should be superseded by the Protocol to the Constitutive Act of the African Union Relating to the Pan-African Parliament (27 Jun. 2014), https://www.au.int/en/treaties, not yet in force.
931. *See also* PSC Protocol Art. 12.
932. *See also* PSC Protocol Art. 13.
933. *See also* PSC Protocol Art. 14.
934. *See also* PSC Protocol Art. 15.
935. Note that under the African Charter on Democracy, Elections and Governance Art. 38(2) (30 Jan. 2007), https://www.au.int/en/treaties, Heyns & Killander, 125 (African Charter on Democracy), in force 15 Feb. 2012, State Parties undertake to support the conflict prevention and resolution initiatives of the PSC.
936. Viljoen, 210–211.

prevention, but generally in the promotion and maintenance of peace, security and stability in Africa.[937] The Panel is composed of five members,[938] who are appointed by the AU Assembly, on the recommendation of the Chair of the Commission, for a three-year period., The Panel may act at the request of the PSC, the Chair of the Commission, or at its own initiative. In 2010 the AU Assembly supported enhancing the Panel's role by establishing the Friends of the Panel of the Wise.[939] The Friends, composed of five to ten eminent African personalities, supports the Panel in its activities, particularly fact-finding missions and negotiations. Of particular importance is the African Standby Force (ASF), a multidisciplinary force composed of military, civilian and police elements, regionally located for rapid deployment in crisis situations. Its responsibilities include peace support missions.[940] However, while the ASF became fully operational, the AU set up, as an interim mechanism, the African Capacity for Immediate Response to Crises (ACIRC).[941] The ACIRC is a rapid deployment military force designed to respond swiftly to emergency situations. Agenda 2063 aims to ensure that all these initiatives are established and fully operational within a couple of years.[942]

204. The African Peace Facility (APF), which is a multidisciplinary force with military, police and civilian components for deployment in crisis situations, channels political support and resources from the EU for PSOs.[943] In 2009 the Early Response Mechanism (ERM) was established to support the APF with funding, presently until mid-2018. The ERM's areas of activities include mediation, human rights and post-conflict building. Recent initiatives include the AU High-Level Implementation Panel on Sudan and South Sudan in 2014 and the appointment of the AU High Representative for Libya in 2016.[944]

205. It has long been an article of faith that African States have little confidence in international third-party adjudication.[945] However, that received wisdom needs to be challenged given the fact that over the last twenty years African States have 'ranked

937. In 2016 the Panel of the Wise was involved in defusing a constitutional crisis in Madagascar, Report of the UN Secretary-General on strengthening the partnership between the United Nations and the African Union on issues of peace and security in Africa, UN Doc. S/2016/780, para. 27.
938. '[H]ighly respected African personalities…who have made outstanding contributions to the cause of peace, security and development' in Africa, PSC Protocol Art. 11(2).
939. Assembly, *Decision on the Appointment of the Members of the Panel of the Wise,* AU Doc. Assembly/AU/Dec. 310 (XV) (25–27 Jul. 2010).
940. PSC Protocol Art. 13(1). A number of such missions have been deployed over the years, often in association with the UN, including AMISOM and UNAMID.
941. Assembly, *Decision on the Establishment of an African Capacity for Immediate Response to Crises,* AU Doc. Assembly/AU/Dec. 489(XXI) (26–27 May 2013).
942. Assembly, *Decision on the Report of the Commission on Development of the African Union Agenda 2063*, AU Doc. Assembly/AU/Dec. 565(XXIV) (30–31 Jan. 2015).
943. Assembly, *Decision on the Establishment by the European Union of a Peace Support Operation Facility for the African Union*, AU Doc. Assembly/AU/Dec.21(II) (10–12 Jul. 2003); *The Africa-EU Partnership: 2 unions, 1 vision*, 9.
944. Report of the UN Secretary-General on strengthening the partnership between the United Nations and the African Union on issues of peace and security in Africa, UN Doc. S/2016/780, para. 26.
945. Maluwa, International Law in Post-Colonial Africa, 236, 305–307.

high as a source of cases' before the ICJ.[946] Furthermore, recourse has been had to other international tribunals.[947] In light of recent developments it can be safely asserted that African States have come to accept judicial settlement as an accepted means of dispute resolution. Particular note should be taken of the fact that the Constitutive Act makes provision for a Court of Justice.[948]

206. The AU's Court seems to have finally emerged in the form of the ACJHR.[949] Since the ACJHR is discussed elsewhere[950] it is unnecessary to enter into detail here except to recall that the ACJHR is composed of two divisions, a General Affairs Section and a Human Rights Section. The Human Rights Section is considered below and therefore will not be discussed further.[951] Under Article 29(1) of the Statute the applicants entitled to submit cases to the General Affairs Section fall into three categories, only two of which have relevance here: first, the contracting parties to the 2008 Protocol; second, the Assembly, the PAP and other AU organs authorized by the Assembly (e.g., the EX or the PSC). Member States must take the conscious decision to sign up to the Protocol since the ACJHR's jurisdiction does not extend automatically over states merely by virtue of participation in the AU.[952] Article 29(2) of the Statute makes it clear that the ACJHR does not have jurisdiction over disputes involving AU Member States that have not ratified the Protocol.[953] Since the ACJHR is the 'main judicial organ' of the AU it is submitted that it ought to have been conferred automatic jurisdiction over the whole membership. Nonetheless, in one circumstance the ACJHR's decisions bind all Member States regardless of whether or not they have ratified the Protocol: according to Article 50(3) of the Statute, decisions on the Constitutive Act's interpretation and application are binding on all Members. The Statute does not extend *locus standi* to non-AU Member States even if a dispute should arise with the AU itself or a Member

946. Judge Stephen Schwebel, then President of the ICJ, in a speech to the UN General Assembly, ICJ Communiqué No. 98/33. For a recent example *see Maritime Delimitation in the Indian Ocean (Somalia v. Kenya)*, Preliminary Objections, I.C.J. Reports 2017.

947. Including the International Tribunal on the Law of the Sea, *see M.V. Saiga (No. 2) (Saint Vincent and the Grenadines v. Guinea)* 37 I.L.M. 1202 (1998), and *The M/V 'Virginia G' (Panama/ Guinea-Bissau)*, Judgment, 14 Apr. 2014, ITLOS Case No. 19; and international arbitral tribunals, *see Chagos Marine Protected Area Arbitration (Mauritius v. United Kingdom)*, Award, 18 Mar. 2015) PCA Case No. 2011-03. A significant number of African States, thirty-four, have ratified the Rome Statute of the International Criminal Court (17 Jul. 1998), 2187 U.N.T.S. 91, 37 I.L.M. 999 (1998) (Rome Statute). It is interesting to note that many of the cases on the ICC's docket or under examination relate to Africa, Report of the International Criminal Court on its activities in 2015/16., UN Doc. A/71/342.

948. *See* Constitutive Act Arts 5(1), 18. It should be further observed that African regional organizations, such as COMESA, ECOWAS, and SADC, have established courts for the settlement of disputes.

949. Protocol on the Statute of the African Court of Justice and Human Rights (1 Jul. 2008), https://www.au.int/en/treaties, 48 I.L.M. 337 (2009) (2008 Protocol). As of June 2017, the 2008 Protocol has been ratified by six Member States.

950. *See supra* , paras 122–135.

951. *See infra* , Ch. 2 s. 5.

952. While according to the UN Charter Art. 93(1), all UN Member States are *ipso facto* parties to the ICJ Statute, acceptance of its compulsory jurisdiction is dependent on a declaration to that effect pursuant to the ICJ Statute Art. 36(2).

953. The Statute, Art. 28(f), rules out the possibility of a non-party submitting a case to the ACJHR by special agreement. Compare ICJ Statute Art. 36(1).

State. Such disputes would have to be resolved by some other body. The ACJHR's contentious jurisdiction is set out in Article 28 of the Statute, which reflects Article 36(2) of the ICJ Statute although the former has a specifically African perspective and is considerably broader in scope. The ACJHR is competent to hear all cases and legal disputes submitted to it concerning, *inter alia*, the interpretation and application of the Constitutive Act, the interpretation, application or validity of other AU treaties and subsidiary legal instruments, any question of international law, all secondary legislation adopted by AU organs, all matters specifically provided for in other agreements that the contracting parties to the Statute may conclude among themselves or with the AU which confer jurisdiction on the ACJHR, the existence of any fact which, if established, would constitute a breach of an obligation owed to a State Party or to the AU, and the nature or extent of the reparation to be made for the breach of an obligation. Whether the drafters of the 2008 Protocol intended to establish an alternative, regional, forum to the ICJ for African States is unclear but a solid argument can be made that the primary responsibility for determining general questions of international law should lie with the ICJ which, as 'the principal judicial organ of the United Nations', is uniquely placed to examine such issues.[954] Of course, it could simply be that it was merely intended to ensure that the ACJHR has the specific authorization to consider a wide range of international law issues. In the absence of such a provision, the ACJHR, as an institutionalized judicial body, would nevertheless have had the inherent right to consider international law issues as they arose. In fact, it should be noted that the ICJ is not mentioned at all in the Statute, which does not contain a savings clause. Therefore, the important question of the relationship between these two bodies is not addressed.

207. Since its founding the OAU put in place mechanisms for the peaceful settlement of disputes. Subsequently various initiatives were adopted, particularly the Mechanism for Conflict Prevention, Management, and Resolution, to promote the OAU's capacity for dispute resolution. These were almost exclusively diplomatic or political rather than legal. Some modest attempts were made to deploy observers in conflict situations. However, OAU peacemaking and conflict management was hampered by a lack of adequate resources and a lack of confidence. For too long the emphasis had been on short-term conflict prevention measures. Although the OAU had some successes there were also too many failures. Recourse was more often had to non-African settlement mechanisms, with the onus often on the UN.[955] The claim that a practice had evolved in Africa whereby disputes should initially be submitted for resolution to the regional organization[956] did not seem to stand scrutiny. To its credit, the OAU/AU recognized that the root causes of conflict had to be addressed. The

954. In recent years fears have been expressed that the proliferation of international judicial bodies could lead to the fragmentation of international law, *see* , e.g., G. Guillaume, 'The Future of International Judicial Institutions', *I.C.L.Q.*44 (1995): 848.

955. In recent years the UN and the AU have established a collaborative relationship in the maintenance of peace and security under the Ten-Year Capacity-Building Programme for the African Union, UN Doc. A/61/630 (2006). *See* further *infra* , Part IV, Ch. 2 s. 1.

956. *Land and Maritime Boundary between Cameroon and Nigeria (Cameroon v. Nigeria)*, Preliminary Objections, I.C.J. Reports 1998, paras 48–60. Compare, *contra*, Maluwa, International Law in Post-Colonial Africa, 249.

establishment of the PSC, which mirrors the UN's preventive diplomacy and conflict resolution initiatives, has been a significant step forward. The ACJHR may add another dimension for dispute resolution. The willingness of ECOWAS to assume a proactive and determined regional role in peace-enforcement is significant.[957] But it is important for the international community to continue to support the AU and ECOWAS with the necessary resources and capacity to meet the difficult challenges that it is facing in Mali, Somalia, and elsewhere.[958] Without the political willingness to provide the resources necessary to support a more resolute approach by the AU its chances of providing successfully the means for dispute resolution will remain haphazard.

957. *See* generally C. Gray, *International Law and the Use of Force*(3rd edn, Oxford: Oxford University Press, 2008), 392–396, 400–407, 411–417.
958. *See infra* , Part IV, Ch. 2.

Chapter 2. Human Rights

§1. The African Union and Human Rights

208. The transformation of the OAU into the AU propelled human rights to the top of the agenda. Unlike the OAU Charter, express references to human rights and democratic values are made in the Constitutive Act of the AU. The AU not only reinforces the OAU's endeavours in these fields[959] but places respect for human rights at the forefront of its policies in the knowledge that progress in development, poverty eradication and conflict resolution are dependent on the guaranteeing of human rights. Significantly, through the PSC the AU has armed itself with the capacity to take concrete action to promote and protect human rights. The express commitments to democracy and human rights are especially desirable developments and constitute welcome improvements on the OAU Charter, which was silent on these matters. The wording of the relevant provisions in the Constitutive Act would indicate that they create binding obligations for the Member States. The AU would thus appear to have a democratic legitimacy that the discredited OAU had always lacked. Yet human rights and democratic values can only be enhanced if the AU takes its pertinent pledges seriously. If so, the frequently abysmal human rights record in certain African States should be ameliorated.[960]

209. The AU's commitment to these ideals is clearly established in the Constitutive Act's Preamble where the AU undertakes to 'promote and protect human and peoples' rights, consolidate democratic institutions and culture, and to ensure good governance and the rule of law'. Significantly, these norms have not remained at a theoretical level but effect has been given to them by enshrining them in the operative sections of the Act, and subsequently reinforced by the Protocol on the PAP and the PSC Protocol. Among the AU's objectives, as set out in Article 3 of the Constitutive Act, are the promotion of democratic principles and institutions, popular participation and good

959. *See* in particular the African Charter on Human and Peoples' Rights, *infra* , s. 2.

960. The human rights record of African States varies widely. The Mo Ibrahim Foundation, a civil society organization, rated Cape Verde as the clear leader in its Rights sub-category in the Participation & Rights index for 2015, with Mauritius, Namibia and Ghana following, *2016 Ibrahim Index of African Governance: Summary* http//:moibrahimfoundation.org/en. Equatorial Guinea and Eritrea had the dubious honour of worst rated countries, with Somalia, Sudan and South Sudan close behind.

governance,[961] and the promotion and protection of human rights in accordance with the African Charter on Human and Peoples' Rights and other relevant human rights instruments.[962] It is also interesting to observe that the statement of the AU's objectives reveal the realization by the African States that the attainment of sustainable economic development cannot be achieved without respecting and encouraging the principles of democracy, popular participation, and good governance, and the protection of human rights. By making a direct connection between sustainable economic development and human rights, the Constitutive Act acknowledges that a human rights culture is indispensable in fostering economic growth.

210. The objectives are to be attained through the strict observance of a number of fundamental principles, in accordance with which the AU shall function. Included among these principles is respect for democratic principles, human rights, the rule of law, and good governance.[963] Particularly noteworthy is the inclusion of a 'democracy clause' whereby unconstitutional changes of government are condemned and rejected.[964] This appears to follow rationally from the objectives of promoting democratic principles and institutions, and good governance throughout the continent. Crucially, the AU can reinforce democracy among Member States through the imposition of punitive measures. Article 30 stipulates that regimes coming to power through unconstitutional means shall be prohibited from participating in the activities of the AU.[965] Its proper and consistent application should hopefully act as a deterrent to attempts at unconstitutional removals of legitimate governments. Of significant interest also is the fact that war crimes, genocide and crimes against humanity are viewed so seriously that the AU is authorized to intervene in a Member State where these atrocities are being perpetrated.[966] Also worthy of note is the commitment to the promotion of gender equality.[967] Given

961. Constitutive Act of the African Union Art. 3(g) (26 May 2001), 2158 U.N.T.S. 3. *See* further Protocol Establishing the African Economic Community relating to the Pan-African Parliament Art. 3(3) (2 Mar. 2001), https://www.au.int/en/treaties, C. Heyns & M. Killander (eds), *Compendium of Key Human Rights Documents of the African Union*(6th edn, Pretoria: Pretoria University Law Press, 2016), 14, (PAP Protocol), and Protocol Relating to the Establishment of the Peace and Security Council of the African Union Art.3(f) (9 Jul. 2002), https://www.au.int/en/treaties, Heyns & Killander, 17 (PSC Protocol). An important development in this regard, reinforcing the AU's commitments to these values, is the adoption of the African Charter on Democracy, Elections and Governance (30 Jan. 2007), https://www.au.int/en/treaties, Heyns & Killander, 125, which entered into force 15 Feb. 2012. *See also* Fifteenth Anniversary Solemn Declaration para. F, Assembly, Twenty-First Ordinary Session, 26 May 2013.

962. Constitutive Act Art. 3(h). *See* further PSC Protocol Art. 3(f), and African Charter on Democracy Art. 2(1).

963. Constitutive Act Art. 4(g). *See* further PAP Protocol Art. 3(2), PSC Protocol Art. 4(c), and African Charter on Democracy Arts 3 and 4(1).*See Actions pour la Protection des Droit de l'Homme (APDH) v. Côte d'Ivoire*, African Court of Human and Peoples' Rights, App. No. 001/2014 (18 Nov. 2016).

964. Constitutive Act Art. 4(p). *See* further African Charter on Democracy Arts 2(4), 3(10) and 5.

965. *See also* African Charter on Democracy Art. 25(1). In addition, under the Constitutive Act Art. 23(2) the failure by any Member State to comply with the decisions and policies of the AU may lead to the imposition of sanctions. *See* further PSC Protocol Art. 7(g), and African Charter on Democracy Art. 23.

966. Constitutive Act Art. 4(h). *See* further PSC Protocol Art. 7(e).

967. Constitutive Act Art. 4(l). *See* further African Charter on Democracy Art. 3(6).

that the crises affecting many African countries often manifest themselves through ethnic and cultural tensions and conflicts it seems regrettable that non-discrimination is not expressly made a key element of the Constitutive Act.

§2. The African Charter on Human and Peoples' Rights

211. The adoption of the African Charter on Human and Peoples' Rights (hereinafter the African Charter) in 1981 gave rise to expectations that human rights in Africa would be adequately promoted and protected.[968] It is only in recent years, however, that these expectations, after many false starts, are beginning to be fulfilled. One of the reasons why the road to the effective protection of human rights in Africa has been laboured may lie with the African Charter itself which many commentators have considered as fatally flawed.[969] The features of the African Charter which have given cause for concern will initially be considered.

I. Is the African Charter Fundamentally Flawed?

212. The African Charter is distinctive, unique even, for providing in a sole binding legal document all three categories of human rights.[970] Civil and political rights, essentially corresponding to those protected by the familiar human rights treaty texts, are guaranteed by Articles 3–14 and include the right to life, the prohibition of torture and other forms of ill-treatment, the prohibition of arbitrary deprivations of liberty, the right to a fair trial, the freedom of conscience, expression, association and

968. African Charter on Human and Peoples' Rights (17 Jun. 1981), 1520 U.N.T.S. 217, 21 I.L.M. 58 (1982). The African Charter entered into force on 21 Oct. 1986 and has been ratified by all of the AU's Member States with the sole exception of Morocco which joined the AU in 2017.
969. The African Charter has been described as 'modest in its objectives and flexible in its means', *see* B. Obinna Okere, 'The Protection of Human Rights in Africa and the African Charter on Human and Peoples' Rights: A Comparative Analysis with the European and American Systems', *Human Rights Quarterly* 6 (1984): 141, 158. For other sceptical assessments, *see* R. Gittleman, 'The African Charter on Human and Peoples' Rights: A Legal Analysis', *Virginia J.I.L.* 22 (1981–1982): 667; P. Amoah, 'The African Charter on Human and Peoples' Rights – An Effective Weapon for Human Rights?', *R.A.D.I.C.* 4 (1992): 226; G. Robertson, *Crimes Against Humanity: The Struggle for Global Justice*(London: Penguin, 1999), 57–58.
970. In *Good v. Botswana*, Communication No. 306/2005, 28th Activity Report 2009–2010, paras 227–234, the African Commission on Human and Peoples' Rights dismissed Botswana's submission that the African Charter was not a legally binding treaty.

assembly, and the right to property.[971] Second generation rights are set out in Articles 15–18 and include the right to work, the right to health, the right to education and to culture, and the rights of the family.[972] Third generation or peoples' rights are listed in Articles 19–24 and include the right of self-determination, the right to peace and security, the right to environment, the right to natural resources, and the right to development.[973] The African Commission on Human and Peoples' Rights[974] (Commission) considers these categories of rights as indivisible and has stated that States parties are under a 'duty to respect, protect, promote, and fulfil' all the Charter obligations,

971. For an in-depth analysis of the specific rights, *see* A.H. Ankumah, *The African Commission on Human and Peoples' Rights* (The Hague: Martinus Nijhoff, 1996), 111–142; H.B. Jallow, *The Law of the African (Banjul) Charter on Human and Peoples' Rights* (Victoria, BC: Trafford Publishing, 2007), 178–291; C. Heyns, 'Civil and Political Rights in the African Charter', in *The African Charter on Human and Peoples' Rights: The System in Practice, 1986–2000*, M. Evans & R. Murray (eds), (Cambridge: Cambridge University Press, 2002), 137–177; B. Manby, 'Civil and Political Rights in the African Charter on Human and Peoples' Rights: Arts 1–7', in *The African Charter on Human and Peoples' Rights: The System in Practice, 1986–2006*, M. Evans & R. Murray (eds), (2nd edn, Cambridge: Cambridge University Press, 2008), 171–212; K. Olaniyan, 'Civil and Political Rights in the African Charter on Human and Peoples' Rights: Arts 8–17', in *The African Charter on Human and Peoples' Rights: The System in Practice, 1986–2006*, Evans & Murray (eds), (2nd edn, Cambridge: Cambridge University Press, 2008), 213–243; U.O. Umozurike, *The African Charter on Human and Peoples' Rights* (The Hague: Martinus Nijhoff, 1997), 29–43.
972. For an in-depth analysis of the specific rights, *see* Ankumah, 143–159; Jallow, 293–305; C.A. Odinkalu, 'Implementing Economic, Social and Cultural Rights under the African Charter on Human and Peoples' Rights', in *The African Charter on Human and Peoples' Rights: The System in Practice, 1986–2000*, Evans & Murray (eds), (Cambridge: Cambridge University Press, 2002),178–218.
973. The Commission has stated that the inclusion of third generation rights in the African Charter constitutes one of its main distinctive features, *Bissangou v. Republic of Congo*, Communication No. 253/2002, 21st Activity Report 2005–2006, para. 80. For an in-depth analysis of the specific rights, *see* Ankumah, 160–170; Jallow, 305–323; C. Baldwin & C. Morel, 'Group Rights', in *The African Charter on Human and Peoples' Rights: The System in Practice, 1986–2006*, Evans & Murray (eds), (2nd edn, Cambridge: Cambridge University Press, 2008), 244–288.
974. The Commission has the responsibility under the African Charter of promoting and protecting human and peoples' rights, *see infra* , paras 235–273. The Commission's decisions on communications can be consulted at the following sources: the Commission's website, http://www.achpr.org, the website of the University of Pretoria's Centre for Human Rights, http://www.up.ac.za/chr/ahrdb/acomm_decisions.html, and the website of the University of Minnesota's Human Rights Library, http://www1.umn.edu/humanrts/africa; International Human Rights Reports (I.H.R.R.); R. Murray & M. Evans (eds), *Documents of the African Commission on Human and Peoples' Rights* (Oxford: Hart Publishing, 2001), and Vol. II (Oxford: Hart Publishing, 2008).

entailing a combination of negative and positive duties.[975] More so than other comparable human rights treaty texts the substantive provisions of the African Charter are equivocally or broadly phrased.[976] This on occasion has led the Commission to develop unenumerated rights that are not explicitly mentioned in provisions which are nevertheless considered to embody them implicitly.[977]

213. The perceived inadequate protection of civil and political rights has attracted considerable criticism.[978] The statist bias of the African Charter is manifest. In particular, extensive use is made of 'clawback' clauses that appear to make the rights subject to municipal law, or at the discretion of the national authorities. They seek to provide a justification for a violation.[979] There are numerous examples. Thus, Article 8, which guarantees the freedom of conscience and religion, states that '[n]o one may, *subject to law and order*, be submitted to measures restricting the exercise of these freedoms' (emphasis added). Article 9(2) guarantees the freedom of expression 'within the law'. Article 10(1) guarantees individuals the right of association 'provided that he abides by the law'. Article 13(1) guarantees the right to participate in government 'in accordance with the provisions of the law'. Clawback clauses are therefore especially insidious because, through their vagueness, they 'do not provide the required external control over State behaviour'.[980] It has therefore been observed that the 'legal reasons and conditions for invoking these limitations are not defined in the Charter'.[981]

214. Commentators have been critical of the wording of these provisions. Ankumah has observed that they 'could render previously granted rights meaningless'.[982] Gittleman has written that the African Charter is 'incapable of supplying even a scintilla of external restraint upon a government's power to create laws contrary to the spirit

975. *The Social and Economic Rights Action Center and the Center for Economic and Social Rights v. Nigeria*, Communication No. 155/96, 15th Activity Report 2001–2002, paras 43–48. Briefly, the Commission explained that the obligation to respect 'entails that the State should refrain from interfering in the enjoyment of all fundamental rights'; the obligation to protect requires, *inter alia*, the creation and maintenance of an environment based on an effective framework of laws and regulations where individuals can realize their rights and freedoms; the obligation to promote requires States to ensure an environment of tolerance and awareness that allows that individuals can exercise their rights and freedoms; and the obligation to fulfil requires States to secure the realization of these rights. *See* further *Association of Victims of Post Electoral Violence & INTERIGHTS v. Cameroon*, Communication No. 272/2003, 27th Activity Report 2009, paras 87–92.

976. Gittleman, 685; R.M. D'Sa, 'The African Charter on Human and Peoples' Rights: Problems and Prospects for Regional Action', *Australian Y.B.I.L.* 10 (1981/1983): 101, 107–108.

977. Examples include elements of the right to a fair trial, *infra* paras 230–239, and a right to shelter or housing, *The Social and Economic Rights Action Center and the Center for Economic and Social Rights v. Nigeria*, Communication No. 155/96, 15th Activity Report 2001–2002, para. 60.

978. *See* , e.g., Gittleman.

979. Jallow, 163. According to Higgins, clawback clauses permit 'in normal circumstances, breach of an obligation for a specified number of published reasons', R. Higgins, 'Derogations under Human Rights Treaties', *B.Y.B.I.L.* 48 (1976–1977): 281.

980. Gittleman, 692. *See also* D'Sa, 110.

981. E. Bello, 'The African Charter on Human and Peoples' Rights', *Hague Recueil* 194 (1985/1986): 13, 70.

982. Ankumah, 176.

of the rights granted'.[983] Kunig has expressed the view that since 'there are no provisions to ensure that a core of the human rights guarantees prevails against legislative restrictions, this represents a considerable structural defect'.[984] And Murray has commented that '[t]he limitations are not defined exactly in the Charter, arguably leaving it purely to the discretion of states, and thus, in effect, allowing rights to be denied'.[985] The African Commission itself has stated that 'if "law" is interpreted to mean any domestic law regardless of its effect, States Parties to the Charter would be able to negate the rights conferred upon individuals by the Charter'.[986]

215. It is interesting to observe, however, that the practice of the Commission clearly demonstrates that it will not uphold the legality of a restraint that leaves its precise scope and nature to the whim of the State.[987] Indeed, the Commission has cautioned against a 'too easy resort to the limitation clauses in the African Charter'.[988] In *Media Rights Agenda and Constitutional Rights Project v. Nigeria*, which was mainly concerned with the proscription of various publications critical of the Nigerian military regime, the Commission gave a comprehensive reasoned explanation of its interpretation of the nature and scope of clawback clauses in the Charter. It stated:

> Governments should avoid restricting rights, and have special care with regard to those rights protected by constitutional or international human rights law. No situation justifies the wholesale violation of human rights. In fact, general restrictions on rights diminish public confidence in the rule of law and are often counter-productive.
>
> According to Article 9(2) of the Charter, dissemination of opinions may be restricted by law. This does not mean that national law can set aside the right to disseminate one's opinions; this would make the protection of the right to express one's opinions ineffective. To allow national law to have precedent over the international law of the Charter would defeat the purpose of the rights and freedoms enshrined in the Charter. International human rights standards must always prevail over contradictory national law. Any limitation on the rights of the Charter must be in conformity with the provisions of the Charter.

---

983. Gittleman, 694.
984. P. Kunig, 'The Protection of Human Rights by International Law in Africa', *German Y.B. I. L.* 25 (1982): 138, 155.
985. R. Murray, *The African Commission on Human and Peoples' Rights and International Law*(Oxford: Hart Publishing, 2000), 127.
986. *Article 19 v. Eritrea*, Communication No. 275/2003, 22nd Activity Report 2006–2007, para. 91.
987. *See* further, G.J. Naldi, 'Limitation of Rights under the African Charter on Human and Peoples' Rights: The Contribution of the African Commission on Human and Peoples' Rights', *S.A.J.H.R.* 17 (2001): 109.
988. *Amnesty International v. Zambia*, Communication No. 212/98, 12th Activity Report 1998–1999, para. 42.

> The only legitimate reasons for limitations to the rights and freedoms of the African Charter are found in Article 27(2), that is that the rights of the Charter 'shall be exercised with due regard to the rights of others, collective security, morality and common interest.'
>
> The reasons for possible limitations must be founded in a legitimate state interest and the evils of limitations of rights must be strictly proportionate with and absolutely necessary for the advantages which are to be obtained.
>
> Even more important, a limitation may never have as a consequence that the right itself become illusory.[989]

216. The Commission has cautioned against reliance on clawback clauses as a means of 'giving credence' to violations of the African Charter. In the alternative, it has interpreted clawback clauses as 'constituting a reference to international law, meaning that only restrictions on rights which are consistent with the Charter and with States Parties' international obligations should be enacted by the relevant national authorities'.[990] It has therefore made it manifest that the applicable standard is that of International Human Rights Law, which prevails over any inconsistent municipal law.[991] The Commission has thus held that where a State claims to be acting under legislation 'previously laid down by law', it must show that such law is consistent with its obligations under the African Charter.[992] Moreover, a limitation can be justified only by reference to the criteria listed in Article 27(2) of the African Charter.[993] Consequently, in relation to the protection of the freedoms of assembly and expression, the Commission stated that these 'actions and expressions are among the most important exercises of human rights and as such should be given substantial protection that do

989. Communication Nos 105/93, 128/94, 130/94, 152/96, 12th Activity Report 1998–1999, paras 65–70. *See also Constitutional Rights Project, Civil Liberties Organisation and Media Rights Agenda v. Nigeria*, Communication Nos 140/94, 141/94, 145/95, 13th Activity Report 1999–2000, para. 42; *Interights, Institute for Human Rights and Development in Africa, and Association Mauritaniene des Droits de l'Homme v. Mauritania*, Communication No. 242/2001, 17th Activity Report 2003–2004, paras 76–79. And *see Tanganyika Law Society et al. v. Tanzania*, African Court of Human and Peoples' Rights, App. Nos 009/2011 and 011/2011 (14 Jun. 2013), para. 107.

990. *Article 19 v. Eritrea*, Communication No. 275/2003, 22nd Activity Report 2006–2007, para. 92.

991. *Amnesty International v. Mauritania*, Communication No. 61/91, 13th Activity Report 1999–2000, para. 102.

992. *Sir Dawda K. Jawara v. Gambia*, Communication Nos 147/95 and 149/96, 13th Activity Report 1999–2000, paras 43, 58–59.

993. Heyns, 140–141; *Tanganyika Law Society et al. v. Tanzania*, African Court of Human and Peoples' Rights, App. Nos 009/2011 and 011/2011 (14 Jun. 2013), para. 107. In *Legal Resources Foundation v. Zambia*, Communication No. 211/98, 14th Activity Report 2000–2001, para. 70, the Commission stated that the African Charter must be interpreted holistically and all provisions must reinforce each other.

not allow the State to suspend these rights for frivolous reasons and in a manner that is thus disproportionate to the interference with the exercise of these fundamental rights'.[994] In addition, the Commission has further extended the scope of a State's obligation by placing upon it the burden of proof, stating in *Amnesty International v. Zambia* that the 'onus is on the State to prove that it is justified to resort to the limitation clause'.[995] Nevertheless, the Commission, in common with other human rights systems, accepts that the doctrine of margin of appreciation informs the African Charter.[996]

217. While the wording of the African Charter with respect to clawback clauses leaves much to be desired, it is encouraging to observe that through its jurisprudence the Commission has interpreted the relevant provisions to conform with international human rights standards. And it should be observed that the Commission's approach has been approved by the African Court of Human and Peoples' Rights.[997] Given in addition the fact that the African Charter omits a derogation clause[998] there is every cause to be optimistic that the protection of human rights will prove effective

218. A salient feature of the African Charter is the fact that it incorporates a list of duties owed by the individual.[999] The individual's obligations towards 'his family and society, the State and other legally recognized communities and the international community' are emphasized.[1000] While this section of the African Charter has been inspired by traditional African values it is apparent that the scope and extent of these obligations goes considerably further than those imposed by other international documents.[1001] This aspect of the African Charter is difficult to reconcile with the individualistic approach of liberal democratic thought but it should not be overlooked that even the European Convention on Human Rights (ECHR) recognizes that individuals have responsibilities, implied or otherwise, towards their social environment. The African Charter is more explicit in articulating elements of the social contract but the danger lies in their sweeping nature which could adversely affect the enjoyment of

---

994. *The Law Office of Ghazi Suleiman v. Sudan*, Communication No. 228/99, 16th Activity Report 2002–2003, para. 62.
995. Communication No. 212/98, 12th Activity Report 1998–1999, para. 42.
996. *Garreth Anver Prince v. South Africa*, Communication No. 255/2002, 18th Activity Report 2002–2003, paras 51–52. *See also Tanganyika Law Society et al. v. Tanzania*, African Court of Human and Peoples' Rights, App. Nos 009/2011 and 011/2011 (14 Jun. 2013), para. 112.
997. *Tanganyika Law Society et al. v. Tanzania*, African Court of Human and Peoples' Rights, App. Nos 009/2011 and 011/2011 (14 Jun. 2013), paras 107.3–110.
998. In *Media Rights Agenda and Constitutional Rights Project v. Nigeria*, Communication Nos 105/93, 128/94, 130/94, 152/96, 12th Activity Report 1998–1999, para. 67, the Commission stated accordingly that 'limitations on the rights and freedoms enshrined in the Charter cannot be justified by emergencies or special circumstances', not even the existence of war or other turmoil, *Commission Nationale des Droits de l'Homme et des Libertés v. Chad*, Communication No. 74/92(1995); *Article 19 v. Eritrea*, Communication No. 275/2003, 22nd Activity Report 2006–2007, para. 87. In *Groupe de Travail sur les Dossiers Judiciaires Stratégiques v. Democratic Republic of Congo*, Communication No. 259/2002 (2011) para. 66, the Commission explained that this omission was based on a desire to avoid abusive restrictions of rights.
999. African Charter Arts 27–29. *See* further Ankumah, 170–172; Umozurike, 63–65.
1000. African Charter Art. 27(1).
1001. *See* , e.g., Universal Declaration of Human Rights Art. 29(1), UN General Assembly Res. 217A (III) (UDHR).

rights protected by the African Charter.[1002] Questions arise as to whether legally binding obligations have been imposed upon the individual and to what extent these duties are enforceable. By definition many of these duties are of a general nature which place a moral rather than a legal obligation upon the individual but answers to these questions are particularly important, for example, can an individual be prosecuted under municipal law because s/he has not placed her/his physical and intellectual abilities at the service of the community as required by Article 29(2)? What is the relationship between such an obligation and the guarantee against forced labour or the right to (intellectual) property? How can the Commission seek to enforce these duties when individuals cannot be arraigned before the Commission? Could a complaint be brought against a State that did not seek to enforce these duties? During the drafting conference it was stated that not all the duties were expected to be carried out to the letter but reference was made to principles acceptable to the community but whose immediate application is not envisaged.[1003] Nevertheless, some duties are considered enforceable and the individual who failed in her/his duty would be answerable under municipal law.[1004] It may be that the concept of duties as a whole serves as a code of good citizenship for the people of Africa.[1005]

219. In addition to the general obligation to give effect to the African Charter in accordance with Article 1 thereof, and the fact that rights, by implication, impose duties on States the African Charter curiously sets forth a number of State duties.[1006] These include the duty to promote and ensure awareness of and respect for rights guaranteed in the African Charter through teaching, education and publication, and the duty to guarantee the independence of the courts.[1007]

220. The African Charter attracted criticism for incorporating all three categories of rights. In its Preamble, the African Charter justifies its approach by indicating that civil and political rights cannot be dissociated from economic, social, and cultural rights and that to guarantee the former the latter must be satisfied. In this the African Charter reflects the position adopted by the Universal Declaration on Human Rights (UDHR) regarding the universality and indivisibility of all human rights.[1008] But it should not be overlooked that the African Charter is also inspired by the African philosophy of rights which emphasizes the nexus between the individual and the wider

---

1002. Ankumah, 171; Umozurike, 65.

1003. International Commission of Jurists, *Human and Peoples' Rights in Africa and the African Charter* (International Commission of Jurists: Geneva, 1986), 54–55.

1004. Enforceable duties would appear to include the obligation under Art. 28 to respect other individuals without discrimination; the duty under Art. 29(1) to maintain one's parents in case of need; the duty under Art. 29(3) not to compromise the security of the State; the duty under Art. 29(5) to contribute to the defence of one's country, which would appear to include military service; and the duty under Art. 29(6) to pay taxes.

1005. D'Sa, 77.

1006. African Charter Arts 25–26.

1007. The Commission has found the independence of the courts to have been compromised in a number of cases concerning Nigeria, *see* , e.g., *International Pen, Constitutional Rights Project, Interights on behalf of Ken Saro-Wiwa Jr. and Civil Liberties Organisation v. Nigeria*, Communication Nos 137/94, 139/94, 154/96, 161/97, 12th Activity Report 1998–1999.

1008. T. Buergenthal, D. Shelton & D. Stewart, *International Human Rights* (3rd edn, St. Paul: West Group, 2002, 35–43).

community.[1009] The OAU/AU reaffirmed its comprehensive stance on the subject in the Grand Bay Declaration 1999, proclaiming 'the principle that human rights are universal, indivisible, interdependent and inter-related' and calling for parity to be given to economic, social, and cultural rights.[1010] The Grand Bay Declaration goes on to hold third generation rights as 'universal and inalienable rights which form an integral part of fundamental human rights'.[1011] The Commission has stressed the 'uniqueness' of the African situation and the 'special qualities' of the African Charter, which obliges international human rights to be responsive to African needs,[1012] commenting that 'collective rights, environmental rights, and economic and social rights are essential elements of human rights in Africa'.[1013]

221. A frequently voiced criticism is that the implementation of second generation rights is programmatic, requiring State intervention. Critics therefore consider them purely aspirational, social, and political desiderata to be progressively realized as resources permit but incapable of enforcement. In addition, it is argued that the State is under no legal duty to provide these societal goals. The extent to which a State provides social assistance to its citizens is viewed as a political and not a legal matter. Yet these views do not take account of the growing awareness of the importance of these 'rights' and of the work of international bodies to achieve their full realization. It is instructive to note that the Commission has stressed that once ratified States Parties are legally bound by the provisions of the African Charter.[1014] In *Commission Nationale des Droits de l'Homme et des Libertés v. Chad* the Commission stated:

> The Charter specifies in Article 1 that the States Parties shall not only recognize the rights, duties and freedoms adopted by the Charter, but they should also 'undertake…measures to give effect to them'. In other words, if a state neglects to ensure the rights in the African Charter, this can constitute a violation.[1015]

1009. Umozurike, 17–18.

1010. Grand Bay (Mauritius) Declaration and Plan of Action 1999 para. 1, Heyns & Killander, 155. *See also* African Charter on Democracy Art. 6.

1011. Grand Bay Declaration para. 2.

1012. In *Constitutional Rights Project and Civil Liberties Organisation v. Nigeria*, Communication Nos 143/95, 150/96, 13th Activity Report 1999–2000, para. 26, the Commission expressed the view that the African Charter 'should be interpreted in a culturally sensitive way'.

1013. *The Social and Economic Rights Action Center and the Center for Economic and Social Rights v. Nigeria*, Communication No. 155/96, 15th Activity Report 2001–2002, para. 68.

1014. *International Pen, Constitutional Rights Project, Interights on behalf of Ken Saro-Wiwa Jr. and Civil Liberties Organization v. Nigeria*, Communication Nos 137/94, 139/94, 154/96, 161/97, 12th Activity Report 1998–1999.

1015. Communication No. 74/92, 9th Activity Report 1995–1996. Furthermore, the Commission considers that each State is under a 'minimum core obligation' to ensure the satisfaction of, at the very least, minimum essential levels for each right under the Charter and that concerted action is sometimes required from States to ensure meaningful enjoyment of these rights, *The Social and Economic Rights Action Center and the Center for Economic and Social Rights v. Nigeria*, Communication No. 155/96, 15th Activity Report 2001–2002, para. 48.

According to Odinkalu, 'the obligations that States Parties assume with respect to these rights are clearly stated as being of immediate application'.[1016] Significantly, it is no longer true that second generation rights are non-justiciable. There is an increasing acceptance of the justiciability of positive obligations.[1017] Indeed, the Commission has taken the stance that 'there is no right in the African Charter that cannot be made effective' and that it will apply any of the diverse rights contained' therein.[1018] Crucially, as will be considered more fully below, the Commission has pronounced on these areas.[1019]

222. The importance of third generation rights, or 'peoples' or group rights, as an element of the African concept of human rights is illustrated by its inclusion in the African Charter, specifically in Articles 19–24.[1020] African traditional life has focused on collective, rather than individual, responsibility. It is the well-being of the community as a whole that is important; by protecting the community the individual is thereby also protected. However, the problem with this argument is that it is difficult to reconcile with any classical theory of human rights, with its emphasis on an individualistic approach. It is therefore still unusual in legal and political theory to view peoples' rights as human rights. The criticisms made of second generation rights apply equally here, and the Commission has spoken of 'gradual implementation' although immediate obligations may also arise.[1021] But it is interesting to note that more recently the Commission has expressed the view that 'peoples' rights are not 'solely or exclusively collective' but can also have an individual dimension and that the two can converge.[1022] The safer conclusion is that at the present stage of development of international law the majority of States are unwilling to accept the concept of peoples' rights.[1023] However, in practice, there has been widespread recognition of some of these rights, for example,

1016. Odinkalu, 196.

1017. Thus Hatem Kotrane, independent expert on the question of a draft optional protocol to the International Covenant on Economic, Social and Cultural Rights has expressed the view that, 'In light of the experience gained in recent years from the application of international, regional and national human rights instruments and mechanisms, the independent expert notes that there is no longer any doubt about the essentially justiciable nature of the rights guaranteed by the [International Covenant on Economic, Social and Cultural Rights], UN Doc. E/CN.4/2003/53, para. 2.

1018. *International Pen, Constitutional Rights Project, Interights on behalf of Ken Saro-Wiwa Jr. and Civil Liberties Organization v. Nigeria*, Communication Nos 137/94, 139/94, 154/96, 161/97, 12th Activity Report 1998–1999, para. 68.

1019. *See infra* paras 262–266.

1020. Ankumah, 159–170; Umozurike, 51–61; *Bissangou v. Republic of Congo*, Communication No. 253/2002, 21th Activity Report 2005–2006, para. 80.

1021. *Open Society Justice Initiative v. Côte d'Ivoire*, Communication No. 318/06 (2015) para. 183.

1022. *Ibid.*

1023. Although the International Commission of Jurists has expressed the view that these provisions of the African Charter impose a positive obligation upon States parties to realize these rights, 29.

relating to the protection of the environment.[1024] The jurisprudence of the Commission in relation to these rights will be discussed below.

II. The Application of the African Charter

223. Article 1 of the African Charter imposes a binding legal obligation on States Parties to recognize and uphold the rights, duties and freedoms therein.[1025] In so doing, the Commission assumes the task of being able to examine the extent to which domestic law complies with the provisions of the African Charter.[1026] States that have ratified the African Charter have a clear responsibility to incorporate the treaty

1024. *Legality of the Threat or Use of Nuclear Weapons*, Advisory Opinion, I.C.J. Reports 1996, 266, para. 29; *Gabcíkovo-Nagymaros Project Case (Hungary v. Slovakia)* I.C.J. Reports 1997, 7, paras 53, 111–114.

1025. *Sir Dawda K. Jawara v. Gambia*, Communication Nos 147/95 and 149/96, 13th Activity Report 1999–2000, para. 46; *International Pen, Constitutional Rights Project, Interights on behalf of Ken Saro-Wiwa Jr. and Civil Liberties Organisation v. Nigeria*, Communication Nos 137/94, 139/94, 154/96 and 161/97, 12th Activity Report 1998–1999, para. 116. Or as the Commission put it in *Association of Victims of Post Electoral Violence & INTERIGHTS v. Cameroon*, Communication No. 272/2003, 27th Activity Report 2009, para. 87, to respect, protect, promote and implement the rights. In *Purohit and Moore v. The Gambia*, Communication No. 241/2001, 16th Activity Report 2002–2003, para. 43, the Commission stated that if this were not true the significance of ratifying a human rights treaty would be seriously defeated. The Commission has therefore described it as an obligation of means and of result, *Mbianku v. Cameroon*, Communication No. 389/10 (2015) para. 126. *See also African Commission on Human and Peoples' Rights v. Libya*, African Court of Human and Peoples' Rights, App. No. 002/2013 (3 Jun. 2016), Separate Opinion of Judge Ouguergouz, para. 12.

1026. *Purohit and Moore v. The Gambia*, Communication No. 241/2001, 16th Activity Report 2002–2003, para. 43; *Good v. Botswana*, Communication No. 306/2005, 28th Activity Report 2009–2010, para. 240. In *Legal Resources Foundation v. Zambia*, Communication No. 211/98, 14th Activity Report 2000–2001, paras 59, 61, the Commission stated that it has no jurisdiction in interpreting and applying domestic law or adjudicating on its validity, but it can examine a State's compliance with the African Charter; 'the point of the exercise is to interpret and apply the African Charter rather than to test the validity of domestic law for its own sake'. In *Garreth Anver Prince v. South Africa*, Communication No. 255/2002, 18th Activity Report 2002–2003, paras 50–52, the Commission expressed the view that its mandate incorporated the principle of subsidiarity and the doctrine of margin of appreciation.

in national law by adopting legislative or other measures to give effect to it.[1027] This should result in its practical implementation producing tangible results.[1028] In *Malawi African Association et al. v. Mauritania*, the Commission stated that the 'entry into force of the Charter in Mauritania created for that country an obligation of consequence, deriving from the customary principle *pacta sunt servanda*. It consequently has the duty to adjust its legislation to harmonize it with its international obligations'.[1029] In *Lawyers for Human Rights v. Swaziland*, the Commission found that by ratifying the African Charter without at the same time taking appropriate measures to bring domestic laws in conformity with it, Swaziland was defeating the object and spirit of the African Charter, violating Article 1 thereof.[1030] Where a domestic law is found to be incompatible with the African Charter the State has the obligation to restore harmony.[1031] In keeping with fundamental principles of international law, the Human Rights Court has held that a State cannot seek to evade its international obligations by reference to its municipal law.[1032] However, the Commission has decided that the effect of Article 1 goes further, expressing the view that, 'Any violation of the provisions of the African

1027. In *Purohit and Moore v. The Gambia*, Communication No. 241/2001, 16th Activity Report 2002–2003, para. 41, the Commission stated that, 'When States ratify…the African Charter, they do so voluntarily and very much awake to their responsibilities to implement' its provisions. Whether a State adheres to the dualist or monist tradition is immaterial, *Good v. Botswana*, Communication No. 306/2005, 28th Activity Report 2009–2010, paras 236–239. In *Civil Liberties Organisation v. Nigeria*, Communication No. 129/94, 9th Activity Report 1995–1996, the Commission condemned Nigeria's purported revocation of the domestic effect of the African Charter, describing it as a 'serious irregularity'. It held that Nigeria could not negate the effects of its ratification of the African Charter through domestic action. In an Extraordinary Session the Commission proceeded to maintain that the African Charter remained legally binding on Nigeria, *Account of the Internal Legislation of Nigeria and the Disposition of the African Charter on Human and Peoples' Rights*, Communication Nos 129/94 and 101/93, in Murray & Evans, Documents Vol. I, 468. *See also Sir Dawda K. Jawara v. Gambia*, Communication Nos 147/95 and 149/96, 13th Activity Report 1999–2000, para. 49. It should be observed that the African Charter does not contain a denunciation clause but it is accepted that States do have a right to withdraw from the African Charter subject to reasonable notice in accordance with the terms of the Vienna Convention on the Law of Treaties Art. 56(2) (22 May 1969), 1155 U.N.T.S. 331, *see Civil Liberties Organisation v. Nigeria*, Communication No. 129/94, 9th Activity Report 1995–1996, para. 12.

1028. *Association of Victims of Post Electoral Violence & INTERIGHTS v. Cameroon*, Communication No. 272/2003, 27th Activity Report 2009, para. 108.

1029. Communication Nos 54/91, 61/91, 98/93, 164/97–196/97, 210/98, 13th Activity Report 1999–2000, para. 84.

1030. Communication No. 251/2002, 18th Activity Report 2004–2005, para. 51.

1031. *Legal Resources Foundation v. Zambia*, Communication No. 211/98, 14th Activity Report 2000–2001, para. 68. In *Women's Legal Aid Centre (on behalf of Sophia Moto) v. Tanzania*, Communication No. 243/2001, 18th Activity Report 2002–2003, paras 45–46, the Commission stated that the substantive rights enshrined in the African Charter rely on domestic procedural rules for their effective enjoyment but that their application may sometimes result in a negation of these rights. Domestic procedures to implement the African Charter must not frustrate the obligations Member States assumed in ratifying the treaty.

1032. *Tanganyika Law Society et al. v. Tanzania*, African Court of Human and Peoples' Rights, App. Nos 009/2011 and 011/2011 (14 Jun. 2013), paras 108–109. *See* , e.g., *Treatment of Polish Nationals in Danzig Case*, Advisory Opinion, P.C.I.J., Series A/B, No. 44 (1931).

Charter automatically means a violation of Article 1 and that goes to the root of the African Charter since the obligations imposed by Article 1 of the African Charter are peremptory.'[1033] Consequently, any violation additionally engages automatically the responsibility of the State.[1034]

224. Failure to secure the rights in the African Charter can give rise to a violation of Article 1.[1035] In *Zimbabwe Human Rights NGO Forum v. Zimbabwe*, the Commission held that an amnesty given to the perpetrators of violent crimes committed in the run up to elections in Zimbabwe in 2000, thus preventing victims from seeking redress and encouraging impunity, amounted to a violation of Article 1.[1036] The Commission stated further that Article 1 requires States Parties to ensure that 'effective and enforceable remedies are available'.[1037] In order to guarantee effective protection of human rights States are under a positive obligation to ensure that rights and freedoms are additionally protected from unwarranted interference by third parties and, in accordance with the principle of due diligence, must carry out proper investigations of alleged violations.[1038] But according to the Commission, this obligation extends additionally to one of result, giving the State the freedom of choice and action to achieve the required result.[1039]

1033. *Zimbabwe Human Rights NGO Forum v. Zimbabwe*, Communication No. 245/2002, 21st Activity Report 2005–2006, para. 78. *See also Sir Dawda K. Jawara v. Gambia*, Communication Nos 147/95 and 149/96, 13th Activity Report 1999–2000, *ibid.* The Commission's jurisprudence has been endorsed by the Human Rights Court, *Alex Thomas v. Tanzania*, African Court of Human and Peoples' Rights, App. No. 005/2013 (20 Nov. 2015), paras 135–136.

1034. *Sudan Human Rights Organization and Sudan Centre for Housing Rights and Evictions v. Sudan* Communication Nos 279/03, 296/05, 28th Activity Report, 2010, para. 227; *Monim Elgak, Osman Hummeida and Amir Suleiman (represented by FIDH and OMCT) v. Sudan*, Communication No. 379/09 (2014) para. 140.

1035. *Commission Nationale des Droits de l'Homme et des Libertés v. Chad*, Communication No. 74/92, 9th Activity Report 1995–1996, para. 20; *Gunme et al. v. Cameroon,* Communication No. 266/2003, 26th Activity Report 2008–2009, para. 213.

1036. *Zimbabwe Human Rights NGO Forum v. Zimbabwe*, Communication No. 245/2002, 21st Activity Report 2005–2006, para. 215. *See also Mouvement Ivorien des Droits Humains (MIDH) v. Côte d'Ivoire*, Communication No. 246/2002, 25th Activity Report 2008, para. 98.

1037. *Zimbabwe Human Rights NGO Forum v. Zimbabwe*, Communication No. 245/2002, 21st Activity Report 2005–2006, para. 171.

1038. *Amnesty International et al. v. Sudan*, Communication Nos 48/90, 50/91, 52/91, 89/93, 13th Activity Report 1999–2000, para. 50; *Zimbabwe Human Rights NGO Forum v. Zimbabwe*, Communication No. 245/2002, 21st Activity Report 2005–2006; *Association of Victims of Post Electoral Violence & INTERIGHTS v. Cameroon*, Communication No. 272/2003, 27th Activity Report 2009, para. 110; *Institute for Human Rights and Development in Africa v. Angola*, Communication No. 292/2004, 24th Activity Report 2008, para. 83; *Egyptian Initiative for Personal Rights and INTERIGHTS v. Egypt*, Communication No. 323/2006 (2011), para. 166.

1039. *Association of Victims of Post Electoral Violence & INTERIGHTS v. Cameroon*, Communication No. 272/2003, 27th Activity Report 2009, para. 111.

225. Article 2 of the African Charter enshrines the 'fundamental' principle of non-discrimination;[1040] it guarantees every individual[1041] the rights and freedoms guaranteed in the Charter without distinction on a wide number of specified grounds, including race, ethnic or national origin,[1042] language,[1043] sex,[1044] political opinion,[1045] or religion.[1046] However, the term 'or any status' means this list is neither 'absolute

---

1040. *Good v. Botswana*, Communication No. 306/2005, 28th Activity Report 2009–2010, para. 218.
1041. According to the Commission States are obliged to secure the rights protected by the African Charter to all persons within their jurisdiction, nationals and non-nationals alike, *Rencontre Africaine pour la Defense des Droits de l'Homme v. Zambia*, Communication No. 71/92, 10th Activity Report, 1996–1997, para. 22. *See also African Institute for Human Rights and Development (on behalf of Sierra Leonean refugees in Guinea) v. Republic of Guinea*, Communication No. 249/2002, 20th Activity Report 2005–2006, para. 68; *Institute for Human Rights and Development in Africa v. Angola*, Communication No. 292/2004, 24th Activity Report 2008, para. 80.
1042. *Organisation Mondiale contre la Torture et al. v. Rwanda*, Communication Nos 27/89, 46/91, 49/91, 99/93, 10th Activity Report 1993–1994, para. 22; *Zimbabwe Lawyers for Human Rights and the Institute for Human Rights and Development (on behalf of Andrew Barclay Meldrum) v. Zimbabwe*, Communication No. 294/2004, 26th Activity Report 2008–2009, paras 93–94; *Open Society Justice Initiative v. Côte d'Ivoire*, Communication No. 318/06 (2015) para. 146; *The Nubian Community in Kenya v. Kenya*, Communication No. 317/06 (2015), paras 134–135. *See also* African Charter on Democracy Art. 8(1).
1043. *Gunme et al. v. Cameroon,* Communication No. 266/2003, 26th Activity Report 2008–2009, para. 108.
1044. *Egyptian Initiative for Personal Rights and INTERIGHTS v. Egypt*, Communication No. 323/2006 (2011), paras 121–122, 137. It should be observed that under the African Charter Art. 18(3) States Parties are under an obligation to eliminate discrimination against women. In *Egyptian Initiative for Personal Rights and INTERIGHTS v. Egypt*, Communication No. 323/2006 (2011), paras 142–153, the Commission found that acts of violence carried out on a number of women was based on their sex only and was therefore gender-specific and discriminatory.
1045. *Zimbabwe Human Rights NGO Forum v. Zimbabwe*, Communication No. 245/2002, 21st Activity Report 2005–2006; *Good v. Botswana*, Communication No. 306/2005, 28th Activity Report 2009–2010, paras 220–221. *See also* African Charter on Democracy Art. 8(1).
1046. In *Zimbabwe Human Rights NGO Forum v. Zimbabwe*, Communication No. 245/2002, 21st Activity Report 2005–2006, para. 170, the Commission defined discrimination as 'applying any distinction, exclusion, restriction or preference' based on grounds such as 'race, colour, sex, language, religion, political or other opinion, national or social origin, property, birth or other status, and which has the purpose or effect of nullifying or impairing the recognition, enjoyment or exercise by all persons, on equal footing, of all rights and freedoms'. Accordingly, a 'universal 'composite concept of discrimination' can contain the following elements, stipulates a difference in treatment, has a certain effect and is based on a certain prohibited ground.' In *Malawi African Association et al. v. Mauritania*, Communication Nos 54/91, 61/91, 98/93, 164/97–196/97, 210/98, 13th Activity Report 1999–2000, para. 131, the Commission described discrimination on the basis of colour as an 'unacceptable' attitude that violated the very spirit of the African Charter and of the letter of the provision. *See also* African Charter on Democracy Art. 8(1).

nor comprehensive.'[1047] According to the Commission, Article 2 'guarantees that those in the same circumstances are dealt with equally in law and practice'.[1048] However, it 'does not stipulate a general banning of discrimination; it only prohibits discrimination where it affects the enjoyment of a right or freedom guaranteed by the Charter'.[1049] Its aim is 'to ensure equality of treatment for individuals irrespective' of the specified grounds.[1050] Certain differential practices will be considered permissible as long as some rational and objective basis, proportionate to the legitimate aim pursued, exists.[1051]

226. Article 2 of the African Charter has been described as a 'non-derogable' provision that must be respected in all circumstances.[1052] This is because the rights guaranteed in Article 2 'are an important entitlement as the availability or lack of them affects the capacity of one to enjoy many other rights';[1053] they 'provide the foundation for the enjoyment of all human rights'.[1054] Consequently, Article 2 will often be considered in conjunction with other provisions of the African Charter.[1055] In *Legal Resources Foundation v. Zambia*, the Commission drew attention to the political instability caused in recent years by the adoption of discriminatory practices based on

1047. *Open Society Justice Initiative v. Côte d'Ivoire*, Communication No. 318/06 (2015) para. 145. In *African Commission on Human and Peoples' Rights v. Kenya*, African Court of Human and Peoples' Rights, App. No. 006/2012 (26 May 2017) para. 138, the Human Rights Court held that Art. 2 encompasses other types of discrimination not foreseen when the African Charter was adopted.

1048. *Good v. Botswana*, Communication No. 306/2005, 28th Activity Report 2009–2010, para. 218. An intention to discriminate is not required so that an apparently neutral law or measure that results in an unjustified distinction is covered, *Open Society Justice Initiative v. Côte d'Ivoire*, Communication No. 318/06 (2015) para. 144.

1049. *Bissangou v. Republic of Congo*, Communication No. 253/2002, 21st Activity Report 2005–2006, para. 69. However, in *Malawi African Association et al. v. Mauritania*, Communication Nos 54/91, 61/91, 98/93, 164/97–196/97, 210/98, 13th Activity Report 1999–2000, para. 131, the Commission stated that, 'Article 2 of the Charter lays down a principle that is essential to the spirit of this convention, one of whose goals is the elimination of all forms of discrimination and to ensure equality among all human beings…it is apparent that international human rights law and the community of States accord a certain importance to the eradication of discrimination in all its guises.' *See also Purohit and Moore v. The Gambia*, Communication No. 241/2001, 16th Activity Report 2002–2003, para. 49.

1050. *Legal Resources Foundation v. Zambia*, Communication No. 211/98, 14th Activity Report 2000–2001, para. 63; *Zimbabwe Human Rights NGO Forum v. Zimbabwe*, Communication No. 245/2002, 21st Activity Report 2005–2006, para. 169.

1051. *Good v. Botswana*, Communication No. 306/2005, 28th Activity Report 2009–2010, para. 219; *African Commission on Human and Peoples' Rights v. Kenya*, African Court of Human and Peoples' Rights, App. No. 006/2012 (26 May 2017) para. 139.

1052. *Purohit and Moore v. The Gambia*, Communication No. 241/2001, 16th Activity Report 2002–2003, para. 49.

1053. *Zimbabwe Human Rights NGO Forum v. Zimbabwe*, Communication No. 245/2002, 21st Activity Report 2005–2006, paras 81, 169; *Legal Resources Foundation v. Zambia*, Communication No. 211/98, 14th Activity Report 2000–2001, para. 63; *The Nubian Community in Kenya v. Kenya*, Communication No. 317/06 (2015), paras 150, 168.

1054. *Zimbabwe Human Rights NGO Forum v. Zimbabwe*, Communication No. 245/2002, 21st Activity Report 2005–2006, para. 169.

1055. *See* , e.g., *Ivorien Human Rights Movement (MIDH) v. Côte d'Ivoire*, Communication No. 262/2002, 26th Activity Report 2008–2009, paras 74–78.

birth and social origin which excluded a section of the citizenry from participating in the democratic process and which therefore undermined the legitimacy of elections. The Commission held such practices to breach Article 2.[1056]

227. In *Zimbabwe Human Rights NGO Forum v. Zimbabwe*, it was alleged that the Zimbabwean Government had encouraged a deliberate policy of violence against the political opposition, consequently discriminating against persons holding an alternative political opinion. This was denied by the State which argued that it was not responsible for the actions of non-State actors and that it had in fact taken steps to try to deal with the situation. The Commission found that the legislative and other measures taken by the government to contain the violence did not suggest a discriminatory pattern against the complainants.[1057] However, by way of contrast, in *Association of Victims of Post Electoral Violence & INTERIGHTS v. Cameroon*, the failure of the State to take adequate measures to protect the victims from post electoral violence did violate their rights under Article 2.[1058]

III. Civil and Political Rights

228. Article 3 of the African Charter guarantees the individual's right to equality before the law and the right to equal protection before the law, complementing the prohibition on discrimination set out in Article 2.[1059] The Commission has expressed the view that Article 3 is necessarily important 'because it guarantees fair and essential treatment of individuals within a legal system of a given country'.[1060] According to the Commission, equality before the law, under Article 3(1), 'relates to the status of individuals before the law', that everyone is subject to the same laws, whereas equal

1056. Communication No. 211/98, 14th Activity Report 2000–2001, paras 63–64. *See also Mouvement Ivorien des Droits Humains (MIDH) v. Côte d'Ivoire*, Communication No. 246/2002, 26th Activity Report 2008–2009, para. 86.

1057. Communication No. 245/2002, 21st Activity Report 2005–2006, para. 172.

1058. Communication No. 272/2003, 27th Activity Report 2009, paras 122–126.

1059. *Bissangou v. Republic of Congo*, Communication No. 253/2002, 21st Activity Report 2005–2006, para. 70; *Egyptian Initiative for Personal Rights and INTERIGHTS v. Egypt*, Communication No. 323/2006 (2011), para. 175. The Human Rights Court has stated that equality in law 'presupposes that the law protects everyone without discrimination', *Actions pour la Protection des Droit de l'Homme (APDH) v. Côte d'Ivoire*, African Court of Human and Peoples' Rights, App. No. 001/2014 (18 Nov. 2016) para. 146. In *Open Society Justice Initiative v. Côte d'Ivoire*, Communication No. 318/06 (2015) para. 155, the Commission was of the view that a violation of Art. 2 would inexorably lead to a violation of Art. 3. In *Purohit and Moore v. The Gambia*, Communication No. 241/2001 16th Activity Report 2002–2003, para. 49, the Commission described Art. 3 as a 'non-derogable' provision that must be respected in all circumstances. *See also* African Charter on Democracy Art. 10 (3).

1060. *Purohit and Moore v. The Gambia*, Communication No. 241/2001, 16th Activity Report 2002–2003, para. 49.

protection by the law, under Article 3(2), reflects a 'fundamental fairness'[1061] that 'relates to the implementation of the law and is applicable where the rights of the Complainant are implemented unequally'.[1062] More specifically, the Commission has described this right as guaranteeing persons the same access to the law and courts and the same treatment in procedure and substance by the law and courts.[1063] The Human Rights Court has referred to the principle of equality of arms.[1064]

229. The Commission has stated that for Article 3 to apply, the inequality 'should follow from the "law"'.[1065] It has expressed the view that a violation of Article 3 would occur if a State exercised a power or judgment conferred by law in a discriminatory or arbitrary manner.[1066] It must be established that the State must have treated the complainants differently from others in the same position.[1067] The outbreak of politically motivated violence in Zimbabwe since 2000 gave rise to the African Commission having to consider the submission in *Zimbabwe Human Rights NGO Forum v. Zimbabwe* that in refusing to investigate complaints of attacks on members of the political opposition the police selectively enforced the law to the detriment of the victims, amounting to unequal protection of the law in breach of Article 3(2) of the African

---

1061. *Zimbabwe Lawyers for Human Rights and the Institute for Human Rights and Development v. Zimbabwe*, Communication No. 293/2004, 24th Activity Report 2008, para. 124. In *Zimbabwe Human Rights NGO Forum v. Zimbabwe*, Communication No. 245/2002, 21st Activity Report 2005–2006, para. 174, the Commission stated that for 'there to be equal protection of the law, the law must not only be fairly applied but must be seen to be fairly applied'.

1062. *Bissangou v. Republic of Congo*, Communication No. 253/2002, 21st Activity Report 2005–2006), para. 70. *See* also *Zimbabwe Lawyers for Human Rights and the Institute for Human Rights and Development (on behalf of Andrew Barclay Meldrum) v. Zimbabwe*, Communication No. 294/2004, 26th Activity Report 2008–2009, para. 96. In *Open Society Justice Initiative v. Côte d'Ivoire*, Communication No. 318/06 (2015) para. 153, the Commission considered Art. 3(1) to refer to 'equality in law or legal equality inherent to any individual subject of law as a result of his human nature and which places him on equal legal terms with other human persons', whereas Art. 3(2) refers to the 'guarantees introduced in order to give substance to the subjective law deriving from equality before the law or in law.'

1063. *Zimbabwe Lawyers for Human Rights and the Institute for Human Rights and Development v. Zimbabwe*, Communication No. 293/2004, 24th Activity Report 2008, para. 124; *Zimbabwe Lawyers for Human Rights and the Institute for Human Rights and Development (on behalf of Andrew Barclay Meldrum) v. Zimbabwe*, Communication No. 294/2004, 26th Activity Report 2008–2009, para. 99; *Egyptian Initiative for Personal Rights and INTERIGHTS v. Egypt*, Communication No. 323/2006 (2011), para. 177. In *Dino Noca v. Democratic Republic of the Congo*, Communication No. 286/2004 (2012), para. 203, a violation of Art. 3 was found on the ground that only the case put by one party was taken into account by the court.

1064. *Mohamed Abubakri v. Tanzania*, African Court of Human and Peoples' Rights, App. No. 007/2013 (3 Jun. 2016), para. 193.

1065. *Bissangou v. Republic of Congo*, Communication No. 253/2002, 21st Activity Report 2005–2006, para. 71.

1066. *Ibid.*; *Zimbabwe Lawyers for Human Rights and the Institute for Human Rights and Development (on behalf of Andrew Barclay Meldrum) v. Zimbabwe*, Communication No. 294/2004, 26th Activity Report 2008–2009, para. 96.

1067. *Zimbabwe Lawyers for Human Rights and the Institute for Human Rights and Development v. Zimbabwe*, Communication No. 293/2004, 24th Activity Report 2008, para. 127.

Charter. However, the Commission was unable to make a determination on the evidence available to it.[1068]

230. Article 4 of the African Charter guarantees the right to life. It was initially believed that this was not an absolute right; that it was the 'arbitrary' deprivation of life that was proscribed.[1069] In *Forum of Conscience v. Sierra Leone*, the Commission emphasized the essential importance of this right, stating that it 'is the fulcrum of all other rights. It is the fountain through which other rights flow, and any violation of this right without due process amounts to arbitrary deprivation of life'.[1070] In fact, the Commission has expressed the view that the right to life is a norm of customary law.[1071] But in an important development, in *Groupe de Travail sur les Dossiers Judiciaires Stratégiques v. Democratic Republic of Congo* the Commission went further and stressed that the right to life was inviolable and permitted no limitations.[1072] State Parties are under an obligation to provide a reasonably secure environment and to take effective measures not only to prevent and punish the loss of life[1073] but to desist from

1068. Communication No. 245/2002, 21th Activity Report 2005–2006, paras 175–176. However, in *Kazeem Aminu v. Nigeria*, Communication Nos 205/97, 13th Activity Report 1999–2000, para. 15, the Commission found that repeated arrests and detention of the victim which led him to go into hiding for fear of his life violated this provision.

1069. General Comment No. 3 on the African Charter on Human and Peoples' Rights: The Right to Life (Art. 4), paras 12–14, in Heyns & Killander, 379 (General Comment 3); *Sudan Human Rights Organization and Sudan Centre for Housing Rights and Evictions v. Sudan* Communication Nos 279/03, 296/05, 28th Activity Report, 2010, para. 147; *African Commission on Human and Peoples' Rights v. Kenya*, African Court of Human and Peoples' Rights, App. No. 006/2012 (26 May 2017) para. 152., In *Kazeem Aminu v. Nigeria*, Communication Nos 205/97, 13th Activity Report 1999–2000, the Commission was confronted with the problem whether the victim's going into hiding for fear of his life violated this provision. It stated, at para. 18, that, 'It would be a narrow interpretation to this right to think that it can only be violated when one is deprived of it. It cannot be said that the right to respect for one's life…would be protected in a state of constant fear and/or threats.'

1070. Communication No. 223/98, 14th Activity Report 2000–2001, para. 19. In *Sudan Human Rights Organization and Sudan Centre for Housing Rights and Evictions v. Sudan* Communication Nos 279/03, 296/05, 28th Activity Report, 2010, para. 146, the Commission described the right to life as 'the supreme right of the human being. It is basic to all human rights and without it all other rights are without meaning'. In *Kasingachire et al. v. Zimbabwe*, Communication No. 295/04 (2012), para. 138, the Commission stated that the right to life was the 'foundational, or bedrock human right'. The Human Rights Court has described it as 'the cornerstone on which the realisation of all other rights and freedoms depend', *African Commission on Human and Peoples' Rights v. Kenya*, African Court of Human and Peoples' Rights, App. No. 006/2012 (26 May 2017) para. 152. The Court proceeded to observe that Art. 4 refers to 'the physical rather than the existential understanding of the right to life', *ibid.*, para. 154.

1071. *Kasingachire et al. v. Zimbabwe*, Communication No. 295/04 (2012), para. 137.

1072. Communication No. 259/2002 (2011) para. 68. The Commission has described it as 'non-derogable', General Comment 3, para. 1.

1073. *Sudan Human Rights Organization and Sudan Centre for Housing Rights and Evictions v. Sudan* Communication Nos 279/03, 296/05, 28th Activity Report, 2010, para. 147; *Kasingachire et al. v. Zimbabwe*, Communication No. 295/04 (2012), para. 123.

the excessive or inappropriate use of force.[1074] Moreover, States are under a procedural obligation to investigate suspicious deaths[1075] and provide redress, including fair compensation if necessary.[1076] Extra-judicial killings have also been condemned by the Commission.[1077] In *Organisation Mondiale contre la Torture et al. v. Rwanda*, the Commission found that large numbers of Rwandan villagers had been massacred by the Rwandan military for membership of a particular ethnic group.[1078] In *Zimbabwe Human Rights NGO Forum v. Zimbabwe*, the Commission expressed the view that extra-judicial killings are 'caused by the State or through its agents or acquiescence'.[1079] The responsibility of the State can extend to killings by non-State actors where the State has failed to be diligent in taking adequate measures of protection.[1080] In this instance, the Commission found no violation of Article 4 because it accepted the State's submissions that it bore no responsibility for the terror gangs and suspicious deaths were investigated and perpetrators prosecuted for murder.[1081] Indeed, the Commission requires that extra-judicial killings must be investigated 'by entirely independent individuals, provided with the necessary resources, and their findings must be made public and prosecutions initiated in accordance with the information uncovered'.[1082] Thus, in *Sudan Human Rights Organization and Sudan Centre for Housing Rights and Evictions v. Sudan*, arising out of the violence in the Darfur region, the Commission found a violation of Article 4 because of the State's failure to conduct effective investigations.[1083]

1074. Such as in *Krischna Achutan (on behalf of Aleke Banda) v. Malawi*; *Amnesty International on behalf of Orton and Vera Chirwa v. Malawi*, Communication Nos 64/92, 68/92, 78/92, 8th Activity Report 1994–1995, where the police opened fire on workers on a peaceful strike. *See also Kasingachire et al. v. Zimbabwe*, Communication Nos 295/04 (2012), paras 105–123. *See also* General Comment 3, paras 27–31.

1075. *Gunme et al. v. Cameroon,* Communication No. 266/2003, 26th Activity Report 2008–2009, para. 112; *Kasingachire et al. v. Zimbabwe*, Communication No. 295/04 (2012), para. 133; General Comment 3, paras 15–17.

1076. *Zimbabwe Human Rights NGO Forum v. Zimbabwe*, Communication No. 245/2002, 21st Activity Report 2005–2006; *Association of Victims of Post Electoral Violence & INTERIGHTS v. Cameroon*, Communication No. 272/2003, 27th Activity Report 2009, para. 136; *Kasingachire et al. v. Zimbabwe*, Communication No. 295/04 (2012), paras 127–128; General Comment 3, para. 19.

1077. *Free Legal Assistance Group v. Zaire*, Communication No. 25/89, 9th Activity Report 1995–1996; *Sudan Human Rights Organization and Sudan Centre for Housing Rights and Evictions v. Sudan* Communication Nos 279/03, 296/05, 28th Activity Report, 2010.

1078. Communication Nos 27/89, 46/91, 49/91, 99/93, 10th Activity Report 1993–1994, para. 24.

1079. Communication No. 245/2002, 21st Activity Report 2005–2006, para. 181.

1080. *Ibid.*; General Comment 3, paras 38–39.

1081. Communication No. 245/2002, 21st Activity Report 2005–2006, *ibid.*

1082. *Amnesty International et al. v. Sudan*, Communication Nos 48/90, 50/91, 52/91, 89/93, 13th Activity Report 1999–2000, para. 51.

1083. Communication Nos 279/03, 296/05, 28th Activity Report, 2010, paras 150–153.

231. The imposition of the death penalty in accordance with the law was believed to be sanctioned by Article 4,[1084] although the Commission has repeatedly called for its suspension.[1085] However, in *Groupe de Travail sur les Dossiers Judiciaires Stratégiques v. Democratic Republic of Congo*, the Commission cast doubt on this position, intimating that the death penalty was not admitted under Article 4.[1086] It based its conclusion chiefly on the fact that there is no mention of the death penalty in Article 4.[1087] But in a later case, *Interights & Ditshwanelo v. Botswana*, the Commission backed away from this radical position, indicating that given its previous rulings on the matter, it would be improper if it were suddenly to hold that the death penalty 'would in all cases' constitute a violation of Article 4.[1088] However, given the evolution of human rights law, the Commission regarded it as 'increasingly difficult to envisage a case in which the death penalty can be found to have been applied in a way that is not in some way arbitrary. As a result it is difficult to conceive that, if called upon in future to do so, the Commission will find that the death penalty, however it is executed, is any longer compatible with the African Charter.'[1089] What is beyond question is that the method of execution may be incompatible with the obligation to uphold human dignity

---

1084. Although the death penalty cannot be imposed on a child, *see* African Charter on the Rights and Welfare of the Child Art. 5(3), (1 Jul. 1990), https://www.au.int/en/treaties, 28 I.L.M. 1456 (1989), *Groupe de Travail sur les Dossiers Judiciaires Stratégiques v. Democratic Republic of Congo*, Communication No. 259/2002 (2011), para. 71, or carried out on pregnant or nursing women, *see* Protocol to the African Charter on Human and Peoples' Rights on the Rights of Women in Africa Art. 4(j), (11 Jul. 2003), https://www.au.int/en/treaties, Heyns & Killander, 65. As of December 2016 sixteen African States were classified as retentionist countries, including Botswana, Egypt, Nigeria, Sudan, Uganda and Zimbabwe, while eighteen were abolitionist in practice, including Algeria, Ghana, Kenya, Tanzania and Zambia. Countries that are completely abolitionist include Angola, Benin, Cape Verde, Mauritius, Mozambique, Namibia, Senegal, Seychelles and South Africa. *See* Amnesty International, Abolitionist and Retentionist Countries as of 19 Dec. 2016, Index: ACT 50/3831/2016, http://www.amnesty.org. In *S v. Makwanyane and Mchunu* 1995 (3) SA 391 (CC) the Constitutional Court of South Africa ruled that capital punishment was unconstitutional as violating, *inter alia*, the right to life. Compare, contra, *Catholic Commission for Justice and Peace in Zimbabwe v. Attorney-General, Zimbabwe* 1993 (4) SA 239 (ZS); *Mbushuu and Another v. Republic* [1995] 1 L.R.C. 216 (Tanzania Court of Appeal); *Ntesang and Others v. State* [1995] B.L.R. 151 (Botswana Court of Appeal); *Kigula and Others v. Attorney-General* (2005) A.H.R.L.R. 197 (Constitutional Court of Uganda) para. 49.

1085. The Commission's obiter dictum in *Interights (on behalf of Mariette Sonjaleen Bosch) v. Botswana*, Communication No. 240/2001, 17th Activity Report 2003–2004, para. 52, is worth noting. It drew attention to the trend towards the abolition of the death penalty in international law, including the Second Optional Protocol to the International Covenant on Civil and Political Rights Aiming at the Abolition of the Death Penalty, 15 Dec. 1989, 1642 U.N.T.S. 414, and the Commission's own Resolution Urging States to envisage a Moratorium on the Death Penalty, adopted at the Twenty-Sixth Ordinary Session of the African Commission, 1999, and therefore encouraged all States Parties to refrain from exercising the death penalty and calling for it abolition. *See also Interights & Ditshwanelo v. Botswana*, Communication No. 319/06 (2015).

1086. Communication No. 259/2002 (2011), para. 69.

1087. *Ibid.*, para. 68.

1088. Communication No. 319/06 (2015) para. 66.

1089. *Ibid.*

under Article 5.[1090] The Commission has therefore proceeded to hold that hanging as a method of execution causes excessive suffering and is inhuman and degrading.[1091] However, it is imperative that due process in capital cases is scrupulously observed, including the holding of a trial, an adequate defence, a right of appeal and a right to seek pardon or commutation of sentence.[1092] This requirement is exemplified by the notorious case concerning the poet and human rights activist Ken Saro-Wiwa who was found guilty of murder in a travesty of justice by a special military tribunal which lacked the most elementary standards of a fair trial, and who was later judicially murdered by the Nigerian military regime in defiance of international public opinion. The Commission found that since the trial itself violated the right to a fair trial guaranteed by Article 7 of the African Charter the resultant implementation of the death sentence was rendered arbitrary and in violation of Article 4.[1093]

232. Article 5 of the African Charter protects human dignity, extending to the physical and mental integrity of the individual.[1094] It occupies a central place in the African Charter.[1095] In *Purohit and Moore v. The Gambia*, the Commission defined human dignity as an:

1090. *Spilg and Mack & Ditshwanelo (on behalf of Lehlohonolo Bernard Kobedi) v. Botswana*, Communication No. 277/2003(2011), paras 167, 169; *Interights & Ditshwanelo v. Botswana*, Communication No. 319/06 (2015) para. 84. In *Interights (on behalf of Mariette Sonjaleen Bosch) v. Botswana*, Communication No. 240/2001, 17th Activity Report, 2003–2004, para. 41, the Commission expressed the view that a criminal justice system must have 'a human face in matters of execution of death sentences'. The Commission has also expressed the view that the 'death row' phenomenon is incompatible with Art. 5, *Interights & Ditshwanelo v. Botswana*, Communication No. 319/06 (2015) para. 93. *See also Catholic Commission for Justice and Peace in Zimbabwe v. Attorney-General, Zimbabwe* 1993 (4) SA 239 (ZS); *Kigula and Others v. Attorney-General* (2005) A.H.R.L.R. 197 (Constitutional Court of Uganda) paras 116–120.

1091. *Interights & Ditshwanelo v. Botswana*, Communication No. 319/06 (2015) para. 87. In *S v. Makwanyane and Mchunu* 1995 (3) SA 391 (CC) the Constitutional Court of South Africa ruled that the death penalty was cruel, inhuman and degrading punishment. *See also Mbushuu and Another v. Republic* [1995] 1 L.R.C. 216. Compare, contra, *Catholic Commission for Justice and Peace in Zimbabwe v. Attorney-General, Zimbabwe* 1993 (4) SA 239 (ZS) para. 4; *Kigula and Others v. Attorney-General* (2005) A.H.R.L.R. 197 (Constitutional Court of Uganda) para. 49.

1092. *Forum of Conscience v. Sierra Leone,* Communication No. 223/98, 14th Activity Report 2000–2001, para. 19; *Interights (on behalf of Mariette Sonjaleen Bosch) v. Botswana*, Communication No. 240/2001, 17th Activity Report, 2003–2004, para. 43. Clemency procedures are not in themselves arbitrary, *Interights & Ditshwanelo v. Botswana*, Communication No. 319/06 (2015) para. 81.

1093. *International Pen, Constitutional Rights Project, Interights on behalf of Ken Saro-Wiwa Jr. and Civil Liberties Organisation v. Nigeria*, Communication Nos 137/94, 139/94, 154/96 and 161/97, 12th Activity Report 1998–1999, para. 103. *See also Malawi African Association et al. v. Mauritania*, Communication Nos 54/91, 61/91, 98/93, 164/97–196/97, 210/98, 13th Activity Report 1999–2000, para. 120; *Interights & Ditshwanelo v. Botswana*, Communication No. 319/06 (2015) paras 64–65.

1094. *Sudan Human Rights Organization and Sudan Centre for Housing Rights and Evictions v. Sudan* Communication Nos 279/03, 296/05, 28th Activity Report 2010, para. 155.

1095. *Open Society Justice Initiative v. Côte d'Ivoire*, Communication No. 318/06 (2015) para. 139.

> inherent basic right to which all human beings, regardless of their mental capabilities or disabilities are entitled to without discrimination. It is therefore an inherent right which every human being is obliged to respect by all means possible and on the other hand it confers a duty on every human being to respect this right.[1096]

In *Open Society Justice Initiative v. Côte d'Ivoire*, the Commission described it thus:

> Dignity is consubstantial, intrinsic and inherent to the human person…when the individual loses his dignity, it is his human nature itself which is called into question, to the extent that it is likely to interrogate the validity of continuing to belong to human society.[1097]

The Commission added that the right to enjoy a decent life, as normal and full as possible, lay at the core of the right to human dignity.[1098] It also provides for recognition of an individual's legal status. This denotes the ability to have rights and obligations.[1099] Nationality has been held to be a fundamental component of this right.[1100] The provision additionally prohibits all forms of exploitation and degradation, including slavery, torture, cruel, inhuman or degrading punishment and treatment,[1101] for which there is no justification.[1102] This list is not exhaustive, however. In *International Pen, Constitutional Rights Project, Interights on behalf of Ken Saro-Wiwa Jr. and Civil Liberties Organisation v. Nigeria*, the Commission held that the prohibition in Article 5 included 'not only

---

1096. Communication No. 241/2001, 16th Activity Report 2002–2003, para. 57. The Commission held that branding people with mental illness as 'lunatics' and 'idiots' dehumanized them and denied them dignity, para. 59. *See also Sudan Human Rights Organization and Sudan Centre for Housing Rights and Evictions v. Sudan* Communication Nos 279/03, 296/05, 28th Activity Report, 2010, para. 163. It should be observed that in 2016 the Commission adopted a draft Protocol to the African Charter on the Rights of Persons with Disabilities in Africa.

1097. Communication No. 318/06 (2015) para. 139.

1098. *Purohit and Moore v. The Gambia*, Communication No. 241/2001, 16th Activity Report 2002–2003, para. 61.

1099. *Open Society Justice Initiative v. Côte d'Ivoire*, Communication No. 318/06 (2015) para. 96.

1100. *Ibid.*, para. 97. In *The Nubian Community in Kenya v. Kenya*, Communication No. 317/06 (2015), para. 151, non-recognition of the legal status of the Nubian community, resulting in discriminatory and arbitrary measures for the acquisition of identity documents, constituted a violation of Art. 5.

1101. According to the Commission, the phrase 'cruel, inhuman or degrading punishment and treatment' should be interpreted 'so as to extend to the widest possible protection against abuses, whether physical or mental', *Purohit and Moore v. The Gambia*, Communication No. 241/2001, 16th Activity Report 2002–2003, para. 58. *See also Huri-Laws v. Nigeria*, Communication No. 225/98, 14th Activity Report 2000–2002, para. 40.

1102. Even combating terrorism, *Gunme et al. v. Cameroon,* Communication No. 266/2003, 26th Activity Report 2008–2009, paras 113–114.

actions which cause serious physical or psychological suffering, but also actions which humiliate the individual or force him or her to act against his will or conscience'.[1103]

233. The Commission has adopted the definition of torture contained in the UN Convention Against Torture[1104] and has described its prohibition as being a norm *jus cogens.*[1105] It has taken the reasonable stance that the phrase 'cruel, inhuman or degrading punishment and treatment' must be interpreted so as to provide the widest possible protection against abuse.[1106] It has thus observed that, '[p]ersonal suffering and indignity can take many forms, and will depend on the particular circumstances of each communication brought before the Commission'.[1107] An analysis of the Commission's jurisprudence can assist in determining what type of ill-treatment can amount to violations of Article 5. Included are beatings,[1108] applying physical violence to individuals

---

1103. Communication Nos 137/94, 139/94, 154/96 and 161/97, 12th Activity Report 1998–1999, para. 79. *See* further, *Egyptian Initiative for Personal Rights and INTERIGHTS v. Egypt*, Communication No. 323/2006 (2011), paras 187–196. In *Huri-Laws v. Nigeria*, Communication No. 225/98, 14th Activity Report 2000–2001, para. 40, the Commission stated that not knowing the reason or duration of detention constituted mental trauma.

1104. Convention Against Torture and Other Cruel, Inhuman or Degrading Treatment or Punishment Art. 1(1) (10 Dec. 1984), 1465 U.N.T.S. 85. *See Sudan Human Rights Organization and Sudan Centre for Housing Rights and Evictions v. Sudan* Communication Nos 279/03, 296/05, 28th Activity Report, 2010, paras 155–156; *Monim Elgak, Osman Hummeida and Amir Suleiman (represented by FIDH and OMCT) v. Sudan*, Communication No. 379/09 (2014) para. 98.

1105. *Mohamed Abdullah Saleh al-Asad v. Djibouti*, Communication No. 383/10 (2014), para. 179.

1106. *Sudan Human Rights Organization and Sudan Centre for Housing Rights and Evictions v. Sudan* Communication Nos 279/03, 296/05, 28th Activity Report, 2010, para. 158.

1107. *Purohit and Moore v. The Gambia*, Communication No. 241/2001, 16th Activity Report 2002–2003, para. 58.

1108. *Krischna Achutan (on behalf of Aleke Banda) v. Malawi*; *Amnesty International on behalf of Orton and Vera Chirwa v. Malawi*, Communication Nos 64/92, 68/92, 78/92, 8th Activity Report 1994–1995; *International Pen, Constitutional Rights Project, Interights on behalf of Ken Saro-Wiwa Jr. and Civil Liberties Organisation v. Nigeria*, Communication Nos 137/94, 139/94, 154/96 and 161/97, 12th Activity Report 1998–1999; *Malawi African Association et al. v. Mauritania*, Communication Nos 54/91, 61/91, 98/93, 164/97–196/97, 210/98, 13th Activity Report 1999–2000; *Rights International v. Nigeria*, Communication No. 215/98, 13th Activity Report 1999–2000, para. 26.

in the form of public lashings,[1109] rape,[1110] poor conditions of detention or incarceration,[1111] including excessive solitary confinement,[1112] no or poor quality food,[1113] shackling within a cell,[1114] overcrowded or unhygienic cells,[1115] denial of access to medical care,[1116]

1109. *Doebbler v. Sudan*, Communication No. 236/2000, 16th Activity Report 2002–2003, para. 42, which the Commission said would be 'tantamount to sanctioning State sponsored torture under the Charter and contrary to the very nature of this human rights treaty'.

1110. *Krischna Achutan (on behalf of Aleke Banda) v. Malawi*; *Amnesty International on behalf of Orton and Vera Chirwa v. Malawi*, Communication Nos 64/92, 68/92, 78/92, 8th Activity Report 1994–1995; *Malawi African Association et al. v. Mauritania*, Communication Nos 54/91, 61/91, 98/93, 164/97–196/97, 210/98, 13th Activity Report 1999–2000).

1111. *Institute for Human Rights and Development in Africa v. Angola*, Communication No. 292/2004, 24th Activity Report 2008, para. 51. In *Zegveld and Ephrem v. Eritrea*, Communication No. 250/2002, 17th Activity Report 2003–2004, para. 55, the Commission expressed the view that 'all detentions must be subject to basic human rights standards. There should be no secret detentions and States must disclose the fact that someone is being detained as well as the place of detention. Furthermore, every detained person must have prompt access to a lawyer and to their families and their rights with regards to physical and mental health must be protected as well as entitlement to proper conditions of detention.' *See Civil Liberties Organisation v. Nigeria*, Communication No. 151/96, 13th Activity Report 1999–2000, para. 25.

1112. *Krischna Achutan (on behalf of Aleke Banda) v. Malawi*; *Amnesty International on behalf of Orton and Vera Chirwa v. Malawi*, Communication Nos 64/92, 68/92, 78/92, 8th Activity Report 1994–1995; *Malawi African Association et al. v. Mauritania*, Communication Nos 54/91, 61/91, 98/93, 164/97–196/97, 210/98, 13th Activity Report 1999–2000; *Zegveld and Ephrem v. Eritrea*, Communication No. 250/2002, 17th Activity Report 2003–2004, para. 55.

1113. *Krischna Achutan (on behalf of Aleke Banda) v. Malawi*; *Amnesty International on behalf of Orton and Vera Chirwa v. Malawi*, Communication Nos 64/92, 68/92, 78/92, 8th Activity Report 1994–1995; *Malawi African Association et al. v. Mauritania*, Communication Nos 54/91, 61/91, 98/93, 164/97–196/97, 210/98, 13th Activity Report 1999–2000); additionally a violation of Art. 4, *Malawi African Association et al. v. Mauritania*, Communication Nos 54/91, 61/91, 98/93, 164/97–196/97, 210/98, 13th Activity Report 1999–2000, para. 120.

1114. *Ibid.*; *International Pen, Constitutional Rights Project, Interights on behalf of Ken Saro-Wiwa Jr. and Civil Liberties Organisation v. Nigeria*, Communication Nos 137/94, 139/94, 154/96 and 161/97, 12th Activity Report 1998–1999.

1115. *Ibid.*

1116. *Ibid.*; additionally, a violation of Art. 4, *International Pen, Constitutional Rights Project, Interights on behalf of Ken Saro-Wiwa Jr. and Civil Liberties Organisation v. Nigeria*, Communication Nos 137/94, 139/94, 154/96 and 161/97, 12th Activity Report 1998–1999, para. 104, where the Commission stated that the State was under a duty not to let persons in their custody deliberately die. Also a violation of the right to health under Art. 17, *Monim Elgak, Osman Hummeida and Amir Suleiman (represented by FIDH and OMCT) v. Sudan*, Communication No. 379/09 (2014) paras 136–137. The Commission has held that there must be prompt access to medical personnel, *Egyptian Initiative for Personal Rights and INTERIGHTS v. Egypt*, Communication No. 334/06 (2011), paras 172–177.

repeated deportations,[1117] separation from one's family,[1118] forced evictions,[1119] and disappearances.[1120] By way of contrast, the prohibition on the possession and use of drugs does not violate human dignity.[1121] Acts that appear to constitute torture include the application of electric shocks and weights to particularly sensitive parts of the body,[1122] 'water boarding',[1123] and being burnt and buried in sand and left to die a slow death.[1124] In addition, a State is prohibited from deporting, expelling or extraditing a person to another State where s/he is will or is likely to face torture.[1125] Certainly the Human Rights Court, in keeping with international standards, has taken the view that cruel, inhuman and degrading punishment and treatment must meet a threshold of 'severity, intention, and severe humiliation'.[1126]

234. As with other protective rights under the African Charter above-mentioned the State is under an obligation to take timely and appropriate steps to deal with allegations of torture. The State is therefore under an obligation to prove that the allegations are unfounded.[1127] In *The Law Office of Ghazi Suleiman v. Sudan*, the Commission stated that it was important for the State 'to take preventive measures', to take legal action proportionate to the abuses against those who have committed torture, to 'search for effective solutions in a transparent legal system', and to investigate allegations of torture.[1128]

235. The right to liberty and security of the person is guaranteed by Article 6 of the African Charter and applies to all deprivations of liberty and not solely in relation to the criminal law.[1129] The Commission has defined the right to liberty as 'the right

---

1117. *Modise v. Botswana*, Communication No. 97/93, 14th Activity Report 2000–2001, para. 91.

1118. *Modise v. Botswana*, Communication No. 97/93, 10th Activity Report 1996–1997, para. 32; *Amnesty International et al. v. Sudan*, Communication Nos 48/90, 50/91, 52/91, 89/93 13th Activity Report 1999–2000, para. 54; *The Law Office of Ghazi Suleiman v. Sudan*, Communication Nos 222/98 and 229/99, 16th Activity Report 2002–2003, para. 44.

1119. *Sudan Human Rights Organization and Sudan Centre for Housing Rights and Evictions v. Sudan* Communication Nos 279/03, 296/05, 28th Activity Report 2010, para. 164.

1120. *Mouvement Burkinabé des Droits de l'Homme et des Peuples v. Burkina Faso*, Communication No. 204/97, 14th Activity Report 2000–2001, para. 44.

1121. *Garreth Anver Prince v. South Africa*, Communication No. 255/2002, 18th Activity Report 2002–2003, para. 49.

1122. *Malawi African Association et al. v. Mauritania*, Communication Nos 54/91, 61/91, 98/93, 164/97–196/97, 210/98, 13th Activity Report 1999–2000.

1123. *Ibid.*

1124. *Ibid.*, additionally a violation of Art. 4.

1125. *Mohamed Abdullah Saleh al-Asad v. Djibouti*, Communication No. 383/10 (2014), para. 179.

1126. *Alex Thomas v. Tanzania*, African Court of Human and Peoples' Rights, App. No. 005/2013 (20 Nov. 2015), para. 146.

1127. *Egyptian Initiative for Personal Rights and INTERIGHTS v. Egypt*, Communication No. 334/06 (2011), paras 169–170.

1128. Communication Nos 222/98 and 229/99, 16th Activity Report 2002–2003, para. 46. *See also Amnesty International et al. v. Sudan*, Communication Nos 48/90, 50/91, 52/91, 89/93, 13th Activity Report 1999–2000, para. 56.

1129. *Purohit and Moore v. The Gambia*, Communication No. 241/2001, 16th Activity Report 2002–2003, para. 64; *Sudan Human Rights Organization and Sudan Centre for Housing Rights and Evictions v. Sudan* Communication Nos 279/03, 296/05, 28th Activity Report, 2010, para. 179.

to be free…freedom from restraint…in accordance with established law', whereas security of the person includes national and individual security.[1130] As the Commission has indicated, 'this is not an absolute right because the African Charter allows the deprivation of this right through lawful means'.[1131] The Commission has added that deprivation of liberty 'is only acceptable if it is authorised by law and is compatible with the obligations of States Parties under the African Charter'; it does not mean that any domestic law may justify the loss of a person's freedom.[1132] While 'an arrest or detention may be legal according to the letter of domestic law' it may nonetheless be 'arbitrary and therefore illegal by reason of its inappropriate, unjust or unpredictable nature'.[1133] Certainly, what are specifically prohibited are arbitrary arrests and detentions.[1134] In *Purohit and Moore v. The Gambia*, the Commission stated that, 'Prohibition against arbitrariness requires among other things that deprivation of liberty shall be under the authority and supervision of persons procedurally and substantively competent to certify it.'[1135] In *Amnesty International et al. v. Sudan*, the Commission said that Article 6 had to be interpreted 'in such a way as to permit arrests only in the exercise of powers normally granted to the security forces in a democratic society'. The Commission found Article 6 to have been breached because the decree allowed individuals to be arrested 'for vague reasons, and upon suspicion, not proven acts'.[1136]

236. Article 6 fails to specify the guarantees against loss of liberty in any detail. This is regrettable because deprivation of liberty by the State constitutes one of the most serious infringements of a person's fundamental rights and it would therefore have been appropriate to have enumerated some of these guarantees. Significantly, the Commission has found that the right of habeas corpus comes within the scope of Article

1130. *Sudan Human Rights Organization and Sudan Centre for Housing Rights and Evictions v. Sudan* Communication Nos 279/03, 296/05, 28th Activity Report, 2010, paras 172–175.

1131. *Zegveld and Ephrem v. Eritrea*, Communication No. 250/2002, 17th Activity Report 2003–2004, para. 52; *Alex Thomas v. Tanzania*, African Court of Human and Peoples' Rights, App. No. 005/2013 (20 November 2015), para. 150.

1132. *Purohit and Moore v. The Gambia*, Communication No. 241/2001, 16th Activity Report 2002–2003, para. 64. *See Amnesty International et al. v. Sudan*, Communication Nos 48/90, 50/91, 52/91, 89/93, 13th Activity Report 1999–2000, para. 59; *African Commission on Human and Peoples' Rights v. Libya*, African Court of Human and Peoples' Rights, App. No. 002/2013 (3 Jun. 2016) paras 80–83.

1133. *Article 19 v. Eritrea*, Communication No. 275/2003, 22nd Activity Report 2006–2007, para. 93.

1134. *Constitutional Rights Project, Civil Liberties Organisation and Media Rights Agenda v. Nigeria*, Communication Nos 140/94, 141/94, 145/95, 13th Activity Report 1999–2000, para. 51; *Zegveld and Ephrem v. Eritrea*, Communication No. 250/2002, 17th Activity Report 2003–2004, para. 52; *Institute for Human Rights and Development in Africa v. Angola*, Communication No. 292/2004, 24th Activity Report 2008, para. 54; *Monim Elgak, Osman Hummeida and Amir Suleiman (represented by FIDH and OMCT) v. Sudan*, Communication No. 379/09 (2014) paras 104–107., In *Organisation Mondiale contre la Torture et al. v. Rwanda,* Communication Nos 27/89, 46/91, 49/91, 99/93, 10th Activity Report 1993–1994, para. 28, the Commission held that the arrests and detentions of people on grounds of ethnic origin alone constituted arbitrary deprivation of liberty in clear violation of Art. 6.

1135. Communication No. 241/2001, 16th Activity Report 2002–2003, para. 65.

1136. Communication Nos 48/90, 50/91, 52/91, 89/93, 13th Activity Report 1999–2000, para. 59.

6.[1137] Nevertheless, the Commission has partially addressed this omission by adopting the Resolution on the Right to Recourse Procedure and Fair Trial which reflects accepted international human rights standards,[1138] such as the right to be informed at the time of the arrest for the reasons of the arrest,[1139] the right to be brought promptly before a judicial officer, and the right to challenge the lawfulness of the detention before a court[1140] and to be released if the lawfulness is not established. This soft law instrument has influenced the Commission's jurisprudence which has held that detention without charge or trial for a prolonged period of time constitutes an arbitrary deprivation of liberty.[1141] In *Zegveld and Ephrem v. Eritrea*, the Commission stated that the:

> lawfulness and necessity of holding someone in custody must be determined by a court or other appropriate judicial authority. The decision to keep a person in detention should be open to review periodically so that the grounds justifying the detention can be assessed. In any event, detention should not continue beyond the period for which the State can provide appropriate justification. Therefore, persons suspected of committing any crime must be promptly charged with

---

1137. *Constitutional Rights Project and Civil Liberties Organisation v. Nigeria*, Communication Nos 143/95, 150/96, 13th Activity Report 1999–2000, paras 22–27. *See also Constitutional Rights Project v. Nigeria*, Communication No. 153/96, 13th Activity Report 1999–2000, para. 18.

1138. Adopted at the Commission's Eleventh Ordinary Session, 1992, 5th Activity Report, 1991–1992.

1139. *Media Rights Agenda and Constitutional Rights Project v. Nigeria*, Communication Nos 105/93, 128/94, 130/94, 152/96, 12th Activity Report 1998–1999, para. 84; *The Law Office of Ghazi Suleiman v. Sudan*, Communication Nos 222/98 and 229/99, 16th Activity Report 2002–2003, para. 49.

1140. *Krischna Achutan (on behalf of Aleke Banda) v. Malawi*; *Amnesty International on behalf of Orton and Vera Chirwa v. Malawi*, Communication Nos 64/92, 68/92, 78/92, 8th Activity Report 1994–1995, para. 9; *International Pen, Constitutional Rights Project, Interights on behalf of Ken Saro-Wiwa Jr. and Civil Liberties Organisation v. Nigeria*, Communication Nos 137/94, 139/94, 154/96 and 161/9712th Activity Report 1998–1999, para. 83. In *Amnesty International et al. v. Sudan*, Communication Nos 48/90, 50/91, 52/91, 89/93, 13th Activity Report 1999–2000, para. 60, found a breach of Art. 6 in relation to a situation where the 'appeal in the case of arrest lies to the body whose president orders the arrests. Such a remedy provides no guarantee of good administration of justice and is more akin to an appeal for clemency than a judicial appeal'.

1141. *Free Legal Assistance Group v. Zaire*, Communication No. 25/89, 9th Activity Report 1995–1996, para. 42; *Constitutional Rights Project and Civil Liberties Organisation v. Nigeria*, Communication No. 102/93, 12th Activity Report 1998–1999, para. 55; *International Pen, Constitutional Rights Project, Interights on behalf of Ken Saro-Wiwa Jr. and Civil Liberties Organisation v. Nigeria*, Communication Nos 137/94, 139/94, 154/96 and 161/97, 12th Activity Report 1998–1999, para. 83; *The Law Office of Ghazi Suleiman v. Sudan*, Communication Nos 222/98 and 229/99, 16th Activity Report 2002–2003, para. 50; *Zegveld and Ephrem v. Eritrea*, Communication No. 250/2002, 17th Activity Report 2003–2004, paras 94–95; *Article 19 v. Eritrea*, Communication No. 275/2003, 22nd Activity Report 2006–2007, para. 94; *Institute for Human Rights and Development in Africa v. Angola*, Communication No. 292/2004, 24th Activity Report 2008, para. 54; *Jean-Marie Atangana Mebara v. Cameroon*, Communication No. 416/12 (2015) para. 119.

> legitimate criminal offences and the State should initiate legal proceedings that should comply with fair trial standards.[1142]

Furthermore, the Human Rights Court has had recourse to the guarantees enumerated in Article 9 International Covenant on Civil and Political Rights (ICCPR).[1143] It has therefore held that incommunicado detention constitutes a 'gross violation of human rights'.[1144]

237. The right to a fair trial is enshrined in Article 7 of the African Charter,[1145] described by the Commission as 'fundamental tenets of any democratic state'.[1146] The Human Rights Court has identified it as a fundamental human right which 'implies that every individual accused of a crime or an offence shall receive all the guarantees under the procedure'.[1147] Attention should be drawn to the use of the noun 'cause' which suggests a wider application to encompass not only civil actions[1148] and criminal cases but also non-judicial disputes and traditional dispute settlement by village or tribal elders. Thus, in *Purohit and Moore v. The Gambia*, a case concerning the rights of mental health patients, the Commission stated that the 'guarantees in Article 7(1) extend beyond hearings in the normal context of judicial determinations or proceedings'.[1149] According to the Commission in *Zimbabwe Human Rights NGO Forum v. Zimbabwe* Article 7:

> encompasses the right of every individual to access the relevant judicial bodies competent to have their causes heard and be granted adequate relief. If there appears to be any possibility of an alleged victim succeeding at a hearing, the

1142. *Zegveld and Ephrem v. Eritrea*, Communication No. 250/2002, 17th Activity Report 2003–2004, para. 56.
1143. *African Commission on Human and Peoples' Rights v. Libya*, African Court of Human and Peoples' Rights, App. No. 002/2013 (3 Jun. 2016) paras 82–83.
1144. *Ibid.*, para. 684.
1145. In *Civil Liberties Organisation, Legal Defence Centre, Legal Defence and Assistance Project v. Nigeria*, Communication No. 218/98, 14th Activity Report 2000–2001, para. 27, the Commission described the provisions of Art. 7 as 'non-derogable'. *See also Good v. Botswana*, Communication No. 306/2005, 28th Activity Report 2009–2010, para. 175, where the Commission stated that the right to a fair trial is absolute and cannot be derogated from in any circumstance.
1146. *Gunme et al. v. Cameroon,* Communication No. 266/2003, 26th Activity Report 2008–2009, para. 126.
1147. *African Commission on Human and Peoples' Rights v. Libya*, African Court of Human and Peoples' Rights, App. No. 002/2013 (3 Jun. 2016) para. 89.
1148. *Zimbabwe Lawyers for Human Rights and the Institute for Human Rights and Development v. Zimbabwe*, Communication No. 293/2004, 24th Activity Report 2008, para. 130.
1149. Communication No. 241/2001, 16th Activity Report 2002–2003, para. 72.

> applicant should be given the benefit of the doubt and allowed to have their matter heard.[1150]

Furthermore, the 'right of access to judicial protection to ensure respect for a legal right requires available and effective recourse for the violation of a right protected under the Charter or the Constitution of the country concerned'.[1151] The Commission therefore found that the amnesty law, which prohibited the prosecution of, and set free, perpetrators of politically motivated acts, prevented victims from seeking an effective remedy and eroded their opportunity to have their complaint heard, rendering them helpless and depriving them of justice.[1152] It held that the amnesty law breached Article 7(1) because it:

> foreclosed access to any remedy that might be available to the victims to vindicate their rights, and without putting in place alternative adequate legislative or institutional mechanisms to ensure that perpetrators...were punished, and victims...duly compensated or given other avenues to seek effective remedy.[1153]

In a similar vein, the Commission has condemned ouster clauses. In *International Pen, Constitutional Rights Project, Interights on behalf of Ken Saro-Wiwa Jr. and Civil Liberties Organisation v. Nigeria*, the Commission stated that ouster clauses 'render local remedies non-existent, ineffective or illusory. They create a legal situation in which the judiciary can provide no check on the executive branch of government'.[1154] In *Civil Liberties Organization v. Nigeria*, the Commission was outspoken in its criticism, describing the ousting of the jurisdiction of the courts as 'an attack of incalculable proportions on Article 7 ... . An attack of this sort on the jurisdiction of

---

1150. Communication No. 245/2002, 21th Activity Report 2005–2006, para. 213; *Good v. Botswana*, Communication No. 306/2005, 28th Activity Report 2009–2010, paras 162–163. The right to be heard is protected by Art. 7, *Bissangou v. Republic of Congo*, Communication No. 253/2002, 21st Activity Report 2005–2006, para. 75. In *Sudan Human Rights Organization and Sudan Centre for Housing Rights and Evictions v. Sudan* Communication Nos 279/03, 296/05, 28th Activity Report, 2010, para. 181, the Commission stated that the right to be heard gives complainants 'unfettered access to a tribunal of competent jurisdiction'. *See also Zimbabwe Lawyers for Human Rights and the Institute for Human Rights and Development (on behalf of Andrew Barclay Meldrum) v. Zimbabwe*, Communication No. 294/2004, 26th Activity Report 2008–2009, paras 106–107, where the deportation of the victim effectively prevented him from being heard. The Commission has held the nullification of court cases in progress by the Nigerian military regime breached Art. 7(1)(a), *Constitutional Rights Project, Civil Liberties Organisation and Media Rights Agenda v. Nigeria*, Communication Nos 140/94, 141/94, 145/95, 13th Activity Report 1999–2000, para. 27.

1151. Communication No. 245/2002, 21th Activity Report 2005–2006, para. 213. In *Bissangou v. Republic of Congo*, Communication No. 253/2002, 21th Activity Report 2005–2006, para. 75, the Commission stated that Art. 7 included the right to the execution of a judgment.

1152. Communication No. 245/2002, 21th Activity Report 2005–2006, paras 211, 213.

1153. *Ibid.*, para. 215. *See also Mouvement Ivorien des Droits Humains (MIDH) v. Côte d'Ivoire*, Communication No. 246/2002, 25th Activity Report 2008, para. 98.

1154. Communication Nos 137/94, 139/94, 154/96 and 161/97, 12th Activity Report 1998–1999, para. 76. *See also Good v. Botswana*, Communication No. 306/2005, 28th Activity Report 2009–2010, para. 179.

the courts is especially invidious, because while it is a violation of human rights itself, it permits other violations of rights to go unredressed'.[1155]

238. The right to a fair trial set out in Article 7 consists of four elements.[1156] First, the right of access or to appeal to a competent national organ.[1157] Accordingly, in *Purohit and Moore v. The Gambia*, the Commission recognized that the provision necessitated a legal remedy[1158] and that 'in circumstances where persons are to be detained, such persons should at the very least be presented with the opportunity to challenge the matter of their detention before the competent jurisdictions that should have ruled on their detention'.[1159] Moreover, the Commission has held that the impossibility of 'any avenue of appeal to "competent national organs" in criminal

1155. Communication No. 129/94, 9th Activity Report, 1995–1996, para. 13. *See also Lawyers for Human Rights v. Swaziland*, Communication No. 251/2002, 18th Activity Report 2002–2003. In *Civil Liberties Organisation v. Nigeria*, Communication No. 151/96, 13th Activity Report 1999–2000, para. 17, the Commission recommended an end to the use of ouster clauses.

1156. All of these provisions are mutually dependent or interlinked and infringement of the right to be heard can lead to other violations, *Amnesty International et al. v. Sudan*, Communication Nos 48/90, 50/91, 52/91, 89/93, 13th Activity Report 1999–2000, para. 62; *The Law Office of Ghazi Suleiman v. Sudan*, Communication Nos 222/98 and 229/99, 16th Activity Report 2002–2003, para. 52.

1157. African Charter Art. 7(1)(a). In *Amnesty International et al. v. Sudan*, Communication Nos 48/90, 50/91, 52/91, 89/93, 13th Activity Report 1999–2000, para. 37, the Commission described the right of appeal as 'a general and non-derogable principle of international law'. This includes the right to be heard, *Women's Legal Aid Centre (on behalf of Sophia Moto) v. Tanzania*, Communication No. 243/2001, 18th Activity Report 2002–2003, para. 44, and the right to a second hearing, *Groupe de Travail sur les Dossiers Judiciaires Stratégiques v. Democratic Republic of Congo*, Communication No. 259/2002 (2011) para. 75. *See* further *Egyptian Initiative for Personal Rights and INTERIGHTS v. Egypt*, Communication No. 334/06 (2011), paras 220–222. Denial of a right of access to a national court constitutes a 'definite and inexcusable violation' of Art. 7(1)(a), *Tembani and Freeth v. Angola and Thirteen Others*, Communication No. 409/12 (2013) para. 138.

1158. In *Zongo and Others v. Burkina Faso*, African Court of Human and Peoples' Rights, App. No. 013/2011 (28 Mar. 2014) para. 156, the Court found that the Respondent had failed to act with due diligence in dealing with the murder of the victim.

1159. Communication No. 241/2001, 16th Activity Report 2002–2003, para. 72. *See also Krischna Achutan (on behalf of Aleke Banda) v. Malawi*; *Amnesty International on behalf of Orton and Vera Chirwa v. Malawi*, Communication Nos 64/92, 68/92, 78/92(1995), para. 9; *Rencontre Africaine pour la Defense des Droits de l'Homme v. Zambia*, Communication No. 71/92, 10th Activity Report, 1996–1997, para. 29; *Union Interafricaine des Droits de l'Homme et al. v. Angola*, Communication No.159/96, 11th Activity Report 1997–1998, para. 19; *International Pen, Constitutional Rights Project, Interights on behalf of Ken Saro-Wiwa Jr. and Civil Liberties Organisation v. Nigeria*, Communication Nos 137/94, 139/94, 154/96 and 161/97, 12th Activity Report 1998–1999, para. 93; *Amnesty International v. Zambia*, Communication No. 212/98, 12th Activity Report 1998–1999, para. 53; *Institute for Human Rights and Development in Africa v. Angola*, Communication No. 292/2004, 24th Activity Report 2008, para. 58.

cases' constitutes a clear violation of this provision.[1160] This is imperative where the accused is facing the death penalty.[1161] In fact, the Commission has expressed the view that the right to appeal is a right recognized by international law.[1162] In addition, it is important to note that the Commission has held that the appeal process must be authentic and effective. In *Malawi African Association et al. v. Mauritania*, it found that the appeal court:

> simply confirmed the sentences without considering all the elements of fact and law. Such a practice can not be considered a genuine appeal procedure. For an appeal to be effective, the appellate jurisdiction must, objectively and impartially, consider both the elements of fact and of law that are brought before it.[1163]

In *Amnesty International et al. v. Sudan* the Commission stated further:

> An effective appeal is one that, subsequent to the hearing by the competent tribunal of first instance, may reasonably lead to a reconsideration of the case by a superior jurisdiction, which requires that the latter should, in this regard, provide all necessary guarantees of good administration of justice.[1164]

239. What constitutes a 'competent organ' in such instances raises another point. The Commission has defined a competent tribunal as one having the power to hear the case by law, having 'jurisdiction over the subject matter and the person, and the trial is being conducted within any applicable time limit prescribed by law'.[1165] One other aspect refers to 'facets such as the expertise of the judges and the inherent justice

1160. *Constitutional Rights Project (in respect of Waheb Akamu, G. Adega and Others) v. Nigeria*, Communication No. 60/91, 8th Activity Report, 1994–1995, para.7; *Constitutional Rights Project (in respect of Zamani Lakwot and Others) v. Nigeria*, Communication No. 87/93, 8th Activity Report 1994–1995, para. 8; *The Law Office of Ghazi Suleiman v. Sudan*, Communication Nos 222/98 and 229/99, 16th Activity Report 2002–2003, para. 53. *See also Sudan Human Rights Organization and Sudan Centre for Housing Rights and Evictions v. Sudan* Communication Nos 279/03, 296/05, 28th Activity Report, 2010, para. 182.

1161. *Civil Liberties Organisation, Legal Defence Centre, Legal Defence and Assistance Project v. Nigeria*, Communication No. 218/98, 14th Activity Report 2000–2001, para. 33; *Forum of Conscience v. Sierra Leone,* Communication No. 223/98, 14th Activity Report 2000–2001, para. 17; *Egyptian Initiative for Personal Rights and INTERIGHTS v. Egypt*, Communication No. 334/06 (2011), para. 221; *Groupe de Travail sur les Dossiers Judiciaires Stratégiques v. Democratic Republic of Congo*, Communication No. 259/2002 (2011) para. 75.

1162. *Egyptian Initiative for Personal Rights and INTERIGHTS v. Egypt*, Communication No. 323/2006 (2011), para. 220.

1163. Communication Nos 54/91, 61/91, 98/93, 164/97–196/97, 210/98, 13th Activity Report 1999–2000, para. 94.

1164. Communication Nos 48/90, 50/91, 52/91, 89/93, 13th Activity Report 1999–2000, para. 37. *See also Women's Legal Aid Centre (on behalf of Sophia Moto) v. Tanzania*, Communication No. 243/2001, 18th Activity Report 2002–2003, para. 43, where the Commission stated that the principle of natural justice underlies Art. 7(1)(a).

1165. *Sudan Human Rights Organization and Sudan Centre for Housing Rights and Evictions v. Sudan* Communication Nos 279/03, 296/05, 28th Activity Report, 2010, para. 181; *Good v. Botswana*, Communication No. 306/2005, 28th Activity Report 2009–2010, para. 169.

of the laws under which they operate'.[1166] Another includes 'the duty of everyone, including the state, to respect and follow' the judgments of the courts.[1167] The Commission has expressed its unhappiness at military courts exercising jurisdiction over civilians.[1168] In *The Law Office of Ghazi Suleiman v. Sudan* the Commission found that 'the fact that the decisions of the military court are not subject to appeal and that civilians are brought to a military court constitutes a de jure procedural irregularity'.[1169]

240. Second, the presumption of innocence,[1170] which the Commission has described as 'a fundamental principle which protects everybody against being treated by public officials as if they were guilty of an offence … No guilt should be presumed until a charge has been proved beyond reasonable doubt. It is, therefore, a duty for all public authorities to refrain from prejudging the outcome of a trial'.[1171] In *Malawi African Association et al. v. Mauritania*, the Commission found that this presumption had been violated when the presiding judge had declared that the refusal of the accused to defend themselves was tantamount to an admission of guilt.[1172] The same conclusion was reached with regard to the fact that the court had based its verdict on statements coerced from the accused by the police.[1173] The Commission has further held that negative pre-trial publicity by the State aimed at casting guilt on the victims before a competent court has had the opportunity of ruling on the matter violates the presumption

1166. *Amnesty International et al. v. Sudan*, Communication Nos 48/90, 50/91, 52/91, 89/93, 13th Activity Report 1999–2000, para. 62.

1167. *Media Rights Agenda and Constitutional Rights Project v. Nigeria*, Communication Nos 105/93, 128/94, 130/94, 152/96, 12th Activity Report 1998–1999, para. 62.

1168. *Gunme et al. v. Cameroon,* Communication No. 266/2003, 26th Activity Report 2008–2009, paras 127–128; *Koso and Others v. Democratic Republic of Congo*, Communication No. 281/2003, 26th Activity Report 2008–2009, paras 83–87; *Egyptian Initiative for Personal Rights and INTERIGHTS v. Egypt*, Communication No. 334/06 (2011), paras 199–200.

1169. Communication Nos 222/98 and 229/99, 16th Activity Report 2002–2003, para. 53. *See also Civil Liberties Organisation v. Nigeria*, Communication No. 151/96, 13th Activity Report 1999–2000, paras 2, 22, where the decisions of a special military tribunal could not be appealed but was only subject to confirmation by the highest decision-making body of the Nigerian military regime, the Provisional Ruling Council.

1170. African Charter Art. 7(1)(b); *Haregewoin Gabre-Selassie and IHRDA (on behalf of former Dergue officials) v. Ethiopia*, Communication No. 301/05 (2011) paras 184–194. *See Civil Liberties Organisation, Legal Defence Centre, Legal Defence and Assistance Project v. Nigeria*, Communication No. 218/98, 14th Activity Report 2000–2001, para. 40, where the Commission went on to state that this extended to the right to silence, i.e., the right not to incriminate oneself, nor to testify against oneself, nor to confess under duress.

1171. *Haregewoin Gabre-Selassie and IHRDA (on behalf of former Dergue officials) v. Ethiopia*, Communication No. 301/05 (2011) para. 190; *Tsikata v. Ghana*, Communication No. 322/2006 (2014), paras 116–119. In *Jean-Marie Atangana Mebara v. Cameroon*, Communication No. 416/12 (2015) paras 97–103, the Commission stated that the decision of the trial or appeals courts must not be influenced by members of the executive.

1172. Communication Nos 54/91, 61/91, 98/93, 164/97–196/97, 210/98, 13th Activity Report 1999–2000, para. 95.

1173. *Ibid.*; *Egyptian Initiative for Personal Rights and INTERIGHTS v. Egypt*, Communication No. 334/06 (2011), paras 212–219.

of innocence.[1174] The same applies to the media.[1175] Detention on mere suspicion also violates this provision,[1176] as does prolonged imprisonment without conviction.[1177] The Human Rights Court has held that criminal sentences must be based on 'strong and credible evidence'.[1178]

241. Third, the right to a defence, including the right to be defended by counsel of choice.[1179] The Commission stressed the importance of this right in *Amnesty International et al. v. Sudan* where doubts existed as to whether the accused could choose their own lawyers and whether the tribunal could bar certain lawyers from the court. The Commission stated that:

> the right to freely choose one's counsel is essential to the assurance of a fair trial. To give the tribunal the power to veto the choice of counsel of defendants is an unacceptable infringement of this right. There should be an objective system for licensing advocates, so that qualified advocates cannot be barred from appearing in particular cases. It is essential that the national bar be an independent body which regulates legal practitioners, and that the tribunals themselves not adopt this role, which will infringe the right to defence.[1180]

1174. *International Pen, Constitutional Rights Project, Interights on behalf of Ken Saro-Wiwa Jr. and Civil Liberties Organisation v. Nigeria*, Communication Nos 137/94, 139/94, 154/96 and 161/97, 12th Activity Report 1998–1999, para. 96; *Media Rights Agenda v. Nigeria*, Communication No. 224/98, 14th Activity Report 2000–2001, paras 47–48; *The Law Office of Ghazi Suleiman v. Sudan*, Communication Nos 222/98 and 229/99, 16th Activity Report 2002–2003, paras 54, 56.

1175. *Tsikata v. Ghana*, Communication No. 322/2006 (2014), para. 116.

1176. *Annette Pagnoulle (on behalf of Abdoulaye Mazou) v. Cameroon*, Communication No. 39/90, 10th Activity Report 1996–1997, para. 21.

1177. *Haregewoin Gabre-Selassie and IHRDA (on behalf of former Dergue officials) v. Ethiopia*, Communication No. 301/05 (2011) para. 209.

1178. *Mohamed Abubakri v. Tanzania*, African Court of Human and Peoples' Rights, App. No. 007/2013 (3 Jun. 2016), para. 174.

1179. African Charter Art.7(1)(c). The right to defence applies at each stage of the criminal proceedings and implies the accused's presence throughout, *Avocats Sans Frontières (on behalf of Gaëtan Bwampamye) v. Burundi*, Communication No. 231/99, 14th Activity Report 2000–2001, para. 28; *Egyptian Initiative for Personal Rights and INTERIGHTS v. Egypt*, Communication No. 334/06 (2011), para. 209; *African Commission on Human and Peoples' Rights v. Libya*, African Court of Human and Peoples' Rights, App. No. 002/2013 (3 Jun. 2016) paras 89, 93; *Alex Thomas v. Tanzania*, African Court of Human and Peoples' Rights, App. No. 005/2013 (20 Nov. 2015), para. 96.

1180. *Amnesty International et al. v. Sudan*, Communication Nos 48/90, 50/91, 52/91, 89/93, 13th Activity Report 1999–2000, para. 64. *See also Civil Liberties Organisation v. Nigeria*, Communication No. 151/96, 13th Activity Report 1999–2000, para. 24; *Groupe de Travail sur les Dossiers Judiciaires Stratégiques v. Democratic Republic of Congo*, Communication No. 259/2002 (2011) para. 81.

Where the accused cannot afford legal counsel the Commission has urged that they be represented by counsel at state expense.[1181] The Commission has stressed that the right to legal assistance is a fundamental element of the right to a fair trial.[1182] Indeed, the Human Rights Court has emphasized that legal aid is a right designed to ensure a fair judicial process and avoid miscarriages of justice and should be available automatically in appropriate cases.[1183] The Commission found violations of this provision in *Krischna Achutan (on behalf of Aleke Banda) v. Malawi*; *Amnesty International on behalf of Orton and Vera Chirwa v. Malawi*, where the applicants had been tried without counsel,[1184] *Constitutional Rights Project (in respect of Zamani Lakwot) v. Nigeria*, where the defence counsel had been harassed and intimidated into resigning from a trial,[1185] *Media Rights Agenda and Constitutional Rights Project v. Nigeria*, where the applicant had been denied access to a lawyer,[1186] and *Civil Liberties Organisation, Legal Defence Centre, Legal Defence and Assistance Project v. Nigeria*, where the accused had been assigned military lawyers.[1187]

242. Although not expressly spelt out in the provision it has been established by the Commission that the right to a fair trial includes other guarantees, including the right to prepare adequately one's defence.[1188] In *William A. Courson v. Equatorial Guinea*, the Commission held that the right to defence 'includes the right to be informed of the charges…as well as the evidence of the said charges; all sorts of elements required to prepare his defence', and that failure to bring those elements to the knowledge

1181. *Civil Liberties Organisation, Legal Defence Centre, Legal Defence and Assistance Project v. Nigeria*, Communication No. 218/98, 14th Activity Report 2000–2001, para. 29; *Groupe de Travail sur les Dossiers Judiciaires Stratégiques v. Democratic Republic of Congo*, Communication No. 259/2002 (2011) para. 82.

1182. *Avocats Sans Frontières (on behalf of Gaëtan Bwampamye) v. Burundi*, Communication No. 231/9914th Activity Report 2000–2001, para. 30.

1183. *Alex Thomas v. Tanzania*, African Court of Human and Peoples' Rights, App. No. 005/2013 (20 Nov. 2015), paras 114–124; *Wilfred Onyango Nganyi & 9 Others v. Tanzania*, African Court of Human and Peoples' Rights, App. No. 006/2013 (18 Mar. 2016), paras 156–184; *Mohamed Abubakri v. Tanzania*, African Court of Human and Peoples' Rights, App. No. 007/2013 (3 Jun. 2016), paras 138–139.

1184. Communication Nos 64/92, 68/92, 78/92, 8th Activity Report 1994–1995, para. 10.

1185. Communication No. 87/93, 8th Activity Report, 1994–1995, para. 9. *See also International Pen, Constitutional Rights Project, Interights on behalf of Ken Saro-Wiwa Jr. and Civil Liberties Organisation v. Nigeria*, Communication Nos 137/94, 139/94, 154/96 and 161/97, 12th Activity Report 1998–1999, para. 101.

1186. Communication Nos 105/93, 128/94, 130/94, 152/96, 12th Activity Report 1998–1999, para. 88. *See also Constitutional Rights Project and Civil Liberties Organisation v. Nigeria*, Communication Nos 143/95, 150/96, 13th Activity Report 1999–2000, para. 29.

1187. Communication No. 218/98, 14th Activity Report 2000–2001, para. 31.

1188. *See African Commission on Human and Peoples' Rights v. Libya*, African Court of Human and Peoples' Rights, App. No. 002/2013 (3 Jun. 2016) para. 94.

of the accused resulted in a breach of Article 7(1)(c).[1189] Access to case files and documents is also an essential factor.[1190] There is a right to call witnesses, although subject to certain limitations.[1191] Manifest errors in national proceedings have also been taken to undermine the right to a fair trial.[1192] Another guarantee is the right to equal treatment. In *Avocats Sans Frontiéres (on behalf of Gaëtan Bwampamye) v. Burundi*, the Commission explained what this right meant, especially in criminal cases. It stated that, firstly:

> both the defence and the public prosecutor shall have equal opportunity to prepare and present their pleas and indictment during the trial. Simply put, they should argue their cases before the jurisdiction on an equal footing. Secondly it entails the equal treatment of all accused persons by jurisdictions charged with trying them. This does not mean that identical treatment should be meted to all accused. The idea here is the principle that when objective facts are alike, the response of the judiciary should also be similar. There is a breach of the principle of equality if judicial or administrative decisions are applied in a discriminatory manner.[1193]

243. And fourth, the right to a trial within a reasonable time by an impartial court or tribunal,[1194] said by the Commission to be a cardinal element.[1195] Insofar as

---

1189. Communication No. 144/95, 11th Activity Report, 1997–1998, para. 21. *See also International Pen, Constitutional Rights Project, Interights on behalf of Ken Saro-Wiwa Jr. and Civil Liberties Organisation v. Nigeria*, Communication Nos 137/94, 139/94, 154/96 and 161/97, 12th Activity Report 1998–1999, para. 101. In *Mohamed Abubakri v. Tanzania*, African Court of Human and Peoples' Rights, App. No. 007/2013 (3 Jun. 2016), para. 158, the Human Rights Court stated that the right to be informed of the charges was a 'key element' of the right to a fair trial. In *Tsikata v. Ghana*, Communication No. 322/2006 (2014), para. 138, the Commission explained that the State 'must clearly outline the arraigned acts and the law under which the accused…is being charged.'

1190. *Jean-Marie Atangana Mebara v. Cameroon*, Communication No. 416/12 (2015) paras 104–109; *African Commission on Human and Peoples' Rights v. Libya*, African Court of Human and Peoples' Rights, App. No. 002/2013 (3 Jun. 2016) para. 94.

1191. *Tsikata v. Ghana*, Communication No. 322/2006 (2014), paras 144–145.

1192. *Alex Thomas v. Tanzania*, African Court of Human and Peoples' Rights, App. No. 005/2013 (20 Nov. 2015), paras 125–131. In *Mohamed Abubakri v. Tanzania*, African Court of Human and Peoples' Rights, App. No. 007/2013 (3 Jun. 2016), para. 194, the Court opined that alibi claims had to be properly investigated.

1193. Communication No. 231/99, 14th Activity Report 2000–2001, para. 28.

1194. African Charter Art. 7(1)(d). This right also applies to the appeals process, *Alex Thomas v. Tanzania*, African Court of Human and Peoples' Rights, App. No. 005/2013 (20 Nov. 2015), paras 100–110.

1195. *Haregewoin Gabre-Selassie and IHRDA (on behalf of former Dergue officials) v. Ethiopia*, Communication No. 301/05 (2011) para. 215. In *Tsikata v. Ghana*, Communication No. 322/2006 (2014), para. 146, the Commission stated that this was an absolute right with no exceptions. In *Wilfred Onyango Nganyi & 9 Others v. Tanzania*, African Court of Human and Peoples' Rights, App. No. 006/2013 (18 Mar. 2016), para. 127, the Court stressed the importance of a 'speedy judicial process'.

the concept of 'a reasonable time' is concerned, in the absence of a standard period[1196] three criteria have been adopted: the complexity of the case, the conduct of the applicant, and the conduct of the relevant national authorities.[1197] It has proceeded to state that in 'a criminal case, especially one in which the accused is detained until trial, the trial must be held with all possible speed to minimize the negative effects on the life of a person who, after all, may be innocent.'[1198] It has therefore held that indefinite detention,[1199] detention without trial,[1200] unclear indictments,[1201] or the passage of a number of years before the matter is brought to trial breach this provision.[1202] Certainly, the Human Rights Court has held that any individual arrested or detained for a criminal offence must be brought before a judge with 'minimum delay'.[1203] In relation to civil actions, a case pending for more than five years was deemed in breach of this provision.[1204]

244. The requirement of 'an impartial court or tribunal' is considered one of the 'pillars' of a fair trial.[1205] The Commission has drawn links with Article 26 of the

---

1196. *Wilfred Onyango Nganyi & 9 Others v. Tanzania*, African Court of Human and Peoples' Rights, App. No. 006/2013 (18 Mar. 2016), para. 135.

1197. *Article 19 v. Eritrea*, Communication No. 275/2003 (2007), paras 97–100; *Wilfred Onyango Nganyi & 9 Others v. Tanzania*, African Court of Human and Peoples' Rights, App. No. 006/2013 (18 Mar. 2016), paras 136–155.

1198. *Constitutional Rights Project v. Nigeria*, Communication No. 153/96, 13th Activity Report 1999–2000, para. 19; *Haregewoin Gabre-Selassie and IHRDA (on behalf of former Dergue officials) v. Ethiopia*, Communication No. 301/05 (2011) para. 215.

1199. *Krischna Achutan (on behalf of Aleke Banda) v. Malawi*; *Amnesty International on behalf of Orton and Vera Chirwa v. Malawi*, Communication Nos 64/92, 68/92, 78/92, 8th Activity Report 1994–1995, para. 9. In *Sir Dawda K. Jawara v. Gambia*, Communication Nos 147/95 and 149/96, 13th Activity Report 1999–2000, para. 61, the Minister was authorized to extend the period of detention *ad infinitum*.

1200. *Constitutional Rights Project and Civil Liberties Organisation v. Nigeria*, Communication Nos 143/95, 150/96, 13th Activity Report 1999–2000, para. 28.

1201. *Haregewoin Gabre-Selassie and IHRDA (on behalf of former Dergue officials) v. Ethiopia*, Communication No. 301/05 (2011) paras 231–232.

1202. *Annette Pagnoulle (on behalf of Abdoulaye Mazou) v. Cameroon*, Communication No. 39/90, 10th Activity Report 1996–1997, para. 19 (two years); *Alhassan Abubakar v. Ghana*, Communication No. 103/93, 10th Activity Report 1996–1997, para. 12 (seven years); *Constitutional Rights Project v. Nigeria*, Communication No. 153/96, 13th Activity Report 1999–2000, para. 20 (two years); *Mouvement Burkinabé des Droits de l'Homme et des Peuples v. Burkina Faso*, Communication No. 204/97, 14th Activity Report 2000–2001, para. 40 (fifteen years); *Haregewoin Gabre-Selassie and IHRDA (on behalf of former Dergue officials) v. Ethiopia*, Communication No. 301/05 (2011) paras 233–239; *Jean-Marie Atangana Mebara v. Cameroon*, Communication No. 416/12 (2015) paras 113–115. *See also Odjouoriby Cossi Paul v. Benin*, Communication No. 199/97, 17th Activity Report, 2003–2004.

1203. *African Commission on Human and Peoples' Rights v. Libya*, African Court of Human and Peoples' Rights, App. No. 002/2013 (3 Jun. 2016) para. 91.

1204. *Association of Victims of Post Electoral Violence & INTERIGHTS v. Cameroon*, Communication No. 272/2003, 27th Activity Report 2009, para. 130.

1205. *Mohamed Abubakri v. Tanzania*, African Court of Human and Peoples' Rights, App. No. 007/2013 (3 Jun. 2016), para. 110.

African Charter which guarantees the independence of the judiciary.[1206] As a general principle the Commission has stated that it covers the subjective impartiality of a judge and the objective impartiality of a court.[1207] It has deemed the following criteria to be essential elements: to be established by law with adjudicative functions on the basis of the rule of law; no interference with the judicial function; no review of decisions except through judicial review; independence from the executive branch which the government must respect; and decisions based on objective evidence, arguments and facts before it.[1208] The fact that judicial appointments may be made by the executive does not in itself undermine the independence of the judiciary but it depends on context. If a judicial appointment is made seemingly to deal with a specific case, the appearance of independence and impartiality is brought into question.[1209] In *Lawyers for Human Rights v. Swaziland*, the Commission held that vesting judicial power in the king, including the authority to appoint and dismiss judges, not only violated Article 7 but also compromised the independence of the judiciary guaranteed by Article 26 of the African Charter.[1210] It has taken the view that such courts or tribunals must meet judicial standards.[1211] It has therefore held that military tribunals with jurisdiction over civilians cannot be considered impartial, stating that their 'composition alone, creates the

---

1206. *Zimbabwe Lawyers for Human Rights and the Institute for Human Rights and Development v. Zimbabwe*, Communication No. 293/2004, 24th Activity Report 2008, paras 138–41; *Koso and Others v. Democratic Republic of Congo*, Communication No. 281/2003, 26th Activity Report 2008–2009, paras 76–77; *Egyptian Initiative for Personal Rights and INTERIGHTS v. Egypt*, Communication No. 323/2006 (2011), paras 216–218; *Tembani and Freeth v. Angola and Thirteen Others*, Communication No. 409/12 (2013) para. 144.

1207. *Jean-Marie Atangana Mebara v. Cameroon*, Communication No. 416/12 (2015) para. 116.

1208. *Egyptian Initiative for Personal Rights and INTERIGHTS v. Egypt*, Communication No. 323/2006 (2011), para. 223; *Egyptian Initiative for Personal Rights and INTERIGHTS v. Egypt*, Communication No. 334/06 (2011), para. 197.

1209. In *Tsikata v. Ghana*, Communication No. 322/2006 (2014), paras 158–159, the reconstitution of the Supreme Court panel suggested tacit interference with its independence.

1210. Communication No. 251/2002, 18th Activity Report 2002–2003, para. 54; *Amnesty International et al. v. Sudan*, Communication Nos 48/90, 50/91, 52/91, 89/93, 13th Activity Report 1999–2000, para. 69.

1211. *Constitutional Rights Project v. Nigeria*, Communication No. 153/96, 13th Activity Report 1999–2000, para. 15; *Egyptian Initiative for Personal Rights and INTERIGHTS v. Egypt*, Communication No. 334/06 (2011), paras 206–207.

appearance, if not actual lack of impartiality'.[1212] Similarly, review panels composed of presidential appointees and representatives of the executive branch,[1213] or special tribunals.[1214]

245. Article 7(2) of the African Charter enshrines the principle of non-retroactivity of the criminal law and criminal penalties.[1215] In addition, punishment is declared to be personal and may only be imposed on the offender.[1216] In *Media Rights Agenda and Constitutional Rights Project v. Nigeria*, the Commission expressed what it believed was at the core of this principle. It stated that:

> Article 7(2) must be read to prohibit not only condemnation and infliction of punishment for acts which did not constitute crimes at the time they were committed, but retroactivity itself. It is expected that citizens must take the laws seriously. If laws change with retroactive effect, the rule of law is undermined since individuals cannot know at any moment if their actions are legal. For a law-abiding citizen, this is a terrible uncertaintly, regardless of the likelihood of eventual punishment.

1212. *Constitutional Rights Project (in respect of Waheb Akamu, G. Adega and Others) v. Nigeria*, Communication No. 60/91, 8th Activity Report, 1994–1995, para. 8; *Constitutional Rights Project (in respect of Zamani Lakwot) v. Nigeria*, Communication No. 87/93, 8th Activity Report, 1994–1995, para. 10; *Amnesty International et al. v. Sudan*, Communication Nos 48/90, 50/91, 52/91, 89/93, 13th Activity Report 1999–2000, para. 68; *Centre for Free Speech v. Nigeria*, Communication No. 206/97, 13th Activity Report 1999–2000, paras 15–16; *Malawi African Association et al. v. Mauritania*, Communication Nos 54/91, 61/91, 98/93, 164/97–196/97, 210/98, 13th Activity Report 1999–2000, para. 98; *The Law Office of Ghazi Suleiman v. Sudan*, Communication Nos 222/98 and 229/99, 16th Activity Report 2002–2003, paras 61–67; *Egyptian Initiative for Personal Rights and INTERIGHTS v. Egypt*, Communication No. 334/06 (2011), paras 199–200. In *Media Rights Agenda v. Nigeria*, Communication No. 224/98, 14th Activity Report 2000–2001, para. 60, the breach was caused by the fact that the members of the tribunal were serving military officers with little or no knowledge of the law. Compare *Civil Liberties Organisation, Legal Defence Centre, Legal Defence and Assistance Project v. Nigeria*, Communication No. 218/98, 14th Activity Report 2000–2001, para. 44, where the Commission expressed the view that military tribunals per se were not contrary to the terms of the African Charter if they met the requirements of fairness, openness, justice, independence and due process.

1213. *Constitutional Rights Project v. Nigeria*, Communication No. 153/96, 13th Activity Report 1999–2000, para. 15. In *Sir Dawda K. Jawara v. Gambia*, Communication Nos 147/95 and 149/96, 13th Activity Report 1999–2000, para. 61, the Commission found that the discretion vested in the Minister to extend detention 'will render favour rather than vindicating a right'.

1214. *Civil Liberties Organisation v. Nigeria*, Communication No. 151/96, 13th Activity Report 1999–2000, para. 21.

1215. *Civil Liberties Organization in respect of Nigerian Bar Association v. Nigeria*, Communication No. 101/93, 8th Activity Report 1994–1995, para. 12; *Sir Dawda K. Jawara v. Gambia*, Communication Nos 147/95 and 149/96, 13th Activity Report 1999–2000, para. 63; *Tsikata v. Ghana*, Communication No. 322/2006 (2014), para. 128.

1216. *See Mohamed Abubakri v. Tanzania*, African Court of Human and Peoples' Rights, App. No. 007/2013 (3 Jun. 2016), para. 105.

The Commission was underwhelmed at the State's defence that the retroactive law was not actually enforced, declaring that, 'Potential prosecution is a serious threat. An unjust but unenforced law undermines…the sanctity in which the law should be held.'[1217]

246. It should be observed that Article 7 omits a number of internationally accepted express elements of a fair trial, although some are listed in the Resolution on the Right to Recourse Procedure and Fair Trial,[1218] but misgivings over their omission has been lessened by the fact that the Commission considers them as implicit constituents of the right. These include the requirement that cases be heard in public,[1219] the right to examine witnesses, the right to be present at one's trial, the right not to be retried according to the principle of *ne bis in idem*, the right to understand the charges,[1220] the right to be informed promptly of any charges,[1221] and the right to the free assistance of an interpreter in court.

247. Article 8 of the African Charter protects freedom of conscience, the profession and the free practice of religion. The freedom of conscience and of religion allows people to gather together to worship, to establish and maintain places of worship, and to celebrate ceremonies in connection thereto.[1222] The Commission has accepted the symbiotic relationship between practice and religious freedom.[1223] While it has stated that while the right to hold religious beliefs is absolute, the right to act on those

1217. Communication Nos 105/93, 128/94, 130/94, 152/96, 12th Activity Report 1998–1999, paras 59–60.

1218. Adopted at the Commission's Eleventh Ordinary Session, 1992, 5th Activity Report, 1991–1992. *See Lawyers for Human Rights v. Swaziland*, Communication No. 251/2002, 18th Activity Report 2002–2003, para. 53.

1219. In *Civil Liberties Organisation, Legal Defence Centre, Legal Defence and Assistance Project v. Nigeria*, Communication No. 218/98, 14th Activity Report 2000–2001, paras 35–39, the Commission held that hearings in public were an important safeguard and that holding trials in secret therefore violated the right to a fair hearing enshrined in the African Charter Art. 7. *See also Media Rights Agenda v. Nigeria*, Communication No. 224/98, 14th Activity Report 2000–2001, paras 50–53.

1220. In *Malawi African Association et al. v. Mauritania*, Communication Nos 54/91, 61/91, 98/93, 164/97–196/97, 210/98, 13th Activity Report 1999–2000, para. 97, the Commission held this right should come within the scope of the African Charter Art. 7(1)(c). *See also Gunme et al. v. Cameroon,* Communication No. 266/2003, 26th Activity Report 2008–2009, paras 129–130.

1221. In *Huri-Laws v. Nigeria*, Communication No. 225/98, 14th Activity Report 2000–2001, para. 44, the Commission found a violation of the right to a fair trial following the State's failure to give reasons for arrest and failure to bring charges. *See also Media Rights Agenda v. Nigeria*, Communication No. 224/98, 14th Activity Report 2000–2001, paras 42–44.

1222. *Free Legal Assistance Group, Lawyers Committee for Human Rights, Union Interafricaine des Droits de l'Homme, and Les Temoins Jehoves v. Zaire*, Communication Nos 25/89, 47/90, 59/91, 100/93, 9th Activity Report 1995–1996, para. 45; *Centre for Minority Rights Development (Kenya) and Minority Rights Group International on behalf of Endorois Welfare Council v. Kenya*, Communication No. 276/2003, 27th Activity Report 2009, paras 165–168. The Human Rights Court has given Art. 8 a broad interpretation that extends to non-belief, *African Commission on Human and Peoples' Rights v. Kenya*, African Court of Human and Peoples' Rights, App. No. 006/2012 (26 May 2017) para. 163.

1223. *Amnesty International et al. v. Sudan*, Communication Nos 48/90, 50/91, 52/91, 89/93, 13th Activity Report 1999–2000, paras 71–76.

beliefs is not since the latter right must sometimes yield to the overriding interests of society, such as protecting the health, welfare, and safety of children.[1224] However, any restriction 'must be based on exceptionally good reasons', must be proportionate and reasonable, and minimal.[1225] The Commission has found violations of Article 8 where the State has harassed, oppressed and persecuted religious believers.[1226] It has also held that the forceful removal of indigenous peoples from their ancestral lands sacred to their religion constituted an unjustified interference with their religious practices.[1227] In a finding of especial significance the Commission has addressed the application of religious laws to non-adherents. It has held such situations to be 'fundamentally unjust' and that individuals should have the right to be tried by secular courts.[1228]

248. These freedoms are, however, limited. In *Garreth Anver Prince v. South Africa*, the Commission had to consider whether the State's prohibition on the possession and use of cannabis infringed the freedom of the complainant, a Rastafari, to practice his religion.[1229] The Commission held that the State had a legitimate interest in addressing the problems associated with drugs and that the law in place was both proportionate and necessary, coming therefore within the scope of the limitations in Articles 8 and 27(2) of the African Charter.[1230]

249. Article 9 of the African Charter guarantees what is one of the fundamental pillars of a free and democratic society, the right to receive information (paragraph 1), and to express and disseminate opinion (paragraph 2).[1231] The Commission has stated that these two elements are indivisible concepts that must be guaranteed simultaneously.[1232] It is interesting to note that the Commission has established a link between the right to receive information and the right to a fair trial, so that a person has a right to be

1224. *Garreth Anver Prince v. South Africa*, Communication No. 255/2002, 18th Activity Report 2002–2003, paras 41–42.

1225. *Centre for Minority Rights Development (Kenya) and Minority Rights Group International on behalf of Endorois Welfare Council v. Kenya*, Communication No. 276/2003, 27th Activity Report 2009, para. 172; *African Commission on Human and Peoples' Rights v. Kenya*, African Court of Human and Peoples' Rights, App. No. 006/2012 (26 May 2017) para. 167.

1226. *Free Legal Assistance Group, Lawyers Committee for Human Rights, Union Interafricaine des Droits de l'Homme, and Les Temoins Jehoves v. Zaire*, Communication Nos 25/89, 47/90, 59/91, 100/93, 9th Activity Report 1995–1996, para. 45; *Amnesty International et al. v. Sudan*, Communication Nos 48/90, 50/91, 52/91, 89/93, 13th Activity Report 1999–2000, paras 71–76.

1227. *Centre for Minority Rights Development (Kenya) and Minority Rights Group International on behalf of Endorois Welfare Council v. Kenya*, Communication No. 276/200327th Activity Report 2009, para. 173.

1228. *Amnesty International et al. v. Sudan*, Communication Nos 48/90, 50/91, 52/91, 89/93, 13th Activity Report 1999–2000, para. 73.

1229. Communication No. 255/2002, 18th Activity Report 2002–2003.

1230. *Ibid.*, para. 43.

1231. *See International Pen, Constitutional Rights Project, Interights on behalf of Ken Saro-Wiwa Jr. and Civil Liberties Organisation v. Nigeria*, Communication Nos 137/94, 139/94, 154/96 and 161/97, 12th Activity Report 1998–1999, para. 110; *Sir Dawda K. Jawara v. Gambia*, Communication Nos 147/95 and 149/96, 13th Activity Report 1999–2000, para. 65; *Egyptian Initiative for Personal Rights and INTERIGHTS v. Egypt*, Communication No. 323/2006 (2011), para. 250.

1232. *Scanlen and Holderness v. Zimbabwe*, Communication No. 297/2005, 26th Activity Report 2009, para. 108.

informed of the reasons for the actions taken against him/her.[1233] Although freedom of speech or other forms of expression are not explicitly mentioned per se it is clear that they come within the scope of the provision.[1234] Thus, in *Media Rights Agenda and Constitutional Rights Project v. Nigeria*, the Commission stated that Article 9 'reflects the fact that freedom of expression is a basic human right, vital to an individual's personal development, his political consciousness, and participation in the conduct of public affairs in his country'.[1235] Furthermore, in its Declaration of Principles on Freedom of Expression in Africa the Commission asserts the 'fundamental importance of freedom of expression and information as an individual human right, as a cornerstone of democracy and as a means of ensuring respect for all human rights and freedoms'.[1236] A blanket restriction on the freedom of expression breaches Article 9(2).[1237]

250. The reach of the provision extends to the freedom of political expression.[1238] Hence in *The Law Office of Ghazi Suleiman v. Sudan*, the Commission stated that speech that contributed to political debate had to be protected.[1239] The essential role played by the press in society has been emphasized by the Commission. In *Constitutional Rights Project, Civil Liberties Organisation and Media Rights Agenda v. Nigeria*, the Commission found that the military regime had been harassing the press by proscribing specified newspapers and sealing their premises arbitrarily which gave rise to the danger of self-censorship.[1240] In *Article 19 v. Eritrea*, the Commission found that a wholesale ban on the press and the imprisonment of those holding views contrary to those of the State violated the spirit and purpose of Article 9. Banning 'the entire press on the grounds that it constitutes a threat to the...government is a violation of the right to freedom of expression, and is the type of action that Article 9 is intended to proscribe. A free press is one of the tenets of a democratic society, and a valuable check on potential excesses by government'.[1241] Furthermore, the imprisonment of journalists

1233. *Good v. Botswana*, Communication No. 306/2005, 28th Activity Report 2009–2010, paras 193–194.

1234. *Ibid.*, paras 186–187; *Scanlen and Holderness v. Zimbabwe* Communication No. 297/2005, 26th Activity Report 2009, para. 81; *Egyptian Initiative for Personal Rights and INTERIGHTS v. Egypt*, Communication No. 323/2006 (2011), para. 243.

1235. Communication Nos 105/93, 128/94, 130/94, 152/96, 12th Activity Report, 1998–1999, para. 54. *See also Constitutional Rights Project, Civil Liberties Organisation and Media Rights Agenda v. Nigeria*, Communication Nos 140/94, 141/94, 145/95, 13th Activity Report 1999–2000, para. 36; *Egyptian Initiative for Personal Rights and INTERIGHTS v. Egypt*, Communication No. 323/2006 (2011), para. 244. *See also* African Charter on Democracy Art. 27(8).

1236. Adopted at the Commission's Thirty-Second Ordinary Session on 23 Oct. 2002, 16th Activity Report, 2002–2003. *See Zegveld and Ephrem v. Eritrea*, Communication No. 250/2002, 17th Activity Report 2003–2004, para. 59.

1237. *Amnesty International et al. v. Sudan*, Communication Nos 48/90, 50/91, 52/91, 89/93, 13th Activity Report 1999–2000, para. 80.

1238. *Good v. Botswana*, Communication No. 306/2005, 28th Activity Report 2009–2010, para. 197; *Egyptian Initiative for Personal Rights and INTERIGHTS v. Egypt*, Communication No. 323/2006 (2011), paras 246–247.

1239. Communication No. 228/99, 16th Activity Report 2002–2003, para. 53.

1240. Communication Nos 140/94, 141/94, 145/95, 13th Activity Report 1999–2000, para. 37.

1241. Communication No. 275/2003, 22nd Activity Report 2006–2007, paras 105, 107. *See also Constitutional Rights Project and Civil Liberties Organisation v. Nigeria*, Communication No. 102/93, 12th Activity Report 1998–1999, para. 59.

'deprives not only the journalists of their rights to freely express and disseminate their opinions, but also the public, of their right to information'.[1242] It constitutes a disproportionate interference in the exercise of the freedom of expression.[1243] Does a law that requires newspapers to register with a licensing authority and pay a registration fee interfere with the freedom of expression? The Commission addressed this question in *Media Rights Agenda and Constitutional Rights Project v. Nigeria* and held that in itself it did not. However, the fee should not be so excessive as to constitute a disincentive or restriction. In addition, the licensing authority should not be the puppet of the government giving it the power to prohibit the publication of any periodical they choose since this would invite censorship.[1244] However, in *Konaté v. Burkina Faso* the Human Rights Court was of the view that the licensing of journalists was unwarranted under Article 9 which guaranteed the freedom of expression to *all* citizens and not just journalists.[1245] Similarly, in *Scanlen and Holderness v. Zimbabwe*, the Commission held that the compulsory accreditation of journalists was incompatible with the freedom of expression.[1246]

251. Moreover, politicians, who thereby assume a public position, or other public figures must accept a wide degree of criticism.[1247] The press has a role as a public watchdog in politics and to restrict or prevent the press from passing legitimate comment, criticizing the government or making value judgments would amount to censorship.[1248] A prohibition on the publication of 'falsehoods' has also been found to be excessive.[1249]

1242. *Article 19 v. Eritrea*, Communication No. 275/2003, 22nd Activity Report 2006–2007, para. 106; *Sir Dawda K. Jawara v. Gambia*, Communication Nos 147/95 and 149/96, 13th Activity Report 1999–2000, para. 63. *See also Constitutional Rights Project and Civil Liberties Organisation v. Nigeria*, Communication No. 102/93, 12th Activity Report 1998–1999.

1243. *Konaté v. Burkina Faso*, African Court of Human and Peoples' Rights, App. No. 004/2013 (5 Dec. 2014), para. 164. *See M.J. Duffy, Konaté v. Burkina Faso: An Analysis of a Landmark Ruling on Criminal Defamation in Africa*, 6 J. Int'l Media & Entertainment Law (2015–2016) 1.

1244. Communication Nos 105/93, 128/94, 130/94, 152/96, 12th Activity Report, 1998–1999, paras 54–57.

1245. App. No. 004/2013 (5 Dec. 2014), paras 57–58.

1246. Communication No. 297/200526th Activity Report 2009, paras 84–98.

1247. *Media Rights Agenda and Constitutional Rights Project v. Nigeria*, Communication Nos 105/93, 128/94, 130/94, 152/96, 12th Activity Report 1998–1999, para. 74; *Good v. Botswana*, Communication No. 306/2005, 28th Activity Report 2009–2010, para. 198; *Konaté v. Burkina Faso*, African Court of Human and Peoples' Rights, App. No. 004/2013 (5 Dec. 2014), paras 155–156. A number of cases have been heard in Zimbabwe concerning 'insulting' the President, *see* , e.g., *Mwonzora v. State* (Constitutional Court of Zimbabwe, Judgment No. CCZ 17/2016, 23 Nov. 2016).

1248. *Media Rights Agenda and Constitutional Rights Project v. Nigeria*, Communication Nos 105/93, 128/94, 130/94, 152/96, 12th Activity Report 1998–1999, paras 73–75.

1249. *Scanlen and Holderness v. Zimbabwe*, Communication No. 297/2005, 26th Activity Report 2009, para. 117.

252. A distinction seems to be drawn between the two rights. Thus, while the right to receive information seems to be absolute[1250] the freedom to express an opinion must be exercised 'within the law'. It is generally accepted that the freedom of expression entails duties and responsibilities[1251] and therefore that some interference may be necessary, for example, to deal with libel or national security, but such restrictions must be provided for by laws that meet international human rights standards.[1252] Consequently restrictions must be provided by law, serve a legitimate interest and be necessary in a democratic society.[1253] If the exercise of the freedom of expression appears to offend the law then 'there should be due process and all affected persons should be allowed to seek redress in a court of law'.[1254] This limitation appears to be no more sweeping than that contained in comparable international documents where the limitation constitutes the exception to the general rule and the Commission has interpreted it in such a way that governments are not allowed to enact arbitrary or punitive measures which would unnecessarily curb these freedoms or amount to prior censorship.[1255] It has therefore stated that while according to Article 9(2), dissemination of opinions may be restricted by law, this 'does not mean that national law can set aside the right to disseminate one's opinions; this would make the protection of the

---

1250. *Constitutional Rights Project, Civil Liberties Organisation and Media Rights Agenda v. Nigeria*, Communication Nos 140/94, 141/94, 145/95, 13th Activity Report 1999–2000, para. 38; *Good v. Botswana*, Communication No. 306/2005, 28th Activity Report 2009–2010, para. 193. Compare *Scanlen and Holderness v. Zimbabwe*, Communication No. 297/2005, 26th Activity Report 2009, para. 121.

1251. *Zegveld and Ephrem v. Eritrea*, Communication No. 250/2002, 17th Activity Report 2003–2004, para. 59; *Scanlen and Holderness v. Zimbabwe*, Communication No. 297/2005, 26th Activity Report 2009, para. 108.

1252. *Zegveld and Ephrem v. Eritrea*, Communication No. 250/2002, 17th Activity Report 2003–2004, paras 59–60; *Good v. Botswana*, Communication No. 306/2005, 28th Activity Report 2009–2010, paras 187–189. Note also African Charter Art. 27(2). In *Constitutional Rights Project and Civil Liberties Organisation v. Nigeria*, Communication No. 102/93, 12th Activity Report 1998–1999, para. 59, the Commission found that given that Nigerian law made provision for a law of libel 'a government proscription of a publication, by name, is of particular concern.' *See also Media Rights Agenda and Constitutional Rights Project v. Nigeria*, Communication Nos 105/93, 128/94, 130/94, 152/96, 12th Activity Report 1998–1999, para. 71.

1253. *Egyptian Initiative for Personal Rights and INTERIGHTS v. Egypt*, Communication No. 323/2006 (2011), para. 248; *Monim Elgak, Osman Hummeida and Amir Suleiman (represented by FIDH and OMCT) v. Sudan*, Communication No. 379/09 (2014) para. 114. According to the Human Rights Court any criminal sanctions must be subject to the criteria of necessity and proportionality, *Konaté v. Burkina Faso*, African Court of Human and Peoples' Rights, App. No. 004/2013 (5 Dec. 2014), para. 166.

1254. *Zegveld and Ephrem v. Eritrea*, Communication No. 250/2002, 17th Activity Report 2003–2004, para. 60. *See also Scanlen and Holderness v. Zimbabwe*, Communication No. 297/2005, 26th Activity Report 2009, para. 102.

1255. *See supra* para. 248 where the Commission has stated that limitations must be both proportionate and necessary.

right to express one's opinions ineffective'.[1256] Criminal sanctions should be contemplated only for 'serious and very exceptional circumstances', such as incitement to international crimes, or incitement to hatred or violence.[1257]

253. Article 10 of the African Charter protects in broad terms the right of free association. This implies that individuals must be free to come together[1258] and to create and join political parties,[1259] trades unions, and professional bodies.[1260] It is therefore both an individual and a collective right.[1261] Thus, in *Civil Liberties Organisation in respect of Nigerian Bar Association v. Nigeria*, the African Commission held that, 'Freedom of association is enunciated as an individual right and is first and foremost a duty for the State to abstain from interfering with the free formation of associations. There must always be a general capacity for citizens to join, without State interference, in association in order to attain various ends.'[1262] Accordingly, the dissolution of a political party was deemed an excessive sanction since it had the right to hold public debates in accordance with democratic rules.[1263]

254. Again this provision is subject to limitations. As in Article 9, Article 10 contains a general exception in that the right is conditional on the individual abiding by the law. While concern had been expressed that the freedom guaranteed could be

---

1256. *Media Rights Agenda and Constitutional Rights Project v. Nigeria*, Communication Nos 105/93, 128/94, 130/94, 152/96, 12th Activity Report 1998–1999, para. 66; *Article 19 v. Eritrea*, Communication No. 275/2003, 22nd Activity Report 2006–2007, para. 105; *Scanlen and Holderness v. Zimbabwe*, Communication No. 297/2005, 26th Activity Report 2009, para. 121.

1257. *Malawi African Association et al. v. Mauritania*, Communication Nos 54/91, 61/91, 98/93, 164/97–196/97, 210/98, 13th Activity Report 1999–2000, para. 102; *Konaté v. Burkina Faso*, African Court of Human and Peoples' Rights, App. No. 004/2013 (5 Dec. 2014), para. 165. However, a number of judges were of the view that no criminalization of speech by criminal defamation laws could be justified under African Charter Art. 27(2), *ibid.* Separate Opinion of Judge Thompson, Judge Akuffo, Judge Ngoepe and Judge Tambala, para. 4.

1258. *The Law Office of Ghazi Suleiman v. Sudan*, Communication No. 228/99, 16th Activity Report 2002–2003, para. 56.

1259. *Amnesty International v. Zambia*, Communication No. 212/98, 12th Activity Report 1998–1999, para. 49; *Lawyers for Human Rights v. Swaziland*, Communication No. 251/2002, 18th Activity Report 2002–2003, para. 62.

1260. In *Ouko v. Kenya*, Communication No. 232/99, 14th Activity Report 2000–2001, para. 29, the Commission upheld a violation of Art. 10 with regard to the political persecution of a student union leader. In *Huri-Laws v. Nigeria*, Communication No. 225/98, 14th Activity Report 2000–2001, paras 47–48, the persecution of employees of a NGO amounted to violations of the African Charter Arts 9 and 10.

1261. *Monim Elgak, Osman Hummeida and Amir Suleiman (represented by FIDH and OMCT) v. Sudan*, Communication No. 379/09 (2014) para. 118.

1262. Communication No. 101/93, 8th Activity Report 1994–1995, para. 14. *See also International Pen, Constitutional Rights Project, Interights on behalf of Ken Saro-Wiwa Jr. and Civil Liberties Organisation v. Nigeria*, Communication Nos 137/94, 139/94, 154/96 and 161/97, 12th Activity Report 1998–1999, para. 108.

1263. *Interights, Institute for Human Rights and Development in Africa, and Association Mauritaniene des Droits de l'Homme v. Mauritania*, Communication No. 242/2001, 17th Activity Report 2003–2004, para. 80. In *Sir Dawda K. Jawara v. Gambia*, Communication Nos 147/95 and 149/96, 13th Activity Report 1999–2000, para. 68, the Commission condemned the banning of political parties.

rendered worthless the Commission has nevertheless held that limitations must be compatible with the obligations of States under the African Charter so that the right is not rendered illusory. It has expressed the view that while States may regulate the exercise of this right under domestic law such regulation must conform to the provisions of the African Charter which requires legitimate and proportionate reasons for any restrictions.[1264] Consequently, any national law on associations 'should include an objective description that makes it possible to determine the criminal nature' of an organization.[1265]

255. Article 10(2) contains a correlative right in that 'no one may be compelled to join an association'. As the African Court on Human and Peoples' Rights has observed, the freedom of association implies the freedom not to associate.[1266] However, this guarantee is made subject to the obligation of solidarity contained in Article 29 of the African Charter which imposes upon the individual duties towards the family, the community and the State. While the sentiment of these obligations may be laudable in that they reflect traditional African values and attempt to imbue the individual with civic values the potential for abuse exists. For example, individuals may be compelled to join a political party not of their choice under the guise that it preserves and strengthens social and national solidarity.

256. Article 11 of the African Charter guarantees the right of assembly, which includes demonstrations or rallies,[1267] subject to certain restrictions and limitations. The right of assembly cannot be absolute because it impacts on the rights of others and because of the threat of disorder and these reasonable restrictions can be found in all democratic societies. At the same time States must do their utmost to uphold this right.[1268] As has already been discussed in relation to other limitations, the African Commission has sought to ensure that restrictions on this right are objectively justified

1264. *Interights, Institute for Human Rights and Development in Africa, and Association Mauritaniene des Droits de l'Homme v. Mauritania*, Communication No. 242/2001, 17th Activity Report 2003–2004, paras 76–79; *Monim Elgak, Osman Hummeida and Amir Suleiman (represented by FIDH and OMCT) v. Sudan*, Communication No. 379/09 (2014) para. 118. *See supra* paras 213–217, for fuller discussion of this topic.

1265. *Malawi African Association et al. v. Mauritania*, Communication Nos 54/91, 61/91, 98/93, 164/97–196/97, 210/98, 13th Activity Report 1999–2000, para. 107.

1266. *Tanganyika Law Society et al. v. Tanzania*, African Court of Human and Peoples' Rights, App. Nos 009/2011 and 011/2011 (14 Jun. 2013), para. 113.

1267. *International Pen, Constitutional Rights Project, Interights on behalf of Ken Saro-Wiwa Jr. and Civil Liberties Organisation v. Nigeria*, Communication Nos 137/94, 139/94, 154/96 and 161/97, 12th Activity Report 1998–1999, para. 106; *The Law Office of Ghazi Suleiman v. Sudan*, Communication No. 228/99, 16th Activity Report 2002–2003, para. 56.

1268. *Gunme et al. v. Cameroon,* Communication No. 266/2003, 26th Activity Report 2008–2009, para. 138.

and are not excessive or arbitrary.[1269] A blanket ban on the formation of political parties thus violated the right of assembly.[1270]

257. The Commission has stressed the close relationship between the freedom of expression, the right of association and the right of assembly,[1271] considering expression as one of the objectives of the latter.[1272] This affinity is considered particularly important in the case of political parties, given 'their essential role for the maintenance of pluralism and the proper functioning of democracy'.[1273]

258. Article 12 of the African Charter secures various aspects of the right of free movement, described by the Commission as 'a fundamental human right to all individuals within States',[1274] including the right to enter and leave a country.[1275] First, under paragraph 1, individuals, of whatever nationality, can move freely within the State.[1276] Second, they can elect where they wish to reside, both important considerations

---

1269. *Malawi African Association et al. v. Mauritania*, Communication Nos 54/91, 61/91, 98/93, 164/97–196/97, 210/98, 13th Activity Report 1999–2000, para. 111; *Lawyers for Human Rights v. Swaziland*, Communication No. 251/2002, 18th Activity Report 2002–2003, para. 60; *Gunme et al. v. Cameroon,* Communication No. 266/2003, 26th Activity Report 2008–2009, para. 138; Resolution on the Right to Freedom of Association, adopted at the Commission's Eleventh Ordinary Session, 1992, 5th Activity Report, 1991–1992. *See supra* paras 213–217 for fuller discussion of this topic.

1270. *Sir Dawda K. Jawara v. Gambia*, Communication Nos 147/95 and 149/96, 13th Activity Report 1999–2000, para. 69; *Lawyers for Human Rights v. Swaziland*, Communication No. 251/2002, 18th Activity Report 2002–2003, para. 60.

1271. *International Pen, Constitutional Rights Project, Interights on behalf of Ken Saro-Wiwa Jr. and Civil Liberties Organisation v. Nigeria*, Communication Nos 137/94, 139/94, 154/96 and 161/97, 12th Activity Report 1998–1999, para. 110.

1272. *Interights, Institute for Human Rights and Development in Africa, and Association Mauritaniene des Droits de l'Homme v. Mauritania*, Communication No. 242/2001, 17th Activity Report 2003–2004, para. 80.

1273. *Ibid.*

1274. *Sudan Human Rights Organization and Sudan Centre for Housing Rights and Evictions v. Sudan* Communication Nos 279/03, 296/05, 28th Activity Report, 2010, para. 187. In principle, Art. 12 can also be invoked by refugees, *Doebbler v. Sudan*, Communication No. 235/2000, 27th Activity Report 2009), para. 167.

1275. *Sudan Human Rights Organization and Sudan Centre for Housing Rights and Evictions v. Sudan* Communication Nos 279/03, 296/05, 28th Activity Report, 2010, para. 187. In *Sir Dawda K. Jawara v. Gambia*, Communication Nos 147/95 and 149/96, 13th Activity Report 1999–2000, para. 70, the Commission held that travel restrictions violated Art. 12. This was also the case in *Open Society Justice Initiative v. Côte d'Ivoire*, Communication No. 318/06 (2015) para. 161, where the difficulties of the Dioula community in obtaining identity and travel documents interfered with their freedom of movement. *See also Ouko v. Kenya*, Communication No. 232/99, 14th Activity Report 2000–2001, para. 31. For a national decision *see Nyirongo v. Attorney-General* (1990–1992) Z.R. 92 (SC).

1276. *The Law Office of Ghazi Suleiman v. Sudan*, Communication No. 228/99, 16th Activity Report 2002–2003, para. 60.

in view of apartheid's restrictions on these rights.[1277] Flight because of fear of persecution is incompatible with this right.[1278] Particularly important has been the Commission's condemnation of forced evictions and population displacement as a result of the violence in Darfur.[1279] The individual's right to freedom of movement or residence is guaranteed provided the person 'abides by the law'. This not only suggests that the individual must be lawfully within the territory, having complied with immigration requirements, but that their continued presence is contingent on observing domestic law, a requirement that seems to be wholly legitimate.[1280]

259. Article 12(2) grants the individual the right to leave and return to a State subject to restrictions imposed by law for the protection of national security, law and order, public health or morality.[1281] In principle, therefore, a person should not be denied a passport but inability to leave as a result of having to serve a lawful prison sentence would not violate this right. In *Amnesty International v. Zambia*, the African Commission held that the State must prove that it is justified in invoking these conditions and that the rules of natural justice must apply.[1282] With specific reference to the limitation on the ground of law and order the Commission stated that the State had to prove that the individuals were indeed a danger to law and order; that they posed a 'likely' danger was too vague.[1283] The right of an individual to enter their own State

---

1277. In *Malawi African Association et al. v. Mauritania*, Communication Nos 54/91, 61/91, 98/93, 164/97–196/97, 210/98, 13th Activity Report 1999–2000, para. 126, the Commission found that the mass eviction of people from their property violated Art. 12(1). The compulsory mass transfer of people from one State to another has been held to breach this provision, *Democratic Republic of Congo v. Burundi, Rwanda and Uganda*, Communication No. 227/99, 20th Activity Report 2005–2006, para. 81.

1278. *Sudan Human Rights Organization and Sudan Centre for Housing Rights and Evictions v. Sudan* Communication Nos 279/03, 296/05, 28th Activity Report, 2010, para. 190; *Monim Elgak, Osman Hummeida and Amir Suleiman (represented by FIDH and OMCT) v. Sudan*, Communication No. 379/09 (2014) para. 123.

1279. *Sudan Human Rights Organization and Sudan Centre for Housing Rights and Evictions v. Sudan* Communication Nos 279/03, 296/05, 28th Activity Report, 2010, paras 188–190.

1280. But *see Modise v. Botswana*, Communication No. 97/93, 14th Activity Report 2000–2001, para. 93. In *Rencontre Africaine pour la Defense des Droits de l'Homme v. Zambia*, Communication No. 71/92, 10th Activity Report 1996–1997, para. 31, the Commission stated that it would not dispute the right of the State to bring legal action against illegal migrants and to deport them if justified.

1281. *Mouvement Burkinabé des Droits de l'Homme et des Peuples v. Burkina Faso*, Communication No. 204/97, 14th Activity Report 2000–2001, para. 47. In *Rights International v. Nigeria*, Communication No. 215/98, 13th Activity Report 1999–2000, para. 30, the Commission held that the fact that the victim had been forced to flee his country for his safety violated Art. 12(1)–(2). *See Nyirongo v. Attorney-General* (1990–1992) Z.R. 92 (SC).

1282. Communication No. 212/98, 12th Activity Report 1998–1999, para. 42.

1283. *Ibid.*

is also guaranteed[1284] but the African Charter, in accordance with international law, restricts the right of entry to nationals only.[1285] However, it should be observed that the African Charter is unique in seemingly making the nationals' right to enter their own country subject to the restrictions. This provision would appear to be incompatible with international law.[1286]

260. A positive feature is Article 12(3) which grants a right to seek and obtain asylum. This provision is inspired by, and is a complement to, the OAU Convention on Refugees 1969 and is considered in more detail below.[1287] Nevertheless, it is worth observing that the Commission has stated that this provision includes 'a general protection of all those who are subject to persecution, that they may seek refuge in another state'.[1288]

261. Article 12(4) protects a non-national who is legally within another State from summary expulsion as such sanctions can only be legitimate by virtue of a decision taken in accordance with the law. While this provision is too broadly worded and fails to stipulate any procedural guarantees, such as the right to be given reasons against expulsion, the jurisprudence of the Commission requires that the provision must be interpreted to prevent arbitrary expulsions.[1289] Consequently, expulsions must be consistent with the due process of law;[1290] States must have laws in place to regulate this area which must meet international standards.[1291] Furthermore, if the procedure

---

1284. *Democratic Republic of Congo v. Burundi, Rwanda and Uganda*, Communication No. 227/99, 20th Activity Report, 2005–2006, para. 81. In *Huri-Laws v. Nigeria*, Communication No. 225/98, 14th Activity Report 2000–2001, paras 50–51, the Commission held that harassment and arrests at re-entry points infringed the freedom of movement. Fear of persecution upon return also constitutes a violation of Art. 12(2), *Monim Elgak, Osman Hummeida and Amir Suleiman (represented by FIDH and OMCT) v. Sudan*, Communication No. 379/09 (2014) para. 126.

1285. General comment 15, UN Doc. HRI/GEN/1/Rev.2, para. 5. However, this right may also extend to family members who are aliens, *Dow v. Attorney-General* [1992] L.R.C. (Const) 623 (Botswana Court of Appeal); *Rattigan and Others v. Chief Immigration Officer of Zimbabwe* 1995 (2) SA 182 (ZS).

1286. Compare International Covenant on Civil and Political Rights Art. 12(4) (16 Dec. 1966), 999 U.N.T.S. 171, American Convention on Human Rights Art. 22(5) (22 November 1969), O.A.S.T.S. No. 36, ECHR Fourth Protocol 4 Art. 3(2) (16 Sept. 1963), E.T.S. No. 46; *East African Asians v. United Kingdom*, 3 E.H.R.R. 76 (1981); D.J. Harris, M. O'Boyle & C. Warbrick, *Law of the European Convention on Human Rights* (2nd edn, Oxford: Oxford University Press, 2009), 743–744.

1287. *See infra* Ch. 3, para. 404.

1288. *Organisation Mondiale contre la Torture et al. v. Rwanda,* Communication Nos 27/89, 46/91, 49/91, 99/93, 10th Activity Report 1993–1994, para. 30.

1289. *Organisation Mondiale contre la Torture et al. v. Rwanda*, Communication Nos 27/89, 46/91, 49/91, 99/93, 10th Activity Report 1993–1994, para. 30.

1290. *Institute for Human Rights and Development in Africa v. Angola*, Communication No. 292/2004, 24th Activity Report 2008, paras 63–65; *Zimbabwe Lawyers for Human Rights and the Institute for Human Rights and Development (on behalf of Andrew Barclay Meldrum) v. Zimbabwe*, Communication No. 294/2004, 26th Activity Report 2008–2009, paras 114–115.

1291. *Good v. Botswana*, Communication No. 306/2005, 28th Activity Report 2009–2010, paras 203–204.

for expulsion entails arrest, the safeguards relating to deprivation of liberty are applicable, as is the right to have the case reviewed.[1292]

262. Finally, Article 12(5) prohibits the mass expulsion of non-nationals aimed at national, racial, ethnic or religious groups. Expulsion based purely on nationality is therefore forbidden.[1293] A link thus exists between this provision and Article 2 of the African Charter that enshrines the principle of non-discrimination.[1294] The rationale for the proscription contained in Article 12(5) was that 'the drafters of the Charter believed that mass expulsions presented a special threat to human rights'.[1295] In *Rencontre Africaine pour la Defense des Droits de l'Homme v. Zambia*, which concerned the expulsion of over five hundred illegal residents, the Commission stated that while the African Charter did not prohibit deportations as such Zambia's right to deport people did not justify the manner in which it had done so.[1296] Again the Commission requires that due process be observed.[1297]

263. Article 13(1) of the African Charter broadly guarantees the right to participate freely in the government of one's country, either directly or through freely chosen representatives.[1298] A right to participate, and stand,[1299] in elections on the basis of

---

1292. *Organisation Mondiale contre la Torture et al. v. Rwanda*, Communication Nos 27/89, 46/91, 49/91, 99/93, 10th Activity Report 1993–1994, para 34; *Good v. Botswana*, Communication No. 306/2005, 28th Activity Report 2009–2010, para. 205; *Amnesty International v. Zambia*, Communication No. 212/98, 12th Activity Report 1998–1999.

1293. *Rencontre Africaine pour la Defense des Droits de l'Homme v. Zambia*, Communication No. 71/92, 10th Activity Report, 1996–1997; *Organisation Mondiale contre la Torture et al. v. Rwanda*, Communication Nos 27/89, 46/91, 49/91, 99/93, 10th Activity Report 1993–1994; *African Institute for Human Rights and Development (on behalf of Sierra Leonean refugees in Guinea v. Republic of Guinea*, Communication No. 249/2002, 20th Activity Report 2005–2006.

1294. *Rencontre Africaine pour la Defense des Droits de l'Homme v. Zambia*, Communication No. 71/92, 10th Activity Report, 1996–1997, para. 21; *Organisation Mondiale contre la Torture et al. v. Rwanda*, Communication Nos 27/89, 46/91, 49/91, 99/93, 10th Activity Report 1993–1994, para. 32; *African Institute for Human Rights and Development (on behalf of Sierra Leonean refugees in Guinea v. Republic of Guinea*, Communication No. 249/2002, 20th Activity Report 2005–2006, para. 69.

1295. *Rencontre Africaine pour la Defense des Droits de l'Homme v. Zambia*, Communication No. 71/92, 10th Activity Report 1996–1997, para. 20; *Institute for Human Rights and Development in Africa v. Angola*, Communication No. 292/2004, 24th Activity Report 2008, para. 68.

1296. *Rencontre Africaine pour la Defense des Droits de l'Homme v. Zambia*, Communication No. 71/92, 10th Activity Report 1996–1997, para. 23. *See also African Institute for Human Rights and Development (on behalf of Sierra Leonean refugees in Guinea v. Republic of Guinea*, Communication No. 249/2002, 20th Activity Report, 2005–2006.

1297. *Institute for Human Rights and Development in Africa v. Angola*, Communication No. 292/2004, 24th Activity Report 2008, para. 70.

1298. *See also* the African Charter on Democracy. Independent and impartial electoral bodies are also required, *Actions pour la Protection des Droit de l'Homme (APDH) v. Côte d'Ivoire*, African Court of Human and Peoples' Rights, App. No. 001/2014 (18 Nov. 2016) paras 135–136.

1299. *Modise v. Botswana*, Communication No. 97/93, 14th Activity Report 2000–2001, para. 95; *Mouvement Ivorien des Droits Humains (MIDH) v. Côte d'Ivoire*, Communication No. 246/2002, 25th Activity Report 2008, para. 77. *See also Open Society Justice Initiative v. Côte d'Ivoire*, Communication No. 318/06 (2015) paras 165–169.

universal adult suffrage and a right to elected representative government[1300] seems to be secured by this provision according to the Commission. Indeed, the Commission has proceeded to describe this right as 'a fundamental civil liberty and human right, and should be enjoyed by citizens without discrimination'.[1301] Thus the right to 'participate freely in government entails, among other things, the right to vote for the representative of one's choice. An inevitable corollary of this right that the results of free expression of the will of the voters are respected; otherwise, the right to vote freely is meaningless'.[1302] The right to vote has been described as the 'bedrock of modern democratic systems'.[1303] In addition, citizens can participate in governance through political parties.[1304] Hence a ban on individuals or political parties from participating in political activity contravenes this provision.[1305] Similarly, the annulment of the results of democratic elections.[1306] These opinions are important in light of recent events which witnessed the manipulation of the electoral process in Kenya in 2007 and Zimbabwe in 2008 and the extreme reluctance of the respective Governments to accept the outcome of the people's decision. Too many ruling regimes in Africa simply pay lip service to the values of liberal democracy. They observe the trappings of democracy and expect that merely holding elections, neither free nor fair necessarily, will suffice.[1307] They therefore lack popular support or genuine democratic mandate.[1308]

1300. *See also* African Charter on Democracy Art. 3(3) and Art. 4(2). Under Arts 17 and 32(7) thereof State Parties commit themselves to holding regular, transparent free and fair elections.

1301. *Mouvement Ivorien des Droits Humains (MIDH) v. Côte d'Ivoire*, Communication No. 246/2002, 25th Activity Report 2008, para. 77.

1302. *Constitutional Rights Project and Civil Liberties Organisation v. Nigeria*, Communication No. 102/93, 12th Activity Report 1998–1999, para. 50.

1303. *Open Society Justice Initiative v. Côte d'Ivoire*, Communication No. 318/06 (2015) para. 164.

1304. *Lawyers for Human Rights v. Swaziland*, Communication No. 251/2002, 18th Activity Report 2002–2003, para. 63. *See also* African Charter on Democracy Arts 3(11), 27(1) and 32(6).

1305. *Sir Dawda K. Jawara v. Gambia*, Communication Nos 147/95 and 149/96, 13th Activity Report 1999–2000, paras 66–67; *Lawyers for Human Rights v. Swaziland*, Communication No. 251/2002, 18th Activity Report 2002–2003, paras 62–63. In *Tanganyika Law Society et al. v. Tanzania*, African Court of Human and Peoples' Rights, App. Nos 009/2011 and 011/2011 (14 Jun. 2013), para. 109, the African Court on Human and Peoples' Rights held that a prohibition on individual candidatures in elections was in breach of the African Charter Art. 13(1).

1306. *Constitutional Rights Project and Civil Liberties Organisation v. Nigeria*, Communication No. 102/93, 12th Activity Report 1998–1999, para. 53.

1307. *See* the UK Foreign and Commonwealth Office's critique of the disputed 2008 election in Zimbabwe, conducted in an atmosphere of intimidation and violence, *United Kingdom Foreign & Commonwealth Office Annual Report on Human Rights 2008* http://www.gov.uk/government/publications/systems/annual-report-on-human-rights-2008. In a landmark decision, the Supreme Court of Kenya annulled the result of the presidential election held in August 2017 as a result of numerous irregularities and illegalities on the part of the Electoral Commission, *Odinga and Others v. Independent Electoral and Boundaries Commission and Others* Supreme Court of Kenya, Judgment of 20 Sept. 2017.

1308. The OAU acknowledged the relationship between poor governance and human rights abuses, *see* Grand Bay Declaration para. 8(g)–(i), (p)(r). The UN Commission on Human Rights has declared that democracy fosters the full realization of human rights, Res. 1999/57, UN Doc. E/CN.4/1999/167, 194. *See* further R. Murray, *Human Rights in Africa: From the OAU to the African Union* (Cambridge: Cambridge University Press, 2004), 235–266.

The Commission has affirmed that the best form of government is one elected by and accountable to the people.[1309] It has therefore condemned military seizures of power as a clear violation of the fundamental principle of democracy that governments should be based on the consent of the people and has called upon military governments to respect the right of free participation in government and, additionally, to hand over political power to democratically elected governments.[1310] In fact, the Commission has pronounced that one of its roles is that of promoting democracy in Africa.[1311] It may be that the Commission was emboldened to adopt this stance by the AU's explicit commitment to an agenda of democracy, human rights, and good governance.[1312] The Commission has held that the right contained in Article 13(1) can be denied only in limited circumstances, either by reason of legal incapacity or because the individual is not a citizen of the State.[1313] However, while the Commission has accepted that restrictions on the basis of nationality are understandable in the context of high offices of the nation it considers it unjustifiable and discriminatory to impose such restrictions on citizens by virtue of descent.[1314]

264. It should be noted that the right in Article 13(1) contains a limitation in that participation in government must be in accordance with the law. Consequently, States have the right to legislate to regulate elections, to determine voting age, criteria for eligibility, etc. but these must be objective, reasonable, and justifiable and must not negate the essence of the right.[1315] In *Interights, Institute for Human Rights and*

1309. Resolution on Electoral Process and Participatory Governance, adopted at the Commission's Nineteenth Ordinary Session, 1996, 9th Activity Report, 1995–1996. In *Mouvement Ivorien des Droits Humains (MIDH) v. Côte d'Ivoire*, Communication No. 246/2002, 25th Activity Report 2008, para. 77, the Commission expressed the view that a freely elected government 'provide the soundest guarantee that the basic human rights will be observed and protected'. In *Constitutional Rights Project and Civil Liberties Organisation v. Nigeria*, Communication No. 102/93, 12th Activity Report 1998–1999, para. 48, the Commission stated that the 'criteria for what constitutes free and fair elections are internationally agreed upon, and international observers are put in place to apply these criteria. It would be contrary to the logic of international law if a national government with a vested interest in the outcome of an election, were the final arbiter of whether the election took place in accordance with international standards'.

1310. Resolution on the Human Rights Situation in Africa, Resolution on The Gambia, and Resolution on Nigeria, adopted at the Commission's Sixteenth Ordinary Session, 1994, 8th Activity Report, 1994–1995.

1311. *The Law Office of Ghazi Suleiman v. Sudan*, Communication No. 228/99, 16th Activity Report 2002–2003, para. 53.

1312. Among the AU's objectives and principles, as set out in the Constitutive Act Arts 3(g) and 4(m), are the promotion of, and respect for, democratic principles and institutions, popular participation and good governance, human rights, and the rule of law. These aims are reinforced by the African Charter on Democracy.

1313. *Purohit and Moore v. The Gambia*, Communication No. 241/2001, 16th Activity Report 2002–2003, para. 75. The Commission proceeded to find that mentally disabled persons could be excluded from political participation only on the basis of objective and reasonable criteria established by law, *ibid.*, para. 76.

1314. *Mouvement Ivorien des Droits Humains (MIDH) v. Côte d'Ivoire*, Communication No. 246/2002, 25th Activity Report 2008, paras 80–87.

1315. *Mouvement Ivorien des Droits Humains (MIDH) v. Côte d'Ivoire*, Communication No. 246/2002, 25th Activity Report 2008, para. 83.

Development in Africa, and Association Mauritanienne des Droits de l'Homme v. Islamic Republic of Mauritania, the Commission accepted that there were circumstances in which restrictions could be imposed upon political parties, for example, if they incited violence or threatened public order, but that any restrictions had to be proportionate, based on a legitimate public purpose and conform to international human rights standards.[1316] While some regimes may no doubt be tempted to invoke this limitation to undermine the political opposition it is nevertheless gratifying to observe that the Commission itself is committed to democratic principles and pluralism.[1317]

265. Article 13(2) gives the citizen the right of equal access to the public service of one's country but the concept of 'public service' is not defined.[1318] It is unclear whether this refers to use of social services such as educational or health facilities,[1319] and/or employment opportunities.[1320] However, the Commission has adopted the view that it refers to political participation.[1321] Article 13(3) grants every individual, thereby including non-nationals, the right of equal access to public property and services before the law.

266. Article 14 of the African Charter guarantees the right to property, which is one enjoyed by every individual.[1322] The Commission has described the right to property as 'a fundamental right in democratic and liberal societies'.[1323] According to the Commission it includes 'the principle of ownership and peaceful enjoyment of property',[1324] the 'right to use, enjoy and dispose of something in an exclusive and absolute manner'[1325] and the effective benefit of this right 'necessarily includes a right to have access to property of one's own and the right not for one's property to be

1316. Communication No. 242/2001, 17th Activity Report 2003–2004.

1317. *Ibid.*, para. 84.

1318. Compare the European Court of Justice's interpretation of 'public service' in Treaty on the Functioning of the European Union Art. 45(4) (13 Dec. 2007), [2010] O.J. C 83/47, as referring to activities which involve participation in the exercise of powers conferred by public law or safeguard the general interests of the State, such as the armed forces, the police, or the judiciary, Case 149/79 *Commission v. Belgium* [1980] ECR 3881; Case 225/85 *Commission v. Italy* [1987] ECR 2625.

1319. Note that the African Charter on Democracy Art. 41, requires States Parties to provide and enable access to basic social services.

1320. Compare *Glasenapp v. Germany* Series A, Vol. 104 (1986) and *Kosiek v. Germany* Series A, Vol. 105 (1986) where the European Court of Human Rights held that the ECHR does not recognize a right of recruitment to the civil service.

1321. *Modise v. Botswana*, Communication No. 97/93, 14th Activity Report 2000–2001, para. 96.

1322. *Dino Noca v. Democratic Republic of the Congo*, Communication No. 286/2004 (2012), para. 128. However, the Human Rights Court has held that the right to property may additionally be a collective right, *African Commission on Human and Peoples' Rights v. Kenya*, African Court of Human and Peoples' Rights, App. No. 006/2012 (26 May 2017) para. 123.

1323. *Interights et al. v. Mauritania*, Communication No. 373/2006, 28th Activity Report 2009–2010, para. 43.

1324. *Ibid.*, para. 44.

1325. *Mbianku v. Cameroon*, Communication No. 389/10 (2015) para. 106.

removed'.[1326] Property has been given a wider interpretation to include other assets,[1327] including land.[1328] Traditional lands belonging to indigenous communities also constitute property.[1329] As a necessary corollary, and in association with other rights, it extends to housing.[1330] A burning question that arises concerns the compatibility of African customary laws or religious law, where women are often disadvantaged in terms of family law and succession, with this provision in association with Article 2 of the African Charter.[1331] A curious decision is that of *Rabah v. Mauritania* where the Commission held that for a mother to deprive her children of their inheritance for the benefit of a third party with no specific reason contravened Article 14.[1332] This conclusion led to what appears to be a unique occurrence in the Commission's practice, the appending of a dissenting opinion.[1333] Commissioner El Hassan could not see how the law in Mauritania, which gave the owner of property, a rational and mature person, the freedom to dispose of property as she saw fit, could be considered incompatible with the African Charter. In fact, in his view, the Commission was in essence restraining the owner from disposing freely of her property and depriving the recipient of property he had lawfully inherited.

1326. *Media Rights Agenda and Constitutional Rights Project v. Nigeria*, Communication Nos 105/93, 128/94, 130/94, 152/96, 12th Activity Report 1998–1999, para. 77. *See also Constitutional Rights Project, Civil Liberties Organisation and Media Rights Agenda v. Nigeria*, Communication Nos 140/94, 141/94, 145/95, 13th Activity Report 1999–2000, para. 54. The Commission has also referred to 'the right to undisturbed possession, use and control of...property however the owner(s) deem fit', *Centre for Minority Rights Development (Kenya) and Minority Rights Group International on behalf of Endorois Welfare Council v. Kenya*, Communication No. 276/2003, 27th Activity Report 2009, para. 186.

1327. In *Bissangou v. Republic of Congo*, Communication No. 253/2002, 21st Activity Report 2005–2006, para. 76, the Commission found that monetary compensation awarded by a court judgment was to be considered an asset.

1328. *Malawi African Association et al. v. Mauritania*. Communication Nos 54/91, 61/91, 98/93/164/97–196/97, 210/98, 13th Activity Report 1999–2000, para. 128; *Centre for Minority Rights Development (Kenya) and Minority Rights Group International on behalf of Endorois Welfare Council v. Kenya*, Communication No. 276/2003, 27th Activity Report 2009, para. 186.

1329. *Centre for Minority Rights Development (Kenya) and Minority Rights Group International on behalf of Endorois Welfare Council v. Kenya*, Communication No. 276/2003, 27th Activity Report 2009, para. 187. The Commission proceeded to state that special measures may be necessary to secure such property, and that at the very least, traditional possession of land is equivalent to full title, *ibid.*, paras 187–209. *See also African Commission on Human and Peoples' Rights v. Kenya*, African Court of Human and Peoples' Rights, App. No. 006/2012 (26 May 2017) paras 126–128.

1330. *Mbianku v. Cameroon*, Communication No. 389/10 (2015) paras 121–123.

1331. *See* the controversial judgment of the Supreme Court of Zimbabwe in *Magaya v. Magaya* [1999] 3 L.R.C. 35, noted in 43 J.A.L. 248 (1999). However, in *Bhe and Others v. The Magistrate, Khayelitsha and Others* 2005 (1) SA 580 (CC) the Constitutional Court of South Africa held that the African customary rule of male primogeniture in relation to the inheritance of property discriminated against women and illegitimate children.

1332. Communication No. 197/97, 17th Activity Report, 2003–2004.

1333. Neither the African Charter nor the Commission's Rules of Procedure make explicit provision for dissenting opinions. According to the Rules, revised in 2010, one Rapporteur is appointed for each Communication, Rule 97(1).

267. The right to property is not absolute[1334] and its enjoyment of may be limited or encroached upon 'in the interest of public need or in the general interest of the community' in accordance with the law, which means that interference with, or deprivation of, property must not be arbitrary or without good reason.[1335] The Commission has held that this test is conjunctive[1336] and must meet a higher threshold with regard

1334. *Institute for Human Rights and Development in Africa v. Angola*, Communication No. 292/2004, 24th Activity Report 2008, para. 73; *Dino Noca v. Democratic Republic of the Congo*, Communication No. 286/2004 (2012), para. 143.

1335. *Media Rights Agenda and Constitutional Rights Project v. Nigeria*, Communication Nos 105/93, 128/94, 130/94, 152/96, 12th Activity Report, 1998–1999, para. 77; *Constitutional Rights Project, Civil Liberties Organisation and Media Rights Agenda v. Nigeria*, Communication Nos 140/94, 141/94, 145/95, 13th Activity Report 1999–2000, para. 54; *African Institute for Human Rights and Development (on behalf of Sierra Leonean refugees in Guinea v. Republic of Guinea*, Communication No. 249/2002, 20th Activity Report, 2005–2006; *Scanlen and Holderness v. Zimbabwe*, Communication No. 297/2005, 26th Activity Report 2009, para. 179; *Interights et al. v. Mauritania*, Communication No. 373/2006, 28th Activity Report 2009–2010, para. 45; *Open Society Justice Initiative v. Côte d'Ivoire*, Communication No. 318/06 (2015) para. 174; *The Nubian Community in Kenya v. Kenya*, Communication No. 317/06 (2015), para. 165. The Commission has further stated that any limitation must be proportionate to a legitimate need, *Centre for Minority Rights Development (Kenya) and Minority Rights Group International on behalf of Endorois Welfare Council v. Kenya*, Communication No. 276/2003, 27th Activity Report 2009, paras 213–215; *Dino Noca v. Democratic Republic of the Congo*, Communication No. 286/2004 (2012), para. 145. Property can be regulated by the State to meet, for example, environmental standards, health and safety standards, building and planning regulations, and rent controls, UN Doc. E/CN.4/1993/15, pp. 75–76. The jurisprudence of the European Court of Human Rights demonstrates that the State has wide powers to take and to control the use of property, Harris, O'Boyle, Warbrick, 677–692. The policy of land redistribution pursued by the Zimbabwean Government in recent years has proven disastrous. The expropriation of farms in Zimbabwe for the purpose of social equity was held to be legitimate in the public interest, *Davies v. Minister of Land, Agriculture and Water Development* 1997 1 SA 228 (ZS). However, the Zimbabwean Government was either unable or unwilling to abide by its own laws and follow proper procedure, permitting or instigating the infamous violent farm invasions. This anarchical situation was condemned by the Supreme Court, which found that resettlement in such circumstances was unconstitutional, being incompatible with the right to property and the protection from arbitrary search or entry, *Commercial Farmers Union v. Minister of Lands, Agriculture and Rural Resettlement and Others* 2001 2 SA 925 (ZS). The Supreme Court's defence of constitutionalism in turn led to the ousting of the firmly independent justices referred to *infra* , para. 286. The reconstituted Supreme Court subsequently upheld the constitutionality of the land resettlement programme, *Minister of Lands, Agriculture and Rural Resettlement & Others v. Commercial Farmers Union* (SC 111/01). *See also Mike Campbell (Pvt) Ltd. v. Minister of National Security Responsible for Land, Land Reform and Resettlement & Others* (SC 49/07). However, in *Mike Campbell (Pvt) Ltd. et al. v. The Republic of Zimbabwe* the SADC Tribunal, in its first judgment, held that Zimbabwe's land reform programme was in breach of the SADC Treaty, SADC (T) Case No. 2/2007 (2008), http://www.saflii.org/sa/cases/SADCT/2008/2.pdf.

1336. *Centre for Minority Rights Development (Kenya) and Minority Rights Group International on behalf of Endorois Welfare Council v. Kenya*, Communication No. 276/2003, 27th Activity Report 2009, para. 211.

to encroachment on traditional lands.[1337] If evictions are contemplated then prior, bona fides consultation is required.[1338] The fact that only a limited number of people may be affected is immaterial.[1339] It should be observed that the African Charter makes no express reference as to the appropriate level of compensation for the expropriation of property.[1340] However, in *Centre for Minority Rights Development (Kenya) and Minority Rights Group International on behalf of Endorois Welfare Council v. Kenya*, the Commission held that where it is not possible to return land, the dispossessed owners should, *inter alia*, receive compensation at full replacement cost prior to their the dispossession.[1341] The Commission found a violation of this provision in *Malawi African Association et al. v. Mauritania* where the property of black Mauritanians had been confiscated and looted as part of a campaign of harassment.[1342] Another violation was found in *Union Interafricaine des Droits de l'Homme et al. v. Angola* where the mass expulsion of West Africans resulted in the loss of property.[1343]

268. It is interesting to note that the right to property does not extend to tax evasion since Article 29(6) of the African Charter, in another cultural variation, imposes an obligation upon the individual to pay taxes according to the law in the interest of society.

IV. Social and Economic Rights

269. Articles 15–18 of the African Charter provide for economic, social and cultural rights, otherwise classified as second generation rights. Some of these rights

1337. *Ibid.*, para. 212. *See also African Commission on Human and Peoples' Rights v. Kenya*, African Court of Human and Peoples' Rights, App. No. 006/2012 (26 May 2017) para. 130.

1338. *Ibid.*, para. 226; *The Nubian Community in Kenya v. Kenya*, Communication No. 317/06 (2015), para. 165.

1339. *Ivorien Human Rights Movement (MIDH) v. Côte d'Ivoire*, Communication No. 262/2002, 26th Activity Report 2008–2009, para. 77.

1340. At present international law requires compensation to be prompt, adequate and effective but developing States maintain that the less rigid standard of adequate compensation is appropriate, *see Texaco v. Libya* 17 I.L.M. 1 (1978) where the arbitrator observed that developed States regarded the latter formulation as *contra legem*. In *Institute for Human Rights and Development in Africa v. Angola*, Communication No. 292/2004, 24th Activity Report 2008, para. 73, and in *Dino Noca v. Democratic Republic of the Congo*, Communication No. 286/2004 (2012), para. 147, the Commission referred to 'adequate compensation'. Note that in *Lithgow v. United Kingdom* Series A, Vol. 102 (1986) the European Court of Human Rights declared that under the ECHR First Protocol Art. 1 (20 Mar. 1952), E.T.S. No. 9, the taking of property without payment of an amount reasonably related to its value would normally constitute a disproportionate interference which could not be considered justifiable.

1341. Communication No. 276/2003, 27th Activity Report 2009, paras 234–237.

1342. Communication Nos 54/91, 61/91, 98/93/164/97–196/97, 210/98, 13th Activity Report 1999–2000, para. 128.

1343. Communication No. 159/96, 11th Activity Report, 1997–1998; *African Institute for Human Rights and Development (on behalf of Sierra Leonean refugees in Guinea v. Republic of Guinea*, Communication No. 249/2002, 20th Activity Report 2005–2006; *Institute for Human Rights and Development in Africa v. Angola*, Communication No. 292/2004, 24th Activity Report 2008, para. 73.

have a plural nature, transcending both first and second generation rights; the right to property and the rights of the family are but two examples of rights which may be said to have a dual nature.[1344] The Commission has stated that States must respect the free use of resources owned or at the disposal of individuals for the purpose of rights-related needs.[1345] Additionally, the obligation on States to promote and fulfil these rights could amount to the provision of basic needs such as food or social security.[1346]

270. The right to work is guaranteed by Article 15 of the African Charter. This does not equate to an 'absolute and unconditional right to obtain employment', rather 'the State has the obligation to facilitate employment through the creation of an environment conducive to the full employment of individuals within society under conditions that ensure the realisation of the dignity of the individual'.[1347] It 'implies the right to enter employment, and the right not to be deprived of employment unfairly'.[1348] The Commission has stated that one of the purposes of this provision is 'to ensure that States respect and protect the right of everyone to have access to the labour market without discrimination. The protection should be construed to allow certain restrictions depending on the type of employment'.[1349] While the Commission has found violations of Article 15 on various occasions,[1350] in *Garreth Anver Prince v. South Africa*, the Commission found no violation because the complainant was deemed to have disqualified himself from pursuing his occupation through his use of drugs, which the State had a legitimate interest in controlling.[1351]

1344. *See The Social and Economic Rights Action Center and the Center for Economic and Social Rights v. Nigeria*, Communication No. 155/96, 15th Activity Report 2001–2002.

1345. *Ibid.*, para. 45.

1346. *Ibid.*, para. 47.

1347. *Monim Elgak, Osman Hummeida and Amir Suleiman (represented by FIDH and OMCT) v. Sudan*, Communication No. 379/09 (2014) para. 129.

1348. *Ibid.*, para. 130.

1349. *Garreth Anver Prince v. South Africa*, Communication No. 255/2002, 18th Activity Report 2002–2003, para. 46.

1350. *Annette Pagnoulle (on behalf of Abdoulaye Mazou) v. Cameroon*, Communication No. 39/90, 10th Activity Report 1996–1997; *Institute for Human Rights and Development in Africa v. Angola*, Communication No. 292/2004, 24th Activity Report 2008, para. 76; *Scanlen and Holderness v. Zimbabwe*, Communication No. 297/2005, 26th Activity Report 2009, para. 179; *Open Society Justice Initiative v. Côte d'Ivoire*, Communication No. 318/06 (2015) paras 176–177.

1351. *Garreth Anver Prince v. South Africa*, Communication No. 255/2002, 18th Activity Report 2002–2003, para. 46.

271. Other second generation rights include the right to health enshrined in Article 16,[1352] and the right to education guaranteed by Article 17(1).[1353] In an important case on the right to health, *Purohit and Moore v. The Gambia*, the Commission upheld a number of complaints against the legislation governing mental health.[1354] The Commission emphasized the significance of the right to health describing it as 'vital to all aspects of a person's life and well-being, and is crucial to the realisation of all the other fundamental human rights and freedoms'.[1355] In *Egyptian Initiative for Personal Rights and INTERIGHTS v. Egypt*, the Commission underlined its significance, stating that the right to health 'is an entitlement which is derived from specific obligations claimed by individuals from States, and it is very fundamental to the exercise of other human rights enshrined in the African Charter…States have a legal obligation to protect the right to health of its citizens, including…taking concrete and targeted steps towards the full realization of the right, and adopting legislation or other measures to ensure equal access to health-related services and health care'.[1356] It extends to the right to control one's health and body and to be free from intrusions.[1357] With specific reference to mental health patients the Commission in *Purohit and Moore v. The Gambia* clarified the standard of care that they were entitled to expect; failure to meet these standards breached Articles 16 and 18.[1358] But in an important passage the Commission spelt out its position on this issue:

> The African Commission would…like to state that it is aware that millions of people in Africa are not enjoying the right to health maximally because African countries are generally faced with the problem of poverty which renders them incapable to provide the necessary amenities, infrastructure and resources that facilitate the full enjoyment of this right. Therefore, having due regard to this

---

1352. *Union Interafricaine des Droits de l'Homme v. Zaïre*, Communication 100/93, (failure by the State to provide safe drinking water, electricity and medicines); *Media Rights Agenda and Constitutional Rights Project v. Nigeria*, Communication Nos 105/93, 128/94, 130/94, 152/96, (denial of medical assistance to detainee in deteriorating health); *International Pen, Constitutional Rights Project, Interights on behalf of Ken Saro-Wiwa Jr. and Civil Liberties Organisation v. Nigeria*, Communication Nos 137/94, 139/94, 154/96, 161/97, 12th Activity Report 1998–1999 (denial of medical assistance to detainee); *Malawi African Association et al. v. Mauritania*, Communication Nos 54/91, 61/91, 98/93/164/97–196/97, 210/98, 13th Activity Report 1999–2000 (lack of medical attention for detainees); *Democratic Republic of Congo v. Burundi, Rwanda and Uganda*, Communication No. 227/99, 20th Activity Report, 2005–2006 (stopping essential services in a hospital).

1353. *Union Interafricaine des Droits de l'Homme v. Zaïre*, Communication No. 100/93, (closure of universities and secondary schools for a number of years); *Democratic Republic of Congo v. Burundi, Rwanda and Uganda*, Communication No. 227/99, 20th Activity Report, 2005–2006.

1354. Communication No. 241/2001, 16th Activity Report 2002–2003.

1355. *Ibid.*, para. 80.

1356. Communication No. 323/2006 (2011), para. 264.

1357. *Monim Elgak, Osman Hummeida and Amir Suleiman (represented by FIDH and OMCT) v. Sudan*, Communication No. 379/09 (2014) para. 134.

1358. Communication No. 241/2001, 16th Activity Report 2002–2003, para. 84. *See also* African Charter on Democracy Art. 41 according to which State Parties undertake to provide and enable access to basic social services.

> depressing but real state of affairs, the African Commission would like to read into Article 16 the obligation on part of States…to take concrete and targeted steps, while taking full advantage of its available resources, to ensure that the right to health is fully realized in all its aspects without discrimination of any kind.[1359]

A seminal case is that of *The Social and Economic Rights Action Center and the Center for Economic and Social Rights v. Nigeria*, where the Commission considered these rights in some detail.[1360] The Ogoni people claimed that a number of their fundamental rights had been violated by the Nigerian military regime, acting through the state oil company, which had failed to take measures to protect the local population from acts harmful to the environment. The Commission found violations of, *inter alia*, the right to health, the right to protection of the family, the right to housing and the right to food. The Commission's approach to this case is particularly interesting because it found that a number of rights protected by different provisions were in fact mutually dependent and mutually reinforcing. In addition, by adopting a broad view of the combined effect of a number of provisions it was able to read into the African Charter a right that was not explicitly guaranteed, namely, a right to shelter or housing.[1361]

272. The right to cultural life assured by Article 17(2) requires the State to tolerate cultural diversity and to protect minority groups.[1362] Given the challenges faced by indigenous peoples, the State is under a higher duty to take positive steps to promote their culture and way of life.[1363] Culture in this context has been defined by the Commission as 'that complex whole which includes a spiritual and physical association with one's ancestral land, knowledge, belief, art, law, morals, customs, and any other capabilities and habits acquired by humankind as a member of society – the sum total of the material and spiritual activities and products of a given social group that distinguish it from other similar groups'.[1364] It has a dual dimension in that it has individual and collective elements, ensuring the individual's participation in cultural life and required state protection of traditional community values.[1365] In *Malawi African Association et al. v. Mauritania*, the Commission considered stating that language is an integral part of cultural expression that enables the individual to take an active part in the life of the community. Preventing individuals expressing themselves in a particular

1359. *Ibid.*, paras 81–83.

1360. Communication No. 155/96, 15th Activity Report 2001–2002. For comment, *see* G. Bekker, 'The Social and Economic Rights Action Center and the Center for Economic and Social Rights/ Nigeria', *J.A.L.* 47(2003): 126.

1361. Communication No. 155/96, 15th Activity Report 2001–2002, para. 60. *See also Mbianku v. Cameroon*, Communication No. 389/10 (2015) paras 121–123.

1362. *Centre for Minority Rights Development (Kenya) and Minority Rights Group International on behalf of Endorois Welfare Council v. Kenya*, Communication No. 276/2003, 27th Activity Report 2009, para. 246.

1363. *Ibid.*, para. 248; *African Commission on Human and Peoples' Rights v. Kenya*, African Court of Human and Peoples' Rights, App. No. 006/2012 (26 May 2017) paras 177–179.

1364. *Centre for Minority Rights Development (Kenya) and Minority Rights Group International on behalf of Endorois Welfare Council v. Kenya*, Communication No. 276/2003, 27th Activity Report 2009, para. 241.

1365. *Ibid.*

language deprives them of their identity.[1366] However, the right to cultural life is not absolute, and restrictions may legitimately be imposed on certain cultural practices, such as the use of drugs, for the overall good of society.[1367]

273. The rights of the family is guaranteed by Article 18 of the African Charter. According to the Commission, Article 18 imposes both positive and negative obligations upon the State, in that the State must protect the family and assist it in meeting its needs and interests, while refraining from unwarranted interference with the family.[1368] In this latter context the State must avoid separating arbitrarily family members.[1369] The Commission has found violations of Article 18 on numerous occasions[1370] but an important decision is that of *Sudan Human Rights Organization and Sudan Centre for Housing Rights and Evictions v. Sudan.*[1371] Here, the Commission found that the failure of the State to protect the victims from the Janjaweed militia who killed and forcibly evicted people from their homes, while others fled for their lives, violated Article 18.[1372] It stated that this state of affairs threatened the very foundation of the family and rendered enjoyment of the right difficult.[1373]

V. Peoples' Rights

274. The significance attributed to the concept of the rights of 'peoples', or third generation rights, as an component of African human rights philosophy is illustrated by its inclusion in the African Charter, specifically in Articles 19–24.[1374] It requires States to respect the resources belonging to a collective group.[1375] The definition of

1366. Communication Nos 54/91, 61/91, 98/93/164/97–196/97, 210/98, 13th Activity Report 1999–2000.
1367. *Garreth Anver Prince v. South Africa*, Communication No. 255/2002, 18th Activity Report 2002–2003, para. 48.
1368. *Good v. Botswana*, Communication No. 306/2005, 28th Activity Report 2009–2010, para. 212.
1369. *Ibid.*; *Open Society Justice Initiative v. Côte d'Ivoire*, Communication No. 318/06 (2015) para. 179.
1370. *Union Interafricaine des Droits de l'Homme et al. v. Angola*, Communication No. 159/96, 11th Activity Report, 1997–1998; *Amnesty International v. Zambia*, Communication No. 212/98, 12th Activity Report 1998–1999; *Malawi African Association et al. v. Mauritania*, Communication Nos 54/91, 61/91, 98/93/164/97–196/97, 210/98, 13th Activity Report 1999–2000; *Constitutional Rights Project and Civil Liberties Organisation v. Nigeria*, Communication Nos 143/95, 150/96, 14th Activity Report 1999–2000; *Modise v. Botswana*, Communication No. 97/93, 14th Activity Report 2000–2001; *Democratic Republic of Congo v. Burundi, Rwanda and Uganda*, Communication No. 227/99, 20th Activity Report, 2005–2006; *Article 19 v. Eritrea*, Communication No. 275/2003, 22nd Activity Report 2006–2007; *Good v. Botswana*, Communication No. 306/2005, 28th Activity Report 2009–2010; *Egyptian Initiative for Personal Rights and INTERIGHTS v. Egypt*, Communication No. 323/2006 (2011), paras 142–153.
1371. Communication Nos 279/03, 296/05, 28th Activity Report 2010.
1372. *Ibid.*, para. 216.
1373. *Ibid.*
1374. *Bissangou v. Republic of Congo*, Communication No. 253/2002, 21st Activity Report 2005–2006, para. 80. *See* Baldwin & Morel.
1375. *The Social and Economic Rights Action Center and the Center for Economic and Social Rights v. Nigeria*, Communication No. 155/96, 15th Activity Report 2001–2002, para. 45.

the concept of 'peoples' is troublesome because there is little consensus and it is difficult to identify the peoples or groups entitled to these rights as well as the entities that owe them these rights.[1376] The African Charter does not provide a definition of the African notion of a 'people',[1377] but depending on context it appears capable of either referring to the national community as a whole, or the State itself,[1378] or collective, as in distinct ethnic or tribal, communities.[1379] However, in *Gunme et al. v. Cameroon*, the Commission engaged with this controversial question.[1380] The central argument in this case centred on the claim that the people of southern Cameroon had been denied the right of self-determination at the time of decolonization and continued to be denied that right. The respondent government argued that the people of southern Cameroon were not a 'separate and distinct' people entitled to self-determination. The Commission interpreted the concept of 'people' broadly, combining both objective and subjective elements. It took the view that the following characteristics were crucial: a common historical tradition, a racial or ethnic identity, cultural homogeneity, linguistic unity, religious and ideological affinities, territorial connections, and a common economic life. Additionally, the group may consider itself a 'people' by virtue of their consciousness that they constitute a people.[1381] Identity, said the Commission, 'is an innate characteristic within a people' and the fact that a group sees itself as having a separate and distinct identity was important, as was its recognition by others. Ethno-anthropological attributes, while important, were not determinative, except in the case of indigenous peoples.[1382] Significantly, the Commission expressed the view that the African Charter applied to all peoples in Africa, regardless of origin, including therefore, communities of Asian or European descent.[1383] In *Sudan Human Rights Organization and Sudan Centre for Housing Rights and Evictions v. Sudan*, an added feature was that of 'mixed racial composition'.[1384] In such cases the Commission stated that race became a determinant

1376. A. Kiss, 'The Peoples' Right to Self-Determination', *H.R.L.J.* 7 (1986): 165, 172–173; T. van Boven, 'The Relations Between Peoples' Rights and Human Rights in the African Charter', *H.R.L.J.*7 (1986): 183; J.-B. Marie, 'Relations Between Peoples' Rights and Human Rights: Semantic and Metholodogical Distinctions', *H.R.L.J.*7(1986): 195.

1377. A. Kiwanuka, 'The Meaning of 'People' in the African Charter of Human and Peoples' Rights', *A.J.I.L.* 82 (1988): 80.

1378. *Katangese Peoples' Congress v. Zaire,* Communication No. 75/92, 8th Activity Report 1994–1995; *African Commission on Human and Peoples' Rights v. Kenya*, African Court of Human and Peoples' Rights, App. No. 006/2012 (26 May 2017) para. 198.

1379. *Malawi African Association et al. v. Mauritania*, Communication Nos 54/91, 61/91, 98/93, 164/97–196/97, 210/98, 13th Activity Report 1999–2000; *African Commission on Human and Peoples' Rights v. Kenya*, African Court of Human and Peoples' Rights, App. No. 006/2012 (26 May 2017) *ibid.*

1380. Communication No. 266/2003, 26th Activity Report 2008–2009.

1381. *Ibid.*, para. 170. *See also Centre for Minority Rights Development (Kenya) and Minority Rights Group International on behalf of Endorois Welfare Council v. Kenya*, Communication No. 276/2003, 27th Activity Report 2009, para. 151. Self-identification as a factor is stressed by the I.L.O. Convention No. 169 on Indigenous and Tribal Peoples in Independent Countries Art. 1(2) (27 Jun. 1989) 1650 U.N.T.S. 28383.

1382. *Ibid.*, para. 178.

1383. *Ibid.*

1384. Communication Nos 279/03, 296/05, 28th Activity Report 2010, para. 220.

factor, just as ethnic identity could also play a part.[1385] The Commission took the opportunity to celebrate Africa's rich diversity.[1386]

275. The African Charter does not expressly recognize indigenous peoples, partly due to a fear that to have done so could have had a destabilizing effect.[1387] However, in 2000 the Commission established a Working Group on Indigenous Populations/Communities, thus recognizing the existence of indigenous peoples in Africa.[1388] But it was the case of *Centre for Minority Rights Development (Kenya) and Minority Rights Group International on behalf of Endorois Welfare Council v. Kenya* that advanced the rights of indigenous people.[1389] In this case the Endorois community alleged multiple violations of the African Charter, complaining that they had been forcibly removed from their ancestral lands without proper consultation or compensation, thereby separating them from their spiritual, cultural, and economic ties to the land. The Commission identified four criteria for recognizing indigenous peoples: the occupation and use of a specific territory; the voluntary perpetuation of cultural distinctiveness; self-identification as a distinct collectivity, as well as its recognition by others; and a history of subjugation, marginalization, dispossession or discrimination.[1390] The Commission found that the Endorois culture, religion, and traditional way of life was intimately linked to their ancestral lands and that without access thereto they could not fully exercise their cultural and religious rights.[1391]

276. Article 19 of the African Charter puts in context the rights that are elaborated further in the subsequent provisions. It extends the principle of non-discrimination to the community as a whole by proclaiming the equality of all peoples. Considering the African notion of 'peoples' as a national community this provision would appear to refer to the principles of equal rights and sovereign equality contained in Articles 1(2) and 2(1) of the UN Charter. Moreover, the total prohibition on the domination of one people over another would appear to be a reference to the principles of political independence and political and economic self-determination. In addition, it can also be interpreted as Africa's rejection of the policies of racial oppression and intolerance, not only as characterized by apartheid and white-minority rule, but also the ethnic and tribal hatreds that have descended into massacres in parts of Africa.[1392]

1385. *Ibid.*

1386. *Ibid.*, para. 221.

1387. Viljoen, 279–281.

1388. Resolution on Indigenous Populations/Communities, Twenty-Eighth Ordinary Session 2000. *See* further Baldwin & Morel, 248–249.

1389. Communication No. 276/2003, 27th Activity Report 2009.

1390. *Ibid.*, para. 150. These criteria were endorsed by the Human Rights Court in *African Commission on Human and Peoples' Rights v. Kenya*, African Court of Human and Peoples' Rights, App. No. 006/2012 (26 May 2017) para. 107.

1391. *Ibid.*, para. 156. Note *Sesana and Others v. Attorney-General* (2006) A.H.R.L.R. 183, where the High Court of Botswana held that the San people (Bushmen) had been evicted illegally from their ancestral lands and that they had the right to live on such land.

1392. *See Malawi African Association et al. v. Mauritania*, Communication Nos 54/91, 61/91, 98/93, 164/97–196/97, 210/98, 13th Activity Report 1999–2000, para. 142, where discriminatory practices against the Black population of Mauritania was condemned. *See also Sudan Human Rights Organization and Sudan Centre for Housing Rights and Evictions v. Sudan*, Communication Nos. 279/03, 296/05, 28th Activity Report, 2010, para. 223.

277. Article 20 of the African Charter enshrines a principle of international law long cherished by the OAU/AU, the inalienable right to political and economic self-determination. Because this right can assume different manifestations the precise the content and scope of self-determination is still the subject of considerable debate. Nevertheless, one facet of self-determination is as a corollary of sovereignty, necessarily associated with the principle of non-intervention.[1393] Paragraph 1 enshrines the right of peoples to determine freely their political status. The Commission has therefore been able to rely on the internal dimension of self-determination to uphold democratic values and to condemn military coups. In *Sir Dawda K. Jawara v. Gambia*, the Commission held that the military coup that overthrew Gambia's democratic system 'was a grave violation of the right of the Gambian people to freely choose their government as entrenched in Article 20(1)'.[1394]

278. The right to self-determination extends to colonized and oppressed people.[1395] This is apparent from paragraphs 2 and 3 of the provision, and the practice and *opinio juris* of African States and the OAU/AU. In this context self-determination, in its external manifestation, is synonymous with decolonization.[1396] However, if self-determination is a right of all people does this mean that secession is legitimized? The international community is reluctant generally to accept such a possibility. African States are adamantly opposed to any interpretation of self-determination that involves

1393. *Democratic Republic of Congo v. Burundi, Rwanda and Uganda*, Communication No. 227/99, 20th Activity Report, 2005–2006, para. 68.

1394. Communication Nos 147/95 and 149/96, 13th Activity Report 1999–2000, para. 73.

1395. The reference to 'oppressed peoples' was designed to include the majority of the inhabitants of Rhodesia, South Africa, and Namibia who were labouring under unrepresentative minority governments.

1396. It is now established that the inhabitants of non-self-governing territories have a legal right freely to determine their future political, economic and cultural status; independence must be an available choice. *See* in particular UN General Assembly Res. 1514(XV) 1960, Declaration on the Granting of Independence to Colonial Countries and Peoples, Res. 1541(XV) 1960, and Res. 2625(XXV) 1970, Declaration on Friendly Relations Among States in Accordance with the Charter of the United Nations, the relevant jurisprudence of the ICJ, in particular *Legal Consequences for States of the Continued Presence of South Africa in Namibia (South West Africa) notwithstanding Security Council Res. 276 (1970)*, Advisory Opinion, I.C.J. Reports 1971, 16, *Western Sahara Case*, Advisory Opinion, I.C.J. Reports 1975, 12, and *East Timor Case (Portugal v. Australia)* I.C.J. Reports 1995, 90. *See* further General comment 12 paras 6–7, UN Doc. HRI/GEN/1/Rev.2. In Africa it is arguable that the Sahrawis of Western Sahara have not yet exercised their right of self-determination. This conclusion has been implicitly recognized by the CJEU, Case C-104/16 P, *Council v. Front Polisario*, Judgment of 21 Dec. 2016, C:2016:973. Mauritius and the United Kingdom are locked in a dispute as to whether the decolonization of Mauritius was carried out in conformity with international law in light of the separation of the Chagos Archipelago from Mauritius. In *Chagos Marine Protected Area Arbitration (Mauritius v. United Kingdom)*, Award, 18 Mar. 2015) PCA Case No. 2011-03, paras 70–72, Dissenting and Concurring Opinion of Judges Kateka and Wolfrum, the view was expressed that this fact was contrary to the principles of decolonization and self-determination. The UN General Assembly has now referred the matter to the ICJ for an advisory opinion, Press Release No. 2017/27 (29 Jun. 2017).

a threat of unilateral, or contested, secession.[1397] The Commission has therefore held that it is obliged to uphold the sovereignty and territorial integrity of States and that self-determination must be exercised in a manner compatible with the sovereignty and territorial integrity of states.[1398] Accordingly, 'secession is not recognised as a variant of the right of self-determination within the context of the African Charter'.[1399] It has therefore stated that it 'cannot envisage, condone or encourage secession, as a form of self-determination'.[1400] In this sense, self-determination operates 'externally' and once independence is attained no further recourse to the right is permissible. Nevertheless, the internal dimension of self-determination must be complied with, by proving for autonomy or some form of self-government.[1401] it should be observed that there exists considerable support for the view, known as the 'remedial theory', that internal self-determination requires good and democratic governance and that in extreme cases of oppression and persecution of minorities secession is justified.[1402] A link with Article 13 of the African Charter may thereby be established.[1403]

279. Paragraphs 2 and 3 of Article 20 confer on colonized and oppressed people the right to free themselves by resorting to any means recognized by the international community, and the right to the assistance of African States in their liberation struggle

---

1397. Constitutive Act Art. 3(b), PSC Protocol Art. 4(e). *See also* AHG/Res. 51(IV) (1967) whereby the OAU condemned secession in Member States, reaffirmed its support for the principle of territorial integrity and declared that the right of self-determination did not apply to cases of secession. The AU continues to refuse recognition to the Republic of Somaliland, which declared its independence in May 1991, despite meeting the criteria of statehood. *See* B.R. Farley, 'Calling a State a State: Somaliland and International Recognition', *Emory I.L.R.* 24 (2010): 777. *See* generally G.J. Naldi, 'Secession: The African Experience', in *Shielding Humanity: Essays in International Law and Policy in Honour of Abdul Koroma*, C. C. Jalloh & O. Elias (eds) (The Hague: Martinus Nijhoff Brill, 2015), 873–902.

1398. *Katangese Peoples' Congress v. Zaire*, Communication No. 75/92, 8th Activity Report 1994–1995, para. 4; *Gunme et al. v. Cameroon,* Communication No. 266/2003, 26th Activity Report 2008–2009, paras 190, 200.

1399. *Gunme et al. v. Cameroon*, Communication No. 266/2003, 26th Activity Report 2008–2009, para. 200. *See also African Commission on Human and Peoples' Rights v. Kenya*, African Court of Human and Peoples' Rights, App. No. 006/2012 (26 May 2017) para. 199.

1400. *Ibid.* The Commission thus rejected a secessionist claim to independence from Senegal by Casamance separatists, *Report on the Mission of Good Offices to Senegal of the African Commission on Human and Peoples' Rights* (1–7 Jun. 1996), 10th Activity Report 1996–1997, in Murray & Evans, Documents Vol. I, 530.

1401. *Katangese Peoples' Congress v. Zaire*, Communication No. 75/92, 8th Activity Report 1994–1995, para. 4; *Gunme et al. v. Cameroon*, Communication No. 266/2003, 26th Activity Report 2008–2009, para. 190.

1402. *Katangese Peoples' Congress v. Zaire,* Communication No. 75/92, 8th Activity Report 1994–1995, para. 6; *Gunme et al. v. Cameroon*, Communication No. 266/2003, 26th Activity Report 2008–2009, paras 197, 199; *Reference Re Secession of Quebec* 37 I.L.M. 1340 (1998); A. Cassese, *Self-Determination of Peoples: A Legal Reappraisal* (Cambridge: Cambridge University Press, 1995), 108–125.

1403. *Katangese Peoples' Congress v. Zaire,* Communication No. 75/92, 8th Activity Report 1994–1995, para. 6; *Gunme et al. v. Cameroon*, Communication No. 266/2003, 26th Activity Report 2008–2009, para. 190.

against foreign domination.[1404] Developing States have traditionally argued that the use of force in furtherance of wars of national liberation[1405] is valid on the grounds that these conflicts are being waged in support of a norm of international law, the principle of self-determination, and because the forcible deprivation of a people's right to self-determination constitutes a breach of international law. Material aid, including that of a military nature, is therefore justified. The generally adopted stance of Western States has been that aid to nature liberation movements is limited to humanitarian assistance and political and moral support.[1406] These rights have less contemporary relevance with the virtual elimination of colonialism from Africa.

280. As has been stated Article 20 includes economic self-determination and the content of this right assumes various manifestations. Article 21 of the African Charter clearly refers to the concept of permanent sovereignty over natural resources and must be viewed in the context of the negative legacy of the colonial era[1407] and the attempts of the Developing States over the last fifty years to create a New International Economic Order.[1408] The Commission has clarified that Article 21 refers to a group right and not an individual right.[1409] The firm language in which this provision is couched reflects the strength of feeling among African States that true economic and political independence was largely dependent on exercising control over their natural resources. Thus, paragraph 1 declares that '[a]ll peoples shall freely dispose of their wealth and natural resources', a right that must be exercised in their exclusive interest and of which they cannot be deprived. In *The Social and Economic Rights Action Center and the Center for Economic and Social Rights v. Nigeria*, the Commission found that the 'destructive and selfish role' played by oil development in Ogoniland, which did not involve the local population in any decision-making and which failed to bring them any material benefits, constituted a violation of this Article.[1410] If the

---

1404. *See also* UN General Assembly Res. 3103 (XXVIII) 1973 Basic Principles on the Legal Status of the Combatants Struggling Against Colonial and Alien Domination and Racist Regimes, para. 1.

1405. Wars of national liberation have been defined as 'armed conflicts in which peoples are fighting against colonial domination and alien occupation and against racist regimes in the exercise of their right to self-determination', Protocol I Additional to the Geneva Conventions relating to the Protection of Victims of International Armed Conflicts, Art. 1(4) 1977, 1125 U.N.T.S. 3. *See* generally N. Ronzitti, 'Wars of National Liberation - A Legal Definition', *Italian Y.B.I.L.* 1 (1975): 192; H. Wilson, *International Law and the Use of Force by National Liberation Movements* (Oxford: Oxford University Press, 1988).

1406. In *Military and Paramilitary Activities in and against Nicaragua (Nicaragua v. United States)* (Merits) I.C.J. Reports 1986, 14, 351, Judge Schwebel stated that 'it is lawful for a foreign State or movement to give to a people struggling for self-determination moral, political and humanitarian assistance'.

1407. *The Social and Economic Rights Action Center and the Center for Economic and Social Rights v. Nigeria*, Communication No. 155/96, 15th Activity Report 2001–2002, para. 56.

1408. *See* UN General Assembly Res. 1803(XVII) 1962, Declaration on Permanent Sovereignty over Natural Resources, 3201 (S-VI) 1974, Declaration on the Establishment of a New International Economic Order, and 3281(XXIX) 1974, Charter on the Economic Rights and Duties of States.

1409. *Bissangou v. Republic of Congo*, Communication No. 253/2002, 21st Activity Report 2005–2006, para. 81.

1410. Communication No. 155/96, 15th Activity Report 2001–2002, paras 55–58.

natural resources are in the land of indigenous peoples the Commission has held that the right also vests in them, but in this instance limited to such resources put to traditional, cultural and religious uses.[1411] Paragraph 4 extends this right to the States themselves, with the added obligation of strengthening African unity and solidarity.[1412] Moreover, in order for their people to benefit fully from the riches of their natural resources paragraph 5 obliges Member States to eliminate all forms of foreign economic exploitation, particularly that practiced by international monopolies.[1413] Paragraph 2 is of special interest because it states that in cases of spoliation the dispossessed people shall have the right to the lawful recovery of their property and adequate compensation.[1414] It is not altogether clear by whom the compensation will be payable, or what appropriate levels of compensation should be, but in *The Social and Economic Rights Action Center and the Center for Economic and Social Rights v. Nigeria*, the Commission asked the respondent State to pay compensation.[1415] This provision must be read in light of the moderating influence of paragraph 3 which imposes an obligation to 'promote international cooperation based on mutual respect, equitable exchange and the principles of international law'.

281. Article 22(1) of the African Charter enshrines the right to economic, social and cultural development.[1416] This appears to refer to factors such as opportunities for the advancement of the individual, and is designed to address problems such as poverty, housing, and illiteracy. The Commission has stated that the right to development is comprised of two indivisible elements, constitutive and instrumental, or 'useful both

---

1411. *The Social and Economic Rights Action Center and the Center for Economic and Social Rights v. Nigeria*, Communication No. 155/96, 15th Activity Report 2001–2002, paras 56–58; *Centre for Minority Rights Development (Kenya) and Minority Rights Group International on behalf of Endorois Welfare Council v. Kenya*, Communication No. 276/2003, 27th Activity Report 2009, paras 255, 263. *See also African Commission on Human and Peoples' Rights v. Kenya*, African Court of Human and Peoples' Rights, App. No. 006/2012 (26 May 2017) para. 201.

1412. In *Democratic Republic of Congo v. Burundi, Rwanda and Uganda*, Communication No. 227/99, 20th Activity Report 2005–2006, para. 94, the Commission held that the illegal exploitation and looting of the Congo's natural resources, including minerals, lumber coffee and livestock, by neighbouring States breached Art. 21.

1413. On the relationship between the enjoyment of human rights and the activities of transnational corporations, *see* the reports of the UN Secretary-General, UN Docs. E/CN.4/Sub.2/1995/11 and E/CN.4/Sub.2/1996/12. *See also The Social and Economic Rights Action Center and the Center for Economic and Social Rights v. Nigeria*, Communication No. 155/96, 15th Activity Report 2001–2002, para. 58, where the Commission found that Nigeria had facilitated the destruction of Ogoniland in league with oil companies.

1414. In *Bissangou v. Republic of Congo*, Communication No. 253/2002, 21st Activity Report 2005–2006, paras 80–82, the Commission made clear that this provision referred to the wealth and natural resources of a group or a population, and not to the assets of any individual.

1415. Communication No. 155/96, 15th Activity Report 2001–2002. *See also Centre for Minority Rights Development (Kenya) and Minority Rights Group International on behalf of Endorois Welfare Council v. Kenya*, Communication No. 276/2003, 27th Activity Report 2009, para. 268.

1416. In *Democratic Republic of Congo v. Burundi, Rwanda and Uganda*, Communication No. 227/99, 20th Activity Report, 2005–2006, para. 87, the Commission held that the indiscriminate dumping of and mass burial of victims of massacres by occupying forces violated the peoples' right to cultural development.

as a means and an end'.[1417] Five principal criteria must be fulfilled: it must be equitable, non-discriminatory, participatory, accountable and transparent, with equity and choice as overarching themes.[1418] If developments projects that are likely to have a major impact are undertaken, the people affected must be consulted and their prior informed consent must be obtained.[1419] Paragraph 2 thereof imposes a concomitant duty upon States individually or collectively to ensure the exercise of this right. This reflects the view that development can only take place in the context of a favourable and equitable economic order, both national and international.

282. Article 22(1) additionally declares the right of peoples to the equal enjoyment of the common heritage of humankind. The common heritage of humankind is a concept that has received some limited recognition by the international community right and which seeks to bring about its realization by having fair access to natural resources beyond national jurisdiction.[1420]

283. Article 23(1) of the African Charter promotes a principle fundamental to the stability of the international community, that of national and international peace and security. It may seem a trite observation that the optimum realization of human rights is dependent on the maintenance of peace and security.[1421] While the African Charter does not explicitly define what is meant by the term 'peace and security'[1422] it does refer to the principles of solidarity and friendly relations affirmed by the UN and the OAU. Additionally it would seem that the principles contained in the UN Declaration on the Principles of International Law Concerning Friendly Relations and Cooperation Among States in Accordance with the UN Charter are directly relevant.[1423] In *Democratic Republic of Congo v. Burundi, Rwanda and Uganda* the African Commission established a link between this provision and the principle of the peaceful settlement of disputes, Article 33 and Chapter VII of the UN Charter, and Article III of the OAU Charter.[1424] It proceeded to hold that the occupation of the DRC by the armed forces of neighbouring States was 'impermissible' and a violation of Article 23.[1425]

1417. *Centre for Minority Rights Development (Kenya) and Minority Rights Group International on behalf of Endorois Welfare Council v. Kenya*, Communication No. 276/2003, 27th Activity Report 2009, para. 277.

1418. *Ibid.*

1419. *Ibid.*, para. 291. *See also African Commission on Human and Peoples' Rights v. Kenya*, African Court of Human and Peoples' Rights, App. No. 006/2012 (26 May 2017) para. 210.

1420. *See* Agreement Governing the Activities of States on the Moon and other Celestial Bodies Art. 11(1) (5 Dec. 1979), 1363 U.N.T.S. 3, and UN Convention on the Law of the Sea Art. 136 (10 Dec. 1982), 1833 U.N.T.S. 3. An alternative interpretation is that the concept of common heritage of humankind refers to the protection for posterity of the cultural heritage of a nation or the wonders of nature, a species of international conservation law.

1421. This nexus is acknowledged by the African Charter on Democracy Arts 38 and 39.

1422. In *Malawi African Association et al. v. Mauritania*, Communication Nos 54/91, 61/91, 98/93, 164/97–196/97, 210/98, 13th Activity Report 1999–2000, para. 140, the Commission held that unprovoked attacks on villages amounted to a denial of the right to live in peace and security.

1423. *Democratic Republic of Congo v. Burundi, Rwanda and Uganda*, Communication No. 227/99, 20th Activity Report, 2005–2006, para. 73.

1424. *Ibid.*, paras 66, 74–75.

1425. *Ibid.*, para. 76.

284. The African Charter pioneered the environment as a human right.[1426] The right to environment is not defined in Article 24 but coming within its scope is protection of the environment from, *inter alia*, pollution and polluting activities.[1427] Thus, in *The Social and Economic Rights Action Center and the Center for Economic and Social Rights v. Nigeria*, the African Commission found a violation of the right of peoples to a clean and safe environment protected by Article 24 of the African Charter when Nigerian exploitation of oilfields polluted the environment of the Ogoni people.[1428] A complementary measure is the Bamako Convention banning the import of toxic waste into Africa.[1429]

285. Article 26 of the African Charter obliges States parties to guarantee the independence of the courts[1430] and, additionally, to allow the establishment and improvement of appropriate national institutions entrusted with the promotion and protection of the rights and freedoms enshrined in the Charter. An independent judiciary is vital to the existence of a State governed by the rule of law and committed to human rights and many African countries have fallen short in upholding this guarantee.[1431] The campaign of threats and harassment against the robustly independent justices of the Supreme Court of Zimbabwe,[1432] and other members of the judiciary, in 2000–2001 by state-sponsored thuggery that eventually led to the resignations of the justices is common knowledge. The African Commission has stated that this provision 'speaks of the institutions which are essential to give meaning and content' to the rights protected by Article 7 of the African Charter and 'clearly envisions the protection of the courts which have traditionally been the bastion of protection of the individual's rights against the abuses of State power'.[1433] Moreover, its mandate on this issue is to consider complaints of 'undue interference by the executive with judicial independence'.[1434] In *Lawyers for Human Rights v. Swaziland*, the Commission found that vesting all judicial

---

1426. Ankumah, 168–70.

1427. *See also* African Charter on Democracy Art. 42, under which States commit themselves to implement policies to protect the environment to achieve sustainable development for the benefit of present and future generations.

1428. Communication No. 155/96, 15th Activity Report 2001–2002.

1429. *See infra* Ch. 5.

1430. 'Courts' in this context refers to national judicial organs and not international courts, *Tembani and Freeth v. Angola and Thirteen Others*, Communication No. 409/12 (2013) para. 144.

1431. *See Amnesty International et al. v. Sudan*, Communication Nos 48/90, 50/91, 52/91, 89/93, 13th Activity Report 1999–2000, para. 69, where over one hundred judges opposed to special and military tribunals were dismissed. In *Sir Dawda K. Jawara v. Gambia*, Communication Nos 147/95 and 149/96, 13th Activity Report 1999–2000, para. 74, the Commission found that the military regime ignored court judgments and ousted the competence of the ordinary courts to consider human rights cases. But *see* African Charter on Democracy Art. 32(3).

1432. The years 1985–2001 have been rightly described as the 'golden era of human rights litigation' in Zimbabwe, A. de Bourbon, 'Human Rights Litigation in Zimbabwe: Past, Present and Future', *A.H.R L.J.* 3 (2003): 195, 206.

1433. *Civil Liberties Organization v. Nigeria*, Communication No. 129/94, 9th Activity Report 1995–1996, para. 14. *See also* African Charter on Democracy Art. 32(3).

1434. *Tsikata v. Ghana*, Communication No. 322/2006, 21st Activity Report 2005–2006, para. 32. *See also* Resolution on the Respect and Strengthening on the Independence of the Judiciary, adopted at the Commission's Nineteenth Ordinary Session, 1996.

powers in the Head of State, with the capability of hiring and firing judges, directly threatened the independence of the judiciary.[1435] In addition, the Commission held this situation to undermine the doctrine of separation of powers.[1436] However, in *Article 19 v. Eritrea,* the Commission dismissed the argument that the removal of the Chief Justice in a manner inconsistent with international standards rendered domestic remedies ineffective.[1437] The Commission has held that 'ouster clauses' are incompatible with Article 26,[1438] as are the creation of special courts to try civilians.[1439]

§3. The African Commission on Human and Peoples' Rights

286. The African Commission on Human and Peoples' Rights (hereinafter the Commission) is one of the bodies entrusted with the implementation of the rights enshrined in the African Charter. By virtue of Article 30 it is mandated with promoting human and peoples' rights and ensuring their protection.[1440] The Commission is an 'autonomous treaty body working within the framework of the African Union'.[1441] It has described itself as 'an international quasi-judicial institution established to promote and protect the rights enshrined in the African Charter'.[1442] It is composed of eleven members, serving in their personal capacities, from amongst African personalities of the highest reputation with legal experience and competence in the field of human rights.[1443] The odd number of commissioners facilitates the taking of decisions in that a tie in voting may thus be avoided but in the event of a tie Article 64 provides that

1435. Communication No. 251/2002, 18th Activity Report 2004–2005, para. 58.

1436. *Ibid.*, para. 56. On the commitment to the doctrine of separation of powers, *see* African Charter on Democracy Art. 3(5).

1437. Communication No. 275/2003, 22nd Activity Report 2006–2007, paras 66–67.

1438. *Civil Liberties Organization v. Nigeria*, Communication No. 129/94, 9th Activity Report 1995–1996.

1439. *International Pen, Constitutional Rights Project, Interights on behalf of Ken Saro-Wiwa Jr. and Civil Liberties Organisation v. Nigeria*, Communication Nos 137/94, 139/94, 154/96 and 161/97, 12th Activity Report 1998–1999, para. 95; *Media Rights Agenda v. Nigeria*, Communication No. 224/98, 14th Activity Report 2000–2001, para. 66.

1440. *See also* Rule 3 of the Commission's Rules of Procedure, hereinafter 'Rules', which entered into force in 2010; Heyns & Killander, 182. The Commission, which became operational in 1987, is based in Banjul, The Gambia. The Commission is assisted by a secretariat, Art. 41 and Rules 17–22.

1441. Rule 3. In *Good v. Botswana*, Communication No. 306/2005, 28th Activity Report 2009–2010, paras 53–55, Botswana argued that the Commission had ceased to exist along with the OAU. The Commission dismissed this submission on the ground that only the termination of the African Charter could affect the Commission's existence. The continuing operation of the African Charter amounted to an acceptance of the Commission's jurisdiction. Furthermore, as a body working within the framework of the OAU, it devolved to the AU, *ibid.*, paras 75–79.

1442. *Interights, Institute for Human Rights and Development in Africa, and Association Mauritaniene des Droits de l'Homme v. Islamic Republic of Mauritania*, Communication No. 373/2009 (formerly 242/2001), 28th Activity Report 2010, para. 83.

1443. Article 31. *See also* Rule 4. Art. 38 and Rule 9 require the members of the Commission upon their election to make a solemn declaration that they will discharge their duties impartially and faithfully.

the Chairperson has the casting vote.[1444] Article 34 stipulates that the members of the Commission must be the nationals of one of the State parties to the African Charter. Each State party may nominate a maximum of two candidates who must not be of the same nationality. In addition, according to Article 32, the Commission may not include more than one national of the same State. The size of the Commission is supposed to correspond to an equitable geographic distribution.[1445] The members of the Commission enjoy diplomatic privileges and immunities in the performance of their duties.[1446]

287. The members of the Commission are elected by secret ballot by the, now, AU Assembly from a list of persons nominated by the States parties to the African Charter.[1447] They serve a renewable six-year term.[1448] The Commission's Chairperson and Vice-Chairperson are elected by its members for a renewable two-year term,[1449] who together constitute the bureau.[1450] It should be noted that the Chairperson has few executive powers.[1451]

288. In the event of the death or resignation of a member the seat is declared vacant by what is now the Chair of the AU Commission.[1452] The Chair of the AU Commission can additionally declare the seat vacant if, in the unanimous opinion of colleagues, a member ceases to fulfil his/her functions or is incapable of continuing to fulfil them, unless such failure is of a temporary nature.[1453] In either case the AU Assembly shall fill that seat unless the remaining period of office is less than six months, in which event the seat will be filled in due course. A member of the Commission elected to replace another member shall complete their predecessor's mandate.[1454] In order to avoid conflicts of interest a member of the Commission must not be present or participate in any communication where s/he is a national of the respondent State, has a personal interest in the case, has previously been involved in the case, has expressed public pronouncements that may give rise to a perception of impartiality, or is engaged in any activity that may lead his/her impartiality and independence to be questioned.[1455]

1444. *See also* Rule 51(3).
1445. According to Ankumah, 17–18, the important consideration is ensuring the representation of the different legal and language traditions from across Africa.
1446. Article 43.
1447. Article 33.
1448. Article 36 and Rule 5(1).
1449. Article 42(1) and Rule 11(1). Election is by secret ballot, Rule 11(2). *See also* Rule 56.
1450. Rule 10.
1451. Rule 14.
1452. Article 39(1) and Rule 8.
1453. Article 39(2) and Rule 16.
1454. Article 39(3) and Rule 5(3).
1455. Rule 101. In *Interights, Institute for Human Rights and Development in Africa, and Association Mauritaniene des Droits de l'Homme v. Mauritania*, Communication No. 373/2009, 28th Activity Report, 2009–2010, paras 47–62, a challenge to the impartiality of the Commission because a Commissioner who was a national of the respondent State was present during the deliberations was dismissed on the ground that he 'did not take part in the deliberations'. Under the new Rules this case would be decided differently.

289. The Chairperson may convene the Commission whenever necessary but at least once a year.[1456] In addition, extraordinary sessions may be convened.[1457] The Commission's sessions are normally held in public.[1458] At least seven members must be present to be quorate[1459] and decisions are taken by a majority of the voting members,[1460] with the Chairperson having the casting vote in the event of a tie.[1461] However, decisions may be taken by consensus.[1462]

290. The Commission's mandate is defined by a number of guidelines set out in Article 45. It should be noted at the outset that while the Commission was created to promote and protect human rights[1463] in Africa its competence in the field of protection is not exclusive but is shared not only with the African Court on Human and Peoples' Rights[1464] but also with the AU Assembly which has a supervisory role.[1465] However, the Commission does perform a quasi-judicial function and it possesses jurisdiction to interpret the African Charter and to carry out tasks conferred upon it by the AU Assembly.[1466] It is therefore necessary to consider separately the various functions of the Commission, which may be divided into three categories: promotion; protection; and other areas of competence.

291. The first, and fundamental, function of the Commission, as provided for by the African Charter is to promote human rights in Africa, which it is doing with the assistance of partners such as National Human Rights Institutions and NGOs.[1467] There appear to be three elements to its promotional function: a studies and information function; a quasi-legislative function; and cooperative functions.[1468]

292. Article 45(1)(a) requires the Commission to perform its study and information function in several ways.[1469] Thus the Commission acts as a documentation centre. It therefore gathers and classifies information on human rights in Africa. In addition, it is responsible for disseminating information, either systematically or in response to inquiries, and one method of achieving this is by organizing conferences or seminars.

1456. Article 64(2). However, Rule 26(1) requires at least two ordinary sessions a year of two weeks' duration.
1457. Rule 27.
1458. Rule 25(2). However, private sessions may also be held, Rule 31.
1459. Article 42(3) and Rule 30.
1460. Rule 52(1).
1461. Article 42(4) and Rule 51(3).
1462. Rule 51(1).
1463. Article 30 and Rule 3; *Bissangou v. Republic of Congo*, Communication No. 253/2002, 21st Activity Report 2005–2006, para. 47.
1464. Rule 114(1). *See* further *infra* paras 322–363.
1465. Under Rule 125(1) the Commission may ask the Assembly to take measures to implement its decisions.
1466. Article 45(4).
1467. Rules 67–68.
1468. Article 45(1) and Rules 69–72. *See* Ankumah, 21–22; Murray, African Commission on Human and Peoples' Rights, 14–15. *See* further V. Dankwa, 'The Promotional Role of the African Commission on Human and Peoples' Rights', in *The African Charter on Human and Peoples' Rights: The System in Practice, 1986–2000*, Evans & Murray (eds), (Cambridge: Cambridge University Press, 2002), 335–352.
1469. *See also* Rules 69–72.

Furthermore, the Commission can undertake studies and conduct research. The Commission is also entrusted with encouraging national and local institutions concerned with human and peoples' rights. Finally, the Commission can advise governments.

293. Article 45(1)(b) endows the Commission with a quasi-legislative function by giving it responsibility for developing principles and rules aimed at solving legal problems relating to human rights generally upon which governments may base their legislation.

294. Finally, Article 45(1)(c) requires the Commission to cooperate with other African and international institutions concerned with human rights.[1470] The Commission has thus cooperated with non-governmental agencies, such as the United Nations High Commission for Refugees (UNHCR), and NGOs such as Amnesty International and IGOs.

295. The Commission has two other areas of competence in this regard. According to Article 45(3) it can interpret the provisions of the African Charter at the request of a State party, the AU, or an African organization recognized by the AU,[1471] and it has additionally adopted the practice of interpreting some Charter provisions at its own initiative.[1472] The Commission's powers in this context are important given that it is performing a quasi-judicial function, similar to the advisory jurisdiction of international judicial bodies, in defining and declaring the extent of fundamental freedoms and duties. The Commission has therefore adopted resolutions on general human rights concerns or specific problems and countries.[1473] In view of the fact that the Court has also been given such a power it may be that this particular function of the Commission will fall into disuse.

296. In this context the State reporting system should be mentioned. Under Article 62 States parties must submit every two years a report on legislative or other measures taken to give effect to the rights and freedoms guaranteed by the African Charter.[1474] The system is designed to reveal the extent of implementation through 'constructive dialogue'.[1475] The Commission can thereby identify the issues that require urgent attention by States.[1476] This system is virtually identical to the supervisory

1470. *See also* Rule 65.

1471. *See also* Rule 116.

1472. Ankumah, 26.

1473. The resolutions are listed in the Activity Reports.

1474. Although Art. 62 does not make it clear that the Commission has been expressly assigned this supervisory role it assumed this responsibility, Ankumah, 79. *See also* Rule 73. The Commission has issued guidelines to assist States parties in drafting their reports, amended in 1998, in Murray & Evans, Documents Vol. I, 49–81. *See* generally M. Evans, T. Ige & R. Murray, 'The Reporting Mechanism of the African Charter on Human and Peoples' Rights', in *The African Charter on Human and Peoples' Rights: The System in Practice, 1986–2000*, Evans & Murray (eds) , (Cambridge: Cambridge University Press, 2002), 36–60.

1475. Ankumah, 80.

1476. Rule 78(1).

functions that exist under the UN control machinery. To date the record of compliance is unsatisfactory.[1477]

297. The Commission has an extremely important role to play in the protection of human rights[1478] and its mandate is set out in Articles 46–58, as supplemented by the Rules of Procedure. The Commission has broad investigative powers in that it may resort to any appropriate method of investigation in accordance with international law and the African Charter.[1479] Its primary function seems to be to uncover the facts and attempt to reach an amicable settlement based on respect for human rights.[1480] It appears that the Commission has used these powers creatively by appointing thematic rapporteurs and sending missions to conduct on-site investigations.[1481] The latter, known as 'protection missions', is now specifically provided for in the Rules.[1482] Additionally, special provision is made for the Commission to refer 'matters of emergency' to the AU policy organs under Article 58(3)[1483] or the African Court of Human and Peoples' Rights.[1484]

298. In *Bissangou v. Republic of Congo* the respondent State argued that Article 45 had established a non-jurisdictional mechanism and that the Commission's decisions were not binding but simply had a moral significance.[1485] It is certainly the case that there is nothing in the African Charter to indicate that the Commission's decisions

1477. Evans, Ige & Murray, 41–42. By January 2013 only eight States were up to date with their reporting obligations, Commission's Combined Thirty-second and Thirty-third Activity Report 2013, pt. IV. There is little that the Commission can do except to remind States of their obligations, Rule 76.

1478. Article 45(2). In this context the Commission has therefore stated that 'its role consists precisely in pronouncing on allegations of violations of the human rights protected by the Charter', *Malawi African Association et al. v. Mauritania*, Communication Nos 54/91, 61/91, 98/93, 164/97–196/97, 210/98, 13th Activity Report 1999–2000, para. 83. *See also Good v. Botswana*, Communication No. 306/2005, 28th Activity Report 2009–2010, paras 80–82.

1479. Article 46.

1480. *See* Rule 90(1). This role has become an established part of the Commission's mandate, F. Viljoen, 'Communications under the African Charter: Procedure and Admissibility', in *The African Charter on Human and Peoples' Rights: The System in Practice, 1986–2006*, Evans & Murray (eds), (Cambridge: Cambridge University Press, 2008), 80–85.

1481. Murray, 21–24. *See* Rule 23.

1482. Rules 81–82.

1483. *See also* Rules 79–80, 84(1).

1484. Rule 84(2).

1485. Communication No. 253/2002, 21st Activity Report 2005–2006, para. 46.

have the binding force of a ruling of a court of law;[1486] at best they may be said to have a persuasive authority akin to the Opinions of the HRC. However, an expectation of compliance does appear to have been engendered.[1487]

299. An important tool in the Commission's protective mandate is the capacity to examine interstate complaints and 'other communications'. Articles 47–54 govern interstate complaints.[1488] Provision is made for a negotiation procedure and a complaint procedure. Under Article 47, which is a permissive not mandatory procedure,[1489] the complainant State can draw the attention of the accused State to possible violations of the African Charter through a written communication. This requirement, according to the Commission, 'is to avoid a situation of springing surprises on the States involved'. It also 'enables the Respondent States to decide whether to settle the complaint amicably or not'.[1490] At the same time this communication is also submitted to the Chair of the AU Commission and the Chairperson of the Commission, providing a detailed account

1486. *See* Art. 59 and Rule 110; Ankumah, 24, 74–75. However, in its Introduction to the first volume of law reports published by the Commission available on the website of the University of Pretoria, the Commission has stated that, 'As the only existing body with the power to examine communications, mandated by Article 45.2 to ensure the protection of human and peoples' rights under the conditions laid down by the present Charter, the Commission considers that its decisions with regard to these communications are legally binding upon the states parties concerned,' http://www.up.ac.za/chr/ahrdb/acomm_decisions.html. One commentator writes that the Commission has relied on these provisions to declare that there have been violations of the Charter, R. Murray, 'Decisions by the African Commission on Individual Communications under the African Charter on Human and Peoples' Rights,' *I.C.L.Q.* 46 (1997): 412, 428. A 'decision' may be procedurally distinct from a 'judgment', M.O. Hudson, *The Permanent Court of International Justice 1920-1942* (New York: MacMillan, 1943), 583–584. *See also Ekollo Moundi Alexandre v. Republic of Cameroon and Federal Republic of Nigeria*, African Court of Human and Peoples' Rights, App. No. 008/2011 (23 Sept. 2011) paras 3–4.

1487. This approach would appear to be required under the African Charter, Art. 1, *see Civil Liberties Organization v. Nigeria*, Communication No. 129/94, 9th Activity Report 1995–1996. *See* further C. Anyangwe, 'Obligations of States Parties to the African Charter on Human and Peoples' Rights', *R.A.D.I.C.* 10 (1998): 625. It may be that the Commission has come to regard its decisions on communications as binding, *see International Pen, Constitutional Rights Project, Interights on behalf of Ken Saro-Wiwa Jr. and Civil Liberties Organisation v. Nigeria*, Communication Nos 137/94, 139/94, 154/96 and 161/97, 12th Activity Report 1998–1999, paras 113–116; Murray, The African Commission on Human and Peoples' Rights and International Law, 53–55.

1488. Ankumah, 23–24. *See also* Rules 83, 86–92. In *Interights (on behalf of Pan-African Movement and Citizens for Peace in Eritrea) and Interights (on behalf of Pan-African Movement and Inter Africa Group) v. Eritrea*, Communication Nos 233/99, 234/99, 16th Activity Report 2002–2003, para. 44, the Commission stated that the 'initiation of an interstate complaint is dependent on the voluntary exercise of the sovereign will of a State party to the Charter, which decision can only be made by States in accordance with the Charter'. Individual communications cannot be converted into interstate communications, *ibid.* To date only one complaint has been submitted, *Democratic Republic of Congo v. Burundi, Rwanda and Uganda*, Communication No. 227/99, 20th Activity Report 2005–2006.

1489. *Democratic Republic of Congo v. Burundi, Rwanda and Uganda*, Communication No. 227/99, 20th Activity Report 2005–2006, para. 58.

1490. *Ibid.*, para. 60.

of the facts denounced and the Charter provisions allegedly violated.[1491] The accused State then has three months in which to respond in writing, providing information on the relevant laws and administrative measures applied or applicable and any redress given or the course of action available.[1492] If the complainant State is not satisfied with this statement or if no reply is forthcoming and the question is not settled through bilateral negotiation or 'any other peaceful procedure' either State may submit the matter to the Commission.[1493] The phrase 'any other peaceful procedure' appears to refer to 'regional or international procedures of settlement or good offices'.[1494] According to the Commission these provisions are aimed at conciliation.[1495]

300. Alternatively, a State can submit a complaint directly to the Commission.[1496] It is interesting to note that the jurisdiction of the Commission is not dependent upon a State party's prior acceptance of its competence, that is, a State automatically accepts the compulsory jurisdiction of the Commission upon ratification or accession to the African Charter.

301. The Commission's jurisdiction *ratione materiae* is broad since Article 47 clearly indicates that its attention may be drawn to any violation, whether by omission or commission, of the African Charter. Its jurisdiction *ratione personae* extends to acts committed by, or imputable to, a State party in accordance with the doctrine of state responsibility. In relation to its jurisdiction *ratione loci* it is clear from the wording of the African Charter that many of the rights guaranteed are available not only to the nationals of State parties but also to *any* individual under their jurisdiction.

302. Article 50 requires the exhaustion of all existing local remedies. However, States cannot profit by deliberately delaying redress since the Commission can ignore this stricture if it is apparent that exhausting those remedies would entail an inordinate length of time or do not exist.[1497]

303. The Commission's investigative powers are contained in Articles 51 and 52. Once an issue has been referred to it the Commission can request the States concerned to provide it with all relevant information.[1498] However, it is not clear whether the States are obliged to supply this information although any lack of cooperation will doubtless feature in the Commission's report. During this stage the States concerned may be represented before the Commission and may submit written or oral observations.[1499] In addition, the Commission can approach 'other sources' for any information it deems

1491. Rule 86.

1492. *See also* Rule 88(1).

1493. Article 48 and Rules 87–92.

1494. Rule 87(2)(b).

1495. *Democratic Republic of Congo v. Burundi, Rwanda and Uganda*, Communication No. 227/99, 20th Activity Report 2005–2006, para. 57.

1496. Article 49. *See also* Rule 87. According to the Commission, Art. 49 allows the States to avoid engagement where 'such contacts will not be diplomatically either effective or desirable', *Democratic Republic of Congo v. Burundi, Rwanda and Uganda*, Communication No. 227/99, 20th Activity Report 2005–2006, para. 61.

1497. *Democratic Republic of Congo v. Burundi, Rwanda and Uganda*, Communication No. 227/99, 20th Activity Report 2005–2006, paras 62–63.

1498. *See also* Rule 88(3)(a).

1499. *See also* Rule 88(5)–(6).

necessary[1500] and this would appear to include other States, individuals, NGOs, the AU and other international organizations. Nonetheless, during this time the Commission must attempt by all possible means to reach an amicable settlement based on respect for human and peoples' rights.[1501]

304. If no settlement is forthcoming the Commission is required to draft a report stating the facts and its findings which it must subsequently submit to the States concerned and the AU Assembly.[1502] The Commission may make such recommendations as it considers necessary to the AU Assembly when submitting the report, so that it could recommend that the matter be closed and no further action be taken, or that the report be published.[1503] The ultimate responsibility however, lies with the AU Assembly.

305. The African Charter also envisages complaints, or 'communications', 'other than those of State parties' under Article 55. Rule 93(1) refers to 'natural or legal persons' and Rule 93(2)(a) confirms that individuals and NGOs have standing to approach the Commission as complainants.[1504] It is interesting to note that the *locus standi* requirements before the Commission are comparatively broad since individuals and organizations other than the victim can submit a complaint.[1505] In fact, the

1500. Rule 85 employs the noun 'parties' and appears to be narrower in scope than the parent treaty provision.

1501. *See also* Rule 90.

1502. *See also* Rules 91–92. Rule 92(1) requires the Commission to adopt its report within twelve months.

1503. Article 53.

1504. It was clearly established in the Commission's practice that it was competent to receive complaints from individuals and NGOs, *see* , e.g., *Sir Dawda K. Jawara v. Gambia*, Communication Nos 147/95 and 149/96, 13th Activity Report 1999–2000, paras 41–42. In *Bissangou v. Republic of Congo*, Communication No. 253/2002, 21st Activity Report 2005–2006, para. 47, described this aspect of its promotional and protective function, that 'in seizing the Commission, the complainant does not have any other intention than to request the latter to play its role by controlling the conformity to...the Charter of an action...of a State party'.

1505. Rule 93(2)(a); *Zitha & Zitha v. Mozambique*, Communication No. 361/08, 29th Activity Report 2010, para. 106; *Haregewoin Gabre-Selassie and IHRDA (on behalf of former Dergue officials) v. Ethiopia*, Communication No. 301/05 (2011) paras 61–62. This includes NGOs such as Amnesty International and International Pen; *see* further Viljoen, Communications under the African Charter, 76. Nor need the applicant be a national or registered in the Respondent State, *Spilg and Mack & Ditshwanelo (on behalf of Lehlohonolo Bernard Kobedi) v. Botswana*, Communication No. 277/2003, paras 83–84; *Haregewoin Gabre-Selassie and IHRDA (on behalf of former Dergue officials) v. Ethiopia*, Communication No. 301/05 (2011) para. 64. In *Interights (on behalf of Pan-African Movement and Citizens for Peace in Eritrea) and Interights (on behalf of Pan-African Movement and Inter Africa Group) v. Eritrea*, Communication Nos 233/99, 234/99, 16th Activity Report 2002–2003, paras 32, 34, Ethiopia questioned the neutrality, credibility and integrity of the NGO but the Commission expressed the view that such a matter did not fall within the conditions of admissibility under Art. 56. In *Malawi African Association et al. v. Mauritania*, Communication Nos 54/91, 61/91, 98/93, 164/97–196/97, 210/98, 13th Activity Report 1999–2000, para. 78, the Commission justified this situation thus, 'This characteristic of the African Charter reflects sensitivity to the practical difficulties that individuals can face in countries where human rights are violated. The national or international channels of remedy may not be accessible to the victims themselves or may be dangerous to pursue.'

Commission has stated that it has adopted an *actio popularis* approach.[1506] A number of procedural hurdles have to be initially overcome before the Commission will consider the substance of a communication, which it will do by a simple majority of its members.[1507] Article 56 enumerates seven admissibility requirements and although similar criteria are to be found in comparable international instruments the African Charter goes further in introducing unique and, in theory, more restrictive requirements of admissibility.[1508] It is important to take cognizance of the fact that the admissibility requirements are cumulative, or 'conjunctive, meaning that if any one of them is absent, the communication will be declared inadmissible'.[1509] Consequently, all seven conditions must generally be fulfilled.[1510] The conditions are designed 'to sieve frivolous and vexatious communications before they reach the merits stage'.[1511] This provision takes into account the conditions *ratione materiae, loci, personae* and *temporis*.[1512] It is important to note that no prescribed form of submission of a communication is required.[1513]

306. The first condition of admissibility is that the communication must indicate the author, even if the author requests anonymity, so that 'adequate information with

1506. *Article 19 v. Eritrea*, Communication No. 275/2003, 22nd Activity Report 2006–2007, para. 65; 'wisely allowed', *see The Social and Economic Rights Action Center and the Center for Economic and Social Rights v. Nigeria*, Communication No. 155/96, 15th Activity Report 2001–2002, para. 49; *Spilg and Mack & Ditshwanelo (on behalf of Lehlohonolo Bernard Kobedi) v. Botswana*, Communication No. 277/2003, para. 81; *Haregewoin Gabre-Selassie and IHRDA (on behalf of former Dergue officials) v. Ethiopia*, Communication No. 301/05 (2011) para. 61. In *The Law Office of Ghazi Suleiman v. Sudan*, Communication Nos 222/98 and 229/99, 16th Activity Report 2002–2003, para. 39, the Commission stated that States' obligations were of an *erga omnes* nature not dependent on individuals, an apparent reference to the special character of human rights treaties. It should be observed that the Commission may receive amicus curiae briefs on communications, Rule 99(16).

1507. Article 55(2); *Amnesty International v. Zambia*, Communication No. 212/98, 12th Activity Report 1998–1999, para. 24.

1508. Ankumah, 61–67.

1509. Rule 106; *Article 19 v. Eritrea*, Communication No. 275/2003, 22nd Activity Report 2006–2007, para. 43; *Zimbabwe Lawyers for Human Rights & Associated Newspapers of Zimbabwe v. Zimbabwe*, Communication No. 284/2003, 26th Activity Report 2008–2009, para. 81. *See also Omary and Others v. Tanzania*, African Court of Human and Peoples' Rights, App. No. 001/2012 (28 Mar. 2014), para. 86.

1510. *Zimbabwe Human Rights NGO Forum v. Zimbabwe*, Communication No. 245/2002, 21st Activity Report 2005–2006, para. 36.

1511. *Chinhamo v. Zimbabwe*, Communication No. 307/2005, 23rd Activity Report 2007, para. 45; *Majuru v. Zimbabwe*, Communication No. 308/2005, 25th Activity Report 2008, para. 70.

1512. Viljoen, Communications under the African Charter, 69; Murray, Decisions by the African Commission on Individual Communications, 418–421.

1513. *Haregewoin Gabre-Selassie and IHRDA (on behalf of former Dergue officials) v. Ethiopia*, Communication No. 301/05 (2011) paras 119–120.

a certain degree of specificity concerning the victim' must be provided.[1514] However, the names of the victims where they are not complainants must also be provided.[1515] The Commission has stated that the 'existence of a direct interest (like being a victim) to bring the matter before the Commission is not a requirement under the African Charter'.[1516] This situation has been justified on the grounds that the 'African Charter reflects sensitivity to the practical difficulties that individuals can face in countries where human rights are violated. The national or international channels of remedy may not be accessible to the victims themselves or may be dangerous to pursue.'[1517] The Commission has therefore held that in the context of grave and massive violations there is no need for all the victims to be identified and named by the complainants.[1518] If there are fears of reprisals, a real fear in much of Africa, or other dangers the Commission can protect the author's identity.[1519]

307. The second condition is that the communication must be compatible with the AU Constitutive Act or the African Charter. It has been held by the Human Rights Court that these instruments should be read independently.[1520] It cannot be that mere submission of a complaint in itself gives rise to incompatibility. In a general sense 'compatibility' signifies 'in compliance with' or 'in conformity with'.[1521] As the Commission has observed, this procedure is designed to protect human rights and States are duty bound to adhere to the obligations they have assumed.[1522] However, a claim that the people of Katanga had a right to secede from Zaïre in accordance with the right to self-determination raised the question of compatibility with the basic principles of the OAU regarding territorial integrity.[1523] The Commission has summarized the requirements of this condition: that the communication be brought against a State Party to the African Charter; that it claims prima facie violations of the African Charter; that the communication be brought in respect of violations that occurred after ratification of the African Charter, or in relation to continuing violations if they commenced before ratification of the African Charter; and that the communication contain a degree of

---

1514. *Centre for Independence of Judges and Lawyers v. Algeria*, Communication Nos 104/94, 109–126/94, 8th Activity Report 1994–1995, para. 5. *See also* Rule 93(2)(a), (d). Email addresses appear to suffice, *Spilg and Mack & Ditshwanelo (on behalf of Lehlohonolo Bernard Kobedi) v. Botswana*, Communication No. 277/2003, para. 98. Communications can be rejected on the grounds that they are vague or unclear, *Bakweri Land Claims Committee v. Cameroon,* Communication No. 260/02, 18th Activity Report 2002–2003, para. 47.

1515. Rule 93(2)(e).

1516. *Bakweri Land Claims Committee v. Cameroon,* Communication No. 260/02, 18th Activity Report 2002–2003, para. 46.

1517. *Ibid.*, para. 78.

1518. *Ibid.*, para. 79.

1519. *Ibid.*, paras 78–79. *See also* Rule 93(2)(b).

1520. *Omary and Others v. Tanzania*, African Court of Human and Peoples' Rights, African Court of Human and Peoples' Rights, App. No. 001/2012 (28 Mar. 2014), paras 74, 93.

1521. *Mohamed Abdullah Saleh al-Asad v. Djibouti*, Communication No. 383/10 (2014), para. 128.

1522. *Sudan Human Rights Organization and Sudan Centre for Housing Rights and Evictions v. Sudan* Communication Nos 279/03, 296/05, 28th Activity Report, 2010, paras 90–91.

1523. *Katangese Peoples Congress v. Zaire*, Communication No. 75/92, 8th Activity Report 1994–1995.

specificity.[1524] In *Omary and Others v. Tanzania*, Tanzania argued that the Court lacked jurisdiction because the application failed to cite either instrument.[1525] However, the Court ruled that an application could not be adjudged inadmissible on this ground as long as the rights alleged to have been violated were guaranteed by the African Charter or some other human rights instrument ratified by the State.[1526]

308. It has been established that this particular provision should be interpreted as a reference to the conditions *ratione materiae, loci, personae,* and *temporis*.[1527] With regard to subject matter, it is not necessary to list in a communication which specific articles of the African Charter are alleged to have been violated[1528] as long as the substance of the issue at stake is raised[1529] and a prima facie case is established,[1530] in that the complaint 'should be one that compels the conclusion that a human rights violation has occurred'[1531] There is no need for evidence of systematic violations to prove a prima facie case.[1532] In *Katangese Peoples Congress v. Zaïre*, the Commission found no evidence of violations of human rights which could justify secession and was therefore without 'merit' under the African Charter.[1533] Vague complaints about the general political climate cannot suffice either.[1534]

309. Complaints can only be submitted against States parties.[1535] In fact, quite a number of communications have been declared inadmissible on the ground of being

1524. *Gunme et al. v. Cameroon,* Communication No. 266/2003, 26th Activity Report 2008–2009, para. 38.
1525. *Omary and Others v. Tanzania*, African Court of Human and Peoples' Rights, App. No. 001/2012 (28 Mar. 2014), para. 55. *See also Wilfred Onyango Nganyi & 9 Others v. Tanzania*, African Court of Human and Peoples' Rights, App. No. 006/2013 (18 Mar. 2016), para. 57.
1526. *Ibid.,* paras 74–76, 92–93.
1527. *Mohamed Abdullah Saleh al-Asad v. Djibouti*, Communication No. 383/10 (2014), paras 129–137.
1528. Rule 93(2)(g); *Haregewoin Gabre-Selassie and IHRDA (on behalf of former Dergue officials) v. Ethiopia*, Communication No. 301/05 (2011) para. 106; *Wilfred Onyango Nganyi & 9 Others v. Tanzania*, African Court of Human and Peoples' Rights, App. No. 006/2013 (18 March 2016), para. 58.
1529. *Majuru v. Zimbabwe*, Communication No. 308/2005, 25th Activity Report 2008, para. 73; *Muzerengwa and 110 Others (represented by Zimbabwe Lawyers for Human Rights) v. Zimbabwe*, Communication No. 306/2005, 29th Activity Report 2010, para. 56; *Southern Africa Human Rights NGO Network and Others v. Tanzania*, Communication No. 333/200, 28th Activity Report 2009–2010, para. 51. Rule 93(2)(d) requires that an account of the act or situation complained of be provided.
1530. *Wilfred Onyango Nganyi & 9 Others v. Tanzania*, African Court of Human and Peoples' Rights, App. No. 006/2013 (18 Mar. 2016), para. 79.
1531. *Chinhamo v. Zimbabwe*, Communication No. 307/2005, 23rd Activity Report 2007, para. 48. *See also Uhuru Kenyatta and William Ruto (represented by Innocence Project Africa) v. Kenya*, Communication No. 464/14 (2014), para. 20.
1532. *Priscilla Njeri Echaria (represented by Federation of Women Lawyers, Kenya and International Center for the Protection of Human Rights) v. Kenya*, Communication No. 375/09 (2011), para. 35.
1533. Communication No. 75/92, 8th Activity Report 1994–1995.
1534. *Centre for Independence of Judges and Lawyers v. Algeria*, Communication Nos 104/94, 109–126/94, 8th Activity Report 1994–1995.
1535. *See* Rule 93(2)(g).

lodged against non-State parties, including States beyond Africa.[1536] The alleged violation must have occurred within the territorial jurisdiction of a State party.[1537]

310. Finally, as regards the time of the alleged violation, communications must be submitted against African States that were parties to the African Charter at the time the violations were alleged to have occurred.[1538] However, it should be observed that both the Commission and the Human Rights Court have expressed approval of the concept of 'continuing violations', that is, that they will assume jurisdiction even though the violation had taken place before the State had become a party to the African Charter because its effects continued after that time. Thus in *Amnesty International et al. v. Sudan*, the Commission made it plain that continuing violations fall within its competence.[1539] In *Annette Pagnoulle (on behalf of Abdoulaye Mazou) v. Cameroon*, the Commission expressed the view that if 'irregularities in the original sentence have consequences that constitute a continuing violation of any of the Articles of the African Charter, the Commission must pronounce on these'.[1540] In *Zitha & Zitha v. Mozambique*, the Commission held that the phenomenon of forced disappearances constitutes a continuing violation of human rights which continued to occur after the State party had ratified the African Charter even though the initial fact had taken place before the date of ratification.[1541] In the Commission's view, this principle 'presupposes the failure by the State party to adopt measures, as required by Article 1 of the African Charter to redress the violations and their effects'.[1542]

311. The third condition is that the communication must not be disparaging or insulting towards the State concerned, its institutions or the AU.[1543] The Commission has stated that while it must strike a balance between the freedom of expression and the reputation of others vital state institutions must not be exposed to comments which

1536. *See* generally 7th Activity Report 1993–1994.

1537. *Muzerengwa and 110 Others (represented by Zimbabwe Lawyers for Human Rights) v. Zimbabwe*, Communication No. 306/2005, 29th Activity Report 2010, para. 58; *Mohamed Abdullah Saleh al-Asad v. Djibouti*, Communication No. 383/10 (2014), paras 151–177.

1538. *See* generally 7th Activity Report; *Malawi African Association et al. v. Mauritania*, Communication Nos 54/91, 61/91, 98/93, 164/97–196/97, 210/98, 13th Activity Report 1999–2000, paras 104, 109.

1539. Communication Nos 48/90, 50/91, 52/91, 89/93, 13th Activity Report 1999–2000, para. 40; *Wilfred Onyango Nganyi & 9 Others v. Tanzania*, African Court of Human and Peoples' Rights, App. No. 006/2013 (18 Mar. 2016), para. 66; *African Commission on Human and Peoples' Rights v. Kenya*, African Court of Human and Peoples' Rights, App. No. 006/2012 (26 May 2017) para. 65.

1540. Communication No. 39/90, 10th Activity Report 1996–1997, para. 15.

1541. Communication No. 361/08, 29th Activity Report 2010, paras 85–94.

1542. *Gunme et al. v. Cameroon,* Communication No. 266/2003, 26th Activity Report 2008–2009, para. 96.

1543. *See Ligue Camerounaise des Droits de l'Homme v. Cameroon*, Communication No. 65/92, 10th Activity Report 1996–1997; *Bakweri Land Claims Committee v. Cameroon,* Communication No. 260/02, 18th Activity Report 2002–2003, para. 48; *Ahmed Ismael and 528 Others v. Egypt*, Communication No. 467/14 (2015) paras 141–145. *See* further Viljoen, Communications under the African Charter, 78–80.

bring them into disrepute or undermine their effectiveness.[1544] Hence it has the authority to dismiss patently absurd complaints that amount to an abuse of the right of petition. It is important that the adjectives 'disparaging' and 'insulting' should not be interpreted too broadly, and can be dependent on context,[1545] but abusive language is not acceptable.[1546] The Commission has accepted that this provision imposes an objective test.[1547]

312. The fourth condition is that the communication must not be based exclusively on information obtained from the mass media. The rationale for this requirement seems to be that communications should not be based on secondary and unsubstantiated allegations given the African Charter's relaxed requirements of individual standing[1548] but on primary evidence although events reported by the media have been taken into account by the Commission. Thus, in *Sir Dawda K. Jawara v. Gambia*, the Commission stated that, 'While it would be dangerous to rely *exclusively* on news disseminated from the mass media, it would be equally damaging if the Commission were to reject a communication because some aspects of it are based on news disseminated through

1544. *Ilesanmi v. Nigeria*, Communication No. 268/2003, 18th Activity Report 2002–2003, para. 40. *See also Zimbabwe Lawyers for Human Rights and the Institute for Human Rights and Development v. Zimbabwe*, Communication No. 293/2004, 24th Activity Report 2008, paras 46–56; *Zimbabwe Lawyers for Human Rights & Associated Newspapers of Zimbabwe v. Zimbabwe*, Communication No. 284/2003, 26th Activity Report 2008–2009, paras 83–97.

1545. The applicant's subjective opinion about the regime or its leaders cannot per se be considered insulting, *Bakweri Land Claims Committee v. Cameroon,* Communication No. 260/02, 18th Activity Report 2002–2003, para. 48; *Jean-Marie Atangana Mebara v. Cameroon*, Communication No. 416/12 (2015) para. 55. In *Ivorien Human Rights Movement (MIDH) v. Côte d'Ivoire*, Communication No. 262/2002, 26th Activity Report 2008–2009, para. 47, the terms 'xenophobia' and 'discriminatory' were accepted as accurate descriptions of the state of affairs.

1546. Statements such as 'regime of torturers' and 'government barbarisms' were considered insulting by the Commission in *Ligue Camerounaise des Droits de l'Homme v. Cameroon*, Communication No. 65/92, 10th Activity Report 1996–1997, para. 15. Other unacceptable terms include 'sickening' and 'charade', *Uhuru Kenyatta and William Ruto (represented by Innocence Project Africa) v. Kenya*, Communication No. 464/14 (2014), para. 18. *See also Ilesanmi v. Nigeria*, Communication No. 268/2003, 18th Activity Report 2002–2003, paras 22–29. The Commission has stated that the language used must 'unequivocally demonstrate the intention of the Complainant to bring the State and its institutions into disrepute', *Eyob B. Asemie v. Lesotho*, Communication No. 435/12 (2014), para. 59. Facts or allegations of African Charter violations are not deemed incompatible with this provision, *Tsikata v. Ghana*, Communication No. 322/2006, 21st Activity Report 2005–2006, paras 32–33.

1547. *Ahmed Ismael and 528 Others v. Egypt*, Communication No. 467/14 (2015) para. 142. Although in a previous case, *Gunme et al. v. Cameroon,* Communication No. 266/2003, 26th Activity Report 2008–2009, para. 75, the Commission had suggested the provision had a subjective character.

1548. Viljoen, Communications under the African Charter, 80.

the mass media' (emphasis added).[1549] The Commission went on to state that the test was not whether the information had been obtained from the media but whether it was correct. The crucial question was whether the applicant had tried to verify the truth and whether it was possible for him to have done so in the circumstances.[1550]

313. The fifth condition requires the exhaustion of existing domestic, or local or internal, remedies.[1551] This provision reflects a general principle of international law granting the State the initial opportunity to right any wrongdoing[1552] and exists in all major human rights instruments. The Commission has pointed out that the international system plays a subsidiary and complementary role and that access to an international

---

1549. Communication Nos 147/95 and 149/96, 13th Activity Report 1999–2000, para. 24. In *Zimbabwe Human Rights NGO Forum v. Zimbabwe*, Communication No. 245/2002, 21st Activity Report 2005–2006, para. 43, the Commission stressed the 'operative term being "exclusively"'. In *Ahmed Ismael and 528 Others v. Egypt*, Communication No. 467/14 (2015), para. 151, the applicants had relied on sources derived from NGOs. In *Sudan Human Rights Organization and Sudan Centre for Housing Rights and Evictions v. Sudan* Communication Nos 279/03, 296/05, 28th Activity Report 2010, paras 92–93, the Commission accepted the fact that the conflict in Darfur had attracted the attention of the mass media.

1550. *Sir Dawda K. Jawara v. Gambia*, Communication Nos 147/95 and 149/96, 13th Activity Report 1999–2000, para. 26. Security risks and difficulties in obtaining access to documents and victims were accepted as legitimate reasons by the Commission, *Ahmed Ismael and 528 Others v. Egypt*, Communication No. 467/14 (2015) para. 150.

1551. *See also* Rule 93(2)(i). The emphasis is on the availability of remedies in the State where the violation allegedly occurred and not in other jurisdictions, *Crawford Lindsay von Abo v. Zimbabwe*, Communication No. 477/14 (2015) para. 97.

1552. *See* generally C.F. Amerasinghe, *Local Remedies in International Law* (2nd edn, Cambridge: Cambridge University Press, 2004). The principle of exhaustion of local remedies has been described as the 'cornerstone of the Commission's adjudicatory function…which safeguard prevents the Commission from acting as a court of first instance', *Crawford Lindsay von Abo v. Zimbabwe*, Communication No. 477/14 (2015) para. 66. In *Free Legal Assistance Group, Lawyers Committee for Human Rights, Union Interafricaine des Droits de l'Homme, and Les Temoins Jehoves v. Zaïre*, Communication Nos 25/89, 47/90, 59/91, 100/93, 9th Activity Report 1995–1996, para. 36, the Commission reaffirmed this principle, stating that, 'The requirement of exhaustion of local remedies is founded on the principle that a government should have notice of a human rights violation in order to have the opportunity to remedy such violations before being called before an international body.' In *Haregewoin Gabre-Selassie and IHRDA (on behalf of former Dergue officials) v. Ethiopia*, Communication No. 301/05 (2011) para. 113, the Commission referred to the State being given ample time and notice to redress the situation. *See also Rencontre Africaine pour la Defense des Droits de l'Homme v. Zambia*, Communication No. 71/92, 10th Activity Report 1996–1997, para. 11; *Mohammed Lamine Diakité v. Gabon*, Communication No. 73/92, 13th Activity Report 1999–2000, para. 16; *Malawi African Association et al. v. Mauritania*, Communication Nos 54/91, 61/91, 98/93, 164/97–196/97, 210/98, 13th Activity Report 1999–2000, para. 80; *Sir Dawda K. Jawara v. Gambia*, Communication Nos 147/95 and 149/96, 13th Activity Report 1999–2000, para. 31; *Anuak Justice Council v. Ethiopia*, Communication No. 299/05, 20th Activity Report 2005–2006, para. 47; *Muzerengwa and 110 Others (represented by Zimbabwe Lawyers for Human Rights) v. Zimbabwe*, Communication No. 306/2005, 29th Activity Report 2010, para. 65; *Zimbabwe Lawyers for Human Rights & Associated Newspapers of Zimbabwe v. Zimbabwe*, Communication No. 284/2003, 26th Activity Report 2008–2009, para. 100. In *Mbianku v. Cameroon*, Communication No. 389/10 (2015) para. 71, the Commission stated that Art. 56(5) was an expression of the principle of subsidiarity.

organ is a last, rather than initial, resort.[1553] It is of the view that this condition is one of the most important and is invariably the first requirement to be examined.[1554] Its 'essential characteristic' is its 'demonstrable effectiveness in redressing a particular violation.'[1555] The Commission has held that domestic remedies refer to 'the ordinary remedies of common law',[1556] or 'those normally available in the domestic court system and excluding those available only as a pure discretionary matter from the executive'.[1557] Moreover, it 'must operate in strict observance of the procedural guarantees of a fair hearing by a competent, independent and impartial organ…[and] must be based on enforceable law from which the relief it offers earns its mandatory or coercive force, as opposed to being merely discretionary.'[1558] The remedy should therefore be primarily

---

1553. *Anuak Justice Council v. Ethiopia*, Communication No. 299/05, 20th Activity Report 2005–2006, para. 48, though the Commission went on to state that this condition 'should not constitute an unjustifiable impediment to access to international remedies', para. 49. However, in *Crawford Lindsay von Abo v. Zimbabwe*, Communication No. 477/14 (2015) para. 99, the Commission explained that its role was subsidiary to that of the respondent State and it was not a 'last resort' while the applicant pursued remedies in other jurisdictions.

1554. *Amnesty International v. Zambia*, Communication No. 212/98, 12th Activity Report 1998–1999, para. 24; *Sir Dawda K. Jawara v. Gambia*, Communication Nos 147/95 and 149/96, 13th Activity Report 1999–2000, para. 30; *The Law Office of Ghazi Suleiman v. Sudan*, Communication No. 228/99, 16th Activity Report, 2002–2003, para. 29.

1555. *Human Rights Council and Others v. Ethiopia*, Communication No. 445/13 (2015) para. 59; *Groupe de Travail sur les Dossiers Judiciaires Stratégiques v. Democratic Republic of Congo*, Communication No. 259/2002 (2011) para. 46.

1556. *Interights, Institute for Human Rights and Development in Africa, and Association Mauritaniene des Droits de l'Homme v. Mauritania*, Communication No. 242/2001, 17th Activity Report, 2003–2004, para. 27; *Koso and Others v. Democratic Republic of Congo*, Communication No. 281/2003, 26th Activity Report 2008–2009, para. 51. Approved by the Human Rights Court, *Alex Thomas v. Tanzania*, African Court of Human and Peoples' Rights, App. No. 005/2013 (20 Nov. 2015), para. 64. The Court proceeded to state that constitutional remedies or applications for review constitute 'exceptional remedies' which the applicant is not expected to use, *ibid.*, paras 63–64. In *Socio-Economic Rights and Accountability Project v. Nigeria*, Communication No. 300/2005, 25th Activity Report 2008, para. 69, the question was whether socio-economic rights could be litigated in Nigerian courts.

1557. *Account of the Internal Legislation of Nigeria and the Disposition of the African Charter on Human and Peoples' Rights*, Communication Nos 129/94 and 101/93, in Murray & Evans, Documents Vol. I, 468. *See also Amnesty International et al. v. Sudan*, Communication Nos 48/90, 50/91, 52/91, 89/93, 13th Activity Report 1999–2000, para. 31; *Ilesanmi v. Nigeria*, Communication No. 268/2003, 18th Activity Report 2002–2003, para. 42; *Bissangou v. Republic of Congo*, Communication No. 253/2002, 21st Activity Report 2005–2006, paras 56, 61; *Good v. Botswana*, Communication No. 306/2005, 28th Activity Report 2009–2010, para. 89; *Muzerengwa and 110 Others (represented by Zimbabwe Lawyers for Human Rights) v. Zimbabwe*, Communication No. 306/2005, 29th Activity Report 2010, para. 74.

1558. *Human Rights Council and Others v. Ethiopia*, Communication No. 445/13 (2015) para. 59.

a judicial one[1559] which is not 'subordinated to the discretionary power of public authorities'.[1560] In *Article 19 v. Eritrea*, the Commission expanded on the necessary criteria:

> (i) the existence of domestic procedures for dealing with the claim; (ii) the justiciability or otherwise, domestically, of the subject-matter of the complaint; (iii) the existence under the municipal legal order of provisions for redress of the type of wrong being complained of; and (iv) available effective local remedies, that is, remedies sufficient or capable of redressing the wrong complained of.[1561]

1559. In *Zimbabwe Lawyers for Human Rights and the Institute for Human Rights and Development (on behalf of Andrew Barclay Meldrum) v. Zimbabwe*, Communication No. 294/2004, 26th Activity Report 2008–2009, para. 51, the Commission stated that, 'Administrative or quasi judicial remedies which do not operate impartially are…inadequate and ineffective.' *See also Alfred B. Cudjoe v. Ghana*, Communication No. 221/98, 12th Activity Report 1998–1999, para. 13; *Constitutional Rights Project (in respect of Waheb Akamu, G. Adega and Others) v. Nigeria*, Communication No. 60/91, 8th Activity Report 1994–1995, para. 5. Administrative remedies have also been discounted unless they are capable and effective under domestic law, *Ilesanmi v. Nigeria*, Communication No. 268/2003, 18th Activity Report 2002–2003, para. 42; *Article 19 v. Eritrea,* Communication No. 275/2003, 22nd Activity Report 2006–2007, para. 70; *Mbianku v. Cameroon*, Communication No. 389/10 (2015) para. 66. Diplomatic protection does not constitute a judicial remedy, *Crawford Lindsay von Abo v. Zimbabwe*, Communication No. 477/14 (2015) para. 94. In *Zimbabwe Human Rights NGO Forum v. Zimbabwe*, Communication No. 245/2002, 21st Activity Report 2005–2006, para. 45, the Commission rejected the State's argument that the complainant could have pursued a remedy with the Ombudsman, who was mandated to investigate human rights violations, holding that the Ombudsman did not provide a judicial remedy. The Commission has therefore established a nexus between this remedy and Art. 7 African Charter which guarantees the right to a fair trial, *Amnesty International et al. v. Sudan*, Communication Nos 48/90, 50/91, 52/91, 89/93, 13th Activity Report 1999–2000, para. 31. In a number of cases concerning Nigeria the Commission has held that ouster clauses remove the possibility of a local remedy, *see* , e.g., *Constitutional Rights Project and Civil Liberties Organisation v. Nigeria*, Communication Nos 143/95, 150/96, 13th Activity Report 1999–2000, paras 16–19.
1560. *Good v. Botswana*, Communication No. 306/2005, 28th Activity Report 2009–2010, para. 88. *See also Amnesty International et al. v. Sudan*, Communication Nos 48/90, 50/91, 52/91, 89/93, 13th Activity Report 1999–2000, para. 31; *Groupe de Travail sur les Dossiers Judiciaires Stratégiques v. Democratic Republic of Congo*, Communication No. 259/2002 (2011) para. 43.
1561. Communication No. 275/2003, 22nd Activity Report 2006–2007, para. 47. *See also Ivorien Human Rights Movement (MIDH) v. Côte d'Ivoire*, Communication No. 262/2002, 26th Activity Report 2008–2009, para. 55. Denial in general terms by the government of human rights violations does not mean the matter had been considered by the domestic courts, *International Pen (in respect of Kemal al-Jazouli) v. Sudan*, Communication No. 92/93, 8th Activity Report, 1994–1995. The Commission has held that the applicant need not be physically present in the country in order to access local remedies, *Chinhamo v. Zimbabwe*, Communication No. 307/2005, 23rd Activity Report 2007, para. 82.

An obvious example would be to approach the highest court of the land with the grievance and fail to obtain a remedy.[1562] The burden of proof is initially on the applicant[1563] but if met the onus shifts on to the State.[1564]

314. The Commission has declared a large number of communications inadmissible on the ground of failure to exhaust local remedies. The reasons are various and include the fact that the case was pending before the domestic courts,[1565] failure to institute legal proceedings,[1566] failure to appeal to a higher court,[1567] making general and uncorroborated allegations,[1568] and that denial of human rights violations by the government in general terms did not mean that the matter had been exhausted before the domestic courts.[1569]

315. The Commission has pointed out that this condition is not a strict requirement that must always be satisfied.[1570] It has, for instance, adopted the principle of 'constructive' exhaustion of local remedies where the complainant is prevented from accessing

---

1562. *Zimbabwe Lawyers for Human Rights & Associated Newspapers of Zimbabwe v. Zimbabwe* Communication No. 284/2003, 26th Activity Report 2008–2009, para. 113; *Lawyers for Human Rights (Swaziland) v. Swaziland*, Communication No. 414/12, (2013), para. 40.

1563. *See Rule 93(2)(i)* and further, e.g., *Nziwa Buyingo v. Uganda*, Communication No. 8/88, 8th Activity Report 1994–1995; *Sana Dumbuya v. The Gambia*, Communication No. 127/94, 8th Activity Report 1994–1995; *Mouvement des Réfugiés Mauritaniens in Senegal v. Senegal*, Communication No. 254/02, 16th Activity Report 2002–2003, para. 21; *Chinhamo v. Zimbabwe*, Communication No. 307/2005, 23rd Activity Report 2007, para. 62. In *Anuak Justice Council v. Ethiopia*, Communication No. 299/05, 20th Activity Report 2005–2006, para. 50, the Commission stated, *inter alia*, that applicants 'must provide some prima facie evidence of an attempt to exhaust local remedies'.

1564. *Rencontre Africaine pour la Defense des Droits de l'Homme v. Zambia*, Communication No. 71/92, 10th Activity Report 1996–1997, para. 13.

1565. *El Hadj Boubacare Diawara v. Benin*, Communication No. 18/88 joined with Nos 16/88 and 17/88, 8th Activity Report, 1994–1995; *Kenya Human Rights Commission v. Kenya*, Communication No. 135/94, 9th Activity Report 1995–1996; *Tsikata v. Ghana*, Communication No. 322/2006, 21st Activity Report 2005–2006, para. 35. As the Commission has observed, 'exhaustion' refers to the conclusion of an action, *Mbianku v. Cameroon*, Communication No. 389/10 (2015) para. 71.

1566. *Alfred B. Cudjoe v. Ghana*, Communication No. 221/98, 12th Activity Report 1998–1999. However, this requirement is dependent on circumstances and where the State is aware of the situation but fails to act the complainants may not be obliged to exhaust local remedies, *Monim Elgak, Osman Hummeida and Amir Suleiman (represented by FIDH and OMCT) v. Sudan*, Communication No. 379/09 (2014) paras 60–63.

1567. *Paul S. Haye v. The Gambia*, Communication No. 90/93, 8th Activity Report, 1994–1995; *Darfur Relief and Communication Centre v. Sudan*, Communication No. 310/2005, 27th Activity Report 2009, para. 73.

1568. *Chinhamo v. Zimbabwe*, Communication No. 307/2005, 23rd Activity Report 2007, para. 76; *Majuru v. Zimbabwe*, Communication No. 308/2005, 25th Activity Report 2008, para. 92; *Socio Economic Rights and Accountability Project (SERAP) v. Nigeria*, Communication No. 338/07, 29th Activity Report 2010, para. 66.

1569. *International Pen (in respect of Kemal al-Jazouli) v. Sudan*, Communication No. 92/93, 8th Activity Report 1994–1995.

1570. *Institute for Human Rights and Development in Africa v. Angola*, Communication No. 292/2004, 24th Activity Report 2008, para. 39.

existing remedies.[1571] Domestic remedies must therefore exist not just in theory but in practice, otherwise it is not accessible, and their exhaustion is not required where it is apparent that such procedures would be 'unduly prolonged'.[1572] It has been held that this test applies to local remedies 'in their entirety as utilised or likely to be utilised by those concerned.'[1573] Although the wording of the African Charter may appear prima facie restrictive[1574] the practice of the Commission demonstrates a more liberal approach.[1575] In determining the rule on the exhaustion of domestic remedies the Commission has resolved on three principal elements: the remedy must be available, effective and sufficient.[1576] It has therefore held that a remedy is 'considered *available* if the petitioner can pursue it without impediment, it is deemed *effective* if it offers a

1571. *Rights International v. Nigeria*, Communication No. 215/98, 13th Activity Report 1999–2000, para. 24; *Doebbler v. Sudan*, Communication No. 236/2000, 16th Activity Report 2002–2003, para. 27. In *Zimbabwe Lawyers for Human Rights and the Institute for Human Rights and Development (on behalf of Andrew Barclay Meldrum) v. Zimbabwe*, Communication No. 294/2004, 26th Activity Report 2008–2009, paras 52–56, the victim was deported in defiance of court orders which in itself amounted to a violation of the African Charter Art. 26.

1572. There are no standard criteria to determine this particular point but is dependent on a variety of factors, *Zimbabwe Lawyers for Human Rights and the Institute for Human Rights and Development v. Zimbabwe*, Communication No. 293/2004, 24th Activity Report 2008, paras 58–61; *Jean-Marie Atangana Mebara v. Cameroon*, Communication No. 416/12 (2015) paras 60–73. The Commission has stated that if it is proven that a State has had ample time and notice to remedy the situation the State will be deemed to have been properly informed and will be expected to take the necessary steps to rectify the violation, *Article 19 v. Eritrea,* Communication No. 275/2003, 22nd Activity Report 2006–2007, para. 77. *See also Wilfred Onyango Nganyi & 9 Others v. Tanzania*, African Court of Human and Peoples' Rights, App. No. 006/2013 (18 March 2016), paras 90–95.

1573. *Zongo and Others v. Burkina Faso*, African Court of Human and Peoples' Rights, App. No. 013/2011 (28 Mar. 2014) para. 90.

1574. Ankumah, 67–69.

1575. In *Malawi African Association et al. v. Mauritania*, Communication Nos 54/91, 61/91, 98/93, 164/97–196/97, 210/98, 13th Activity Report 1999–2000, para. 85, the Commission stated that it 'interprets the provisions of Article 56(5) in the light of its duty to protect human and peoples' rights as stipulated in the Charter'. Moreover, in *Bakweri Land Claims Committee v. Cameroon,* Communication No. 260/02, 18th Activity Report 2002–2003, para. 55, the Commission stated that this requirement 'should be interpreted liberally so as not to close the door on those who have made at least a modest attempt to exhaust local remedies. Under this Article [56(5)], all the African Commission wishes to hear from the complainant is that it has approached either local or national judicial bodies'.

1576. *Anuak Justice Council v. Ethiopia*, Communication No. 299/05, 20th Activity Report 2005–2006, para. 51; *African Commission on Human and Peoples' Rights v. Libya*, African Court of Human and Peoples' Rights, App. No. 002/2013 (3 Jun. 2016) para. 67. Additionally, the remedy must be both 'theoretical and practical', *Institute for Human Rights and Development in Africa (on behalf of Jean Simbarakiye) v. Democratic Republic of Congo*, Communication No. 247/2002, 16th Activity Report 2002–2003, para. 26.

prospect of success, and it is found *sufficient* if it is capable of redressing the complaint'.[1577] In addition, the 'existence of a remedy must be sufficiently certain, not only in theory but also in practice, failing which, it will lack the requisite accessibility and effectiveness'.[1578] Thus remedies do not need to be exhausted if they are 'unavailable,

1577. *Sir Dawda K. Jawara v. Gambia*, Communication Nos 147/95 and 149/96, 13th Activity Report 1999–2000, para. 32; *Ahmed Ismael and 528 Others v. Egypt*, Communication No. 467/14 (2015), paras 155–169. In *Zongo and Others v. Burkina Faso*, African Court of Human and Peoples' Rights, App. No. 013/2011 (28 Mar. 2014) para. 68, the Human Rights Court held that an effective remedy refers to 'that which produces the expected result…the effectiveness of a remedy is therefore measured in terms of its ability to solve a problem raise by the Applicant'. In *Kazeem Aminu v. Nigeria*, Communication No. 205/97, 13th Activity Report 1999–2000, paras 11–13, the Commission decided that it would not insist on the exhaustion of domestic remedies given the fact that the complainant's life was in danger in the chaotic situation prevailing under the military regime. *See also African Institute for Human Rights and Development (on behalf of Sierra Leonean refugees in Guinea v. Republic of Guinea*, Communication No. 249/2002, 20th Activity Report, 2005–2006, para. 33, where the victims were in constant danger.

1578. *Sir Dawda K. Jawara v. Gambia*, Communication Nos 147/95 and 149/96, 13th Activity Report 1999–2000, para. 35; *Zimbabwe Lawyers for Human Rights & Associated Newspapers of Zimbabwe v. Zimbabwe*, Communication No. 284/2003, 26th Activity Report 2008–2009, para. 119; *Justice Thomas S. Masuku v. Swaziland*, Communication No. 444/13 (2014) paras 58–59. In *Article 19 v. Eritrea*, Communication No. 275/2003, 22nd Activity Report 2006–2007, para. 73, the Commission found that merely listing remedies *in abstracto* without showing how they might provide effective redress did not prove domestic remedies existed. In *Ivorien Human Rights Movement (MIDH) v. Côte d'Ivoire*, Communication No. 262/2002, 26th Activity Report 2008–2009, paras 50–51, remedies could be pursued only by certain classes of citizen.

ineffective or unreasonably prolonged',[1579] are 'certain to yield no results',[1580] are

---

1579. *Alberto Capitao v. Tanzania*, Communication No. 53/91, 8th Activity Report, 1994–1995, para. 3; *Mohammed Lamine Diakité v. Gabon*, Communication No. 73/92, 13th Activity Report 1999–2000, para. 16; *Lawyers for Human Rights v. Swaziland*, Communication No. 251/2002, 18th Activity Report 2002–2003, para. 27; *Bissangou v. Republic of Congo*, Communication No. 253/2002, 21st Activity Report 2005–2006, para. 61; *Zimbabwe Lawyers for Human Rights & Associated Newspapers of Zimbabwe v. Zimbabwe*, Communication No. 284/2003, 26th Activity Report 2008–2009, para. 118. In *Haregewoin Gabre-Selassie and IHRDA (on behalf of former Dergue officials) v. Ethiopia*, Communication No. 301/05 (2011) paras 111–112, the complainants could not access the courts. Similarly, *African Commission on Human and Peoples' Rights v. Libya*, African Court of Human and Peoples' Rights, App. No. 002/2013 (3 Jun. 2016) paras 68–70, where the victim was kept in secret detention by rebels without access to lawyers. In *Monim Elgak, Osman Hummeida and Amir Suleiman (represented by FIDH and OMCT) v. Sudan*, Communication No. 379/09 (2014) paras 54–55, fear of persecution meant that domestic remedies were unavailable. In *Modise v. Botswana*, Communication No. 97/93, 10th Activity Report 1996–1997, para. 20, the Commission found that the complainant had instituted domestic legal proceedings sixteen years previously but that they had been repeatedly interrupted and wifully obstructed. In *Bakweri Land Claims Committee v. Cameroon,* Communication No. 260/02, 18th Activity Report 2002–2003, para. 24, the Commission found that the State had had forty years in which to address the grievances of the complainants. In *Association of Victims of Post Electoral Violence & INTERIGHTS v. Cameroon*, Communication No. 272/2003, 27th Activity Report 2009, paras 63–68, the case had been before the court for five years. Moreover, the Commission found an ad hoc body set up to settle the dispute amicably 'highly inefficient' for its failure to produce a report after twelve years of existence, *ibid.,* paras 64, 69. In *Article 19 v. Eritrea,* Communication No. 275/2003, 22nd Activity Report 2006–2007, para. 48, the Commission also referred to situations where no justice is available, e.g., where the judiciary is not independent, or where the wrong is due to an executive act which is not justiciable. *See also Mouvement Ivorien des Droits Humains (MIDH) v. Côte d'Ivoire*, Communication No. 246/2002, 25th Activity Report 2008, para. 49. However, simply maintaining that local remedies are not likely to be effective is not a persuasive argument, *Bakweri Land Claims Committee v. Cameroon,* Communication No. 260/02, 18th Activity Report 2002–2003, para. 55; *Anuak Justice Council v. Ethiopia*, Communication No. 299/05, 20th Activity Report 2005–2006, para. 58; *Chinhamo v. Zimbabwe*, Communication No. 307/2005, 23rd Activity Report 2007, para. 84.
1580. *Constitutional Rights Project and Civil Liberties Organisation v. Nigeria*, Communication Nos 143/95, 150/96, 13th Activity Report 1999–2000, para. 17. In an interesting decision, *Konaté v. Burkina Faso*, African Court of Human and Peoples' Rights, App. No. 004/2013 (5 Dec. 2014), paras 108–115, the Human Rights Court found an exception to the requirement of the exhaustion of local remedies when it held that the Applicant could not have expected a ruling in his favour from the highest court of the land which was not in a position to annul the impugned law. *See also*, e.g., *Actions pour la Protection des Droit de l'Homme (APDH) v. Côte d'Ivoire*, African Court of Human and Peoples' Rights, App. No. 001/2014 (18 Nov. 2016) para. 103, where the Human Rights Court held that there is 'no need to go through the same judicial process the outcome of which was known'.

'non-existent'[1581] or 'impractical or undesirable', or impossible.[1582] However, if there is some prospect of success the remedies must be pursued.[1583] Neither can a remedy be deemed sufficient if it meets only part of the claim rather than the full claim.[1584] Furthermore, if the availability of the remedies is not obvious, they 'cannot be invoked by the State to the detriment of the complainant'.[1585] In *Ilesanmi v. Nigeria*, the Commission set the applicable procedure where it was argued that local remedies were unavailable as follows: first, the complainant submits that the remedy is ineffective, unavailable or insufficient this does not have to be proven; second, the Respondent State must then demonstrate that the remedy is available, effective and sufficient; if the Respondent State establishes this fact, the complainant must then either show that s/he did exhaust the remedy, or that it could not have been effective in this specific case even if effective in general.[1586] Account has also been taken of the circumstances of the complainant, for example, refugees, who because of their vulnerability, deprivation and fear may not have the means or wherewithal to pursue local remedies.[1587] But generally it is important that the complainant takes all necessary steps to exhaust, or attempt to exhaust, domestic remedies as s/he may otherwise find that the case will be dismissed.[1588] Since it is not necessary for the complainant to be physically present in the territory of the Respondent State to exhaust local remedies,[1589] the onus is on

---

1581. *Centre for Free Speech v. Nigeria*, Communication No. 206/97, 13th Activity Report 1999–2000, para. 10. In *Malawi African Association et al. v. Mauritania*, Communication Nos 54/91, 61/91, 98/93, 164/97–196/97, 210/98, 13th Activity Report 1999–2000, para. 85, the Commission held that the amnesty law adopted by the State rendered all domestic remedies obsolete.
1582. *Free Legal Assistance Group, Lawyers Committee for Human Rights, Union Interafricaine des Droits de l'Homme, and Les Temoins Jehoves v. Zaïre*, Communication Nos 25/89, 47/90, 59/91, 100/93, 9th Activity Report 1995–1996, para. 37; *Article 19 v. Eritrea,* Communication No. 275/2003, 22nd Activity Report 2006–2007, para. 48; *Malawi African Association et al. v. Mauritania*, Communication Nos 54/91, 61/91, 98/93, 164/97–196/97, 210/98, 13th Activity Report 1999–2000, para. 85 (large number of victims); *African Institute for Human Rights and Development (on behalf of Sierra Leonean refugees in Guinea v. Republic of Guinea*, Communication No. 249/2002, 20th Activity Report, 2005–2006, para. 34 (large number of potential complainants required to return to Guinea). In *Koso and Others v. Democratic Republic of Congo*, Communication No. 281/2003, 26th Activity Report 2008–2009, para. 53, the fact that no appeal was possible from the rulings of the Military Tribunal meant that the exhaustion of local remedies was 'impossible'. In *Purohit and Moore v. The Gambia*, Communication No. 241/2001, 16th Activity Report 2002–2003, paras 32–38, the Commission found that the remedies available, in the absence of legal aid, were not realistic for poor mental health patients.
1583. *Anuak Justice Council v. Ethiopia*, Communication No. 299/05, 20th Activity Report 2005–2006, para. 58; *Nixon Nyikadzino (represented by Zimbabwe Human Rights NGO Forum) v. Zimbabwe*, Communication No. 340/07 (2012), paras 89–91.
1584. *Crawford Lindsay von Abo v. Zimbabwe*, Communication No. 477/14 (2015) para. 86.
1585. *Sir Dawda K. Jawara v. Gambia*, Communication Nos 147/95 and 149/96, 13th Activity Report 1999–2000, para. 34.
1586. Communication No. 268/2003, 18th Activity Report 2002–2003, para. 46. *See also Zimbabwe Lawyers for Human Rights & Associated Newspapers of Zimbabwe v. Zimbabwe*, Communication No. 284/2003, 26th Activity Report 2008–2009, para. 102.
1587. *Doebbler v. Sudan*, Communication No. 235/2000, 27th Activity Report 2009, para. 116.
1588. *Chinhamo v. Zimbabwe*, Communication No. 307/2005, 23rd Activity Report 2007, para. 86.
1589. *Mbianku v. Cameroon*, Communication No. 389/10 (2015) para. 75.

the complainant to explain why it was not possible to institute legal proceedings or have them started on his or her behalf.[1590]

316. It is important to note that the Commission has established that the requirement of exhaustion of local remedies will not apply in cases of serious or massive violations of human rights under Article 58 of the African Charter.[1591] This is because given the scale and nature of the alleged violations and the number of people involved the remedies are deemed not to be available or effective in such extreme circumstances.[1592]

317. The sixth condition is that the communication must be submitted within a reasonable period from the time local remedies were exhausted or from the date the Commission was seized of the matter.[1593] This is to ensure that the complainant is 'vigilant and to discourage tardiness'.[1594] No indication is given as to what constitutes 'reasonable' but the Commission seems to have considerable flexibility[1595] and the reasonableness of time is considered in each case on its own merits.[1596] In *Tsikata v. Ghana*, the Commission held that this provision was related to the previous paragraph which meant that the 'Commission estimates the timeliness of a Communication from the date that the last available local remedy is exhausted by the Complainant. In the case of unavailability or prolongation of local remedies, it will be from the date of the

---

1590. *Zitha & Zitha v. Mozambique*, Communication No. 361/08, 29th Activity Report 2010, paras 108–109; *Nixon Nyikadzino (represented by Zimbabwe Human Rights NGO Forum) v. Zimbabwe*, Communication No. 340/07 (2012), paras 81–82.

1591. *See* , e.g., *Free Legal Assistance Group, Lawyers Committee for Human Rights, Union Interafricaine des Droits de l'Homme, and Les Temoins Jehoves v. Zaïre*, Communication Nos 25/89, 47/90, 59/91, 100/93, 9th Activity Report 1995–1996, para. 37; *Open Society Justice Initiative v. Côte d'Ivoire*, Communication No. 318/06 (2015) paras 42–50.

1592. *Article 19 v. Eritrea*, Communication No. 275/2003, 22nd Activity Report 2006–2007, para. 71; *Doebbler v. Sudan*, Communication No. 235/2000, 27th Activity Report 2009, para. 117; *Sudan Human Rights Organization and Sudan Centre for Housing Rights and Evictions v. Sudan* Communication Nos 279/03, 296/05, 28th Activity Report 2010, paras 97–102. *See also* Viljoen, Communications under the African Charter, 86–88.

1593. *See also* Rule 93(2)(h).

1594. *Darfur Relief and Communication Centre v. Sudan*, Communication No. 310/2005, 27th Activity Report 2009, para. 78. In *Crawford Lindsay von Abo v. Zimbabwe*, Communication No. 477/14 (2015) para. 97, the Commission held that the applicant had not been diligent in pursuing alternative remedies in other jurisdictions when there was no such requirement under the African Charter.

1595. *See* Ankumah, 65–66, who writes that the Commission should take account of factors 'such as the general nature of the case, the continuity or lack thereof of the alleged violation, the seriousness of the alleged violation and the domestic remedies procedure in the country concerned.' In *Tsikata v. Ghana*, Communication No. 322/2006, 21st Activity Report 2005–2006, para. 38, the Commission stated that despite the fact that no time period is specified that early submission is advisable.

1596. *Darfur Relief and Communication Centre v. Sudan*, Communication No. 310/2005, 27th Activity Report 2009, para. 74; *Article 19 and Others v. Zimbabwe*, Communication No. 305/05, 29th Activity Report 2010, para. 91. This stance has been approved by the Human Rights Court, *Mohamed Abubakri v. Tanzania*, African Court of Human and Peoples' Rights, App. No. 007/2013 (3 Jun. 2016), para. 91.

Complainant's notice thereof.'[1597] This should ensure that any imputed State does not profit from delaying tactics. Nevertheless, the Commission considers the six-month rule applied by the European and American systems as a useful guide unless there is a 'good and compelling reason' or justification to the contrary or to ensure 'fairness and justice'.[1598] Periods of eleven years[1599] and thirteen years[1600] have been deemed unreasonable unsurprisingly but so have periods of two years[1601] and two years and five months.[1602]

318. The seventh and final condition is that the communication must not be concerned with cases that have previously been settled in accordance with the principles of the UN Charter, the OAU/AU Charter/Act or the African Charter.[1603] According to the Commission the rationale for this requirement 'is to desist from faulting Member States twice for the same alleged violations of human rights…the *non bis in idem* rule'.[1604] To come within the ambit of this provision the communication should involve 'the same parties, the same issues…and must have been settled by an international or regional mechanism'.[1605] The Commission can therefore reject communications which

---

1597. Communication No. 322/2006, 21st Activity Report 2005–2006, para. 37. In *Centre for Minority Rights Development (CEMIRIDE) and Truth be Told Network v. Kenya*, Communication No. 332/06 (2014) para. 103, the Commission added that the Communication must be brought within a reasonable time from the time the alleged violation occurred. The time period often applied by the Human Rights Court is the date on which the State accepted the jurisdicition of the Court to receive individual communications and the date it was seized of the case, *Mohamed Abubakri v. Tanzania*, African Court of Human and Peoples' Rights, App. No. 007/2013 (3 Jun. 2016), para. 93.

1598. *Chinhamo v. Zimbabwe*, Communication No. 307/2005, 23rd Activity Report 2007, paras 88–89; *Majuru v. Zimbabwe*, Communication No. 308/2005, 25th Activity Report 2008, paras 109–110; *Darfur Relief and Communication Centre v. Sudan*, Communication No. 310/2005, 27th Activity Report 2009, paras 75–79; *Article 19 and Others v. Zimbabwe*, Communication No. 305/05, 29th Activity Report 2010, paras 95–97. The Human Rights Court has not discouted the six-month rule, *Mohamed Abubakri v. Tanzania*, African Court of Human and Peoples' Rights, App. No. 007/2013 (3 Jun. 2016), paras 86–94.

1599. *Southern Africa Human Rights NGO Network and Others v. Tanzania*, Communication No. 333/200, 28th Activity Report 2009–2010, paras 74–76.

1600. *Zitha & Zitha v. Mozambique*, Communication No. 361/08, 29th Activity Report 2010, para. 113.

1601. *Article 19 and Others v. Zimbabwe*, Communication No. 305/05, 29th Activity Report 2010, para. 96.

1602. *Darfur Relief and Communication Centre v. Sudan*, Communication No. 310/2005, 27th Activity Report 2009, para. 77.

1603. *See also* Rule 93(2)(j). *See Amnesty International v. Tunisia*, Communication No. 69/92, 7th Activity Report 1993–1994. In *Interights (on behalf of Pan-African Movement and Citizens for Peace in Eritrea) and Interights (on behalf of Pan-African Movement and Inter Africa Group) v. Eritrea*, Communication Nos 233/99, 234/99, 16th Activity Report 2002–2003, paras 52–56, the Commission found that the Claims Commission established under the Peace Agreement of 2000 between Ethiopia and Eritrea came within the scope of this provision.

1604. *Bakweri Land Claims Committee v. Cameroon,* Communication No. 260/02, 18th Activity Report 2002–2003, para. 52.

1605. *Gunme et al. v. Cameroon,* Communication No. 266/2003, 26th Activity Report 2008–2009, para. 86.

have been determined by the HRC for example, or some other international human rights adjudicatory body.[1606] The critical element is that this provision envisages mechanisms 'capable of granting declaratory or compensatory relief to victims, not mere political resolutions and declarations' by bodies such as the UN Security Council.[1607] However, the Commission has held that it is not precluded from receiving communications identical to those *submitted* to another international body so long as a decision on the merits has not been reached.[1608] The fact that the case has been discussed is not fatal.[1609] This amounts to recognition of the principle of res judicata.[1610] This provision also refers to cases where an amicable settlement has been reached. But there is another issue that the Commission has had to address, namely, whether a government is deemed responsible for the misdeeds of its predecessors. Relying on the principle of state responsibility the Commission's established practice is that successor governments do indeed inherit the responsibility for their predecessors' wrongdoings.[1611]

319. No other formal conditions of admissibility are required and it appears that these criteria are exhaustive. However, prior to the substantive examination of any communication accepted Article 57 requires that the State concerned be notified by the Commission.[1612] The complainant then has two months in which to present evidence and arguments on admissibility[1613] while the respondent State is then given a further two months in which to respond to the allegations.[1614] The complainant can exercise a right of reply within a month.[1615]

320. Failure of a Respondent State to appear does not prevent the Commission from proceeding with the case nor does it absolve the State from the Commission's

1606. *Sudan Human Rights Organization and Sudan Centre for Housing Rights and Evictions v. Sudan* Communication Nos 279/03, 296/05, 28th Activity Report 2010, para. 104.

1607. *Ibid.*, para. 105. Nor, it would appear, the I.C.J., *Gunme et al. v. Cameroon,* Communication No. 266/2003, 26th Activity Report 2008–2009, para. 86.

1608. *Bob Ngozi Njoku v. Egypt*, Communication No. 40/90, 11th Activity Report 1997–1998, paras 54–56; *Bakweri Land Claims Committee v. Cameroon,* Communication No. 260/02, 18th Activity Report 2002–2003, paras 49–53.

1609. *Haregewoin Gabre-Selassie and IHRDA (on behalf of former Dergue officials) v. Ethiopia,* Communication No. 301/05 (2011) para. 117.

1610. *Bakweri Land Claims Committee v. Cameroon,* Communication No. 260/02, 18th Activity Report 2002–2003, para. 52; *Sudan Human Rights Organization and Sudan Centre for Housing Rights and Evictions v. Sudan* Communication Nos 279/03, 296/05, 28th Activity Report 2010, para. 104.

1611. *See* , e.g., *Krischna Achutan (on behalf of Aleke Banda) v. Malawi*; *Amnesty International on behalf of Orton and Vera Chirwa v. Malawi*, Communication Nos 64/92, 68/92, 78/92, 8th Activity Report 1994–1995, para. 12; *Civil Liberties Organisation, Legal Defence Centre, Legal Defence and Assistance Project v. Nigeria*, Communication No. 218/98, 14th Activity Report 2000–2001, para. 21; *Media Rights Agenda v. Nigeria*, Communication No. 224/98, 14th Activity Report 2000–2001, paras 36–38.

1612. *See also* Rule 105(1).

1613. *Ibid., See SERAP (on behalf of Daniel Nso for and Osayindwinde Agbomien) v. Nigeria*, Communication No. 427/12 (2015).

1614. Rule 105(2). Note further Rule 113 which allows for a single extension of one month.

1615. Rule 105(3).

decision.[1616] The new Rules do not address the possibility of a State failing to respond but the Commission's practice has established that in such instances it must decide on the facts provided by the complainant.[1617]

321. The Commission has the power to reconsider communications that have been declared inadmissible in the light of new evidence[1618] if, for example, local remedies that had not been exhausted at the time of the communication turn out subsequently not to be available.[1619] In *Interights, Institute for Human Rights and Development in Africa, and Association Mauritaniene des Droits de l'Homme v. Mauritania*, the Commission held that review was appropriate where the application introduced a 'new or compelling element, the failure to consider which would be an affront to fairness, justice and good conscience.'[1620] At greater length it has stated:

> the application would be granted where it is proved that some facts have been discovered which intrinsically might have had a decisive influence on the judgment had it been brought to the attention of the Commission at the time the decision was made, but which at the time was unknown to both the Commission and the party making the application and also which could not, with reasonable diligence, have been discovered by the party before the judgment was made or on account of some mistake, fraud or error on the face of the record or because an injustice has been done.[1621]

However, the Commission cannot dismiss a communication once it has been declared admissible.[1622]

1616. *Organisation Mondiale contre la Torture et al. v. Rwanda*, Communication Nos 27/89, 46/91, 49/91, 99/93, 10th Activity Report 1993–1994, para. 20. The established practice of the Commission in such instances is that the burden of proof lies with the State, *see*, e.g., *Amnesty International et al. v. Sudan*, Communication Nos 48/90, 50/91, 52/91, 89/93, 13th Activity Report 1999–2000, para. 52. There the Commission stated that, 'If the government provides no evidence to contradict an allegation of human rights allegation made against it, the Commission will take it as proven, or at the least probable or plausible.'

1617. *Democratic Republic of Congo v. Burundi, Rwanda and Uganda*, Communication No. 227/99, 20th Activity Report 2005–2006, paras 52–53.

1618. Rule 107(4). *See Modise v. Botswana*, Communication No. 97/93, 14th Activity Report 2000–2001, para. 69. The Rules do not specify who is entitled to submit the evidence nor within what time limits.

1619. *S.O.S. – Esclaves v. Mauritania*, Communication No. 198/97, 12th Activity Report 1998–1999, para. 18; *Bakweri Land Claims Committee v. Cameroon,* Communication No. 260/02 (2014), paras 1–9.

1620. Communication No. 373/2009 (2010), para. 11.

1621. *Bakweri Land Claims Committee v. Cameroon,* Communication No. 260/2002 (2014),para. 17, citing *Kevin Ngwang Gumne v. Cameroon,* Communication No. 384/09 (2012), para. 37 (unreported).

1622. *Zegveld and Ephrem v. Eritrea*, Communication No. 250/2002, 17th Activity Report 2003–2004, paras 43–45; *Article 19 v. Eritrea*, Communication No. 275/2003, 22nd Activity Report 2006–2007, para. 85.

322. The Commission may also review its decisions on the merits, either *proprio motu* or at the request of one of the parties.[1623] The request must be submitted within six months of new facts coming to light[1624] but in any case no later than three years after the decision.[1625] The request must be based on the discovery of a fact of a decisive factor which was not known at the time to the Commission and the party requesting revision, provided that such ignorance was not due to negligence, presumably on the part of the party claiming revision.[1626] In the alternative, and of significance, for any other compelling reason or situation which the Commission finds convincing in order to ensure fairness, justice and respect for human rights.[1627] In *Interights, Institute for Human Rights and Development in Africa, and Association Mauritaniene des Droits de l'Homme v. Mauritania*, decided before the adoption of the new Rules, the Commission revised its decision on the ground that it had been *infra petita*, that is, that it had failed to address all the allegations in the original complaint.[1628] Allegations of bias were also considered by the Commission but dismissed on the facts.[1629]

323. The Rules make provision for parties to file preliminary objections, a common feature of international litigation, both at the stage of admissibility or at the merits stage.[1630] An objection must be raised within thirty days after notification to submit on admissibility or on the merits.[1631] Any objection must be determined before any other question.[1632]

324. Provision is made under Article 58 for exceptional cases where communications reveal 'the existence of a series of serious or massive violations of human and peoples' rights'. This phrase is not defined but specific, isolated violations, however serious, lie beyond the scope of this provision; instead it refers to a pattern of large-scale violations.[1633] However, the Commission has proceeded to define 'massive' in terms of scale as 'where a significant number of people are targeted either within a specific

1623. Rule 111; *Interights, Institute for Human Rights and Development in Africa, and Association Mauritaniene des Droits de l'Homme v. Mauritania*, Communication No. 373/2009, 28th Activity Report, 2009–2010, paras 8–12.

1624. Rule 111(2)(b).

1625. Rule 111(3).

1626. Rule 111(2)(a).

1627. Rule 111(2)(c).

1628. Communication No. 373/2009, 28th Activity Report 2009–2010, paras 16–39.

1629. *Ibid.*, paras 47–62.

1630. Rule 103. *See Interights & Ditshwanelo v. Botswana*, Communication No. 319/06 (2015) paras 37–38.

1631. *Ibid.*

1632. Rule 103(4).

1633. *See Anuak Justice Council v. Ethiopia*, Communication No. 299/05, 20th Activity Report 2005–2006, para. 61. Compare *Jean Yaovi Degli (au nom du Caporal N. Bikagni), Union Interafricaine des Droits de l'Homme, Commission Internationale de Juristes v. Togo* Communication Nos 83/92, 88/93, 91/93, 8th Activity Report 1994–1995, where torture and ill-treatment, extortion and killings, electoral irregularities, and a general breakdown in law and order, amounted to grave and massive violations. *See also Malawi African Association et al. v. Mauritania*, Communication Nos 54/91, 61/91, 98/93/164/97–196/97, 210/98, 13th Activity Report 1999–2000, para. 80; *Amnesty International et al. v. Sudan*, Communication Nos 48/90, 50/91, 52/91, 89/93 13th Activity Report 1999–2000, para. 32. Rule 79(1)(b) also refers to 'the danger of irreparable harm' or 'irreparable damage'.

area or across the territory of a State', whereas in terms of nature where it is 'the product of a consistent and predetermined action that impacts on a right or...rights guaranteed under the African Charter.'[1634] Widespread allegations of human rights violations lead the Commission to presume a series of serious or massive violations as established.[1635] It has adopted the stance that 'the state will be presumed to have notice of the violations within its territory and the State is expected to act accordingly to deal with whatever human rights violations'.[1636] The Commission has determined that it must act promptly in such cases.[1637]

325. Under Article 58(2) the AU Assembly may request the Commission to undertake in-depth studies of such cases and present factual reports with findings and recommendations. In addition, under paragraph 3 thereof a case of emergency duly noted by the Commission shall be submitted to the AU Chairman who may request an in-depth study. The Commission may also take 'any appropriate action'.[1638]

326. An important protective power is the Commission's ability to issue provisional, or interim, measures of protection.[1639] The purpose of interim measures is to 'prevent irreparable damage to the victim...as urgently as the situation demands' and/or to protect the interests of the parties or the proper conduct of the proceedings.[1640] An important safeguard is the requirement on States to report back on the implementation of the measures within fifteen days.[1641] They do not prejudge the case on the merits.[1642] The Commission is competent to decide on its own motion, or at the request of a party, whether interim measures should be indicated in any particular case.[1643]

1634. *Ahmed Ismael and 528 Others v. Egypt*, Communication No. 467/14 (2015) para. 172; *The Kenyan Section of the International Commission of Jurists v. Kenya*, Communication No. 385/10 (2013) paras 63–64.

1635. *Free Legal Assistance Group, Lawyers Committee for Human Rights, Union Interafricaine des Droits de l'Homme, and Les Temoins Jehoves v. Zaïre*, Communication Nos 25/89, 47/90, 59/91, 100/93, 9th Activity Report 1995–1996.

1636. *Anuak Justice Council v. Ethiopia*, Communication No. 299/05, 20th Activity Report 2005–2006, para. 60.

1637. *Free Legal Assistance Group, Lawyers Committee for Human Rights, Union Interafricaine des Droits de l'Homme, and Les Temoins Jehoves v. Zaïre*, Communication Nos 25/89, 47/90, 59/91, 100/93, 9th Activity Report 1995–1996.

1638. Rule 80(2).

1639. Rule 98. *See* G.J. Naldi, 'Interim Measures of Protection in the African System for the Protection of Human and Peoples' Rights', *A.H.R.L.J.* 2 (2002): 1.

1640. *Association pour la Defence des Droits de l'Homme et des Libertés v. Djibouti*, Communication No. 133/94, 13th Activity Report 1999–2000, para. 5; *Constitutional Rights Project, Civil Liberties Organisation and Media Rights Agenda v. Nigeria*, Communication Nos 140/94, 141/94, 145/95, 13th Activity Report 1999–2000, para. 17. *See also International Pen, Constitutional Rights Project, Interights on behalf of Ken Saro-Wiwa Jr. and Civil Liberties Organisation v. Nigeria*, Communication Nos 137/94, 139/94, 154/96 and 161/97, 12th Activity Report 1998–1999, para. 114.

1641. Rule 98(4).

1642. Rule 98(5).

1643. Rule 98(1). *See* further *Constitutional Rights Project, Civil Liberties Organisation and Media Rights Agenda v. Nigeria*, Communication Nos 140/94, 141/94 and 145/95, 13th Activity 1999–2000, para. 17.

327. Although there is nothing in the African Charter nor the Rules to assert that interim measures are considered as binding on the parties to the case,[1644] the case of *International Pen, Constitutional Rights Project, Interights on behalf of Ken Saro-Wiwa Jr. and Civil Liberties Organisation v. Nigeria*, which concerned the detention and trial of the writer Ken Saro-Wiwa and others, would appear to suggest otherwise. Here the Commission observed that Nigeria was bound by Article 1 of the African Charter and that one of the Commission's functions was to assist States parties to implement their obligations under the Charter.[1645] In its reasoning the Commission found that the trial and implementation of the death sentence were in violation of the African Charter. Moreover, the:

> violation is compounded by the fact that there were pending communications before the African Commission at the time of the executions, and the Commission had requested the government to avoid causing any 'irreparable prejudice' to the subjects of the communications before the Commission had concluded its consideration. Executions had been stayed in Nigeria in the past on the invocation by the Commission of its rules on provisional measures...and the Commission had hoped that a similar situation will obtain in the case of Ken Saro-Wiwa and others. It is a matter of deep regret that this did not happen.[1646]

The Commission therefore held that the Nigerian Government had, 'in ignoring its obligations to institute provisional measures', violated Article 1 of the Charter.[1647] The Commission added that:

> To have carried out the execution in the face of pleas to the contrary by the Commission and world opinion is something which we pray will never happen again. That it is a violation of the Charter is an understatement' (emphasis added).[1648]

1644. In *Anuak Justice Council v. Ethiopia*, Communication No. 299/05, 20th Activity Report 2005–2006, para. 18, the complainant explicitly asked the Commission to declare interim measures binding but the request was not addressed by the Commission.

1645. *International Pen, Constitutional Rights Project, Interights on behalf of Ken Saro-Wiwa Jr. and Civil Liberties Organisation v. Nigeria*, Communication Nos 137/94, 139/94, 154/96 and 161/97, 12th Activity Report 1998–1999, paras 113–114. *See* similarly *Piandiong, Morallos and Bulan v. The Philippines* Communication No. 869/1999, UN Doc CCPR/C/70/D/869/1999 (19 Oct. 2000) (UN Human Rights Committee).

1646. *Ibid.*, para. 103.

1647. *Ibid.*, p. 285.

1648. *Ibid.*, para. 115.

328. Under Articles 60 and 61 of the African Charter the Commission is authorized to draw inspiration from various sources of law.[1649] The primary sources include international human rights law, such as the UDHR[1650] and the ICCPR[1651] which many African States have ratified. Other sources include other international treaties, such the ACHR and the ECHR, insofar as they reflect rules expressly recognized by the AU Member States, customs generally accepted as law, general principles of law and legal precedents and doctrines.[1652] While the Commission may look to other treaties it has stated that it is not tasked with ensuring the monitoring of their implementation nationally.[1653]

1649. *Civil Liberties Organisation, Legal Defence Centre, Legal Defence and Assistance Project v. Nigeria*, Communication No. 218/98, 14th Activity Report 2000–2001, para. 24; *African Institute for Human Rights and Development (on behalf of Sierra Leonean refugees in Guinea v. Republic of Guinea*, Communication No. 249/2002, 20th Activity Report 2005–2006, paras 37–38. The Human Rights Court has also relied on these provisions, *African Commission on Human and Peoples' Rights v. Kenya*, African Court of Human and Peoples' Rights, App. No. 006/2012 (26 May 2017) para. 108.

1650. *See* , e.g., *Zimbabwe Human Rights NGO Forum v. Zimbabwe*, Communication No. 245/2002, 21st Activity Report 2005–2006, para. 180.

1651. International Covenant on Civil and Political Rights (16 Dec. 1966), 999 U.N.T.S. 171. *See* , e.g., *Civil Liberties Organisation, Legal Defence Centre, Legal Defence and Assistance Project v. Nigeria*, Communication No. 218/98, 14th Activity Report 2000–2001; *Purohit and Moore v. The Gambia*, Communication No. 241/2001, 16th Activity Report 2002–2003, para. 76; *Garreth Anver Prince v. South Africa*, Communication No. 255/2002, 18th Activity Report 2002–2003, para. 42; *African Commission on Human and Peoples' Rights v. Libya*, African Court of Human and Peoples' Rights, App. No. 002/2013 (3 Jun. 2016) paras 89, 92.

1652. *See* , e.g., *Democratic Republic of Congo v. Burundi, Rwanda and Uganda*, Communication No. 227/99, 20th Activity Report 2005–2006, paras 70, 78, where the Commission invoked the Geneva Conventions 1949 and the Additional Protocols 1977 as general principles of law recognized by African States. The case of *Zimbabwe Human Rights NGO Forum v. Zimbabwe*, Communication No. 245/2002, 21st Activity Report 2005–2006, is an especially interesting illustration because of the extensive references to international law, including the jurisprudence of the European Court of Human Rights, the Inter-American Court of Human Rights and the International Criminal Tribunal for the Former Yugoslavia. *See also Zitha & Zitha v. Mozambique*, Communication No. 361/08, 29th Activity Report 2010, paras 89–92, where the Commission made extensive references to the jurisprudence of the Inter-American Court of Human Rights in relation to the issue of forced disappearances. In *Centre for Minority Rights Development (Kenya) and Minority Rights Group International on behalf of Endorois Welfare Council v. Kenya*, Communication No. 276/2003, 27th Activity Report 2009, the Commission made extensive references to the jurisprudence of the Inter-American Court of Human Rights on the rights of indigenous peoples. In *Purohit and Moore v. The Gambia*, Communication No. 241/2001, 16th Activity Report 2002–2003, and *Lawyers for Human Rights v. Swaziland*, Communication No. 251/2002, 18th Activity Report 2002–2003, the Commission relied on UN soft law in the form of the UN Principles for the Protection of Persons with Mental Illness and the Improvement of Mental Illnesses and the Improvement of Mental Health Care, and the UN Basic Principles on the Independence of the Judiciary respectively. Such inspiration also extends to procedural points of law, *Darfur Relief and Communication Centre v. Sudan*, Communication No. 310/2005, 27th Activity Report 2009, paras 75–76.

1653. *Groupe de Travail sur les Dossiers Judiciaires Stratégiques v. Democratic Republic of Congo*, Communication No. 259/2002 (2011) para. 59.

329. There is an important omission in the African Charter and that is on a right to reparation, although the Human Rights Court is empowered to award remedies under Article 27(1) of the Protocol. Nevertheless, in its early jurisprudence the Commission adopted the view that the State was 'rcsponsible for the reparation' of its abuses[1654] and accepted the principle of compensatory damages as a form of indemnity.[1655] In subsequent cases a right to reparation has become established and has been applied in different forms, spanning administrative and judicial measures, such as reform of the law and prosecution of the perpertrators, *restitution in integrum* to monetary compensation.[1656] Significant in the latter context was the case of *Egyptian Initiative for Personal Rights and INTERIGHTS v. Egypt*, where the Commission for the first time requested the payment of a specific sum of money.[1657] In *Jean-Marie Atangana Mebara v. Cameroon*, the Commission itself assessed the appropriate amount of monetary compensation.[1658] Ultimately, the Commission's stance is that the reparation has to be 'fair, adequate, effective, sufficient, appropriate, satisfactory to the victim and proportionate to the damage suffered.'[1659]

§4. THE AFRICAN COURT ON HUMAN AND PEOPLES' RIGHTS

330. In a historic decision at its Thirty-Fourth Ordinary Session in Burkina Faso in June 1998 the OAU Assembly adopted the Protocol on the African Court on Human

1654. *Krischna Achutan (on behalf of Aleke Banda) v. Malawi*; *Amnesty International on behalf of Orton and Vera Chirwa v. Malawi*, Communication Nos 64/92, 68/92, 78/92, (1995), para. 12.
1655. *See* , e.g., African Commission on Human and Peoples' Rights, *Malawi African Association, Amnesty International, Ms Sarr Diop, Union Interafricaine des Droits de l'Homme and RADDHO, Collectif des Veuves et Ayant-droit, and Association Mauritanienne des Droits de l'Homme v. Mauritania*, Communication Nos. 54/91, 61/91, 98/93, 164/97-196/97, and 210/98, (2000). *See* further G. Naldi, 'Reparations in the Practice of the African Commission on Human and Peoples' Rights', *Leiden Journal International Law* 14 (2001) 681.
1656. *See* , e.g., *Good v. Botswana*, Communication No. 306/2005, 28th Activity Report 2009–2010, para. 245; *Egyptian Initiative for Personal Rights and INTERIGHTS v. Egypt*, Communication No. 323/2006 (2011), para. 275; *Jean-Marie Atangana Mebara v. Cameroon*, Communication No. 416/12 (2015) para. 137.
1657. Communication No. 323/2006 (2011), para. 275.
1658. Communication No. 416/12 (2015) paras 141–142.
1659. *Jean-Marie Atangana Mebara v. Cameroon*, Communication No. 416/12 (2015) para. 135.

and Peoples' Rights.[1660] The adoption of the Protocol corrects the gravest omission in the African Charter, namely the failure to make provision for a court to interpret, apply and enforce the rights guaranteed thereunder. The lack of a judicial remedy attracted considerable criticism as undermining the effective application and enforcement of human rights in Africa.[1661] Consequently, continued opposition to the establishment of a court could no longer be credibly maintained as compatible with respect for human rights. But it was a few years before the Human Rights Court became operational, its first ruling on a matter of substantive law was delivered in 2013.[1662]

331. The seat of the Human Rights Court is Arusha, Tanzania,[1663] but if the Court deems it desirable it may convene in the territory of any AU Member State with its prior permission.[1664] The official and working languages of the Human Rights Court are those of the AU.[1665] The Human Rights Court meets four times a year, each session lasting a fortnight[1666] but extraordinary sessions may also be convened.[1667]

332. The general role of the Human Rights Court is to reinforce the work of the Commission. Thus, according Article 2 of the Protocol the Human Rights Court is to complement the protective mandate of the Commission in accordance with the

---

1660. Protocol to the African Charter on Human and Peoples' Rights on the Establishment of an African Court on Human and Peoples' Rights (10 Jun. 1998) http://www.au.int/en/treaties, Heyns & Killander, 41 (Protocol). The Protocol entered into force on 25 Jan. 2004. As of April 2014 it had been ratified by thirty States. The Protocol cites the OAU but such references must now be taken to indicate the AU. For analysis *see* J. Harrington, 'The African Court on Human and Peoples' Rights,' in *The African Charter on Human and Peoples' Rights: The System in Practice, 1986–2000*, Evans & Murray (eds), (Cambridge: Cambridge University Press, 2002), 305–334; V.O. Nmehielle, *The African Human Rights System: Its Laws, Practice and Institutions* (The Hague: Martinus Nijhoff, 2001), 259–308; F. Viljoen, *International Human Rights Law in Africa* (Oxford: Oxford University Press, 2007), 418–475; G.J. Naldi & K.D. Magliveras, 'Reinforcing the African System of Human Rights: The Protocol on the Establishment of a Regional Court on Human and Peoples' Rights,' *N.Q.H.R.* 16 (1998): 431; N.J. Udombana, 'Toward the African Court on Human and Peoples' Rights: Better Late than Never', *Yale H.R. & Dev. Law Journal* 3 (2000): 45. As with the African Charter the Protocol does not contain a denunciation clause but the view has been expressed that the Vienna Convention on the Law of Treaties Art. 56(2) is applicable, *Ingabire Victoire Umuhoza v. Rwanda*, African Court of Human and Peoples' Rights, App. No. 003/2014 (5 Sept. 2016) para. 54, Corrigendum.
1661. D'Sa, African Charter on Human and Peoples' Rights; Gittleman.
1662. *Tanganyika Law Society et al. v. Tanzania*, App. Nos 009/2011 and 011/2011 (14 Jun. 2013). Its first judgment was handed down on 15 Dec. 2009 in the case of *Michelot Yogogombaye v. Senegal*, African Court of Human and Peoples' Rights, App. No. 001/2008. Its case law can be accessed at http://www.african-court.org/en/.
1663. Assembly, *Decision on the Activity Report of the African Court on Human and Peoples' Rights for 2006*, AU Doc. Assembly/AU/Dec. 144(VIII) (29-30 -1-2007).
1664. Protocol Art. 25(1).
1665. Rule of Court 18(1)-(2). Compare Constitutive Act Art. 25. The Rules of Court are available at http://www.african-court.org, Heyns & Killander, 404.
1666. Rule of Court 14(1).
1667. Rule of Court 15(1).

terms of the African Charter.[1668] However, with many questions between the two bodies left unanswered,[1669] it was important that their working relationship be clarified through rules of procedure. Pursuant to Article 33 of the Protocol the Human Rights Court and the Commission set to work on drafting a harmonized set of rules and on 2 June 2010 the Court's Rules of Procedure came into force.[1670] Thus the two bodies are to meet at least once a year or whenever considered necessary in order to ensure a good working relationship between them.[1671] A potential source of conflict arises in relation to the Commission's quasi-judicial function under Article 45(3) of the African Charter to interpret the provisions of the African Charter at the request of a State party, the AU, or an African organization recognized by the AU. The Commission retains this power notwithstanding the creation of the Human Rights Court. It is unclear what effect the establishment of the Court will have in practice since the potential for duplication exists, although it needs to be observed that the Commission's interpretative mandate is narrower than the Human Rights Court's.[1672] One can only speculate that it may be that this specific role of the Commission will fall into desuetude or it may be that the Human Rights Court will be asked to review the Commission's interpretations and provide definitive comment.[1673]

333. It is self-evident that the effective guarantee of human and peoples' rights will be largely dependent on the jurisdiction conferred upon, and assumed by, the Human Rights Court. The Protocol provides for both contentious and advisory jurisdiction. Under Article 3(1) and Rule of Court 26(1)(a) the jurisdiction of the Human Rights Court thus extends to all cases and disputes submitted to it concerning the interpretation and application of the African Charter, the Protocol and any other relevant human rights instrument which a State has ratified.[1674] This final clause is particularly interesting because of its innovative character. It is extremely broad in scope and has been described as conferring upon the Human Rights Court an 'almost unlimited substantive jurisdiction'.[1675] It extends the jurisdiction of the Court over not only other OAU/AU human rights treaties, for example, the African Charter on the

1668. *See also* Rule 114(1) of Commission. This principle enables the Commission to refer any matter to the Human Rights Court, *African Commission on Human and Peoples' Rights v. Kenya*, African Court of Human and Peoples' Rights, App. No. 006/2012 (26 May 2017) para. 53.

1669. Harrington, 316–317; Nmehielle, 261–262; Udombana, 97.

1670. Rule of Court 76.

1671. Rule of Court 29(1)(a); Rule 115(1) of Commission.

1672. Protocol Art. 3.

1673. Nmehielle, 262.

1674. *See Femi Falana v. African Union*, African Court of Human and Peoples' Rights, App. No. 001/2011 (26 Jun. 2012) para. 63; *Ingabire Victoire Umuhoza v. Rwanda* African Court of Human and Peoples' Rights, App. No. 003/2014 (5 Sept. 2016) para. 52. The Human Rights Court has stressed that it does not have appellate jurisdiction, *Ernest Francis Mtingwi v. Malawi*, African Court of Human and Peoples' Rights, App. No. 001/2013 (15 Mar. 2015) para. 14. In *Mohamed Abubakri v. Tanzania*, African Court of Human and Peoples' Rights, App. No. 007/2013 (3 Jun. 2016), para. 28, the Human Rights Court stated that scrutinizing the national courts for compliance with the State's human rights obligations did not amount to exercising appellate jurisdiction.

1675. Harrington, 318.

Rights and Welfare of the Child,[1676] but also ECOWAS treaties[1677] and UN treaties such as the ICCPR.[1678] The Human Rights Court has interpreted the term 'instrument' broadly, enabling it to consider the UDHR.[1679] This particular power of the Human Rights Court is an interesting development, seemingly justified by a desire to promote the effective protection of human rights in Africa.[1680]

334. Given the traditional reluctance among African States to submit to third-party adjudication, the power of the Human Rights Court to *apply* the law is a welcome and necessary development if human rights are to have any meaningful protection in Africa.[1681] The concern that the jurisdiction of the Human Rights Court might have been restricted to issuing declaratory judgments only, similar to that of the Commission under Article 45(3) of the African Charter described above, has been allayed. However, the composition of the Human Rights Court assumes added significance if the judges are prepared to interpret the law in a dynamic and teleological fashion so as to make it truly effective.[1682] Nevertheless, this provision has the potential of giving the Human Rights Court ample opportunities to develop a significant and distinctive human rights jurisprudence.

1676. *Request for Advisory Opinion by the African Committee of Experts on the Rights and Welfare of the Child on the Standing of the African Committee of Experts on the Rights and Welfare of the Child before the African Court of Human and Peoples' Rights*, African Court of Human and Peoples' Rights, Request No. 002/2013 (5 Dec. 2014) para. 97. In *Actions pour la Protection des Droit de l'Homme (APDH) v. Côte d'Ivoire*, African Court of Human and Peoples' Rights, App. No. 001/2014 (18 Nov. 2016) paras 49–65, the Human Rights Court held that the African Charter on Democracy was a human rights instrument. The Human Rights Court stated that in answering this question it was necessary to consider the purpose of the instrument, reflected either by an express enunciation of rights or by binding obligations on States for the enjoyment of those rights, *ibid.* para. 57. The Human Rights Court has also held that it is competent to consider the human rights provisions of the Constitutive Act, *Mohamed Abubakri v. Tanzania*, African Court of Human and Peoples' Rights, App. No. 007/2013 (3 Jun. 2016), para. 51.

1677. *Zongo and Others v. Burkina Faso*, African Court of Human and Peoples' Rights, App. No. 013/2011 (28 Mar. 2014) para. 48; *Actions pour la Protection des Droit de l'Homme (APDH) v. Côte d'Ivoire*, African Court of Human and Peoples' Rights, App. No. 001/2014 (18 Nov. 2016) para. 65.

1678. *Zongo and Others v. Burkina Faso*, African Court of Human and Peoples' Rights, App. No. 013/2011 (28 Mar. 2014) *ibid.*; *Actions pour la Protection des Droit de l'Homme (APDH) v. Côte d'Ivoire*, African Court of Human and Peoples' Rights, App. No. 001/2014 (18 Nov. 2016) paras 107, 145; *Wilfred Onyango Nganyi & 9 Others v. Tanzania*, African Court of Human and Peoples' Rights, App. No. 006/2013 (18 Mar. 2016), para. 165.

1679. *Omary and Others v. Tanzania*, African Court of Human and Peoples' Rights, App. No. 001/2012 (28 Mar. 2014), paras 71–73.

1680. Nmehielle, 264.

1681. *See* further Protocol Arts 7 and 27.

1682. In *Request for Advisory Opinion by the African Committee of Experts on the Rights and Welfare of the Child on the Standing of the African Committee of Experts on the Rights and Welfare of the Child before the African Court of Human and Peoples' Rights* Request No. 002/2013 (5 Dec. 2014) para. 98, the Human Rights Court rejected the use of the purposive approach to override the clear and unambiguous intention of the legislators discernible from the plain and ordinary meaning of the text. This approach would be in keeping with the Vienna Convention on the Law of Treaties Art. 31(1).

335. If the jurisdiction of the Human Rights Court is disputed Article 3(2) of the Protocol and Rule of Court 26(2) declare that the matter shall be settled by the decision of the Human Rights Court.[1683] This corresponds to a fundamental principle of international law, namely, 'the inherent power of a tribunal to interpret the text establishing its jurisdiction'.[1684]

336. The Protocol itself does not make express provision for parties to file preliminary objections,[1685] rather this important procedure is governed by Rule of Court 52.[1686] A preliminary objection is admissible only when proceedings are begun through an application,[1687] and must be raised by the objector before it files its first set of pleadings.[1688] As a rule, objections will not operate so as to suspend the proceedings on the merits.[1689] Objections may be decided upon separately by the Human Rights Court in what would be a preliminary judgment or joined to the merits.[1690] The Human Rights Court's rulings on preliminary objections must be reasoned.[1691] The fact that under Rule 39(1) the Human Rights Court must at the outset satisfy itself that it has jurisdiction and that the application is admissible would suggest that the party entering an objection has to make a compelling case to convince the Court.

337. Article 5 of the Protocol governs the contentious jurisdiction of the Human Rights Court. According to Article 5(1) the following are entitled to submit contentious cases: (a) the Commission; (b) a State Party which has lodged a complaint to the Commission; (c) a State Party against which a complaint has been lodged at the Commission; (d) a State Party whose citizen is a victim of a human rights violation;

1683. *See Femi Falana v. African Union*, African Court of Human and Peoples' Rights, App. No. 001/2011 (26 Jun. 2012); *Ingabire Victoire Umuhoza v. Rwanda*, African Court of Human and Peoples' Rights, App. No. 003/2014 (5 Sept. 2016) para. 52.

1684. *Nottebohm (Liechtenstein v. Guatemala)*, Preliminary Objection, I.C.J. Reports 1953, 111; *Constitutional Court v. Peru*, Competence, Ser. A, No. 55 (1999) paras 33–34.

1685. Although Art. 3(2) would appear to envisage this procedure by envisaging challenges to the Human Rights Court's jurisdiction.

1686. *See Michelot Yogogombaye v. Senegal*, African Court of Human and Peoples' Rights, App. No. 001/2008 (15 Dec. 2009) para. 38.

1687. Rule of Court 52(1).

1688. Rule of Court 52(2).

1689. Rule of Court 52(3).

1690. *Ibid.* This was the case in *Tanganyika Law Society et al. v. Tanzania*, African Court of Human and Peoples' Rights, App. Nos 009/2011 and 011/2011 (14 Jun. 2013) paras 79–88; *Wilfred Onyango Nganyi & 9 Others v. Tanzania*, African Court of Human and Peoples' Rights, App. No. 006/2013 (18 Mar. 2016), paras 69–103. However, in *Zongo and Others v. Burkina Faso*, Preliminary Objection, African Court of Human and Peoples' Rights, App. No. 013/2011 (21 Jun. 2013, unreported), the Court for the first time considered a number of objections to its jurisdiction in a separate phase.

1691. Rule of Court 52(7). *See Tanganyika Law Society et al. v. Tanzania*, African Court of Human and Peoples' Rights, App. Nos 009/2011 and 011/2011 (14 Jun. 2013) *ibid.*

and (e) African IGOs.[1692] These, in contrast to applicants under Article 5(3), could be described as privileged applicants since access is automatic upon ratification of the Protocol and is not dependent on further declarations by State Parties. The wording of this provision suggests that only the Commission and, somewhat unusually, African IGOs have unlimited access to the Human Rights Court. It appears that States do not have direct access to the Human Rights Court but must come within one of the categories specified in subparagraphs (b)–(d). It is certainly curious that African IGOs should have unrestricted access to the Human Rights Court but not States.

338. In certain instances the Protocol envisages a two-tier system comparable to that currently operating under the ACHR with the Commission as the preliminary jurisdictional body, acting as a filter mechanism.[1693] Where the Commission submits a case to the Human Rights Court in accordance with Article 5(1)(a) of the Protocol and Rule of Court 33(1)(a) the application must be accompanied by the Commission's Report and other documents.[1694] The Human Rights Court may hear the Commissioners[1695] or the individual or NGO that initiated the communication to the Commission.[1696] Cases referred to the Human Rights Court can include those of serious or massive violations of human rights under Article 58 of the African Charter perpetrated by a State Party to the Protocol.[1697] Rule of Court 29(6) provides that a communication before the Commission must be withdrawn if the case submitted to the Human Rights Court relates to issues in said communication. This is an expression of the *lis pendens* principle.

339. The Protocol also recognizes the *locus standi* of other applicants under Article 5(3). Thus, the Human Rights Court *may* allow individuals and NGOs with observer status before the Commission to bring cases directly before it.[1698] Clearly the Human Rights Court has a discretion whether to accept an application, jurisdiction is

1692. In *Request for Advisory Opinion by the African Committee of Experts on the Rights and Welfare of the Child on the Standing of the African Committee of Experts on the Rights and Welfare of the Child before the African Court of Human and Peoples' Rights* Request No. 002/2013 (5 Dec. 2014) paras 60–76,94, the Human Rights Court had to consider whether the Committee on the Rights of the Child had the capacity to bring contentious cases. Since the Committee was not specifically listed in Art. 5(1) it was submitted that it qualified as an IGO under indent (e). However, the Court, with reluctance given that it felt that it would be 'highly desirable' that the Committee did have access, concluded that the Committee did not meet the definition of an IGO.

1693. Udombana, 98.

1694. Rule of Court 29(3)(a). *See also* Rule 121 of Commission.

1695. Rule of Court 29(3)(b). *See also* Rule 120 of Commission.

1696. Rule of Court 29(3)(c).

1697. Rule 118(3) of Commission. *See In the Matter of the African Commission on Human and Peoples' Rights v. Libyan Arab People's Jamahiriya (Provisional Measures)*, African Court of Human and Peoples' Rights, App. No. 004/2011 (3 Mar. 2011); *African Commission on Human and Peoples' Rights v. Kenya*, African Court of Human and Peoples' Rights, App. No. 006/2012 (26 May 2017) para. 53.

1698. *See* , e.g., *Zongo and Others v. Burkina Faso*, African Court of Human and Peoples' Rights, App. No. 013/2011 (28 Mar. 2014) para. 49.

optional in this instance.[1699] Moreover, the competence of the Human Rights Court to entertain an application against a particular State is dependent on that State's prior acceptance of the Human Rights Court's jurisdiction in accordance with Article 34(6) of the Protocol.[1700] Under this provision States must make a separate declaration accepting the competence of the Human Rights Court to receive petitions from these complainants.[1701] This position is regrettable since it is likely that some of the worst perpetrators of serious human rights abuses will not be brought to account given that it is improbable that they will accept the Human Rights Court's exceptional jurisdiction under Article 5(3).[1702] These issues came to the fore in its first case, *Michelot Yogogombaye v. Senegal*. For the Human Rights Court to exercise jurisdiction it was necessary that the respondent State Party, Senegal, must have deposited said declaration under Article 34(6) of the Protocol accepting the competence of the Human Rights Court to receive applications from individuals in accordance with Article 5(3) thereof.[1703] However, in the absence of such declaration the Human Rights Court was unable to entertain the

1699. Udombana, 87. Thus in *Tanganyika Law Society et al. v. Tanzania*, African Court of Human and Peoples' Rights, App. Nos 009/2011 and 011/2011 (14 Jun. 2013) para. 86, the Human Rights Court used the term 'can consider'.

1700. *Mohamed Abubakri v. Tanzania*, African Court of Human and Peoples' Rights, App. No. 007/2013 (3 Jun. 2016), para. 33. The Human Rights Court has made it plain that Art. 34(6) does not apply to the Commission, *African Commission on Human and Peoples' Rights v. Kenya*, African Court of Human and Peoples' Rights, App. No. 006/2012 (26 May 2017) para. 60.

1701. *Femi Falana v. African Union*, African Court of Human and Peoples' Rights, App. No. 001/2011 (26 Jun. 2012) para. 73; *Omary and Others v. Tanzania*, African Court of Human and Peoples' Rights, App. No. 001/2012 (28 Mar. 2014), para. 80. The applicants do not have to be nationals of the respondent State, *Wilfred Onyango Nganyi & 9 Others v. Tanzania*, African Court of Human and Peoples' Rights, App. No. 006/2013 (18 Mar. 2016), para. 63. And only States may be respondents, Separate Opinion by Judge Mutsinzi, *Femi Falana v. African Union*, African Court of Human and Peoples' Rights, App. No. 001/2011 (26 Jun. 2012). Eight States have made this declaration, Benin, Burkina Faso, Côte d'Ivoire, Ghana, Malawi, Mali, Tanzania and Tunisia. Rwanda withdrew its declaration with effect from 1 Mar. 2017. The Human Rights Court upheld the legality of the withdrawal as a legitimate exercise of state sovereignty, *Ingabire Victoire Umuhoza v. Rwanda*, African Court of Human and Peoples' Rights, App. No. 003/2014 (5 Sept. 2016) paras 57–59.

1702. On the controversy surrounding the drafting history of these provisions, *see* Harrington, 320–321; Nmehielle, 266–267; Udombana, 87–88.

1703. *Michelot Yogogombaye v. Senegal*, African Court of Human and Peoples' Rights, App. No. 001/2008 (15 Dec. 2009) paras 35–37. *Tanganyika Law Society et al. v. Tanzania*, African Court of Human and Peoples' Rights, App. Nos 009/2011 and 011/2011 (14 Jun. 2013) para. 86.

case.[1704] In *Association Juriste d'Afrique pour la Bonne Gouvernance v. Ivory Coast* the problem was that the applicant NGO did not have observer status with the Commission as required by Article 5(3) of the Protocol.[1705] Another peculiar attribution is that while the Human Rights Court decides on the admissibility of a case under Article 5(3) it may, according to Article 6(1) of the Protocol, request an opinion from the Commission. The Commission is obliged to respond promptly and under Rule of Court 29(4) the Human Rights Court will indicate the time limit within which it wishes to receive the Commission's opinion. For its part, the Commission will consider the matter in light of the conditions of admissibility.[1706] No indication is given as to the sort of circumstances that might prompt the Human Rights Court to invoke this provision. Nevertheless, the wisdom of introducing any delay in such urgent circumstances appears questionable. It should also be noted that individuals and NGOs must overcome hurdles of admissibility.

340. The Human Rights Court must initially satisfy itself that it has jurisdiction and that the application is admissible.[1707] The Human Rights Court therefore needs to

---

1704. *Ibid.*, para. 37. *See also Soufiane Ababou v. Algeria*, African Court of Human and Peoples' Rights, App. No. 002/2011 (16 Jun. 2011) paras 5–11; *Daniel Amare and Mulugeta Amare v. Republic of Mozambique and Mozambique Airlines*, African Court of Human and Peoples' Rights, App. No. 005/2011 (16 Jun. 2011) paras 6–8; *Ekollo Moundi Alexandre v. Cameroon and Nigeria*, African Court of Human and Peoples' Rights, App. No. 008/2011 (23 Sept. 2011) paras 5–9; *National Convention of Teachers Trade Union v. Republic of Gabon*, African Court of Human and Peoples' Rights, App. No. 012/2011 (15 Dec. 2011); *Delta International Investments SA, Mr AGL de Lange and Mrs M. de Lange v. Republic of South Africa*, African Court of Human and Peoples' Rights, App. No. 002/2012 (30 Mar. 2012); *Amir Adam Timan v. Republic of Sudan*, African Court of Human and Peoples' Rights, App. No. 005/2012 (30 Mar. 2012). Judge Ouguergouz has argued that in such circumstances applications should not be dealt with by the Human Rights Court but should be 'dismissed *de plano* by a simple letter from the Registry' on grounds of time and resources, *see* , e.g., his Separate Opinion in *Amir Adam Timan v. Republic of Sudan*, African Court of Human and Peoples' Rights, App. No. 005/2012 (30 Mar. 2012); *Baghdadi Ali Mahmoudi v. Republic of Tunisia*, African Court of Human and Peoples' Rights, App. No. 007/2012 (30 Mar. 2012).

1705. *Association Juriste d'Afrique pour la Bonne Gouvernance v. Ivory Coast*, African Court of Human and Peoples' Rights, App. No. 006/2011 (16 Jun. 2011) paras 7–9. *See also National Convention of Teachers Trade Union v. Republic of Gabon*, African Court of Human and Peoples' Rights, App. No. 012/2011 (15 Dec. 2011). Compare contra *Tanganyika Law Society et al. v. Tanzania*, African Court of Human and Peoples' Rights, App. Nos 009/2011 and 011/2011 (14 Jun. 2013) para. 86.

1706. Rule 119(1) of Commission. According to Judge Ouguergouz's Dissenting Opinion in *Ekollo Moundi Alexandre v. Cameroon and Nigeria*, African Court of Human and Peoples' Rights, App. No. 008/2011 (23 Sept. 2011) para. 17, it is a condition precedent that the Human Rights Court should determine that it has jurisdiction over the case.

1707. Rule of Court 39(1). *See Michelot Yogogombaye v. Senegal*, African Court of Human and Peoples' Rights, App. No. 001/2008 (15 Dec. 2009) para. 40; *Wilfred Onyango Nganyi & 9 Others v. Tanzania*, African Court of Human and Peoples' Rights, App. No. 006/2013 (18 Mar. 2016), para. 51.

ensure that the complaint impleads a State Party,[1708] that it possesses jurisdiction *ratione materiae,*[1709] that the applicants have *locus standi* or that domestic remedies have been exhausted. In *Tanganyika Law Society et al. v. Tanzania* the Respondent argued that the Human Rights Court lacked jurisdiction *ratione temporis* because the violation occurred before the Protocol had entered into force. Dismissing this challenge to its jurisdiction the Human Rights Court found that the rights in question were protected by the African Charter which had been in force for Tanzania at the material time. Moreover, the alleged violation was of a continuing nature which continued when the Protocol was ratified and the optional declaration made.[1710] It must be observed that absent this latter contingency, the better view seems to be that the crucial date is that of the State's ratification of the Protocol.[1711] Article 6(2) of the Protocol states that the Human Rights Court shall rule on the admissibility of cases taking account of Article 56 of the African Charter, which governs communications submitted by individuals and NGOs to the Commission.[1712] Rule of Court 40 makes it clear that applications *must* satisfy the hurdles of admissibility, which in every material respect are identical to those listed in Article 56 of the African Charter with the exception of sub-rule (6) which makes the necessary adjustment in that the case must be filed within a reasonable period from the time local remedies were exhausted[1713] or from the date set by the Human Rights Court as being the commencement of the time limit within which it shall be seized of the matter. The Human Rights Court has endorsed the Commission's

---

1708. In *Youseff Ababou v. Kingdom of Morocco*, African Court of Human and Peoples' Rights, App. No. 007/2011 (2 Sept. 2011) para. 12, the Human Rights Court found it lacked jurisdiction because Morocco was not then a member of the AU and thus not a party to the Protocol. *See also Femi Falana v. African Union*, African Court of Human and Peoples' Rights, App. No. 001/2011 (26 Jun. 2012) where the applicant sought to implead, unsuccessfully, the AU itself. In *African Commission on Human and Peoples' Rights v. Libya*, African Court of Human and Peoples' Rights, App. No. 002/2013 (3 Jun. 2016) paras 49–50, the Human Rights Court held Libya responsible for the actions of rebels within its territory.

1709. *See Efoua Mbozo'o Samuel v. Pan-African Parliament*, African Court of Human and Peoples' Rights, App. No. 010/2011 (30 Sept. 2011) para. 6, where the Human Rights Court found it lacked jurisdiction on the ground that the application was based exclusively upon breach of an employment contract. But *see* Judge Ouguergouz's Dissenting Opinion, *ibid.*, para. 12.

1710. App. Nos 009/2011 and 011/2011 (14 Jun. 2013) para. 84; *Mkandawire v. Malawi,* African Court of Human and Peoples' Rights, App. No. 003/2011 (21 Jun. 2013) para. 32.

1711. *See Mkandawire v. Malawi,* African Court of Human and Peoples' Rights, App. No. 003/2011 (21 Jun. 2013), Joint Dissenting Opinion of Judge Niyungeko and Judge El Hadji Guisse, paras 5–8.

1712. *See Mkandawire v. Malawi,* African Court of Human and Peoples' Rights, App. No. 003/2011 (21 Jun. 2013) para. 38.1; *African Commission on Human and Peoples' Rights v. Libya*, African Court of Human and Peoples' Rights, App. No. 002/2013 (3 Jun. 2016) para. 63. *See* further *supra* paras 305–318. The Human Rights Court has held that while the rules of admissibility of the Commission of the Court are very similar they are in fact distinct and should not be conflated, *African Commission on Human and Peoples' Rights v. Kenya*, African Court of Human and Peoples' Rights, App. No. 006/2012 (26 May 2017) para. 78.

1713. In *Tanganyika Law Society et al. v. Tanzania*, African Court of Human and Peoples' Rights, App. Nos 009/2011 and 011/2011 (14 Jun. 2013) para. 83, the Human Rights Court found that one year was not an unreasonable period of time.

jurisprudence on this question.[1714] The Human Rights Court will dismiss applications without merit (manifestly ill-founded) giving reasons for its decision.[1715]

341 Individuals and NGOs may be further disadvantaged by the fact that under Article 6(3) the Human Rights Court is not compelled to entertain an admissible case but has the discretion of referring it to the Commission. Rule of Court 29(5)(a) makes a passing reference to this procedure but no indication is given as to what factors may motivate the Human Rights Court to take such a step. However, the Human Rights Court's case law is providing some answers to this question. In instances where it has found that it does not possess jurisdiction because a complainant under Article 5(3) of the Protocol lacks standing, either because a State Party has not made a declaration under Article 34(6) of the Protocol or an NGO does not have observer status with the Commission, in light of the claims made it has transferred them to the Commission.[1716] The Human Rights Court appears to be guided by a desire to avoid a denial of justice. However, such emergent practice has attracted strong disapproval from Judge Ouguergouz who has argued that it 'is not founded in law' and that the Human Rights Court has 'deviated from the original purpose of that provision'.[1717] Implicit in his criticism is the opinion that the issues of jurisdiction and admissibility have not been determined correctly.[1718] In his view, this procedure 'applies primarily to the consideration of the admissibility of a case over which the jurisdiction of the Court has already been established'.[1719] Judge Ouguergouz additionally contends that the principle of legal certainty demands that clear reasoned objective criteria should guide the Human Rights Court in its practice of referrals to the Commission since the current policy was haphazard and unpredictable and was in danger of becoming 'systematic'.[1720] In his view the Human Rights Court could play 'the role of an "early warning mechanism" for the Commission' and that the procedure in question should be reserved for those

1714. *Tanganyika Law Society et al. v. Tanzania*, African Court of Human and Peoples' Rights, App. Nos 009/2011 and 011/2011 (14 Jun. 2013) para. 82.3, where the Human Rights Court rejected the notion of parliamentary process, a political process which was discretionary and could be abandoned at any time, as adequate.

1715. Rule of Court 38. *See Amare v. Republic of Mozambique and Mozambique Airlines*, African Court of Human and Peoples' Rights, App. No. 005/2011 (16 Jun. 2011) para. 8. Judge Ouguergouz has argued that in such circumstances the application should not be 'considered judicially by the Court' but should be 'dismissed *de plano* by a simple letter from the Registry' on grounds of time and resources, *see* , e.g., his Separate Opinion in *Michelot Yogogombaye v. Senegal*, African Court of Human and Peoples' Rights, App. No. 001/2008 (15 Dec. 2009), and his Dissenting Opinion in *Ekollo Moundi Alexandre v. Cameroon and Nigeria*, African Court of Human and Peoples' Rights, App. No. 008/2011 (23 Sept. 2011) para. 7.

1716. *Amare v. Mozambique and Mozambique Airlines*, African Court of Human and Peoples' Rights, App. No. 005/2011 (16 Jun. 2011) para. 9; *Ekollo Moundi Alexandre v. Cameroon and Nigeria* App. No. 008/2011 (23 Sept. 2011) para. 11; *Association Juriste d'Afrique pour la Bonne Gouvernance v. Ivory Coast*, African Court of Human and Peoples' Rights, App. No. 006/2011 (16 Jun. 2011) para. 10.

1717. *Ekollo Moundi Alexandre v. Cameroon and Nigeria*, African Court of Human and Peoples' Rights, App. No 008/2011 (23 Sept. 2011), Dissenting Opinion of Judge Ouguergouz, paras 12, 20.

1718. *Ibid.*, paras 14–19.

1719. *Ibid.*, para. 13.

1720. *Ibid.*, paras 21–26.

cases where the former lacks jurisdiction displaying 'exceptional circumstances' such as those envisaged by Article 58 of the African Charter.[1721] He sees no reason why the Human Rights Court should not use its discretion to transfer cases over which it has jurisdiction to the Commission to rule on the merits.[1722] He advocates such a policy in order to lessen the workload on the Human Rights Court.[1723] His suggestions seem eminently sensible if the Human Rights Court is to avoid the significant delays caused by a backlog of cases.

342. Article 5(2) enshrines what appears to be a welcome development in human rights instruments in that it permits a State Party that has an interest in a case to request the Human Rights Court to be permitted to join, essentially to intervene. The decision whether to grant a request for intervention naturally rests with the Human Rights Court; the views of the applicant or the parties to the case cannot bind it. While Rule of Court 53(2)(a) makes it clear that the interest must be one of a 'legal' nature no further guidance is provided as to the meaning of the noun 'interest' but the Human Rights Court may choose to be guided by the practice of other tribunals.[1724] Nonetheless, it could include situations not envisaged by Article 5(1) of the Protocol.[1725] Intervening States must additionally state the precise object of the intervention and the basis of jurisdiction that exist between them and the parties to the case.[1726] Any possible delays to the proceedings should be minimized by the fact that the Human Rights Court will fix a time limit within which the intervening State must submit its written observations.[1727]

343. Article 26(1) of the Protocol obliges the Human Rights Court to hear submissions by all parties and if necessary hold an enquiry. Rule of Court 45(3) provides the Human Rights Court with the discretion to conduct an enquiry at any time during the proceedings by one or more of the judges, to carry out visits to scenes or gather evidence in any other manner. Considering the often uncooperative and obstructive behaviour of impugned States in such circumstances the Human Rights Court's ability to visit scenes or conduct enquiries is of considerable importance in marshalling the facts and attempting to arrive at the truth.

344. By virtue of Article 26(2) of the Protocol and Rule of Court 27 the Human Rights Court may receive written and oral evidence including expert testimony. Evidence may be obtained by the Human Rights Court *propio motu*, at the request of a party or the Commission.[1728] No new evidence may be submitted by the parties after

1721. *Ibid.*, paras 22–29.
1722. *Ibid.*, paras 31–33.
1723. *Ibid.*, para. 35.
1724. ICJ practice under its Statute Art. 62 reveals that it has applied a very strict policy in this area, *see* C. Chinkin, 'Third Party Intervention Before the International Court of Justice,' *A.J.I.L.* 80 (1986): 495. The European Convention on Human Rights Art. 36(2) (4 Nov. 1950) (as amended), E.T.S. No. 155, which is limited under para. 1 thereof to cases where a national of a contracting party is an applicant, requires the intervention to be in the interest of the proper administration of justice. *See* further Harris, O'Boyle & Warbrick, 853–856.
1725. Nmehielle, 270.
1726. Rule 53(2)(b), (c) of the Court. This is contrary to the practice of the ICJ where a 'jurisdictional link' by the intervening party is not required, *Land and Maritime Boundary (Cameroon v. Nigeria) (Equatorial Guinea Intervening)* I.C.J. Reports 1999, 1029.
1727. Rule of Court 53(5).
1728. Rule of Court 45(1).

the closure of pleadings save with the leave of the Human Rights Court.[1729] That the Human Rights Court has a wide discretion as to the evidence and witnesses it will admit is confirmed by its rules. Hence Rule of Court 45(1) states that the Human Rights Court may 'obtain any evidence which in its opinion may provide clarification of the facts of a case'.[1730] To this end it can 'decide to hear as a witness or expert or in any other capacity any person whose evidence, assertions or statements it deems likely to assist it'. Moreover, the Human Rights Court 'may ask any person or institution of its choice to obtain information, express an opinion or submit a report to it on any specific point'.[1731] *Amici curiae* would therefore seem to be allowed and the effective protection of human rights in Africa could only be enhanced if the Human Rights Court were to allow representations from a broad category of *amici curiae,* especially NGOs. It is evident, although not set out in explicit terms, that parties may object to a witness or expert given that the Human Rights Court is authorized to rule on any such challenge.[1732] Questions may be put by the Human Rights Court to witnesses, experts or other persons appearing before it.[1733] They may be examined, cross-examined and re-examined by the parties and the Commission.[1734]

345. The possibility of failure of witnesses to appear, of contempt of court or of perjury are not addressed by either the Protocol or the Rules of Court. Article 10(3) guarantees protection to any person, witness or representative of parties who appears before the Human Rights Court necessary for the proper discharging of their functions and duties before the Human Rights Court. Individuals and others should therefore be able to appear before the Human Rights Court without fear of retribution, and is a welcome development since arbitrary detention and disappearances are all too common in parts of Africa for defying the authorities. It is unclear therefore, how, if at all, individuals are to be effectively protected within the jurisdiction of a State party to the Protocol but it is submitted that this guarantee could be strengthened were the Human Rights Court to use creatively its competence to indicate provisional measures under Article 27(2). In addition, explicit provision should have been made for the imposition of sanctions on States that failed to protect effectively or persecuted such people.

346. The rules contain a reaffirmation of the principle *pacta sunt servanda* in that States Parties to a case are under an obligation to cooperate with the Human Rights Court so that all notices, communications and summonses addressed to persons in their territory or under their jurisdiction are executed.[1735] This is also true for any proceeding that the Human Rights Court holds in the territory of a State Party to a

1729. Rule of Court 50.

1730. Judge Ouguergouz has stressed the importance of the Court satisfying itself as to the veracity of facts by making full use of its ability to gather evidence and question witnesses, *African Commission on Human and Peoples' Rights v. Libya*, African Court of Human and Peoples' Rights, App. No. 002/2013 (3 Jun. 2016), Separate Opinion of Judge Ouguergouz, paras 16–25.

1731. Rule of Court 45(2).

1732. Rule of Court 46(5).

1733. Rule of Court 47(1).

1734. Rule of Court 47(2).

1735. Rule of Court 32(1).

case.[1736] This duty extends also to other States.[1737] Given a real fear of retribution for challenging State authorities the Human Rights Court, in providing some protection for applicants, witnesses, or legal representatives, is seeking to preserve the integrity of the proceedings; a State that failed to protect such individuals could ultimately be found to be in breach of its treaty obligations.

347. Under Article 27(2) the Human Rights Court must adopt such interim, or provisional, measures as it deems necessary in cases of 'extreme gravity and urgency', and 'to avoid irreparable harm to persons'.[1738] They are also designed to preserve the *status quo ante* pending the determination of the case.[1739] Stringent requirements must therefore be met. The Human Rights Court found that 'circumstances…of great urgency' relating especially to the rights to life and physical integrity during the revolution in Libya in early 2011 compelled it to order such measures.[1740] This capacity is supplemented by Rule 51(1) of the Court which refers to 'the interest of the parties', no doubt corresponding to the preservation of their respective rights, or 'of justice', thus conferring upon the Human Rights Court a sweeping discretion. In *African Commission on Human and Peoples' Rights v. Kenya (Provisional Measures)* the Human Rights Court took notice of prejudice to the substantive matter before it.[1741] In cases of extreme urgency an extraordinary session of the Human Rights Court may be convened to decide on measures to be taken.[1742]

348. Interim measures can be given at the request of a party to the case, the Commission[1743] or the Human Rights Court on its own accord. In *African Commission on Human and Peoples' Rights v. Libya (Provisional Measures)*, the Human Rights

1736. Rule of Court 32(2).

1737. Rule of Court 32(3).

1738. The Human Rights Court has described provisional measures as 'a consequence of the right to protection under the [African] Charter', *African Commission on Human and Peoples' Rights v. Libya (Order of Provisional Measures)*, African Court of Human and Peoples' Rights, App. No. 002/2013 (15 Mar. 2013) para. 13. In *General Kayumba Nyamwasa and Six Others v. Rwanda (Order of Provisional Measures)*, African Court of Human and Peoples' Rights, App. No. 016/2015 (24 Mar. 2017) para. 35, the Human Rights Court declined to grant interim measures since the object of the request had been overtaken by events.

1739. *African Commission on Human and Peoples' Rights v. Republic of Kenya (Order of Provisional Measures)*, African Court of Human and Peoples' Rights, App. No. 006/2012 (15 Mar. 2013) para. 23.

1740. *In the Matter of the African Commission on Human and Peoples' Rights v. Libyan Arab People's Jamahiriya (Provisional Measures)*, African Court of Human and Peoples' Rights, App. No. 004/2011 (25 Mar. 2011) paras 22–23.

1741. *African Commission on Human and Peoples' Rights v. Republic of Kenya (Order of Provisional Measures)*, African Court of Human and Peoples' Rights, App. No. 006/2012 (15 Mar. 2013) para. 22.

1742. Rule 51(2) of Court.

1743. *See*, e.g., *African Commission on Human and Peoples' Rights v. Republic of Kenya (Order of Provisional Measures)*, African Court of Human and Peoples' Rights, App. No. 006/2012 (15 Mar. 2013).

Court ordered measures *proprio motu*.[1744] The fact that the Human Rights Court can order any measures 'it deems necessary' suggests that they could be 'in whole or in part other than those requested'. The Human Rights Court need not satisfy itself that it has jurisdiction on the merits but simply that prima facie jurisdiction exists.[1745] This it can do by establishing that the applicant is an entity entitled to submit a case to the Human Rights Court and that the Respondent has ratified the African Charter and the Protocol.[1746] There is certainly no need to engage in prior consideration of the substantive issues in the case.[1747] The Human Rights Court has stated that the indication of interim measures does not prejudge the question of jurisdiction, the admissibility or merits of the case.[1748]

349. A number of questions remain unaddressed however. Can a request for interim measures be submitted to the Human Rights Court at any time of the proceedings pending final decision, including at the same time as the institution of proceedings? What will the Human Rights Court's approach be towards interim measures adopted by the Commission? Furthermore, no explicit provision is made for the revocation or modification of interim measures. However, a surprising omission, given significant developments elsewhere, is any explicit guidance to the question whether interim measures have binding effect.[1749] The language of the relevant provisions of the Rules of the Court is unclear on this point;[1750] the use of the verb 'prescribe' in Rule 51(1) is capable of being interpreted as an order or a recommendation. However, favouring the sense of a legal duty is the Human Rights Court's capacity under Rule 51(4) to 'make all such recommendations as it deems appropriate' in instances of non-compliance

---

1744. *African Commission on Human and Peoples' Rights v. Libyan Arab People's Jamahiriya (Provisional Measures)*, African Court of Human and Peoples' Rights, App. No. 004/2011 (25 Mar. 2011) paras 9–12; *African Commission on Human and Peoples' Rights v. Libya (Order of Provisional Measures)*, African Court of Human and Peoples' Rights, App. No. 002/2013 (15 Mar. 2013).

1745. *African Commission on Human and Peoples' Rights v. Libya (Provisional Measures)*, African Court of Human and Peoples' Rights, App. No. 004/2011 (25 Mar. 2011) para. 15; *African Commission on Human and Peoples' Rights v. Republic of Kenya (Order of Provisional Measures)*, African Court of Human and Peoples' Rights, App. No. 006/2012 (15 Mar. 2013) para. 16.

1746. *African Commission on Human and Peoples' Rights v. Libya (Provisional Measures)*, African Court of Human and Peoples' Rights, App. No. 004/2011 (25 Mar. 2011) paras 17–18.

1747. *African Commission on Human and Peoples' Rights v. Republic of Kenya (Order of Provisional Measures)*, African Court of Human and Peoples' Rights, App. No. 006/2012 (15 Mar. 2013) para. 19.

1748. *African Commission on Human and Peoples' Rights v. Republic of Kenya (Order of Provisional Measures)*, African Court of Human and Peoples' Rights, App. No. 006/2012 (15 Mar. 2013) para. 24; *African Commission on Human and Peoples' Rights v. Libya (Order of Provisional Measures)*, African Court of Human and Peoples' Rights, App. No. 002/2013 (15 Mar. 2013) para. 19.

1749. *LaGrand Case* (*Germany v. United States of America*) I.C.J. Reports 2001, 466, paras 99–103; *Application of the Convention on the Prevention and Punishment of the Crime of Genocide (Bosnia and Herzegovina v. Serbia and Montenegro)* I.C.J. Reports 2007, 1, paras 452, 468; *Constitutional Court v. Peru (Provisional Measures)*, Ser. E, No. 3 (2000); *Mamatkulov and Abdurasulovic v. Turkey*, European Court of Human Rights, App. Nos 46827/99, 46951/99, Judgment of 6 Feb. 2003).

1750. Rule 61(5) of the Court states that 'judgments' have a legally binding effect on the parties.

by States.[1751] The Human Rights Court should follow the international trend and it could do worse than adopt the Commission's approach declaring that a contracting party that has failed to abide by its indication of interim measures is in breach of the principle of *pacta sunt servanda* enshrined in Article 1 of the African Charter.[1752]

350. While the Protocol does not address the possibility of a non-appearing State party Rule 55 allows the Human Rights Court to proceed with the case and give its judgment at the request of the other party. However, the Human Rights Court must first satisfy itself that it has jurisdiction, that the claim is well-founded in fact and in law, that the case is admissible and that due notice was given to the defaulting party.[1753] This is designed to ensure the proper administration of justice and preserve the principle of equality of the parties.[1754]

351. The Applicant can discontinue a case by informing the Registrar to that effect.[1755] However, the Respondent's consent to discontinue is required if it has already taken measures to proceed with the case. The Human Rights Court itself is not explicitly empowered to strike out cases from its list at any stage of the proceedings. No provision is made for restoring a case to the Court's list even if circumstances appear to so dictate.

352. The procedure in contentious cases consists primarily of written proceedings, but oral proceedings only if considered necessary.[1756] Cases are heard in open court[1757] although it may decide, *propio motu* or at the request of the parties, that they be held in camera in the interests of public morality, safety or public order.[1758] A safeguard exists in that the Human Rights Court must provide a reasoned explanation based on the listed grounds for its decision.[1759] At any stage of the pleadings the Human Rights Court may order the joinder of interrelated cases and pleadings if considered

1751. The Human Rights Court brought Libya's non-compliance with an Order to the attention of the AU Assembly, *African Commission on Human and Peoples' Rights v. Libya*, African Court of Human and Peoples' Rights, App. No. 002/2013 (3 Jun. 2016) para. 18.

1752. *See supra* paras 223–224.

1753. *See African Commission on Human and Peoples' Rights v. Libya*, African Court of Human and Peoples' Rights, App. No. 002/2013 (3 Jun. 2016) paras 38–43. In his Separate Opinion, Judge Ouguergouz stated that the Court should have been guided by the jurisprudence of the ICJ and Inter-American Court of Human Rights in this area. He proceeded to express the view that the Court had failed to carry out a proper examination of the facts and law which had seemingly resulted in the Court pronouncing itself 'automatically' in favour of the Applicant, *ibid.*, *African Commission on Human and Peoples' Rights v. Libya*, African Court of Human and Peoples' Rights, App. No. 002/2013 (3 Jun. 2016), Separate Opinion of Judge Ouguergouz, paras 3–4, 27–28.

1754. *African Commission on Human and Peoples' Rights v. Libya*, African Court of Human and Peoples' Rights, App. No. 002/2013 (3 Jun. 2016), Separate Opinion of Judge Ouguergouz, paras 26–27.

1755. Rule 58 of the Court.

1756. Rule 27(1) of the Court. The Human Rights Court may put questions to the parties, Rule 47(1) of the Court.

1757. Protocol Art. 10(1); Rule 43(1) of the Court.

1758. Rule 43(2) of the Court.

1759. Rule 43(3) of the Court.

appropriate.[1760] The use of the term 'pleadings' rather than 'proceedings' suggests the Human Rights Court enjoys a narrower discretion in this field. Following the conclusion of the hearings the Human Rights Court deliberates in private[1761] and then delivers its judgment in open Court.[1762] Judgments must be taken by majority, and shall be final and not subject to appeal.[1763] Moreover, judgments must be reasoned,[1764] and separate and dissenting opinions may be attached.[1765] The Rules make provision for the publication of the Human Rights Court's judgments, advisory opinions, orders, etc.[1766] It seems implicit in the Rules that corrections may be made to insignificant errors or omissions in judgments or opinions.[1767] It is interesting to note that Article 28(1) of the Protocol requires the Human Rights Court to render its judgment within ninety days of having completed its deliberations. This does not seem an unreasonable expectation in the context of the protection of human rights.

353. The judgments of the Human Rights Court are binding;[1768] thus States parties to cases decided by the Human Rights Court 'undertake to comply with the judgment…and to guarantee its execution'.[1769] International practice suggests that the Human Rights Court's jurisprudence will have a persuasive effect on other States. However, the Human Rights Court has no power to enforce its judgments, although it can draw the Assembly's attention to any cases in which a State has not complied with a judgment in its annual report under Article 31 of the Protocol. Under Article 29(2) of the Protocol and Rule 64(2) of Court the EX (previously Council of Ministers) is entrusted with the task of monitoring the execution of judgments on the Assembly's behalf. Absent further clarification it is unlikely that the EX will have any powers to ensure compliance. In principle, there appears to be no legal obstacle to the Assembly imposing sanctions on a recalcitrant State pursuant to Article 23 of the Constitutive Act for breach of its obligations under the Protocol. Moreover, a creative interpretation of Article 27(1) could allow the Human Rights Court to award punitive damages in

1760. Rule 54 of the Court. This it did in *Tankanyika Law Society and The Legal and Human Rights Law Centre and Reverend Christopher Mtikila v. Tanzania*, African Court of Human and Peoples' Rights, App. No. 009 & 011/2011 (22 Sept. 2011), where the subject matter and the defendants were the same in both cases.

1761. Rules 59(1) and 60(1) of the Court.

1762. Protocol, Art. 28(5); Rule 61(3) of the Court. According to the Human Rights Court, 'publicity of a judgment is assured as long as it is rendered in a premises or open area; provided the public is notified of the place and…can have free access to the same', *Mohamed Abubakri v. Tanzania*, African Court of Human and Peoples' Rights, App. No. 007/2013 (3 Jun. 2016), para. 225. However, this conclusion was criticized by the dissenting judges who argued that judgments in judges' chambers could not amount to 'open court'.

1763. Protocol, Art. 28(2); Rule 60(3) of the Court.

1764. Protocol, Art. 28(6); Rule 61(1) of the Court.

1765. Protocol, Art. 28(7); Rule 60(5) of the Court.

1766. Rules 25(2)(i) and 65 of the Court. Also available at the Court's website, http://www.african-court.org.

1767. Rule 25(2)(i) of the Court.

1768. Rule 61(5) of Court. *See also* Protocol Art. 28(2) and Rule 61(4) of Court which describe the Human Rights Court's judgments as 'final'.

1769. Protocol Art. 30.

cases where the applicant establishes that a State has flouted a judgment of the Human Rights Court and has failed to make reparation to a victim.

354. Although the Human Rights Court's judgments are final and not subject to appeal,[1770] the Human Rights Court can review its decisions in the light of new evidence.[1771] According to Rule 67(1) of Court the new evidence must not have been known at the time the judgment was delivered to the party. There is no explicit requirement that the new evidence should have played a decisive factor in the case. A limitation period of no more than six months of the new fact's discovery is imposed. In addition, the Human Rights Court has the power to interpret its decisions.[1772] Under Rule 66(1) of Court the Human Rights Court is competent to interpret a judgment on application by any party. Significantly, the Court's power in this regard is narrow, limited 'for the purpose of *executing a judgment*' (emphasis added).[1773] The rationale seems to be in order 'to prevent a new dispute being submitted to the Human Rights Court in the guise of a request to interpret an earlier judgment'.[1774] A deadline of twelve months from the date of judgment is set unless the interests of justice dictate otherwise.

355. It is interesting to note with regard to both these procedures that while the Protocol refers to 'decisions' the corresponding Rules of Court employ the noun 'judgment'. It should not be assumed that the two terms are coterminous[1775] but it is not clear whether the use of the different nouns is supposed to make a substantive procedural distinction.

356. The Protocol bestows a broad advisory jurisdiction upon the Human Rights Court. Article 4(1) thus confers upon the Human Rights Court competence to give advisory opinions on any legal matter relating to the African Charter or other relevant human rights instrument[1776] at the request of a Member State of the AU, any AU organ,

1770. Protocol Art. 28(2); Rule 61(4) of Court.

1771. Protocol Art. 28(3); Rule 26(1)(e) of Court. An application for revision does not stay the execution of a judgment unless the Human Rights Court decides otherwise, Rule 67(5) of Court.

1772. Protocol Art. 28(4); Rule 26(1)(e) of Court.

1773. An application for interpretation does not stay the execution of a judgment unless the Human Rights Court decides otherwise, Rule 66(5) of Court.

1774. S. Rosenne, *The World Court: What It is and How It Works* (5th edn, Dordrecht: Martinus Nijhoff, 1995), 151. Rosenne was writing about the ICJ but his comment seems equally valid with regard to the Human Rights Court.

1775. Hudson, 583–584. *See also Ekollo Moundi Alexandre v. Cameroon and Nigeria*, African Court of Human and Peoples' Rights, App. No. 008/2011 (23 Sept. 2011), Dissenting Opinion of Judge Ouguergouz, paras 3–4.

1776. *See also* Rule 68(1)–(2) of the Court. However, the Human Rights Court seems to have cast doubt on whether it could consider the Rome Statute of the International Criminal Court (17 Jul. 1998), 2187 U.N.T.S. 91, 37 I.L.M. 999 (1998) (Rome Statute), *Request for Advisory Opinion by the Coalition for* the *International Criminal Court, the Legal Defence & Assistance Project (LEDAP), the Civil Resource Development & Documentation Center (CIRDDOC) and the Women Advocates Documentation Center (WARDC)*, African Court of Human and Peoples' Rights, Request No. 001/2015 (29 Nov. 2015) para. 18.

or any African organization recognized by the AU.[1777] In another application of the *lis pendens* principle the request must not relate to an application pending before the Commission.[1778] The fact that all Member States of the AU are able to request an opinion, whether or not they are parties to the Protocol, is noteworthy. The recognition of a broad range of applicants and wide-ranging subject matter could give rise to problems similar to those discussed above in relation to its contentious jurisdiction. However, such a wide jurisdiction has the potential of strengthening the commitment to human rights and giving rise to a rich jurisprudence.

357. It is important to note that the power of the Human Rights Court to render advisory opinions is discretionary, as evidenced by the inclusion of the word 'may' in Article 4(1).[1779] It remains to be seen in what circumstances, other than that specifically relating to an issue being examined by the Commission, the Human Rights Court may choose to decline to exercise its advisory jurisdiction.

358. In matters of procedure it is important to note that Rule 72 of the Court assimilates the advisory procedure to contentious procedure. Preliminary objections to advisory proceedings are therefore permitted. Furthermore, it is an established practice for States to raise objections to the advisory jurisdiction of the ICJ.[1780]

359. The rules make it clear that advisory proceedings consist of written[1781] and, if necessary, oral stages.[1782] Of particular interest is the fact that any State Party is allowed to enter written submissions on any of the issues raised in the request for an opinion.[1783] The same holds true for any other 'interested entity' authorized by the Human Rights Court. Such entities would appear to be those such as AU organs or African organizations recognized by the AU as listed in Article 4(1) of the Protocol and Rule 68(1) of the Court. However, it is submitted that in the interests of justice

1777. The Human Rights Court has held that the Committee on the Rights of the Child is an AU organ with *locus standi*, *Request for Advisory Opinion by the African Committee of Experts on the Rights and Welfare of the Child on the Standing of the African Committee of Experts on the Rights and Welfare of the Child before the African Court of Human and Peoples' Rights*, African Court of Human and Peoples' Rights, Request No. 002/2013 (5 Dec. 2014), paras 56–57. The potential for duplication again arises since, as has been observed, the Commission has the power of interpretation under the African Charter Art. 45(3), which has been described by an eminent author as amounting to authorization 'to issue what are in effect advisory opinions', A.H. Robertson & J.G. Merrills, *Human Rights in the World*(3rd edn, Manchester: Manchester University Press, 1992), 221. It is likely that the Court will assume primary competence, Nmehielle, 273.

1778. Rule 68(3) of the Court. *See Request for Advisory Opinion by Pan-African Lawyers' Union and Southern African Litigation Center*, African Court of Human and Peoples' Rights, Request No. 002/2012 (15 Mar. 2013).

1779. *Request for Advisory Opinion by the African Committee of Experts on the Rights and Welfare of the Child on the Standing of the African Committee of Experts on the Rights and Welfare of the Child before the African Court of Human and Peoples' Rights*, African Court of Human and Peoples' Rights, Request No. 002/2013 (5 Dec. 2014), para. 40.

1780. For example, Spain in the *Western Sahara Case* (Advisory Opinion) I.C.J. Reports 1975, 14; Israel in the *Legal Consequences of the Construction of a Wall in the Occupied Palestinian Territory Case* (Advisory Opinion) I.C.J. Reports 2004, 136.

1781. Rule 70 of the Court.

1782. Rule 71 of the Court.

1783. Rule 70(2) of the Court.

the Human Rights Court should be prepared to accept NGOs and individuals as 'interested entities'. Other procedures are identical, *mutatis mutandis*, to those in contentious cases.[1784]

360. Article 4(2) requires the Human Rights Court to give reasons for its advisory opinions and enables the judges to deliver separate or dissenting opinions. This appears to be standard international judicial practice. Opinions must be read in open court unless circumstances dictate otherwise.[1785] This situation hardly seems consonant with basic notions of justice which demands openness, particularly in contemporary times when an expectation of transparency has arisen. It is difficult to conceive of circumstances where a 'secret opinion' may be justified. Regrettably the rules are silent as to whether a 'secret opinion' could be made public at some future stage or whether it would remain 'secret' in perpetuity, or which body would be entitled ultimately to take a decision on this issue.

361. It is a trite observation that advisory opinions are not legally binding but it would be surprising if the Human Rights Court's opinions were not to acquire an authoritative status.

362. The Human Rights Court is given the power under Article 9 to attempt amicable settlements in accordance with the African Charter.[1786] Both Article 9 of the Protocol and the Rules of the Court envisage a proactive role, which is discretionary, for the Human Rights Court in reaching amicable, or friendly, settlements.[1787] It may therefore contact the parties and take suitable measures to facilitate an amicable settlement based on respect for human and peoples' rights.[1788] Rule 56 of the Court provides for the possibility of the parties settling their dispute amicably out of court. The agreement to settle in this instance must be mutual. A settlement may be reached at any time before the Human Rights Court renders judgment. The Human Rights Court will then deliver a judgment limited to a brief statement of the facts and the solution adopted.[1789] Notwithstanding such an agreement the Human Rights Court may decide to proceed with the case.[1790] Although the rationale for doing so is not explicated it is likely to be for reasons regarding the good administration of justice or for upholding human rights.[1791]

363. Under Article 10(2) and Rule 29 of Court any party to a case can be represented by a legal representative of their choice. Free legal representation may be provided in the interests of justice.[1792] Given the abject poverty in many parts of Africa this circumstance appears significant but it will only prove effective if proper funding

1784. Rule 72 of the Court.
1785. Rule 73(1) of the Court.
1786. *See also* Rule 26(1)(c) of the Court.
1787. Rule 26(1)(c) and 57 of the Court.
1788. Rule 57(1) of the Court.
1789. Rule 56(2) of the Court.
1790. Rule 56(3) of the Court.
1791. By analogy with Rule 57(1) of the Court.
1792. *See also* Rule 30 of Court.

is forthcoming. As a general rule states that each party will bear its own costs unless the Human Rights Court decides otherwise.[1793]

364. According to Article 7 the Court shall apply the provisions of the African Charter and other human rights instruments ratified by the States concerned. The Human Rights Court can thus draw inspiration from the wealth of general and particular international law, including the ICCPR, the ECHR and the ACHR.[1794] No express mention is made of the norms of general international law but they should undoubtedly influence the Human Rights Court. It will be interesting to see if the Human Rights Court builds a distinctive jurisprudence emphasizing the second and third generation rights championed by the African Charter.

365. Article 11(1) states that the Human Rights Court consists of eleven judges. This is only a fraction of the actual membership of the AU and should ensure that the bench does not become unwieldly. Cases are heard by the full Court; Article 23 of the Protocol provides that the Human Rights Court must consist of at least seven judges to be quorate.[1795] Neither the Protocol nor the Rules make provision for the creation of chambers. The judges must be nationals of AU Member States; it is not specified that a judge must be a national of a State that has ratified the Protocol.[1796] However, only States Parties to the Protocol may nominate candidates,[1797] and in a welcome innovation, consideration must be given to 'adequate gender representation'.[1798] How this is to be achieved is unclear. Rule 13 of Court states, *inter alia*, that 'the Members of the Court, shall pursue to the greatest extent possible, a policy aimed at securing a balanced representation of gender'. There is an element of discretion therefore. No two judges can be nationals of the same State.[1799] As is standard practice in international tribunals, judges may be drawn from a varied background.

366. Judges are elected by secret ballot by the AU Assembly,[1800] which requires a two-thirds majority, a not inconsiderable hurdle. Again, adequate gender representation must be observed,[1801] which implies that the candidatures of certain women must survive the nomination process. Article 14(2) requires that Africa's main regions and its principal legal traditions (civil, Roman-Dutch, common, and Islamic law, but is customary law included?) are represented on the Human Rights Court.[1802] It is curious that no similar direction is required at the nomination stage.

1793. Rule 30 of Court. *See Michelot Yogogombaye v. Senegal*, African Court of Human and Peoples' Rights, App. No. 001/2008 (15 Dec. 2009) paras 41–45.

1794. *See* , e.g., *Wilfred Onyango Nganyi & 9 Others v. Tanzania*, African Court of Human and Peoples' Rights, App. No. 006/2013 (18 Mar. 2016), paras 169–179.

1795. *See also* Rule 17(1) of Court.

1796. Compare African Charter Art. 34, which stipulates that members of the Commission 'must have the nationality of one of the States Parties to the present Charter'.

1797. Protocol Art. 12(1), which stipulates that each State may propose up to three candidates, at least two of whom must be nationals of that State.

1798. Protocol Art. 12(2). *See also* Protocol Art. 14(3).

1799. *Ibid.* Art. 11(2).

1800. *Ibid.* Art. 14(1). *See* http://www.aict-ctia.org/courts_conti/achpr/achpr_bios.html.

1801. Protocol Art. 14(3).

1802. Rule 13 of Court.

367. The judges' term of office is six years with the possibility of one further renewable period.[1803] All judges, except for the President,[1804] shall be part-time.[1805] A judge may be suspended or removed from office when the other members of the Human Rights Court are unanimously of the view that s/he no longer fulfils the requirements of office.[1806] The judge in question must be informed in writing by the President of the Court. The impugned judge will be able to defend himself/herself at a specially convened private session of the Human Rights Court and a decision will be reached by the rest of the Court at a further special private session.[1807] The Human Rights Court's decision can be overturned by the AU Assembly.[1808]

368. The judges are elected in an individual capacity, that is, they must not follow instructions from any State or other agency. They must therefore desist from any activity that is incompatible with their independence or impartiality or the demands of their office.[1809] Exactly what activities come within the scope of a prohibited activity was left to the Rules of Court to determine. Rule 5(2) specifically lists political, diplomatic or administrative positions or function as government legal advisers at the national level but the use of the adverb 'in particular' indicates that other occupations are not excluded.[1810] This requirement should also be read in conjunction with Article 17(1) of the Protocol which guarantees the independence of the judges. A general obligation exists to ensure that judges consider all cases impartially, free from inducements, pressure, influence, threats or other interference.[1811] Additionally, the judges enjoy all immunities extended to diplomatic agents under international law during their term of office.[1812] Article 17(2) seeks to avoid conflicts of interest by requiring a judge who has previously been involved in a case to recuse himself/herself. However, the rules of Court go further. Thus a judge who has a personal interest in the case, who has expressed public pronouncements, through the media or academic writings perhaps, or '*for any other reason*' (emphasis added), that may undermine or lead his/her impartiality and independence to be questioned is disqualified from the case.[1813] The President of the Court has no power to exclude a judge from a case. No provision is made for replacing a judge in such circumstances with an interim or substitute judge. In fact, the Protocol makes no provision whatsoever for the appointment of ad hoc judges. In order to avoid any semblance of partiality, Article 22 of the Protocol

---

1803. Protocol Art. 15(1). At the end of two years following the first election, the terms of office shall expire after two years and the terms of four more judges shall expire at the end of four years.
1804. *Ibid.* Art. 21(2). The President serves a term of office of two years and may be re-elected once, *ibid.*, Art. 20(1).
1805. *Ibid.* Art. 15(4). However, the Assembly may alter this arrangement; such circumstance might arise if the Human Rights Court develops a busy docket.
1806. *Ibid.*, Art. 19(1).
1807. Rule 7(1) of Court.
1808. Protocol Art. 19(2).
1809. Protocol Art. 18; Rule 5(1) of Court.
1810. *See* further Rule 5(3) of Court.
1811. *See also* Protocol Art. 16 and Rule 4(1) of Court on the oath of office.
1812. Vienna Convention on Diplomatic Relations (24 Apr. 1961) 500 U.N.T.S. 95; General Convention on the Privileges and Immunities of the OAU (25 Oct. 1965) 1000 U.N.T.S. 393.
1813. Rule 8(4)(b)–(d) of Court.

does not allow a judge who is a national of a State that is a party to a case to hear it.[1814] Additionally, a judge is also prohibited from hearing a case concerning the State that elected him/her.[1815]

369. If the Human Rights Court concludes that human rights have been violated, Article 27(1) of the Protocol requires that it 'shall make appropriate orders to remedy the violation, including the payment of fair compensation or reparation'. Rule 34(5) of Court requires the Applicant to submit a request for reparation in the application commencing proceedings and allows him/her to submit a request for the amount of the reparation. The Human Rights Court will rule on the request for reparation either in the judgment or, as has become its practice, in a separate decision.[1816]

370. What constitutes 'fair compensation' or 'reparation' is undefined but the Human Rights Court has held that it can take the form of restitution, compensation and satisfaction.[1817] Awards of a pecuniary nature are clearly envisaged because of the use of the noun 'amount' in Rule 34(5) of Court and by definition 'fair compensation' must include awards of a pecuniary nature, and this interpretation has been upheld by the Court which in the case of *Zongo and Others v. Burkina Faso* awarded monetary sums.[1818] The concept of 'reparation' extends to ordering consequential measures requiring States to take certain positive steps.[1819] In relation to the quantification of reparation, the Human Rights Court has held that the applicable principle is that of 'full reparation, commensurate with the prejudice suffered.'[1820]

371. In the case of *Zongo and Others v. Burkina Faso*, the Human Rights Court considered the issue of reparations at length.[1821] The first point of interest is that the Court will only consider awarding reparations where an application to that effect has been submitted and arguments made.[1822] The Court recalled that it is a basic principle of international law that a State must make reparation for a breach of its obligations,[1823]

1814. *See also* Rule 8(2) of Court. In consequence Judge El Hadj Guissé, a national of Senegal, recused himself from hearing the case of *Michelot Yogogombaye v. Senegal*, African Court of Human and Peoples' Rights, App. No. 001/2008 (15 Dec. 2009). *See also*, e.g., *Association Juriste d'Afrique pour la Bonne Gouvernance v. Ivory Coast*, African Court of Human and Peoples' Rights, App. No. 006/2011 (16 Jun. 2011).

1815. Rule 8(3) of Court. Presumably this refers to a State party that nominated the judge.

1816. Rule 63 of Court. *See Zongo and Others v. Burkina Faso*, Judgment on Reparations, African Court of Human and Peoples' Rights, App. No. 013/2011 (5 Jun. 2015).

1817. *Zongo and Others v. Burkina Faso*, Judgment on Reparations, African Court of Human and Peoples' Rights, App. No. 013/2011 (5 Jun. 2015), para. 29.

1818. *Ibid.*, para. 111(ii).

1819. *See Zongo and Others v. Burkina Faso*, Judgment on Reparations, African Court of Human and Peoples' Rights, App. No. 013/2011 (5 Jun. 2015), para. 111(x), where the Court ordered the Respondent to reopen the investigation into the murder of the victim. On the Commission's practice *see supra* para. 298.

1820. *Zongo and Others v. Burkina Faso*, Judgment on Reparations, African Court of Human and Peoples' Rights, App. No. 013/2011 (5 Jun. 2015), para. 60.

1821. *Zongo and Others v. Burkina Faso*, Judgment on Reparations, African Court of Human and Peoples' Rights, App. No. 013/2011 (5 Jun. 2015).

1822. *Ibid.*, para. 2.

1823. *Case concerning the Factory at Chorzow (Germany v. Poland)*, Indemnity, Merits, P.C.I.J., Series A, No. 17 (1928).

reflected in Article 27(1).[1824] But this was limited to 'identified wrongful acts'.[1825] The Court recognized two categories of damage, material and moral.[1826] In relation to moral prejudice, the Court first considered whether the Applicants, Zongo's beneficiaries, were 'victims' entitled to reparations. The Court opined that international human rights law did not restrict the notion of victim to direct heirs but extends to close relatives.[1827] In relation to proof of causal link between the wrongful act and the moral prejudice, the Court was of the view that such a link may result automatically from a violation of a human right without any need to prove otherwise.[1828]

372. The future of the Human Rights Court is currently subject to a degree of uncertainty, however. In July 2004 the AU decided that the Human Rights Court should be merged with the Court of Justice.[1829] While valid arguments may exist on practical grounds for reducing the number of AU organs, including a desire for rationalization,[1830] and the potential problem of overlapping jurisdiction between the two courts,[1831] the decision was not favourably received. Thus Amnesty International criticized it on the ground that it undermines the effective functioning of the Human Rights Court.[1832] Academics were also critical, drawing attention to the different roles played by the courts, particularly the fact that the Court of Justice has no explicit human rights mandate and its judges do not have to have expertise in human rights, and the different rules on *locus standi*.[1833] The Commission also expressed serious concern, fearing the 'negative impact' that the decision could have on the effectiveness of the Human Rights Court and drew attention to the different mandates and litigants of the two courts.[1834] These criticisms notwithstanding, in 2008 the Assembly adopted the Protocol on the

---

1824. *Zongo and Others v. Burkina Faso*, Judgment on Reparations, African Court of Human and Peoples' Rights, App. No. 013/2011 (5 Jun. 2015), paras 20–22.
1825. *Ibid.*, para. 25.
1826. *Ibid.*, para. 27. The Court adopted the IACHR's definition of moral damage in *Cantoral Benevides v. Peru*, Reparations, Series C, No. 88 (2001).
1827. *Zongo and Others v. Burkina Faso*, Judgment on Reparations, African Court of Human and Peoples' Rights, App. No. 013/2011 (5 Jun. 2015), paras 46–49.
1828. *Ibid.*, para. 55.
1829. *Decision on the Merger of the African Court of Human and Peoples' Rights and the Court of Justice of the African Union*, AU Doc. Assembly/AU/Dec.83 (V). *See* Protocol of the Court of Justice of the African Union, AU Doc. Assembly/AU/Dec.25 (II).
1830. N.J. Udombana, 'An African Human Rights Court and an African Union Court: A Needful Duality or a Needless Duplication?', *Brooklyn J.I.L.* 28 (2003): 811.
1831. The Human Rights Court appears to have the capacity to pronounce on the Constitutive Act on the basis that the promotion and protection of human rights are stated as core principles and objectives, under the Protocol, Art. 3(1), whereas the Court of Justice would seem to have had jurisdiction over the African Charter under the Protocol of the Court of Justice Art. 18(1)(b).
1832. *African Union: Assembly's decision should not undermine the African Court*, http://web.amnesty.org/library/print/ENGIOR300202004.
1833. F. Viljoen & E. Baimu, 'Courts for Africa: Considering the Co-Existence of the African Court on Human and Peoples' Rights and the African Court of Justice', *N.Q.H.R.* 22 (2004): 241; K.D. Magliveras & G.J. Naldi, 'The African Court of Justice', *Z.a.ö.R.V.* 66 (2006): 187, 212–213.
1834. Resolution on the Establishment of an Effective African Court on Human and Peoples' Rights, ACHPR/Res.76 (XXXVII) 05 (2005) http://www1.umn.edu/humanrts/africa/resolutions/rec81.html.

ACJHR (2008 Protocol) establishing the ACJHR.[1835] Nevertheless, pending the merger the AU decided to allow the Human Rights Court to become operational.[1836] The 2008 Protocol contains transitional arrangements regarding the Human Rights Court. First, according to Article 4, the term of office of the judges of the Human Rights Court shall end when the judges of the ACJHR have been elected but shall remain in office until the latter have been sworn-in. Second, pursuant to Article 5, any cases pending before the Human Rights Court which have not been concluded before the 2008 Protocol enters into force, will be transferred to the Human Rights Section and will continue to be considered pursuant to the rules of the 1998 Protocol. Third, according to Article 7, once the 2008 Protocol has entered into force, the 1998 Protocol will remain in operation for a period of one year to allow for the assets and liabilities of the Human Rights Court to be transferred to the ACJHR. It is not inconceivable that the Human Rights Court may have a long life pending the entry into force of the 2008 Protocol.

§5. The Human Rights Section of the African Court of Justice and Human Rights

373. The AU sidestepped the potential difficulties thrown up by the proposed merger by creating two sections, one of which is the Human Rights Section with jurisdiction over alleged violations of human rights.[1837] Nonetheless, it appears true to say that one of the effects of the merger is that the distinctive identity of the Human Rights Court is diminished. According to the Preamble of the 2008 Protocol, the Human Rights Section's task is to secure the objectives of the African Charter, and to supplement and strengthen the mission of the Commission as well as of the African Committee of Experts on the Rights and Welfare of the Child.[1838] While this could simply be considered a statement of the intent to boost the existing protective system, it could also be seen as a reference to the fact that these two bodies have an enhanced role to play since, as is explained later, they have direct access to the Human Rights Section. Indeed, Article 27(2) of the Statute refers to the complementarity that the ACJHR maintains with the African Commission and the Committee of Experts.[1839]

374. Under Article 28(c) of the Statute the Human Rights Section[1840] has jurisdiction relating to the interpretation and application of the African Charter, the African Charter on the Rights of the Child, the Protocol on the Rights of Women in Africa, or of any other legal instrument pertaining to human rights. The inclusion of the latter clause is especially noteworthy because of its sweeping nature. The Human Rights Section appears to have been conferred jurisdiction to pronounce on multilateral instruments such as the International Covenants on Human Rights 1966 and the Convention on the Rights of the Child 1989, and on the constituent treaties of RECs

1835. *See supra* para. 215.
1836. AU Doc. Assembly/AU/Dec.83 (V), para. 3.
1837. Statute of the African Court of Justice and Human Rights Art. 17(2) (Statute).
1838. *See infra* paras 369–370.
1839. *See also* Rule 114 of the Commission.
1840. Article 28 of the Statute setting out the ACJHR's contentious jurisdiction does not address the separate Sections but their discrete competences should be borne in mind.

with human rights commitments, for example, ECOWAS[1841] and the SADC.[1842] Given that the Constitutive Act contains general provisions on human rights there appears to be no valid reason why the Human Rights Section should not assume the authority to examine it, either under this provision or paragraph (a) thereof.[1843] The Human Rights Section is expressly granted jurisdiction over OAU/AU treaties, such as the Convention on Refugees, under Article 28(b) of the Statute. It is interesting to note that in this particular instance the jurisdiction of the Human Rights Section extends to judging the *validity* of the treaties.

375. The following parties possess standing according to Article 30 of the Statute to submit cases to the Human Rights Section alleging human rights violations: (a) States Parties to the Protocol; (b) the African Commission on Human and Peoples' Rights; (c) the Committee of Experts on the Rights of the Child; (d) African IGOs; (e) African national human rights institutions; and (f) individuals and NGOs accredited to the AU or to its organs. Although not explicitly set out in the Statute it is likely that interstate cases are permissible. Whether States will be allowed to appeal adverse opinions issued by the Commission and by the Committee of Experts on the Rights of the Child is by no means certain but the language of the Statute suggests that it is likely to be so. That African IGOs, such as ECOWAS, and national human rights institutions have been listed as applicants is especially interesting. National human rights institutions could play a significant role if sufficiently independent. The fact that, in principle, the standing of duly accredited individuals and NGOs has been recognized is encouraging, although the requirement of accreditation may have a restrictive effect.[1844] Whether standing is afforded to associations and legal persons as is the case under the European system remains to be seen.[1845] An added difficulty is that the standing of NGOs and individuals is subject to the condition set out in Article 8(3) of the 2008 Protocol, the substantive section of which states that, '[a]ny Member

1841. *See* Revised ECOWAS Treaty 1993 Art. 4(g), 35 I.L.M. 663 (1996). Thus, in *Hadijatou Mani Koraou v. Niger*, ECOWAS Community Court of Justice, Judgment No. ECW/CCJ/JUD/06/08, (27 Oct. 2008) paras 41–42, http://www.unhcr.org/refworld/docid/496b41fa2.html (accessed 16 Jan. 2013), the ECOWAS Community Court of Justice invoked this particular treaty provision to state that it was charged with protecting human rights.

1842. Amended SADC Treaty 2001 Art. 4(c). In *Mike Campbell (Pvt) Ltd. et al. v. The Republic of Zimbabwe*, SADC (T) Case No. 2/2007, http://www.saflii.org/sa/cases/SADCT/2008/2.pdf (accessed 16 Jan. 2013), the SADC Tribunal held similarly that the SADC Treaty Art. 4(c) conferred upon it the competence to rule on human rights issues.

1843. The Human Rights Court has assumed the jurisdiction to consider the human rights provisions of the Constitutive Act, *Mohamed Abubakri v. Tanzania*, African Court of Human and Peoples' Rights, App. No. 007/2013 (3 Jun. 2016), para. 51.

1844. S. Sceats, *Africa's New Human Rights Court: Whistling in the Wind?*, Chatham House Briefing Paper IL BP 09/01. In *Association Juriste d'Afrique pour la Bonne Gouvernance v. Ivory Coast,* African Court of Human and Peoples' Rights, App. No. 006/2011 (16 Jun. 2011), the Human Rights Court dismissed the case as the applicant NGO did not have observer status with the Commission as required by the 1998 Protocol Art. 5(3). In July 2005, the Executive Council updated the criteria for accreditation which apply to NGOs only, Executive Council, *Criteria for Granting Observer Status and for a System of Accreditation within the AU* (EX.CL/Dec.195 (VII)).

1845. Harris, O'Boyle, Warbrick, 788–796.

State may … make a declaration accepting the competence of the Court to receive cases under Article 30(f) [of the Statute] *involving a State which has not made such a declaration*' (emphasis added). That this provision lacks clarity is a matter of regret. If the intention is to make the jurisdiction of the Human Rights Section in this instance contingent upon States making a separate optional declaration,[1846] it would have made more sense to repeat verbatim Article 34(6) of the 1998 Protocol which is a model of simplicity. If, as is apparently the case, a separate declaration is required, then the situation is highly unfortunate because States with a poor human rights record are unlikely to accept the jurisdiction of the Human Rights Section in this regard. Whereas the Statute could be said to provide for what may amount to public interest litigation, it is regrettable that this will only prove possible in extremely restrictive circumstances.[1847] Applicants who are unable to proceed because of a contracting party's refusal to accept this head of jurisdiction will need to rely on other parties, the Commission or national human rights institutions for example, to champion their complaints before the Human Rights Section. However, another avenue may emerge for an applicant found not to have standing, *forum prorogatum*.[1848] Under the Statute, a complainant is not required to be the victim of the alleged violation. It is commendable that the African system has opted for an expansive approach which can be justified on grounds such as poverty and lack of legal assistance.[1849] It should be observed that the Statute is silent on the issue of hurdles of admissibility. It must be assumed that detailed conditions governing admissibility will be laid down in the Rules of the Court.

§6. The African Charter on the Rights and Welfare of the Child

376. The rights of the child are not adequately addressed by the African Charter.[1850] In later years, however, the issue of children's rights came to the fore with the adoption of the UN Convention on the Rights of the Child (CRC) in 1989.[1851] Although the CRC attracted the support of many African States[1852] there was a consensus that the African child was exposed to particular dangers[1853] which demanded additional measures of

1846. Sceats, 9–10; *Interights*, http://www.interights.org/africansingleprotocoladopted/index.html (accessed 15 Jan. 2013).

1847. According to *Interights*, this limitation 'renders access to justice illusory for human rights victims', *ibid.*

1848. *Michelot Yogogombaye v. Senegal*, African Court of Human and Peoples' Rights, App. No. 001/2008 (15 Dec. 2009), Separate Opinion of Judge Ouguergouz, paras 31–39.

1849. F. Viljoen, 'Admissibility under the African Charter', in *The African Charter on Human and Peoples' Rights: The System in Practice, 1986–2000*, Evans & Murray (eds), (Cambridge: Cambridge University Press, 2002), 61, 75.

1850. *See* African Charter Art. 18(3).

1851. UN Convention on the Rights of the Child (20 Nov. 1989) 1577 U.N.T.S. 3, 28 I.L.M. 1448 (1989).

1852. Somalia is the only African State not to have ratified the CRC.

1853. K.C.J.M. Arts, *The International Protection of Children's Rights in Africa: The 1990 OAU Charter on the Rights and Welfare of the Child*, 5 R.A.D.I.C. 139, 141–143 (1993).

protection in an African perspective.[1854] The result was the African Charter on the Rights and Welfare of the Child 1990.[1855]

377. The Charter on the Rights of the Child complements the CRC. It guarantees a number of civil, political, economic, social, and cultural rights largely comparable to those protected by the CRC,[1856] although it would seem that such protection is not on paper as forceful as under the CRC.[1857] However, this should not be considered a fundamental weakness since the Charter on the Rights of the Child contains a safeguard clause and yields in those situations where it may not equal national or international standards.[1858] It should also be noted that the AU Protocol on the Rights of Women 2003 supplements some of the substantive rights enshrined in the Charter on the Rights of the Child. In keeping with the African concept of rights, the Charter on the Rights of the Child imposes responsibilities on the child towards his/her family, the community and the State.[1859] At the same time the family is stated to be the 'natural unit and basis of society'[1860] and the child is entitled to parental care and protection.[1861] The Charter on the Rights of the Child contains progressive features that have attracted praise.

1854. A. Lloyd, 'A Theoretical Analysis of the Reality of Children's Rights in Africa: An Introduction to the African Charter on the Rights and Welfare of the Child', *A.H.R.L.J.* 2 (2002): 11, 14–15; B. Thompson, 'Africa's Charter on Children's Rights: A Normative Break with Cultural Traditionalism', *I.C.L.Q.* 41 (1992): 434.

1855. African Charter on the Rights and Welfare of the Child (1 Jul. 1990), https://www.au.int/en/treaties, 28 I.L.M. 1456 (1989). The Charter entered into force on 29 Nov. 1999. As of January 2017, it had been ratified by forty-seven States. *See* further Arts; Lloyd; Viljoen, International Human Rights Law in Africa, 260–266.

1856. According to the African Committee of Experts on the Rights and Welfare of the Child (ACERWC) the obligation under the African Charter on the Rights of the Child Art. 1(1) to adopt legislative and other measures to give effect to said Charter 'is subject neither to progressive realization, nor to available resources', *Michelo Hunsungule and Others (on behalf of Children in Northern Uganda) v. Uganda* Communication No. 1/2005 (2013) para. 37. It proceeded to state that 'effective implementation of laws with due diligence is part of States parties obligation under the Charter', *ibid.* para. 38.

1857. Arts 147–149, identifies the freedom of expression and of thought, conscience and religion, the right to privacy, the right of access to information, the right to benefit from social security, and rights for minorities as especially problematic since they are made subordinate to the rights of parents, legal guardians or the State. Compare *contra* Lloyd, 14–15, who asserts that the level of protection is higher under the African Charter on the Rights of the Child. It should be noted that under the African Charter on Democracy Art. 31(1), State Parties commit themselves to promoting Youth in the governance process. It should be observed that as with the rights protected by the African Charter, the African Charter on the Rights of the Child are considered indivisible, *IHRDA and Open Society Justice Initiative (OSJI)(on behalf of children of Nubian descent in Kenya) v. Kenya* Communication No. 2/09 (2011) para. 58.

1858. African Charter on the Rights of the Child Art. 1(2); Arts 154–155.

1859. African Charter on the Rights of the Child Art. 31. *See* Arts 153–154. However, it has been emphasized that children's rights are 'not contingent upon them fulfilling their "duties"', since duties co-exist inter-dependently with rights, *Michelo Hunsungule and Others (on behalf of Children in Northern Uganda) v. Uganda* Communication No. 1/2005 (2013) para. 59.

1860. African Charter on the Rights of the Child Art. 18(1). Compare African Charter Art. 18(1).

1861. African Charter on the Rights of the Child Art. 19. *See* further *ibid.*, Art. 20 on parental responsibilities.

Crucially a child is defined as a person below the age of 18 years.[1862] The best interests of the child is *the* primary consideration.[1863] The right of non-discrimination applies.[1864] Children with disabilities are entitled to special measures of protection.[1865] The child has an inherent right to life and States Parties are under a positive obligation to do their utmost to ensure the survival, protection and development of the child.[1866] The participation and recruitment of children in armed conflicts, which has been a problem in a number of African countries such as Burundi, the DRC, Liberia, Sierra Leone,

1862. African Charter on the Rights of the Child Art. 2. Compare CRC Art. 1, which is somewhat ambiguous. *See* Lloyd, 20.

1863. African Charter on the Rights of the Child Art. 4. According to the CRC Art. 3(1), the best interests of the child is simply *a* primary consideration. *See* Lloyd, 17–19. In *Request for Advisory Opinion by the African Committee of Experts on the Rights and Welfare of the Child on the Standing of the African Committee of Experts on the Rights and Welfare of the Child before the African Court of Human and Peoples' Rights* Request No. 002/2013 (5 Dec. 2014) para. 95, the Human Rights Court emphasized the paramount nature of the best interests of the child which should take priority over technical points that could obstruct accessibility of justice for children. *See also IHRDA and Open Society Justice Initiative (OSJI)(on behalf of children of Nubian descent in Kenya) v. Kenya* Communication No. 2/09 (2011) para. 42. In *The Centre for Human Rights (University of Pretoria) v. Senegal* Communication No. 001/2012 (2014) paras 37–39, ACERWC found Senegal to be in breach of the African Charter on the Rights of the Child Art. 4 for failing to take the necessary measures against those forcing children into begging.

1864. African Charter on the Rights of the Child Arts 3, 26. *See IHRDA and Open Society Justice Initiative (OSJI)(on behalf of children of Nubian descent in Kenya) v. Kenya* Communication No. 2/09 (2011) paras 55–57, relating to discrimination in acquisition of nationality. This obligation could prove problematic in Islamic societies where females do not have equal rights of inheritance.

1865. African Charter on the Rights of the Child Art. 13. Note the draft Protocol on the Rights of Persons with Disabilities in Africa Art. 23.

1866. African Charter on the Rights of the Child Art. 5(1)–(2). In *The Centre for Human Rights (University of Pretoria) v. Senegal* Communication No. 001/2012 (2014) paras 40–45, ACERWC stressed the significance of these principles in reinforcing the other rights guaranteed under the Charter.

Somalia, and Uganda, is prohibited.[1867] Harmful social and cultural practices, which

1867. African Charter on the Rights of the Child Art. 22(2).The prohibition extends to voluntary recruitment, *Michelo Hunsungule and Others (on behalf of Children in Northern Uganda) v. Uganda* Communication No. 1/2005 (2013) paras 42, 58. *See also* Convention on the Protection and Assistance to Internally Displaced Persons in Africa (23 Oct. 2009) Arts 7(5)(e), 9(1)(d), https://www.au.int/en/treaties, 49 I.L.M. 83 (2010)(Kampala Convention); Rome Statute Art. 8(2)(b)(xxvi) describing such an activity as a 'war crime', I.L.O. Convention No. 182 on the Worst Forms of Child Labour Art. 3(a) (17 Jun. 1999), 2133 U.N.T.S. 161, 38 I.L.M. 1207 (1999), and the Optional Protocol to the Convention on the Rights of the Child on the involvement of children in armed conflict (25 May 2000), 2173 U.N.T.S. 222, 39 I.L.M. 1285 (2000). In *Decision on Preliminary Motion Based on Lack of Jurisdiction (Child Recruitment)*, SCSL-2004-14-AR72(E), (31 May 2004), a majority of the Special Court for Sierra Leone (SCSL) held that child recruitment was a crime under customary international law. Abduction of children in order to force them into combat has been a serious problem in Uganda where the Lord's Resistance Army has abducted thousands of children, *see Michelo Hunsungule and Others (on behalf of Children in Northern Uganda) v. Uganda* Communication No. 1/2005 (2013) and, till 2003, Liberia where again thousands of children were coerced into joining armed gangs, UN Doc. E/CN.4/2005/74, pp. 5–7. UN Security Council Res. 1460 (2003) adopted definitive targets, the 'Era of Application', to end this pernicious practice. Under UN Security Council Res. 1612 (2005) a Monitoring and Reporting Mechanism (MRM) was established to focus on grave violations of the rights of war-afflicted children, including abduction. UN Security Council Res. 2068 (2012) emphasized the importance of the comprehensive protection of children in situations of armed conflict. In *Prosecutor v. Charles Ghankay Taylor*, SCSL-03-1-T, Trial Chamber II, Judgment of 26 Apr. 2012, the former President of Liberia was found guilty by the SCSL of aiding and abetting and planning the crime of conscripting or enlisting child soldiers, or using them to take an active part in hostilities. These findings were upheld by the Appeals Chamber, *Prosecutor v. Charles Ghankay Taylor*, SCSL-03-1-A, Judgment of 26 Sept. 2013.

appears to include female genital mutilation,[1868] are to be eliminated.[1869] Children are to be protected from all forms of abuse, torture and ill-treatment.[1870] The sexual exploitation and abuse of children is prohibited[1871] as is the sale, trafficking and

---

1868. Arts 151. This practice has been condemned by the UN Fourth World Conference on Women (Beijing Platform for Action) para. 283(d), 35 I.L.M. 401 (1996). *See also* UN General Assembly Res. (2012). It has been reported that female genital mutilation, a practice which includes female circumcision and varying degrees of excision, exists in at least twenty-six countries in Africa, Report of Ms Halima Embarek Warzazi, Special Rapporteur, on traditional practices affecting the health of women and the girl child 10, UN Doc. E/CN.4/Sub.2/2005/36. According to this report in West Africa this practice is usually performed at the age of puberty, whereas in East Africa it is carried out at the earlier age of 7 or 8, UN Doc. E/CN.4/Sub.2/2005/36, 11. It is encouraging to note that in recent years the practice has been, or is being, prohibited by law and made a criminal offence in a number of African countries, Report of Ms Radhika Coomaraswamy, Special Rapporteur, on violence against women, its causes and consequences para. 17, UN Doc. E/CN.4/2002/83; *see also* UN Doc. E/CN.4/Sub.2/2005/36, 13. Western countries are also determined to eradicate this practice, *see* e.g., the UK's Female Genital Mutilation Act 2003 which not only makes it illegal in the UK but additionally makes it an offence to take girls to another country for female genital mutilation.

1869. African Charter on the Rights of the Child Art. 21(1). Begging, specifically prohibited by Art. 29(b), is one such practice, *see The Centre for Human Rights (University of Pretoria) v. Senegal* Communication No. 001/2012 (2014) paras 69–73. *See also* African Charter on the Rights of the Child Art. 1(3) which states that any custom, tradition, cultural or religious practice inconsistent with the Charter shall to the extent of the inconsistency be discouraged. *See also* UN General Assembly Res. 52/99. According to a UN report little has been done to address these issues although Ghana has criminalized the practice of *trokosi*, the giving of 'virgin girls to priests as appeasement for past crimes committed by family members', UN Doc. E/CN.4/Sub.2/2005/36, para. 49. The report identifies traditional birth practices, which jeopardizes both mother and child, as prevalent throughout Africa, *ibid.*, paras 75–76. *See* I.L.O. Maternity Protection Convention 2000 No. 183. The problem of forced marriage, for instance, is not addressed expressly by the Charter.

1870. African Charter on the Rights of the Child Art. 16(1). *See The Centre for Human Rights (University of Pretoria) v. Senegal* Communication No. 001/2012 (2014) paras 62–68. In *Michelo Hunsungule and Others (on behalf of Children in Northern Uganda) v. Uganda* Communication No. 1/2005 (2013) para. 76, ACERWC held that acts of sexual violence in armed conflicts were not only in violation of international criminal law but the African Charter on the Rights of the Child.

1871. African Charter on the Rights of the Child Art. 27. *See also ibid.*, Art. 16(1), CRC Art. 34, I.L.O. Convention No. 182 on the Worst Forms of Child Labour Art. 3(b), and the Optional Protocol to the Convention on the Rights of the Child on the sale of children, child prostitution and child pornography (25 May 2000) 2171 U.N.T.S. 227, 39 I.L.M. 1285 (2000). For a national measure *see* Kenya's Children's Act 2001.

abduction of children.[1872] Child, or early, marriages are expressly prohibited[1873] and the fact that eighteen years is specified as the minimum age at which marriage can be lawfully entered into is noteworthy.[1874] The prohibition on child labour is rather equivocal, however.[1875] Requiring States Parties to take legislative and administrative measures only to combat this problem has been criticized as inadequate.[1876] Yet the action required of States Parties is more extensive than under the CRC.[1877] Special provision is made for children caught up in the criminal justice system, including separation from adults in places of detention or imprisonment, a prohibition on torture, inhuman or degrading treatment or punishment,[1878] legal guarantees such as the presumption of innocence, and an age of capacity.[1879] The imposition of the death penalty on children is outlawed.[1880] The Charter on the Rights of the Child also makes

---

1872. African Charter on the Rights of the Child Art. 29. *See also* Kampala Convention Art. 7(5)(f), CRC Art. 35, the Optional Protocol to the Convention on the Rights of the Child on the sale of children, child prostitution and child pornography, and the Protocol to Prevent, Suppress and Punish Trafficking in Persons, Especially Women and Children, supplementing the UN Convention against Transnational Organized Crime (15 Nov. 2000) 2237 U.N.T.S. 319. In *The Centre for Human Rights (University of Pretoria) v. Senegal* Communication No. 001/2012 (2014) paras 74–81, ACERWC found that the children engaged in forced begging were victims of such practices.
1873. African Charter on the Rights of the Child Art. 21(2).
1874. Arts 149.
1875. African Charter on the Rights of the Child Art. 15. Compare CRC Art. 32. *See also* I.L.O. Convention No. 182 on the Worst Forms of Child Labour. In *The Centre for Human Rights (University of Pretoria) v. Senegal* Communication No. 001/2012 (2014) paras 57–61, ACERWC found that forced begging amounted to a worst form of child labour. In this case ACERWC interpreted the African Charter on the Rights of the Child Art. 15 in conjunction with other international law such as I.L.O. Convention No. 182.
1876. Arts 149–150. By comparison, CRC Art. 32(2) additionally requires social and educational measures. In *The Centre for Human Rights (University of Pretoria) v. Senegal* Communication No. 001/2012 (2014) paras 59–61, ACERWC found that in failing to take appropriate enforcement measures against begging Senegal had violated the African Charter on the Rights of the Child Art. 15(2). I.L.O. Convention No. 182 on the Worst Forms of Child Labour Art. 7(1), envisages the imposition of penal sanctions if appropriate.
1877. Arts 150.
1878. The imposition of judicial corporal punishment on juveniles has been condemned by the highest courts of various African States, including Namibia, *Ex Parte Attorney-General, Namibia: In re Corporal Punishment by Organs of State* 1991 (3) SA 76 (NmS), South Africa, *S v. Williams and Others* 1995 (CC), and Zimbabwe, *S v. Juvenile* 1990 (4) SA 151 (ZS).
1879. African Charter on the Rights of the Child Art. 17.
1880. *Ibid.,* Art. 5(3); *Groupe de Travail sur les Dossiers Judiciaires Stratégiques v. Democratic Republic of Congo*, Communication No. 259/2002 (2011), para. 71. Compare CRC Art. 37(a), and UN General Assembly Res. 59/261. It would appear that this prohibition may have acquired the status of customary international law at the very least, Report of the Secretary-General, Capital punishment and implementation of the safeguards guaranteeing protection of the rights of those facing the death penalty, UN Doc. E/2005/3, para. 76.

provision for other important rights, that to education[1881] and to health.[1882] Furthermore, children have the right to leisure, recreational and cultural activities.[1883] Although not mentioned in the Charter itself it has been held that States Parties must provide a remedy which includes a right to reparation.[1884]

378. The Charter on the Rights of the Child sets up a monitoring and implementation mechanism, the African Committee of Experts on the Rights and Welfare of the Child,[1885] (ACERWC) composed of eleven independent members,[1886] which, while it must meet at least once a year, can be convened whenever necessary.[1887] ACERWC's mandate is to promote and protect the rights and welfare of the child, especially to collect and document information, assess problems relating to children, organize meetings, encourage national, and local institutions concerned with child welfare and to advise governments, to formulate and draft rules aimed at protecting children, to cooperate with African, regional and international institutions and organizations concerned with the rights and welfare of children, to monitor the implementation and ensure protection of the rights enshrined in the Charter, and to perform any other tasks entrusted to it by the AU,[1888] and has been praised as broader and better defined than

---

1881. African Charter on the Rights of the Child Art. 11. *See IHRDA and Open Society Justice Initiative (OSJI)(on behalf of children of Nubian descent in Kenya) v. Kenya* Communication No. 2/09 (2011) paras 63–65; *The Centre for Human Rights (University of Pretoria) v. Senegal* Communication No. /2012 (2014) para. 50; *Michelo Hunsungule and Others (on behalf of Children in Northern Uganda) v. Uganda* Communication No. 1/2005 (2013) paras 72–73. *See* further African Charter on Democracy Art. 43(1). In parts of Africa, almost half of all girls are excluded from formal education, Report of Mr Muñoz Villalobos, Special Rapporteur, on the right to education para. 45, UN Doc. E/CN.4/2005/45.

1882. African Charter on the Rights of the Child Art. 14. *See IHRDA and Open Society Justice Initiative (OSJI)(on behalf of children of Nubian descent in Kenya) v. Kenya* Communication No. 2/09 (2011) paras 59–62, where it was held that the health needs of Nubian children had not been adequately recognized or provided for.

1883. African Charter on the Rights of the Child Art. 12.

1884. *Michelo Hunsungule and Others (on behalf of Children in Northern Uganda) v. Uganda* Communication No. 1/2005 (2013) para. 51. African Charter on the Rights of the Child Art. 46, which allows ACERWC to draw inspiration from the international law of human rights, appears to provide an explicit legal basis for this decision.

1885. African Charter on the Rights of the Child Art. 32. *See* Lloyd, 23–30. ACERWC has been held to be an AU organ with a quasi-judicial function, *Request for Advisory Opinion by the African Committee of Experts on the Rights and Welfare of the Child on the Standing of the African Committee of Experts on the Rights and Welfare of the Child before the African Court of Human and Peoples' Rights* Request No. 002/2013 (5 December 2014) paras 56–57, 87.

1886. African Charter on the Rights of the Child Art. 33.

1887. *Ibid.,* Art. 37(3). Rule 2(1) specifies two ordinary sessions annually.

1888. African Charter on the Rights of the Child Art. 42. ACERWC considers that its 'primary mandate' is to 'interpret and monitor the implementation' of the African Charter on the Rights of the Child, *Michelo Hunsungule and Others (on behalf of Children in Northern Uganda) v. Uganda* Communication No. 1/2005 (2013) para. 39. ACERWC's mandate is supplemented by its Rules of Procedure, *see* http://www.acerwc.org/rules-of-procedure/ (Rules). The African Charter on the Rights of the Child cites the OAU but such references must now be taken to indicate the AU.

that of the UN Committee on the Rights of the Child.[1889] As part of its monitoring activities, a reporting procedure requires States to submit a report to ACERWC every three years.[1890]

379. A potentially effective enforcement weapon possessed by ACERWC, which the UN Committee on the Rights of the Child lacks, is jurisdiction to entertain communications relating to the Charter on the Rights of the Child from persons, groups or NGOs.[1891] This provision allows ACERWC to consider individual complaints in the manner of the African Commission. In 2014 ACERWC adopted Guidelines on Communications, akin to rules of procedure, setting out the governing procedure.[1892] Any individual, including children, or group of natural or legal persons; a State Party, any IGO or NGO recognized in an AU Member State, a State Party or the UN; any specialized AU or UN organ or agency, have *locus standi.*[1893] It can be seen that this is a very broad category, patently designed to afford children the best possible representation. Communications may be submitted on their own behalf or on behalf of third parties.[1894] However, an interesting development is the fact that a communication can be brought on a child's behalf without his or her consent on condition that the complainant can demonstrate that the case is in 'the supreme interest of the child.'[1895] Given that children are the focus of this system, it is not a surprise that ACERWC's jurisdiction is conditional on the child's age at the time of the alleged violation, and ACERWC retains jurisdiction over a communication that is submitted but not concluded before the child's eighteenth birthday.[1896] The latter provision takes notice of the concept of 'continuing violations' which is well-established in international human rights law.[1897] ACERWC has made an important clarification of this provision. It has held, as an 'exceptional measure' in the best interests of the child, that the fact that the victim was over the age of eighteen at the time of the submission of the complaint does not render it inadmissible.[1898] This interpretation seems correct; the crucial issue must be

1889. Arts 155–157; Lloyd, 24.

1890. African Charter on the Rights of the Child Art. 43(1)(b); Rules 65–75. *See* online, http://www.acerwc.org/member-states/.

1891. African Charter on the Rights of the Child Art. 44(1). *See IHRDA and Open Society Justice Initiative (OSJI)(on behalf of children of Nubian descent in Kenya) v. Kenya* Communication No. 2/09 (2011).

1892. Revised Guidelines for the Consideration of Communications Provided For in Article 44 of the African Charter on the Rights and Welfare of the Child, http://www. acerwc.org/.

1893. Guideline s.I(1).

1894. *Ibid. See Michelo Hunsungule and Others (on behalf of Children in Northern Uganda) v. Uganda* Communication No. 1/2005 (2013) para. 16.

1895. Guideline s.I(3).

1896. Guideline s.I(1)(4).

1897. *Loizidou v. Turkey*, 23 E.H.R.R. 513GC (1996); *Blake v. Guatemala*, Ser. C, No. 27 (1996); *Zitha & Zitha v. Mozambique*, Communication No. 361/08 (2010) paras 85–94. The principle was applied by ACERWC in *African Centre of Justice and Peace Studies (ACJPS) and Peoples' Legal Aid Centre (PLACE) v. Sudan* Communication No. 005/Com/001/2015, Decision on Admissibility No. 003/1016 (2016) paras 35–37.

1898. *African Centre of Justice and Peace Studies (ACJPS) and Peoples' Legal Aid Centre (PLACE) v. Sudan* Communication No. 005/Com/001/2015, Decision on Admissibility No. 003/1016 (2016) para. 38.

the age of the person at the time of the alleged violations. Communications must comply with Requirements of Form, to all intents and purposes conditions of admissibility.[1899] Accordingly, the communication must not be anonymous and must be written in one of the official languages.[1900] Radically, a complaint against a non-State Party need not prove fatal if ACERWC considers the case to be in the 'overall best interests of the child'.[1901] Should a respondent State fail to appear ACERWC can proceed to consider the case on admissibility or the merits based on the complainant's submissions.[1902] Six conditions of admissibility must be satisfied, largely identical to those listed in Article 56 of the African Charter. However, a communication must additionally not be 'manifestly groundless'.[1903] The Guidelines have adopted the principle of 'constructive' exhaustion of local remedies[1904] while ACERWC has invoked the practice of the African Commission in its decisions.[1905]

380. The Guidelines also make provision for a number of other procedural matters. Thus a party may raise a preliminary objection before ACERWC takes a decision on the merits,[1906] which it must rule upon before considering any other matters in the communication.[1907] Third parties may be allowed to intervene if ACERWC considers that they may provide it with relevant information.[1908] It is noteworthy that ACERWC can solicit such intervention.[1909] The third party is required to state its interest in the case and the object of its intervention.[1910] These requirements extend to *amicus curiae* who may petition to submit briefs.[1911] ACERWC may review its decisions *proprio motu* or at the request of a party.[1912] The grounds justifying review are: the emergence of a decisive fact or evidence which was not known to ACERWC or the party;[1913] that ACERWC erred egregiously in its interpretation and application of the Charter on the Rights of the Child or other relevant instrument;[1914] any other compelling reason ACERWC deems appropriate in the interests of justice.[1915] An application for

1899. Guideline s.II(2).
1900. Guideline s.II(2)(a), (b).
1901. Guideline s.II(2)(c), (ii).
1902. Guideline s.XI(1).
1903. Guideline s.IX(1)(b). This condition appears to be identical to that of 'manifestly groundless' in the European Convention on Human Rights Art. 35(3) (4 Nov. 1950), C.E.T.S. No. 204 (as amended).
1904. Guideline s.IX(1)(d).
1905. *Michelo Hunsungule and Others (on behalf of Children in Northern Uganda) v. Uganda* Communication No. 1/2005 (2013) paras 19–21. *See also African Centre of Justice and Peace Studies (ACJPS) and Peoples' Legal Aid Centre (PLACE) v. Sudan* Communication No. 005/Com/001/2015, Decision on Admissibility No. 003/1016 (2016) paras 22–33.
1906. Guideline Section XVI(1).
1907. Guideline Section XVI(4).
1908. Guideline Section XVII(1)(i).
1909. *Ibid.*
1910. Guideline Section XVII(1)(i)(b)(c).
1911. Guideline Section XVII(2).
1912. Guideline Section XX(1).
1913. Guideline Section XX(2)(a).
1914. Guideline Section XX(2)(c).
1915. Guideline Section XX(2)(d).

review must be made within six months of the new fact's discovery, unless it is in the best interests of the child.[1916]

381. The Guidelines's provisions on provisional measures are of particular interest because of their innovative nature. In cases of urgency, serious or massive violations of the Charter on the Rights of the Child and the likelihood of irreparable harm to children ACERWC is authorized to indicate, *proprio motu* or at the request of a litigant party, provisional measures to prevent grave or irreparable harm to victims.[1917] Unlike other similar jurisdictions, there is no mention of preserving the respective rights of the parties, this is purely about protecting the victims. In considering a request for provisional measures ACERWC can take account of a number of factors, namely, the gravity and urgency of the situation, the irreparable nature and imminence of the harm in question, whether the situation or harm has been brought to the attention of the authorities or the reasons why not, whether the beneficiaries of the provisional measures can be individually or collectively identified, and whether the beneficiaries' consent has been obtained.[1918] In order to verify the facts ACERWC may conduct on-site investigations.[1919] Nonetheless, ACERWC's decision must be taken within twenty-one days at most.[1920] The Guidelines are silent on whether provisional measures are considered binding but in case of non-compliance ACERWC is empowered to take all necessary steps it considers appropriate.[1921] In a different but associated context, in cases where there are reasonable grounds to believe that the life or personal integrity of a child or children is in danger, ACERWC can request the speediest reply from the State Party.[1922]

382. As is usual, the Guidelines envisage amicable settlements. These may be arranged between the parties themselves at any time prior to a decision,[1923] or under ACERWC's auspices. In both instances, amicable settlements must be based on respect for human rights.[1924] However, in the former case, ACERWC may decide to proceed with the communication despite the settlement,[1925] presumably because ACERWC may be of the view that justice is not being served or that important issues of public interest are at stake. While ACERWC has a mission to promote amicable settlements it may terminate its facilitation of such on various grounds. These are: if the issues are not susceptible to amicable settlement; if any party does not consent to an amicable settlement; of if it chooses not to continue with an amicable settlement; if any party is unwilling to reach an amicable settlement based on respect for children's rights and welfare; if serious or massive violations of children's rights are at issue.[1926]

1916. Guideline Section XX(2)(b).
1917. Guideline Section VII(1)(i). The Secretariat must notify ACERWC immediately should a communication reveal serious or massive violations or in cases of emergency so that it can consider provisional measures, Guideline Section III(2).
1918. Guideline Section VII(2).
1919. Guideline Section VII(3)(i).
1920. Guideline Section VII(2)(iv).
1921. Guideline Section VII(4)(iv).
1922. Guideline Section IX(2)(v).
1923. Guideline Section XIII(1)(i).
1924. Guideline Section XIII(1)(ii), (2)(i).
1925. Guideline Section XIII(1)(iv).
1926. Guideline Section XIII(2)(iv).

383. In addition, ACERWC has been conferred broad powers of investigation.[1927] It may therefore 'resort to any appropriate method of investigating any matter falling within the ambit of the…Charter', including measures a State Party has taken to implement the Charter on the Rights of the Child, and 'request from the States Parties any information relevant to the implementation of the Charter'. ACERWC also possesses the weapon of publicity.[1928] ACERWC hence has at its disposal considerable powers to hold States to account. If exercised properly, the Committee could become a formidable guardian of children's rights. The few cases ACERWC has decided certainly suggest a robust approach. It should not be overlooked that alleged violations of the Charter on the Rights of the Child can be referred to the African Court on Human and Peoples' Rights.[1929]

384. The Charter on the Rights of the Child must be viewed as a positive development. It is the first regional document of its type.[1930] ACERWC's mandate compares favourably with that of the UN Committee. In substantive terms it complements the CRC. However, a potential disadvantage is that for many African States the Charter on the Rights of the Child may simply be too radical and progressive to attract widespread support since it challenges established traditions and customary and religious laws.[1931]

§7. The Protocol on the Rights of Women

385. On 11 July 2003 the AU, meeting in Maputo, Mozambique, adopted a Protocol to the African Charter on women's rights.[1932] Although the African Charter

1927. African Charter on the Rights of the Child Art. 45(1).

1928. *Ibid.*, Art. 45(2)–(4).

1929. Although ACERWC itself does not have standing to bring an action before the Human Rights Court, a fact confirmed in *Request for Advisory Opinion by the African Committee of Experts on the Rights and Welfare of the Child on the Standing of the African Committee of Experts on the Rights and Welfare of the Child before the African Court of Human and Peoples' Rights* Request No. 002/2013 (5 Dec. 2014). However, the Court expressed the view that there was no apparent reason why ACERWC was denied this capacity which may have been a mere oversight, *ibid.*, para. 75.

1930. Lloyd, 13.

1931. In particular, family law, Arts 158; Thompson, 438–442.

1932. Protocol to the African Charter on Human and Peoples' Rights on the Rights of Women in Africa (11 Jul. 2003), https://www.au.int/en/treaties, Heyns & Killander, 65. The Protocol entered into force on 25 Nov. 2005. As of Jan. 2017, it had been ratified by thirty-seven States. *See* generally F. Banda, 'Blazing a Trail: The African Protocol on Women's Rights Comes into Force', *J.A.L.* 50 (2006): 72; F. Banda, 'Protocol to the African Charter on the Rights of Women in Africa', in *The African Charter on Human and Peoples' Rights: The System in Practice, 1986–2006*, Evans & Murray (eds), (Cambridge: Cambridge University Press, 2008),441–474; C. Ocran, 'The Protocol to the African Charter on Human and Peoples' Rights on the Rights of Women in Africa', *R.A.D.I.C.* 15 (2007): 147; Viljoen, International Human Rights Law in Africa, 266–277.

enshrines the principle of non-discrimination on the grounds of, *inter alia*, sex[1933] and additionally calls specifically for the elimination of every discrimination against women and the protection of women's rights,[1934] women nevertheless continued to face considerable disadvantages.[1935] A patriarchal gender order meant that women in many African countries are legally considered minors, often described as 'junior males', and routinely encountered discrimination in areas such as succession, marriage and divorce.[1936] One of the least recognized rights is the right to an equal share of an inheritance. Such adverse treatment can be compounded in traditional societies by resort to customary or religious laws that confer upon women a hierarchically inferior status.[1937] The Protocol is the most obvious manifestation of the OAU/AU's promotion of gender perspective and thereby seeks to promote gender equality.[1938] More specifically, it seeks to extend 'the substantive scope of the existing law', 'to improve quasi-legal and legal means of ensuring compliance', and 'to extend the use of non-legal forms of implementation'.[1939] But the Protocol may be considered ground-breaking in that it is the first regional instrument that seeks to deal with women's rights in a comprehensive manner.

1933. African Protocol on Women's Rights Art. 2. *See Egyptian Initiative for Personal Rights and INTERIGHTS v. Egypt*, Communication No. 323/2006 (2011), para. 121. For national decisions *see Ephraim v. Pastory* [1990] L.R.C. (Const) 757 (Tanzania High Court) para. 10; *Dow v. Attorney-General* [1992] L.R.C. (Const) 623 (Botswana Court of Appeal).
1934. African Protocol on Women's Rights Art. 18(3).
1935. According to the Report of Mrs Halima Embarek Warzazi, Special Rapporteur, on the situation regarding the elimination of traditional practices affecting the health of women and the girl child para. 66, UN Doc. E/CN.4/2002/83, the African Charter is not considered to be gender neutral. It does not give sufficient emphasis to women's fundamental rights to liberty, equality and dignity, and reflects a paternalistic conception of women that reduces them to the status of minors.
1936. *See* Report of Ms Radhika Coomaraswamy, Special Rapporteur, on violence against women, its causes and consequences paras 65–69, UN Doc. E/CN.4/2002/83. In many African countries the husband, or other male relative, is considered the custodian of the wife's person and property, Ankumah, 153–154. *See* the controversial judgment of the Supreme Court of Zimbabwe in *Magaya v. Magaya* [1999] 3 L.R.C. 35. However, in recent years many African countries have enacted or amended legislation to strengthen the rights of women, and the girl child, though traditional attitudes may still persist, *see* UN Doc. E/CN.4/2004/SR.37. In *Bhe and Others v. The Magistrate, Khayelitsha and Others* 2005 (1) SA 580 (CC) the Constitutional Court of South Africa held that the African customary rule of male primogeniture in relation to the inheritance of property discriminated against women. *See also Ephraim v. Pastory* [1990] L.R.C. (Const) 757 (Tanzania High Court) para. 42.
1937. *See Magaya v. Magaya* [1999] 3 L.R.C. 35. Note also the *cause célèbre* of Amina Lawal who in September 2003 was finally acquitted by an Islamic Court of Appeal in Nigeria on charges of adultery, UN Doc. E/CN.4/2004/66/Add.1, para. 131.
1938. One of the guiding principles of the AU is the promotion of gender equality, Constitutive Act Art. 4(l). Note that the Protocol on Amendments to the Constitutive Act Art. 3, additionally seeks to 'ensure the effective participation of women in decision-making, particularly in the political, economic and socio-cultural areas' as one of the objectives of the AU. *See also* African Charter on Democracy Art. 3(6).
1939. Viljoen, International Human Rights Law in Africa, 268.

386. Like the African Charter the Protocol asserts different categories of rights, first, second, and third generation rights. Under it States Parties undertake to combat all forms of discrimination against women[1940] and to include the principle of sex equality in municipal law.[1941] Significantly provision is made for 'corrective and positive action'.[1942] Other salient features of the Protocol which are particularly worthy of note include a prohibition on the execution of pregnant or nursing women,[1943] a prohibition on the exploitation and degradation of women,[1944] and the adoption of measures to tackle trafficking in women,[1945] so that forced prostitution should be covered, the elimination of practices harmful to women, including a prohibition on female genital mutilation,[1946] protection of women against all forms of violence,[1947] including sexual violence and rape which if perpetrated in times of armed conflict should be considered war crimes, genocide and/or crimes against humanity,[1948] the principle of marriage based on consent,[1949] a minimum age of 18 years for a valid marriage,[1950] thus proscribing

---

1940. African Protocol on Women's Rights Art. 2(1). *See also* African Charter on Democracy Art. 8(1).

1941. African Protocol on Women's Rights Art. 2(1)(a). *See also ibid.*, Art. 8 ensuring equal protection before the law. And further African Charter on Democracy Art. 8(2).

1942. African Protocol on Women's Rights Art. 2(1)(d). Compare UN Convention on the Elimination of Discrimination against Women Art. 4 (18 Dec. 1979) 1249 U.N.T.S. 13 (CEDAW). *See* Viljoen, International Human Rights Law in Africa, 272. It appears that the term 'positive action' is equivalent to positive differentiation, or affirmative action, Progress Report submitted by Mr Bossuyt, Special Rapporteur, on the concept and practice of affirmative action paras 6–8, UN Doc. E/CN.4/Sub.2/2001/15.

1943. African Protocol on Women's Rights Art. 4(j). *See also* African Charter on the Rights of the Child Art. 30(e).

1944. African Protocol on Women's Rights Art. 3(3). *See also ibid.*, Art. 13(m).

1945. *Ibid.*, Art. 4(g). *See* , e.g., the Protocol to Prevent, Suppress and Punish Trafficking in Persons, Especially Women and Children (15 Nov. 2000), UN General Assembly Res. 55/25, which reinforces the Convention for the Suppression of the Traffic in Persons and of the Exploitation of the Prostitution of Others (21 Mar. 1950) 96 U.N.T.S. 271.

1946. African Protocol on Women's Rights Art. 5(b). It has been stated *supra* para. 377, that many African States are legislating to prohibit and criminalize this practice.

1947. African Protocol on Women's Rights Arts 3(4), 4(2) and 5(d). There appears to be a strong correlation between violence against women and HIV/AIDS, Report of Yakin Ertürk, Special Rapporteur, on violence against women, UN Doc. E/CN.4/2005/72.

1948. African Protocol on Women's Rights Art. 11(3). *See also* Kampala Convention Arts 7(5)(f),9(1)(d). Compare Rome Statute Arts 7(1)(g) and 8(2)(xxii) and (2)(e)(vi). *See Prosecutor v. Akayesu* 37 I.L.M. 1399 (1998) para. 31, where the ICTR found as established a campaign of systematic rapes and other forms of sexual violence perpetrated by extremist Hutu militias. *See* further *Prosecutor v. Furundzija* 38 I.L.M. 317 (1999) paras 165–186 (ICTY). In *Prosecutor v. Charles Ghankay Taylor*, SCSL-03-1-T, Trial Chamber II, Judgment of 26 Apr. 2012, the accused was found guilty of aiding and abetting and planning the crimes of rape, sexual slavery and other crimes of a sexual nature. These findings were upheld by the Appeals Chamber, *Prosecutor v. Charles Ghankay Taylor*, SCSL-03-1-A, Judgment of 26 Sept. 2013.

1949. African Protocol on Women's Rights Art. 6(a).

1950. *Ibid.*, Art. 6(b). *See also* African Charter on the Rights of the Child Art. 21(2). The practice of early marriage is prevalent in parts of Africa, UN Doc. E/CN.4/Sub.2/1991/6, 7.

early marriage, the encouragement of monogamy as the preferred form of marriage,[1951] the right to be regarded as equal partners in marriage,[1952] the right of a married woman to retain and use her maiden name,[1953] the right to own and administer property,[1954] the right to divorce, separation or annulment,[1955] reciprocal rights and responsibilities with respect to the children upon divorce or separation,[1956] equitable sharing of joint property of the marriage,[1957] a widow's right to her children[1958] and to remarry,[1959] a widow's right to live in the matrimonial home[1960] and to an equitable share in the inheritance of her husband's property,[1961] a woman's right to participate equally in the political process,[1962] rights to education and training,[1963] employment rights, including equal remuneration,[1964] and reproductive rights,[1965] including termination of pregnancy in certain circumstances, for example, in cases of rape or incest, or where the mother's health or life is endangered.[1966] Vulnerable groups, such as elderly women, women with disabilities, and women in distress, are entitled to special measures of protection.[1967]

387. Although no provision is made for a dedicated enforcement or regulatory mechanism,[1968] the African Commission on Human and Peoples' Rights has a supervisory

---

1951. African Protocol on Women's Rights Art. 6(c). Polygamy, associated both with customary practices and Islam, is prevalent in many African countries. Note *Bhewa v. Government of Mauritius* (1990) MR 79, where the Supreme Court of Mauritius upheld the exclusive status of monogamous marriages.

1952. African Protocol on Women's Rights Art. 6.

1953. *Ibid.*, Art. 6(f). *See Müller and Engelhard v. Namibia*, Communication No. 919/2000, UN Doc A/57/40, Vol II, Annex IX, CC, where the UN HRC found that differentiation on the basis of sex relating to the right of persons to assume the surname of the spouse on marriage amounted to discrimination in violation of ICCPR Art. 26.

1954. African Protocol on Women's Rights Art. 6(j). *See* further *supra* , paras 266, 385. But *see Rabah v. Mauritania,* Communication No. 197/97, 17th Activity Report, 2003–2004.

1955. African Protocol on Women's Rights Art. 7(b).

1956. *Ibid.*, Art. 7(c). *See also* Charter on the Rights of the Child Arts 18(2) and 19(2).

1957. African Protocol on Women's Rights Art. 7(d).

1958. *Ibid.*, Art. 20(b). *See also* Charter on the Rights of the Child Art. 18(2).

1959. African Protocol on Women's Rights Art. 20(c).

1960. *Ibid.*, Art. 21(a).

1961. *Ibid.* Customary law often adversely affects the woman's rights to succession, *see* further *supra* paras 266, 385.

1962. African Protocol on Women's Rights Art. 9. *See also* Protocol on Amendments to the Constitutive Act Art. 3(i), and African Charter on Democracy Arts 2(11), 3(6) and 29.

1963. African Protocol on Women's Rights Art. 12. *See also* African Charter on Democracy Art. 43(2).

1964. African Protocol on Women's Rights Art. 13(b). Equal opportunities in education has traditionally been problematic in many African countries, *see* G.J. Naldi, *The Organization of African Unity* (London & New York: Mansell, 1989), 195, n. 223.

1965. African Protocol on Women's Rights Art. 14.

1966. *Ibid.*, Art. 14(2)(c).

1967. *Ibid.*, Arts 22, 23, 24. Note the draft Protocol on the Rights of Persons with Disabilities in Africa Art. 22.

1968. Compare the Committee on the Elimination of Discrimination against Women established under CEDAW which has a supervisory capacity, receiving national reports. An Optional Protocol (10 Dec. 1999), 38 I.L.M. 763 (1999), enables the Committee to consider individual petitions and to investigate reports of systematic violations.

role in that States Parties must account for the measures taken to realize the rights recognized by the Protocol in their periodic reports.[1969] Significantly the Protocol can be interpreted and applied by the African Court on Human and Peoples' Rights.[1970] A feature is the requirement on States Parties to provide appropriate remedies to women whose rights have been violated.[1971] Another important element is the obligation upon States Parties to implement the protocol at national level.[1972]

388. The Protocol on Women's Rights seeks to bridge the 'gender gap'. In terms of substantive rights, the protocol is comprehensive and progressive in many respects and generally seems to reflect current developments in international human rights law, enshrined in documents such as UN Convention on the Elimination of Discrimination Against Women (CEDAW) and the Beijing Platform for Action.[1973] But it could also be considered revolutionary because it challenges many entrenched traditional, cultural, societal and religious values, although some of the more radical proposals submitted in the draft did not survived unscathed. States Parties are required to implement appropriate national measures to further the rights of women. The Protocol requires extensive law reform in many African countries, and while progress has been made in this regard in a number of countries women are still very vulnerable in others. Furthermore, the political will to transform entrenched attitudes must be found. The plight of women living with HIV/AIDS also requires urgent practical action. However, the fact that it is now in force should provide an added incentive.

§8. The Protocol on the Rights of Older Persons

389. Until recent times the rights of older persons in international law were set out in a number of soft law documents. In 1991 the UN General Assembly had adopted a resolution, the UN Principles for Older Persons, setting out a number of basic principles to which States should adhere.[1974] In 2002 the Madrid Plan of Action on Ageing became the foremost standard-setter in the field, and, *inter alia*, addressed ageing issues from a human rights perspective.[1975] However, it was under the auspices of the OAS that the first treaty on the rights of older persons was adopted, in 2015.[1976]

1969. African Protocol on Women's Rights Art. 26(1). *See* further Viljoen, International Human Rights Law in Africa, 275–276.

1970. African Protocol on Women's Rights Art. 27.

1971. *Ibid.*, Art. 25.

1972. *Ibid.*, Art. 26(1).

1973. According to Murray, Human Rights in Africa, 151, the Protocol goes further than CEDAW in terms of substance. *See also* Viljoen, International Human Rights Law in Africa, 271–272, who additionally argues that the Protocol brings crucial 'specificity' to a number of areas. *See* Viljoen, International Human Rights Law in Africa, 272–273.

1974. UN General Assembly Res. 46/91.

1975. Madrid International Plan of Action on Ageing, http://www.un.org/en/events/pastevents/pdfs/Madrid_plan.pdf.

1976. Inter-American Convention on Protecting the Human Rights of Older Persons (A-70) (15 Jun. 2015), 55 I.L.M. 989 (2016).

390. An ageing population poses its own set of challenges to Africa.[1977] Despite various initiatives older persons cannot be said to have been at the forefront of vulnerable groups that the African Charter on Human and Peoples' Rights sought to protect in any meaningful way.[1978] The African Charter makes provision for the rights of the aged in a generalized way, stating that they have the right to 'special measures of protection in keeping with their physical or moral needs.'[1979] A similar provision can be found in Article 22 of the Protocol on Women's Rights. In addition, it seems that the principle of non-discrimination contained in Article 2 of the African Charter extends to the aged as they come within the scope of 'other status'. As with other vulnerable groups such as women and children it was felt in time that the rights of the aged would be better protected through an instrument that specifically addressed their needs and concerns. Accordingly, in 2016 the AU adopted a Protocol on the Rights of Older Persons.[1980]

391. The Protocol sets out a framework of the obligations of States regarding the rights of older persons. It enables States Parties to recognize, promote and protect older persons 'rights. Older persons are defined as persons aged 60 years and above[1981] and extends to persons with disabilities.[1982] The Protocol is framed in terms of duties and responsibilities upon States Parties which are required to implement appropriate national measures to further older persons 'rights.[1983] States will be required to adopt affirmative measures and allocate resources, for example, in relation to social security. The Protocol requires programmes that raise awareness on ageing and prepare persons for the challenges of old age.[1984] States Parties are placed under a general duty to gather and analyse national data and develop a national mechanism with the task of integrating and implementing older persons' rights in national policies and legislation.[1985]

392. The Protocol enshrines a number of rights which States Parties must either protect or provide. A general obligation upon States Parties is the necessity to prohibit discrimination against older persons and eliminate social and cultural stereotypes.[1986] However, no definition of age discrimination is provided which might have proved useful. Protection from gender discrimination against older women is a specific requirement, however.[1987] Discrimination against older persons relating to access to

---

1977. *See* I. Doron, B. Spannier & O. Lazar, 'The Rights of Older Persons Within the African Union', *Elder Law Review* 10 (2016): 1.
1978. *Ibid.*
1979. African Charter Art. 18(4).
1980. Protocol to the African Charter on Human and Peoples' Rights of Older Persons in Africa (31 Jan. 2016), https://www.au.int/en/treaties. The Protocol, not yet in force, requires fifteen ratifications to enter into force, Art. 26(1).
1981. Protocol on Older Persons Art. 1.
1982. Protocol on Older Persons Art. 13. Note the draft Protocol on the Rights of Persons with Disabilities in Africa Art. 25.
1983. Protocol on Older Persons Art. 2(1).
1984. *Ibid.*, Art. 19.
1985. *Ibid.*, Art. 21.
1986. *Ibid.*, Art. 3.
1987. *Ibid.*, Art. 9(1) Protocol on Older Persons. *See also* Protocol on Women's Rights Art. 2(1). The importance of gender equality has been stressed by the European Court of Human Rights, *see Carvalho Pinto de Sousa Morais v. Portugal*, European Court of Human Rights, Appl. No. 17484/15, Judgment of 25 Jul. 2017.

employment must be removed.[1988] However, the Protocol has nothing to say on guaranteeing the same rights and benefits for all workers for equal work, regardless of age. Another general obligation is that of equal protection before the law and access to justice.[1989] This extends to the provision of legal assistance to protect their rights.[1990]

393. More specifically, the Protocol seeks to guarantee the autonomy of older persons by ensuring their rights to make decisions regarding their well-being without undue interference from other persons or entities and to appoint a party of their choice to carry out their wishes and instructions.[1991] In the case of incapacity older persons are to be provided with assistance in order to make decisions in their best interests.[1992] States must ensure that persons who retire have adequate pensions and other social security and must additionally ensure some form of universal social protection is in place for those who may not have contributed to any social security scheme.[1993] In addition, States should ensure that older persons can access buildings and public transport.[1994]

394. With respect to care and support the Protocol acknowledges the role of family members through the provision of incentives for family carers.[1995] It also seeks the promotion and strengthening of traditional support systems to enhance the ability of families and communities to care for older persons.[1996] Residential care should also be an affordable option for older persons.[1997] However, there is no explicit mention of long-term care. But the needs of older persons in palliative care are not overlooked.[1998] The Protocol does not in fact provide for a right to health as such, that is guaranteed by the African Charter, but it does oblige States Parties to grant older persons access to health services.[1999] In order to foster a healthy environment older persons should have access to education, cultural programmes, leisure and sports.[2000] Older persons taking care of vulnerable children should be provided with financial, material and other support but this support is limited to those who are 'indigent'.[2001]

395. Older women are deemed in need of special protection. Protection from discrimination has been previously noted but it also extends to property and land rights, and inheritance rights.[2002] Older women should be protected from violence and sexual abuse,[2003] including harmful traditional practices.[2004] Protection from violence is not

1988. Protocol on Older Persons Art. 6(1).
1989. *Ibid.*, Art. 4(1).
1990. *Ibid.*, Art. 4(2).
1991. *Ibid.*, Art. 5(1).
1992. *Ibid.*, Art. 5(2).
1993. *Ibid.*, Art. 7(1)–(2).
1994. *Ibid.*, Art. 18.
1995. *Ibid.*, Art. 10(1).
1996. *Ibid.*, Art. 10(2).
1997. *Ibid.*, Art. 11(1).
1998. *Ibid.*, Art. 11(3).
1999. *Ibid.*, Art. 15(1)–(2).
2000. *Ibid.*, Arts 16 and 17.
2001. *Ibid.*, Art 12.
2002. *Ibid.*, Art. 9(2)–(3). *See also* Protocol on Women's Rights Art. 21(a).
2003. Protocol on Older Persons Art. 9(1).
2004. *Ibid.*, Art. 8. *See also* Protocol on Women's Rights Art. 5(b).

defined but it can take many different forms and it is submitted that the Protocol should have made it clear that older persons, of either sex since men can also be at risk, have a right to a life free of violence of any kind.[2005]

396. The plight of older persons in conflict and disaster situations is not overlooked and the Protocol seeks to ensure that they are a prioritized group in such situations.[2006]

397. Inspired by traditional cultural values and in keeping with the African Charter, the Protocol incorporates a short list of duties owed by older persons towards their 'families, communities, the wider society, the state and the international community'.[2007] These responsibilities include mentoring and passing on knowledge to the younger generations and playing a role in mediation and conflict resolution.

398. In terms of implementation, States Parties are under an express obligation to implement the Protocol and they must give account for the measures taken to realize the rights recognized therein in their periodic reports to the African Commission on Human and Peoples' Rights.[2008] Both the African Commission and the African Court on Human and Peoples' Rights have the mandate to interpret and settle disputes over the Protocol.[2009] There is no discrete committee.

399. The Protocol on the Rights of Older Persons is the second regional instrument on this subject and in the absence of any global treaty is especially welcome. However, in some respects it seems like a missed opportunity. It cannot be described as a comprehensive document; it is not as detailed as the Inter-American Convention on the Human Rights of Older Persons. This may be due to the fact that the Protocol is a framework treaty that allows considerable latitude to States Parties as to how they achieve and implement their obligations. Neither are the rights protected in the Protocol as extensive as those in the Inter-American Convention on the Human Rights of Older Persons. For instance, the Protocol does not explicitly stipulate protection of the right to life and dignity in old age, a right not to be subjected to inhuman or degrading treatment, a right to give free and informed consent in medical matters, a right to personal liberty, a right to privacy and intimacy or a right to housing. Since States Parties are under an obligation to incorporate the UN Principles for Older Persons into national law,[2010] some of these rights, such as dignity, may be indirectly applicable but there is no guarantee in so far as other rights which do not feature therein. A potential weakness is evident. However, a positive attribute is that the Protocol contains a safeguard clause and must not therefore derogate from relevant 'instruments', which seems to be a reference to international treaties, realizing rights for older persons.[2011]

2005. Compare Inter-American Convention on Protecting the Human Rights of Older Persons Art. 9.
2006. Protocol on Older Persons Art. 14.
2007. *Ibid.*, Art. 20.
2008. *Ibid.*, Art. 22(1).
2009. *Ibid.*, Art. 22(2)–(4).
2010. *Ibid.*, Art. 2(1).
2011. *Ibid.*, Art. 24(1).

Chapter 3. Refugees

§1. The OAU Convention on Refugees

400. The plight of Africa's refugees remains an ongoing tragedy. Conflict, environmental degradation,[2012] impoverishment, crop failures and famine, political unrest, and abuses of human rights,[2013] have all contributed to the displacement of millions of people.[2014] As the flow of refugees has shown little sign of decreasing in recent years[2015] and mass exoduses have occurred from places such as Sudan,[2016] Somalia,[2017] and the Great Lakes region of Central Africa,[2018] the reception of refugees has led to serious problems for host States which, lacking the necessary resources and

2012. *See* Progress Achieved Towards Meeting Objectives of the Earth Summit, UN General Assembly Res. A/RES/S-19/2.

2013. The UN has established links between human rights violations and population displacements, *see* e.g., Vienna Declaration and Programme of Action, adopted by the World Conference on Human Rights in June 1993, pt. I, para. 23(2), 32 I.L.M. 1661 (1993); Report of the UN Secretary-General on Human Rights and Mass Exoduses, UN Doc. E/CN.4/1996/42, 4-12, 25. *See also* UN Commission on Human Rights Res. 2003/52, Human rights and mass exoduses. The UN Secretary-General identified weak national systems of human rights protection as being a significant contributing factor in mass displacement and argued that national systems of human rights protection had to be established and/or strengthened, UN Doc. A/57/387. The OAU also acknowledged this nexus, *see* Grand Bay (Mauritius) Declaration and Plan of Action 1999, para. 9, C. Heyns & M. Killander (eds), *Compendium of Key Human Rights Documents of the African Union* (6th edn, Pretoria: Pretoria University Law Press, 2016), 149.

2014. Report of the UN Secretary-General on the causes of conflict and the promotion of durable peace and sustainable development in Africa, UN Doc. A/52/871-S/1998/318 (1998) paras 7–15; T. Maluwa, *International Law in Post-Colonial Africa* 171–176 (The Hague: Kluwer Law International 1999). At the end of 2015 there were over five million refugees in Africa, *UNHCR Global Trends 2015*, http://www.unhcr.org/globaltrends/ (accessed 26 Apr. 2017).

2015. In 2015 the top countries of origin of refugees in Africa included the Central African Republic, Democratic Republic of Congo, Somalia, South Sudan and Sudan, *UNHCR Global Trends 2015*, http://www.unhcr.org/globaltrends/ (accessed 26 Apr. 2017). Note UN Security Council Res. 2349 (2017).

2016. The civil war between north and south in Sudan that lasted from 1983–2005 is said to have caused the internal displacement of four million southerners, while the more recent conflict in Darfur has displaced over two million people, UN Doc. E/CN.4/2006/71/Add.6, paras 6, 9. According to UN Security Council Res. 1556 (2004) the conflict in Darfur had led to two hundred thousand refugees fleeing to neighbouring Chad. *See also Sudan Human Rights Organization and Sudan Centre for Housing Rights and Evictions v. Sudan* Communication Nos 279/03, 296/05, 28th Activity Report 2010. By the end of 2015 there were over seven hundred thousand refugees in South Sudan and over six hundred thousand refugees in Sudan, *UNHCR Global Trends 2015*, http://www.unhcr.org/globaltrends/ (accessed 26 Apr. 2017).

2017. At the end of 2015 there were over three million refugees in the East and Horn of Africa, *UNHCR Global Trends 2015*, http://www.unhcr.org/globaltrends/ (accessed 26 Apr. 2017).

2018. At the end of 2015 there were over one and a half million refugees in the Great Lakes region, *ibid.*

infrastructure, have expressed concern about the security and environmental implications caused by large population movements. Although the financial and material resources of African States to cope with the refugee burden is limited[2019] it is perhaps ironic that the African States have contributed significantly to the progressive development of international refugee law.

401. In 1969 the OAU adopted the Convention on Refugees.[2020] The OAU believed a regional treaty was necessary because the existing law, enshrined in the UN Convention on Refugees 1951,[2021] which seeks to protect the individual refugee and is not deemed applicable to flight *en masse*, was deemed inadequate.[2022] Such a narrow definition failed to take account of the particular difficulties facing Africa, such as wars of national liberation and natural disasters, which had given rise to mass exoduses and displaced whole populations. However, the OAU Convention does not seek to exclude the operation of the UN Convention from Africa;[2023] it simply seeks to solve the refugee problem in an African context. It is innovative in a number of respects.

402. The first item of significance is the broadening of the concept of the refugee. The OAU Convention on Refugees incorporates the UN Convention definition in Article 1(1) but it extends the definition in paragraph 2 to include those in need of complementary international protection based either on humanitarian grounds or human

2019. In Res. 2003/52 the Commission on Human Rights stressed the responsibility of States and international organizations to cooperate with States with large numbers of refugees to ensure that assistance and protection needs are addressed.

2020. Convention Governing the Specific Aspects of Refugee Problems in Africa (10 Sept. 1969), 1001 U.N.T.S. 45, 8 I.L.M. 1288 (1969). The Convention entered into force on 20 Jan. 1974 and by June 2017 had been ratified by forty-six Member States. *See* generally P. Weis, *The Convention of the Organization of African Unity Governing the Specific Aspects of Refugee Problems*, 3 Revue de Droits de l'Homme 449 (1970); R.M. D'Sa, 'The African Refugee Problem, Relevant International Conventions and Recent Activities of the Organization of African Unity', *N.I.L.R.* 31 (1984): 378; F. Hofman, 'Refugee Law in an African Context', *Z.a.ö.R.V.* 52 (1992): 318; E.O. Awuku, 'Refugee Movements in Africa and the OAU Convention on Refugees', *J.A.L.* 39 (1995): 79; B.T. Mukirya-Nyanduga, 'Refugee Protection under the 1969 OAU Convention Governing the Specific Aspects of Refugee Problems in Africa', *German Y.B.I.L.* 47 (2004): 85. According to the African Commission on Human and Peoples' Rights States Parties are under an obligation to secure the rights protected by the African Charter to all persons within their jurisdiction, nationals and non-nationals alike, *Rencontre Africaine pour la Defense des Droits de l'Homme v. Zambia*, Communication No. 71/92, 10th Activity Report 1996–1997, para. 22, which extends to protecting the human rights of refugees, *African Institute for Human Rights and Development (on behalf of Sierra Leonean refugees in Guinea v. Republic of Guinea*, Communication No. 249/2002, 20th Activity Report 2005–2006, para. 68.

2021. Convention Relating to the Status of Refugees (28 Jul. 1951), 189 U.N.T.S. 137.

2022. *See* Weis. UN Convention on Refugees Art. 1(a)(2), defines a refugee as, *inter alia*, a person having a 'well-founded fear of being persecuted for reasons of race, religion, nationality, membership of a particular social group or political opinion'.

2023. OAU Convention on Refugees Art. 8(2), states that it is the effective regional complement to the UN Convention on Refugees. The preamble additionally acknowledges that the UN Convention on Refugees constitutes the basic instrument relating to the status and treatment of refugees. *See also Doebbler v. Sudan*, Communication No. 235/2000, 27th Activity Report 2009, para. 125.

rights law, namely, internationally, or externally, displaced persons and humanitarian or de facto refugees,[2024] stating that:

> The term 'refugee' shall also apply to every person who, owing to external aggression, occupation, foreign domination or events seriously disturbing public order in either part or the whole of his country of origin or nationality, is compelled to leave his place of habitual residence in order to seek refuge in another place outside his country of origin or nationality.

Excluded from acquiring refugee status are persons guilty of acts contrary to the purposes and principles of the OAU/AU.[2025]

403. The OAU definition therefore intended to cover mass exoduses brought about by the struggle for liberation. Although population displacement as a result of famine or other natural disasters may not have been originally envisaged as coming within the protective scope of the definition, it has subsequently been accepted that such displaced persons would qualify as refugees for the purposes of the Convention.[2026] This broader and more liberal regime was motivated, as stated in the Preamble to the OAU Convention, by 'the need for an essentially humanitarian approach towards solving the problems of refugees', and was therefore a step that was welcomed. It has nevertheless been suggested that the concept of the 'refugee' should be extended in line with the non-discrimination clause of Article 2 of the African Charter,[2027] to cover every person who fears being persecuted for belonging to an ethnic group, or for

2024. Hofman, 323; *Hirsi Jamaa and Others v. Italy*, Concurring Opinion of Judge Pinto de Albuquerque, European Court of Human Rights, Appl. No. 27765/09, Judgment of 23 Feb. 2012, http://www.echr.coe.int (accessed 24 Feb. 2012). According to the African Commission on Human and Peoples' Rights (Commission), 'International protection is granted to refugees because they do not enjoy the protection of their own home countries', *Doebbler v. Sudan*, Communication No. 235/2000, 27th Activity Report 2009, para. 149.

2025. OAU Convention on Refugees Art. 1(5). This provision would seem to be applicable to those militants implicated in the genocide in Rwanda.

2026. C. d'Orsi, 'Sub-Saharan Africa: Is a New Special Regional Refugee Law Regime Emerging?', *Z.a.ö.R.V.* 68 (2008), 1057, 1065–1069. This conclusion is supported by the African Charter on the Rights and Welfare of the Child Art. 23(4) (1 Jul. 1990), 28 I.L.M. 1456 (1989). And *see* Vienna Declaration and Programme of Action pt. I, para. 23(5). *See also Hirsi Jamaa v. Italy*, Concurring Opinion of Judge Pinto de Albuquerque, European Court of Human Rights, Appl. No. 27765/09, Judgment of 23 Feb. 2012, who states, 'Groups of refugees cannot be subject to a diminished status based on an "inherent" mass-influx exception to "genuine" refugee status. To provide reduced, subsidiary protection…for people who arrive as part of a mass influx would be unjustified discrimination.' A simpler definition that reflects such causes is those who have fled for reasons 'traceable to conflicts, or radical political, social or economic changes', quoted in E.-I.A. Daes, *Status of the Individual and Contemporary International Law: Promotion, Protection and Restoration of Human Rights at National, Regional and International Levels* (New York: United Nations, 1992), 34.

2027. African Charter on Human and Peoples' Rights (17 Jun. 1981), 1520 U.N.T.S. 217, 21 I.L.M. 58 (1982).

reasons of colour, sex, social origin, fortune, birth or other status.[2028] The ethnic conflict in the Great Lakes region of Central Africa from 1994–1996 in particular makes a compelling case for the extension of this definition.

404. Article 2 of the OAU Convention on Refugees notably enshrines a right of asylum,[2029] which is reinforced by Article 12(3) of the African Charter.[2030] However, it must be stressed that there is no automatic right to asylum; the use of the term 'best endeavours' is recommendatory rather than mandatory.[2031] States retain an absolute discretion and ultimately the granting of asylum remains their prerogative.[2032] Furthermore, the granting of asylum is declared to be a peaceful and humanitarian act which must not be regarded as an unfriendly gesture by other OAU/AU Member States. Provision is made for burden sharing if a State finds difficulty in continuing to grant asylum to

2028. D'Sa, 378. This is because the OAU Convention on Refugees Art. 4, is narrower in scope, stating that the provisions of the Convention are to be applied to all refugees without discrimination as to, *inter alia*, race, religion, or nationality. However, note should be taken of the African Charter on Democracy Art. 8(2), (30 Jan. 2007), https://www.au.int/en/treaties, Heyns & Killander, 125, whereby State Parties are required to guarantee, *inter alia*, the rights of refugees and displaced persons. Nevertheless, the Commission has made this connection, *see Rencontre Africaine pour la Defense des Droits de l'Homme v. Zambia*, Communication No. 71/92, 10th Activity Report, 1996–1997, paras 21–22; and *Union Interafricaine des Droits de l'Homme et al. v. Angola*, Communication No. 159/96, 11th Activity Report 1997–1998, paras 16–17, where the Commission stated that, 'Mass expulsions of any category of persons, whether on the basis of nationality, religion ethnic, racial or other considerations "constitute a special violation of human rights".' Similarly, in *African Institute for Human Rights and Development (on behalf of Sierra Leonean refugees in Guinea v. Republic of Guinea*, Communication No. 249/2002, 20th Activity Report 2005–2006, para. 69, the Commission held that mass expulsion of refugees amounted to discriminatory action contrary to the OAU Convention on Refugees Art. 4. It is interesting to note that in 2013 the CJEU held in relation to three African asylum seekers that sexual orientation could be a valid basis for having a well-founded fear of persecution, Case C-199/12, C-200/12, C-201/12 *X, Y, Z v. Minister voor Immigratie en Asiel*, Judgment of 7 Nov. 2013, C:2013:720.

2029. Hofman, 318. At the very least it goes beyond that provided for in the UN Convention on Refugees, A.M. Rifaat, *Refugees and the right of asylum: an African perspective*, 40 Revue Egyptienne de droit international 71, 106 (1984). It should be observed that the right of asylum is a conventional right and not a customary right, *Asylum Case (Colombia v. Peru)* I.C.J. Reports 1950, 266; G.S. Goodwin-Gill, *The Refugee in International Law* (Oxford: Clarendon Press, 1996), Ch. 5. For a discussion on how Africa has contributed to the evolution of the law of asylum, *see* G.J. Naldi & C. d'Orsi, 'The Multi-Faceted Aspects of Asylum Law Applicable to Africa: Analysis for Reflection', *Loyola of Los Angeles International& Comparative Law Review* 36 (2014), 115–152.

2030. It appears that this provision applies a more restrictive approach to the granting of asylum in that asylum seekers are required to have suffered actual persecution rather than having a well-founded fear of persecution. In *Organisation Mondiale Contre La Torture and the Association Internationale des Juristes Democrates and Others v. Rwanda* Communication Nos 27/89, 46/91, 49/91, 99/93, 10th Activity Report 1993–1994, para. 30, the Commission expressed the view that this provision included 'a general protection of all those who are subject to persecution, that they may seek refuge in another state'.

2031. Weis, 457; Hofman, 324; Awuku, 82–83.

2032. D'Sa, 387; Hofman, 324; R. Murray, *Human Rights in Africa: From the OAU to the African Union* (Cambridge: Cambridge University Press, 2004), 221.

refugees. A State may thus appeal directly to other States or through the AU for appropriate measures to be taken in the spirit of African solidarity and international cooperation to lessen that burden.

405. The OAU Convention on Refugees further emphasizes its humanitarian credentials by affirming in Article 2(3) the principle of *non-refoulement*,[2033] seemingly having a wider scope than that contained in its corresponding provision of the UN Convention on Refugees, Article 33(1).[2034] In essence, the *non-refoulement* obligation in the OAU Convention amounts to an obligation to admit and host humanitarian refugees. Unlike the UN Convention on Refugees, no express reference is made to exceptions in the interests of national security or public order, or incidents of international crime.[2035] It would therefore seem that a bona fide refugee cannot be expelled.[2036] It has additionally been suggested that the OAU Convention on Refugees guarantees the principle of *non-refoulement* without exception.[2037] However, it has been argued to the contrary that this is not in fact the case since this provision must be read in the context of the Convention as a whole.[2038] Hence, according to Article 1(4)–(5) of the OAU Convention on Refugees, a person may lose their refugee status on various grounds of incompatibility.[2039] Since according to Article 3(1) thereof a refugee is under a duty to abide by the laws of the country of asylum, including measures taken for the maintenance of public order, any breach thereof may result in the loss of refugee status

2033. According to the UNHCR *non-refoulement* is, in addition to a binding treaty obligation, a rule of customary international law and a human right, quoted in *M.S.S. v. Belgium and Greece*, European Court of Human Rights, Appl. No. 30696/09, Judgment of 21 Jan. 2011, para. 56. *See also* Daes, 34; Goodwin-Gill, 167–168. According to the Commission *non-refoulement* is a principle 'which has taken an increasingly fundamental character, as one of the cornerstones of international refugee law', *Doebbler v. Sudan*, Communication No. 235/2000, 27th Activity Report 2009, para. 150.

2034. *See* D'Sa, 387–389; Goodwin-Gill, 140; Hofman, 320–321; d'Orsi, 1059-1065. But only if the UN Convention on Refugees is interpreted restrictively. In practice there may be little difference, Goodwin-Gill, 170–171. However, it appears that there is a lack of uniformity in the interpretation and scope of the principle in state practice, *see* generally E.F. D'Angelo, 'Non-refoulement: The Search for a Consistent Interpretation of Article 33', *Vanderbilt Journal Transnational Law* 42 (2009): 279.

2035. Such individuals do not qualify for, or lose, the status of refugees or protected person, UN Convention on Refugees Arts 32, 33(2); *see* generally Goodwin-Gill, Ch. 4. In *African Institute for Human Rights and Development (on behalf of Sierra Leonean refugees in Guinea v. Republic of Guinea*, Communication No. 249/2002, 20th Activity Report 2005–2006, paras 69, 72, the Commission held that the State was entitled to prosecute persons that posed a threat to the State. *See* further Cases C-57/09 and C-101/09 *Federal Republic of Germany v. B & D* [2010] E.C.R. I-10979, para. 101.

2036. Indeed, expelling refugees and refuge seekers to high-risk countries can constitute *arbitrary* repatriation, *Hirsi Jamaa v. Italy*, European Court of Human Rights, Appl. No. 27765/09, Judgment of 23 Feb. 2012, paras 153–156.

2037. Goodwin-Gill, 140.

2038. D'Sa, 388; Murray, 189. Awuku, 82, is of the view that the OAU's exclusion clause is stricter than that of the UN Convention on Refugees.

2039. Which would appear to extend to terrorist acts, Cases C-57/09 and C-101/09 *Federal Republic of Germany v. B & D* [2010] E.C.R. I-10979, paras 81–84; Case C-573/14. *Commissaire générale aux réfugiés et aux apatrides v. Mostafa Lounani*, Judgment of 31 Jan. 2017, C:2017:71.

and expulsion may ensue. Nevertheless, a safeguard is provided by Article 12(4) of the African Charter which protects against arbitrary expulsions, stating that an alien lawfully in the territory of a State may be expelled only in accordance with the due process of law.[2040] It is significant that the principle of *non-refoulement* must be observed even in cases of mass influx of displaced persons, and this obligation is complemented by Article 12(5) of the African Charter which prohibits the mass expulsion of aliens.[2041] However, events in the Great Lakes region of Central Africa highlighted the difficulties faced by African States in coping with the reception of large numbers of refugees. In apparent defiance of their treaty obligations borders were closed and more than one million Rwandan and Burundian refugees were forced to leave Zaïre and Tanzania and return to their country of origin where they faced an uncertain future. However, these events may be explicable against a background of violence and infiltration by armed gangs as opponents of the new regimes in Rwanda and Burundi, many with complicity in the massacres perpetrated in those countries, used the refugee camps for subversive activities.[2042]

406. Note should be taken of the fact that under Article 2(6) of the OAU Convention on Refugees States granting the right of asylum are, for reasons of security, under an obligation to settle refugees a reasonable distance from the frontier of their country of origin. This requirement may appear, prima facie, to be incompatible with Article 26 of the UN Convention on Refugees and Article 12(1) of the African Charter which states that every individual shall have the right of freedom of movement and residence within the borders of a State. Nevertheless, States are under an obligation

---

2040. *Organisation Mondiale Contre La Torture and the Association Internationale des Juristes Democrates and Others v. Rwanda*, Communication Nos 27/89, 46/91, 49/91, 99/93, 10th Activity Report 1993–1994, para. 30; *Union Interafricaine des Droits de l'Homme et al. v. Angola*, Communication No.159/96, 11th Activity Report 1997–1998, paras 19–20.

2041. In *Doebbler v. Sudan*, Communication No. 235/2000, 27th Activity Report 2009, para. 146, the question whether the principle of *non-refoulement* applied to 14,000 Ethiopian refugees residing in Sudan was central to the case. Mass expulsions have been described as 'a special threat to human rights', *Rencontre Africaine pour la Defense des Droits de l'Homme v. Zambia*, Communication No. 71/92, 10th Activity Report, 1996–1997, para. 20. *See also African Institute for Human Rights and Development (on behalf of Sierra Leonean refugees in Guinea v. Republic of Guinea*, Communication No. 249/2002, 20th Activity Report 2005–2006, para. 69.

2042. UN Doc. E/CN/4/1997/61. Whilst the Commission will take note of the legitimate national security concerns of States their freedom of action is not unlimited however. In *Organisation Mondiale Contre La Torture and the Association Internationale des Juristes Democrates and Others v. Rwanda*, Communication Nos 27/89, 46/91, 49/91, 99/93, 10th Activity Report 1993–1994, the Commission found that the expulsion of Burundi nationals from Rwanda because they were considered to be a security risk amounted to a violation of, *inter alia*, the African Charter Art. 12(5). *See alsoAfrican Institute for Human Rights and Development (on behalf of Sierra Leonean refugees in Guinea v. Republic of Guinea*, Communication No. 249/2002, 20th Activity Report 2005–2006. In *Democratic Republic of Congo v. Burundi, Rwanda and Uganda*, Communication No. 227/99, 20th Activity Report 2005–2006, para. 76, the Commission rejected as 'impermissible' Uganda's argument that it had launched operations in the DRC's territory in order to safeguard its national security interests since armed rebel groups hostile to Burundi, Rwanda and Uganda had sanctuary in the DRC. *See also Case concerning Armed Activities on the Territory of the Congo* (*Democratic Republic of Congo v. Uganda*) I.C.J. Reports 2005, 168.

to ensure effective protection of refugees within their borders[2043] and the wisdom of this provision has been substantiated by events in the Great Lakes region of Central Africa during 1996 when refugees along the Rwanda/Zaïre border often fell victims to acts of atrocities committed by different parties and refugee camps were used to increase tension along the border.

407. A further distinguishing feature of the OAU Convention on Refugees is the prohibition on refugees engaging in subversive activities contained in Article 3. This principle is in keeping with Article 4(o) of the Constitutive Act,[2044] Article 23(2) of the African Charter and the OAU Declaration on the Problem of Subversion.[2045] Accordingly a refugee is under a duty to abide by the laws of the country in which s/he finds herself/himself and to refrain from any subversive activities against any OAU/AU Member State. By restricting the prohibition towards OAU/AU Member States only, the national liberation struggle was left unhindered. A problem of definition may nevertheless arise. If the host-State adopts a restrictive approach legitimate political dissent or agitation in support of human rights could be suppressed, at variance with the freedom of expression enshrined in Article 9(2) of the African Charter.[2046] However, restrictions may be understandable to prevent unrest, acts of terror and incitement to violence.[2047] A person who does not abide by such a prohibition could lose his/her refugee status in accordance with Article 1(4)–(5) of the OAU Convention on Refugees and face expulsion. State parties are under a similar obligation to prohibit refugees residing in their territories from attacking, or engaging in any subversive activities, against any OAU/AU Member State.[2048] The political upheaval in the Great Lakes Region of Central Africa in recent years has highlighted the difficulties that these provisions seek to address. Mass population movements mingled genuine asylum seekers with armed gangs and individuals who had committed serious crimes, including crimes against humanity.[2049] Unrest was fomented in refugee camps which were used as bases from which to launch attacks against neighbouring territories. As a result

2043. *See* Res. 2003/52 of the UN Commission on Human Rights.

2044. And the OAU Charter Art. III(5), (25 May 1963), 479 U.N.T.S. 39, 2 I.L.M. 766 (1963), before it. *See* further Protocol on Amendments to the Constitutive Act, Art. 4(r), (9 Jul. 2002), https://www.au.int/en/treaties, Heyns & Killander, 12.

2045. In G.J. Naldi, *Documents of the Organization of African Unity* (London & New York: Mansell, 1992), 57.

2046. The term 'subversive activities' has been criticized for vagueness and the possibility that it could be invoked to curb legitimate activities, Weis, 457; Awuku, 83.

2047. In Res. 1161 the UN Security Council acknowledged the threat posed to the stability of the Great Lakes Region of Central Africa posed by malicious propaganda. *See also* Report of the UN Secretary-General on the causes of conflict and the promotion of durable peace and sustainable development in Africa, UN Doc. A/52/871-S/1998/318 (1998) para. 53.

2048. Under the Arusha Accords, the Governments of Burundi, Tanzania, Uganda and Zaïre agreed to the non-use of territories as bases for destabilizing Rwanda, UN Doc. E/CN.4/1995/50/Add. 2, para. 42.

2049. Report of the UN Secretary-General on the causes of conflict and the promotion of durable peace and sustainable development in Africa, UN Doc. A/52/871-S/1998/318 (1998) para. 53.

some refugee camps were stormed and refugees killed and dispersed.[2050] In order to protect bona fide refugees in these dangerous circumstances the UNHCR reached agreement with the governments of the region on security measures to ensure the civilian nature of the refugee camps.[2051] Accordingly, the UNCHR put forward what it described as a 'ladder of options' identifying proportionate measures to perceived threats.[2052]

408. Article 5 of the OAU Convention on Refugees contains another distinctive right in making provision for voluntary repatriation.[2053] It is clear that repatriation must be voluntary and, in light of the principle of *non-refoulement*, it declares that no refugee shall be repatriated against his/her will.[2054] If a refugee does wish to be repatriated the country of origin and the country of asylum are obliged to collaborate to ensure the refugee's safe return. Neither should returning refugees be victimized for having left. In addition, refugees who freely decide to return to their homeland on their own initiative or as the result of assurances must have their return facilitated by the country of origin, the country of asylum, voluntary agencies, NGOs, and international organizations. While voluntary repatriation may offer one of the best solutions to the refugee crisis[2055] it is apparent that unless the root causes that created the displacement in the first place are not remedied the prospects of voluntary repatriation will prove negligible. Consequently, the return of relative stability and security to parts of Africa such as Liberia and Sierra Leone has led to the large-scale repatriation of refugees.[2056] Moreover, voluntary repatriation can only be made more effective if human rights are protected, the rule of law is respected, property restitution is addressed and the safety of returnees can be assured.[2057]

409. It needs to be recalled that according to international human rights norms a person cannot be arbitrarily deprived of the right to return to his/her country. The

---

2050. UN Doc. E/CN.4/1995/50/Add.4. Similar problems arose in West Africa; in *African Institute for Human Rights and Development (on behalf of Sierra Leonean refugees in Guinea v. Republic of Guinea*, Communication No. 249/2002, 20th Activity Report 2005–2006, para. 71, the Commission acknowledged that Guinea held legitimate concerns about 'threats to its national security posed by the attacks from Sierra Leone and Liberia with a flow of rebels and arms across the borders.'

2051. UN Doc. E/CN.4/1997/61.

2052. The 'ladder of options' includes the following measures: (a) enhancing existing national law enforcement mechanisms; (b) international support for national security forces; (c) deployment of international fact-finding missions and observers; (d) deployment of international/regional police forces; (e) deployment of international/regional military forces under Ch. VI or Ch. VII UN Charter, UN Doc. E/CN.4/2005/80, para. 41.

2053. *See* d'Orsi, 1069–1076.

2054. *See* d'Orsi who highlights a number of cases of 'forced' repatriation, *ibid.*, 1077–1079.

2055. Awuku, 85. In Res. 2003/52 the UN Commission on Human Rights makes the point that return is not and should not be perceived as the only solution to forcible displacement but that resettlement and local integration are policies that should also be considered. *See* further Murray, 210–216. In 2015 one hundred and thirty thousand refugees in Africa returned, *UNHCR Global Trends 2015*, http://www.unhcr.org/globaltrends/ (accessed 26 Apr. 2017).

2056. UN Doc. E/CN.4/2005/80, para. 56. In *Doebbler v. Sudan*, Communication No. 235/2000, 27th Activity Report 2009, para. 161, the Commission found that thousands of Ethiopian refugees repatriated voluntarily following the end of the Ethiopian-Eritrean war.

2057. *See* the Kigali Declaration 2003 para. 14, Heyns & Killander, 154.

OAU Convention on Refugees does not address this issue but under general international law a national cannot be denied entry to his or her country of origin.[2058] Furthermore, according to Article 12(2) of the African Charter, an individual has the right to leave any country and to return to his or her country subject to the law of public order and security.[2059]

410. The importance of the OAU Convention on Refugees to international law lies in its progressive nature, setting a legal standard to which the international community should aspire.[2060] Particularly worthy of note are the extension of the definition of the concept of the refugee, the implementation of voluntary repatriation programmes and its provision of a right of asylum. Motivated in part by problems peculiar to Africa these humanitarian developments were nonetheless welcome. These commitments have been subsequently endorsed by the OAU/AU and the UN in a number of special conferences convened to discuss the challenges posed by the refugee crises in Africa, which have also sought to address their root causes and offer practical proposals.[2061] Although these recommendations have no binding legal force, although they may have an impact as soft law, they nevertheless, in urging OAU/AU Member States to comply more effectively with their international obligations, constitute an important expression of the political will of OAU/AU Member States to reaffirm their legal and humanitarian obligations in accordance with the UN and OAU Conventions. However, in light of later developments, particularly the EU, it seems fair comment to suggest that the African response, once pioneering, now seems behind the times. For example, unlike the EU, there exists no uniform set of procedures for determination of refugee status and appeals.[2062] Yet the African Commission on Human and Peoples' Rights is having a positive influence on the development of the law in this area. The fact that the African Charter is deemed applicable to refugees is highly significant as it means, amongst other things, that refugees are entitled to basic rights and must be

2058. Universal Declaration of Human Rights Art. 13(2), UN General Assembly Res. 217A (III); International Covenant on Civil and Political Rights Art. 12(2) (16 Dec. 1966), 999 U.N.T.S. 171, European Convention on Human Rights Fourth Protocol 4 Art. 3 (16 Sept. 1963), E.T.S. No. 46.

2059. *Alhassan Abubakar v. Ghana*, Communication No. 103/93, 10th Activity Report 1996–1997.

2060. The OAU Convention on Refugees has been described as creating 'an impressive normative framework', F. Viljoen, *International Human Rights Law in Africa* (Oxford: Oxford University Press, 2007), 258.

2061. Particular mention should be made of the Pan-African Conference on the Situation on Refugees in Africa held at Arusha, Tanzania, in May 1979, the Arusha Conference, which adopted a series of recommendations on 'The Situation of Refugees in Africa and Prospective Solutions to the Problem in the 1980s', *see* UN General Assembly Res. 34/61; the Addis Ababa Recommendations 1994; and the Conakry Comprehensive Action Plan 2000. *See* further Murray, 190–192.

2062. *Doebbler v. Sudan*, Communication No. 235/2000, 27th Activity Report 2009, para. 165. *See* EU Council Directive 2004/83 of 29 Apr. 2004 on minimum standards for the qualification and status of third country nationals or stateless persons as refugees or as persons who otherwise need international protection and the content of the protection granted, O.J. L 304/12, 30 Sept. 2004.

treated with dignity.[2063] However, in practical terms much remains to be done as African States generally lack the financial, logistical and material resources to deal with the challenges posed by refugee crises. But, as recent events in Europe have demonstrated, even Western States can struggle to cope with large numbers of refugees. It is clear that African States must acquire and develop early warning and early-action systems, as called for by resolution 2003/52 of the UN Commission on Human Rights, to react more promptly to evolving crises. Timely donor assistance, properly spent, is also important. But unless the root causes of mass displacement are effectively addressed, to be replaced by peace, security and stability, the international community is dealing in palliatives and the plight of refugees will continue to blight Africa.[2064]

411. The situation in Darfur is therefore of particular interest in this respect because it demonstrates the capacity of the international community to respond to threats to international peace and security in a collectively forceful manner when the political will exists. Since 2001 the conflict in the Darfur region of Sudan has engaged the international community. The Janjaweed militia especially had been carrying out attacks, and perpetrating atrocities, on civilian populations that led to forced displacement. The UN Security Council found that this conflict posed a threat to international peace and security.[2065] In demanding that the Sudanese Government put a stop to these attacks and disarm the militia the UN Security Council also called for measures to prevent or mitigate the humanitarian catastrophe.[2066] An international presence was initially established by the AU in 2004 as a monitoring mission in the form of the AMIS which was mandated, *inter alia*, to contribute to a secure environment for the delivery of humanitarian aid and the return of refugees and the internally displaced, or IDPs.[2067] A UN presence followed in the form of the UNMIS, established under Security Council resolution 1590(2005), which was additionally given the task of facilitating the voluntary return of IDPs and refugees by helping to establish the necessary security conditions.

2063. *African Institute for Human Rights and Development (on behalf of Sierra Leonean refugees in Guinea v. Republic of Guinea*, Communication No. 249/2002, 20th Activity Report 2005–2006, paras 66–67.

2064. *See* Murray, 206–209. One important factor that is being addressed is ending impunity for human rights and humanitarian law violations. This has happened in relation to the conflict in Darfur, *see infra* para. 420 for fuller discussion. In 2004 the UN Secretary-General, pursuant to Security Council Res. 1564 (2004) acting under Ch. VII UN Charter, established an International Commission of Inquiry on Darfur with a view investigating alleged violations of human rights law and international humanitarian law in Darfur. The Commission found as established that the Government of Sudan and the Janjaweed were responsible for serious violations of human rights law and international humanitarian law amounting to crimes under international law and recommended that the Security Council refer the Darfur conflict to the ICC, UN Doc. S/2005/60. Under Res. 1593 (2005) the Security Council duly referred this matter to the ICC.

2065. Resolution 1556 (2004), adopted pursuant to Chapter VII UN Charter, which imposed sanctions on Sudan. *See also*, e.g., Res. 1784 (2007).

2066. Resolutions 1556 (2004) and 1591 (2005), adopted pursuant to Ch. VII UN Charter. The African Commission on Human and Peoples' Rights has also expressed its concern at the situation in Darfur, *see* , e.g., Resolution on the Situation of Human Rights in the Darfur Region in Sudan, 20th Activity Report, 2006.

2067. Communiqué of the Seventeenth Meeting of the Peace and Security Council of the AU, AU Doc. PSC/PR/Comm.(XVII), endorsed by UN Security Council Res. 1556 (2004).

However, the numerous difficulties encountered by AMIS, which included suffering casualties from militia attacks and obstruction to humanitarian access, exposed its limitations but this led to an extraordinary development, the creation of a hybrid AU/UN peacekeeping operation, AU/UN Hybrid Operation in Darfur (UNAMID).[2068] Furthermore, due to the destabilizing effect the Darfur conflict has been having on neighbouring countries the UN has authorized, pursuant to Chapter VII of the UN Charter, the deployment of an EU operation in eastern Chad and north-eastern CAR with a view, *inter alia*, to protecting refugees and IDPs.[2069]

412. In 1964 the OAU set up as a permanent organ the Commission on Refugees with the task of considering all aspects of refugee problems in Africa and devising appropriate policies.[2070] With the advent of the AU, this body was transformed into the Sub-Committee on Refugees, Returnees and IDPs in Africa. Its expanded mandate includes assisting AU organs in formulating, developing and coordinating policy on issues affecting refugees, returnees and IDPs, promoting humanitarian law in Africa, examining the plight and needs of refugees, returnees and IDPs and providing policy recommendations, and collaborating with UN humanitarian agencies, RECs and NGOs.[2071]

§2. The AU Convention on Internally Displaced Persons

413. The OAU Convention on Refugees is not alone in having failed to address a problem of significant magnitude in Africa, of people who as a result of forced or involuntary movement find themselves in a refugee-like situation but do not legally qualify for refugee status because they remain within national frontiers, namely, IDPs. According to the UNHCR there were over eleven million IDPs in Africa at the end of 2015.[2072] The UN has stressed the importance of humanitarian aid and securing access to civilians.[2073] Although the OAU took some action to deal with the plight of IDPs[2074] it was only in 2009 that a Convention on IDPs in Africa (Kampala Convention) was adopted by the AU.[2075] The Kampala Convention may be considered ground-breaking due to the fact that currently it is the only existing specific universal or regional legal

2068. UN Security Council Res. 1769 (2007).

2069. UN Security Council Res. 1778 (2007). In January 2008 the Council of the EU adopted a Decision on the launching of operation EUFOR Tchad/RCA, Press Release 5625/08.

2070. *See* G.J. Naldi, *The Organization of African Unity* (London & New York: Mansell, 1989), 97.

2071. *African Union Handbook 2014*, 98–99, https://www.au.int.

2072. *UNHCR Global Trends 2015*, http://www.unhcr.org/globaltrends/ (accessed 26 Apr. 2017).

2073. Vienna Declaration and Programme of Action pt. I, para. 23(4); Report of the High-Level Panel on Threats, Challenges and Change, A More Secure World: Our Shared Responsibility, UN Doc. A/59/565 (2004) paras 231–238.

2074. Murray, 222–225.

2075. Convention on the Protection and Assistance to Internally Displaced Persons in Africa (23 Oct. 2009), 49 I.L.M. 83 (2010). The Convention entered into force on 6 Dec. 2012 and by June 2017 had been ratified by twenty-seven Member States.

instrument providing for the comprehensive protection of IDPs.[2076] But the Kampala Convention is notable for a host of other reasons, including the comprehensive obligations owed by States and others, including humanitarian agencies and armed groups, towards IDPs, and human rights guarantees. Its basic premise may be said to that all persons have a right to be protected against arbitrary displacement.[2077]

414. The Kampala Convention defines IDPs as, 'persons or groups of persons who have been forced or obliged to flee or to leave their homes or places of habitual residence, in particular as a result of or in order to avoid the effects of armed conflict, situations of generalized violence, violations of human rights or natural or human-made disasters, and who have not crossed an internationally recognized State border'.[2078] The broad scope of the definition adopted by the Kampala Convention is noteworthy; it expressly takes into consideration factors such as natural disasters that either were implicit in the OAU Convention on Refugees or became accepted due to subsequent practice. But especially significant is the fact that account is taken of human impact such as development projects, for example, the building of dams[2079] or the exploitation of natural resources.[2080] A definition of internal displacement is also provided, 'the involuntary or forced movement, evacuation or relocation of persons or groups of persons within internationally recognized state borders'.[2081] But the Kampala Convention protects against *arbitrary* displacement. Such displacement includes displacement caused by what may be termed 'ethnic cleansing',[2082] displacement caused by armed conflict,[2083] displacement caused by generalized violence or violations human rights,[2084] and displacement used as a collective punishment.[2085] Consequently, evacuations necessitated by imperative military reasons in accordance with international humanitarian law,[2086] or for health and safety reasons,[2087] for example, to protect a population at risk of drowning in floods, do not come within the scope of the definition.

415. The Kampala Convention imposes a series of general obligations upon States Parties,[2088] a number of which have special relevance to the lawlessness that

2076. However, the UN has drafted a 'soft law' document, Guiding Principles on Internal Displacement, setting out the humanitarian and human rights standards applicable to IDPs, which have been widely adopted, UN Doc. E/CN.4/1999/79. It has been described as 'an important international framework', UN General Assembly Resolution 60/1 (2005) on the 2005 World Summit Outcome, para. 132. *See* further F.M. Deng, 'The International Protection of the Internally Displaced', *International Journal of Refugee Law* 7 (1995): 7. The Kampala Convention closely mirrors the Guiding Principles on Internal Displacement.
2077. Kampala Convention Art. 4(4).
2078. *Ibid.*, Art. 1(k). It essentially repeats verbatim the description provided by the Guiding Principles on Internal Displacement, 5.
2079. Kampala Convention Art. 10.
2080. *Ibid.*, Art. 3(l)(i).
2081. *Ibid.*, Art. 1(l).
2082. *Ibid.*, Art. 4(4)(a).
2083. *Ibid.*, Art. 4(4)(b)–(c).
2084. *Ibid.*, Art. 4(4)(d).
2085. *Ibid.*, Art. 4(4)(g).
2086. *Ibid.*, Art. 4(4)(b).
2087. *Ibid.*, Art. 4(4)(f).
2088. *Ibid.*, Art. 3.

has affected Somalia and Darfur. These include preventing arbitrary displacement,[2089] ensuring respect for human rights and international humanitarian law relating to IDPs,[2090] ensuring individual responsibility for acts of arbitrary displacement, including those of non-State actors,[2091] and meeting the basic needs of IDPs.[2092] More specifically, States Parties are required to ensure respect for human rights and international humanitarian law as a means of preventing situations giving rise to arbitrary displacement,[2093] and to set up early warning systems.[2094] The Kampala Convention reiterates the basic principle of international law that the primary duty and responsibility, though not exclusive, for providing protection and humanitarian assistance to IDPs within their territory or jurisdiction rests with States.[2095] This extends to taking measures to protect and assist IDPs,[2096] including assessing the needs and vulnerabilities of IDPs,[2097] and taking the necessary steps to organize relief action.[2098] Where appropriate States Parties shall turn to international organizations and humanitarian agencies for assistance.[2099] They undertake to respect the mandates of the AU, UN, and humanitarian organizations to assist IDPs,[2100] and must therefore protect and refrain from attacking or harming humanitarian personnel and resources.[2101] However, in keeping with the traditional view that the legality of the delivery of humanitarian aid is contingent on the consent of the recipient State[2102] it is made clear that the sovereignty and territorial integrity of States remains unaffected.[2103]

416. More detailed obligations are set out in Article 9 of the Kampala Convention. These include preventing and refraining from violations of international humanitarian

---

2089. *Ibid.*, Art. 3(l)(a)–(b).
2090. *Ibid.*, Art. 3(l)(c)–(e).
2091. *Ibid.*, Art. 3(l)(g)–(h). In addition, acts of arbitrary displacement that amount to genocide, war crimes or crimes against humanity shall be deemed offences punishable by law. *See also ibid.*, Arts 7(4), (5)(a). Such violations of international criminal law could therefore be prosecuted before the ICC.
2092. *Ibid.*, Art. 3(l)(k).
2093. *Ibid.*, Art. 4(l).
2094. *Ibid.*, Art. 4(2).
2095. *Ibid.*, Art. 5(1). *See* Goodwin-Gill, 265.
2096. Kampala Convention Art. 5(4).
2097. *Ibid.*, Art. 5(5).
2098. *Ibid.*, Art. 5(7).
2099. *Ibid.*, Art. 5(6).
2100. *Ibid.*, Art. 5(3). *See also ibid.*, Art. 8(2) which reiterates the rights of States to request intervention from the AU in light of security problems caused by displacement.
2101. *Ibid.*, Art. 5(10). *See* UN Convention on Safety of United Nations and Associated Personnel (9 Dec. 1994) 2051 U.N.T.S. 363.
2102. *See* UN General Assembly Res. 46/182 (1991), Annex: Strengthening of the Coordination of Humanitarian Emergency Assistance of the United Nations, para. 3. However, at the same time it was acknowledged that victims of natural disasters are of concern to the international community. Moreover, UN practice has established that it can authorize enforcement action on humanitarian grounds, *see* , e.g., UN Security Council Res. 794 (1992) on Somalia. *See also Military and Paramilitary Activities in and against Nicaragua (Nicaragua v. United States)* I.C.J. Reports 1986, paras 242–243.
2103. Kampala Convention Art. 5(12).

law, including genocide, war crimes or crimes against humanity,[2104] serious human rights violations, such as arbitrary killings, enforced disappearances and torture,[2105] all forms of sexual and gender based violence,[2106] and starvation.[2107] States Parties must therefore ensure that IDPs live in satisfactory conditions so adequate humanitarian assistance, food, water, shelter, sanitation, medical care, must be provided.[2108] Those with special needs, children, mothers, the elderly, must be provided for.[2109] States must do their utmost to trace and reunify separated families.[2110] The property of IDPs must be protected.[2111] The civilian nature of the camps must be maintained and protected against armed groups.[2112]

417. In light of events in Somalia and Darfur in particular where armed groups have attacked IDPs and disrupted the provision of humanitarian assistance, the Kampala Convention seeks to address the situation of IDPs in instances of armed conflict. It is made clear that there is nothing in the Kampala Convention that prevents a State from defending its sovereignty or re-establishing law and order by legitimate means,[2113] nor can the Kampala Convention be construed as affording legal status or recognition to armed groups.[2114] Members of armed groups are specifically prohibited from, *inter alia*, carrying out arbitrary displacement,[2115] from obstructing and impeding humanitarian assistance and resources to IDPs,[2116] attacking or harming humanitarian personnel,[2117] abduction and hostage taking, people trafficking and sexual slavery, as is forcible recruitment, including of children.[2118] Members of armed groups who violates the rights of IDPs will be held criminally liable under national and international law.[2119]

418. The Kampala Convention provides certain guarantees in relation to movement and settlement. IDPs have a right of freedom of movement, which is not absolute,[2120] and States must make provision for voluntary return, local integration or relocation.[2121] IDPs must be able to make a free and informed choice as to their resettlement.[2122] Significantly, States must create appropriate mechanisms to resolve

---

2104. *Ibid.*, Art 9(1)(b). It should be recalled that under Res. 1593 (2005) the UN Security Council referred the situation in Darfur to the ICC, resulting in the prosecution of the sitting President of Sudan, Omar Al-Bashir, *The Prosecutor v. Omar Hassan Ahmad Al Bashir* ICC-02/05-01/09.
2105. Kampala Convention Art. 9(1)(c).
2106. *Ibid.*, Art. 9(1)(d).
2107. *Ibid.*, Art. 9(1)(e).
2108. *Ibid.*, Art. 9(2)(b).
2109. *Ibid.*, Art. 9(2)(c)–(d).
2110. *Ibid.*, Art. 9(2)(h).
2111. *Ibid.*, Art. 9(2)(i).
2112. *Ibid.*, Art. 9(2)(g). *See also ibid.*, Art. 7(5)(i).
2113. *Ibid.*, Art. 7(2).
2114. *Ibid.*, Art. 7(1).
2115. *Ibid.*, Art. 7(5)(a).
2116. *Ibid.*, Art. 7(5)(b), (g).
2117. *Ibid.*, Art. 7(5)(h).
2118. *Ibid.*, Art. 7(5)(e), (f).
2119. *Ibid.*, Art. 7(4).
2120. *Ibid.*, Art. 9(2)(f). *See also* African Charter Art. 12(1).
2121. Kampala Convention Art. 11(1).
2122. *Ibid.*, Art. 11(2).

property disputes and must, where possible, restore the lands of communities with 'special dependency and attachment to such lands'.[2123]

419. A particularly interesting feature of the Kampala Convention is the fact that it makes provision for effective remedies.[2124] States Parties must provide 'just and fair compensation and other forms of reparations' to IDPs for damage occurred as a result of dislocation where appropriate.[2125] In addition, a State incurs liability when it fails to protect and assist IDPs in cases of natural disasters.[2126] The question arises as to what is meant by fair compensation, which by definition must include awards of a pecuniary nature as one option. Restitution in kind could be another possibility. But it could extend to ordering consequential measures requiring certain positive steps to be taken. However, the Kampala Convention may not be limited solely to material redress but appears to be open to the possibility of some form of amends for mental distress.

420. The AU has been the first organization of its type to tackle the significant predicament posed by IDPs. The Kampala Convention is a welcome development in that it seeks to establish a legal framework for resolving the causes of displacement and the problems arising in its wake. It sets out the rights of IDPs and the obligations of States towards them. In this respect, the fact that obligations are imposed on States towards humanitarian agencies and international organizations is important. Non-State actors, in the form of armed groups, are also under obligations towards IDPs but how these are to be enforced is a matter of some doubt.[2127] The strengthening of the prohibition on arbitrary displacement is noteworthy. Its provisions on remedies are innovative but their effectiveness is to a degree dependent on the creation of appropriate mechanisms. Concern has been expressed that the human rights guarantees are imperfect but the fact that the African Charter is deemed applicable to IDPs makes this critique less plausible. All in all the Kampala Convention constitutes a creditable effort at dealing with the problem of IDPs.

2123. *Ibid.*, Art. 11(4)–(5). *See Centre for Minority Rights Development (Kenya) and Minority Rights Group International on behalf of Endorois Welfare Council v. Kenya*, Communication No. 276/2003 (2009).

2124. Kampala Convention Art.e 12(1).

2125. *Ibid.*, Art. 12(2).

2126. *Ibid.*, Art. 12(3).

2127. In general, a diligent State cannot be held responsible for the acts of rebels or insurrectionists, D.J. Harris, *Cases and Materials on International Law* (7th edn, London: Sweet & Maxwell, 2010), 430–431.

Chapter 4. Economic Cooperation

§1. The African Economic Community (AEC)

421. For many years after independence most African States largely experienced general economic decline. Economic growth tended to be uneven or unreliable. A combination of internal and external factors was responsible for this poor economic performance. The former include the pursuit of unsuccessful economic policies, lack of financial resources, deficiencies in institutional and physical infrastructures, insufficient managerial/administrative capacity, often leading to rampant corruption, kleptocracy, inadequate human resource development, and political instability. A business friendly environment often did not exist. External factors include adverse terms of trade, a decline in financial flows, overreliance on commodities, a decline in commodity prices and high debt and debt-servicing obligations.[2128] In a radical attempt to break the cycle of economic despair the African States came to the conclusion that a domestic solution, based on collective economic self-reliance, was not only necessary to reverse this trend and to ensure economic growth and prosperity but also feasible. The founding by the OAU of an AEC in 1991 represented one of the most ambitious developments in this field.[2129]

422. The AEC or Abuja, Treaty was adopted in June 1991 and entered into force in May 1994.[2130] Its objectives are: to promote economic, social, and cultural development and the integration of African economies in order to increase economic self-reliance and promote development; to harness and develop Africa's human and material resources; and to promote cooperation so as to raise the standard of living and enhance economic stability, foster peaceful relations among Member States and contribute to the progress, development and economic integration of Africa.[2131] These are to be achieved by, *inter alia*, the liberalization of trade through the abolition of customs duties on imports and exports and non-tariff barriers in order to establish a free trade

2128. *See* The Causes of Conflict and the Promotion of Durable Peace and Sustainable Development in Africa: Report of the Secretary-General, UN Doc. A/52/871-S/1998/318.

2129. Another significant initiative to promote economic and social development and to advance the economic integration of Africa was the Lagos Plan of Action for the Economic Development of Africa 1980, which sought to create favourable conditions to encourage economic growth in Africa. It also envisaged the creation of the AEC by the millennium. *See* R.M. D'Sa, 'The Lagos Plan of Action – Legal Mechanisms for Cooperation Between the Organization of African Unity and the United Nations Economic Commission for Africa', *J.A.L.* 27 (1983): 4.

2130. Treaty Establishing an African Economic Community (3 Jun. 1991), 30 I.L.M. 1241 (1991). As of January 2017, it has been ratified by forty-nine States. For analysis, *see* N.L. Lumu, *De la Nature de la Communauté Economique Africaine*, 8 R.A.D.I.C. 51 (1996); G.J. Naldi & K.D. Magliveras, 'The African Economic Community: Emancipation for African States or Yet Another Glorious Failure?', *North Carolina J. Int'l Law & Comm. Reg.* 24 (1999): 601; M. Ndulo, 'Harmonisation of Trade Laws in the African Economic Community', *I.C.L.Q.* 42 (1993): 101; B. Thompson, 'Economic Integration Efforts in Africa', *R.A.D.I.C.* 5 (1993): 743.

2131. AEC Treaty Art. 4(1).

area, the adoption of a common trade policy vis-à-vis third States, the harmonization of national policies in agriculture, industry, transport and communications, energy, trade, money and finance and science and technology, the establishment of a common external tariff, the removal of obstacles to the free movement of persons, goods, services and capital and the right of residence and establishment, and the establishment of a common market.[2132] Not unlike the EU, the AEC has the features of a supranational organization and foresees a role beyond the economic sphere, in the social and political worlds, leading eventually to political union, since achieved with the creation of the AU.[2133] The AEC Treaty is best described as a framework treaty setting down general policies with much of the detail to be provided in subsequent protocols.

423. The AEC Treaty seeks to regulate various areas of economic activity at both the regional and continental levels. The first important area concerns liberalization of trade and the creation of a customs union. Article 29 requires the progressive establishment of a customs union involving the elimination of customs duties, quota restrictions, other restrictions or prohibitions and administrative trade barriers, as well as all other non-tariff barriers, and the adoption of a common external customs tariff.[2134] The experience of the EU demonstrates that States are ingenious in developing barriers to the free movement of goods and it may therefore have been sensible to insert the phrase 'and measures of equivalent effect' where appropriate in the relevant provisions of the AEC Treaty.

424. Article 35 allows for derogation from the application of these provisions in a number of circumstances, none of which can be used as a means of arbitrary discrimination or a disguised restriction on trade. The grounds of derogation, which appear to be exhaustive, include national security, the control of arms and military equipment, protection of health and life of humans, animals and plants, public morality, protection of national treasures of artistic or archaeological value, protection of industrial, commercial and intellectual property, exports of strategic minerals and precious stones, the protection of infant industries, the control of hazardous and radioactive wastes and products and nuclear materials, the control of strategic products, balance of payment difficulties, and serious economic difficulties arising from imports from a Member State.[2135] It is submitted that the derogations should be subject to the principle of proportionality.

425. Another essential element of economic integration is the free movement of persons.[2136] Pursuant to Article 43 Member States undertake progressively to secure for their nationals the free movement of persons and the rights of residence and

2132. *Ibid.*, Art. 4(2).

2133. *See supra* Part II. Note that according to the Constitutive Act Art. 33(2) (26 May 2001), 2158 U.N.T.S. 3, its provisions take precedence over or supersede any inconsistent provisions of the AEC Treaty.

2134. The manner in which these objectives are to be achieved are specified in AEC Treaty Arts 30–34.

2135. This final exception is reinforced by AEC Treaty Art. 36 which prohibits the practice of 'dumping'.

2136. *See also ibid.*, Art. 71(2)(a). The free movement of persons is described as one of the 'fundamental freedoms' of EU Law, *see* , e.g., Case 53/81 *Levin v. Staatssecretaris van Justicie* [1982] E.C.R. 1035. Thompson, 753–754, laments the lack of reference to 'Community citizenship' unlike the experience of ECOWAS, since she regards a common position on this issue as imperative for the accomplishment of the AEC's goals.

establishment within the AEC.[2137] By analogy with the EU experience,[2138] the issues that will need to be addressed include rights of entry and residence, the right to take up offers of employment, the right to look for employment,[2139] employment and associated rights, including equality in employment, unemployment and incapacity to work, the right to remain after employment, family rights, including schooling for dependants, the rights of non-AEC national dependants, entitlement to social security,[2140] public service employment, access to the professions, including the mutual recognition of qualifications, the rights of legal persons,[2141] and derogation on grounds of public policy, public security or public health, and the appropriate safeguards for persons whose rights of free movement may be restricted on such grounds.[2142]

426. Another crucial area is that of money and finance. Member States are to harmonize their monetary, financial and payment policies, including the insurance and banking sectors, with the eventual aim of establishing an African Monetary Union.[2143] Furthermore, the free movement of capital is to be achieved through the elimination of restrictions on the transfer of capital funds between Member States. The opening of bank accounts or the obtaining of loans from a financial institution in another Member State should therefore be facilitated. If the free movement of persons is to be properly secured then restrictions on the movement of capital belonging to persons resident in other Member States must be reduced. However, the very real risk exists that the liberalization of monetary controls, particularly exchange controls, could lead to the flight of money.

427. Other areas of cooperation addressed by the AEC Treaty include: agricultural development and food production;[2144] industrial development, science and technology, energy and natural resources, and the environment;[2145] transport and communications (post, telecommunications and broadcasting), including an integrated network;[2146] tourism;[2147] education, training and culture;[2148] and human resources, social affairs, health and population.[2149]

2137. The details as to how this freedom is to be guaranteed have been left to a later protocol. No express provision is made for the freedom to provide services, compare Treaty on the Functioning of the European Union (13 Dec. 2007), Art. 56 [2010] O.J. C 83 (30 Mar. 2010) 47, although the scope of the provision seems broad enough to encompass this freedom.

2138. A.M. Arnull, A.A. Dashwood, M.G. Ross & D.A. Wyatt, *European Union Law* (4th edn, London: Sweet & Maxwell, 2000), 380–494.

2139. *See also* AEC Treaty Art. 71(2)(b), (e).

2140. *See also ibid.*, Art. 72(2)(b).

2141. The application of this provision must be deemed to extend to legal persons, or the policy to be pursued would be substantially impeded.

2142. *See also* AEC Treaty Art. 72(2)(g).

2143. *Ibid.*, Art. 44.

2144. *Ibid.*, Arts 46–47.

2145. *Ibid.*, Arts 48–60.

2146. *Ibid.*, Arts 61–64.

2147. *Ibid.*, Art. 65.

2148. *Ibid.*, Arts 68–70.

2149. *Ibid.*, Arts 71–76.

428. The AEC's goals were to be effected gradually in six stages over a transitional period not exceeding forty years.[2150] While the AU seemed determined to accelerate the process of establishing the AEC[2151] progress was initially slow.[2152] It was only in 2012 that the AU adopted the First Plan of Action of the Minimum Integration Programme requesting that Member States speed up the integration process and initiate programmes to promote, *inter alia*, the free movement of persons, goods, services and capital.[2153] The AU also endorsed the Framework Road Map and Architecture for Fast Tracking the establishment of the CFTA and the Action Plan for Boosting Intra-African Trade.[2154] In its fiftieth anniversary Solemn Declaration in 2013 the AU reiterated its commitment to speed up the process of achieving the objectives of the AEC and implement promptly the CFTA.[2155] The vehicle for delivering these goals was Agenda 2063, considered more fully below.

§2. NEPAD

429. The transition to the AU presented African leaders with the opportunity to relaunch their campaign for economic development as progress on furthering the goals of the AEC Treaty stagnated. Economic cooperation is expressly listed as one of the purposes of the AU.[2156] The means chosen to this end was the New Partnership for Africa's Development (NEPAD) adopted in 2001.[2157] NEPAD is an AU 'strategic framework for pan-African socio-economic development' within the context of the AU.[2158] It seeks to eradicate poverty, promote sustainable growth and development, and integrate Africa into the global economy. One of the significant aspects of NEPAD is that it is based on an integrated approach, it accepts that a variety of factors, peace

2150. *Ibid.*, Art. 6. *See* Thompson, 750–751; Y. Omorogbe, 'Economic Integration and African National Development', Proceedings African Social International & Comparative Law', 7 (1995): 279, 284–285.

2151. Constitutive Act, preamble.

2152. Assembly, *Decision on Economic Integration*, AU Doc. Assembly/AU/Dec.178(X) (31 Jan.– 2 Feb. 2008).

2153. Assembly, *Decision on African Integration*, AU Doc. Assembly/AU/Dec.392(XVIII) (29–30 Jan. 2012).

2154. Assembly, *Decision on Boosting Intra-African Trade and Fast Tracking the Continental Free Trade Area*, AU Doc. Assembly/AU/Dec.394(XVIII) (29–30 Jan. 2012).

2155. Assembly, *Solemn Declaration on the 50th Anniversary of the OAU/AU*, AU Doc. Assembly/AU/Decl. 3 (XXI) (26 May 2013) para. C.

2156. Constitutive Act Art. 2(b).

2157. The New Partnership for Africa's Development (NEPAD) Declaration 2001, C. Heyns & M. Killander (eds), *Compendium of Key Human Rights Documents of the African Union* (5th edn, Pretoria: Pretoria University Law Press, 2013), 486. *See* R. Murray, *Human Rights in Africa: From the OAU to the African Union* (Cambridge: Cambridge University Press, 2004), 38–42.

2158. In 2010 NEPAD was integrated into the AU structure, Assembly, *Decision on the Integration of the Transformation of the New Partnership for Africa's Development (NEPAD) into the Structures and Processes of the African Union including the Establishment of the NEPAD Planning and Co-ordinating Agency (NPCA)*, AU Doc. Assembly/AU/Dec. 283(XIV) (31 Jan.–2 Feb. 2010).

and security, democracy, good governance and human rights, are essential conditions for sustainable development.[2159] It seeks to enhance the adoption of shared values and standards, policies, and good practice in these areas amongst its members. The RECs play an important role in its implementation.

430. But probably NEPAD's single most important practical feature is the peer review mechanism, the African Peer Review Mechanism (APRM), whereby a country's democratic and political governance, economic governance and management, corporate governance, and socio-economic development record is subjected to periodic scrutiny in light of a number of benchmarks.[2160] Established in 2003, this self-monitoring and voluntary system allows for weaknesses to be identified and corrected.[2161] Member States' compliance with African and international standards in the areas of political and democratic governance, economic governance and good management, corporate governance, and socio-economic development, is assessed. Crucially, any shortcomings identified by a review must be addressed by the State in question.

431. NEPAD's governing structure is based on three bodies: the AU Assembly, the NEPAD Heads of State and Government Orientation Committee (HGSOC), and the NEPAD Steering Committee. The AU Assembly is the body with ultimate responsibility; it oversees NEPAD and considers and adopts recommendations from the HGSOC Chair. The HGSOC sets policies and programmes of action. It is composed of twenty States, five permanent members (Algeria, Egypt, Nigeria, Senegal, South Africa) and fifteen others representing Africa's regions elected for a two-year period. The NEPAD Steering Committee develops the terms of reference for projects and programmes of action. It is made up of representatives nominated by the HGSOC from its members. A Sub-Committee, established in 2010, manages and supports activities promoting NEPAD. Mention must also be made of the NEPAD Planning and Co-ordinating Agency, an AU technical body. Its principal function is to facilitate and coordinate the implementation of the projects and programmes of action. To this end it co-operates actively with the UN.

432. Although NEPAD was welcomed by the UN[2162] it has nevertheless attracted some criticism, pointing to a lack of clear priorities[2163] or a lack of appreciation of the significance of human rights in realizing developmental goals.[2164] But these are surmountable problems. The one fundamental flaw that remains is that participation in the APRM is voluntary.

2159. NEPAD para. 71.

2160. Heyns & Killander, 497, 500; F. Viljoen, *International Human Rights Law in Africa* (Oxford: Oxford University Press, 2007), 211–216. Thirty-five AU Member States have joined the APRM.

2161. Although the APRM operated as an independent body, in 2014 it was integrated into the AU structure as an autonomous body, Assembly, *Decision on the Integration of the APRM into the African Union*, AU Doc. Assembly/AU/Dec. 527(XXIII) (26–27 Jun. 2014).

2162. World Summit Outcome, UN General Assembly Res. 60/1, UN Doc. A/Res/60/1, para. 68.

2163. Murray, 264.

2164. Viljoen, 216.

§3. AGENDA 2063

433. In 2015 the AU adopted Agenda 2063, a bold strategic people-driven plan for pan-African renewal of an 'integrated, prosperous and peaceful Africa' based on, *inter alia*, the structural transformation and integration of African economies through growth and sustainable socio-economic development, peace, human rights and good governance, building upon the Lagos Plan of Action, the AEC Treaty and NEPAD.[2165] It reflects deeply held desires for unity and integration, peace and improved human security, progress and development, and a meaningful voice for Africa on the global stage. Its projects, or 'aspirations', are to be secured by a series of five ten year plans over fifty years and the First Ten-Year Implementation Plan, a medium-term development plan involving Member States, RECs and the AU, has since been launched.[2166] It covers a number of areas, including sustainable economic growth, human capital development, employment creation, social protection, gender and youth development, infrastructure development, good governance, science and technology, peace and security, and culture, sports and arts. More specifically, it seeks to achieve these goals by, *inter alia*, encouraging private-public sector partnerships and greater involvement of the private sector, improving the public sector, preventing and combatting corruption, developing tax policies, increasing investment in agriculture, education, health and urban settlement, alleviating poverty and raising living standards, generating employment, providing basic social services, and sustainable natural resource management. Other goals include entrenching human rights, the rule of law and good governance, and bringing conflicts to an end. The achievement of many of these goals requires the establishment of financial institutions, such as the AIB, the Pan-African Stock Exchange and the African Central Bank, and of a regulatory framework. Among its foremost projects pertinent here are the CFTA and the African Passport and the free movement of persons. It is intended the CFTA will be launched in 2018, to be followed in later years by an African Customs Union, an African Common Market and African Monetary Union by 2023. The aim is to enhance free movement of persons by 2018.

434. The AEC Treaty, NEPAD and Agenda 2063 are ambitious projects that typify the global trends towards regional economic integration. But they additionally signify a concrete expression of the ultimate objective of economic integration.[2167] However, the future of these long-term projects face considerable hurdles. Political instability remains a major obstacle. The historical weakness and mismanagement of many African economies are obvious difficulties. In this regard, the African Charter on Democracy made a start in addressing these weaknesses by seeking to advance good and efficient economic governance. And Agenda 2063 recognizes these barriers

2165. Assembly, *Decision on the Report of the Commission on Development of the African Union Agenda 2063*, AU Doc. Assembly/AU/Dec. 565(XXIV) (30–31 Jan. 2015).

2166. African Union Commission, *Agenda 2063, The Africa We Want: First Ten-Year Implementation Plan* (2015).The Africa Progress Panel, a civil society organization, has stressed the need to secure universal access to energy across Africa, Africa Progress Panel, *Africa Progress Report 2013*, 14–19, http://www.africaprogresspanel.org (accessed 15 May 2013).

2167. *See*, e.g., Assembly, *Decision on the Progress Report on the Transformation of the African Union Commission into the African Union Authority*, AU Doc. Assembly/AU/Dec. 454(XX) (27–28 Jan. 2013) para. 3.

to progress and acknowledges that they must be confronted and overcome. NEPAD is also important as it provides a structured framework that lays the foundations for development. More importantly, African States appear to take their NEPAD commitments seriously. But Agenda 2063 is especially significant. It brings together the aims and objectives set out in the earlier instruments and sets out new goals for both the immediate and longer terms. In light of the challenges facing Africa Agenda 2063 may be overambitious and some of its goals may not be attainable in the time frame without serious political commitment. Africa is, of course, exposed to global economic forces. Although much of Africa is resource-rich in terms of much sought-after commodities, oil and gas, minerals, etc. they are subject to the vagaries of the market. The last decade has witnessed economic growth and improvement in economic opportunities, and despite the economic downturn of recent years Africa's economic outlook remains optimistic.[2168] Wealth is being distributed more equitably, although the gap between the wealthy and the poor, the majority, is still enormous. If the African continent can sustain a peaceful and stable environment then economic development is likely to follow.

2168. *ECA Economic Report on Africa 2017* http://www.uneca.org/publications/economic-report-africa-2017 (accessed 10 May 2017). The Mo Ibrahim Foundation, a civil society organization, rated Mauritius as the clear leader in its Sustainable Economic Opportunity index for 2015, with South Africa, Morocco and Botswana some way behind, *2016 Ibrahim Index of African Governance: Sustainable Economic Opportunity*, http//:moibrahimfoundation.org/en (accessed 8 Mar. 2017). Mauritius, Rwanda and Botswana were the top three rated countries in its Business Environment index.

Chapter 5. Environment

435. Africa has been particularly susceptible to environmental degradation in recent times.[2169] That Africa suffers from drought and desertification,[2170] and the spoliation of natural resources, is common knowledge. Yet the OAU had been an early convert to conservation and the need to protect the environment. In 1968, the OAU had adopted the Convention on the Conservation of Nature and Natural Resources, according to which the parties undertake to conserve, utilize and develop soil, water, flora and fauna resources.[2171] Development is also a central element of this treaty.[2172] In 2003, this Convention was superseded by the Revised African Convention on the Conservation of Nature and Natural Resources.[2173] The objectives of the Revised Convention are, *inter alia*, to enhance environmental protection, and to foster the conservation and sustainable use of natural resources.[2174] Its guiding principles are the right to a sustainable environment and the right to development and the ensuing duty on States to ensure that both these needs are met in a sustainable, fair and equitable manner.[2175] Significantly, States agree as a fundamental obligation to take all necessary measures to achieve its objectives, especially through preventive measures and the application of the precautionary principle.[2176] Other important aspects of the Revised Convention are the inclusion of procedural rights,[2177] and an acknowledgement, albeit decidedly limited, of indigenous rights.[2178] Under Article 58(1) of the AEC Treaty,

---

2169. *See* UN General Assembly Res. A/RES/S-19/2 on Progress Achieved Towards Meeting Objectives of the Earth Summit, 36 I.L.M. 1639 (1997).

2170. Note the UN Convention to Combat Desertification (15 Sept. 1994), 1954 U.N.T.S. 3, 33 I.L.M. 1328 (1994), which, *inter alia*, establishes a regional programme for Africa to fight land degradation. Africa is vulnerable to climate change, Africa Progress Panel, *Africa Progress Report 2015*, 20–21, http://www.africaprogresspanel.org (accessed 29 Apr. 2017). Many African countries have therefore been supportive of the Paris Agreement (12 Dec. 2015) which seeks to impose reductions on greenhouse gas emissions.

2171. OAU Convention on the Conservation of Nature and Natural Resources (15 Sept. 1968), 1001 U.N.T.S. 3. The Convention was wide-ranging and innovative, F. Viljoen, *International Human Rights Law in Africa* (Oxford: Oxford University Press, 2007), 289. *See* further M. van der Linde, 'A Review of the African Convention on Nature and Natural Resources', *A.H.R.L.J.* 2 (2002): 33. It should be noted that fifty-three African States have ratified the Convention on International Trade in Endangered Species of Wild Fauna and Flora and Fauna (3 Mar. 1973), 993 U.N.T.S. (CITES). Poaching remains a significant problem.

2172. OAU Convention on Nature and Natural Resources Art. 7.

2173. African Convention on the Conservation of Nature and Natural Resources (Revised) (11 Jul. 2003), https://www.au.int/en/treaties, C. Heyns & M. Killander (eds), *Compendium of Key Human Rights Documents of the African Union* (6th edn, Pretoria: Pretoria University Law Press, 2016), 98. As of March 2017, it had been ratified by thirteen States (not yet in force). *See* Viljoen, 289–90.

2174. OAU Revised Convention on Nature and Natural Resources Art. 2(1)–(2).

2175. *Ibid.*, Art. 3. The nexus between the need to protect the environment in order to achieve sustainable development is reaffirmed by the African Charter on Democracy Art. 42.

2176. On the precautionary principle *see* para. 444 n. 2205 *infra.*

2177. OAU Revised Convention on Nature and Natural Resources Art. 16.

2178. *Ibid.*, Art. 17.

Member States commit themselves to promote a healthy environment. The Grand Bay Declaration affirmed the right to a healthy environment as a human right that was infringed by environmental degradation.[2179] But the most notable development is this regard had been the inclusion in the African Charter of the environment as a human, and justiciable, right.[2180] It will be recalled that the African Commission on Human and Peoples' Rights found that Article 24 of the African Charter placed an obligation on States to take reasonable steps, *inter alia*, to prevent polluting activities and ecological degradation, and to promote conservation.[2181] Of particular interest is the tough stance adopted by the Statute on the ACJHR according to which the illegal exploitation of natural resources is classified as a crime over which the ICL Section has jurisdiction.[2182] In this light it is therefore surprising, and regrettable, that the AU Constitutive Act is silent on the issue of the environment.

436. But Africa has also been confronted with another menace, the practice of the illicit dumping of toxic and dangerous substances, with all the attendant risks that that implies for the well-being of local populations and the ecosystem, and which undeniably has adverse effects on the enjoyment of human rights.[2183] The OAU Council of Ministers therefore declared in 1988 that the dumping of nuclear and industrial wastes was 'a crime against Africa and the African people'.[2184] Growing hostility to these dangerous and often illegal practices resulted in international action regulating the movement and disposal of hazardous waste. This section focuses on the attempts of the OAU/AU to deal with the latter problem.[2185]

437. The response of the international community in seeking to police the dumping of toxic wastes was the adoption of the Basel Convention on Hazardous

---

2179. Grand Bay (Mauritius) Declaration and Plan of Action 1999, paras 2, 8(n), Heyns & Killander, 149.

2180. *See* para. 284 *supra.*

2181. *The Social and Economic Rights Action Center and the Center for Economic and Social Rights v. Nigeria*, Communication No. 155/96, 15th Activity Report 2001–2002, para. 52.

2182. Statute on the ACJHR Arts 28A(1)(13), and 28L*bis*.

2183. UN Commission on Human Rights, Adverse effects of the illicit movement and dumping of toxic and dangerous wastes on the enjoyment of human rights, Progress Report of the Special Rapporteur, UN Docs. E/CN.4/1998/10, E/CN.4/2001/55, para. 18. *See* further D. Tladi, *The quest to ban hazardous waste import into Africa: first Bamako and now Basel*, 33 C.I.L.S.A. 210, 211–12 (2000). The reasons why Africa became a dumping ground for hazardous wastes are various, *see* C.N. Eze, *The Bamako Convention on the Ban of the Import into Africa and the Control of the Transboundary Movement and Management of Hazardous Wastes within Africa: A Milestone in Environmental Protection?*, 15 R.A.D.I.C. 208, 209–210 (2007).

2184. Resolution 1153 (XLVIII) of 25 May 1988, Art. 1, 28 I.L.M. 567 (1989). The UN General Assembly also condemned the dumping of such wastes in Africa in Res. 43/75 T. Moreover, in the Vienna Declaration and Programme of Action 1993 pt. I, para. 11, 32 I.L.M. 1661 (1993), the international community recognized 'that the illicit dumping of toxic and dangerous substances and wastes potentially constitutes a serious threat to the human rights to life and health of everyone'. Accordingly, it called upon all States to adopt and implement rigorously existing treaties relating to the dumping of toxic and hazardous wastes and to cooperate in the prevention of illicit dumping.

2185. In the discussion of this section the author has relied considerably on the Progress Reports of the UN Special Rapporteur on Adverse effects of the illicit movement and dumping of toxic and dangerous wastes on the enjoyment of human rights.

Wastes in 1989.[2186] The Basel Convention was a compromise between advocates of a complete ban on transboundary movements of wastes, mainly developing countries, which, often lacking the means to dispose properly of such wastes, argued that regulation was no guarantee against pollution, and those that wanted to establish a regulatory framework for the international transfer and treatment of wastes, ultimately opting for a partial ban on the transboundary movement of wastes.[2187] One commentator has described the Basel Convention as based on the key premise that hazardous waste can be exported from industrialized to developing countries subject to regulation and control.[2188] As such the Basel Convention was a disappointment for the former which considered it inadequate as institutionalizing dangerous practices and hence prompted further action.

438. The Basel Convention required that States Parties prevent the import of hazardous and other wastes where they had reason to believe that such wastes would not be managed in an environmentally sound manner.[2189] However, there was recognition that the transboundary movement of hazardous wastes to developing countries might be problematic since many of these States lacked the means to deal adequately with them. As a result, the decision was taken in 1995 to amend the Basel Convention, as from the end of 1997, in order to prohibit the export of hazardous wastes, even for recycling purposes, from Organization for Economic Cooperation and Development (OECD) member countries to non-member countries, thereby specifically addressing the criticisms of developing countries.[2190] This development came too late for the OAU, however, which, considering the Basel Convention flawed with respect to developing countries, in particular the failure to agree a total ban on the export of hazardous and other wastes to Africa, proceeded with its own initiative to combat the transboundary movement of hazardous wastes.

2186. Basel Convention on the Control of Transboundary Movements of Hazardous Wastes and their Disposal (22 Mar. 1989), 28 I.L.M. 657 (1989). The Basel Convention entered into force on 5 May 1992 and has been ratified by twenty-five African States. For analysis of the Basel Convention, *see* P.W. Birnie & A.E. Boyle, *International Law and the Environment* (Oxford: Clarendon Press, 1992), 332–343; M. Bothé, 'International Regulation of Transboundary Movement of Hazardous Waste', *German Y.B.I.L.* 33 (1990): 422; K. Kummer, 'The International Regulation of Transboundary Traffic in Hazardous Wastes: The 1989 Basel Convention', *I.C.L.Q.* 41 (1992): 530. International efforts to control hazardous chemicals led to the adoption of the Stockholm Convention on Persistent Organic Pollutants (22 May 2001), 2256 U.N.T.S. 119, calling for the reduction and elimination in the release of these chemicals.

2187. According to Basel Convention Art. 4(1) any State has the right to ban the entry or disposal of foreign hazardous wastes and other wastes in its territory, and no State party may permit hazardous wastes to be exported to a party that has prohibited their import. *See* further Birnie & Boyle, 332–333; Tladi, 213–14.

2188. Viljoen, 290.

2189. Basel Convention Art. 4(2)(g).

2190. Third Meeting of the Conference of the Parties to the Basel Convention, Decision 111/1, 18–22 Sept. 1995, UNEP/CHW.3/35. However, States that have not ratified the amendment can continue to export hazardous substances. It seems developing countries believed recycling could provide a loophole for illegal imports, Tladi, 220.

439. The Bamako Convention on Hazardous Wastes was adopted by the OAU in 1991[2191] as the regional complement to the Basel Convention which allows for the establishment of regional agreements of equal or added rigour.[2192] The basic characteristics of the regulatory system set in place by the Bamako Convention may be said to be 'prohibition and control'.[2193]

440. The Bamako Convention has adopted a broad definition of waste.[2194] Wastes are considered hazardous according to Article 2(1) when they are: (a) listed in the Convention's annexes; (b) defined as hazardous by the domestic legislation of a State of export, import or transit; and (c) banned, cancelled or refused registration by a State, or voluntarily withdrawn from registration in the country of manufacture for human health or environmental reasons. Significantly radioactive wastes are included, by virtue of Article 2(2), in the scope of the Bamako Convention.[2195]

441. A distinction is drawn between waste generated outside of Africa and waste generated within Africa. With regard to the former, Parties to the Bamako Convention, 'aware of the risk of damage to human health and the environment caused by transboundary movements of hazardous wastes'[2196] and 'further recognizing the sovereignty of States to ban the importation into, and the transit through, their territory, of hazardous wastes and substances for human health and environmental reasons',[2197] hence introduce, first, a hazardous waste import ban; therefore, in accordance with Article 4(1), 'All Parties shall take appropriate legal, administrative and other measures within the area under their jurisdiction to prohibit the import of all hazardous wastes, for any reason, into Africa from non-Contracting Parties. Such import shall be deemed

2191. Bamako Convention on the Ban of the Import of Hazardous Wastes into Africa and on the Control of their Transboundary Movements within Africa (30 Jan. 1991), https://www.au.int/en/treaties, 30 I.L.M. 773 (1991), entered into force on 22 Apr. 1998. As of June 2017, it had been ratified by twenty-seven States. For analysis, *see* Eze; Tladi& I. Cheyne, 'Africa and the International Trade in Hazardous Wastes', *R.A.D.I.C.* 6 (1994): 493; H.S. Kaminsky, 'Assessment of the Bamako Convention on the Ban of Import into Africa and the Control of Transboundary Movement and Management of Hazardous Wastes Within Africa', *The Georgetown International Environmental Law Review* 5 (1992): 77; F. Ouguergouz, 'The Bamako Convention on Hazardous Waste: A New Step in the Development of the African International Environmental Law', *A.Y.B.I.L.* 1 (1994): 19.

2192. *See* Basel Convention Art. 11(1). The view has been expressed that such a regional initiative is a more pragmatic way of protecting the interests of developing countries than a total international ban, Birnie & Boyle, 341–342.

2193. Ouguergouz, 200. Its features are described as being based upon prior informed consent, the prevention of illegal trade, a duty of re-import and environmentally sound treatment of waste, Birnie & Boyle, 334.

2194. Cheyne, 497–499; Eze, 217, 226; Tladi, 217–18.

2195. Whereas the Basel Convention excludes radioactive wastes, *see* Art. 4(3). The Basel Convention has been described as being essentially limited to household and hazardous wastes, Birnie & Boyle, 335. It has been suggested that the reason for the omission is because radioactive wastes are already subject to control by the International Atomic Energy Agency, Kummer, 543–544.

2196. Bamako Convention preambular para. 3.

2197. *Ibid.*, preambular para. 6.

illegal and a criminal act.'[2198] And second, a ban on dumping of hazardous wastes at sea, internal waters and waterways; accordingly, under Article 4(2)(a), States parties shall 'adopt legal, administrative and other appropriate measures to control all carriers from non-Parties, and prohibit the dumping at sea of hazardous wastes'.[2199] The ban on hazardous wastes meets the basic demands of the African States and is reinforced by Article 59 of the AEC Treaty. And in its relations with the EU-African States have ensured that their concerns over the dumping of such wastes is taken into consideration.[2200]

442. The transboundary movement of wastes produced in Africa, or intra-African movement, is permitted but the Bamako Convention emphasizes the environmentally sound and efficient management of hazardous wastes, and thus prohibits exports to States where this cannot be guaranteed.[2201] It requires that each Party, *inter alia*, 'impose strict, unlimited liability as well as joint and several liability on hazardous wastes generators',[2202] seemingly as a means of encouraging the appropriate disposal of hazardous wastes.[2203] The onus is on the generator because s/he is assumed to exercise effective responsibility.[2204]

2198. According to the Basel Convention Art. 4(3), 'illegal traffic in hazardous wastes or other wastes is criminal'. *See* also the European Convention on the Protection of the Environment Through Criminal Law (4 Nov. 1998), C.E.T.S. No. 172, 38 I.L.M. 259 (1999). According to the Statute on the ACJHR Arts 28A(1)(12), and 28L, trafficking in hazardous wastes is a crime over which the ICL Section has jurisdiction.

2199. It should be observed that by virtue of Bamako Convention Art. 4(4)(c) general rights of navigation under international law through maritime zones subject to national jurisdiction remain unimpaired, *see* further, Birnie & Boyle, 336–337.

2200. Cotonou Agreement (23 Jun. 2000) O.J. L 317, 15 Dec. 2000, Declarations IX-X.

2201. Bamako Convention Art. 4(3)(i), (j), (k), (n), (o), (t); Tladi, 221.

2202. Bamako Convention Art. 4(3)(b). *See* further *ibid.*, Art. 12 which calls for a protocol to establish the appropriate rules and procedures in the field of liabilities and compensation. Again, the Bamako Convention adopts a stricter regime than that of the Basel Convention since the latter, under Art. 12, merely requires Parties to cooperate 'with a view to adopting, as soon as practicable, a protocol setting out appropriate rules and procedures in the field of liability and compensation', *see* Birnie & Boyle, 340–341; Kummer, 554–555. Note that in 1993 the Council of Europe adopted a Convention on Civil Liability for Damage Resulting from Activities Dangerous to the Environment (21 Jun. 1993) E.T.S. No. 150, 32 I.L.M. 1228 (1993). *See* generally S.D. Murphy, 'Prospective Liability Regimes for the Transboundary Movement of Hazardous Wastes', *A.J.I.L.* 88 (1994): 24.

2203. C.R.H. Shearer, *Comparative analysis of the Basel and Bamako Conventions on hazardous waste*, 23 *Environmental Law* 141, 157–158 (1993).

2204. Kaminsky, 87.

443. The Bamako Convention additionally requires Parties to 'strive to adopt and implement the preventive, precautionary approach to pollution problems'.[2205] It should be noted that the Parties are also required to apply clean production methods,[2206] that is, production or industrial systems which avoid or eliminate the generation of hazardous wastes.[2207]

444. Article 6 establishes a system of prior informed consent and notification procedures for proposed transboundary movement of hazardous wastes.[2208] The State of export may not allow the transboundary movement until it has received written consent by the State of import and written confirmation of the existence of a contract between the exporter and the disposer specifying environmentally sound management of the wastes in question.

2205. Bamako Convention Art. 4(3)(f). The Bamako Convention appears to have pioneered the inclusion of the precautionary principle in the operative section of the treaty, Kaminsky, 84. *See* further, Rio Declaration on Environment and Development (Principle 15). The ICJ seems to regard the precautionary principle as having persuasive authority as an emergent norm of international law, *Gabcíkovo-Nagymaros Project Case (Hungary v. Slovakia)* I.C.J. Reports 1997, 7, paras 112–113. And *see Pulp Mills on the River Uruguay (Argentina v. Uruguay)* I.C.J. Reports 2010, 14, para. 164. *See* also the Dissenting Opinions of Judges Weeramantry and Koroma in *Request for an Examination of the Situation in Accordance with paragraph 63 of the Court's Judgment in the 1974 Nuclear Tests Case* I.C.J. Reports 1995, 288, 342–344, and 368 respectively. However, it is instructive to note that the Bamako Convention specifies the 'precautionary approach' and a distinction has been drawn between the precautionary approach and the precautionary principle, the former seeming to possess the advantage of flexibility, *see* the Separate Opinions of Judges Laing and Treves in *Southern Bluefin Tuna Cases* (*New Zealand v. Japan*; *Australia v. Japan*) 38 I.L.M. 1624, 1641–1642, 1645 (1999), respectively. The 'precautionary approach' may now form part of customary law, *Responsibilities and Obligations of States Sponsoring Persons and Entities with respect to Activities in the Area, Advisory Opinion*, I.T.L.O.S. Reports 2011, 10, para. 135.

2206. Bamako Convention Art. 4(3)(f)–(g). *See also ibid.*, Art. 10. However, the attainability of such ambitious goals for many African States in the short term was questioned, Shearer, 176–177.

2207. Bamako Convention Art. 1(5).

2208. Kaminsky, 79–81; Shearer, 167–169. *See also* Bamako Convention Art. 4(3)(u). This is also the case with the Basel Convention, *see* Birnie & Boyle, 336–338; Kummer, 547–551. In addition, Bamako Convention Art. 13(1) provides that the Parties 'shall ensure that in the case of an accident occurring during the transboundary movement of hazardous wastes or their disposal which is likely to present risks to human health and the environment in other States those States are immediately informed'. Note the Rotterdam Convention on the Prior Informed Consent Procedure for Certain Hazardous Chemicals and Pesticides in International Trade (10 Sept. 1998), 2244 U.N.T.S. 337, 38 I.L.M. 1 (1999). By virtue of Bamako Convention Art. 7, Art. 6(2)–(4) applies *mutatis mutandis* to the movement of waste from a Party through a State which is not a Party. It now seems that customary international law requires comprehensive environmental impact assessments to be undertaken with a view to identifying potential threats to the environment and public health, *Gabcíkovo-Nagymaros Project Case* I.C.J. Reports 1997, 7, para. 112; *Pulp Mills on the River Uruguay*, I.C.J. Reports 2010, 14, para. 204; *Responsibilities and Obligations of States Sponsoring Persons and Entities with respect to Activities in the Area*, I.T.L.O.S. Reports 2011, paras 147–148. *See also* the Convention on Environmental Impact Assessment in a Transboundary Context (25 Feb. 1991) 1989 U.N.T.S. 310, 30 I.L.M. 800 (1991). The Libréville Declaration on Health and Environment in Africa, Libréville (29 Aug. 2008) calls for the setting up of systematic health and environmental risk assessments, para. 9.

445. A duty to re-import is imposed by Article 8. Where a legitimate transboundary movement of hazardous wastes cannot be completed in accordance with the terms of the contract, the State of export must ensure the re-import of the wastes by the exporter, if alternative arrangements cannot be made for their disposal in an environmentally sound manner within ninety days from the time the exporting State and the Secretariat have been informed by the importing State. The State of export and any State of transit must not oppose, hinder or prevent the return of the wastes to the State of export.[2209]

446. Article 9 addresses the issue of illegal waste. Hence, any transboundary movement of hazardous wastes:

> (a) if carried out without notification, pursuant to the provisions of this Convention, to all States concerned; or (b) if carried out without the consent, pursuant to the provisions of this Convention, of a State concerned; or (c) if consent is obtained from States concerned through falsification, misrepresentation or fraud; or (d) if it does not conform in a material way with the documents; or (e) if it results in deliberate disposal of hazardous wastes in contravention of this Convention and of general principles of international law is deemed to be illegal.[2210]

447. In addition to the imposition of liability under Article 4(3)(b), Article 9(2) requires States parties to legislate in order to provide for criminal sanctions, which must be sufficiently severe to punish and deter, to be imposed on illegal traffickers.[2211] If a movement is held to be illegal traffic as a result of conduct on the part of the exporter or generator the State of export must ensure that the waste is taken back by the exporter or generator or State of export within thirty days.[2212] The return of the wastes to the State of export shall not be opposed, hindered or otherwise prevented.[2213] Furthermore, if a movement is deemed to be illegal traffic as a result of conduct by the importer or disposer, the State of import must ensure that the wastes are returned to the exporter by the importer.[2214] It is not clear how such States are to be compelled to act in such manner but recourse could be had to the settlement of disputes procedure under the Convention.[2215]

448. The Bamako Convention's regulatory system would be ineffective in the absence of control and monitoring mechanisms. Particularly worthy of mention in this context is the Secretariat which is entrusted with a number of administrative functions.[2216] These include acting as a repository of information and assisting in the identification of cases of illegal traffic. The Secretariat also has the responsibility of verifying

2209. This provision is virtually identical to Art. 8 of the Basel Convention, *see* Kummer, 553–554, who asserts that illegal traffic is excluded from the scope of the provision. Moreover, she draws attention to the fact that no definition of non-completion of the contract is given.

2210. Compare Basel Convention Art. 9(1).

2211. *See also* Bamako Convention Art. 4(4)(a)–(b). Compare Basel Convention Art. 9(5), under which parties are required to 'introduce appropriate national/domestic legislation to prevent and punish illegal traffic'.

2212. Bamako Convention Art. 9(3).

2213. *Ibid.*

2214. *Ibid.*, Art. 9(4).

2215. *Ibid.*, Art. 20.

2216. *Ibid.*, Art. 16. *See* Eze, 221–222.

allegations made by a State Party that another State Party has violated its obligations under the Convention.[2217] For their part, States Parties must establish competent authorities.[2218]

449. It appears safe to conclude that the Bamako Convention is significantly stricter than the Basel Convention in many respects.[2219] Especially noteworthy are the wider scope of the Bamako Convention, the total ban on the importation of waste from outside Africa, and the adoption of the precautionary principle and the use of clean production methods. Given Africa's background as a dumping ground for toxic wastes and the lack of expertise on the part of African States it is understandable why the OAU should have favoured a restrictive approach.[2220] However, such inflexibility has been questioned. The inclusion of radioactive waste may prove problematic with commitments under other treaties.[2221] The total ban on imported waste may hamper the development of African industry.[2222] And the adoption of clean production methods may simply be beyond the capabilities of most African States at present.[2223] Nevertheless, the OAU set a standard for the international community to equal. Despite the acute nature of the problem and the profound feelings of the OAU/AU on the subject the Bamako Convention could prove too complex and too expensive for the majority of African States. The Libréville Declaration acknowledged in 2008 that it was not being implemented.

450. Nonetheless, much still remains to be done since there appears to be little sign of a reduction in the movement of hazardous wastes from industrialized countries to the Third World. Traffickers seem to be able to adapt to the changing international situation. One example is the dumping of toxic wastes in maritime space around Africa.[2224] However, the ban on hazardous wastes will not prove effective unless accompanied by practical measures for the detection of illicit operations. International cooperation, including the provision of financial and technical aid to Africa, seems vital.[2225] African States must be provided with the means of cleaning and remedying existing contamination. The technical capacities of developing countries to detect and prevent illicit traffic must therefore be strengthened. Particularly significant in this regard has been the First Continental Conference for Africa on the Environmentally Sound Management of Unwanted Stocks of Hazardous Wastes and their Prevention, convened by the secretariat of the Basel Convention in Rabat in January 2001. An action programme for Africa had been adopted, *inter alia*, to eliminate existing pesticides

---

2217. Bamako Convention Art. 19.

2218. *Ibid.*, Art. 5.

2219. Eze, 225–229; Ouguergouz, 210–212.

2220. Cheyne, 499–503.

2221. Shearer, 175.

2222. *Ibid.*

2223. *Ibid.*, 176.

2224. Assembly, *Decision on the Report of the Peace and Security Council on its Activities and the State of Peace and Security in Africa* (1–3 Jul. 2009) Thirteenth Ordinary Session, Assembly/AU/Dec. 252(XIII) para. 18.

2225. Some aid is being realized, UN Doc. E/CN.4/1999/SR.21, para. 63. Note the First Continental Conference for Africa on the Environmentally Sound management of Unwanted Stocks of Hazardous wastes and their Prevention, convened by the Secretariat of the Basel Convention in Rabat, 8–12 Jan. 2001.

and the possibilities for international assistance and financing had been examined. The Libréville Declaration, which is not limited to the problem of hazardous waste, recognizes that strategies and policies must be put in place to develop, implement and monitor strategies and policies aimed at health and environmental security. Finally, national legislation to reduce and punish illegal transboundary movements of waste must be enacted and enforced.[2226]

2226. UN Commission on Human Rights, Adverse effects of the illicit movement and dumping of toxic and dangerous wastes on the enjoyment of human rights, Progress Report of the Special Rapporteur, UN Doc. E/CN.4/1998/10.

Chapter 6. Other Areas of Activity

§1. Mercenarism

451. Mercenary activity has been a troubling element of post-colonial Africa. The involvement of mercenaries has been a feature of many of the armed conflicts that have affected Africa. Over many years mercenaries have threatened the sovereignty, independence, territorial integrity and security of many African States, undermining the right of self-determination, destabilizing governments and generally compromising peace and good order.[2227] More recently mercenaries have been departing from traditional mercenary activities, that is, fighting for financial gain in an armed conflict alien to their own nationality, and have diversified into new areas, implicated in the illegal exploitation and trafficking of natural resources such as diamonds and other precious stones in Angola and other conflict zones,[2228] and the provision of private security services, offering military and security services on the international market to governments and non-state actors.[2229]

452. The menace posed by mercenarism led the OAU to adopt in 1977 the Convention for the Elimination of Mercenarism in Africa.[2230] A number of cumulative criteria have to be fulfilled in order to meet the definition of a mercenary, which may be summarized as a private individual who takes a direct part in an armed conflict

2227. UN Commission on Human Rights, The use of mercenaries as a means of violating human rights and impeding the exercise of the right of peoples to self-determination, Report of the Special Rapporteur, UN Doc. E/CN.4/2000/20, 8–15. *See* F. Viljoen, *International Human Rights Law in Africa* (Oxford: Oxford University Press, 2007), 296, 298.

2228. UN Commission on Human Rights, The use of mercenaries as a means of violating human rights and impeding the exercise of the right of peoples to self-determination, Report of the Special Rapporteur 11–15, UN Doc. E/CN.4/2004/15.

2229. *Ibid.,* According to Ms Shameem, Special Rapporteur on the use of mercenaries as a means of violating human rights and impeding the exercise of the right of peoples to self-determination, international private military companies have rendered the existing international legal framework 'totally ineffective', UN Doc. E/CN.4/2005/SR.12, para. 60. *See* J.C. Zarate, 'The Emergence of a New Dog of War: Private International Security Companies, International Law, and the New World Disorder', *Stanford J.I.L.* 34 (1998): 75. Nonetheless, the UN General Assembly has condemned such mercenary-related activities, UN General Assembly Res. 67/159 (2013).

2230. Convention for the Elimination of Mercenarism in Africa (3 Jul. 1977) https://www.au.int/en/treaties, G.J. Naldi, *Documents of the Organization of African Unity* (London & New York: Mansell, 1992), 58. In force 22 Apr. 1985. As of March 2017, it had been ratified by thirty-two States. The commitment to fight mercenarism is reinforced by the Protocol to the OAU Convention on the Prevention and Combating of Terrorism Art. 3(1)(e), (8 Jul. 2004), https://www.au.int/en/treaties; C. Heyns & M. Killander (eds), *Compendium of Key Human Rights Documents of the African Union* (6th edn, Pretoria: Pretoria University Law Press, 2016), 96. In force 2 Jul. 2014. As of March 2017, it had been ratified by seventeen States.

affecting a country of which he is neither a national nor a resident for private gain.[2231] It proceeds to include in its definition of mercenarism individuals, groups or associations with the aim of opposing by armed violence a process of self-determination, and the stability or the territorial integrity of another State.[2232] These definitions suffer from a number of limitations. First, meeting the criteria is extremely difficult, although it must be noted that this is a problem common to other international instruments.[2233] Second, in some crucial respects it is not as extensive as that provided in Article 1(2) of the International Convention against the Recruitment, Use, Financing and Training of Mercenaries 1989. Thus, the International Convention expands the definition of a mercenary to include those having the aim of overthrowing a government or undermining in any way the constitutional order of a State.[2234] Unlike the International Convention, the OAU Convention does not address the use of mercenaries in internal conflicts.[2235] However, the use of the phrase 'armed violence' is of interest because it would seem to extend the application of the concept of mercenarism to situations falling short of armed conflict.[2236] This deficiency was acknowledged by the OAU which in its Declaration on Unconstitutional Changes of Government adopted in 2000 condemned

2231. OAU Convention on Mercenarism Art. 1(1). This definition corresponds in all material respects to those in the Additional Protocol I Relating to the Protection of Victims of International Armed Conflicts Art. 47(2), (8 June 1977), 1125 U.N.T.S. 3, and the International Convention against the Recruitment, Use, Financing and Training of Mercenaries Art. 1(1), (4 Dec. 1989), 2163 U.N.T.S. 75. The Convention entered into force on 20 Oct. 2001.

2232. OAU Convention on Mercenarism Art. 1(2). During the drafting of the International Convention Western States would not accept opposition to the exercise of the right of peoples to self-determination as coming within the definition of mercenary activity, UN Commission on Human Rights, Report of the Meeting of Experts on the Traditional and New Forms of Mercenary Activities as a Means of Violating Human Rights and Impeding the Exercise of the Right of Peoples to Self-Determination para. 36, UN Doc. E/CN.4/2001/18. However, by way of compromise the International Convention Art. 5(2) prohibits, *inter alia*, the use of mercenaries for the purpose of impeding the exercise of the right of self-determination. It appears that 'mercenarism' is a broader concept than that of 'mercenary' which includes the responsibilities of States and non-State actors involved in mercenary activities, para. 19.

2233. UN Commission on Human Rights, The use of mercenaries as a means of violating human rights and impeding the exercise of the right of peoples to self-determination, Report of the Special Rapporteur 22–24, UN Doc. E/CN.4/2000/20; UN Commission on Human Rights, Report of the Meeting of Experts on the Traditional and New Forms of Mercenary Activities as a Means of Violating Human Rights and Impeding the Exercise of the Right of Peoples to Self-Determination 6–7, UN Doc. E/CN.4/2001/18.

2234. International Convention Art. 1(2)(a)(i)(ii).

2235. UN Commission on Human Rights, Report of the Meeting of Experts on the Traditional and New Forms of Mercenary Activities as a Means of Violating Human Rights and Impeding the Exercise of the Right of Peoples to Self-Determination para. 45, UN Doc. E/CN.4/2001/18.

2236. Compare International Convention Art. 1(2)(a) which includes in its definition of mercenary those who are specifically recruited to participate in concerted acts of violence.

the use of mercenaries to overthrow democratic governments.[2237] The reference to individuals, groups or associations is also potentially significant because it is capable of extending the scope of the OAU Convention to contemporary forms of mercenary activities, such as private security services.[2238]

453. Under the terms of the OAU Convention mercenarism, whether committed by individuals or sponsored by a State, is condemned as an international crime.[2239] Indeed, under the AU Non-Aggression and Common Defence Pact 2005 the sending by, or on behalf of a Member State or the provision of mercenaries, to carry out grave hostile acts against a Member State, can amount to aggression.[2240] Mercenarism is punishable by the severest penalties under domestic law, including capital punishment.[2241] Mercenaries are denied the status of combatants and are not entitled to prisoner-of-war

---

2237. In C. Heyns & M. Killander (eds), *Compendium of Key Human Rights Documents of the African Union* (5th edn, Pretoria: Pretoria University Law Press, 2013), 159. *See also* African Charter on Democracy, Elections and Governance, Art. 23(2) (30 Jan. 2007), https://www.au.int/en/treaties, Heyns & Killander, Compendium of Key Human Rights Documents 2016, 125(African Charter on Democracy). In force 15 Feb. 2012. By June 2017 the African Charter on Democracy had been ratified by thirty States.

2238. UN Commission on Human Rights, Report of the Meeting of Experts on the Traditional and New Forms of Mercenary Activities as a Means of Violating Human Rights and Impeding the Exercise of the Right of Peoples to Self-Determination para. 43, UN Doc. E/CN.4/2001/18. The adoption of an additional protocol to regulate the activities of private security services has been mooted, para. 46. It should be observed that the definition of the mercenary as given in the International Convention has been criticized as flawed for failing to take adequate account of the current manifestations of mercenary activities, UN Commission on Human Rights, The use of mercenaries as a means of violating human rights and impeding the exercise of the right of peoples to self-determination, Report of the Special Rapporteur 14–21, UN Doc. E/CN.4/2001/19. The Special Rapporteur has proposed a new comprehensive legal definition, UN Commission on Human Rights, The use of mercenaries as a means of violating human rights and impeding the exercise of the right of peoples to self-determination, Report of the Special Rapporteur paras 37–47, UN Doc. E/CN.4/2004/15. Some of the proposals which are significant include those that mercenary activity must be considered a crime in and of itself and be internationally prosecutable, that States that sponsor mercenary activities should be held accountable, that the concept of the mercenary apply to both international and internal armed conflicts, and that the definition of a mercenary include private companies offering consultancy and security services.

2239. OAU Convention on Mercenarism Art. 1(3). Under Art. 2 thereof assuming command over or giving orders to mercenaries constitutes an aggravating circumstance. According to the International Convention Arts 2 and 3 mercenarism and being a mercenary are offences for the purposes of the Convention. It is not clear whether mercenarism is prohibited by customary international law, J.P. Grant & J.C. Barker, *Parry & Grant Encyclopaedic Dictionary of International Law* (3rd edn, New York: Oxford University Press, 2009), 375, but *see Military and Paramilitary Activities In and Against Nicaragua (Nicaragua v. United States of America)* I.C.J. Reports 1986, 14, 103.

2240. African Union Non-Aggression and Common Defence Pact Art. 1(c)viii (31 Jan. 2005), https://www.au.int/en/treaties, Heyns & Killander, Compendium of Key Human Rights 2016, 111.

2241. OAU Convention on Mercenarism Art. 7.

status.[2242] State parties commit themselves to eradicate mercenarism; they therefore undertake, *inter alia*, to prohibit on their territory any activities promoting mercenarism or using mercenaries against any OAU/AU Member State or African people engaged in a liberation struggle; to prohibit the recruitment, training, financing, and equipping of mercenaries; to prevent their nationals or foreigners on their territory from engaging in mercenarism; and to prevent the entry and passage through their territory of mercenaries or their equipment.[2243] State parties are obliged to establish jurisdiction in order to prosecute or extradite offenders found on their territory (the principle *aut dedere aut judicare*),[2244] and must also provide all necessary assistance to other States in matters of investigation.[2245] These obligations are reinforced by the undertaking under the AU Non-Aggression and Common Defence Pact State Parties to arrest and prosecute mercenaries.[2246]

454. Given the difficulties that Africa faced with regard to mercenary activities, the OAU took the initiative to confront this problem through the adoption of a regional convention, anticipating action by the international community. Its approach to the problem may be said to be largely political rather than legal, which may be understandable against the background of the struggle against colonial domination, racist regimes and asserting political independence. However, this emphasis on external threats undermines the effectiveness of the OAU Convention and, unlike the International Convention, narrows its scope to the extraterritorial, but not internal, deployment of mercenaries.[2247] It has therefore been suggested that the OAU Convention be amended so as extend its field of application to internal conflicts.[2248] However, it needs to be borne in mind that AU Member States have a right to request intervention from the AU to restore peace

2242. OAU Convention on Mercenarism Art. 3. *See also* of Additional Protocol I Art. 47(1). However, this is not to say that a mercenary was wholly unprotected by international humanitarian law, *see* UN Commission on Human Rights, Report of the Meeting of Experts on the Traditional and New Forms of Mercenary Activities as a Means of Violating Human Rights and Impeding the Exercise of the Right of Peoples to Self-Determination 5–6, UN Doc. E/CN.4/2001/18. Furthermore, according to the International Convention Art. 16(b) the 'law of armed conflict and international humanitarian law, including the provisions relating to the status of combatant or of prisoner of war' shall apply. It should additionally be observed that mercenaries are entitled to judicial guarantees, *see* OAU Convention OAU on Mercenarism Art. 11, Additional Protocol I Art. 75, and the International Convention Arts 10(3)–11.

2243. OAU Convention on Mercenarism Art. 6. *See also* AU Non-Aggression and Common Defence Pact Art. 5(c) under which States Parties shall prohibit the use of their territory for the stationing, withdrawal or incursions of mercenaries. Compare International Convention Arts 5–6.

2244. OAU Convention on Mercenarism Arts 8–9. Compare International Convention Arts 10(1), 11–12. In 2004 Zimbabwe broke up an alleged conspiracy by mercenaries to carry out a coup d'état in Equatorial Guinea and extradited one of the alleged main conspirators to Equatorial Guinea para. 59, UN Doc. E/CN.4/2005/SR.12. In 2008, this person was given a sentence of over thirty years' imprisonment by a court in Equatorial Guinea. *See also Kaunda v. President of the Republic of South Africa* 2005 (4) SA 235 (CC). *See* further Viljoen, 298.

2245. OAU Convention on Mercenarism Art. 10. Compare International Convention Art. 13(1).

2246. AU Non-Aggression and Common Defence Pact Art. 6(b).

2247. UN Commission on Human Rights, Report of the Meeting of Experts on the Traditional and New Forms of Mercenary Activities as a Means of Violating Human Rights and Impeding the Exercise of the Right of Peoples to Self-Determination, para. 45, UN Doc. E/CN.4/2001/18.

2248. *Ibid.*, para. 46.

and security which could be invoked to deal with a threat from mercenaries.[2249] The AU could additionally take the initiative where a Member State faces an existential threat from mercenaries.[2250] Contemporary manifestations of mercenary-related activities pose a current threat to Africa and while the OAU Convention may be applicable to such activities again it has been suggested that dedicated legislation may be a preferable means of addressing the phenomenon.[2251] However, acting on such suggestions may be unnecessary as the Protocol on Amendments to the Protocol on the Statute of the ACJHR is adopted as the ICL Section's jurisdiction *ratione materiae* extends to mercenarism[2252] which is classified as a crime thereunder.[2253]

§2. Corruption

455. It is a sad fact that bribery and corruption are serious problems in parts of Africa,[2254] notwithstanding the fact that in Commonwealth Africa stringent criminal legislation has been adopted to curb these insidious practices.[2255] Their malign influence distorts socio-economic development and undermines democracy, human rights and the rule of law. Corruption also puts at risk foreign aid and economic emancipation. The AU has therefore recognized the threat posed by corruption[2256] to Africa's attempts at reform and democratization, and the promotion of good governance has thus risen

2249. Constitutive Act of the African Union Art. 4(j) (26 May 2001), 2158 U.N.T.S. 3; Protocol Relating to the Establishment of the Peace and Security Council of the African Union Art. 4(k) (9 Jul. 2002), https://www.au.int/en/treaties, Heyns & Killander, Compendium of Key Human Rights 2016, 17 (PSC Protocol).

2250. PSC Protocol Art. 7(1)(o).

2251. UN Commission on Human Rights, Report of the Meeting of Experts on the Traditional and New Forms of Mercenary Activities as a Means of Violating Human Rights and Impeding the Exercise of the Right of Peoples to Self-Determination, *ibid.*

2252. Statute on the ACJHR Art. 28H.

2253. *Ibid.*, Art. 28(1)A(7).

2254. It would not be an exaggeration to classify some regimes as kleptocracies. According to Transparency International, a civil society organization, Somalia is listed as the most corrupt country in the world in 2016. Other African countries that are listed as highly corrupt are South Sudan, Sudan, Libya, Guinea-Bissau, Eritrea and Angola, but many others are rated extremely poorly. Botswana, Cape Verde and Mauritius remain the top three cleanest African States, with Rwanda and Namibia close behind. *See Corruptions Perceptions Index* 2016, http://www.transparency.org.

2255. *See* S. Coldham, 'Legal Responses to State Corruption in Commonwealth Africa', *J.A.L.* 39 (1995): 115. The Constitutional Court of South Africa has held that the Constitution imposes an obligation on the State to establish and maintain an independent body to combat corruption and organized crime, *Glenister v. President of the Republic of South Africa & Others* 2011 (3) SA 347 (CC).

2256. Grand Bay (Mauritius) Declaration and Plan of Action 1999 para. 8(g), Heyns & Killander, Compendium of Key Human Rights 2016, 149. NEPAD recognizes the imperative need to combat corruption, para. 83, Heyns & Killander, Compendium of Key Human Rights 2013, 486.

to the top of the political agenda.[2257] To that end the AU adopted in 2003 a Convention on Preventing and Combating Corruption.[2258]

456. The AU Convention provides a framework to address the menace of corruption; it seeks to assist State Parties to put in place or strengthen laws and mechanisms to deal with corruption and related offences and to foster transparency and accountability in public affairs, and thereby promote socio-economic development.[2259] Because of the transnational dimension of the problem cross-border cooperation forms an essential element of the AU Convention. It encourages States Parties to harmonize national laws and policies.[2260] State Parties therefore condemn and reject corruption and related offences and commit themselves to, *inter alia*, human rights, transparency, the rule of law and good governance.[2261] The AU Convention proceeds on the basis of a series of preventive and punitive measures. Corruption is defined as 'the acts and practices including related offences' proscribed therein.[2262] However, 'proceeds of corruption' describe 'assets of any kind corporeal or incorporeal, movable or immovable, tangible or intangible and any document or legal instrument evidencing title to or interests in such assets acquired as a result of an act of corruption'.[2263] Whereas 'benefit' refers to 'gifts, favour, promise or advantage'.[2264] In terms of its scope, the AU Convention applies to the following acts of corruption: direct or indirect solicitation or acceptance by a public official[2265] (passive bribery) of any item with monetary value,

---

2257. Grand Bay Declaration para. 3; Constitutive Act para. 3(g); NEPAD paras 7–15; African Charter on Democracy Arts 2(6), 12(1), 32 and 33. *See also* 50th Anniversary Solemn Declaration para. E (iii), Assembly, Twenty-First Ordinary Session, 26 May 2013. The Mo Ibrahim Foundation, a civil society organization, rated Botswana, Mauritius and Rwanda the top three countries in its Accountability index for 2015, with Somalia, Equatorial Guinea and South Sudan the bottom three, *2016 Ibrahim Index of African Governance*, http//:moibrahimfoundation.org/en.

2258. Convention on Preventing and Combating Corruption (11 Jul. 2003), https://www.au.int/en/treaties, Heyns & Killander, Compendium of Key Human Rights 2016, 101. In force 5 Aug. 2006. By June 2017 it had been ratified by thirty-seven States.

2259. AU Convention on Corruption Art. 2. *See also* Conference on Security, Stability, Development and Cooperation in Africa (2000) para. 12, Heyns & Killander, Compendium of Key Human Rights 2013, 163 (CSSDCA Solemn Declaration); African Charter on Values and Principles of Public Service and Administration Art. 3(8) (31 Jan. 2011), https://www.au.int/en/treaties. In force 23 Jul. 2016. By June 2017 it had been ratified by sixteen States.

2260. AU Convention on Corruption Arts 2(3), 4(2)(f). The commitment to collaborate and cooperate in the fight against transnational crime is reinforced by the AU Non-Aggression and Common Defence Pact Art. 5(a).

2261. AU Convention on Corruption Art. 3. *See also* African Charter on Democracy Arts 3(9), 27(5) and 33(3).

2262. AU Convention on Corruption Art. 1(1). *See ibid.*, Art. 4(1).

2263. *Ibid.*, Art. 1(1).

2264. *Ibid.*, Art. 4(1)(a)–(b).

2265. That is, any official or employee of the State or its agencies who has been selected, appointed or elected to perform a function in the name of or in the service of the State at any level of hierarchy, Art. 1(1). Compare the much broader definition adopted by the UN Convention Against Corruption Art. 2 (31 Oct. 2003), 2349 U.N.T.S. 41 (UNCAC), which includes any person holding a legislative, executive, administrative or judicial State office. UNCAC entered into force on 14 Dec. 2005. At the end of 2012 UNCAC had been ratified by 140 States, forty-seven of them AU Member States.

or other benefit for himself or herself or for another person or entity, in exchange for any act or omission in the performance of his or her public functions.[2266] Any act or omission in the performance of his or her public functions by a public official for the purpose of illicitly obtaining benefits for himself or herself or for a third party also comes within the definition of corruption.[2267] The diversion by a public official of public or private property, monies or securities for purposes unrelated to those for which they were intended also constitutes corruption.[2268] However, the AU Convention does not address bribery of a public official to induce the performance of an unlawful act. In addition, the AU Convention defines a public official as an 'official or employee of the State or its agencies' and its scope does not therefore extend to officials of international and regional organizations.[2269] The latter omission is surprising in view of the fact that the AU Convention seeks to deal with corruption in relation to international trade transactions and aid development.[2270] It is arguable that the AU Non-Aggression and Common Defence Pact could be applicable to corrupt practices given that one of its goals is to combat organized transnational crime,[2271] defined, *inter alia*, as having the purpose to obtain, directly or indirectly, financial and other material benefits.[2272]

457. The AU Convention extends its scope to cover persons working in the private sector.[2273] This includes persons who may be able to exert improper influence over the decision-making of a person performing functions in the public or private sectors.[2274] In addition, the tendering process must remain fair and companies must be prevented from paying bribes to win tenders.[2275] It is worthy of note that the AU Convention applies to private-to private corruption.[2276]

458. The AU Convention makes it plain that acts of corruption are also perpetrated when a direct or indirect offer or grant of a benefit is made to a public official[2277] or to persons who may be able to exert improper influence over the decision-making process (active bribery).[2278]

459. Illicit enrichment, defined as the 'significant increase in the assets of a public official or any other person which he or she cannot reasonably explain in relation to his or her income',[2279] also qualifies as corruption.[2280]

2266. AU Convention on Corruption Art. 4(1)(a).
2267. *Ibid.*, Art. 4(1)(c). Nepotism might come within the scope of this definition.
2268. *Ibid.*, Art. 4(1)(d).
2269. *Ibid.*, Art. 1(1).
2270. *Ibid.*, Art. 19(2), (4).
2271. *Ibid.*, Art. 5(a).
2272. *Ibid.*, Art. 1(x).
2273. *Ibid.*, Art. 4(1)(e). *See* further *ibid.*, Art. 11.
2274. *Ibid.*, Art. 4(1)(f).
2275. *Ibid.*, Art. 11(2).
2276. *Ibid.*, Art. 11.
2277. *Ibid.*, Art. 4(1)(b).
2278. *Ibid.*, Art. 4(1)(f).
2279. *Ibid.*, Art. 1(1).
2280. *Ibid.*, Art. 4(1)(g). *See* further *ibid.*, Art. 8(2). Subject, however, to the caveat of domestic law.

460. Participation as a principal, agent, or accomplice in the commission, attempted commission or conspiracy to commit any of the above acts constitutes an act of corruption in itself.[2281]

461. It should be noted that the AU Convention does not preclude States Parties from applying the AU Convention amongst themselves with respect to other acts or practices of corruption not covered by the AU Convention.[2282]

462. In order to punish corrupt acts and practices a State Party must legislate to designate such as criminal offences.[2283] A State Party will be competent to prosecute in four circumstances: (1) where the offence is committed inside its territory; (2) where the offence is committed by a national or a resident individual; (3) where the alleged criminal is in its territory and it does not extradite such person; and where the offence, if committed abroad, has a prejudicial effect on the State Party.[2284] In light of the criminalization of certain practices the right to a fair trial is reaffirmed.[2285] It should be noted that under the Statute on the ACJHR corruption is listed as a crime[2286] over which the ICL Section has jurisdiction.[2287]

463. The AU Convention contains elaborate provisions on extradition. Said offences will be deemed extraditable offences.[2288] Where extradition is conditional on the existence of a treaty with the requesting State but such treaty does not exist, the AU Convention will serve as the relevant legal basis.[2289] However, extradition shall be carried out in accordance with domestic law or existing extradition treaties.[2290] Where a State Party refuses to extradite on the basis that it has jurisdiction over the offence it must submit the case to the competent authorities for prosecution and report the outcome to the requesting State.[2291] At the request of the requesting State the requested Party may take into custody a person whose extradition is sought or ensure that s/he is present at extradition proceedings, subject to domestic law, a relevant extradition treaty or a finding that the circumstances are urgent and so warrant.[2292] Furthermore, the requested State may seize and hand over to the requesting State objects which may be evidence of the offence or acquired as a result of the offence.[2293]

464. State Parties are additionally required to adopt a series of other measures aimed at discouraging, preventing and eradicating corruption. These include establishing

2281. *Ibid.*, Art. 4(1)(g).
2282. *Ibid.*, Art. 4(2).
2283. *Ibid.*, Art. 5(1). *See also* African Charter on Values and Principles of Public Service and Administration Art. 12(1). Illicit enrichment should also be classified as an offence, AU Convention on Corruption Art. 8(1).
2284. AU Convention on Corruption Art. 13(1). Criminal jurisdiction exercised by a State Party in accordance with its domestic law is not precluded, *ibid.*, Art. 13(2).
2285. *Ibid.*, Art. 14.
2286. Statute on the ACJHR Art. 28I.
2287. *Ibid.*, Art. 28(1)A(8).
2288. AU Convention on Corruption Art. 15(2), (4).
2289. *Ibid.*, Art. 15(3).
2290. *Ibid.*, Art. 15(5).
2291. *Ibid.*, Art. 15(6).
2292. *Ibid.*, Art. 15(7).
2293. *Ibid.*, Art. 16(2).

and strengthening anti-corruption agencies,[2294] which crucially should be independent, establishing and strengthening internal accounting and auditing procedures,[2295] protecting those who report or witness corruption,[2296] requiring public officials to declare their assets before they assume office,[2297] better training for public officials,[2298] the establishment of disciplinary mechanisms,[2299] restricting immunity for public officials,[2300] ensuring transparency in the management of tendering and hiring procedures in the public service,[2301] preventing the financing of political parties by the use of funds acquired through corruption,[2302] combating corruption in the private sector,[2303] establishing as a criminal offence the laundering of the proceeds of corruption,[2304] the confiscation and seizure of products of corruption, including asset recovery,[2305] the confiscation and seizure of bank documents,[2306] the waiver of banking secrecy,[2307] and allowing the media and civil society a role in holding governments to account.[2308] Interestingly, the private sector is also given a role in fighting corruption.[2309] It is therefore significant that access to information must be secured.[2310]

465. The AU Convention additionally contains provisions on mutual legal assistance. States Parties will therefore provide each other the greatest measure of assistance by dealing immediately with requests from appropriate authorities investigating corruption.[2311] Moreover, it seeks to foster international cooperation to prevent corrupt practices.[2312] Noteworthy is the plea to developed countries to take measures to prevent corrupt public officials from enjoying stolen or illegally acquired gains.[2313]

2294. *Ibid.*, Art. 5(3). *See also ibid.*, Art. 20. *See* further African Charter on Values and Principles of Public Service and Administration Art. 12(1); Declaration on Democracy, Political, Economic and Corporate Governance para. 14.
2295. AU Convention on Corruption Art. 5(4).
2296. *Ibid.*, Art. 5(5), (6).
2297. *Ibid.*, Art. 7(1). *See also* African Charter on Values and Principles of Public Service and Administration Art. 13.
2298. AU Convention on Corruption Art. 7(2). *See also* African Charter on Values and Principles of Public Service and Administration Art. 12(2)–(4).
2299. AU Convention on Corruption Art. 7(3).
2300. *Ibid.*, Art. 7(5).
2301. *Ibid.*, Art. 7(4).
2302. *Ibid.*, Art. 10.
2303. *Ibid.*, Art. 11.
2304. *Ibid.*, Art. 6.
2305. *Ibid.*, Art. 16. Note that under the Statute on the ACJHR Art. 28(1)A(9), money laundering is listed as a crime.
2306. AU Convention on Corruption Art. 17(1).
2307. *Ibid.*, Art. 17(3), (4).
2308. *Ibid.*, Art. 12.
2309. *Ibid.*, Art. 11(2).
2310. *Ibid.*, Art. 9. It needs to be recalled that the African Charter Art. 9(1), guarantees the right to receive information.
2311. AU Convention on Corruption Art. 18(1).
2312. *Ibid.*, Art. 19.
2313. *Ibid.*, Art. 19(3).

466. Significantly the AU Convention envisages the creation of a transnational body within the AU, the Advisory Board on Corruption.[2314] Its functions include promoting and encouraging the adoption and application of anti-corruption measures in Africa,[2315] advising governments on how to deal with corruption,[2316] monitoring the behaviour of multinational corporations in Africa,[2317] developing and promoting the adoption of harmonized codes of conduct of public officials,[2318] and to liaise with the African Commission on Human and Peoples' Rights, civil society and IGOs and NGOs to facilitate the fight against corruption.[2319]

467. Later in 2003 the UN adopted UN Convention Against Corruption (UNCAC).[2320] UNCAC's approach in preventing and combating corruption is comprehensive and thus more extensive than that of the AU Convention, while sharing many features in common. UNCAC thus devotes detailed provisions to the issue of asset recovery.[2321] It deals with a number of issues unaddressed by the AU Convention. These include the criminal or civil liability of legal persons,[2322] and compensation for damage suffered by a victim of corruption.[2323] Other issues not explicitly addressed by the AU Convention include a statute of limitations,[2324] the suspension or removal of public officials,[2325] and the disqualification of persons found guilty of corruption from holding public office.[2326] It has been suggested that illegal financial flows should come within the scope of the AU Convention.[2327] Fair recruitment policies is required by the African Charter on Values and Principles of Public Service and Administration.[2328] Only lax restrictions are imposed on former public officials taking up private sector employment so as to prevent conflicts of interest.[2329] But the positive features of the AU Convention should be stressed. These include private-to private corruption, transparency in party political funding, the participation of civil society and the private sector in fighting corruption, and the strengthening of national control measures to ensure that foreign corporations in the territory of States Parties comply with national law.[2330] International, continental and regional cooperation is emphasized. Innovative

---

2314. *Ibid.*, Art. 22(1).
2315. *Ibid.*, Art. 22(5)(a).
2316. *Ibid.*, Art. 22(5)(d).
2317. *Ibid.*, Art. 22(5)(e).
2318. *Ibid.*, Art. 22(5)(f).
2319. *Ibid.*, Art. 22(5)(g).
2320. *See supra* para. 465.
2321. UNCAC Ch. V.
2322. *Ibid.*, Art. 26. But *see* AU Convention on Corruption Art. 19(1) which is of limited scope. Note that the Statute on the ACJHR Art. 46C, provides for corporate criminal liability.
2323. UNCAC Art. 35.
2324. *Ibid.*, Art. 29.
2325. *Ibid.*, Art. 30(6).
2326. *Ibid.*, Art. 30(7).
2327. Africa Progress Panel, *Africa Progress Report 2015*, 151, http://www.africaprogresspanel.org (accessed 29 Apr. 2017).
2328. AU Convention on Corruption Art. 19(2), (4). Compare UNCAC Art. 7.
2329. African Charter on Values and Principles of Public Service and Administration Art. 11(5) requires only that they do not unduly profit from offices they previously occupied.
2330. AU Convention on Corruption Art. 5(2).

is this respect is the undertaking to collaborate with countries of origin of multinationals to criminalize and punish secret commissions and other corrupt practices during international trade transactions.[2331]

468. The AU is supportive of the efforts of other international and regional organizations in seeking to combat corruption.[2332] Given the complexities of the problem it might have been useful for the AU Convention to have made some provision for technical assistance for States that felt it necessary. But UNCAC provides an opportunity to combat corruption more effectively on a global scale. Nevertheless, the AU's acknowledgement that corruption has had, has, and will have a negative and corrosive effect on the development and stability of Africa is an important initial step in dealing with this problem. In tandem with the African Charter on Values and Principles of Public Service and Administration and national strategies it is to be hoped that an enhanced culture of professionalism and ethical behaviour will be fostered and nourished. But corruption is a global problem that demands coordinated anti-corruption responses and policies. Bad corporate governance in other parts of the world, where there are failures to confront and prosecute irresponsible corporate behaviour that extends to bribing foreign officials, must also be addressed.[2333] Corporations and company directors must be made answerable for engaging in corrupt practices. Neither should politicians nor State entities evade responsibility. The inclusion of corporate and individual criminal liability for corruption under the Statute on the ACJHR is an indication that corruption will not be tolerated.[2334] The adoption of the AU Convention will send a powerful message that Africa is serious about dealing with the problem of corruption.

§3. Civil Society

469. Since the turn of the millennium in particular the concept of civil society has come to the fore in the body politic. Civil society refers to social or popular movements, socio-economic organizations and associations independent of the state and can include churches and other religious groups, trade unions, the media, the

2331. *Ibid.*, Art. 19(1).

2332. *See* , e.g., the UN Convention Against Transnational Organized Crime Art. 8 (2000), 2225 U.N.T.S. 209; the Inter-American Convention Against Corruption 1996, http//www.oas.org/juridico/English/treaties/b-58.html. The first African anti-corruption treaty was the SADC Protocol Against Corruption (14 Aug. 2001), http://www.sadc.int. This was followed shortly thereafter by the ECOWAS Protocol on the Fight Against Corruption (21 Dec. 2001), http://www.ecowas.int. Both latter treaties seek, *inter alia*, to criminalize a range of offences, harmonize national laws, and provide for international cooperation.

2333. The US Foreign Corrupt Practices Act 1997 is a stringent piece of legislation that imposes criminal penalties for engaging in foreign corruption. The United Kingdom's Bribery Act 2010 constitutes a modest development in this direction. The case of *SFO v. Rolls Royce plc* (Crown Court, 17 Jan. 2017, unreported) revealed the Respondents to have engaged in bribery and corruption in various countries, including Nigeria.

2334. Statute on the ACJHR Art. 46B and 46C. It should be observed that corruption is also condemned under the African Charter on Democracy Art. 3(9).

private sector, public interest groups, academia, and NGOs, or CSOs.[2335] Civil society contributes to the enhancement of democracy; it promotes citizens' participation in public affairs and the decision-making process, and engages in public advocacy; it is a significant player in democratic accountability and responsiveness, helping to hold governments accountable and applying pressure on them to consider or reconsider particular policies. It can have an input at both national and international levels by developing proposals for legislation and policies. CSOs are thus considered as stakeholders in society. In the field of human rights the development of civil society contributes to the creation of an environment conducive to human rights.[2336] The AU acknowledges the role of civil society, recognizing the participation of the people in its activities as one of its founding principles.[2337]

470. The process of reform and democratization in Africa led the OAU to accept the need to connect with the peoples of Africa and cooperate with African NGOs. The AEC Treaty recognizes this necessity at the socio-economic level.[2338] However, particularly significant is the first OAU Ministerial Conference on Human Rights held in April 1999, resulting in the adoption of the Grand Bay Declaration and Plan of Action, where the OAU expressed a renewed sense of commitment to civil society.

471. The Conference, recognizing that civil society contributes to the advancement of human rights,[2339] stressed the importance of promoting an African civil society, particularly NGOs, as a prerequisite for the healthy development of a State governed by the rule of law.[2340] The Conference therefore sought to safeguard the values that promote civil society. Recognizing the role of the media as a public watchdog, the Conference urged States to guarantee a free and independent press.[2341] Freedom of

---

2335. Compare the definition in the Glossary of the Panel of Eminent Persons on United Nations-Civil Society Relations, 'We the Peoples: Civil Society, the United Nations and Global Governance' (11 Jun. 2004) UN Doc. A/58/817.

2336. The Declaration on the Right and Responsibility of Individuals, Groups and Organs of Society to Promote and Protect Universally Recognized Human Rights and Fundamental Freedoms (Declaration on Human Rights Defenders), UN General Assembly Res. 53/144 (1998), acknowledges the role of individuals and groups. *See also* Vienna Declaration and Programme of Action pt. I, para. 38, 32 I.L.M. 1661 (1993). In relation to Africa *see* the Kigali Declaration paras 27–28, Heyns & Killander, Compendium of Key Human Rights 2016, 154; Resolution on the Protection of Human Rights Defenders in Africa, 17th Activity Report, 2003–2004, Annex IV.

2337. Constitutive Act Art. 4(c). *See also* the Cotonou Declaration on the strengthening and expanding the protection of all Human Rights Defenders in Africa, adopted by the International Symposium of Human Rights Defenders in Africa 2017.

2338. AEC Treaty Arts 90–91.

2339. Grand Bay Declaration para. 10.

2340. *Ibid.*, paras 17–19; preambular para. 13. *See also* Declaration on Democracy, Political, Economic and Corporate Governance para. 15.

2341. Grand Bay Declaration para. 21; preambular para. 8(m). Compare African Charter Art. 9. The African Commission on Human and Peoples' Rights has upheld the freedom of the press in *Constitutional Rights Projects and Civil Liberties Organization v. Nigeria* Communication No. 102/93, 12th Activity Report 1998–1999; *Media Rights Agenda and Constitutional Rights Project v. Nigeria* Communication Nos 105/93, 128/94, 130/94 and 152/96, 12th Activity Report 1998–1999. It has also adopted resolutions to that effect, *see* 8th Activity Report 1994–1995.

association was also emphasized.[2342] These conclusions were later reaffirmed by the Kigali Declaration.[2343] And in the CSSDCA Solemn Declaration the role of civil society in the democratization of Africa is acknowledged.[2344]

472. In this context the OAU held a conference in 2001 to establish a framework to enhance and consolidate cooperation between the OAU and African NGOs. It was accepted that CSOs required wider and more systematic access to the OAU. Furthermore, the preamble to the Constitutive Act recognizes 'the need to build a partnership between governments and all segments of civil society'. This is given expression to in the form of ECOSOCC under Article 22 of the Constitutive Act.[2345] In June 2002 a further conference was held with a view to establishing a mechanism to facilitate links between CSOs and the AU.[2346]

473. It is therefore encouraging to note that the role played by CSOs has been acknowledged by the AU. One of the objectives of the African Charter on Democracy, Elections and Governance 2007 is to foster citizen participation.[2347] State Parties are thus obliged to adopt a series of measures to promote and consolidate good governance, popular participation, accountability, transparency, the rule of law and so forth. For present purposes what is salient is that State Parties must ensure effective participation of citizens in democratic processes and in the governance of public affairs.[2348] They must consolidate a culture of democracy and peace, which can be achieved by creating conducive conditions for CSOs to exist and operate.[2349] They must foster popular participation and partnership with CSOs.[2350] And they must ensure and promote partnership and dialogue between government, civil society and the private sector.[2351] Under the African Charter on Values and Principles of Public Service and Administration civil society is to participate in the planning and delivery of public services.[2352] The Libréville Declaration considers civil society as a partner in health and environmental

2342. Grand Bay Declaration para. 8(m). Compare African Charter Art. 10, and *see Civil Liberties Organization in respect of Nigerian Bar Association v. Nigeria* Communication No. 101/93, 8th Activity Report 1994–1995; *Media Rights Agenda and Constitutional Rights Project v. Nigeria* Communication Nos 105/93, 128/94, 130/94 and 152/96, 12th Activity Report 1998–1999; *Amnesty International v. Zambia* Communication No. 212/98 12th Activity Report 1998–1999.

2343. Kigali Declaration paras 27–28. *See also* the Cotonou Declaration on the strengthening and expanding the protection of all Human Rights Defenders in Africa.

2344. CCSSDCA Solemn Declaration para. 14 (c), Heyns & Killander, Compendium of Key Human Rights 2013, 163. *See also* Declaration on Democracy, Political, Economic and Corporate Governance para. 20.

2345. *See supra* paras 143–146; Viljoen, 226–29.

2346. In November 2003 the African Commission on Human and Peoples' Rights decided to establish a focal point for human rights defenders within the Commission's Secretariat in order to facilitate information on human rights defenders in Africa.

2347. African Charter on Democracy Art. 2(10).

2348. *Ibid.*, Art. 3(7).

2349. *Ibid.*, Art. 12(3).

2350. *Ibid.*, Arts 27(2), 28.

2351. *Ibid.*, Art. 28.

2352. African Charter on Values and Principles of Public Service and Administration Art. 5(4).

issues.[2353] And it has previously been seen that civil society has a role to play in fighting corruption.[2354]

474. Civil society plays an immensely positive role in the promotion and implementation of human rights. One aspect of this role is the relationship of CSOs and NGOs with the African Commission on Human and Peoples' Rights where they have assumed promotional and protective functions.[2355] The Commission has appointed a Special Rapporteur on Human Rights Defenders in Africa to cooperate with States, human rights defenders and NGOs with a view to raising awareness and developing strategies.[2356] But considerable obstacles confront civil society in Africa. Civil society requires an informed and active citizenship, problematic in much of Africa. If the ramifications of poverty are not the problem then repressive regimes that do not tolerate opposition certainly are. Civil society cannot be expected to flourish in countries where the media is cowed, where the activities of NGOs, many of which face arbitrary difficulties in registering, are restricted and its activists subjected to harassment, intimidation, legal proceedings and extra-judicial killings, and where the perpetrators of such violence can act with impunity.[2357] The Commission's Special Rapporteur has had cause on numerous occasions to raise concerns for the safety of human rights defenders and to report on their murders.[2358] The OAU/AU is to be congratulated for recognizing the need for strong partnerships with civil society. However, as is often the norm in Africa, the gap between public rhetoric and reality is immense.[2359]

2353. Libréville Declaration on Health and Environment in Africa, Libréville para. 10 (29 Aug. 2008).

2354. *See supra* paras 466, 467.

2355. *See* N. Mbelle, 'The Role of Non-governmental Organisations and National Human Rights Institutions at the African Commission', in *The African Charter on Human and Peoples' Rights: The System in Practice, 1986–2006,* M. Evans & R. Murray (eds) (2nd edn, Cambridge: Cambridge University Press, 2008), Ch. 8.

2356. Resolution on the Protection of Human Rights Defenders in Africa. *See* R. Murray, *The Special Rapporteurs in the African System* in Evans & Murray, 344, 369–70. *See also* the Cotonou Declaration on the strengthening and expanding the protection of all Human Rights Defenders in Africa.

2357. Note that the UN Declaration on Human Rights Defenders obligates States not to subject human rights defenders to harassment or other adverse measures. *See also* the Cotonou Declaration on the strengthening and expanding the protection of all Human Rights Defenders in Africa. For examples of the violations being committed against human rights defenders in Africa and elsewhere, *see* UN Commission on Human Rights, Human Rights Defenders, Report of the Special Rapporteur, UN Doc. E/CN.4/2004/94.

2358. The Commission's Annual Activity Reports attest to this fact.

2359. According to the Mo Ibrahim Foundation, a civil society organization, the picture across Africa in recent years is mixed, with many countries seeing an improvement in civil society participation and yet many seeing a decline, *2016 Ibrahim Index of African* Governance, http//:moibrahimfoundation.org/en.

§4. Terrorism

475. Terrorism in its different manifestations has become a persistent and significant threat in recent years,[2360] described by the UN Security Council in Resolution 1377(2001) as 'one of the most serious threats to international peace and security in the twenty-first century' and as a 'threat to all states and to all humanity'. Africa has not escaped the blight of international terrorism[2361] with countries in East Africa bearing the brunt of some horrific atrocities.[2362] Some countries, such as Algeria, Uganda and Nigeria, have faced long and brutal campaigns by domestic terrorists.[2363] Failed and weak States, such as Somalia, pose their own set of problems, as breeding grounds and havens for home-grown and international terrorist groups. Groups affiliated to Al-Qaeda of the Islamic Maghreb (AQIM) are active in the Sahel region of northwest Africa. In 2012–2013, the territorial integrity and stability of Mali was gravely at risk from jihadist groups and it was only intervention by France that reversed that threat, which has not been eliminated, however.[2364] The OAU/AU, acknowledging 'the scourge of terrorism as a source of serious human rights violation',[2365] therefore joined the war against terrorism. Hence condemnation of acts of terrorism is one of the guiding principles of the AU.[2366] Although the international community has not yet succeeded in agreeing to a comprehensive treaty dealing with terrorism,[2367] *inter alia*, because developing States had traditionally been reluctant to have wars of national liberation

---

2360. Vienna Declaration and Programme of Action pt. I, para. 17.

2361. Report of the UN Secretary-General on strengthening the partnership between the United Nations and the African Union on issues of peace and security in Africa, UN Doc. S/2016/780, para. 5.

2362. Condemned by the UN Security Council in Res. 1189(1998) and 1450(2002). *See also* the condemnation of the terrorist bombing in Kampala by Al Shabab in 2010, Assembly, *Decision on the Report of the Peace and Security Council on its Activities and the State of Peace and Security in Africa,* AU Doc. Assembly/AU/Dec.294 (XV) para. 7 (25–27 Jul. 2010).

2363. *See* , e.g., UN Security Council Res. 2349(2017) condemning the activities of Boko Haram and ISIL in West Africa and the Sahel. In 2015 the AU mandated the Multi National Joint Task Force (MNJTF) to assist in restoring a safe and secure environment in the areas affected by Boko Haram and other terrorist groups. The Lord's Resistance Army (LRA) presented a persistent threat in Uganda which eventually led the AU to set up the Regional Cooperation Initiative for the Elimination of the Lord's Resistance Army (RCI-LRA) with the mandate to defeat the LRA.

2364. *See* UN Security Council Res. 2085(2012).

2365. Grand Bay Declaration para. 12; Kigali Declaration para. 9. *See also* Protocol to the OAU Convention on Terrorism Art. 1(a) (2 Jul. 2004), https://www.au.int/en/treaties, Heyns & Killander, Compendium of Key Human Rights 2016, 96. In force 26 Feb. 2014. As of June 2017, it had been ratified by twenty-one States. According to the CSSDCA Declaration, para. 11(e), terrorism, 'in all its manifestations, is inimical to stability'.

2366. Constitutive Act Art. 4(o). *See also* PSC Protocol Art. 3(d), 50th Anniversary Solemn Declaration para. E(ii), Assembly, Twenty-First Ordinary Session, 26 May 2013.

2367. Although conventions dealing with specific aspects of terrorism, such as hijacking and financing, have been adopted, *see* A. Cassese, *International Law*(2nd edn, Oxford: Oxford University Press, 2005), 465–468.

categorized as terrorism,[2368] the OAU was able to reach a consensus and at a conference held in Algiers in 1999 adopted a Convention on Terrorism.[2369]

476. The OAU Convention defines a 'terrorist act' as 'any act which is a violation of the criminal laws of a State Party and which may endanger the life, physical integrity or freedom of, or cause serious injury or death to, any person, any number or group of persons or causes or may cause damage to public or private property, natural resources, environmental or cultural heritage'.[2370] Moreover, any act calculated or intended to 'intimidate, put in fear, force, coerce or induce any government, body, institution, the general public or any segment thereof, to do or abstain from doing any act, or to adopt or abandon a particular standpoint, or to act according to certain principles', or to 'disrupt any public service, the delivery of any essential service to the public or create a public emergency', or to 'create general insurrection in a State' also comes within the definition.[2371] Aiding and abetting the commission of any of these acts also amount to terrorism.[2372] This definition is noteworthy for its breadth

2368. A. Cassese, *International Criminal Law*(2nd edn, Oxford: Oxford University Press, 2008), 162, n. 1. However, the UN Security Council's position is that any acts of terrorism are unjustifiable, *see* , e.g., Res. 2178 (2014) preambular para. 1. The AU now shares this stance, *see* , e.g., Assembly, *Decision on the Establishment of an African Union Special Fund on Prevention and Combating Terrorism and Violent Extremism in Africa*, AU Doc. Assembly/AU/Dec.614(XXVII) (17–1 Jul. 2016), para. 3.

2369. Convention on the Prevention and Combating of Terrorism (14 Jul. 1999), https://www.au.int/en/treaties, Heyns & Killander, Compendium of Key Human Rights 2016, 93. In force 26 Dec. 2002. As of June 2017, it had been ratified by forty-three States.

2370. OAU Convention on Terrorism Art. 1(3)(a). Note that the Constitutive Act condemns political assassination Art. 4(o). *See also* OAU Charter Art. III(5).

2371. OAU Convention on Terrorism Art. 1(3)(a)(i)–(iii). The inclusion of the disruption of public services within the definition is problematic as it has the capacity of criminalizing the general public and of undermining freedom of industrial action, such as strikes.

2372. OAU Convention on Terrorism Art. 1(3)(b).

which goes significantly further than any existing international definition.[2373] While the inclusion of acts that damage the environment, for instance, is to be welcomed concern must be expressed at the potential for abuse by authoritarian-minded governments. Thus politically motivated strikes or even workers who strike in a labour dispute could find themselves charged with terrorist offences. It is important to note that wars of national liberation are excluded from the definition of terrorism.[2374] This should come as no surprise given the African stance on the issue. With this notable exception terrorist acts cannot be justified on political, philosophical, ideological, racial, ethnic, religious or other grounds.[2375] One of the consequences of this is that political or other motivation cannot provide a defence for terrorist acts for the purpose of extradition.

477. The OAU Convention also addresses the question of State-sponsored terrorism. This particular issue has assumed greater significance in recent years as a consequence of '9/11' and the threat posed by jihadist groups such as Al-Qaeda. The international community has defined the events of '9/11' as an armed attack setting off the right of self-defence under Article 51 of the UN Charter.[2376] The USA was of the view that the attack involved the state responsibility of the Afghan Taliban regime and force was used both to remove it from power and to eradicate the terrorists which it was believed the Taliban were harbouring.[2377] The well-known fact that certain African States have been accused of supporting terrorism thus gives this debate an

2373. Viljoen, 300. A comprehensive definition has thus far eluded the international community. Many treaties are subject specific, dealing with air safety, maritime navigation, or the suppression of the means by which terrorism can be supported. One specific example is the International Convention for the Suppression of Terrorist Bombings (25 Nov. 1997), 2149 U.N.T.S. 256. More recent treaties, such as the International Convention for the Suppression of the Financing of Terrorism (9 Dec. 1999), 2179 U.N.T.S. 197, and the European Convention on the Prevention of Terrorism (16 May 2005), C.E.T.S. 195, as well as UN Security Council Res. 1566(2004), determine what conduct should be depicted as 'terrorist' by linking it to pre-existing treaties on terrorism. Nevertheless, UN Security Council Res. 1566(2004) has established three cumulative elements: (i) acts, including against civilians, committed with the intention of causing death or serious bodily injury, or the taking of hostages; (ii) irrespective of whether motivated by considerations of a political, philosophical, ideological, racial, ethnic, religious or other similar nature, also committed for the purpose of provoking a state of terror in the general public or in a group of persons or particular persons, intimidating a population, or compelling a Government or an international organization to do or to abstain from doing any act; and (iii) such acts constituting offences within the scope of and as defined in the international instruments relating to terrorism. *See* generally, Report of the UN Special Rapporteur on the promotion and protection of human rights and fundamental freedoms while countering terrorism, UN Doc. E/CN.4/2006/98. Cassese argues that an agreed definition has emerged in customary law comprising three elements: (i) acts normally criminalized under municipal law; (ii) intended to provoke a state of terror in the population or to coerce a State or an international organization to take some action; (iii) are politically or ideologically motivated, Cassese, *International Criminal Law*, 165.

2374. OAU Convention on Terrorism Art. 3(1).

2375. *Ibid.*, Art. 3(2). *See* further UN Security Council Res. 1269(1999) and 1566(2004) which state that acts of terrorism are unjustifiable regardless of motivation.

2376. *See* UN Security Council Res. 1368(2001) and 1373(2001).

2377. *See* Cassese, *International Law*, 473–475.

added relevance.[2378] States must therefore refrain from, *inter alia*, organizing, supporting, financing, inciting or committing terrorist acts or providing havens for terrorists.[2379] States are further required to adopt measures, *inter alia*, to prevent their territories from being used for the preparation of terrorist acts,[2380] to deal with arms smuggling,[2381] to prevent the infiltration of their territory by terrorists,[2382] to promote the exchange of information[2383] and to prevent the establishment of terrorist support networks.[2384] In addition, under the Protocol to the OAU Convention on Terrorism States must prevent the entry into, and the training of terrorist groups on their territories.[2385] These proscriptions are reinforced by the AU Non-Aggression and Common Defence Pact, under which the encouragement, support, harbouring or provision of any assistance for the commission of terrorist acts constitutes aggression.[2386] States Parties must also prohibit the use of their territory for the stationing, withdrawal or incursions of terrorists.[2387] In light of the nihilistic threat posed by jihadist groups, States undertake under the Protocol to the OAU Convention on Terrorism States to ensure that terrorists do not acquire weapons of mass destruction.[2388] Many similar measures are advocated by UN Security Council Resolutions.[2389]

478. The OAU Convention adopts the *aut dedere aut judicare* principle. States are hence bound to arrest and prosecute or extradite perpetrators of terrorist acts.[2390] Terrorist acts as defined in the OAU Convention must become an extraditable offence within all extradition treaties.[2391] Jurisdiction is established on various grounds, principally where the act is committed in the territory of the State[2392] or on board a ship or aircraft registered there.[2393] However, jurisdiction is additionally provided for on the basis of the nationality, or active personality, principle,[2394] the passive personality principle[2395] and the protective principle.[2396] In view of the fact that there are compelling arguments for considering terrorist acts as international crimes or crimes against

2378. *Ibid.,* 468, 470.

2379. OAU Convention on Terrorism Art. 4(1). It should be observed that the AU condemns subversive activities, *see* of the Constitutive Act Art. 4(o). *See also* OAU Charter Art. III(5).

2380. OAU Convention on Terrorism Art. 4(2)(a).

2381. *Ibid.*, Art. 4(2)(b).

2382. *Ibid.*, Art. 4(2)(c).

2383. *Ibid.*, Art. 4(2)(e). *See* further *ibid.*, Art. 5.

2384. *Ibid.*, Art. 4(2)(f).

2385. Protocol to the OAU Convention on Terrorism Art. 3(1)(b).

2386. AU Non-Aggression and Common Defence Pact Art. 1(e)(xi).

2387. *Ibid.*, Article 5(c).

2388. Protocol to the OAU Convention on Terrorism Art. 3(f). *See* further UN Convention for the Supression of Acts of Nuclear Terrorism (13 Apr. 2003), 44 I.L.M. 815 (2005).

2389. *See* , e.g., UN Security Council Res. 1904(2009).

2390. OAU Convention on Terrorism Art. 4(2)(h). *See also ibid.*, Arts 6(4), 7(2) and 8. *See* further AU Non-Aggression and Common Defence Pact Art. 6(b).

2391. OAU Convention on Terrorism Art. 9.

2392. *Ibid.*, Art. 6(1)(a).

2393. *Ibid.*, Art. 6(1)(b). *See* further *ibid.*, Art. 6(2)(d).

2394. *Ibid.*, Art. 6(1)(c). *See* further *ibid.*, Art. 6(2)(c).

2395. *Ibid.*, Art. 6(2)(a).

2396. *Ibid.*, Art. 6(2)(b), (e).

humanity[2397] it seems regrettable that the drafters of the treaty did not have the foresight to make provision for universal jurisdiction. However, this omission loses significance as the Protocol on the Statute of the ACJHR classifies terrorism as a crime thereunder.[2398] The Protocol to the OAU Convention on Terrorism provides an important safety net in that it constitutes an adequate legal basis for extradition for States Parties that do not have extradition arrangements.[2399]

479. Provision is made for mutual legal assistance.[2400] This extends to extraterritorial investigations (commission rogatoire). The parties therefore undertake to assist in, *inter alia*, the examination of witnesses and evidence,[2401] the collection of documents[2402] and serving of judicial documents,[2403] and the execution of searches and seizures.[2404] A commission rogatoire may be refused where each State Party has to execute a commission rogatoire relating to the same terrorist acts,[2405] if the request may affect efforts to expose crimes, impede investigations or the indictment of the accused in the requesting country,[2406] and the execution of a request would affect the sovereignty, security or public order of the requested State.[2407] However, a request for a commission rogatoire may not be refused on the grounds of the principle of confidentiality of bank operations or financial institutions.[2408] It is worth observing that the OAU Convention's provisions on mutual legal assistance do not match the detail of the UN Model Treaty on Mutual Legal Assistance.[2409]

480. The Protocol to the OAU Convention on Terrorism provides an important component in the fight against terrorism, that of the confiscation, freezing, and seizure of funds and assets 'for the purpose of committing a terrorist act'.[2410] It is submitted that the AU should have extended the scope of this provision, in line with UN Security Council Resolution 1373(2001), to cover entities and undertakings owned or controlled by terrorist groups and/or their supporters. Neither do the AU treaties follow the international practice of maintaining a Consolidated List of suspect individuals, groups, entities and undertakings subject to such measures.[2411] Holding hostages to ransom has been a favoured method employed by AQIM to boost its finances. This iniquitous

---

2397. Cassese, *International Criminal Law*, 175–77.
2398. Statute of the ACJHR Art. 28A(1)(6).
2399. Protocol to the OAU Convention on Terrorism Art. 8(1).
2400. OAU Convention on Terrorism Art. 17. *See* further AU Non-Aggression and Common Defence Pact Art. 6(a). The OAU Convention on Terrorism allows States Parties to enter into further arrangements providing for greater specificity, *see* Art. 18.
2401. OAU Convention on Terrorism Art. 14(1)(a).
2402. *Ibid.*, Art. 14(1)(d).
2403. *Ibid.*, Art. 14(1)(g).
2404. *Ibid.*, Art. 14(1)(f).
2405. *Ibid.*, Art. 15(a).
2406. *Ibid.*, Art. 15(b).
2407. *Ibid.*, Art. 15(c).
2408. *Ibid.*, Art. 16.
2409. 30 I.L.M. 1419 (1991).
2410. Protocol to the OAU Convention on Terrorism Art. 3(c). *See* further International Convention for the Supression of the Financing of Terrorism Art. 8; UN Security Council Res. 1904 (2009) para. 1(a).
2411. *See* UN Security Council Res. 1267 (1999), 1333 (2000) and 1904 (2009).

practice has been condemned by the AU[2412] and the UN Security Council.[2413] While neither the OAU Convention nor the Protocol provide for the imposition of sanctions on State sponsors of terrorism it is clear that the AU could impose sanctions under Article 23 of the Constitutive Act.[2414] But the main purpose of the Protocol is to secure the effective implementation of the OAU Convention[2415] and to this end the PSC is given the primary role of harmonizing and coordinating continent-wide efforts in the fight against terrorism.[2416]

481. One final observation on these treaties remains to be made. It is an article of faith of liberal democratic societies that the war against terrorism should not undermine its values[2417] and should therefore be fought in conformity with the principles of international humanitarian law and international human rights.[2418] The OAU Convention enshrines this fundamental position,[2419] reinforced by the Protocol to the OAU Convention on Terrorism, which expressly outlaws torture, inhuman and degrading treatment.[2420]

482. Notwithstanding this normative framework, the AU has continued to take steps to bolster its counter-terrorism efforts. In 2011 the AU adopted the African Model Law on Counter Terrorism to help States harmonize domestic legislation on terrorism.[2421] In 2014 the PSC adopted the so-called Nairobi Communiqué setting out a series of objectives for the AU.[2422] One was an African arrest warrant for persons charged with or convicted of terrorist acts.[2423] Another was the creation of a Counter Terrorism Fund.[2424] And another, pursuant to the Non-Aggression and Common Defence Pact, was a call for the creation of specialized joint counter-terrorism units at the sub-regional level within the structure of the ASF.[2425]

2412. Assembly, *Decision to Combat the Payment of Ransom to Terrorist Groups,* AU Doc. Assembly/AU/Dec.256 (XIII) para. 7 (3 Jul. 2009).

2413. *See* UN Security Council Res. 2085(2012) para. 5.

2414. It needs to be recalled that the UN Security Council has imposed sanctions on State sponsors of terrorism, *see* Cassese, *International Law*, 468.

2415. Protocol to the OAU Convention on Terrorism Art. 2(2).

2416. *Ibid.*, Art. 4. Regional mechanisms also have a role, *ibid.*, Art. 6.

2417. Concern has therefore been expressed about the anti-terrorism legislation of various African States, Viljoen, 302. The Cotonou Declaration on the strengthening and expanding the protection of all Human Rights Defenders in Africa draws attention to the fact that anti-terrorism legislation is often used against human rights defenders.

2418. *Gunme et al. v. Cameroon,* Communication No. 266/2003, 26th Activity Report 2008–2009, paras 113–114.

2419. OAU Convention on Terrorism Art. 22(1). *See also* UN Security Council Res. 1456 (2003) and Res. 2178 (2014).

2420. Protocol to the OAU Convention on Terrorism Art. 3(1)(k).

2421. Assembly, *Decision on the Report of the Peace and Security Council on its Activities and the State of Peace and Security in Africa*, AU Doc. Assembly/AU/Dec.369(XVII) (30 Jun.–1 Jul. 2011), para. 30.

2422. AU Doc. PSC/AHG/Comm.(CDLV).

2423. *Ibid.*, para. 21(i).

2424. *Ibid.*, para. 21(vii).

2425. *Ibid.*, para. 21(iii).

§5. Democratization

483. A global trend that became established in the late twentieth century has been that of democratization and constitutionalism.[2426] Included within these broad tenets are the principles of the rule of law, good governance, participatory, pluralistic and representative democracy and constitutional government.[2427] The causal link between repressive and bad governance, lack of security, underdevelopment and human rights abuses has long been accepted by the UN[2428] which thus maintains that participatory democracy fosters the full realization of peace, development and human rights.[2429] Africa has shared in this phenomenon of democratization.[2430] Of course, it must not be overlooked that mature, stable democracies exist in Africa, Botswana, Cape Verde and Mauritius to name a few. There are newer democracies, with vibrant democratic cultures, such as South Africa.[2431] In 2011 popular revolutions known as the 'Arab Spring' swept through much of North Africa but their outcomes have been largely disappointing, resulting either in chaos, as in Libya, or the restoration of illiberal rule, as in Egypt, with Tunisia arguably the only success story. But too many regimes are of an autocratic and repressive nature, lacking popular support or a genuine democratic

---

2426. Vienna Declaration and Programme of Action pt I, para. 8; UN Millennium Declaration Part V, UN General Assembly Res. 55/2, UN Doc. A/Res/55/2; World Summit Outcome paras 135–137, UN General Assembly Res. 60/1, UN Doc. A/Res/60/1. *See also* Constitutive Act of the African Union Art. 3(g) (26 May 2001), 2158 U.N.T.S. 3. It is increasingly argued that a legal entitlement to democratic rule exists, *see* T. Franck, 'The Emerging Right to Democratic Governance', *A.J.I.L.* 86 (1992): 46.

2427. Described as the essence of a liberal democracy, J. Donnelly, *International Human Rights*(2nd edn, Boulder: Westview Press, 1997), 154–57. *See* World Summit Outcome, paras 119–120, 134.

2428. *See* in particular the Vienna Declaration and Programme of Action pt. I. In the World Summit Outcome, the UN General Assembly declared, *inter alia*, 'We recognize that development, peace and security and human rights are interlinked and mutually reinforcing', A/RES/60/1 para. 9. This fact was also accepted by the OAU, *see* Grand Bay Declaration para. 8; CSSDCA Declaration.

2429. Vienna Declaration and Programme of Action pt. I, para. 8; UN Millennium Declaration pt. I, para. 6.

2430. Vienna Declaration and Programme of Action pt. I, para. 9. *See* generally, J. Hatchard, M. Ndulo & P. Slinn, *Comparative Constitutionalism and Good Governance in the Commonwealth: An Eastern and Southern African Perspective* (Cambridge: Cambridge University Press, 2004), Ch. 3. Under the terms of the Harare Declaration 1991, http://www.thecommonwealth.org, members of the Commonwealth, which includes many African States, committed themselves to an agenda of democratization and human rights. This commitment was strengthened under the Commonwealth Charter 2012, http://www.thecommonwealth.org/files/252053/FileName/Charterof theCommonwealth.pdf. This agenda was accepted by the OAU rather late in the day, *see* CSSDCA Declaration.

2431. According to the *2016 Ibrahim Index of African Governance*, based on four principal categories, Safety & Rule of Law, Participation & Human Rights, Sustainable Economic Opportunity, and Human Development, the top five ranking countries were Mauritius, Botswana, Cape Verde, Seychelles and Namibia.

mandate.[2432] A fundamental principle of liberal democracy is that governments should be based on the consent of, and be representative of, the people who must be free to exercise their democratic rights. In order to acquire legitimacy genuine democratization must occur. A willingness to embrace and abide by the values of democracy must exist and a culture of constitutionalism, pluralism and participatory party politics must be nurtured; governments must be elected by and accountable to the people, transparent, free and fair elections on the basis of universal adult suffrage must be held at regular intervals and their results must be respected; democratic institutions must be established and supported; a free media must be allowed; civil society must be allowed to operate; corruption must be eliminated.[2433] Politicians must learn to respect the rule of law and act within the limitations imposed by the law; the executive must not interfere with judicial independence since an independent judiciary is vital to the existence of a State governed by the rule of law, restraining abuses of State power.[2434]

484. Democratization is a core value of the AU. Explicit references to democratic ideals are made in the Constitutive Act and the fiftieth Anniversary Solemn Declaration reaffirms this commitment. They build upon the right to democratic government enshrined in Article 13(1) of the African Charter.[2435] Democratization is a key policy that will help secure progress in development, peace and social progress. Yet democratization can only be made effective if meaningful reforms are undertaken. Significantly, through the PSC the AU has assumed the capacity to take positive steps to promote and advance democratic values.[2436]

485. The AU's acceptance of these ideals is openly expressed in the Constitutive Act's preamble where the AU undertakes, *inter alia*, to 'consolidate democratic institutions and culture, and to ensure good governance and the rule of law'. These principles are enshrined in the operative sections of the Constitutive Act, and supplemented by the PSC Protocol. One of the AU's objectives is the promotion of democratic

---

2432. *See* Hatchard, Ndulo & Slinn, 99–108. The five bottom ranking countries according to the *2016 Ibrahim Index of African Governance* were Somalia, South Sudan, CAR, Libya and Eritrea. The UK Foreign & Commonwealth Office included CAR, DRC, Eritrea, Libya, Somalia, South Sudan, Sudan and Zimbabwe in its list of countries where there are extensive human rights concerns, *Human Rights and Democracy: The 2015 Foreign & Commonwealth Office Report*, http://www.gov.uk/government/publications.

2433. UNHCR 'General Comment 25' in 'Note by the Secretariat, Compilation of General Comments and General Recommendations adopted by Human Rights Treaty Bodies' (2008) in HRI/GEN/1/Rev.9, vol. I. In 2016 the UN Secretary-General highlighted the fact that recent election-related disputes in countries such as Burundi were undermining democracy, Report of the UN Secretary-General on strengthening the partnership between the United Nations and the African Union on issues of peace and security in Africa, UN Doc. S/2016/780, para. 7.

2434. *See* UN Basic Principles on the Independence of the Judiciary, *Human Rights: A Compilation of International Instruments* vol. I (First Part) 409 (New York & Geneva: United Nations 2002); Kigali Declaration para. 5. *See* generally Hatchard, Ndulo & Slinn, Ch. 8.

2435. *See supra* paras 263–264.

2436. *See supra* paras 201–202. M. Wiebusch, *The Role of Regional Organizations in the Protection of Constitutionalism* (Stockholm: International IDEA Discussion Paper 17, 2016), 19–25.

principles and institutions, popular participation and good governance.[2437] Included among the AU's fundamental principles is respect for democratic values, the rule of law, and good governance.[2438] Attention has already been drawn to the existence of a 'democracy clause' in the Constitutive Act.[2439] But these core values form an essential part of NEPAD.[2440] In its Declaration on Democracy, Political, Economic and Corporate Governance the AU further reaffirmed its commitment to democracy and good political governance.[2441] Clearly the AU has the authority to assist transitional societies among its Member States in strengthening and consolidating democracy and constitutionalism.

486. Whereas the AU's commitment to democratic values is expressed in the Constitutive Act in general terms the African Charter on Democracy provides a detailed and wide-ranging set of values in common and undertakings by States Parties.[2442] Its aims, as set out in Article 2 thereof, include adherence to the principles of democracy, constitutionalism and the rule of law, the promotion of free and fair elections, the promotion and protection of an independent judiciary, securing good governance, and the rejection of unconstitutional seizures of power. States Parties commit themselves to promote and ensure these values.[2443] However, salient features that are particularly worthy of note include the following.

487. First, developing a culture of democracy and peace.[2444] In addition, State Parties will promote a culture of respect, compromise, consensus and tolerance.[2445] To this end public, and inclusive, institutions that promote and support democracy and constitutional order must be established.[2446] Second, a commitment to participatory political systems, including the holding of democratic elections.[2447] To this end the AU Commission may send electoral observer missions.[2448] Third, building upon the commitment in the Constitutive Act, unconstitutional changes of government will attract sanctions from the AU.[2449] In this regard, State Parties must ensure civilian

---

2437. Constitutive Act Art. 3(g). *See also* PSC Protocol Art. 3(f). An important development in this regard, reinforcing the AU's commitments to these values, is the adoption in 2007 of the African Charter on Democracy, Elections and Governance (30 Jan. 2007), https://www.au.int/en/treaties, Heyns & Killander, Compendium of Key Human Rights Documents 2016, 125 (African Charter on Democracy). In force 15 Feb. 2012. The African Charter on Democracy has been ratified by thirty States.

2438. Constitutive Act Art. 4(g). *See also* PSC Protocol Art. 4(c), and African Charter on Democracy Arts 3 and 4(1).

2439. *See supra* para. 202.

2440. The New Partnership for Africa's Development (NEPAD) Declaration 2001, Heyns & Killander, Compendium of Key Human Rights 2013, 486.

2441. Heyns & Killander, Compendium of Key Human Rights 2013, 492.

2442. *See* S.-A. Elvy, 'Towards a New Democratic Africa: The African Charter on Democracy, Elections and Governance', *Emory International Law Review* 27 (2013): 41.

2443. African Charter on Democracy Arts 3–6.

2444. *Ibid.*, Arts 11–13, 38(1).

2445. *Ibid.*, Art. 39.

2446. *Ibid.*, Arts 15, 38(1).

2447. *Ibid.*, Arts 3(4), 3(11), 4(2), 17, 38(1). *See* Hatchard, Ndulo & Slinn, 108–114, 120–122. *See* further *Actions pour la Protection des Droit de l'Homme (APDH) v. Côte d'Ivoire*, African Court of Human and Peoples' Rights, App. No. 001/2014 (18 Nov. 2016).

2448. African Charter on Democracy Art. 19(1). *See* generally Hatchard, Ndulo & Slinn, 114, 120.

2449. African Charter on Democracy Arts 3(10), 23–26. *See also ibid.*, Art. 14(2)–(3).

control over the military and security forces.[2450] Fourth, State Parties commit themselves to a series of measures designed to advance political, economic and social governance.[2451]

488. Other, more specific, commitments to constitutionalism that attract comment include that of the supremacy of the constitution.[2452] The Westminster model of parliamentary sovereignty, which has not served Africa well, is therefore rejected.[2453] Another important pledge is that to the separation of powers.[2454] There is a commitment to local government, in that power should be decentralized to democratically elected local authorities.[2455] The extent of the devolution of such powers, and to which levels of local government, be it federal, district, county, etc. is a matter for the States themselves to determine. And significantly, State Parties undertake to ensure constitutional transfer of power.[2456] In this regard, it may be helpful if limits on continuous terms of office of executive Presidents were adopted by State Parties, and more importantly, adhered to.[2457] These commitments have been renewed in Agenda 2063, which stresses that respect for democratic values and practices, human rights, the rule of law and good governance, and the creation of capable institutions, is essential for sustainable socio-economic development.[2458]

489. The AU has put in place a comprehensive framework to bolster constitutionalism, good governance and participatory democracy which extends to practical measures through AU organs such as the PSC. Significantly, this includes the ability to impose sanctions on unconstitutional regimes.[2459] The AU accepts that progress in these fields is unlikely to be sustained unless socio-economic conditions also improve since impoverishment can lead to apathy or instability and create conditions that undermine the legitimacy of governing regimes, including democratic ones. Recent events, such

---

2450. *Ibid.*, Art. 14(1).
2451. *Ibid.*, Arts 27–43.
2452. *Ibid.*, Art. 10(1). *See* , e.g., Constitution of Namibia Art. 1(6), Constitution of Zimbabwe s. 3.
2453. However, Hatchard, Ndulo & Slinn, 15–19, argue that criticisms of the imposition of inappropriate Westminster-style constitutions have been exaggerated.
2454. African Charter on Democracy Art. 3(5).
2455. *Ibid.*, Art. 34. *See* generally, Hatchard, Ndulo & Slinn, Ch. 9.
2456. African Charter on Democracy Art. 5.
2457. *See* Hatchard, Ndulo & Slinn, 63–66. Violence has often broken out as a result of unconstitutional attempts at extending term limits, as in Burkina Faso in 2014 and Burundi in 2015.
2458. Assembly, *Decision on the Report of the Commission on Development of the African Union Agenda 2063*, AU Doc. Assembly/AU/Dec. 565(XXIV) (30–31 Jan. 2015).
2459. *See supra* paras 85–92.

as those in Mali,[2460] Burkina Faso,[2461] Burundi,[2462] Guinea-Bissau,[2463] and The Gambia,[2464] demonstrate that the AU's work in this field is a challenging one with much remaining to be done. The AU has not always been consistent in its approach to such difficult events.[2465] But in collaboration with other organizations, such as the UN and ECOWAS, the AU is succeeding in its mission to bolster democracy.

§6. International Criminal Law

490. In June 2014 the AU adopted a Protocol on Amendments to the Protocol on the Statute of the ACJHR[2466] (Malabo Protocol) adding an International Criminal Law Section[2467] (ICL Section) to the ACJHR competent to hear all cases relating to

---

2460. In January 2012 a rebellion by a Tuareg rebel group broke out in northern Mali which escalated when jihadi militants joined in, leading to the seizure of the region. In March 2012 disaffected soldiers overthrew the President shortly before scheduled presidential elections. International pressure, including from the AU and ECOWAS, led to the restoration of civilian rule and the election of an interim president in April 2012.

2461. In 2014 Burkina Faso was thrown into political crisis following the President's attempt to amend the Constitution to allow him to stand for another term. In 2015 a section of the military carried out a coup d'état but pressure from the UN, AU and ECOWAS forced the putschists to hand over power, and a successful transition to civilian rule occurred, Report of the UN Secretary-General on strengthening the partnership between the United Nations and the African Union on issues of peace and security in Africa, UN Doc. S/2016/780, para. 22.

2462. In 2015 the political climate in Burundi deteriorated, with a rising tide of violence, when it was announced that the incumbent President would seek a further term of office. The escalating violence, including a failed coup d'état, led the PSC in December 2015 to authorize the deployment of a peacekeeping mission which was called off in face of governmental intransigence which threatened to resist the 'invasion' with force. Regional efforts at mediation continue, Report of the UN Secretary-General on strengthening the partnership between the United Nations and the African Union on issues of peace and security in Africa, UN Doc. S/2016/780, para. 23; Assembly, *Decision on the State of Peace and Security in Africa*, AU Doc. Assembly/AU/Dec.612(XXVII) (17–1 Jul. 2016), para. 1. *See* further UN Security Council Res. 2303 (2016).

2463. *See* UN Security Council Res. 2343 (2016).

2464. The Gambia was confronted with a constitutional crisis when outgoing President Jammeh rejected the result of the presidential election held in December 2016, won lawfully by the opposition candidate, and attempted to extend his term in office. In January 2017 the PSC announced that President Jammeh would no longer be recognized as The Gambia's legitimate ruler, a decision endorsed by the UN Security Council, *see* Res. 2337(2017). President Jammeh's refusal to accept defeat led ECOWAS to intervene militarily in the crisis, ECOWAS Mission in The Gambia (ECOMIG), forcing Jammeh's departure.

2465. Wiebusch, 26.

2466. Protocol on Amendments to the Protocol on the Statute of the African Court of Justice and Human Rights (27 Jun. 2014) https://au.int/en/treaties, Heyns & Killander, Compendium of Key Human Rights 2016, 62. No ratifications to date. For comment, *see* G.J. Naldi &K.D. Magliveras, 'The International Criminal Law Section of the African Court of Justice and Human Rights: An Appraisal', *AYBIL* 21 (2015): 297.

2467. Statute of the African Court of Justice and Human Rights annexed to the Protocol Art. 6 (2014 Statute).

international crimes listed in the amended Statute.[2468] This historic and controversial development appears to have been occasioned by a number of concerns that have emerged in Africa regarding international criminal justice and the AU's consequent disenchantment with the ICC.[2469] In particular, these concerns touch upon the ICC's pursuit of senior African officials, notably Sudanese President Al-Bashir and Kenyan President Uhuru Kenyatta, and the perception that the ICC does not take account of the immunity of incumbent heads of state, contrary to established rules of international law;[2470] and the surrounding controversy on the reach of the Statute of the ICC[2471] (Rome Statute) to non-States Parties and whether the latter are obliged to give effect to ICC arrest warrants.[2472] In addition, because much of the ICC's work has focused on situations in Africa the opinion has formed that the ICC was culpable of selective justice by unjustly targeting Africa. The AU regards the arrest warrants against African Heads of State as undermining international law and as an affront to the 'dignity, sovereignty and integrity of the continent'.[2473] As a consequence, the AU has raised the threat of mass withdrawals by African States from the Rome Statute.[2474] But regardless of the actual reasons, the adoption of the Malabo Protocol could seriously undermine the mandate of the ICC and threaten the integrity of this developing branch of international law.

491. The rest of this section is given over to a discussion of the jurisdiction of the ICL Section. The temporal jurisdiction of the ICL Section extends only to crimes committed after the entry into force of the Malabo Protocol and the annexed Statute.[2475]

2468. 2014 Statute Art. 17(3).

2469. K.D. Magliveras & G.J. Naldi, 'The International Criminal Court's Involvement with Africa: An Evaluation of a Fractious Relationship', *Nordic J.I.L.* 82 (2013): 417; G. Werle, L. Fernandez & M. Vormbaum (eds), *Africa and the International Criminal Court* (The Hague: T.M.C. Asser Press, 2014).

2470. C.C. Jalloh, 'Reflections on the Indictment of Sitting Heads of State and Government and Its Consequences for Peace and Stability and Reconciliation in Africa', *African Journal Legal Studies* 7 (2014): 43. *See Arrest Warrant of 11 April 2000 (DR Congo v. Belgium)* I.C.J. Reports 2002, 3.

2471. Statute of the International Criminal Court (17 Jul. 1998), 2187 U.N.T.S. 3.

2472. *Prosecutor v. Omar Hassan Ahmad Al Bashir* (Decision Pursuant to Art. 87(7) of the Rome Statute on the Failure of the Republic of Malawi to Comply with the Cooperation Requests Issued by the Court with respect to the Arrest and Surrender Omar Hassan Ahmad Al Bashir) [2011] ICC-02/05-01/09, 51 I.L.M.397 (2012). *See* K. Magliveras & G. Naldi, 'The ICC Addresses Non-Cooperation by State Parties in Arresting President Al-Bashir: The Malawi Decision', *African Journal Legal Studies* 6 (2013): 1.

2473. Assembly, *Decision on the Report of the Commission on the Meeting of African States Parties to the ICC Statute of the International Criminal Court (ICC)*, AU Doc. Assembly/AU/Dec. 245 (XIII) (1–3 Jul. 2009).

2474. *See* , e.g., Assembly, *Decision on the International Criminal Court*, AU Doc. Assembly/AU/ Dec. 616 (XXVII) (17–18 Jul. 2016). In 2016 both Burundi and The Gambia gave notice of their withdrawal from the Rome Statute although the latter's was rescinded by the new government in 2017. More serious was South Africa's notice of withdrawal which in 2017 was held to be unconstitutional and invalid without prior parliamentary approval, *Democratic Alliance v. Minister of International Relations and Cooperation and Others* (Case No. 83145/2016, 22 Feb. 2017).

2475. 2014 Statute Art. 46E(1).

AU Member States automatically accept the ICL Section's jurisdiction upon ratification of the Malabo Protocol and Statute.[2476] However, non-contracting parties may accept its jurisdiction in certain circumstances on an ad hoc basis by means of an express declaration.[2477] The ICL Section can thereby exercise jurisdiction over crimes committed in the territory of a non-State party.[2478] Thc bases of jurisdiction are wider than those envisaged in Article 12 of the Rome Statute and extend to crimes committed in the territory of a State, the State of which the accused is a national, the nationality of the victim (passive personality principle) and extraterritorial application, i.e., punishing acts committed abroad by non-nationals prejudicial to a contracting party's vital interests (protective principle).[2479] The latter assertions of jurisdiction are controversial. The passive personality principle has generally enjoyed little support but, since in recent years it has been incorporated into counter-terrorism conventions and finds expression in the African human rights system, it has its defenders. Alternatively, it could be considered an expression of the principle of diplomatic protection which can be found in some human rights treaties. The protective principle has again been applied in relation to terrorism and other serious offences against state security such as espionage, counterfeiting and smuggling.[2480]

492. Equally, the ICL Section's jurisdiction *ratione materiae* is considerably broader than that of the ICC. The 2014 Statute takes an expansive stance; it does not restrict itself solely to the 'most serious crimes', it does not make distinctions based on the gravity of the offences. In contrast, it allows for flexibility by including a number of transnational crimes which are reflected in different legal sources, including the definition of international crimes in the Draft Code of Crimes against the Peace and Security of Mankind of 1996,[2481] as well as some proposals on a wide range of serious crimes considered by the Conference which drafted the Rome Statute.[2482] In addition to the core crimes of genocide, crimes against humanity and war crimes, it includes the crime of unconstitutional changes of government, mercenarism, piracy, terrorism, corruption, money laundering, drug trafficking, people trafficking, trafficking in hazardous wastes, and the illicit exploitation of natural resources.[2483] Many of these practices may be considered as prohibited by customary and/or treaty law, even if regionally. However, several of the 'crimes' listed in the 2014 Statute 'are not as yet fixed in the international criminal law firmament'[2484] since they include offences at an

2476. *Ibid.*, Art. 46E*bis* (1).
2477. *Ibid.*, Art. 46E*bis* (3).
2478. *Ibid.*, Art. 46E*bis* (2)(a).
2479. *Ibid.*, Art. 46E*bis* (2) (c)–(d).
2480. A. Aust, *Handbook of International Law* (Cambridge: Cambridge University Press, 2005), 45.
2481. International Law Commission, 'Draft Code of Crimes against the Peace and Security of Mankind', *Yearbook of the International Law Commission* vol. II(2) (1996).
2482. J. Dugard, 'Obstacles in the Way of an International Criminal Court', *Cambridge Law Journal* 56 (1997): 329; N. Boister, 'The Exclusion of Treaty Crimes from the Jurisdiction of the Proposed International Criminal Court: Law, Pragmatism, Politics', *Journal Armed Conflict Law* 3 (1998): 27, 27–28.
2483. 2014 Statute Art. 28A. *See* G. Werle & M. Vormbaum (eds), *The African Criminal Court: A Commentary on the Malabo Protocol* (The Hague: T.M.C. Asser Press, 2017), Part II.
2484. M. du Plessis, *Implications of the AU Decisions Giving the African Court Jurisdiction over International Crimes* (Institute for Security Studies Paper No. 235, 2012), 7–8.

embryonic state of development, whereas others, e.g., coups d'état and mercenarism, reflect African concerns and priorities. Nevertheless, the question does arise as to whether some of these, again coups d'état and mercenarism, however reprehensible, meet the definition of 'most serious crimes of concern to the International community as a whole' as understood by Article 5(1) of the Rome Statute, or indeed, whether they constitute international crimes at all according to universal international law.[2485] Of course, the drafters of the 2014 Statute are free to classify these practices as international crimes if they so wish. Moreover, the AU has notably succeeded in adopting a definition of the crime of aggression, something that eluded the ICC for many years.[2486] Finally, the list of crimes set out in the 2014 Statute is not exhaustive as the Assembly can add further crimes in line with the development of international law.[2487]

493. Jurisdiction *ratione personae* also merits attention. The question of head of state immunity has been a key concern of the AU in light of the controversy generated by the ICC indictments of Presidents Al-Bashir and Kenyatta, and Colonel Gaddafi.[2488] Fundamental disagreement on this issue was one of the driving forces behind the AU's decision in drafting the Malabo Protocol. Notwithstanding jurisprudence that a rule of customary international law removing immunity from heads of states before international tribunals with respect to international crimes has crystallized,[2489] the AU's consistent position is that heads of state continue to enjoy immunity in accordance with traditional rules of international law unless waived explicitly.[2490] The 2014 Statute therefore makes provision for absolute immunity for serving AU heads of state or government, and senior officials during their term of office.[2491] However, this does not mean that impunity for the perpetrators of human rights abuses is condoned. The 2014 Statute makes provision for the attribution of individual criminal responsibility and establishes that the accused's previous position no longer provides a defence to absolve

2485. Cassese, *International Criminal Law* 12–13.

2486. 2014 Statute Art. 28M. A text defining the crime of aggression was adopted at the ICC Review Conference with a view to entry into force by 2017, 'First ICC Review Conference: Resolutions and Declarations', 49 I.L.M. 1328, 1334–1335 (2010).

2487. 2014 Statute Art. 28A(2).

2488. *The Prosecutor v. Omar Hassan Ahmad Al Bashir* ICC-02/05-01/09; *The Prosecutor v. Uhuru Muigai Kenyatta*, ICC-01/09-02/11; *The Prosecutor v. Muammar Mohammed Abu Minyar Gaddafi, Saif Al-Islam Gaddafi and Abdullah Al-Senussi*, ICC-01/11-01/11.

2489. *Prosecutor v. Omar Hassan Ahmad Al Bashir* (Decision Pursuant to Art. 87(7) of the Rome Statute on the Failure of the Republic of Malawi to Comply with the Cooperation Requests Issued by the Court with respect to the Arrest and Surrender Omar Hassan Ahmad Al Bashir) [2011] ICC-02/05-01/09, 51 I.L.M. 397,405–407 (2012); Special Court of Sierra Leone, *Prosecutor v. Charles Ghankay Taylor*, Decision on Immunity from Jurisdiction, SCSL-2003-01-1 (3014–3039)(31 May 2004) paras 51–53. The ICC's conclusion was described by the AU as fundamentally flawed and contrary to international law, AU Commission, 'On the Decisions of Pre-Trial Chamber I of the International Criminal Court (ICC) Pursuant to Article 87(7) of the ICC Statute', Press Release No. 002/2012 (9 Jan. 2012).

2490. Assembly, 'Decision on the Report of the Second Meeting of States Parties to the ICC Statute of the International Criminal Court (ICC)', Assembly/AU/Dec. 270(XIV) (31 Jan.–2 Feb. 2010) para. 8.

2491. 2014 Statute Art. 46A*bis*. *See* D. Tladi, 'The Immunity Provision in the AU Amendment Protocol: Separating the (Doctrinal) Wheat from the (Normative) Chaff', *Journal International Criminal Justice* 13 (2015): 3.

him/her from responsibility.[2492] This provision is in line with the traditional position that former officials may have to face criminal proceedings before transnational criminal courts.[2493]

494. Another significant innovation is that jurisdiction is extended over legal persons, including corporations.[2494] The inclusion of corporate legal liability may be understandable in the era of globalization and especially in light of the sometimes callous and irresponsible behaviour shown by transnational corporations (TNCs) especially in countries of the South.[2495] Given that international criminal law imposes obligations upon individuals, logic would dictate that, particularly since the 2014 Statute includes corruption and illicit trade in hazardous wastes as core crimes, duties are extended to legal persons such as TNCs. That treaties may impose duties on TNCs is no longer to be considered exceptional and certainly an increasing trend exists to impose human rights standards on TNCs[2496] but a challenging difficulty remains: according to traditional international law corporations are mere objects of international law or at best have limited international personality.[2497] However, in principle there exists no legal impediment to States agreeing to make corporations criminally liable under international law.[2498] There does appear to be an increasing trend toward criminal liability for corporations in international law which the 2014 Statute reflects. But the end result could be to deter TNCs from conducting business in Africa at a time when the Continent is in need of foreign investments and seeks to improve its global image as an enterprise-friendly place.

495. The 2014 Statute contains a complementarity clause.[2499] Accordingly, the jurisdiction of the ICL Section is complementary to national criminal jurisdictions whereby national courts are as a rule given precedence where the State is willing and able to investigate and prosecute the case.[2500] This principle has been understood as

---

2492. 2014 Statute Art. 46B(1)–(2).

2493. *Arrest Warrant of 11 April 2000 (D.R. Congo v. Belgium)* I.C.J. Reports 2002, 3, paras 58–61.

2494. 2014 Statute Art. 46C(1).

2495. *See The Social and Economic Rights Action Center and the Center for Economic and Social Rights v. Nigeria* Communication No. 155/96 (2001).

2496. The UN Norms on the Responsibilities of Transnational Corporations and Other Business Enterprises with Regard to Human Rights, adopted in August 2003 by the UN Sub-Commission on the Promotion and Protection of Human Rights Resolution 2003/16, UN Doc. E/CN.4/Sub.2/2003/12/Rev.2 (2003), provides a set of standard-setting principles for socially responsible corporate behaviour. In 2014 the UN Human Rights Council set up an intergovernmental working group on a legally binding instrument on transnational corporations with respect to human rights, UN Doc. A/HRC/26/L.22/Rev. 1.

2497. P. Malanczuk (ed.), *Akehurst's Modern Introduction to International Law* (7th rev. edn, London: Routledge, 1997), 100–103; Special Tribunal for Lebanon, *New TV S.A.L. v. Karma Mohamed Thasin al Khayat*, STL-14-05/I/CJ/ (31 January 2014) paras 18, 25; *Akhbar Beirut S.A.L. v. Ibrahim Mohamed al Amin*, STL-14-06/I/CJ/ (31 Jan. 2014) paras 18, 25.

2498. *New TV S.A.L. v. Karma Mohamed Thasin al Khayat*, STL-14-05/I/CJ/ (31 Jan. 2014) para. 26; *Akhbar Beirut S.A.L. v. Ibrahim Mohamed al Amin*, STL-14-06/I/CJ/ (31 Jan. 2014) para. 26.

2499. 2014 Statute Art. 46H(1).

2500. *Ibid.*, Art. 46H(2); Cassese, *International Criminal Law*, 342–343. Thus, the ICL Section could assume jurisdiction where the national proceedings constitute a sham, 2014 Statute Art. 46H(3)–(4), 46I(2).

applying solely to national authorities[2501] but intriguingly the 2014 Statute additionally mentions the courts of the Regional Economic Communities (RECs). Regrettably the 2014 Statute is exceptionally vague on the relationship between the ICL Section and the courts of the RECs but references to 'other Court' and 'another Court' in Article 46I would suggest that the ICL Section would relinquish jurisdiction to the courts of the RECs.

496. Despite the fact that over thirty African States have ratified the Rome Statute, the Malabo Protocol does not contain a savings clause, in fact there is no mention of the ICC at all, so that the relationship between the two bodies is not addressed explicitly except to the effect that States that ratify the Malabo Protocol accept the jurisdiction of the Court.[2502] International law, set out in Article 30(3) of the Vienna Convention on the Law of Treaties regarding incompatibility between successive treaties on the same subject matter, indicates that the Malabo Protocol, when it enters into force, would prevail over the Rome Statute for those contracting parties that have ratified the latter if *incompatibility* were deemed to arise. There may be an incentive for some States in accepting the 2014 Protocol, even if on an ad hoc basis, in that its list of crimes is more expansive than that in the Rome Statute. Of course, those unhappiest with the ICC but still keen on expressing support for international criminal justice may denounce the Rome Statute and transfer their allegiance to the African alternative. Such a development would have disturbing implications for the role and standing of the ICC should a significant number of African States withdraw. However, certain African countries, e.g., Botswana, are staunch ICC supporters. In fact, the deep divisions caused by this issue were on display at an extraordinary session of the Assembly that took place in October 2013 on the AU's relationship with the ICC where a call for mass withdrawal from the Rome Statute failed to be carried.[2503] The ICL Section is designed, *inter alia*, as an attractive option for those African regimes that would never contemplate accepting the Rome Statute, although whether some of the worst perpetrators of human rights abuses would choose even this course of action is open to doubt. But it should not be overlooked that the ICC has ruled that jurisdiction has also been conferred to it under the UN Security Council's Chapter VII powers in accordance with Article 13(b) of the Rome Statute.[2504] Therefore, if an African State's obligations under the Malabo Protocol and a suitable ICC decision proved incompatible, the latter would prevail consistent with Article 103 of the UN Charter.

2501. Cassese, *International Criminal Law*, 343.

2502. 2014 Statute Art. 46E*bis* (1).

2503. Assembly, *Decision on Africa's Relationship with the International Criminal Court (ICC)*, AU Doc. Ext/Assembly/AU/Dec. 1 (12 Oct. 2013).

2504. *See* , *inter alia*, *The Prosecutor v. Omar Hassan Ahmad Al Bashir,* Decision Pursuant to Art. 87(7) of the Rome Statute on the Failure of the Republic of Malawi to Comply with the Cooperation Requests Issued by the Court with respect to the Arrest and Surrender Omar Hassan Ahmad Al Bashir, ICC-02/05-01/09.

§7. Cyber Security

497. The challenges posed by the digital age, access to information, the ease in communications, e-commerce, fraud and crime, computer security, data protection, among others, require responses which to be truly effective must be dealt with at a transnational level. This is because, to take one example, cybercrime is borderless, the perpertrators and victims of cybercrimes often located in different national jurisdictions. Europe took the lead in seeking to address these problems, adopting the Convention on Cybercrime in 2001 (Budapest Convention).[2505] The focus of the Budapest Convention is on harmonizing national criminal law with regard to computer offences, providing national criminal law powers for the investigation and prosecution of cybercrime and enhancing international cooperation.[2506] In 2014 the AU followed suit with the adoption of the Convention on Cyber Security, or Malabo Convention.[2507] Unlike the Budapest Convention, the AU Convention on Cyber Security assumes a broader perspective bringing within its scope not only cybercrime but also electronic transactions or e-commerce, personal data protection and cybersecurity and cybercrime.[2508] It therefore borrows considerably from the EU Data Protection Directive. The AU Convention on Cyber Security establishes a standard legal and security framework for all these activities. However, the wisdom of this wide-ranging approach has attracted scepticism as overly ambitious and unrealistic.[2509] On the other hand, in relation to cybercrime and national criminal law powers, the AU Convention is not as far-reaching as the Budapest Convention, nor does it provide a framework for international cooperation.[2510] But it is important to note that the AU Convention is more in the nature of a traité cadre, leaving States with considerable discretion in establishing the detailed

2505. European Convention on Cybercrime (23 Nov.2001), E.T.S. No. 185. It is interesting to note that a number of African States are parties to the Budapest Convention, including Ghana, Mauritius, Senegal and South Africa. However, the EU had already taken the initiative, adopting EU Council Directive 95/46 of 24 Oct. 1995 on the protection of individuals with regard to the processing of personal data and on the free movement of such data, O.J. L 281/31, 24 Oct. 1995 (Data Protection Directive). The Data Protection Directive will be superseded in 2018 by EU Council Regulation 2016/679 of 27 Apr. 2016 on the protection of natural persons with regard to the processing of personal data and on the free movement of such data, O.J. L 119/1, 27 Apr. 2016, an expanded and more coherent, protective framework with enhanced enforcement.

2506. *See* generally A.M. Weber, 'The Council of Europe's Convention on Cybercrime', *Berkeley Technology Law Journal* 18 (2003): 425; M.A. Vatis, *The Council of Europe Convention on Cybercrime*, Proceedings of a Workshop on Deterring Cyberattacks: Informing Strategies and Developing Options for US Policy http://www.nap.edu/catalog/12997.html.

2507. Convention on Cyber Security and Personal Data Protection (27 Jun. 2014) https://au.int/en/treaties, not yet in force.

2508. G. Greenleaf & M. Georges, 'The African Union's Data Privacy Convention: A Major Step Toward Global Consistency?', *Privacy Laws & Business International Report* 131 (2014): 18; E. Tamarkin, *The AU's Cybercrime Response: A Positive Start, but Substantial Challenges Ahead* (ISS Policy Brief 73, Pretoria: Institute for Security Studies, 2015).

2509. Tamarkin, 4.

2510. Glacy+, *Comparative analysis of the Malabo Convention of the African Union and the Budapest Convention on cybercrime* 3–4 http://www.coe.int/cybercrime.

framework.[2511] The question has also been posed as to whether Africa has the practical and technical capacity to address many of these issues.[2512]

498. Article 1 of the AU Convention on Cyber Security contains a list of definitions. However, it has been observed that some crucial definitions, such as 'service provider' and 'traffic data', have been omitted.[2513] But it is also true to say that the list of definitions in the AU Convention is more comprehensive than that of the Budapest Convention.

499. The AU Convention on Cyber Security seeks to ensure security of electronic transactions.[2514] E-commerce is to be exercised freely in the States Parties, the one exception being gambling.[2515] There may be sound public interest reasons for such a prohibition but it may have been preferable to have adopted an approach similar to that of EU Law where cross-border gambling is usually permissible subject to proportionate and non-discriminatory restrictions.[2516]

500. The AU Convention on Cyber Security establishes a legal and regulatory framework on personal data protection and cyber security. With regard to the former, the objective is to strengthen protection of data and punish any violation of privacy but 'without prejudice to the principle of free flow of personal data.'[2517] The AU Convention on Cyber Security extends to the collection, processing,[2518] transmission,

---

2511. Several passages in the Preamble support this interpretation.

2512. *Ibid.* 4–5.

2513. Glacy+, 5.

2514. AU Convention on Cyber Security Art. 7.

2515. *Ibid.*, Art. 2(1)(a).

2516. *See* , e.g., Case C-275/92 *HM Customs & Excise v. Schindler* [1994] E.C.R. I-1039; Case C-243/01 *Criminal proceedings against Piergiorgio Gambelli and others* [2003] E.C.R. I-13031.

2517. AU Convention on Cyber Security Art. 8. Personal data is defined as 'any information relating to an identified or identifiable natural person by which this person can be identified, directly or indirectly…by reference to an identification number or to one or more factors specific to his/her physical, physiological, mental, economic, cultural or social identity', *ibid.*, Art. 1. Compare Data Protection Directive Art. 2(a). Personal data can therefore include names, nationality, gender, ethnicity, religion, telephone numbers, fingerprints, images caught on camera. *See* , e.g., Case C-101/01 *Criminal proceedings against Bodil Lindquist* [2003] E.C.R. I-12971, para. 24; Cases C-141/12 and C-372/12 *Minister voor Immigratie v. M.*, Judgment of 17 Jul. 2014, C:2014:2081, paras 34, 38–41; Case C-291/12 *Schwarz v. Bochum*, Judgment of 17 Oct. 2013, C:2013:670, para. 27; Case C-212/13 *Rynes v. Úřad pro Ochranu Údajů*, Judgment of 11 December 2014, C:2014:2428, para. 22.

2518. Processing is defined as 'any operation … which is performed upon personal data, whether or not by automatic means such as the collection, recording, organization, storage, adaptation, alteration, retrieval, backup, copy, consultation, use, disclosure by transmission, dissemination or otherwise making available, alignment or combination and locking, encryption, erasure or destruction of personal data', AU Convention on Cyber Security Art. 1. Compare Data Protection Directive Art. 2(b). Processing can include loading personal data on an internet page, communication of name and address, taking and storing fingerprints, video surveillance involving the recording and storage personal data. *See* , e.g., Case C-101/01 *Lindquist* para. 25; Case C-461/10 *Bonnier Audio et al. v. Perfect Communication Sweden*, Judgment of 19 Apr. 2012, C:2012:219, para. 52; Case C-291/12 *Schwarz v. Bochum*, Judgment of 17 Oct. 2013, C:2013:670, paras 28–29; Case C-212/13 *Rynes v. Úřad pro Ochranu Údajů*, Judgment of 11 Dec. 2014, C:2014:2428, para. 24.

storage or use of personal data, and the automated or non-automated processing of data, by the public and private sectors.[2519] Data processing relating to public or State security, defence, research, or criminal prosecution is included subject to exceptions.[2520] However, data processing by an individual for his/her personal or household activities is excepted unless for 'systematic communication to third parties or for dissemination'.[2521] Also excepted is personal data processing for journalistic and research purposes and artistic and literary expression.[2522]

501. The processing of personal data is subject to a number of conditions.[2523] The central basic principles include that of consent (subject to certain exceptions);[2524] lawfulness and fairness; accuracy; transparency; and confidentiality and security.[2525] The collection and processing of sensitive data revealing racial and ethnic origin, parental filiation, political opinion, religious and philosophical beliefs, trade union membership, sex life and health is prohibited.[2526] This prohibition is not absolute and does not therefore apply in a variety of circumstances, including where written consent has been given, in the course of legal proceedings, or in the public interest for historical, statistical or scientific purposes.[2527]

2519. AU Convention on Cyber Security Art. 9(1)(a)–(b). It is interesting to note that the CJEU has held that EU Law precludes a general and indiscriminate retention of traffic and location data, Cases C-203/15 and C-698/15 *Tele2 Sverige AB v. Post-och telestyrelsen*, Judgment of 21 Dec. 2016, C:2016:70.

2520. AU Convention on Cyber Security Art. 9(1)(d). Compare Data Protection Directive Art. 3(2). The CJEU has held that national measures providing for the retention of traffic and location data is justified if limited to what is strictly necessary, such as with the objective of fighting serious crime, Cases C-293/12 and C-594/12 *Digital Rights Ireland v. Minister for Communications, Marine and Natural Resources*, Judgment of 8 Apr. 2014, C:2014:238; Cases C-203/15 and C-698/15 *Tele2 Sverige AB v. Post-och telestyrelsen*, Judgment of 21 Dec. 2016, C:2016:70.

2521. AU Convention on Cyber Security Art. 9(2)(a). Compare Data Protection Directive Art. 3(2). *See* Case C-101/01 *Lindquist* paras 45–47.

2522. AU Convention on Cyber Security Art. 14(3). Compare Data Protection Directive Art. 9. In Case C-73/07 *Finnish Data Protection Ombudsman v. Satakunnan Markkinaporssi Oy and Satamedia Oy* [2007] E.C.R. I-7075, para. 61 the ECJ stated that activities may be categorized as journalistic if their sole object is the disclosure to the public of information or opinions irrespective of the medium used to transmit them.

2523. AU Convention on Cyber Security Art. 13.

2524. Data Protection Directive Art. 7(a) requires the consent to be unambiguous. However, circumventing consent may be justified, *inter alia*, in the legitimate interests pursued by the controller, *ibid.*, Art. 7(f), a provision absent from the AU Convention on Cyber Security. A balance of interests is required, Case C-131/12 *Google Spain SL v. AEPD & Mario Costeja Gonzalez*, Judgment of 13 May 2014, C:2014:317, paras 70–75.

2525. *See* Case C-291/12 *Schwarz v. Bochum*, Judgment of 17 Oct. 2013, C:2013:670.

2526. AU Convention on Cyber Security Art. 14(1). Compare Data Protection Directive Art. 8(1). *See* Case C-101/01 *Lindquist* paras 50–51, where the CJEU stated that personal data regarding health must be given a broad interpretation so as to include mental and physical health.

2527. AU Convention on Cyber Security Art. 14(2). Compare Data Protection Directive Art. 8(2).

502. The data subject[2528] is conferred a number of rights which are a right to information,[2529] a right of access,[2530] a right to object,[2531] and a right of rectification or erasure.[2532]

503. The AU Convention on Cyber Security imposes a number of obligations on data controllers.[2533] These include confidentiality, security and storage responsibilities.[2534]

504. The AU Convention on Cyber Security requires States Parties to set up independent national personal data protection authorities (NPA) tasked with protecting personal data.[2535] In ensuring that information technologies do not threaten public freedoms and privacy NPAs have a broad mandate. These include responding to requests for an opinion regarding personal data processing; informing persons and data controllers of their rights and obligations; adjudging claims and complaints regarding the processing of personal data; informing the judicial authorities of offences that have come to their attention; imposing sanctions on data controllers; and authorizing transborder transfer of personal data.[2536] In addition, NPAs can warn and order data controllers to stop breaches of the AU Convention.[2537] Moreover, should a data controller fail to comply the NPAs can withdraw their authorizations and impose monetary penalties.[2538] All decisions and sanctions by NPAs are subject to appeal.[2539] Unlike the

---

2528. According to AU Convention on Cyber Security Art. 1 the data subject refers to any 'natural person that is the subject of personal data processing'.

2529. AU Convention on Cyber Security Art. 16. Compare Data Protection Directive Arts 10–11.

2530. AU Convention on Cyber Security Art. 17. Compare Data Protection Directive Art. 12. *See* Cases C-141/12 and C-372/12 *Minister voor Immigratie v. M.*, Judgment of 17 Jul. 2014, C:2014:2081, paras 44–46, 59–60. The CJEU has held that access must be without constraint, without excessive delay and without excessive expense, Case C-486/12 *X*, Judgment of 12 Dec. 2013, C:2013:836. Access may be subject to reasonable time limits, Case C-553/07 *College van Burgemeester en Wethouders van Rotterdam v. Rijkeboer* [2009] E.C.R. I-3889, paras 55–57.

2531. AU Convention on Cyber Security Art. 18. Compare Data Protection Directive Art. 14.

2532. AU Convention on Cyber Security Art. 19. Compare Data Protection Directive Art. 12(b).*See* Case C-131/12 *Google Spain SL v. AEPD & Mario Costeja Gonzalez*, Judgment of 13 May 2014, C:2014:317, para. 98.

2533. Data controller refers to any natural or legal person, public or private, who collects and processes personal data, AU Convention on Cyber Security Art. 1. Compare Data Protection Directive Art. 2(d). *See* Case C-131/12 *Google Spain SL v. AEPD & Mario Costeja Gonzalez*, Judgment of 13 May 2014, C:2014:317, paras 33–41.

2534. AU Convention on Cyber Security Arts 20–23. Compare Data Protection Directive Arts 16–17. *See* Case C-342/12 *Worten-Equipamentos para o Lar v. Authority for Working Conditions*, Judgment of 30 May 2013, C: 2013: 355, paras 24–25.

2535. AU Convention on Cyber Security Art 11(1). State oversight of NPAs would be incompatible with the principle of independence, Case C-518/07 *Commission v. Germany* [2010] E.C.R. I-1885. *See also* Case C-614/10 *Commission v. Austria*, Judgment of 6 Oct. 2012, C:2012:631; Case C-288/12 *Commission v. Hungary*, Judgment of 8 Apr. 2014, C:2014:237.

2536. AU Convention on Cyber Security Art. 12(2).

2537. *Ibid.*, Art. 12(3).

2538. *Ibid.*, Art. 12(4).

2539. *Ibid.*, Art. 12(6).

Data Protection Directive the AU Convention does not compel States to provide a judicial remedy to persons whose rights may have been violated.[2540]

505. In relation to cybercrime, the AU Convention on Cyber Security requires States Parties to adopt legislative or regulatory measures providing for substantive law criminalizing cybercrime and procedural law powers necessary for the investigation and prosecution of these crimes.[2541] Cybercrime offences should be punishable by 'effective, proportionate and dissuasive criminal penalties' or other 'appropriate penalties', which may also be imposed on legal persons.[2542] National regulatory authorities must be put in place with the specific task of taking a leading role in all aspects of cyber security.[2543] Appropriate institutions to combat cybercrime should also be established.[2544] None of these measures should endanger the rights of individuals under national and international law.[2545]

506. The AU Convention on Cyber Security seeks to enhance international cooperation to combat cybercrime through the harmonization of the legislative or regulatory measures and respect for the principle of double criminal liability.[2546] States are encouraged to sign agreements on mutual legal assistance[2547] as well as information-sharing.[2548] The issue of how to settle competing claims to jurisdiction over an alleged offence between States, a likely eventuality, is thus addressed by implication.[2549]

507. States Parties are required to criminalize the following acts:[2550] attacks on computer systems (such as unauthorized access or entering or deleting data fraudulently);[2551] computerized data breaches (such as fraudulently intercepting data);[2552] content related offences (such as child pornography, racist or xenophobic propaganda, threats or insults based on race, national or ethnic origin or religion, genocide denial);[2553] and property

2540. Data Protection Directive Art. 22. However, States Parties are free to do so, AU Convention on Cyber Security Art. 14(4).

2541. AU Convention on Cyber Security Art. 25(1). *See also ibid.*, Art. 31(3). However, these powers do not appear to be as extensive as those under the Budapest Convention and incline to be somewhat imprecise and contain few safeguards, Glacy+, 4–5.

2542. AU Convention on Cyber Security Art. 31(1).*See also ibid.*, Art. 31(2). Art. 30(2) requires States Parties to enact laws providing for the criminal liability of legal persons.

2543. *Ibid.*, Art. 25(2).

2544. *Ibid.*, Art. 27(2).

2545. *Ibid.*, Art. 25(3).

2546. *Ibid.*, Art. 28(1).

2547. *Ibid.*, Art. 28(2).

2548. *Ibid.*, Art. 28(2)–(4).

2549. Compare Budapest Convention Art. 22(5).

2550. The point has been made that the AU Convention on Cyber Security omits a number of crucial *mens rea* elements, Glacy+, 4.

2551. AU Convention on Cyber Security Art. 29(1).

2552. *Ibid.*, Art. 29(2).

2553. *Ibid.*, Art. 29(3)(1). Compare the Additional Protocol concerning the Criminalization of Acts of a Racist and Xenophobic Nature through Computed Systems (28 Jan. 2003) E.T.S. 189.

offences (such as theft, fraud, money laundering or blackmail).[2554] No express provision is made for offences related to copyright infringement.[2555]

508. While the expectation is that States Parties will prosecute offenders the AU Convention on Cyber Security makes no explicit mention of the extradition of offenders although such a prospect may be envisaged in agreements on mutual legal assistance.

509. The AU Convention on Cyber Security has attracted criticism on human rights grounds.[2556] It is claimed that the criminalization of content related offences relating to hate speech, racist or xenophobic propaganda, or genocide denial, for instance, conflicts with the freedom of expression.[2557] However, it needs to be recalled that international human rights law does not consider the freedom of expression an absolute right but envisages limitations as lawful in certain circumstances[2558] or to prevent abuse.[2559]

510. In theory, these restrictions in the AU Convention do not appear sinister but seem compatible with international standards. More problematic, however, are the exceptions to the prohibitions on personal data processing on grounds of public interest or the exercise of official authority. These concepts are not defined in the AU Convention and could therefore be abused by national authorities. Another worrying provision is that whereby a court is permitted to authorize the search and seizure of computerized date when it is deemed 'useful in establishing the truth'.[2560] There is a certain Orwellian ring to this phrase. And while the AU Convention declares that all legal measures should be compatible with human rights law this guarantee is weakened by the fact that the African Charter on Human and Peoples' Rights does contain a right to privacy

2554. AU Convention on Cyber Security Art. 30(1). Although intellectual property is not specifically mentioned it is submitted that it comes within the scope of the term property, *Anheuser-Busch Inc. v. Portugal*, European Court of Human Rights [GC], 45 E.H.R.R. 830 (2007).

2555. Compare Budapest Convention Art. 10.

2556. Tamarkin, 4–5.

2557. It is clear that the freedom of expression applies to cyberspace, *Animal Defenders International v. United Kingdom*, European Court of Human Rights [GC], 57 E.H.R.R. 21 (2013); *Delfi AS v. Estonia*, European Court of Human Rights [GC], App. No. 64569/09, Judgment of 18 Jun. 2015.

2558. European Convention on Human Rights Art. 10(2) (4 Nov. 1950), C.E.T.S. No. 194, as amended (ECHR); International Covenant on Civil and Political Rights Art. 19(3) (16 Dec. 1966), 999 U.N.T.S. 171 (ICCPR). Such as the protection of intellectual property and copyright, *Neij and Sunde Kolmisoppi v. Sweden,* European Court of Human Rights, App. No. 40397/12, Judgment of 19 Feb. 2013.

2559. ECHR Art. 17; ICCPR Art. 20(2); American Convention on Human Rights Art. 13(5) (22 Nov. 1969), O.A.S.T.S. No. 36; Protocol concerning the Criminalization of Acts of a Racist and Xenophobic Nature. *See Faurisson v. France*, Communication No. 550/1993 (1996). The Grand Chamber has assumed the stance that ECHR Art. 17 applies only on an exceptional basis and in extreme cases, *Paksas v. Lithuania*, European Court of Human Rights [GC], App. No. 34932/04, Judgment of 6 Jan. 2011; *Perinçek v. Switzerland*, European Court of Human Rights [GC], App. No. 27510/08, Judgment of 15 Oct. 2015.

2560. AU Convention on Cyber Security Art. 31(3)(a),(b).

or private life.[2561] However, a safeguard clause provides that the AU Convention must not be interpreted in a manner inconsistent with international law.[2562]

2561. The centrality of a right to private life in accordance with ECHR Art. 8 has been stressed by the ECJ/CJEU, Cases C-465/00 and C-138/01 *Rechsnungshof v. Osterreichisher Rundfunk* [2003] E.C.R. I-4989, paras 70–71. *See also* Cases C-293/12 and C-594/12 *Digital Rights Ireland v. Minister for Communications, Marine and Natural Resources*, Judgment of 8 Apr. 2014, C:2014:238.

2562. AU Convention on Cyber Security Art. 33.

Part IV. The Relationship Between the African Union and Other International Organizations

511. A formal cooperative relationship between the OAU and the UN was first established in 1990 but a similar agreement between the UN and the AU was adopted only in November 2006.[2563] This framework agreement provides for cooperation between the two organizations across a wide range of areas, including economic and social development and peace and security. However, in light of changed circumstances and progress in Africa's political and economic governance, and cause for optimism in its prospects, the UN has recognized that an updated partnership agreement is required.[2564] Accordingly, the New United Nations and African Union Partnership on Africa's Integration and Development Agenda (PAIDA) is designed to provide UN support for the AU as it proceeds with implementing Agenda 2063.

512. Cooperation between the EU and African States dates back to the early days of the European Economic Community (EEC) (Yaoundé Convention 1963) but it was only at the Cairo Summit in 2000 that Africa-EU cooperation was placed on a formal footing. At the Lisbon Summit in December 2007 the Africa-EU Partnership was launched which adopted the Joint Africa-EU Strategy (JAES).[2565] The JAES concentrates on a number of policy areas, including peace and security, democratic governance and human rights, trade and infrastructure, and millennium development goals, and is implemented through action plans. The following Summit, held in November 2010 in Tripoli, built on these same priorities. The current action plan (2014–2017) focuses on five priority areas of cooperation agreed at the 4th EU-Africa Summit in Brussels in 2014.[2566] These are: peace and security; democracy, good governance and human rights; human development; sustainable development, growth and continental integration; and global and emerging issues. Peace and security as essential prerequisites for development and prosperity was stressed. It was agreed to support African capabilities in this area with a focus on capacity-building. In particular,

2563. *Enhancing UN-AU Cooperation: Framework for the ten-year capacity-building programme for the African Union*, UN Doc. A/61/630.

2564. Regional Coordination Mechanism for Africa, *Framework for a renewed United Nations and African Union Partnership on Africa's Integration and Development Agenda 2017-2027*. PAIDA was approved by the AU in 2015, Assembly, *Decision on the Framework for a Renewed UN/AU Partnership on Africa's Integration and Development Agenda [PAIDA] 2017-2027*, AU Doc. Assembly/AU/Dec.587(XXV) (14–15 Jun. 2015).

2565. *The Africa-EU Partnership: 2 unions, 1 vision*, http://www.africa-eu-partnership.org.

2566. *4th EU-Africa Summit 2014 – Roadmap 2014-2017*, http://www.consilium.europa.eu/eudocs/cms_Data/docs/pressdata/en/ec/142094.pdf.

they agreed to strengthen their common effort to fight international terrorism. The Summit pledged to stimulate long-term growth on both continents. The importance of encouraging greater investment and economic development within and between countries, in addition to developing transport, access to drinking water and sustainable and affordable energy was emphasized. It was agreed that a comprehensive approach to tackle the phenomenon of irregular migration was required. A shared commitment to fight human trafficking and to ensure respect of human rights for all migrants was reiterated. Important for African leaders, a commitment was made to enhancing political dialogue on international criminal justice and universal jurisdiction. In practice EU efforts have focused on providing political backing and predictable resources through the APF to African-led Peace Support Operations (PSOs), capacity-building measures and mediation activities at continental and regional levels.

513. The 5th EU-Africa Summit is due to be held in late 2017 and it has been proposed that the EU should pursue key strategic objectives based on increased cooperation in international arenas, increased security and sustainable economic development.[2567]

2567. European Commission, Joint Communication to the European Parliament and the Council for a renewed impetus of the Africa-EU Partnership, JOIN(2017) 17 final (4 May 2017).

Chapter 1. Cooperation on Economic Affairs

§1. The African Union and the United Nations

514. The focus of economic cooperation between the AU and the UN centres on the UN Economic Commission for Africa (ECA), one of the regional economic commissions established by the UN Economic and Social Council (ECOSOC) under Article 68 of the UN Charter.[2568] Based in Addis Ababa, membership of the ECA comprises the UN Member States of the region and thus includes Morocco but excludes the SADR. The EX is the AU's coordinating body.[2569] The ECA's mandate in broad terms is to support the economic and social development of its Members and Africa in general, promote regional integration and support international efforts at development. More specifically, it concentrates on such areas as macroeconomic policy, social development, gender issues, technological development, regional integration and trade, resource management, and good governance. The ECA's sessions are held annually.

515. In the 1980s Africa was faced with a series of serious socio-economic crises which led the UN to adopt a programme of action designed to bolster Africa's economic recovery, the UN PAAERD.[2570] UN PAAERD aimed to assist Africa to achieve self-reliant and self-sustained economic development through a new era of cooperation. The sectors identified for special measures included trade and finance, economic management, food and agriculture, and human resource development. An immediate objective was to boost productivity, especially in the food and agricultural sectors. However, the achievements of UN PAAERD were deemed unsatisfactory and it was replaced by the UN New Agenda for the Development of Africa in the 1990s (UN-NADAF).[2571] UN-NADAF similarly aimed at strengthening African economies, with particular emphasis on integration and infrastructure programmes and projects. Regrettably, UN-NADAF was also deemed a disappointment and it was therefore decided that comprehensive support for NEPAD might bear greater success.[2572]

516. In response to an initiative from the AU, in 2006 the UN General Assembly approved the devising and implementation of a ten-year capacity-building plan for the AU.[2573] This plan came to fruition in the 2006 Declaration, 'Enhancing UN-AU Cooperation: Framework for the ten-year capacity-building programme for the African Union.'[2574] This renewed partnership provided for enhanced cooperation between the

2568. ECOSOC Res. 671A (XXV). ECOSOC is the UN's principal body in the field of economic and social cooperation, UN Charter Art. 62. The ECA has its own website, http://www.uneca.org.
2569. Constitutive Act of the African Union Art. 13 (26 May 2001), 2158 U.N.T.S. 3; Rule 5 of the Rules of Procedure of the Executive Council, 13 R.A.D.I.C. (2005) 55.
2570. UN General Assembly Res. S-13/2 (1986). *See* G.J. Naldi, *The Organization of African Unity* (London & New York: Mansell, 1989), 170–174.
2571. UN Doc. A/46/151 (annex).
2572. UN General Assembly Res. 57/7 (2002).
2573. UN General Assembly Res. 60/1 (2005).
2574. UN Doc. A/61/630.

two organizations across a range of areas, including economic and social development, human rights, conflict prevention, and peace and security.

517. This arrangement has since been superseded by PAIDA, a new strategic partnership intended to provide UN collaboration and support for the AU in its endeavours to enhance economic and social conditions, particularly institutional and resource support. PAIDA is designed to be responsive to Africa's expressed aspirations, needs and priorities and is based on a number of principles, including AU ownership and leadership, accountability, consultation and co-ordination, observance of commitments made, and proactive engagement. The priority areas are: economic transformation; development, infrastructure and trade; regional integration; women's rights; agriculture; private sector development; health and nutrition; education and training; natural resource management; climate change; democracy and governance; human rights and the rule of law; and peace and security.

§2. The African Union and the European Union

518. The relationship between the AU and the EU is an important one. The EU is Africa's largest trading partner and makes substantial contributions to the AU's programme budget. The EU invests significant sums in Africa, on economic and human development, human rights, good governance and migration, energy and infrastructure projects, humanitarian assistance, and agri-food.[2575] This partnership is deepening. Early cooperation between the EEC and African States focused on providing financial support to French-speaking Africa to develop its infrastructure. This provided the basis for a series of agreements between the EC/EU and the African, Caribbean and Pacific (ACP) States (Lomé I-IV, Cotonou),[2576] characterized by non-reciprocal free trade arrangements for ACP States and aid packages designed to reduce and eradicate poverty, consistent with the objectives of sustainable development and the measured integration of the ACP countries into the world economy. The Cotonou Agreement, adopted in 2000, is broader in scope than the previous arrangements and has three principal elements, or pillars: development cooperation; economic and trade cooperation; and a political dimension.[2577] Briefly, the first pillar focuses on financial and technical assistance to support agreed cooperation policies. Under the second pillar the non-reciprocal free trade arrangements have been replaced, where desirable, by Economic Partnership Agreements providing for duty-free access to the markets in question. Under the third pillar political dialogue becomes a key facet and extends to peace and security and migration. Civil society is given a central role. Good governance, and specifically combating corruption, is a 'fundamental element'. Conflict prevention and resolution and peace-building are other important features. It is important to note,

2575. European Commission, The EU-Africa Partnership, MEMO/15/4808 (22 Apr. 2015).

2576. *See* P. Sands & P. Klein, *Bowett's Law of International Institutions* (6th edn, London: Sweet & Maxwell, 2009), 147–148.

2577. Cotonou Agreement (23 Jun. 2000) O.J. L 317, 15 Dec. 2000, revised 25 Jun. 2005, O.J. L 287, 28 Oct. 2005, revised 22 Jun. 2010, O.J. L 287, 4 Nov. 2010. *See* generally K. Arts, 'ACP-EC Relations in a New Era: The Cotonou Agreement', *Common Market Law Review* 40 (2003): 95.

however, that these agreements were not concluded with the AU but with ACP States. Formal relations between the AU and the EU were established only in 2000 when the first Africa-EU Partnership Summit was held. Strengthening the partnership between the two continents led to the adoption of the JAES in 2007. Trade, economic development, growth and integration all form essential elements of the JAES.[2578]

2578. *Supra* para. 512.

Chapter 2. Cooperation on Matters of Peace and Security

§1. The African Union and the United Nations

519. The UN Security Council has primary responsibility for the maintenance of international peace and security in accordance with Article 24(1) of the UN Charter. However, under Chapter VIII of the UN Charter the UN may have recourse to regional arrangements or agencies relating to international peace and security, including enforcement action. The AU, as the OAU before it, comes within the scope of such a regional arrangement or agency.[2579] In fact, the UN has had a long cooperative association with Africa and the OAU.[2580] As has been stated, in 2006 the two organizations adopted the 'Framework for the ten-year capacity-building programme for the African Union' which envisaged greater UN support in areas such as conflict prevention and peace and security.[2581] This partnership is succeeded by PAIDA which in April 2017 resulted in a framework agreement to strengthen the relationship on peace and security issues.[2582] In 2010 the United Nations Office to the African Union (UNOAU) was duly established and acts as a liaison with UN agencies and the AU.[2583] The PSC is the AU organ that liaises with the UN on peace and security matters.[2584]

520. One aspect of this relationship has concerned peacekeeping, the UN has deployed more peacekeeping missions in Africa than any other region;[2585] its involvement in the Congo, conducted by United Nations Operation in the Congo (ONUC), is one of its best known episodes;[2586] its involvement in Somalia is one of its most notorious;[2587]

2579. *Repertoire of the Practice of the Security Council* 16th Supplement (2008–2009), http://www.un.org/en/sc/repertoire (accessed 26 Jul. 2013). *See* UN Security Council Res. 2320(2016).

2580. B. Boutros-Ghali, *Confronting New Challenges* (New York: United Nations, 1995), 340–341.

2581. UN Doc. A/61/630.

2582. The details of this framework agreement were not available at the time of writing.

2583. UN General Assembly Res. 64/288 (2010).

2584. Protocol Relating to the Establishment of the Peace and Security Council of the African Union Art. 17 (9 Jul. 2002), http://www.au.int, C. Heyns & M. Killander (eds), *Compendium of Key Human Rights Documents of the African Union* (5th edn, Pretoria: Pretoria University Law Press, 2013), 17.

2585. *Report of the UN Secretary-General on the causes of conflict and the promotion of durable peace and sustainable development in Africa* para. 29, UN Doc. A/52/871-S/1998/318 (1998).

2586. A. Parsons, *From Cold War to Hot Peace: UN Interventions 1947–1995* (London : Penguin, 1995), 77–93; M. Virally, *Les Nations Unies et l'affaire du Congo*, Annuaire Français de Droit International 557 (1960).

2587. Parsons, 198–207; C. Gray, *International Law and the Use of Force* (3rd edn, Oxford: Oxford University Press, 2008), 286–289.

and its role in Rwanda is considered one of its most shameful.[2588] The UN's efforts to hold a referendum in the Western Sahara, assisted by the MINURSO, have still not borne fruit.[2589] The situation in the DRC is still volatile.[2590] The same can be said for the CAR[2591] and South Sudan.[2592] However, there have been positive outcomes. The UN played a major role in Namibia's struggle for independence; the UN Transitional Group (UNTAG) oversaw the South African departure and successfully organized and monitored the independence election.[2593] The UN facilitated the transition to peace in Mozambique's civil war.[2594] In Sierra Leone, the UN force UN Mission in Sierra Leone (UNAMSIL), with the assistance of British troops, eventually succeeded in bringing peace and stable government to a country wracked by violence since 1991.[2595] Nevertheless, the UN's failures in Africa and elsewhere led to increased calls for

---

2588. G. Robertson, *Crimes Against Humanity: The Struggle for Global Justice* (London : Penguin, 1999), 76–79.

However, Gray, 292–294, highlights the hesitant attitude of UN Member States, whereas Parsons, 213–214, points out that the UN force, UNAMIR, had neither the mandate nor the personnel or matérial to play an active part in suppressing the genocidal violence.

2589. *See* , e.g., UN Security Council Res. 2051(2017). MINURSO was first deployed in the Western Sahara in 1991.

2590. Gray, 316–319. *See* UN Security Council Res. 2293(2016). In an extraordinary development in 2013 the UN Security Council authorized the creation of an 'Intervention Brigade' as part of the UN force UN Organization Stabilization Mission in the DRC (MONUSCO) 'with the responsibility of neutralizing armed groups', UN Security Council Res. 2098(2013) para. 9.

2591. *See* , e.g., UN Security Council Res. 2339(2017). Assembly, *Decision on the Report of the Peace and Security Council on its Activities and the State of Peace and Security in Africa*, AU Doc. Assembly/AU/Dec.583(XXV) (14–15 Jun. 2015), para. 7.

2592. UN Security Council Res. 1996(2011). This resolution created another peacekeeping mission, the United Nations Mission in South Sudan (UNMISS), *inter alia,* to support peace consolidation, protect civilians, and provide security. In 2014 UNMISS was given a renewed mandate geared towards the protection of civilians, the safeguarding human rights and securing humanitarian assistance, UN Security Council Res. 2155(2014). Since independence South Sudan has been wracked by internecine warfare despite mediation by different parties including the AU and IGAD. A peace agreement between the South Sudanese leaders was signed in August 2015 but not implemented and serious fighting broke out again in July 2016. *See* UN Security Council Res. 2327(2016), where the Security Council, acting pursuant to Ch. VII, demanded, *inter alia*, the cessation of fighting throughout South Sudan and the implementation of agreed ceasefires. The Security Council had determined that the situation in South Sudan constituted a threat to international peace and security, UN Security Council Res. 2326(2016).

2593. Parsons, Ch. 7.

2594. *Ibid.*, Ch. 10.

2595. Gray, 312–315. It should be observed that from 1997–1999 an ECOWAS force, EGOMOG, was present in Sierra Leone and ultimately resorted to the use of force to reinstate the legitimate government, *ibid.*, 411–417. In *Prosecutor v. Charles Ghankay Taylor* (Judgment) SCSL-03-1-T, T Ch. II (26 Apr. 2012) the former President of Liberia was found guilty by the SCSL of aiding and abetting and planning a number of crimes committed during the invasion of and retreat from Sierra Leone's capital, Freetown.

increased use of regional and sub-regional organizations under Chapter VIII of the UN Charter.[2596]

521. Increased cooperation with African organizations formed an important part of this agenda.[2597] A cooperative relationship had already been established between the UN and the OAU[2598] and between the UN and ECOWAS.[2599] But the advent of the AU signalled a transformation in this relationship. One of the crucial differences between the OAU and the AU is that the latter has an enhanced capacity for conflict management, mediation and peacemaking.[2600] The UN has expressed its support for the AU but it is accepted that it requires sustained capacity-building.[2601] The Ten-Year Capacity-Building Programme for the AU, adopted in 2006, was an important initiative.[2602] UNOAU is engaged in developing the institutional capacity of the AU, assists in operationalizing AU decisions and coordinating the use of funds. UN support finds expression in several ways, for example, capacity-building for mediation in the development of an AU mediation strategy and in making operational the AU Panel of the Wise. It extends to electoral assistance to AU Member States, including providing election observers, bolstering security, enhancing the rule of law, integrating human rights into the conduct of operations and facilitating the participation of NGOs. The UN continues to provide support to recent peacemaking efforts in political crises in

2596. *Report of the UN Secretary-General on the causes of conflict and the promotion of durable peace and sustainable development in Africa* paras 41–45; 'A More Secure World: Our Shared Responsibility', Report of the High-Level Panel on Threats, Challenges and Change paras 270–273, UN Doc. A/59/565 (2004).

2597. *Report of the UN Secretary-General on the causes of conflict and the promotion of durable peace and sustainable development in Africa ibid.*; UN General Assembly Res. 57/48(2003) on Cooperation between the United Nations and the African Union; UN General Assembly Res. 61/296(2007) on Cooperation between the United Nations and the African Union.

2598. Gray, 375–376.

2599. ECOWAS has played a major role in conflicts in West Africa. The civil war that erupted in Liberia in 1989 destabilized neighbouring States, particularly Sierra Leone, which led ECOWAS to take the pioneering step for an African sub-regional organization to send a peacekeeping force to Liberia, EGOMOG, *see* Parsons, 215–219. EGOMOG also established a presence in Sierra Leone and was instrumental in subduing rebel forces and restoring peace and security. The ECOWAS action in both countries generated legal controversy, focused on whether ECOWAS had prior UN authorization to use force, and whether EGOMOG was engaged in peacekeeping or peace-enforcement action, Gray, 400–407, 411–417. Subsequent missions by ECOWAS in Liberia and Côte d'Ivoire in 2003 were expressly authorized by the UN Security Council, Gray, 419–421. In 2017 ECOWAS intervened to resolve the constitutional crisis in The Gambia, *see* UN Security Council, Res. 2337 (2017). *See* further Report of the UN Secretary-General on strengthening the partnership between the United Nations and the African Union on issues of peace and security in Africa, UN Doc. S/2016/780, pt. VIII.

2600. *See* Protocol Relating to the Establishment of the Peace and Security Council of the African Union (9 Jul. 2002), http://www.au.int, Heyns & Killander, 17.

2601. *See* , e.g., 2005 World Summit Outcome para. 93, UN General Assembly Res. 60/1 (2005); 'A More Secure World: Our Shared Responsibility' para. 272(c). *See* further Gray, 376–378.

2602. UN Doc. A/61/630. The UN organs continued to call for greater involvement with the AU on peace and security, *see* UN Security Council Res. 2033(2012), UN Security Council Res. 2167(2014) and UN General Assembly Res. 67/302 (2012).

Burkina Faso, the Comoros, Libya and Madagascar, amongst others.[2603] But, as has been mentioned, peacekeeping missions have become a high-profile aspect of their collaborative efforts. The AU plays a key role in this respect because host-state consent is sometimes contingent on AU participation since certain African States harbour reservations about the UN's motives.[2604] These operations share certain features in that they have a UN mandate; they are created by a UN Security Council Resolution under Chapter VII of the UN Charter, deployed for a limited period of time before handing over to a UN force, and/or they are established by the AU, through the PSC, but approved by, and answerable to, the UN Security Council.[2605] Significantly, the AU has undertaken a number of high-profile operations.

522. One such operation concerns Somalia. AMISOM is a peacekeeping mission authorized by the UN.[2606] AMISOM was initially set up by the PSC in January 2007[2607] and was approved by the UN Security Council on 21 February 2007.[2608] Its mandate is to support transitional governmental structures, implement a national security plan, train the Somali security forces, and assist in creating a secure environment for the delivery of humanitarian aid.[2609] It also supports the Somali government against militants. AMISOM's mandate continues as the security situation remains precarious.[2610]

523. A fascinating facet of the situation in Somalia has been the extraordinary decision of the UN Security Council to combat piracy in Somali territorial waters which since the mid-2000s has posed a not insignificant threat to international shipping and security. Acting under Chapter VII of the UN Charter the UN Security Council adopted Resolution 1816 (2008) authorizing States, with the permission of the Somali authorities, to take such steps within Somali territorial waters to deal with piratical acts consistent with that permitted by international law on the high seas.[2611]

524. The UN Security Council categorized the conflict in the Darfur region of Sudan as a threat to international peace and security.[2612] It also called for measures to prevent or mitigate a humanitarian catastrophe.[2613] The AMIS was initially established

---

2603. Report of the UN Secretary-General on strengthening the partnership between the United Nations and the African Union on issues of peace and security in Africa, UN Doc. S/2016/780, pt. IV.

2604. Gray, 301.

2605. *See* , e.g., UN Security Council Res. 2085 (2012) para. 10, UN Security Council Res. 2127 (2013) paras 28, 32.

2606. *See* Gray, 378–380.

2607. AU Doc. PSC/PR/Comm (LXIX).

2608. UN Security Council Res. 1744 (2007).

2609. UN Security Council Res. 1772 (2007).

2610. Report of the UN Secretary-General on strengthening the partnership between the United Nations and the African Union on issues of peace and security in Africa, UN Doc. S/2016/780, paras 33–27.

2611. *See also* UN Security Council Res. 1846 and 1851 (2008). UN Security Council Res. 2125(2013) renewed the authorization for another year. *See* generally O. Elagab, 'Somali Piracy and International Law: Some Aspects'. *Australia and New Zealand Maritime Law Journal* 24 (2010): 59.

2612. UN Security Council Res. 1556(2004). *See also*, e.g., UN Security Council Res. 1784(2007).

2613. UN Security Council Res. 1556(2004) and 1591(2005).

by the AU in 2004 as a monitoring mission,[2614] but its mandate was soon expanded, *inter alia*, to improve the security situation in Sudan, to monitor the Darfur Peace Agreement, to contribute to a secure environment for the delivery of humanitarian aid and the return of refugees and IDPs.[2615] In 2005, the UN Security Council established the UN Mission in Sudan (UNMIS), *inter alia*, to support AMIS.[2616] However, the numerous difficulties encountered by AMIS, which included militia attacks and obstruction to humanitarian access, exposed its limitations but this led to an remarkable development, the merger of AMIS into a hybrid AU/UN peacekeeping operation, UNAMID.[2617] The AU's participation was crucial since it is clear that the Sudanese government would never have consented to a purely UN operation. UN and AU mediation led to the signing of a Roadmap Agreement between the Sudanese Government and opposition groups in 2016.[2618] However, the situation remains fraught.[2619]

525. The toppling of Mali's democratic government in a military coup in March 2012 intensified a prolonged period of instability and violence, leading to terrorist and extremist groups taking control of the north of Mali. French military intervention has succeeded in restoring a measure of security, however. Both the AU and ECOWAS became involved in mediation efforts to restore constitutional order and national unity. The UN Security Council found that the situation in Mali posed a threat to international peace and security,[2620] and approved the deployment of an African-led force, the African International Support Mission in Mali (AFISMA).[2621] AFISMA had robust rules of engagement, it was authorized to take 'all necessary measures', that is, use force, *inter alia*, to rebuild the Malian security forces, to support the Malian authorities in recovering territory under terrorist and extremist control, to support the Malian authorities in maintaining security and consolidating State authority, to support the Malian authorities in protecting civilians, and assist in creating a secure environment for the delivery of humanitarian aid.[2622] In 2013 the UN Security Council established the UN Multidimensional Integrated Stabilization Mission in Mali (MINUSMA) to take over from AFISMA from 1 July 2013.[2623] MINUSMA's mandate includes support for the political process, protecting civilians, support for humanitarian assistance, support for cultural protection, and support for international justice.[2624] It also is authorized to take 'all necessary

2614. AU Doc. PSC/PR/Comm.(X).
2615. AU Doc. PSC/PR/Comm.(XVII), endorsed by UN Security Council Res. 1556(2004). *See* further Gray, 380–381.
2616. UN Security Council Res. 1590(2005).
2617. UN Security Council Res. 1769(2007). *See* further Gray, 381–382.
2618. Report of the UN Secretary-General on strengthening the partnership between the United Nations and the African Union on issues of peace and security in Africa, UN Doc. S/2016/780, para. 30.
2619. UN Security Council Res. 2340(2017).
2620. UN Security Council Res. 2085(2012).
2621. AU Doc. PSC/AHG/Comm/2(CCCLIII).
2622. UN Security Council Res. 2085(2012), para. 9.
2623. UN Security Council Res. 2100(2013).
2624. *Ibid.*, para. 16.

measures'.[2625] With a peace agreement signed in June 2015,[2626] the UN and the AU continue to work to bring peace and stability to the country.[2627]

526. The CAR provides another example. The security situation in the CAR had been on the UN Security Council's agenda since the 1990s.[2628] In order to help bring stability to the CAR thc UN set up the UN Integrated Peace-building Office in the Central African Republic (BINUCA) with an initial mandate to help consolidate peace, foster national reconciliation, strengthen democratic institutions, and strengthen the promotion and protection of human rights.[2629] In 2013 the security situation in the CAR deteriorated to a degree where there was a complete breakdown in law and order, leading the UN Security Council to designate the state of affairs as a threat to international peace and security.[2630] The UN Security Council additionally approved the deployment of an African-led force, the African International Support Mission in the Central African Republic (MISCA) which was to cooperate with the UN field office. MISCA's mandate was to help protect civilians, stabilize the country and restore state authority, and create conditions conducive to the provision of humanitarian assistance. It was authorized to take 'all necessary measures'.[2631] However, with a deteriorating security situation the UN Security Council took the decision to subsume BINUCA into the UN Multidimensional Stabilizing Mission in the Central African Republic (MINUSCA), a peacekeeping operation, to which MISCA would transfer its authority[2632] and redeploy as part of that peacekeeping operation.[2633] MINUSCA's mandate includes protecting civilians, supporting the political process and extending state authority, facilitating the delivery of humanitarian assistance, promoting and protecting human rights, and supporting justice and the rule of law.[2634]

527. In 2015 a UN High-level Independent Panel on Peace Operations called for strengthening the UN-AU partnership.[2635] It stressed the importance of early engagement, continued consultation, joint planning and an integrated approach towards conflicts. The importance of sound politics in preventing, managing and resolving conflicts was also accentuated. Predictable financing for AU peace support operations was another important consideration. Support was forthcoming from the UN and in

2625. *Ibid.*, para. 17.

2626. *See* Assembly, *Decision on the Report of the Peace and Security Councilon its Activities and the State of Peace and Security in Africa*, AU Doc. Assembly/AU/Dec.583(XXV) (14–15 Jun. 2015), para. 7.

2627. Report of the UN Secretary-General on strengthening the partnership between the United Nations and the African Union on issues of peace and security in Africa, UN Doc. S/2016/780, para. 25.

2628. *See* Gray, 303–304, 331–332.

2629. BINUCA's mandate was extended by UN Security Council Res. 2088(2013) and 2121(2013).

2630. UN Security Council Res. 2127(2013).

2631. *Ibid.*, para. 28.

2632. UN Security Council Res. 2149(2014) para. 21.

2633. *Ibid.*, para. 26.

2634. *Ibid.*, para. 30.

2635. UN Doc. A/70/95-S/2015/446.

May 2016 a joint UN-AU meeting was held on peace-building in Africa which endorsed many of the Panel's recommendations.[2636]

§2. The African Union and the European Union

528. Since the eve of the millennium a cooperative relationship has been established between the UN and the EU on issues relating to peace and security and conflict management, including Africa.[2637] Under the Africa-EU Partnership, the key objectives on peace and security is to ensure a safe and secure environment, and to further political stability and effective governance. More specifically, to promote political dialogue on peace, justice and reconciliation; to strengthen the operationalization of APSA by training African forces; to address the root causes of conflict; and to consolidate human rights, amongst others. The EU provides funding and deploys civilian, military and election observation missions as part of its Common Security and Defence Policy (CSDP).[2638] The first concrete expression of this cooperative military relationship was Operation Artemis in the DRC following a request from the UN pursuant to UN Security Council Resolution 1484(2003) adopted under Chapter VII of the UN Charter. Operation Artemis, a rapid reaction force, was deployed for a few months in a supporting role to the UN force UN Observer Mission in the Democratic Republic of Congo (MONUC)[2639] to stabilize and strengthen the security and humanitarian conditions in the northern city of Bunia.[2640]

529. Another significant military operation undertaken by the EU was that of EUFOR Tchad/RCA in 2008 in Chad and CAR.[2641] Acting in accordance with Chapter VII of the UN Charter EUFOR's role was to support the UN force MINURCAT in establishing a secure environment[2642] but the problems encountered by MINURCAT meant that EUFOR became a 'first-entry force' paving the way for MINURCAT's eventual deployment.[2643] The deteriorating security situation in the CAR in 2013–2014 led the UN Security Council to authorize the deployment of an EU military force there with a mandate to use force.[2644] In April 2014, EUFOR RCA was launched to assist MISCA in achieving a safe and secure environment in the capital, Bangui.[2645]

2636. Report of the UN Secretary-General on strengthening the partnership between the United Nations and the African Union on issues of peace and security in Africa, UN Doc. S/2016/780, para. 40.

2637. Gray, 340–341; A. Novosseloff, *United Nations - European Union Cooperation in the Field of Peacekeeping: Challenges and Prospects* 6, (GGI Analysis Paper No. 4/2012), 8–12.

2638. Military and civilian missions and operations –European External Action Service https://eeas.europa.eu/headquarters.

2639. *See* Gray, 316–319.

2640. Novosseloff, 12.

2641. EU Council Decision on the launching of operation EUFOR Tchad/RCA, Press Release 5625/08. *See* Gray, *ibid.*, Novosseloff, 14–15.

2642. UN Security Council Res. 1778 (2007).

2643. Novosseloff, 14.

2644. UN Security Council Res. 2134 (2014) paras. 43–44.

2645. EU Council Press Release 7672/14.

530. In collaboration with AMISOM the EU contributes significantly, especially in terms of financial support, to bringing peace and security to Somalia and strengthening its institutions and authorities. In April 2010 it launched a military Training Mission in Somalia (EUTM Somalia) to build up and professionalize its armed forces.[2646] In order to counter piracy off the coast Somalia in December 2008 the EU launched the EU Naval Force (EU NAVFOR) Somalia – Operation Atalanta in accordance with relevant UN Security Council Resolutions.[2647] Operation Atalanta's mandate includes deterring, preventing and repressing acts of piracy and armed robbery at sea off the Somali coast, the protection of ships delivering aid to displaced persons in Somalia, the protection of AMISOM shipping, and protecting vulnerable shipping off the Somali coast on a case by case basis. In 2012 the area of operation was extended to include Somali coastal territory and internal waters.[2648] Operation Atalanta's mandate has been extended until December 2018.[2649]

531. The triple relationship involving the AU took longer to develop, however.[2650] The Peace and Security partnership element of the JAES is based on three specific objectives: enhancing the political dialogue on peace and security; operationalizing APSA; and ensuring predictable funding for African-led peace support operations. A cooperative relationship has now been established, focusing on capacity-building in areas such as logistics, training and material.[2651] This it did with AMIS.[2652] A mission was dispatched to Mali to provide military training and advice to the Malian armed forces,[2653] the EU Training Mission in Mali (EUTM Mali).[2654] A number of other civilian missions in Africa have been undertaken.[2655]

532. Funding of operations is also an important element of the EU's projection of soft-power.[2656] The key EU financial instrument to support the Peace and Security partnership is the African Peace Facility (APF). The APF was established at the request of the AU.[2657] It is a multidisciplinary force made up of military, police and civilian components for deployment in crisis situations.[2658] Capacity-Building forms a large part of its work but funding and technical support is provided for APSA and PSOs such as AMISOM, the MNJTF against Boko Haram and the RCI-LRA.

2646. *See* http://www.eeas.europa.eu/csdp/missions-and operations/eutm-somalia.
2647. *Supra.* para. 523.
2648. Council Decision 2012/174/CFSP, O.J. L 89/69, 27 Mar. 2012.
2649. EU Council Press Release 691/16.
2650. Novosseloff, 23.
2651. *See* UN Security Council Res. 2167 (2014).
2652. *Ibid.*, 20.
2653. UN Security Council Res. 2085 (2012) para. 8.
2654. *See* http://www.eutmmali.eu.
2655. Military and civilian missions and operations – European External Action Service https://eeas.europa.eu/headquarters.
2656. The EU has provided funding for AFISMA in Mali, UN Security Council Res. 2085 (2012) para. 20, AMISOM in Somalia and MISCA in the CAR, UN Security Council Res. 2127 (2013) para. 42; *The Africa-EU Partnership: 2 unions, 1 vision*, 7–9. *See* generally Gray, 377–378.
2657. Assembly, *Decision on the Establishment by the European Union of a Peace Support Operation Facility for the African Union*, AU Doc. Assembly/AU/Dec.21(II) (10–12 Jul. 2003).
2658. *The Africa-EU Partnership: 2 unions, 1 vision*, 9.

Part V. Appraisal

533. In 2013, the AU commemorated the fiftieth anniversary of the founding of the OAU amid much fanfare.[2659] The AU had cause for celebration as progress had been achieved across a number of areas such as peace and security, social and economic development, poverty reduction, human rights, the rule of law and good governance but as it itself acknowledged, such advances were often fragile and much still remained to be done as some problems seem intractable.[2660] These challenges continue to be destabilizing and in turn have given rise in recent years to high levels of forced migration. Nevertheless, in Agenda 2063 the AU has renewed its commitment to an African Renaissance.

534. The AU is geared to deal comprehensively with Africa's development challenges by concentrating on the political and economic integration of the African continent. Respect for human rights and the rule of law, democratic principles and good governance constitute the values sustaining the AU. Africa's commitment to these values is reinforced by NEPAD and Agenda 2063, according to which African countries have pledged to uphold, *inter alia*, human rights and good economic and political governance.[2661]

535. Institutionally the AU has made good progress in enhancing the promotion of human rights. The AU recognizes the importance of democratic institutions. The promotion and protection of human rights, the consolidation of democratic institutions and cultures, and good governance and the rule of law form a core element of the AU. Significantly, the AU has indicated the high regard it has for these values by giving itself the power to deal with violations of these ideals. It can therefore impose sanctions on any Member State that fails to comply with the policies and decisions of the AU. Additionally, the AU contains a 'democracy clause', whereby regimes that take power through unconstitutional means are not allowed to participate in the activities of the AU. In this work, attention has been drawn to a number of instances, the Comoros, Madagascar, Mali and The Gambia where the AU, sometimes in collaboration with the UN or ECOWAS, has taken action to restore constitutional order.

536. A number of important human rights instruments, including the Protocol to the African Charter on Human and Peoples' Rights establishing an African Court

2659. 50th Anniversary Solemn Declaration para. E (iii), Assembly, Twenty-First Ordinary Session, 26 May 2013.

2660. *Ibid.*

2661. The EU has also played an important role in promoting democracy and human rights. Since 1992 a 'human rights clause' has formed part of cooperation agreements between the EU and third countries, emphasizing respect for democracy and human rights as 'essential elements' of the agreements. In 2003 the Cotonou Agreement (as revised) between the EU and African, Caribbean and Pacific (ACP) States entered into force. Article 9 thereof is the 'human rights clause'.

on Human and Peoples' Rights, have either been adopted or come into force under the auspices of the AU. The AU has succeeded in demonstrating its concern about human rights in a manner that the OAU never did. The fact that the African Court on Human and Peoples' Rights has become operational is a very welcome development but the AU's seeming indecision over its judicial organs has left a question mark over its future in its present form. But the AU's deteriorating relationship with the ICC has raised the spectre of the OAU's dark days of closing ranks with despots. But one of the fascinating aspects of this dispute has been the ructions within the organization itself as a significant number of States have been open in their support for the ICC. The wisdom of the Statute on an African Criminal Court must be questioned. However, treaties alone cannot prevent human rights violations. At the end of the day, despite the fact that electoral democracy has made progress in recent times, the fundamental obstacle towards guaranteeing human rights in Africa, in addition to economic underdevelopment, remains the unwillingness of too many regimes to build a State based on pluralist, inclusive democracy and the rule of law. Recent initiatives by the AU and NEPAD, in tandem with other international partners, may facilitate efforts at securing concrete measures towards democratization and good governance.

537. It is also important that the implementation of existing human rights standards be strengthened. The African Commission, mandated under the African Charter with promoting and ensuring protection of human and peoples' rights, attracted criticism as an institutionally weak guardian of rights.[2662] However, such pessimism no longer paints an accurate portrait. An analysis of the Commission's work and decisions in recent years suggests that the Commission is becoming more robust.[2663] Thus, Odinkalu's view that on 'its interpretation of the Charter, the Commission has been mostly positive and sometimes even innovative' appears to reflect the greater reality.[2664] He adds that the Commission has been successfully addressing the deficiencies in the African Charter 'through its practice, evolving procedures, and jurisprudence'.[2665]

538. The AU and NEPAD also strengthen Africa's commitment to conflict resolution. The capacity to adopt conflict prevention measures, such as the deployment of observers or missions of inquiry, is enhanced. With the assistance of the international community, the AU has set up African peacekeeping forces. However, the outlook is not positive. AU peacekeeping seems to be afflicted by the same drawbacks as UN peacekeeping, a lack of human, material and financial resources and a lack of political resolve. And security and instability remain persistent problems. The situation in the CAR is verging on anarchy. Mali is unstable. Somalia's problems seem intractable.

2662. Robertson, 58–59; H.J. Steiner & P. Alston, *International Human Rights in Context*(Oxford: Oxford University Press, 2000), 920.

2663. *See* , e.g., *The Social and Economic Rights Action Center and the Center for Economic and Social Rights v. Nigeria*, Communication No. 155/96, *15th Activity Report 2001–2002*; *Gunme et al. v. Cameroon,* Communication No. 266/2003, 26th Activity Report 2008–2009; *Sudan Human Rights Organization and Sudan Centre for Housing Rights and Evictions v. Sudan* Communication Nos 279/03, 296/05, 28th Activity Report, 2010.

2664. C.A. Odinkalu, 'The Individual Complaints Procedures of the African Commission on Human and Peoples' Rights: A Preliminary Assessment', *Transnational Law & Contemporary Problems* 8 (1998): 359, at p. 402.

2665. *Ibid.*, 398.

The Arab Spring has become the Arab Winter, with Egypt and Libya in particular wracked by political instability. Ultimately the root causes of conflict must be addressed.

539. Poverty and underdevelopment have at one and the same time been both the cause and effect of many of Africa's ills. Poverty reduction and eradication strategies must be made to work. Addressing the root causes of conflict, strengthening democracy and human rights should encourage sustainable economic and human development. The AU, NEPAD and Agenda 2063 provide evidence of the commitment of African States to confront and solve their economic and social problems through indigenous solutions. Under NEPAD in particular, African countries have assumed primary responsibility for promoting sustainable development. However, the challenges are considerable. Globalization is a mixed blessing. While some African economies have shown impressive economic growth too many remain either weak or mismanaged, or both. Futhermore, there is an inequitable distribution of wealth. Corruption is widespread. However, the AU, NEPAD, and Agenda 2063 appear committed to tackling this problem through the principle of transparency. All necessary resources will have to be mobilized to ensure the success of ambitious development initiatives such as the AU, NEPAD and Agenda 2063.

540. Currently, the AU is not fully functional although most of the organs envisaged in the Constitutive Act have been established. Of the principal organs, only the Court of Justice has not yet become operational, subject to the entry into force of the relevant Protocol. The establishment of the Parliament injects a welcome measure of democracy to the project, even if limited. Naturally, the successful completion of a project such as the AU requires time, resources and unlimited quantities of willingness and continued cooperation among the membership. The evolution of the EU, on which the AU is said to be based, is a very good example. Therefore, it could be argued with some persuasion that the transformation still has a long way to go. However, the AU's sense of urgency is encouraging and significant progress has been made in a short period. Many important treaties have been adopted and the machinery for the implementation of the AU project is being put in place. Yet, unless the AU demonstrates a willingness to confront and deal resolutely with Africa's vested interests, the AU will share the fate of the unlamented OAU. Ultimately, in concert with NEPAD, the AU's creative approaches to Africa's challenges deserve success.

Part VI. Addresses and Networks

THE AFRICAN UNION: ORGANS AND OTHER RELATED BODIES

African Union (AU)
African Union Headquarters
P.O. Box 3243
Roosevelt Street
(Old Airport Area)
W21K19
Addis Ababa
Ethiopia
Tel: +251 11 551 77 00
Fax: +251 11 551 78 44
website: http://www.au.int

Economic, Social and Cultural Council
ECOSOCC Secretariat
African Union Headquarters
P.O. Box 3243
Roosevelt Street
(OldAirport Area)
W21K19 Addis Ababa
Ethiopia
Tel: + 251 11 5182152
E-Mail: ECOSOCC@africa-union.org

Pan-African Parliament
Pan-African Parliament
Gallagher Estate

Private Bag X16
Midrand 1685
Johannesburg
Republic of South Africa
Tel: +27 11 545 5000
Fax: +27 11 545 5136
E-mail:secretariat@panafricanparliament.org
Website: http://www.pan-africanparliament.org

New Partnership for Africa's Development (NEPAD)
P.O. Box 1234
Halfway House
Midrand 1685
Johannesburg
South Africa
Tel: +27 11 256 36000 / 2563615
Fax: +27 11 206 3762
E-Mail: media@nepad.org
Website: http://www.nepad.org

African Peer Review Mechanism
PO Box 1234
Halfway House
Midrand 1685
Johannesburg
South Africa
Website: http://aprm-au.org/
33 859 88 00
33 820 70 18

African Commission on Human and Peoples' Rights
31 Bijilo Annex Layout
Kombo North District
Western Region

P.O. Box 673
Banjul
The Gambia
Tel: +220 441 05 05 / 441 05 06
Fax: +220 441 05 04
E-mail: au-banjul@africa-union.org
Website: http://www.achpr.org

African Committee of Experts on the Rights and Welfare of the Child
African Union Commission
Department of Social Affairs
P.O. Box 3243
Roosevelt Street (Old Airport Area)
W21K19, Addis Ababa
Ethiopia
Tel: (+ 251 1) 551 3522
Fax: (+ 251 1) 553 5716
Website: http://acerwc.org

African Court on Human and Peoples' Rights
Dodoma Road
Mwalimu Julius Nyerere Conservation Centre
P.O. Box 6274
Arusha
United Republic of Tanzania
Tel: +255-732-979 509 / +255-732-979 506
Fax: +255-732-979 503
E-mail: registrar@african-court.org
Website: http://www.african-court.org

African Union Commission on International Law
Office of Legal Affairs of the AU Commission
P.O. Box 3243
Roosevelt Street (Old Airport Area)

W21K19 Addis Ababa
Ethiopia
Tel: +251 11 551 7700
Fax: +251 11 551 7844

African Union Advisory Board on Corruption
Arusha International Conference Centre (AICC)
Serengeti Wings, 3rd Floor,
East Africa Road, Sekei
P.O. Box 6071
Arusha
Tanzania
Tel: + 255 27 20 500 30
Fax: +255 27 205 0031
E-mail: info@auanticorruption.org
Website: http://www.auanticorruption.org/auac/en

African Centre for the Study and Research on Terrorism
B.P 141 Bureau
Post El-Mohammadia, Algiers
Algeria
Tel: (+123 21) 520 083
Fax: (+213 21) 520 378
E-mail: admin@caert.org.dz
Website: http://www.caert.org.dz

AFRICAN UNION PERMANENT REPRESENTATIONAL OFFICES:
AU Permanent Observer to the United Nations
3 Dag Hammarskjöld Plaza
305 East 47th Street, 5th Floor
New York, NY10017
United States of America
Tel: (+1 212) 319 5490

Fax: (+1 212) 319 7135 or 319 6509
E-mail: africanunion@un.int

AU Permanent Representative to the United Nations and World Trade Organization

127, Rue des Pâquis 36
CH-1211 Genève 22
Switzerland
Tel: (+41 22) 716 0640
Fax: (+41 22) 731 6818
E-Mail: au-geneva@africa-union.org
mission-observer.au@africanunion.ch

AU Permanent Representative to the United States

1919 Pennsylvania Ave, Suite 7001
Washington, DC20006
United States of America
Tel: (+1 202) 293 8006
Fax: (+1 202) 293 8007
E-mail: au-washington@africa-union.org

Permanent Mission to the European Union (EU) and African, Caribbean and Pacific (ACP) states – Brussels Office

Avenue Molière, 186
B- 1050 Brussels
Belgium
Tel: (+32 2) 346 9747 or 346 9748
Fax: (+32 2) 346 9128
E-mail: au-brussels@africa-union.org
africanunion@skynet.be

Permanent Delegation to the League of Arab States – Cairo Office

7, Maydan Algomhouria Al Motaheda
From Elbatal Ahmed Abdel Aziz Street

Dokki, Cairo

Egypt

Tel: (+20 2) 3762 6154 or 3761 2951

Fax: (+20 2) 3762 6153

E-mail: au-cairo@africa-union.org

AFRICAN UNION SPECIALIZED AGENCIES, OTHER INSTITUTIONS AND REGIONAL ECONOMIC COMMUNITIES:

African Civil Aviation Commission

B.P. 8898

Aéroport International LSS

Dakar-Yoff

Sénégal

Tel: +221 33 859 88 00

Fax: +221 33 820 70 18

E-Mail: secretariat@afcac.org

Website: http://www.afcac.org/en/

African Development Bank Group

(Statutory Headquarters)

Rue Joseph Anoma

01 BP 1387 Abidjan 01

Côte d'Ivoire

Tel: (+225 20) 204 444

Fax: (+225 20) 204 959

(Temporary Relocation Agency (Tunis))

15 Avenue du Ghana

P.O. Box 323-1002

Tunis-Belvedère

Tunisia

Tel: +216 71 10 39 00

Fax: +216 71 35 19 33

E-mail: afdb@afdb.org

Website: http://www.afdb.org

Part VI. Addresses and Networks

African Energy Commission (AFREC)
02 Rue Chenoua
BP 791 Hydra
16035 Algiers
Algeria
Tel: +213 21 694 868
Fax: +213 21 692 083
E-mail: afrec@africa-union.org
afrienergy@yahoo.com
Website: http://afrec-energy.org

African Telecommunication Union
CCKBuilding
Waiyaki Way
P.O. Box 35282 - 00200
Nairobi
Kenya
Tel: +254 20 2322120 / 1
Fax: +254 20 2322124
E-mail: sg@atu-uat.org
Website: http://www.atu-uat.org

Pan African Postal Union
Plot III, Block Z
Golf Course, Sekei
P.O. Box 6026
United Republic of Tanzania
Tel: +255 272543263
Fax: +255 272543265
E-mail: sg@papu.co.tz
Website: http://www.upap-papu.org

Pan African Youth Union

Al Salam Street
Taif
Khartoum
Sudan
Tel: (+249 183) 526 694
Fax: (+249 183) 526 695
Website: http://www.pyu-upj.org

African Bureau of Educational Sciences
29, Avenue de la Justice
B.P. 1764
Kinshasa
Democratic Republic of Congo

African Rehabilitation Institute (ARI)
ARI Headquarters
Cnr Jason Moyo Ave and First St
P.O. Box 4056 Harare
Zimbabwe
Tel: (+263 4) 759 211
Fax: (+263 4) 759 218
E-mail: ari@ecoweb.co.zw

Economic Community of Western African States (ECOWAS)
101, Yakubu Gowon Crescent
Asokoro District
P.M.B. 401
Abuja
Nigeria
Tel: +234 9 3147 6479
Fax: (+234 9) 3143 005 / 3147 646
E-mail: info@ecowas.int
Website: http://www.ecowas.int

Part VI. Addresses and Networks

Common Market of Eastern and Southern Africa (COMESA)
COMESA Centre
Ben Bella Road
P.O. Box 30051
Lusaka
Zambia
Tel: +260 211 229725/32
Fax: +260 211 225107
E-Mail: info@comesa.int
Website: http://www.comesa.int

Southern Africa Development Community (SADC)
SADC House
Plot No. 54385
Central Business District
Private Bag 0095
Gaborone
Botswana
Tel: ++267 395 1863
Fax: +267 397 2848; +267 318 1070
E-mail: registry@sadc.int
Website: http://www.sadc.int

Intergovernmental Authority on Development (IGAD)
IGAD Secretariat
Avenue Georges Clemenceau
P.O. Box 2653Djibouti
Republic of Djibouti
Tel: +253 354050
Fax: +253 356994
E-mail: igad@igad.org
Website: http://www.igad.org

Economic Community of Central African States (ECCAS)
Secrétariat Général de la CEEAC
BP 2112
Libreville
Gabon
Tel: +241-444731
Fax: +241-44732
E-mail: secretariat@ceeac-eccas.org
Website: http://www.ceeac-eccas.org

Part VI. Addresses and Networks

East African Community (EAC)
3 EAC Close
East African Community Headquarters
P.O. Box 1096
Arusha
Tanzania
Tel: +255 27 2162100
Fax: +255 27 2162190
E-mail: eac@eachq.org
Website: http://www.eac.int

Community of Sahel-Saharan States (CEN-SAD)
Secretariat General
P.O. Box 4041
Place D'Algeria
Tripoli
Libya
Tel: (+218 21) 361 4832
Fax: (+218 21) 333 216
E-mail: censadsg@yahoo.com
info@cen-sad.org
Website: http://www.censad.org

Arab Magreb Union (AMU)
AMU Secretariat
73, Rue Tensift Agdal
Rabat
Morocco
Tel: +212 537 6813 71- 4
Fax: +212 537 681 377
Website: http://www.maghrebarabe.org/en/
E-mail: sg.uma@maghrebarabe.org

Appendix 1. The Constitutive Act of the African Union (2000)

We, Heads of State and Government of the Member States of the Organization of African Unity

Inspired by the noble ideals which guided the founding fathers of our Continental Organization and generations of Pan-Africanists in their determination to promote unity, solidarity, cohesion and cooperation among the peoples of Africa and African States;

Considering the principles and objectives stated in the Charter of the Organization of African Unity and the Treaty establishing the African Economic Community;

Recalling the heroic struggles waged by our peoples and our countries for political independence, human dignity and economic emancipation;

Considering that since its inception, the Organization of African Unity has played a determining and invaluable role in the liberation of the continent, the affirmation of a common identity and the process of attainment of the unity of our continent and has provided a unique framework for our collective action in Africa and in our relations with the rest of the world;

Determined to take up the multifaceted challenges that confront our continent and peoples in the light of the social, economic and political changes taking place in the world;

Convinced of the need to accelerate the process of implementing the Treaty establishing the African Economic Community in order to promote the socioeconomic development of Africa and to face more effectively the challenges posed by globalization;

Guided by our common vision of a united and strong Africa and by the need to build a partnership between governments and all segments of civil society, in particular women, youth and the private sector in order to strengthen solidarity and cohesion among our peoples;

Conscious of the fact that the scourge of conflicts in Africa constitutes a major impediment to the socio-economic development of the continent and of the need to promote peace, security and stability as a prerequisite for the implementation of our development and integration agenda;

Determined to promote and protect human and peoples' rights, consolidate democratic institutions and culture, and to ensure good governance and the rule of law;

Further determined to take all necessary measures to strengthen our common institutions and provide them with the necessary powers and resources to enable them discharge their respective mandates effectively;

Recalling the Declaration which we adopted at the Fourth Extraordinary Session of our Assembly in Sirte, the Great Socialist People's Libyan Arab Jamahiriya, on 9.9.

99, in which we decided to establish an African Union, in conformity with the ultimate objectives of the Charter of our Continental Organization and the Treaty establishing the African Economic Community;

Have agreed as follows:

Article 1. Definitions

In this Constitutive Act:

'Act' means the present Constitutive Act; 'AEC' means the African Economic Community; 'Assembly' means the Assembly of Heads of State and Government of the Union; 'Charter' means the Charter of the OAU;

'Committee' means a Specialized Technical Committee of the Union;

'Council' means the Economic, Social and Cultural Council of the Union;

'Court' means the Court of Justice of the Union;

'Executive Council' means the Executive Council of Ministers of the Union;

'MemberState' means a MemberState of the Union;

'OAU' means the Organization of African Unity;

'Parliament' means the Pan-African Parliament of the Union;

'Union' means the African Union established by the present Constitutive Act.

Article 2. Establishment

The African Union is hereby established in accordance with the provisions of this Act.

Article 3. Objectives

The objectives of the Union shall be to:

(a) Achieve greater unity and solidarity between the African counties and the peoples of Africa;
(b) Defend the sovereignty, territorial integrity and independence of its Member States;
(c) Accelerate the political and socio-economic integration of the continent;
(d) Promote and defend African common positions on issues of interest to the continent and its peoples;
(e) Encourage international cooperation, taking due account of the Charter of the United Nations and the Universal Declaration of Human Rights;
(f) Promote peace, security, and stability on the continent;
(g) Promote democratic principles and institutions, popular participation and good governance;
(h) Promote and protect human and peoples' rights in accordance with the African Charter on Human and Peoples' Rights and other relevant human rights instruments;
(i) Establish the necessary conditions which enable the continent to play its rightful role in the global economy and in international negotiations;

(j) Promote sustainable development at the economic, social and cultural levels as well as the integration of African economies;
(k) Promote cooperation in all fields of human activity to raise the living standards of African peoples;
(l) Coordinate and harmonize policies between existing and future Regional Economic Communities for the gradual attainment of the objectives of the Union;
(m) Advance the development of the continent by promoting research in all fields, in particular in science and technology;
(n) Work with relevant international partners in the eradication of preventable diseases and the promotion of good health on the continent.

Article 4. Principles

The Union shall function in accordance with the following principles:

(a) Sovereign equality and interdependence among Member States of the Union;
(b) Respect of borders existing on achievement of independence;
(c) Participation of the African peoples in the activities of the Union;
(d) Establishment of a common defence policy for the African continent;
(e) Peaceful resolution of conflicts among Member States of the Union through such appropriate means as may be decided upon by the Assembly;
(f) Prohibition of the use of force or threat to use force among Member States of the Union;
(g) Non-interference by any Member State in the internal affairs of another;
(h) The right of the Union to intervene in a Member State pursuant to a decision of the Assembly in respect of grave circumstances, namely war crimes, genocide and crimes against humanity;
(i) Peaceful co-existence of Member States and their right to live in peace and security;
(j) The right of Member States to request intervention from the Union in order to restore peace and security;
(k) Promotion of self-reliance within the framework of the Union;
(l) Promotion of gender equality;
(m) Respect for democratic principles, human rights, the rule of law and good governance;
(n) Promotion of social justice to ensure balanced economic development;
(o) Respect for the sanctity of human life, condemnation and rejection of impunity and political assassination, acts of terrorism and subversive activities;
(p) Condemnation and rejection of unconstitutional changes of governments.

Article 5. Organs of the Union

(1) The organs of the Union shall be:

(a) The Assembly of the Union;
(b) The Executive Council;
(c) The Pan-African Parliament;
(d) The Court of Justice;
(e) The Commission;
(f) The Permanent Representatives Committee;
(g) The Specialized Technical Committees;
(h) The Economic, Social and Cultural Council;
(i) The Financial Institutions;

(2) Other organs that the Assembly may decide to establish.

Article 6. The Assembly

(1) The Assembly shall be composed of Heads of States and Government or their duly accredited representatives.
(2) The Assembly shall be the supreme organ of the Union.
(3) The Assembly shall meet at least once a year in ordinary session. At the request of any MemberState and on approval by a two-thirds majority of the Member States, the Assembly shall meet in extraordinary session.
(4) The Office of the Chairman of the Assembly shall be held for a period of one year by a Head of State or Government elected after consultations among the Member States.

Article 7. Decisions of the Assembly

(1) The Assembly shall take its decisions by consensus or, failing which, by a two-thirds majority of the Member States of the Union. However, procedural matters, including the question of whether a matter is one of procedure or not, shall be decided by a simple majority.
(2) Two-thirds of the total membership of the Union shall form a quorum at any meeting of the Assembly.

Article 8. Rules of Procedure of the Assembly

The Assembly shall adopt its own Rules of Procedure.

Article 9. Powers and Functions of the Assembly

(1) The functions of the Assembly shall be to:

(a) Determine the common policies of the Union;
(b) Receive, consider and take decisions on reports and recommendations from the other organs of the Union;
(c) Consider requests for Membership of the Union;
(d) Establish any organ of the Union;
(e) Monitor the implementation of policies and decisions of the Union as well as ensure compliance by all Member States;
(f) Adopt the budget of the Union;
(g) Give directives to the Executive Council on the management of conflicts, war and other emergency situations and the restoration of peace;
(h) Appoint and terminate the appointment of the judges of the Court of Justice;
(i) Appoint the Chairman of the Commission and his or her deputy or deputies and Commissioners of the Commission and determine their functions and terms of office.

(2) The Assembly may delegate any of its powers and functions to any organ of the Union.

Article 10. The Executive Council

(1) The Executive Council shall be composed of the Ministers of Foreign Affairs or such other Ministers or Authorities as are designated by the Governments of Member States.
(2) Council shall meet at least twice a year in ordinary session. It shall also meet in an extraordinary session at the request of any MemberState and upon approval by two-thirds of all Member States.

Article 11. Decisions of the Executive Council

(1) The Executive Council shall take its decisions by consensus or, failing which, by a two-thirds majority of the Member States. However, procedural matters, including the question of whether a matter is one of procedure or not, shall be decided by a simple majority.
(2) Two-thirds of the total membership of the Union shall form a quorum at any meeting of the Executive Council.

Article 12. Rules of Procedure of the Executive Council

The Executive Council shall adopt its own Rules of Procedure.

Article 13. Functions of the Executive Council

(1) The Executive Council shall co-ordinate and take decisions on policies in areas of common interest to the Member States, including the following:

(a) Foreign trade;
(b) Energy, industry and mineral resources;
(c) Food, agricultural and animal resources, livestock production and forestry;
(d) Water resources and irrigation;
(e) Environmental protection, humanitarian action and disaster response and relief;
(f) Transport and communications;
(g) Insurance;
(h) Education, culture, health and human resources development;
(i) Science and technology;
(j) Nationality, residency and immigration matters;
(k) Social security, including the formulation of mother and child care policies, as well as policies relating to the disabled and the handicapped;
(l) Establishment of a system of African awards, medals and prizes.

(2) The Executive Council shall be responsible to the Assembly. It shall consider issues referred to it and monitor the implementation of policies formulated by the Assembly.
(3) The Executive Council may delegate any of its powers and functions mentioned in paragraph 1 of this Article to the Specialized Technical Committees established under Article 14 of this Act.

Article 14. The Specialized Technical Committees: Establishment and Composition

(1) There is hereby established the following Specialized Technical Committees, which shall be responsible to the Executive Council:

(a) The Committee on Rural Economy and Agricultural Matters;
(b) The Committee on Monetary and Financial Affairs;
(c) The Committee on Trade, Customs and Immigration Matters;
(d) The Committee on Industry, Science and Technology, Energy, Natural Resources and Environment;
(e) The Committee on Transport, Communications and Tourism;
(f) The Committee on Health, Labour and Social Affairs; and
(g) The Committee on Education, Culture and Human Resources.

(2) The Assembly shall, whenever it deems appropriate, restructure the existing Committees or establish other Committees.
(3) The Specialized Technical Committees shall be composed of Ministers or senior officials responsible for sectors falling within their respective areas of competence.

Article 15. Functions of the Specialized Technical Committees

Each Committee shall within its field of competence:

(a) Prepare projects and programmes of the Union and submit in to the Executive Council;
(b) Ensure the supervision, follow-up and the evaluation of the implementation of decisions taken by the organs of the Union;
(c) Ensure the coordination and harmonization of projects and programmes of the Union;
(d) Submit to the Executive Council either on its own initiative or at the request of the Executive Council, reports and recommendations on the implementation of the provision of this Act; and
(e) Carry out any other functions assigned to it for the purpose of ensuring the implementation of the provisions of this Act.

Article 16. Meetings

(1) Subject to any directives given by the Executive Council, each Committee shall meet as often as necessary and shall prepare its rules of procedure and submit them to the Executive Council for approval.

Article 17. The Pan-African Parliament

(1) In order to ensure the full participation of African peoples in the development and economic integration of the continent, a Pan-African Parliament shall be established.
(2) The composition, powers, functions and organization of the Pan-African Parliament shall be defined in a protocol relating thereto.

Article 18. The Court of Justice

(1) A Court of Justice of the Union shall be established; *2*. The statute, composition and functions of the Court of Justice shall be defined in a protocol relating thereto.

Article 19. The Financial Institutions

The Union shall have the following financial institutions, whose rules and regulations shall be defined in protocols relating thereto:

(a) The African Central Bank;
(b) The African Monetary Fund;
(c) The African Investment Bank.

Article 20. The Commission

(1) There shall be established a Commission of the Union, which shall be the Secretariat of the Union.
(2) The Commission shall be composed of the Chairman, his or her deputy or deputies and the Commissioners. They shall be assisted by the necessary staff for the smooth functioning of the Commission.
(3) The structure, functions and regulations of the Commission shall be determined by the Assembly.

Article 21. The Permanent Representatives Committee

(1) There shall be established a Permanent Representatives Committee. It shall be composed of Permanent Representatives to the Union and other Plenipotentiaries of Member States.
(2) The Permanent Representatives Committee shall be charged with the responsibility of preparing the work of the Executive Council and acting on the Executive Council's instructions. It may set up such sub-committees or working groups as it may deem necessary.

Article 22. The Economic, Social and Cultural Council

(1) The Economic, Social and Cultural Council shall be an advisory organ composed of different social and professional groups of the Member States of the Union.
(2) The functions, powers, composition and organization of the Economic, Social and Cultural Council shall be determined by the Assembly.

Article 23. Imposition of Sanctions

(1) The Assembly shall determine the appropriate sanctions to be imposed on any Member State that defaults in the payment of its contributions to the budget of the Union in the following manner: denial of the right to speak at meetings, to vote, to present candidates for any position or post within the Union or to benefit from any activity or commitments therefrom.
(2) Furthermore, any MemberState that fails to comply with the decisions and policies of the Union may be subjected to other sanctions, such as the denial of transport and communications links with other MemberStates, and other measures of a political and economic nature to be determined by the Assembly.

Article 24. The Headquarters of the Union

(1) The Headquarters of the Union shall be in Addis Ababa in the Federal Democratic Republic of Ethiopia.
(2) There may be established such other offices of the Union as the Assembly may, on the recommendation of the Executive Council, determine.

Article 25. Working Languages

The working languages of the Union and all its institutions shall be, if possible, African languages, Arabic, English, French and Portuguese.

Article 26. Interpretation

The Court shall be seized with matters of interpretation arising from the application or implementation of this Act. Pending its establishment, such matters shall be submitted to the Assembly of the Union, which shall decide by a two-thirds majority.

Article 27. Signature, Ratification and Accession

(1) This Act shall be open to signature, ratification and accession by the Member States of the OAU in accordance with their respective constitutional procedures.
(2) The instruments of ratification shall be deposited with the Secretary-General of the OAU.
(3) Any MemberState of the OAU acceding to this Act after its entry into force shall deposit the instrument of accession with the Chairman of the Commission.

Article 28. Entry into Force

This Act shall enter into force thirty (30) days after the deposit of the instruments of ratification by two-thirds of the Member States of the OAU.

Article 29. Admission to Membership

(1) Any AfricanState may, at any time after the entry into force of this Act, notify the Chairman of the Commission of its intention to accede to this Act and to be admitted as a member of the Union.
(2) The Chairman of the Commission shall, upon receipt of such notification, transmit copies thereof to all Member States. Admission shall be decided by a simple majority of the Member States. The decision of each MemberState shall be transmitted to the Chairman of the Commission who shall, upon receipt of the required number of votes, communicate the decision to the State concerned.

Article 30. Suspension

Governments which shall come to power through unconstitutional means shall not be allowed to participate in the activities of the Union.

Article 31. Cessation of Membership

(1) Any State which desires to renounce its membership shall forward a written notification to the Chairman of the Commission, who shall inform Member States thereof. At the end of one year from the date of such notification, if not withdrawn, the Act shall cease to apply with respect to the renouncing State, which shall thereby cease to belong to the Union.
(2) During the period of one year referred to in paragraph 1 of this Article, any MemberState wishing to withdraw from the Union shall comply with the provisions of this Act and shall be bound to discharge its obligations under this Act up to the date of its withdrawal.

Article 32. Amendment and Revision

(1) Any MemberState may submit proposals for the amendment or revision of this Act.
(2) Proposals for amendment or revision shall be submitted to the Chairman of the Commission who shall transmit same to Member States within thirty (30) days of receipt thereof.

(3) The Assembly, upon the advice of the Executive Council, shall examine these proposals within a period of one year following notification of Member States, in accordance with the provisions of paragraph 2 of this Article.
(4) Amendments or revisions shall be adopted by the Assembly by consensus or, failing which, by a two-thirds majority and submitted for ratification by all Member States in accordance with their respective constitutional procedures. They shall enter into force thirty (30) days after the deposit of the instruments of ratification with the Chairman of the Commission by a two-thirds majority of the Member States.

Article 33. Transitional Arrangements and Final Provisions

(1) This Act shall replace the Charter of the Organization of African Unity. However, the Charter shall remain operative for a transitional period of one year or such further period as may be determined by the Assembly, following the entry into force of the Act, for the purpose of enabling the OAU/AEC to undertake the necessary measures regarding the devolution of its assets and liabilities to the Union and all matters relating thereto.
(2) The provisions of this Act shall take precedence over and supersede any inconsistent or contrary provisions of the Treaty establishing the African Economic Community.
(3) Upon the entry into force of this Act, all necessary measures shall be undertaken to implement its provisions and to ensure the establishment of the organs provided for under the Act in accordance with any directives or decisions which may be adopted in this regard by the Parties thereto within the transitional period stipulated above.
(4) Pending the establishment of the Commission, the OAU General Secretariat shall be the interim Secretariat of the Union.
(5) This Act, drawn up in four (4) original texts in the Arabic, English, French and Portuguese languages, all four (4) being equally authentic, shall be deposited with the Secretary-General of the OAU and, after its entry into force, with the Chairman of the Commission who shall transmit a certified true copy of the Act to the Government of each signatory State. The Secretary-General of the OAU and the Chairman of the Commission shall notify all signatory States of the dates of the deposit of the instruments of ratification or accession and shall upon entry into force of this Act register the same with the Secretariat of the United Nations.

In witness whereof, we have adopted this Act.

Appendix 1. The Constitutive Act of the African Union

Appendix 2. The Member States of the African Union (as of September 2017)

People's Democratic Republic of Algeria;
Republic of Angola;
Republic of Benin;
Republic of Botswana;
Burkina Faso (formerly, Republic of Upper Volta);
Republic of Burundi;
Republic of Cameroon;
Republic of Cape Verde;
Central African Republic;
Republic of Chad;
Islamic Federal Republic of the Comoros;
Republic of the Congo;
Republic of Côte d'Ivoire;
Democratic Republic of Congo;
Republic of Djibouti;
Arab Republic of Egypt;
State of Eritrea;
Federal Democratic Republic of Ethiopia;
Republic of Equatorial Guinea;
Gabonese Republic;
Republic of The Gambia;
Republic of Ghana;
Republic of Guinea;
Republic of Guinea-Bissau;
Republic of Kenya;
Kingdom of Lesotho;
Republic of Liberia;

State of Libya (formerly, Great Socialist People's Libyan Arab Jamahiriya);
Republic of Madagascar;
Republic of Malawi;
Republic of Mali;
Islamic Republic of Mauritania;
Republic of Mauritius;
Kingdom of Morocco;
Republic of Mozambique;
Republic of Namibia;
Republic of Niger;
Federal Republic of Nigeria;
Republic of Rwanda;
Sahrawi Arab Democratic Republic;
Republic of São Tomé and Príncipe;
Republic of Senegal;
Republic of Seychelles;
Republic of Sierra Leone;
Republic of Somalia;
Republic of South Africa;
Republic of South Sudan;
Republic of Sudan;
Kingdom of Swaziland;
United Republic of Tanzania;
Togolese Republic
Republic of Tunisia;
Republic of Uganda;
Republic of Zambia;
Republic of Zimbabwe.

Appendix 3. Solemn Declaration on the 50th Anniversary of the OAU/AU (2013)

AU Doc. Assembly/AU/Decl. 3 (XXI)

We, Heads of State and Government of the African Union assembled to celebrate the Golden Jubilee of the OAU/AU established in the city of Addis Ababa, Ethiopia on 25 May 1963,

Evoking the uniqueness of the history of Africa as the cradle of humanity and a centre of civilization, and dehumanized by slavery, deportation, dispossession, apartheid and colonialism as well as our struggles against these evils, which shaped our common destiny and enhanced our solidarity with peoples of African descent;

Recalling with pride, the historical role and efforts of the Founders of the Pan-African Movement and the nationalist movements, whose visions, wisdom, solidarity and commitment continue to inspire us;

Reaffirming our commitment to the ideals of Pan-Africanism and Africa's aspiration for greater unity, and paying tribute to the Founders of the Organization of African Unity (OAU) as well as the African peoples on the continent and in the Diaspora for their glorious and successful struggles against all forms of oppression, colonialism and apartheid;

Mindful that the OAU/AU have been relentlessly championing for the complete decolonization of the African continent and that one of the fundamental objectives is unconditional respect for the sovereignty and territorial integrity of each of its Member States;

Stressing our commitment to build a united and integrated Africa;

Guided by the vision of our Union and affirming our determination to '*build an integrated, prosperous and peaceful Africa, driven and managed by its own citizens and representing a dynamic force in the international arena*';

Determined to take full responsibility for the realisation of this vision;

Guided by the principles enshrined in the Constitutive Act of our Union and our Shared Values, in particular our commitment to ensure gender equality and a people centred approach in all our endeavours as well as respect for sovereignty and territorial integrity of our countries.

ACKNOWLEDGE THAT:

I. ***The Organisation of African Unity (OAU)*** overcame internal and external challenges, persevered in the quest for continental unity and solidarity; contributed actively to the liberation of Africa from colonialism and apartheid; provided a political and diplomatic platform to generations of leaders on continental and international matters; and elaborated frameworks for Africa's development and integration agenda through programmes such as NEPAD and APRM.

II. ***The African Union (AU)*** carried forward our struggle for self-determination and drive for development and integration; formulated a clear vision for our Union; agreed that the ultimate goal of the Union is the construction of a united and integrated Africa; instituted the principle of non-indifference by authorizing the right of the Union to intervene in Member States in conformity with the Constitutive Act; and laid the groundwork for the entrenchment of the rule of law, democracy, respect for human rights, solidarity, promotion of gender equality and the empowerment of Women and Youth in Africa.

III. The implementation of the integration agenda; the involvement of people, including our Diaspora in the affairs of the Union; the quest for peace and security and preventing wars and genocide such as the 1994 Rwandan genocide; the alignment between our institutional framework and the vision of the Union; the fight against poverty; inequality and underdevelopment; and, assuring Africa's rightful place in the world, remain challenges.

WE HEREBY DECLARE:

A. On the African Identity and Renaissance

i) Our strong commitment to accelerate the African Renaissance by ensuring the integration of the principles of Pan Africanism in all our policies and initiatives;

ii) Our unflinching belief in our common destiny, our Shared Values and the affirmation of the African identity; the celebration of unity in diversity and the institution of the African citizenship;

iii) Our commitment to strengthen AU programmes and Member States institutions aimed at reviving our cultural identity, heritage, history and Shared values, as well as undertake, henceforth, to fly the AU flag and sing the AU anthem along with our national flags and anthems;

iv) Promote and harmonize the teaching of African history, values and Pan Africanism in all our schools and educational institutions as part of advancing our African identity and Renaissance;

v) Promote people to people engagements including Youth and civil society exchanges in order to strengthen Pan Africanism.

B. The struggle against colonialism and the right to self-determination of people still under colonial rule

i) The completion of the decolonization process in Africa; to protect the right to self-determination of African peoples still under colonial rule; solidarity with people of African descend and in the Diaspora in their struggles against racial discrimination; and resist all forms of influences contrary to the interests of the continent;

ii) The reaffirmation of our call to end expeditiously the unlawful occupation of the Chagos Archipelago, the Comorian Island of Mayotte and also reaffirm the right to self-determination of the people of Western Sahara, with a view to enable these countries and peoples, to effectively exercise sovereignty over their respective territories.

C. On the integration agenda

Our commitment to Africa's political, social and economic integration agenda, and in this regard, speed up the process of attaining the objectives of the African Economic Community and take steps towards the construction of a united and integrated Africa. Consolidating existing commitments and instruments, we undertake, in particular, to:

i) Speedily implement the Continental Free Trade Area; ensure free movement of goods, with focus on integrating local and regional markets as well as facilitate African citizenship to allow free movement of people through the gradual removal of visa requirements;

ii) Accelerate action on the ultimate establishment of a united and integrated Africa, through the implementation of our common continental governance, democracy and human rights frameworks. Move with speed towards the integration and merger of the Regional Economic Communities as the building blocks of the Union.

D. On the agenda for social and economic development

Our commitment to place the African people, in particular women, children and the youth, as well as persons with disabilities, at the centre of our endeavours and to eradicate poverty. In this regard, we undertake to:

i) Develop our human capital as our most important resource, through education and training, especially in science, technology and innovation, and ensure that Africa takes its place and contributes to humanity, including in the field of space sciences and explorations;

ii) Eradicate disease, especially HIV/AIDS, Malaria and Tuberculosis, ensure that no African woman dies while giving life, address maternal, infant and child mortality as well as provide universal health care services to our citizens;

iii) Accelerate Africa's infrastructural development, to link African peoples, countries and economies; and help to drive social, cultural and economic development. In this regard, we commit to meet our strategic targets in transport, ICT, energy and other social infrastructure by committing national, regional and continental resources to this end;

iv) Create an enabling environment for the effective development of the African private sector through meaningfull public-private sector dialogue at all levels, in order to foster socially responsive business, good corporate governance and inclusive economic growth;

v) Take ownership of, use and develop, our natural endowments and resources, through value addition, as the basis for industrialization; promote intra-Africa trade and tourism, in order to foster economic integration, development, employment and inclusive growth to the benefit of the African people;

vi) Also take ownership, preserve, protect and use our oceanic spaces and resources, improve our maritime and transport industries to the benefit of the continent and its peoples, including by contributing to food security;

vii) Preserve our arable land for current and future generations, develop our rural economies, our agricultural production and agro-processing to eradicate hunger and malnutrition, as well as achieve food security and self-sufficiency;

viii) Expand and develop urban infrastructure and develop planned approaches to rapid urbanization and the emergence of new cities;

ix) Make our development agenda responsive to the needs of our peoples, anchored on the preservation of our environment for current and future generations, including in the fight against desertification and mitigation of the effects of climate change, especially with regards to island states and land-locked countries.

E. On peace and security

Our determination to achieve the goal of a conflict-free Africa, to make peace a reality for all our people and to rid the continent of wars, civil conflicts, human rights violations, humanitarian disasters and violent conflicts, and to prevent genocide. We pledge not to bequeath the burden of conflicts to the next generation of Africans and undertake to end all wars in Africa by 2020. In this regard, we undertake to:

i) Address the root causes of conflicts including economic and social disparities; put an end to impunity by strengthening national and continental judicial institutions, and ensure accountability in line with our collective responsibility to the principle of non-indifference;

ii) Eradicate recurrent and address emerging sources of conflict including piracy, trafficking in narcotics and humans, all forms of extremism, armed rebellions, terrorism, transnational organized crime and new crimes such as cybercrime.

iii) Push forward the agenda of conflict prevention, peace-making, peace support, national reconciliation and post-conflict reconstruction and development through the African Peace and Security Architecture; as well as, ensure enforcement of and compliance with peace agreements and build Africa's peacekeeping and enforcement capacities through the African Standby Force;

iv) Maintain a nuclear-free Africa and call for global nuclear disarmament, non-proliferation and peaceful uses of nuclear energy;

v) Ensure the effective implementation of agreements on landmines and the non-proliferation of small arms and light weapons;

vi) Address the plight of internally displaced persons and refugees and eliminate the root causes of this phenomenon by fully implementing continental and universal frameworks.

F. On democratic governance

Our determination to anchor our societies, governments and institutions on respect for the rule of law, human rights and dignity, popular participation, the management of diversity, as well as inclusion and democracy. In this regard, we undertake to:

i) Strengthen democratic governance including through decentralized systems, the rule of law and the capacities of our institutions to meet the aspirations of our people;

ii) Reiterate our rejection of unconstitutional change of government, including through any attempts to seize power by force but recognize the right of our people to peacefully express their will against oppressive systems;

iii) Promote integrity, fight corruption in the management of public affairs and promote leadership that is committed to the interests of the people;

iv) Foster the participation of our people through democratic elections and ensure accountability and transparency.

G. On Determining Africa's Destiny

Our determination to take responsibility for our destiny. We pledge to foster self-reliance and self-sufficiency. In this regard, we undertake to:

i) Take ownership of African issues and provide African solutions to African problems;

ii) Mobilize our domestic resources, on a predictable and sustainable basis to strengthen institutions and advance our continental agenda;

iii) Take all necessary measures, using our rich natural endowments and human resources, to transform Africa and make it a leading continent in the area of innovation and creativity;

H. Africa's place in the world

Our endeavour for Africa to take its rightful place in the political, security, economic, and social systems of global governance towards the realization of its Renaissance and establishing Africa as a leading continent. We undertake to:

i) Continue the global struggle against all forms of racism and discrimination, xenophobia and related intolerances;

ii) Act in solidarity with oppressed countries and peoples;

iii) Advance international cooperation that promotes and defends Africa's interests, is mutually beneficial and aligned to our Pan Africanist vision;

iv) Continue to speak with one voice and act collectively to promote our common interests and positions in the international arena;

v) Reiterate our commitment to Africa's active role in the globalization process and international forums including in Financial and Economic Institutions;

vi) Advocate for our common position for reform of the United Nations (UN) and other global institutions with particular reference to the UN Security Council, in order to correct the historical injustice with Africa as the only region without a permanent seat.

We pledge to articulate the above ideals and goals in our national development plans and in the development of the Continental Agenda 2063, through a people-driven process for the realization of our vision for an integrated, people-centred, prosperous Africa at peace with itself.

Appendix 3. Solemn Declaration on the 50th

As Heads of State and Government, mindful of our responsibility and commitment, we pledge to act together with our Peoples and the African Diaspora to realize our vision of Pan Africanism and African Renaissance.

Adopted by the 21st Ordinary Session of the Assembly of Heads of State and Government of the African Union, at Addis Ababa, on 26 May 2013.

Selected Bibliography

Includes Both Works Which Were Cited in the Monograph and Works Which Were Not Cited.

§1. Books, Book Chapters & Monographs

Adebajo, A. & H. Scanlon (eds). *A Dialogue of the Deaf: Essays on Africa and the United Nations.* Johannesburg: Jacana, 2006.

African Union Panel of the Wise. *Election-Related Disputes and Political Violence: Strengthening the Role of the African Union in Preventing, Managing, and Resolving Conflict.* The African Union Series, New York: International Peace Institute, July 2010.

Akokpari, J., A. Ndinga-Muvumba & T. Murithi (eds). *The African Union and Its Institutions.* Johannesburg: Jacana, 2008.

Amate, C.O.C. *Inside the OAU: Pan-Africanism in Practice.* London: Macmillan. 1986.

Ankumah, A.H. *The African Commission on Human and Peoples' Rights.* The Hague: Martinus Nijhoff, 1996.

Bach, D. 'Regionalism in Africa: Concepts and Context'. In *Routledge Handbook of African Security*, edited by J.J. Hentz. London: Routledge, 2014, 181.

Bach, D. *Regionalism in Africa: Genealogies, Institutions and Trans-State Networks.* London: Routledge, 2015.

Boulden, J. (ed.). *Dealing with Conflict in Africa: The United Nations and Regional Organizations.* New York: Palgrave Macmillan, 2003.

Brown, W. &S. Harman. (eds), *African Agency in International Politics*. Abingdon: Routledge, 2013

Cheeseman, N. *Democracy in Africa: Successes, Failures, and the Struggle for Political Reform*. Cambridge: Cambridge University Press, 2015

El-Ayouty, Y. & I.W. Zartman (eds). *The OAU after Twenty Years.* New York: Praeger Press, 1984.

El-Ayouty, Y. (ed.). *The Organization of African Unity after Thirty Years.* Westport: Praeger, 1994.

Engo, P.B. 'Peaceful Co-existence and Friendly Relations among States: The African Contribution to the Progressive Development of Principles of International Law'. In *Africa and International Organization*, edited by Y. El-Ayouty & H. Brooks. The Hague: Martinus Nijhoff, 1974, 31.

Evans, M. & R. Murray (eds). *The African Charter on Human and Peoples' Rights: The System in Practice, 1986–2006*. 2nd edn. Cambridge: Cambridge University Press, 2008.

Falola, T. *The African Diaspora: Slavery, Modernity, and Globalization.* Rochester, NY: University of Rochester Press, 2013.

Hagmann, T. & F. Reyntjens. (eds), *Aid and Authoritarianism in Africa: Development Without Democracy*. London: Zed Books, 2016.

Hatchard, J., M. Ndulo & P. Slinn. *Comparative Constitutionalism and Good Governance in the Commonwealth: An Eastern and Southern African Perspective.* Cambridge: Cambridge University Press 2004.

Heyns, C. & M. Killander (eds). *Compendium of Key Human Rights Documents of the African Union.* 5th edn. Pretoria: University Law Press, 2013.

Huliaras, A. 'Continuity and Change in French Foreign Policy Towards Africa'. In *Africa in Crisis*, edited by D. Frost, A. Thomson & T. Zack-Williams. London: Pluto Press, 2002, 161.

Huliaras, A. *EU-African Relations: Dealing with the Challenges of the Future.* Brussels: Center for European Studies, 2012.

Jalloh, C. (ed.). *The Sierra Leone Special Court and Its Legacy: The Impact for Africa and International Criminal Law.* Cambridge: Cambridge University Press, 2013.

Jallow, H.B. *The Law of the African (Banjul) Charter on Human and Peoples' Rights.* Victoria, BC: Trafford Publishing, 2007.

Kabati, C. 'NATO Military Operations in Libya in Relation to International Humanitarian Law'. In *AU - NATO Collaboration: Implications and Prospects*, edited by B.A. Smith-Windsor. Rome: NATO Defense College, 2013, 135.

Kunig, P. *Das völkerrechtliche Nichteinmischungsprinzip: Zur Praxis der Organisation der Afrikanischen Einheit und das Afrikanische Staatenverkehrs*. Baden-Baden: Nomos Verlagsgesellschaft, 1981.

Makinda, S.M., F. Wafula Okumu & D. Mickler, *The African Union: Addressing the Challenges of Peace, Security and Governance*. 2nd edn.London: Routledge, 2016.

Maluwa, T. *International Law in Post-Colonial Africa.* The Hague: Kluwer Law International, 1999.

Manga Fombad, C., Z. Kebonang & H. Melber. *African Union, NEPAD and the APRM Democratisation Efforts Explored*, Current African Issues No. 32. Uppsala: Nordiska Afrikainstitutet, 2006.

Martin, G. *Africa in World Politics – A Pan-African Perspective.* Trenton, New Jersey: Africa World Press, 2002.

Mazzeo, D. (ed.). *African Regional Organizations*. Cambridge: Cambridge University Press, 1984.

Mills, K. *International Responses to Mass Atrocities in Africa: Responsibility to Protect, Prosecute, and Palliate*. Philadelphia, PA: University of Pennsylvania Press, 2015.

Murray, R. & M. Evans. *Documents of the African Commission on Human and Peoples' Rights*. Oxford: Hart Publishing, 2001 & Vol. II. Oxford: Hart Publishing, 2008.

Naldi, G.J. *Documents of the Organization of African Unity*. London: Mansell, 1992.

Naldi, G.J. *The Organization of African Unity: An Analysis of Its Role*. London: Mansell, 1999.

Nmehielle, V.O. *The African Human Rights System: Its Laws, Practice and Institutions*. The Hague: Martinus Nijhoff, 2001.

Oche, O. (ed.). *African Legal Theory and Contemporary Problems*. New York: Springer, 2014.

Okoye, F.C. *International Law and the New African States*. London: Sweet & Maxwell, 1972.

Resnick, D. & N. van de Walle. (eds). *Democratic Trajectories in Africa: Unraveling the Impact of Foreign Aid*. Oxford: Oxford University Press, 2013.

Schmidt, E. *Foreign intervention in Africa: From the Cold War to the War on Terror*. Cambridge: Cambridge University Press, 2013.

Taylor, I. *Africa Rising? BRICS – Diversifying Dependency*. Oxford: James Currey, 2014.

Umozurike, U.O. *The African Charter on Human and Peoples' Rights*. The Hague: Martinus Nijhoff, 1997.

Viljoen, F. *International Human Rights in Africa*. 2nd edn. Oxford: Oxford University Press, 2012.

§2. Journal Articles

Abrahamsen, A. 'Africa and International Relations: Assembling Africa, Studying the World'. *African Affairs* (London) 116 (462) (2017): 125.

Ajulo, S.B. 'Temporal Scope of ECOWAS and AEC Treaties: A Case for African Economic Integration'. *RADIC* 8 (1996): 111.

Amoah, P. 'The African Charter on Human and Peoples' Rights – An Effective Weapon for Human Rights?'. *RADIC* 4 (1992): 226.

Anand, R.P. 'Role of the New Asian-African Countries in the Present International Legal Order'. *AJIL* 56 (1962): 383.

Arts, K.C.J.M. 'The International Protection of Children's Rights in Africa: The 1990 OAU Charter on the Rights and Welfare of the Child'. *RADIC* 5 (1993): 139.

Bedjaoui, M. 'Le règlement pacifique des différends africains'. *Annuaire français de droit international* 18 (1972): 85.

Bekker, G. 'Recent Developments in the African Human Rights System 2011/12'. *International Human Rights Law Review* 1 (2012): 158.

Bello, E. 'The African Charter on Human and Peoples' Rights'. *Hague Recueil* 194 (1985/1986): 13.

Bu, Q. 'Chinese Multinational Companies in Africa: The Human Rights Discourse'. *African Journal of Legal Studies* 8 (2015): 33.

Cervenka, Z. 'The Settlement of Disputes among Members of the Organization of African Unity'. *Verfassung und Recht in Uerbersee* 7 (1974): 117.

Cheyne, I. 'Africa and the International Trade in Hazardous Wastes'. *RADIC* 6 (1994): 493.

Cowling, M. 'The African Union – An Evaluation'. *South African Yearbook of International Law* 27 (2002): 193.

d'Orsi, C. 'Sub-Saharan Africa: Is a New Special Regional Refugee Law Regime Emerging?'. ZaöRV 68 (2008): 1057.

D'Sa, R.M. 'The African Charter on Human and Peoples' Rights: Problems and Prospects for Regional Action'. *Australian Yearbook of International Law* 10 (1981/83): 101.

D'Sa, R.M. 'The African Refugee Problem, Relevant International Conventions and Recent Activities of the Organization of African Unity'. *Netherlands International Law Review* 31 (1984): 378.

D'Sa, R.M. 'The Lagos Plan of Action – Legal Mechanisms for Cooperation Between the Organisation of African Unity and the United Nations Economic Commission for Africa'. *JAL* 27 (1983): 4.

Djoyou Kamga S.A. & C. Manga Fombad 'A Critical Review of the Jurisprudence of the African Commission on the Right to Development' *JAL* 57 (2013): 196.

Elias, T.O. 'The Commission of Mediation, Conciliation and Arbitration of the Organisation of African Unity'. *BYBIL* 40 (1964): 336.

Elvy, S.-A. 'Towards a New Democratic Africa: the African Charter on Democracy, Elections and Governance'. *Emory International Law Review* 27 (2013): 41.

Gittleman, R. 'The African Charter on Human and Peoples' Rights: A Legal Analysis'. *Virginia Journal of International Law* 22 (1982): 667.

Hastings, J.V. & Phillips S.G. 'Maritime Piracy Business Networks and Institutions in Africa'. *African Affairs* (London) 114 (457)(2015): 555.

Hofman, F. 'Refugee Law in an African Context'. ZaöRV 52 (1992): 318.

Huliaras, A. 'Qadhafi's Comeback: Libya and Sub-Saharan Africa in the 1990s'. *African Affairs*(London) 100 (2001): 5.

Selected Bibliography

Isanga, J.M. 'The Constitutive Act of the African Union, African Courts and the Protection of Human Rights: New Dispensation?'. *Santa Clara Journal of International Law* 11 (2013): 267.

Jalloh, C.C., 'Reflections on the Indictment of Sitting Heads of State and Government and Its Consequences for Peace and Stability and Reconciliation in Africa'. *African Journal of Legal Studies* (7) 2014: 43.

Jonas, O. 'Neutering the SADC Tribunal by Blocking Individuals' Access to the Tribunal'. *International Human Rights Law Review* 2 (2013): 294.

Jordaan, E. 'The African Group on the United Nations Human Rights Council: Shifting Geopolitics and the Liberal International Order'. *African Affairs* (London) 115(460) (2016): 490.

Kaminsky, H.S. 'Assessment of the Bamako Convention on the Ban of Import into Africa and the Control of Transboundary Movement and Management of Hazardous Wastes Within Africa'. *The Georgetown International Environmental Law Review* 5 (1992): 77.

Kato, L.L. 'Recognition in International Law: Some Thoughts on Traditional Theory, Attitudes and Practice by African States'. *Indian Journal of International Law* 10 (1970): 299.

Krisch, N. 'The Establishment of an African Court on Human and Peoples' Rights'. ZaöRV 58 (1998): 713.

Kunig, P. 'The Protection of Human Rights by International Law in Africa'. *German Yearbook of International Law* 25 (1982): 138.

Kuwali, D. 'From Durable Solutions to Holistic Solutions: Prevention of Displacement in Africa'. *African Journal of Legal Studies* (6) 2013: 265.

Lloyd, A. 'A Theoretical Analysis of the Reality of Children's Rights in Africa: An Introduction to the African Charter on the Rights and Welfare of the Child'. *African Human Rights Law Journal* 2 (2002): 11.

Lumu, N.L. 'De la Nature de la Communauté Economique Africaine'. *RADIC* 8 (1996): 51.

Magliveras, K.D. & G.J. Naldi. 'The African Court of Justice'. *ZaöRV* 66 (2006): 187.

Magliveras, K.D. & G.J. Naldi. 'The African Union: A New Dawn for Africa?'. *ICLQ* 51 (2002): 415.

Magliveras, K.D. & G.J. Naldi. 'The ICC Addresses Non-Cooperation by State Parties in Arresting President Al-Bashir: The *Malawi* Decision'. *African Journal of Legal Studies* 6 (2013): 1.

Magliveras, K.D. & G.J. Naldi. 'The International Criminal Court's Involvement with Africa: Evaluation of a Fractious Relationship'. *Nordic Journal of International Law* 83 (2013): 417.

Magliveras, K.D. & G.J. Naldi. 'The Pan-African Parliament of the African Union: An Overview'. *African Human Rights Law Journal* 3 (2003): 222.

Magliveras, K.D. 'Fighting Impunity Unsuccessfully in Africa: A Critique of the African Union's Handling of the Hissène Habré Affair'. *RADIC* 22, no. 3 (2014): 420.

Majinge, C.R. 'The Future of Peacekeeping in Africa and the Normative Role of the African Union'. *Goettingen Journal of International Law* 2 (2010): 463.

Maluwa, T. 'The Peaceful Settlement of Disputes among African States, 1963–1983: Some Conceptual Issues and Practical Trends'. *ICLQ* 38 (1986): 299.

Martorana, C.S. 'The New African Union: Will It Promote Enforcement of the Decisions of the African Court of Human & Peoples' Rights?'. *George Washington International Law Review* 40 (2008): 583.

Mupangavanhu, Y. 'African Union Rising to the Need for Continental IP Protection? The Establishment of the Pan-African Intellectual Property Organization'. *JAL* 59 (2015) 1.

Murray, R. 'Serious or Massive Violations under the African Charter on Human and Peoples' Rights: A Comparison with the Inter-American and European Mechanisms'. *Netherlands Quarterly on Human Rights* 17 (1999): 109.

Mushkat, M. 'The African Approach to Some Basic Problems of Modern International Law'. *Indian Journal of International Law* 7 (1967): 335.

Naldi, G.J. & K.D. Magliveras. 'Reinforcing the African System of Human Rights: The Protocol on the Establishment of a Regional Court on Human and Peoples' Rights'. *Netherlands Quarterly on Human Rights* 16 (1998): 431.

Naldi, G.J. & K.D. Magliveras. 'The African Court of Justice and Human Rights: A Judicial Curate's Egg'. *International Organizations Law Review* 9 (2012): 387.

Naldi, G.J. & K.D. Magliveras. 'The African Economic Community: Emancipation for African States or Yet Another Glorious Failure?'. *North Carolina Journal of International Law and Commercial Regulation* 24 (1999): 601.

Naldi, G.J. & K.D. Magliveras. 'The Ever Difficult Symbiosis of Africa with the International Criminal Court'. *Revue Hellénique de Droit International* 66 (2013): 59.

Naldi, G.J. & K.D. Magliveras. 'The Proposed African Court of Human and Peoples' Rights: Evaluation and Comparison'. *RADIC* 8 (1996): 944.

Naldi, G.J. 'Interim Measures of Protection in the African System for the Protection of Human and Peoples' Rights'. *African Human Rights Law Journal* 2 (2002): 1.

Naldi, G.J. 'Limitation of Rights under the African Charter on Human and Peoples' Rights: The Contribution of the African Commission on Human and Peoples' Rights'. *South African Journal of Human Rights* 17 (2001): 109.

Naldi, G.J. 'The OAU's Grand Bay Declaration On Human Rights in Africa in Light of the Practice of the African Commission on Human and Peoples' Rights'. *ZaöRV* 60 (2000): 715.

Ndulo, M. 'Harmonization of Trade Laws in the African Economic Community'. *ICLQ* 42 (1993): 101.

Selected Bibliography

O'Shea, E. 'Responsibility to Protect (R2P) in Libya: Ghosts of the Past Haunting the Future'. *International Human Rights Law Review* 1 (2012): 173.

Obinna Okere, B. 'The Protection of Human Rights in Africa and the African Charter on Human and Peoples' Rights: A Comparative Analysis with the European and American Systems'. *Human Rights Quarterly* 6 (1984): 141.

Ocran, C. 'The Protocol to the African Charter on Human and Peoples' Rights on the Rights of Women in Africa'. *RADIC* 15 (2007): 147.

Odinkalu, C.A. 'The Individual Complaints Procedures of the African Commission on Human and Peoples' Rights: A Preliminary Assessment'. *Transnational Law & Contemporary Problems* 8 (1998): 359.

Okongwe, O. 'The OAU Charter and the Principle of Domestic Jurisdiction in Inter-African Affairs'. *Indian Journal of International Law* 13 (1973): 589.

Olugbuo, B.C. 'The African Union, the United Nations Security Council and the Politicisation of International Justice in Africa' *African Journal of Legal Studies* 7 (2014): 351.

Omorogbe, Y. 'A Club of Incumbents? The African Union and Coups d'Etat'. *Vanderbilt Journal of Transitional Law* 44 (2011): 123.

Oppong, R.F. 'The African Union, The African Economic Community and Africa's Regional Economic Communities: Untangling a Complex Web'. *RADIC* 18 (2010): 92.

Ouguergouz, F. 'The Bamako Convention on Hazardous Waste: A New Step in the Development of the African International Environmental Law'. *African Yearbook of International Law* 1 (1994): 195.

Sarkin, J. 'The Role of the United Nations, the African Union and Africa's Sub-Regional Organizations in Dealing with Africa's Human Rights Problems: Connecting Humanitarian Intervention and the Responsibility to Protect'. *JAL* 53 (2009) 1.

Shearer, C.R.H. 'Comparative Analysis of the Basel and Bamako Conventions on Hazardous Waste'. *Environmental Law* 23 (1993): 141.

Ssenyonjo, M. 'Direct Access to the African Court on Human and Peoples' Rights by Individuals and Non- Governmental Organisations: An Overview of the Emerging Jurisprudence of the African Court 2008-2012'. *International Human Rights Law Review* 2 (2013): 294.

Thiam, D. 'L'Afrique demande un droit international nouveau'. *Verfassung und Recht in Uebersee* 1 (1968): 1.

Thompson, B. 'Africa's Charter on Children's Rights: A Normative Break with Cultural Traditionalism'. *ICLQ* 41 (1992): 434.

Thompson, B. 'Economic Integration Efforts in Africa'. *RADIC* 5 (1993): 743.

Tladi, D. 'The Quest to Ban Hazardous Waste Import into Africa: First Bamako and Now Basel'. *CILSA* 33 (2000): 210.

Udombana, N.J. 'Toward the African Court on Human and Peoples' Rights: Better Late than Never'. *Yale Human Rights and Development Law Journal* 3 (2000): 45.

Viljoen, F. & L. Louw. 'State Compliance with the Recommendations of the African Commission on Human and People's Rights 1994–2004'. *American Journal of International Law* 101 (2007): 1.

Williams, P.D. & A. Boutellis. 'Partnership Peacekeeping: Challenges and Opportunities in the United Nations-African Union Relationship'. *African Affairs* 113 (2014): 254.

Index

The numbers here refer to paragraph numbers.

Index

Index

Index

Index

www.ingramcontent.com/pod-product-compliance
Ingram Content Group UK Ltd.
Pitfield, Milton Keynes, MK11 3LW, UK
UKHW020130290926
15471UKWH00003B/389

9 789041 195876